TEAR IT DOWN:
HOW CROSSOVER BRIDGED METAL AND HARDCORE PUNK

Dedicated to Nikoletta, Amaryllis, Ian Glasper and the 1926 Family.

La Lucha 4 Sigue

In loving memory of Michael Gibbons (Leeway), Eddie Sutton (Leeway), Josh Pappe (D.R.I./Gang Green), Steve Hanford (Mayhem/Poison Idea), Anthony Bernardo (The Beast NY), Dale Henderson (Beowülf) and Mike Jensen (Beowülf)

Published by Earth Island Books

Pickforde Lodge

Pickforde Lane

Ticehurst

East Sussex

TN5 7BN

www.earthislandbooks.com

First published by Earth Island Books 2026

No part of this publication may be reproduced, distributed or transmitted by any means, electronic, mechanical, photocopying, or otherwise without written permission from the author.

ISBN 9781916864962 paperback

ISBN 9781916864979 ebook

Printed and bound by Solopress, Southend

Thanks to all the bands that appeared with an interview in Crossover The Edge:

Agnostic Front, Cro-Mags, Crumbsuckers, Ludichrist, Leeway, The Icemen, S.O.D./M.O.D., N.Y.C. Mayhem, The Beast (NY), Carnivore, Loss For Words, Lethal Aggression, Gang Green, Post Mortem, Outpatients, White Pigs, Amazing Grace, Nuclear Assault, Sam Black Church, Dirge, The Six and Violence, Hogan's Heroes, Social Decay, Whiplash, Cerebral Hemorrhage, Norman Bates and The Showerheads, PMS/Wench, At War, Travesty, Castle Blood, Rancid Decay, F.U.'s/Straw Dogs, Prong, D.R.I., Corrosion of Conformity, Manimals, Zoetrope, Metal Onslaught, Lost Cause, Snake Nation, Impulse Manslaughter, Dead Horse, Angkor Wat, Bad Yodelers, Aftermath, Acrophet, Verbal Abuse, Civil Disobedience, Random Conflict, Not-Us, Attitude Adjustment, Sacrilege B.C., Beowülf, Clown Alley, Dr. Know, Dissension, The Brood, Uncle Slam, Wehrmacht, Spazztic Blurr, Excel, Virulence, Crucifix, Proudflesh, Bl'ast!, Powertrip, Septic Death, Final Conflict, Final Warning, Mayhem (Portland), Mace, Cryptic Slaughter, Savior, The Accüsed, No Mercy, The Boneless Ones, Hell's Kitchen, Suicidal Tendencies, The Dehumanizers, NME, A.M.Q.A., Aversion, Subvert, Infamous Sinphony, The Braindead, Beyond Possession, Sudden Impact, D.B.C., Dayglo Abortions, Maniac, Onslaught, English Dogs, Anihilated, Sacrilege, Concrete Sox, Axegrinder, Civilised Society?, Deviated Instinct, Electro Hippies, Legion of Parasites, Metal Duck, Virus, Hellbastard, Broken Bones, Decadence Within, Tortoise Corpse, Ardkore, Alternative Attack, Warfare/The Blood, Lobotomia, Armagedom, Ratos De Porão, Agony, Raw Power, Rumble Militia, Erosion, Drakkar/Draksen, Jingo de Lunch, The Beast (NJ), The Worst, Void, Nasty Savage, Impaler, Mentors, Holy Terror, Détente, Overkill LA, Mind Over Four, The Skeptix, Amebix, Doom and to Discharge who started everything.

Contents

Abstract	1
FOREWORD by Parris Mayhew	3
USA	6
WEST COAST	6
EVOL	6
HIRAX	10
HAYWIRE	15
THE MOFO HOMEBOYS	19
THE END/ THE LIVIND END	25
WASTED YOUTH	29
RESISTANT MILITIA	34
MIDWEST AND MIDDLE AMERICA	40
WHOPPERS TASTE GOOD (W.T.G.)	40
HYPER AS HELL	46
TRANSGRESSION	49
ENVIRONMENTAL HAZZARD	52
SIK MENTALITY	56
UGLY BUT PROUD	61
SCRUFFY TEARAWAYS	66
EAST COAST	71
KILLING TIME	72
EXECUTIONER	77
ANTIDOTE	81
SAM BLACK CHURCH	86
SLAUGHTER SHACK	90
METHEDRINE	94
WRECKING CREW	98
PLASMATICS	102
THE MOB	107
DRESDEN	112
THE CATATONICS	115
McRAD	119
ABSOLUTION	125
DEADSPOT	129
STILLBORN	135
AT ALL COST	139
CONFUSION NYC	142
DARKSIDE NYC	147

UNITED KINGDOM	152
DRIVEN TO DISTRACTION/DEATH WARMED UP	152
CANADA	160
FRATRICIDE	160
SLAUGHTER	164
DISTORTED INFLUENCE	168
SCHIZOID	171
B.A.R.F.	175
CAPITALIST ALIENATION	178
CORRUPTED REPUTATION	181
BRAZIL	185
EXTREME VIOLENCE	185
EUROPE	190
EXTREMITY	190
NEUROOT	192
NEW INTERVIEWS FROM BANDS INCLUDED IN CROSSOVER	
THE EDGE	197
AGNOSTIC FRONT	197
CRUMBSUCKERS	201
LUDICHRIST	206
N.Y.C. MAYHEM	224
LEEWAY	227
GANG GREEN	231
MANIMALS	235
CRYPTIC SLAUGHTER	240
LETHAL AGGRESSION	246
HOGAN'S HEROES	250
OVERKILL L.A.	255
SACRILEGE B.C.	260
IMPULSE MANSLAUGHTER	264
AMAZING GRACE	270
BEYOND POSSESSION	273
D.R.I. (DIRTY ROTTEN IMBECILES)	279
A.M.Q.A.	282
ONSLAUGHT	285
SACRILEGE	288
THE NEW BARBARIANS (Post-2000's Crossover Bands)	291
AGGROS	291
COMBUST	297

STAMPIN' GROUND	300
POWER TRIP	306
TOE TAG/THE ACCÜSED AD	308
HOLIER THAN THOU?	311
THE SHINING	316
DEATH IN YOUR YARD	320
TOXIC SHOCK	323
CLUSTERFUX	328
INHUMAN NATURE	333
THE ONES FOR ALL	**339**
G.B.H.	339
ANTI-NOWHERE LEAGUE	343
OFFENDERS	347
THE LABELS	**352**
GENERATION RECORDS	352
BEER CITY RECORDS	356
F.O.A.D. RECORDS	358
SUPREME ECHO RECORDS	361
ALCHEMY RECORDS	367
THE VISUAL ARTISTS	**372**
SEAN TAGGART	372
VINCENZIO PACKARD	376
THE FANZINES	**380**
METAL CORE	380
xXx	386
THE BLOGGER	**392**
NATE WILSON, True Punk & Metal blogspot	392
WHEN YOU LEAST EXPECT IT	**398**
THE FU's and STRAW DOGS	398
M.O.D. and S.O.D.	400
LOSS FOR WORDS	402
PRE METAL SYNDROME	404
ATTITUDE ADJUSTMENT	406
SNAKE NATION	408
METAL ONSLAUGHT	410
MAYHEM (Portland)	412
FINAL WARNING	414
THE BRAINDEAD	416
ACROPHET	420

N.M.E.	422
CORROSION OF CONFORMITY	424
AFTERMATH	425
THE BEAST (NJ)	428
SEPTIC DEATH	430
VERBAL ABUSE	432
AGONI/AGONY	434
METAL DUCK	435
DR. KNOW	437
RAW POWER	439
HELLBASTARD	441
LOST CAUSE	443
BAD YODELERS	445
DIRGE	447
LOBOTOMIA	448
THE LEGION OF PARASITES	450
THE DEHUMANIZERS	452
POST MORTEM	454
BL'AST!	455
ZOETROPE	457
POWERTRIP	459
THE WORST	460
SAVIOR	463
SUBVERT	464
ANGKOR WAT	466
EXCEL	468
CRUCIFIX	470
IMPALER	472
NOT-US	474
RANDOM CONFLICT	476
DISSENSION	478
THE SIX AND VIOLENCE	480
ELECTRO HIPPIES	483
ANIHILATED	485
OUTPATIENTS	487
CIVIL DISOBEDIENCE	489
DISCHARGE	490
NUCLEAR ASSAULT	494
ARDKORE	496

WHIPLASH/CEREBRAL HEMORRHAGE	499
DÉTENTE	501
RANCID DECAY	503
CONCRETE SOX	504
ENGLISH DOGS	506
D.B.C.	508
DAYGLO ABORTIONS	511
CLOWN ALLEY	513
CASTLE BLOOD/TRAVESTY	514
BROKEN BONES	518
SUDDEN IMPACT	521
SOCIAL DECAY	524
WEHRMACHT	526
AMEBIX	528
MACE	531
INFAMOUS SINPHONY	533
HOLY TERROR	534
THE SKEPTIX	536
ALTERNATIVE ATTACK	538
EROSION	540
MANIAC	542
THE BONELESS ONES	544
THE MENTORS	546
THE ICEMEN	549
DEADHORSE	552
PART TWO: But wait…there's more!	554
USA	554
CANADA	580
UK	581
GERMANY	583
FRANCE	583
ITALY	583
AUSTRIA	584
SWEDEN	585
FINLAND	585
NORWAY	586
DENMARK	586
NETHERLANDS	586
BELGIUM	587

GREECE	587
POLAND	588
SWITZERLAND	589
PORTUGAL	589
SPAIN	589
HUNGARY	590
YUGOSLAVIA	591
SINGAPORE	591
MEXICO	591
PERU	591
ARGENTINA	592
BRAZIL	592
CHILE	593
JAPAN	593
NEW ZEALAND	594
INTERNATIONAL NAMEDROPPING	595
NO INTERVIEW, NO WORRY	599
THE LIST SESSIONS	619
50 You Have To Get	619
Under Their Influence	620
The Ones For Everybody	621
Going Underground	621
There's More List….Part 2	622
EPILOGUE: Final Daze	624

Abstract

Crossover thrash, speedcore, metalpunk, punk metal - all these terms first began appearing in magazines and fanzines during the 1980s. Yet the earliest known use of the word crossover in a punk and/or heavy metal context should be credited to UK journalist Geoff Barton, who described Motörhead as "a veritable crossover of both genres – the first true heavy metal punk crossover" in his 1979 review of *Overkill*.

In 1984, Brian "Pushead" Schroeder of Septic Death was the first to use the term speedcore to define "the crossover, where what is known as heavy metal is mixed with the sounds of punk [...] the outcome naturally is considered heavy metal by the metalheads and punk by the punks." Pushead's article in *Maximum Rocknroll* was the first to outline what crossover truly represented, referencing bands from both the hardcore punk and metal camps. In his view, metal bands such as Slayer, Metallica, Venom, Exciter, Anthrax, Megadeth, Exodus, Dark Angel, Hellhammer, Possessed, Warfare, Sodom, Zoetrope, Voivod, Bulldozer, Iron Angel, Bathory, Sacred Blade and Motörhead shared the same spirit as punk acts like Discharge, English Dogs, G.I.S.M., Corrosion of Conformity, Poison Idea, Raw Power, Execute, General Disaster, Disorder, Chaos U.K. and Outo.

Crossover was more than simply a sonic blend. Pushead portrayed speedcore as the product of metal bands unwilling to follow the corporate path of their contemporaries and rejecting the "rock star" attitude, thus adding a stylistic and ideological dimension to the genre. On the punk side, speedcore emerged from the disillusionment of musicians who sought to push beyond the boundaries of traditional punk.

Crossover quickly gained both passionate supporters and fierce detractors. Some punks accused hardcore bands of "selling out", while certain metalheads viewed crossover as a corrupting force threatening the purity of "true metal". Upon reviewing countless recordings and critiques, crossover was the best thing that ever happened to metal. It is the reason hardcore survived and evolved into the 1990s.

Within the hardcore scene there were, in fact, two types of crossover after 1984: crossover with metal, and crossover with indie rock (explored further in my book *We Can Be The New Wind*). Both routes produced masterpieces, seminal records, and notable disappointments. They all form parts of the rich musical history of hardcore that is forever relevant and continuously re-examining itself.

I grew up as Greek bloke who spent a third of his life living between the UK and Italy who was only four or five years old when crossover exploded in the USA. Crossover was my gateway in the 1990s. I was fourteen, already into hardcore and metal, when I bought D.R.I.'s *4 of a Kind* LP for less than a dollar. It blew my mind. It was 1995, and I had no interest in what was happening in the metal scene at the time. Metal has always been huge in Greece, and although we've traditionally had strong UK punk and crust influences, US hardcore was practically non-existent here in terms of a fanbase. Greece has long been shaped by UK music trends, with only a few exceptions.

I began writing letters to D.R.I., and to my surprise Kurt Brecht replied with a kind letter and old flyers. That correspondence pushed me further to learn more about the US scene and this crossover sound. Then came Cro-Mags' *Age of Quarrel*. I still remember exactly what I was wearing the day I bought the original UK pressing on GWR Records. After that I found: Agnostic Front, Corrosion of Conformity, Beyond Possession, Impulse Manslaughter, Excel, Suicidal Tendencies. Suddenly everything made sense. This was where I belonged.

I started buying records obsessively and travelling wherever I could to see any band remotely connected to this world. Crossover, along with hardcore punk, neo-garage, Oi!, UK82, anarcho-punk with a healthy dose of metal. This music became the soundtrack of my life, in a time and place where none of it was fashionable.

As I write yet another book on crossover, this is not *"Crossover The Edge* 2". I wanted to create something different. I managed to gather around 170 interviews and wrote as many reviews and stories as I could. I interviewed nearly all the bands from *Crossover The Edge*. This time each received only one or two questions and like the music, the interviews were short, sharp shocks. I also spoke with new bands, and included some surprises you'll discover as you turn the pages.

Enjoy!

Alexandros Anesiadis

FOREWORD by Parris Mayhew
Founding member of Cro-Mags, White Devil, Aggros

(Parris Mayhew. Photo courtesy of David Griesbrecht)

As a fan of heavy music of all kinds, crossover, for me was the most natural thing. I see heavy music as a family tree, with say Minor Threat on one end and Mercyful Fate on the other, very distant cousins, but with an unbroken relation to each other, with say Motörhead in the middle, equally related to both. Because anyone can see the connection between Mercyful Fate and Motörhead, or between Motörhead and Minor Threat. With that context it's a lot easier to see the connection between say Metallica and the actual Cro-Mags (accept no cheap imitations). I see a family resemblance in what made Judas Priest's album *Unleashed in the East* and Black Flag's *Damaged* album what they are. Both bands from the same thirst for the power of angry guitars and thundering drums. Listening to Black Sabbath or Black Flag alone because no one you know is into "music like that." After school in basements and bedrooms around the world the same solitary fetishist listening rituals: staring at album covers and reading every word on the liner notes until it's memorized. Each band may dress it up a little different, but you can't help but see the family resemblance, the same flesh and blood, the undeniable shared DNA, between Bon Scott and Johnny Rotten, or me and Tony Iommi!

At 15 years old, I discovered the Sex Pistols, Motörhead and Judas Priest at around the same time. In high school new things presented themselves daily. I was a product of 1970s rock, and unwavering paradigm of excellence: Rush, Led Zeppelin, Van Halen and Aerosmith so I had an idea of what I thought music could/should and had to be and what standard could be expected. Excellence period. Then came the Sex Pistols and wow did that twist my perception. It was raw, reckless and possible. You didn't have to be Eddie Van Halen or Rush to make great music that moved people. Motörhead and Judas Priest had a similar effect on my perception of what music could be. I realized, what was attainable musically was within my reach now, "I could do that!" was something that I suddenly became aware of. But these bands had a polarizing effect on fans, you were either metal or punk and they did not mix at all. Not yet. Or so I thought. It was already brewing. I didn't see punk and metal as so separate, and I remember arguing with a kid in school that Bon Scott and Johnny Rotten were just a haircut away from each other. So, for me these bands were an estranged family. And with that realization, I had been given a new set of musical rules and parameters. And armed with that I began writing the songs that made up the bulk of the first Cro-Mags album *Age of Quarrel*. My new music was embraced first by the hardcore fans only, playing locally on the NYHC scene, but we couldn't help but notice new faces showing up to see what we were doing, like Scott Ian and Dan Lilker. They were learning from us. Then bands like Carnivore began to morph into temporary hardcore bands because they were so excited what was happening in the streets of Manhattan. And once our album *Age of Quarrel* dropped, we went on tour with, of all bands, Motörhead and overnight the metal fans outnumbered our hardcore fans. Cro-Mags were poised to crossover without even trying. My music was on the line in between hardcore and metal, so it was a natural to be taken in by the larger metal scene who had been sniffing around. And as we got swept up in it, Cro-Mags played a role, along with other bands like Suicidal Tendencies in erasing that line between hardcore and metal. Oddly enough hardcore fans will insist *Age of Quarrel* is some variety of "the best hardcore album or the most hardcore, or the seminal hardcore album but definitely not a metal album, of all time." *Age of Quarrel* started as product of the NYHC scene, a beacon or it, that album did and still does scream THIS IS NYHC to the world. We accumulated a fuck-ton of metal fans because of that album, metal fans took us into the fold, and the street corners of NYC were in our rear-view mirror. There was no plan, I never heard the word "crossover" while I wrote those songs, after school in my mother's kitchen. That's just who I was at that age as a songwriter and a fan. By the time we made the second Cro-Mags album *Best Wishes* our original fanbase of "hardcore people" were pointing at the new album and crying "they turned metal." Which was funny because 'Malfunction' and 'Seekers of the Truth' are both on *Age of Quarrel* and looking back; those songs are clearly metal songs by any standards. But that just shows how quickly the definitions appeared and then morphed year by year. I found this whole thing freeing. Because, going forward, I had an arsenal of musical ideas that I was able to add to my songs without restrictions, as the parameters of what the fans wanted and expected also expanded. I didn't have to change, the fans changed. Crossover made that happen for me, as much as I played a role in defining the word 'crossover'. So today, crossover means I can do anything I freakin want now. Since that glass ceiling of genre was smashed, anything goes! Nobody batted an eyelash when I had piano, expansive arrangements and song lengths in the 9-minute range on *Rise of the Aggros*, or even that my record was all instrumental. I heard the moniker "progressive hardcore" thrown into a few reviews, which I love. I'm happy that the impression my music gives now is expansive and not expected. I am still me, so anyone familiar with the real Cro-Mags albums (*Age of Quarrel*, *Best Wishes*, and *Revenge*) will absolutely feel like Aggros is familiar, but with Aggros you get so much more.

So, in closing and in preparation or reading this book, crossover means to me, that I'm free to use any of the things that I think music could and should be, in any song. And being a part of this book feels right to me, no matter what other bands are included, because we are all related, especially if it's Carnivore!!!!

USA

WEST COAST

"To me, I believe 'crossover' evolved in around 1984 or so from the influence of speed & thrash metal that was coming out at the time. Bands like 7 Seconds who we loved was going one way and we weren't embracing that like we were embracing newer bands like Possessed and Slayer etc. Those bands were giving us the speed and brutality that got us into hardcore in the first place, so we started embracing that element into our songwriting. The Accüsed are a prime example of a pioneering West Coast crossover act, and we followed shortly afterwards as well..." (Eric McIntire- Attitude Adjustment, Deface, Neglected, Violent Coercion)

EVOL

(Evol, 1988 in Los Angeles. Courtesy unknown)

One of the unsung heroes of Venice scene, Evol included in their initial lineup two next-door neighbours in Chicago (Robert Sodin and Tim Lancaster) who were members of the classic heavy metal band Wrath (that self-released in 1984 the impossible to find nowadays, *Love Cage / Power on Power* 7-inch). "Evol started in 1986 when Venice bassist Dug Mug answered my ad in L.A.'s Music Connection" guitarist Robert Sodin narrates. "I was a Chicago transplant so was the drummer Tim Lancaster-my childhood friend. We connected with Dug (Mug, bassist) in my Hollywood apartment and started writing music. Dug then introduced us to a kid Jason Brown who worked at Streets of Venice skate and T-shirt shop. Jason became the singer. There were no auditions, the four of us decided to work with what we had. We immediately recorded o four song demo which took off and received a lot of interest. Tim and I were metalheads and Jason and Dug were more skate punk guys".

(D.R.I., Uncle Slam and Evol gig at Jezebel's, Anaheim, CA, 14/01/1990)

"Find it funny or not" Robert adds "I always thought Black Sabbath's *Paranoid* and Zeppelin's *Communication Breakdown* were the first punky metal tunes, but I would have to say Motörhead made it their trademark...so I think that crossover was just musician kids pushing the speed boundaries, taking the speed and aggression to another level. Also, metal bands wanted 'street cred' so they dropped the leather and spandex for shorts and Vans. True punks and metalheads never really, really got along so there was always a tension that added to the music. Back in terms of style, we wore Southern California beachwear sometimes and all black sometimes, we went through fazes. The band had super long 'surfer' hair, but Jason had more spikey punk styles at times. We would often wear the shirts we were selling as marketing".

With Dug playing in No Mercy and Jason in Strapt (both crossover and hardcore bands), and with Robert's and Tim's background in heavy metal, in was inevitable that Evol's sound blended the classic Los Angeles and Venice hardcore punk sound with heavy metal; "It was early D.R.I., early Suicidal, Slayer, Misfits" Rob admits, regarding their influences. "I was a classic metal guitarist, so personally I brought my Randy Rhoads, Glen Tipton spice to it. We were all into everything, we had diverse tastes that had no resemblance to with the music we made as Evol. Evol was an experiment. We wanted to create a pummelling wall of sound that would take your breath away for 45 minutes. I would run 3 -100watt heads full blast in tiny clubs sometimes, same with Doug. We were stupid loud. So, you had this thunder with a character like Jason yelling over the top of it about how life, love can beat the shit out of you...that was Evol".

Although Evol were latecomers to the Venice scene, they managed to find themselves playing gigs quite easily, alongside local greats such as Uncle Slam, Excel and Beowülf or touring bands like D.R.I. and even King Diamond, who wore their T-shirt onstage in their live appearance on Country Club, in 1990 (alongside Cholos on Acid)! "We often played with our favourite crossover bands, so if we were on a mini-tour with D.R.I. or Excel I just loved those memories" Robert recalls with a huge smile on his face. "Unfortunately, violence at shows was there all the time…A lot of blood spilled and even life loss. I hated the violence; I wanted everyone to just get into the music and have fun".

Evol released their first demo (named as *Demo I*) in 1989, as well as their second one (*EVOL II*) in 1990, with both being simply frantic, hard-hitting exercises on crossover-however their songs will be reviewed later on. Their quality was the one that offered Evol the chance to support so many great bands (as aforementioned), and Robert adds that "even though there was never a deep love for each other (punks and metalheads), when you had a blasting fuckin fast punk drummer and an intense metal guitarist creating sonic mayhem (as in Evol) it worked. And that formula not only sounded great but was super fun to play!"

(Excel, Evol and Dead & Bloated at The Country Club, Reseda, CA, 03/03/1990)

Another demo (the 1992 *Experiment in Fear*...) followed, and slightly afterwards Evol felt into obscurity, only to come back in 2017. The early 1990s was a hard time for a crossover band (however great that band might have been), and the explosion of grunge in 1991 led this scene back in the underground hardcore scene.

The resurrection of Evol was marked by the release (at last!) of all their demos into one 10-inch record, the 2016 *Experiments in Fear 1988-1992*. Imagine a more evil-sounding Excel (*Split Image* era), blended with some Beowülf (second LP era) and No Mercy (LP era). Crazy, inspired, fast and full of memorable songs-this was the demo era output of Evol. I love the fact that they also have included some more frantic influences here and there (such as Cryptic Slaughter). Songs like 'Cyco-Self' will make you bounce on the walls, while 'Experiment in Fear' carries a wicked bass line reminiscent of Excel (*Personal Onslaught*); this is just stuff that will turn you into a mosh beast!

"I liked the smaller tighter sounding clubs" Robert confesses when asked what type of places he liked to play. "Hollywood's Anti-Club was a favourite of mine. But there were some epic shows at the Country Club in Reseda and the Hollywood Palace as well. But the Anti-Club on Melrose was a magic spot. I was told we played with a brand-new Nirvana and White Zombie there, but it's all a blur. Seems like we played with so many important bands!"

And what about the fans? Who were the best? "All I can say is the California and Mexico fans were so dedicated and loyal was amazing" Robert mentions. "And that was our region mostly would just do L.A. to Mexico and back. A mini tour would be two Los Angeles shows, then to Orange County for a show, then to Riverside, maybe a Vegas, then down to Mexico and back. That's how we worked. One week mini-tours. It was the 1980s and anything you can imagine pretty much happened. Girls, partying, violence…"

(Evol, Uncle Slam, Butcher Therapy gig at The Anti-Club, Hollywood, 10/01/1992)

The comeback of Evol in 2017 was followed by the digital release of a new song, the excellent 'Collapsion', where they were accompanied by their old-time friend, Dale Henderson of Beowülf. Another great anthem in the Evol catalogue, even though it sounds more pissed and tough guy now!

Evol are still (2026) active, playing local shows from time to time, and it's a damn shame that they don't release any record-who knows why? "Today is not the way it was back in the eighties" Robert concludes our discussion. "Everything is safer now and controlled. There was a real danger back then. We designed our songs to get the place slamming and bring out the beast in you. Even with all these heavy bands out today, there is less edge and rawness compared to what Evol and our peers were creating. Digital age softened and controlled the whole process".

At a glance: Have also to mention that Jeff Rogers was the second drummer of Evol, and right now it's Moyer Smith. Obviously, Evol are a mandatory band if you are into early Excel, Suicidal (*Join the Army* era), No Mercy and the Venice sound in general. Wish there were more new bands playing this style today!

HIRAX

(Hirax 1986 band picture)

Hirax is one of the most long-standing bands in thrash metal, that however went to incorporate crossover elements in their music in their second LP (*Hate, Fear and Power*), something that they keep it up to this day in each release. Formed in Buena Park, California in 1981 as LA Kaos, they released one demo in 1983 of classic heavy metal, before changing their name to K.G.B. in 1983 and then to Hirax. Hirax in 1984 released a four-song demo that fans of obscure and classic heavy/speed metal have high esteem of, while the first hints of a crossover approach are evident on the 'Battlecry' song, that clocks around 1 minute and 30 seconds.

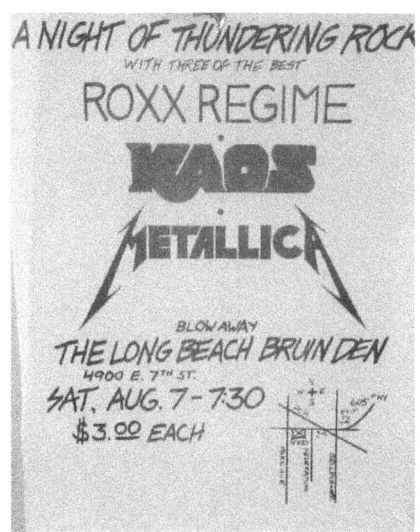

(Hirax as LA Kaos gig flyer with Roxx Regime and Metallica, 07/08/1982)

Guitarist Scott Owen joined Hirax after this demo, and the lineup now included also Katon W. de Pena (vocals), Gary Monardo (bass) and John Tabares (drums). Scott Owen regarding his influences while he joined Hirax narrates that "I was listening to metal exclusively; I liked the attitude and look and beat of punk, but metal was my main interest. This would have been in the early 1980s, so I was listening to things like Iron Maiden, Saxon, Judas Priest, UFO and of course the old classic bands as well. I think the mix of music I was exposed to in California in the 1970s and 1980s was a big part of the way I wrote and wanted to play".

Hirax had contacts with worldwide underground via Katon, who was a fanatic tape-trader, and he was intrigued by both extreme metal of the era, as well as the hardcore and punk scene; you can spot him in photos as early as 1984 wearing a Neos T-shirt! This was always beneficial for Hirax, starting with their inclusion in the UK *Anglican Scrape Attic* Flexi disc 7-inch compilation (1985), that was compiled and distributed by Digby Pearson (later Earache founder) and Heresy's Kalv Piper. Hirax offered their 'Destruction and Terror'; a bombastic thrash metal track with a slight crossover edge, and the operatic/unique vocals of Katon (the compilation also included excellent tracks by Execute, Lip Cream, Concrete Sox and Sacrilege). I have to be honest, initially I couldn't stomach his vocal style, however over the years, I changed my mind! It's definitely a matter of taste, however Katon's vocals make Hirax's music so easily recognizable.

"The band's sound evolved noticeably, from the more traditional heavy metal feel of the early demos to an intense, fast, and aggressive crossover style" Scott admits. "When I was young, I always wanted music to be faster and the guitars to sound more distorted. I always liked live albums because the songs were faster, the music was harder, and more improvised. As far as Hirax the sound of the band in the demo days was established by the first members of the band. The demo is what I learned to try out for the band. Katon had the vision to change the musical direction of Hirax. The band members that were part of the demo days decided that they didn't want to play faster, heavier and more aggressive so they left the band. That's when drummer John Tabares and I entered the picture. That explains the drastic changes in music from demo to *Raging Violence*. Different band members added different styles to the music and more practice also".

Raging Violence was the first full-LP of Hirax, released in 1985 (Metal Blade Records), and inclusions by some already famous underground people are on itn; the record cover was designed by Septic Death's Pushead, while the Hirax logo was created by Celtic Frost's Tom G. Warrior. The music was faster and harder than before, and the lyrics weren't only in the traditional metal style but also focussing on the threat of (nuclear) war. Some of the best Hirax songs are included here, such as the mental 'Blitzkrieg Air Attack', 'Bombs of Death' and 'Destroy', all having a massive hardcore punk influence.

"I would say that my favourite memories from Hirax include the recording of *Raging Violence*" Scott admits. "The process is what I enjoyed. Everything was new because I had never been in a real recording studio or any kind of studio. The Beach Boys recorded music at the same recording studio. Their gold records were hanging on the walls-it was fuckin nuts! I was only 18 when all this was going on. So, those were memories I will never forget. As far as my favourite release was our self-promoted *Blasted in Bangkok*. We were really starting to come into our own as far as writing music".

(Hirax, Excel, Final Conflict, Fatal Vision at the American Legion Hall, Bakersfield, CA, 02/11/1985)

Hirax were already an established name in the West Coast thrash scene, while having musical and general interactions with the hardcore scene. Hirax started playing shows alongside bands like Dark Angel, Excel, Suicidal Tendencies or Megadeth.

"Back then I had a few bands I liked that would fit the crossover description" Scott adds. "Beyond Possession, COC, D.R.I. I also liked a lot of punk bands like Final Conflict, Dayglo Abortions and of course the Bad Brains. The genre crossover wasn't really used then-it's more used now than back in the day. We were just all hard metal or punk, didn't really defined as much as the bands and genres do today… One crazy show regarding crossover that I can think of was a show when we played in our hometown. It was at the beginning of mixing punk and metal crowds together to play. We had a punk band called the Pig Children play before us. They did a great set that I really liked, but our Hirax fans didn't that much so they stayed in the back of the venue and basically didn't give them a chance or support. When we came on, the crowd ran upfront and started going crazy. This really pissed of Pig Children, and they just started beating our fans in the pit along with their fans and it was getting ugly. Katon finally lost it after our friends and fans were getting smacked around so he leaped off the stage and started fighting with the other band. Then our drummer John jumped in the crowd, then me and we were all fighting side by side. Crazy awesome days!".

So, it obviously wasn't all cool back then, and chaos would erupt when the two subcultures would meet- something that would drastically change in the later years. Hirax though continued on with their 'thrash metal with an added hardcore flavour' formula, something that I believe that they perfected it in their next release, the 1986 *Hate, Fear and Power* LP; faster and crazier than before. With Katon's style more into the hardcore, the lyrics focussing mostly on social/political commentary, and the inclusion of the madman Eric Brecht on drums (brother of Kurt of D.R.I., as well as ex-D.R.I., Death and Suburbanites) this is my very favourite Hirax record. Short, fast and sweet. Songs like 'Hate, Fear and Power', 'The Plague' or 'Blind Faith' are just explosion of energy. Did I also mention that the cover artwork got a treatment by the great punk designer Mad Marc Rude?

(Hirax, Aggression, Ons, Habeas Corpus at The Mason Jar, Phoenix, AZ, 15/06/1986)

"Some of my greatest memories then would include visiting the Bay Area and meeting tons of Bay Area musicians" Scott smiles. "Like my old bandmate Paul Baloff of Exodus, the Metallica boys and parting with them at their house. Something that sticks in my mind from those days is smoking a joint with the late great Cliff Burton in an alley next to the Mabuhay Gardens Club in San Francisco. Katon ran up to me and said 'would you like to smoke some bud with the bassist of Metallica?'. I said 'let's fuckin go' and 2 minutes later we were smoking it up. All I remember is being so high!".

The first period of Hirax ends with the excellent *Blasted In Bangkok* 1987 cassette, where Hirax adopted a metal crust sound (like early Concrete Sox), and blended it with some Celtic Frost influences, with political lyrics. 'Beginning Of The End' and 'Dying World' are definitely some the best and most raging songs they ever wrote, total crossover style in both!

Blasted In Bangkok signalled the end of the first period of Hirax, with members moving towards other projects and bands too numerous to mention. Let's just refer to Katon's Phantasm and House of Suffering, Scott's Piranha and currently in Uncivil War, Eric Brecht in Attitude, Gary Monardo in Weapon 13 and Cold Blood alongside John Tavares). Hirax revived in 2000 and since then they are active (2025) and released four LPs and many 7-inchs and split EPs, while now the band's only steady member is Katon, with numerous musicians appearing alongside him.

At a glance: While Hirax are first and foremost a thrash metal band, their 1980s releases had a specific crossover and hardcore influence; in terms of more metal stuff, their *Raging Violence* will appeal to metalheads, while *Hate, Fear and Power* and *Blasted in Bangkok* can have a broader crossover acceptance. I'm definitely more into their hardcore approach.

HAYWIRE

(Haywire band photo 1988)

From California's Orange County, Haywire rooted in the hardcore punk scene and formed in 1988 after the demise of Half Off. Half Off was a good hardcore band with at least one great release, the 1987 *The Truth* LP. Guitarist Rick Greeno narrates their story of formation: "John Bruce (the bassist) and I worked at the same job back in the eighties. We liked a lot of the same music and became friends. He was playing in Half Off, and after they broke up we talked about putting a band together. Vadim Rubin became the drummer, and we started looking for a vocalist. Eventually, Billy Rubin came to one of our band practices and liked what he heard. He ended up being the singer. Everything just clicked".

Before getting into the Haywire story and discography, there's a crazy trivia that must be shared. Drummer Vadim Rubin was the producer in Dark Angel's *We Have Arrived* LP, as well as Overkill's self-titled 1985 EP-Vadim was actually the co-founder of Metal Storm alongside Mike Siegel (a firefighter!). The label was financed by David Thomas Richards, the man behind Azra Records, Iron Works, Trans-Euro Records, World Metal Records, Masque Records and Half Ass Recordings, whose fascinating story you can check out on YouTube, a documentary of Aarol Films channel named as *Hollywood's Weirdest Record Label*.

(Haywire live, courtesy and date unknown)

Haywire's first release was a split 7-inch with fellow Californians Left Insane that contributed two wacky instrumental hardcore songs. The record was included in Al Quint's zine *Suburban Voice*, issue #28. Two powerful offerings from Haywire, and their crossover that was more controlled, like a more metal hardcore version of Motörhead, and "Friend without a Face" is a good tune. "For me it was Motörhead" Rick admits, regarding the first crossover band. "They were one of the bands that was liked by both punks and metal fans in the early days. I knew a lot of punks who started playing in metal bands. They still maintained a punk attitude but changed musically. The speed and aggression were still there, and people seemed to pick up on it".

"When I was young my influences were the hard rock bands my older brother played" Rick confesses. "As I began to discover things on my own, late seventies/early eighties California punk had a huge impact on me. Once I discovered Motörhead, everything changed. I also began listening to bands like Discharge, Slayer and Exodus….in terms of crossover, it seemed like punks were more accepting of it than metalheads. I knew a lot of punks who liked the first Motley Crue album. Keep in mind, my perspective is from living in Southern California".

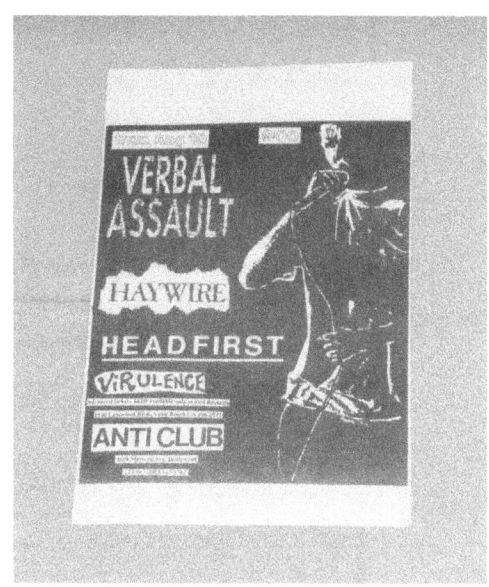

(Haywire, Verbal Assault, Headfirst and Virulence at The Anti Club, Hollywood, CA. 10/08/1989)

In 1990, Haywire were unbelievably prolific, releasing two LPs and two 7-inchs, kicking off with *Private Hell* LP. The LP was a rough and simple, but catchy crossover of thrash with punk, not so much of the hardcore tradition, with a huge Motörhead influence fuelled by their cover of 'Bomber'. I can definitely hear a few Dr. Know or even UK82 elements here and there in songs like 'Latest God' and 'So Good'. My personal favourite is 'Body Politic' the most hardcore song on the record that reminds me of Christ on Parade.

On the other hand, the second LP, *Abominations* had a rougher, heavier edge. Still crossover thrash-punk, only this time the songs were more complex with a weirder edge that isn't as catchy as before. There are a few songs that can catch your attention such as 'Skin Diver' or 'Writer's Cramp'. Overall, *Abominations* is a mid-tempo, heavy crossover. I guess that their shows with Neurosis had a role regarding the influences of this release.

Haywire's final release was the 1990 *Painless Steel* 7-inch where they appeared with NoNoYesNo. Haywire covered Black Sabbath's 'Symptom Of The Universe' and NoNoYesNo covered Judas Priest's 'Breaking the Law'. The live recording was nothing to flip over about; OK stuff, nothing too crucial though.

"I liked the visual style of early punk because people could wear whatever they wanted" Rick mentions. "When hardcore began to take over in the eighties, it seemed like things became a bit more regimented. Some of the thrash bands dressed like punks from the earlier years, but with longer hair. I was into that".

Haywire in their existence played numerous shows, supporting bands like Verbal Assault, 7 Seconds, Neurosis to name a few. Rick admits that "I don't recall seeing a lot of violence at Haywire shows because we formed in the late eighties after crossover had already been accepted. In the early days however, I remember seeing violence at shows over something as trivial as a haircut or T-shirt. There were also instances where a band would be harassed during their set".

"My favourite crossover show in the heyday of crossover is definitely this: D.R.I., Slayer, Overkill, Metal Church and Blast, 1986 at the Olympic Auditorium, Los Angeles. It was wild!" Rick narrates, adding that "however, my favorite place to play was the Country Club in Reseda. The club I miss the most is Bogart's. It was in Long Beach".

Haywire called it a day in early 1991, with Rick coming back to music with Boneshift (post-punk) and Pagan Revenge (stoner-rock). Out of all the other members of Haywire, only Vadim played for a while with the indie/hardcore combo of Ice.

"One story that stands out for me was a small show that took place in a warehouse" Rick offers. "I honestly can't recall what bands played, but there was a rollaway door at one end of the building opposite the stage. One of the bands was playing and suddenly the crowd surged forward, there were bright lights shining on the band. Someone had driven a truck through the rollaway door and it was halfway in the room. People toward the front couldn't hear it due to the volume of the music. Thankfully, no one was hurt. Unfortunately, the show had to be shut down because the door was destroyed and the sound would probably alert police since it wasn't legal".

And concluding his thoughts, Rick adds that "I do think that crossover is still relevant, but it became blurred because of all the different genres you hear about these days. There are a lot of young punk and metal fans who have never heard the name 'crossover'."

At a glance: I think that crossover fans will definitely enjoy the first LP of Haywire (*Private Hell*); for me, it is their brightest moment, full-on assault of thrash punk, not too extreme, but definitely punchy. Pushead art fanatics, get *Abominations* because of Pushead's cover art!

THE MOFO HOMEBOYS

(The Mofo Homeboys band picture 1988, credit unknown)

The Mofo Homeboys was a mystery band for me. They were comprised by members that played already in well-known bands such as Agent Steel, Dragonne and Letchen Grey that in music terms, they were strictly heavy metal. With the exception of Agent Steel, the other bands never enjoyed any exposure even though their musical output was good. Formed in Canoga Park, California, bassist Michael Zaputil narrates their story: "The Mofo Homeboys were formed in 1985 by Tom Baile, vocals and guitar, and Dave Naditch, drums. Their influences were rather typical, Zeppelin and Metallica mostly, I got to know them in 1987 when I was working at Gazzarri's on the Sunset Strip when they were playing their first club shows. Other than Tom and Dave they had a revolving bunch of guys in the band that I also got to know. Finally, they settled on Augusto "Ed" Mendez on lead guitar. It was at this time that the breakup of Agent Steel that I was playing was finalized. Tom then approached me about joining up. I became interested in the change in the band, they were still kind of a metal band but Tom finally got comfortable in his shouting style of vocals, he didn't actually 'sing' really as much as shout the lyrics in rhythm. His prose was also very poetic, not too metal really. Lyrics dealt with insanity, loss, government overreach, world war, the song 'Planets Blues' final verse: 'Stars fell from the sky/as we watched the angels fly/the world was bought by some greedy men/and now it's time for the world to end'. I contributed songs as well, at beginning I was writing Slayer-type thrash metal, but we were changing into more of a punk rock band, our audience was going in that direction as well…The bands we played with at shows were more and more punk than metal bands. We were playing with Wasted Youth, Sick of it All, MX Machine, Dead and Bloated and other hardcore punk bands more than metal bands".

"In my opinion it was the Plasmatics from NYC" Michael replies when asked about the first crossover band. "But I don't think it was a contrived, intentional move, just a progression to what Wendy O. Williams was interested in doing later in her career. I will say this; I loved their music when they were an actual punk band much more than later when crossing over to metal which I thought was a very contrived move to go with the times as they were in the early 1980s. The first two records *New Hope for the Wretched* (1980) and *Beyond the Valley of 1984* (1981) were pure gold, just fan-fucking-tastic! By the time of *Metal Priestess* it was just silly, almost cartoon-ish for children, with all the typical skull and pentagram imagery for all to see, then there was that duet with Lemmy… Speaking of Lemmy, I believe it could be said that Motörhead was one of the earliest punk to metal successes, in the early days in the UK when bands like the Sex Pistols and Generation X were taking off, Lemmy was close to all of them and that scene, he always did say he always considered Motörhead to be a punk band, and never metal, but this can be debated of course. I believe they were one of the first true crossovers in a way, but the music to me was never 100 percent punk rock and metal in the first place…it had also blues rock influences".

Regarding his musical influences, Michael surely surprises: "When I was a kid, it was bands like Cream, Creedence Clearwater and the Strawberry Alarm Clock; yes, I'm that fucking old. But really what influenced me to start playing guitar and bass was Black Sabbath and Rush. And not going to lie, had a school chum into KISS who was a really good guitarist who together we were jamming on their stupid songs. But it was a learning curve like anything else. In 1979 I got into punk rock, mostly Black Flag, the Germs, and the Sex Pistols, but what made me the player I am today is the first Dead Kennedys album *Fresh Fruit for Rotting Vegetables*. So, fast, so sick, so powerful it is still a favourite to this day. The bassist Klause Floride directly influenced how I play, fast picking with psychotic arpeggios, barely in the groove. Geezer Butler is also a big influence; my creativity comes from the likes of him. Most modern metal bass players bore me, you really can see why they are always so buried in the mix…Back in the question, even though I am considered part of the metal community, it was punk and other weird bands like Be-Bop Delux, Oingo Boingo and the old early Alice Cooper band that were my main influences. Dennis Dunaway the bassist of that original Alice Cooper band especially, the dude is amazing, and best matches my own style of play".

(The Mofo Homeboys 1990 gig flyer at The Country Club)

"I believe that the crossover was a natural progression, more and more punk influenced bands wanted to go somewhat heavier, like metal, but wanted to retain punk type vocals without high-pitched screaming, as well as subject contact that was more politically driven, as well as more about real world horrors and protest of the society and government of the time" Michael adds regarding the birth of crossover, adding that " Crossover bands were more interested in serious stuff rather than topics about evil and Satan for instance. The songs were more numerous and shorter, guitar soloing not as prominent. Stranger still was that many of these punks grew longer hair, also many of the lyrics having more of an absurdist sense of humour, where thrash bands were mostly trying to be scary and death centred".

The Mofo Homeboys first release was the 1988 *Mofo-Homeboys* demo, containing four brutal and vicious crossover hardcore songs, that sounded like a thrash metal band that was totally on Discharge, Broken Bones and Dr. Know especially on the vocal delivery. My two favourite songs off it are the opener, a frantic 45-second blast 'The Planets Blues' and 'On Earth as It's in Hell'.

"It was a slow progression between the types of bands that played together, at the beginning metal shows stayed metal, with crossover punk bands in the minority. D.R.I. and Suicidal Tendencies were among the first to jump in shows that were mostly metal, then bands like G.B.H. and The Exploited jumped in. In the audience, punks were in front of the stage for their bands, metalheads came to the front for theirs. Yes, there was violence initially, but things calmed down eventually—somewhat. You never knew how things were going to turn out any particular night. The crossover shows I attended at the Balboa Theater in downtown Los Angeles were generally pretty cool, most of the time. Shows at the Olympic Auditorium also downtown got pretty violent, also I must add it really depended on the promoters putting on the show, some would pay for security, some would not. There was also Fender's Ballroom in Long Beach. Metal used to be a regular feature there, then more and more the shows became almost exclusively hardcore punk bands and the more extreme crossover outfits. Another problem at Fender's were violent street gangs from different factions that would show up and beat the shit out of those they didn't get along with as well as band members jumping into the audience to attack perceived enemies and fans of other bands that they hated. One time I went there with Guy Green, who went on to form Obscene Gesture to see D.R.I. and Hirax play. There were members of the Venice Suicidals there and they wanted to beat Guy up. Finally, I had to get him out of there, but he knew I would fight to the end for him, but he was just too scared to try and hang out, so we left. Eventually the Long Beach police forced the venue to close permanently because of all the fights and brawls spilling out into the streets, the same thing happened to the Cuckoo's Nest in Orange County, the cops had enough of all the violence that continued on outside…"

The Mofo Homeboys through their short-lived existence played numerous shows, alongside bands like MX Machine, Eroti-kill, The Grim; they were definitely a part of the hardcore scene, rather than the metal one. "Favourite venues to play, in California: Cuckoo's Nest in Costa Mesa, Country Club in Reseda, Mabuhay Gardens in San Fran, Olympic Auditorium and Balboa Theater in L.A., Fender's Long Beach, any punk dive in the South Bay" Michael recollects, the favourite places to play throughout his career. "Elsewhere—L'Amours, Brooklyn, New York; Blondies Detroit; Scum Club. I know I'm forgetting a lot of places, but pretty much every place I've played in Europe was a blast. What sucks is we were to go tour South America which I've heard great things about but never got the chance…".

The Mofo Homeboys second and final release was the 1990 *Peace in Anarchy* demo. Sounding now tighter, with the musical output being more crossover/thrash, with less motörpunk influences. This demo contained three vicious songs of their brand once again with a definite Dr Know influence and a cover of Black Flag's 'Six Pack'. Stuff that everyone into the East US crossover sound will like!

(The Mofo Homeboys, MX Machine, Eroti-Kill, Pervert City and Demolition live at the Country Club, 16/03/1990)

"I'd say D.R.I. when they first came to California, also the Crumbsuckers and Agnostic Front, all were badass amazing" Michael narrates, adding a story too: "Quick story, in 1988 D.R.I. were auditioning bassists, Juan Garcia knew their manager and told him they should audition me, that I would be perfect. I was sent a copy of their newest release *Four of a Kind*. Played it and thought wow, they're selling out here big time. Actually, I thought it kind of sucked but learned the whole thing note by note. Went to the audition a couple of weeks later and got a bad vibe immediately. The vocalist Kurt Brecht wasn't even there, and the guitarist Spike and the drummer at that time were there, but acted like they wish they weren't; really full of attitude. So, we went through the motions with my audition, then left. It was really a strange experience...OK, back to the question though regarding my favourite crossover shows, those were Corrosion of Conformity, really early before they became boring sludge metal; Obscene Gesture were always great, after they broke up Guy called me up to restart the band, we were in the process of writing new music and getting tight with our new drummer Lamar, and then he passed on. My wife who is kind of psychic told me the morning he passed she had a vision and Guy told her 'Don't cry for me, I'm ok and in a much better place, love you guys'. Anyway, to move on Sick of It All, Evil Dead, 7 Seconds, Dead and Bloated, Uncle Slam, MX Machine, SOD, and pretty much any outfit Billy Milano threw together were all very impressive to me. Hirax, I never cared for, I know many think they are great but I found them to be mediocre, and never could stand their vocalist Katon's 'singing'...By the way, speaking of terrible vocals, even though I was in his band Agent Steel, I always found John Cyriis's vocals to be silly, preposterous, and over the top in a bad way. That high pitched screamo bullshit was never my thing, even when I was into Judas Priest Halford's vocals bugged me…"

"I have so many crazy stories to offer" Michael laughs, "but let's narrow it down to two: one night I saw 7 Seconds with Uniform Choice and Final Conflict at Fenders in Long Beach. I was pretty close to the front of the stage when 7 Seconds was on, some fuck right up front grabbed the vocalist Kevin Seconds around his neck and pulled him down into our pit, immediately all hell broke loose for a good 10 or 15 minutes, Keven finally was able to get back up onstage, the guy who pulled him down was getting pummelled by the crew relentlessly. I was pretty drunk and don't remember much else, but it was crazy. And then, here's a fun memory I won't ever forget, in 1986 when we were touring Europe with Agent Steel where we played a show in Eindhoven, Holland. A few weeks before, John like the spoiled brat he was, was screaming all these demands to Andre, the promoter there on the phone. The night we played, we were playing a cover of Judas Priest's 'The Ripper', which I thought was cheesy, but not my choice. During the guitar solo Andre ran onstage and shoved John off into the crowd. That was the best laugh I had in that whole tour, and today it's on YouTube for all to see…hahaha!".

The Mofo Homeboys broke up later in 1991, and Chris Amesquita now plays in the techno-thrashers Typhon, while Michael Zaputil adds that "Ten years ago when my wife and I were living in Phoenix, I co-founded a crossover punk band called We Steal Copper, we released CDs and played out a lot, both there in Arizona and back here in L.A. There are videos that Bernie Versailles shot and put together, and are on YouTube, I'm the old grey bastard doing my best Dee Dee Ramone impressions fast downstroking like a motherfucker, and they're still at it today, but it's not the same without me".

"Just before the break-up of the band, in 1991 we met Nirvana. We were rehearsing at Sound City in Van Nuys which was a rundown recording studio with a rehearsal hall. Nirvana was there putting the final touches on their new album *Nevermind*. I don't remember many of the details because Tom said I was getting drunk with Chris Novoselic, Nirvana's bass player. I do remember him keep hugging me because we are both Croatian, but not much else!".

Adding his final touch in our interview, Michael is bittersweet regarding crossover, and its relevance with today's music scene: "To be very honest, and it pains me to say this is no, it's not really relevant. Maybe I'm wrong, but the real thing as I know it isn't existing anymore. Now I know bands like Fear and sometimes the Dead Kennedys are still out there schlepping their poor old asses around, but it is literally a night of senior citizens with some younger guys in the band trying to keep things moving. I've seen recent videos of the DKs and D.R.I. and everything is slowed down to old man tempo…The culture has changed, if punk rock is to go on, new young blood must be there to perform it, and I'm just not seeing it out there, but I'm still hoping, that maybe, just maybe a new, young true punk rock resurrection may come up again. Maybe it's just me, I've been asked by musicians who are younger to start projects, and in my notebook, I have a bunch of songs I'd like to record, but at my age I wouldn't further make punk, metal, thrash, crossover, or any other genre I believe in to be looking silly. I'm 63 years old, this music belongs to the young and pissed off, sexy and energetic, ballsy and pissed off like we all use to be, instead of a bunch of old, tired carcasses going thru the motions".

At a glance: Into Dr Know, with a touch of the Venice scene? The Mofo Homeboys' two demos will be a great soundtrack for you. Let's wish a record label re-releases them!

THE END/ THE LIVIND END

(The Living End band picture, 1987. Courtesy of Adam Seagal)

Talking about obscure bands! The End formed in 1985 in San Jose, California after the first downfall of the classic skate punk band The Faction who everybody should check out at least their excellent *Dark Room* mini album. Adam 'Bomb' Seagal narrates their story: "Right around Halloween 1985, the Faction exchanged some phone calls and decided to break up. I've played music every day since age nine or so, and immediately started a new band The End, later The Living End (not the current Australian band). The first 7" and 12" EPs were really just me playing everything, but I was booking a tour for summer 1986 and got Joe Sib on bass (singer for Frontline and later Wax and 22 Jacks), and Loren Ozaki on drums. We toured in the summer of 1986, including CBGB's. Between then and 1990 we toured quite a bit with different lineups and did two full length albums as The Living End, *The Picture that Came with the Frame* and *Road Shock*, before calling it quits".

The first two releases of Adam's new band under the name The End, were the 1986 *Revenge* 7-inch and 1987 *If You Still Believe* 12-inch. Both were released from Adam's IM Records, that was also the label behind The Faction releases. This time, the approach was different to The Faction's skate rock; pumping, melodic and metal punk, that wasn't crossover in the strict meaning of hardcore-thrash, but more like a blend of metal riffs in punk rock. Both those records rule, and I think that songs like 'No Morals' and 'Innocent' are among the best that Adam ever written.

"In terms of who was the first to cross over, locally in San Jose it was probably Executioner" Adam admits. "In the wider world, Corrosion of Conformity was probably the first time I started hearing about the crossover term, but in hindsight it was probably Motörhead before that crossover term existed. In my band The Faction, on our 1985 record *Dark Room* I was pushing for more metal sounds, like 'Tongue Like a Battering Ram', which was the way I processed early Metallica in context of The Faction. I can only speak to why my songwriting in The Faction started incorporating metal riffs, and that's because I was listening to Judas Priest, Iron Maiden, Metallica and the like, and loved the chunkier, more technical riffs. I assume other punk guitarists responded to those bands as well. Faction singer Gavin O'Brien hated them of course. Did I mention that we broke up soon after *Dark Room*? LOL".

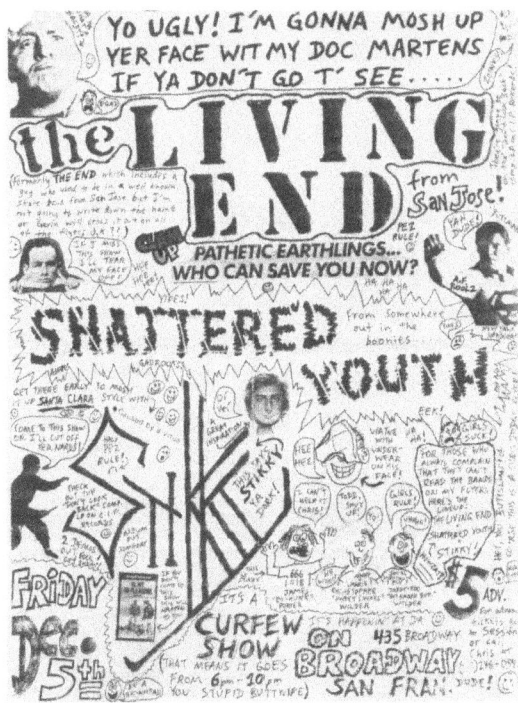

(The Living End, Shattered Youth, Stikky on 435 Broadway SF, 05/12/1988)

Adam then in 1987 recruited John Haugh (guitar), Chris Lentz (bass) and Chris Musgrave (drums) and renamed The End as The Living End, in order to create a proper touring and recording band. "I know there was a lot of tension in some scenes, and even violence. But I will say at some point around 1985 in our scene there was a kinship developing around heavy music. The metalheads could appreciate *My War* and the punks could appreciate *Number of the Beast*. I don't think I witnessed that kind of violence at shows. I remember us skate punks being chased by 'dirt heads', who we associated with metal, but were probably listening to Jethro Tull. Not to harp on 1985, but in Northern California that was the year things really merged. Cliff Burton [of Metallica] came to a Faction show even!".

"I shall say, that overall, in my career I was always influenced by Ramones, AC/DC, Social Distortion, Metallica, Misfits and Iron Maiden" Adam admits. "Plus, visually onstage, it was Angus Young that influenced me, even to switch to guitar. I was primarily a drummer and the first Faction drummer before we ever recorded a record, and when I started seeing pictures of Angus, it really resonated with me that I needed to be in motion when playing music. I even played an SG for awhile, and kept a bit of longer hair to toss it around, which was not punk".

The Living End's first LP release was the excellent *The Picture That Came With The Frame* LP; like a cross between California punk rock of the early 1980s but not hardcore, with classic heavy metal, like Agent Orange gone slightly metal. The songwriting here is just ace. Tracks like the opening 'Sidewalk Home' or the metal-meets-Ramones of 'Do You Remember Rock n' Roll' and 'Can't Stop the Pain' and 'Conscious of Sin' are the highlights of a flawless record. There is actually an indie punk influence creeping in, however the whole thing sounds more like a metal-punk rocker rather than anything else.

"I don't know if, in the moment, I was identifying that change happening" Adam admits regarding the beginning of the crossover. "Certainly *Kill 'Em All* shocked us with its speed for a band that wasn't punk. I do know that Black Flag when I saw them in 1986 was really heavy and showed some Sabbath influence, and I was thinking that at the time - that this wasn't one-two hardcore anymore. They're not thought of as crossover usually. Suicidal Tendencies also had tons of shredding leads at all those punk shows, and that really got people thinking punk didn't need to be devoid of that style of guitar playing".

Next and final release for The Living End was the 1989 *Road Shock* CD on Ossum Possum Records. With the band now heading for a more hard rock-heavy metal approach, with a punk influence, it's still good though, albeit more mellow and reminding me of acts like Warrior Soul. Tracks like 'I am the City' or 'Another Day, Another Dollar' and 'Shot Down' are damn catchy, so if you are a fan of this style, get it!

"CBGB's and CBGB's" Adam smiles when mentioning his favourite place to play. "A total disgusting dive bar, with a massive PA, and a crushing amount of history. I played there in 1984, 1985 and 1986. It was our punk mecca, and we couldn't believe we were doing it. That 1984 Faction show came out on vinyl a couple months ago actually, for the first time".

(The Living End band on tour hanging out with Band Tango and Bad English guys. Courtesy of Adam Seagal)

The Living End ended their career later in 1989, but Adam didn't stop playing great music. In the subsequent years initially, he went on to play with 2¢ Worth (punk rock) in the 1990s, then he returned with The Faction in several reformed versions. In the 2010's he played with Dirk Vermin & The Hostile Talent (punk/rock 'n' roll), Kamikaze Prophet$, The Sonic Saints (alongside Chris Moon of M.I.A./Shattered Faith), and These Roving Years. Currently Adam plays with the excellent Suburban Resistance with Kevin Wilcox of The Dents, UV Rays and War Squad), having released five top-notch full LPs of mighty punk-rock 'n' roll! Post-The Living End John Haugh played with the grunge rockers Shovelhead, releasing one CD.

"There are so many stories to share as you can imagine" Adam adds. "Well as I mentioned, I met Cliff Burton when he came to see The Faction in 1985, and that stuck with me though it was just a brief 'hey what's up?'. In 1984 I think it was Mike Muir had a day off of Suicidal Tendencies' tour and jumped in our van for a show way north in California, Arcata I think, near Oregon. I won't go into all that went on, but I learned that someone I thought was a scary L.A. dude was kind of goofy and fun. Hope that doesn't ruin anyone's image of Mike!".

And what about crossover? Can it still hold up to today's standards? "It is, in the sense that mixing those two energies can be magic. I don't think people draw that 'us vs. them' line anymore, which is good.

Probably for younger people it's hard to imagine that two styles with so much in common were once at war with each other in a way".

At a glance: I love The Living End, and I wholeheartedly believe that *The Picture That Came With The Frame* LP (or the double LP collection) will please every crossover fan, though with a taste for more melodic combinations of metal with punk! That said, get at any cost at least three The Faction records; *Dark Room* and *Epitaph* are my favourite ones. And check out Suburban Resistance too of course!

WASTED YOUTH

(Wasted Youth metal days lineup, 1988. Courtesy of Greg Morgan)

Formed as early as 1979 as L.A.'s Wasted Youth, this Los Angeles, California wild hardcore outfit range amongst the most classic bands of their era and style, alongside Circle Jerks, Fear, Black Flag etc. They went later incorporating more heavy metal stylistic approaches both musically and visually. Wasted Youth gained following of some of the hardest punks in the USA, since the Los Angeles punks of the late 1970s-early 1980s were fearsome to say at least, as mentioned by people that lived that scene or as referenced in books such as *Disco's Out...Murder's In!: The True Story of Frank the Shank and LA's Deadliest Punk Rock Gang*. So, Wasted Youth in their early days performed exclusively with hardcore punk acts such as 45 Grave, Social Unrest, China White, Social Distortion and Breakouts, and so was their musical approach initially.

In 1981 they released on the small indie ICI Sanoblast their first, now classic LP, *Reagan's In.* ICI Sanoblast released only four records. All of them are total prototypes of great L.A. hardcore punk with the other ones being The Lewd's *American Wino*, Eastern Front LP compilation and the glam punk forgotten gem of Zolar X named *Timeless* LP, and *Reagan's In* is just as snotty as you can imagine. Vicious, powerful, nihilistic hardcore punk that sounds like a tighter Germs, a more chaotic Circle Jerks, an obvious influence, since Chett Lehrer was the brother of Keith "Lucky" Lehrer, the drummer and one of the founding members of Circle Jerks or even a darker and simpler Adolescents. With great songs like 'Problem Child' that actually reminds me of Posh Boy bands like Agent Orange too, the crazy 'Born Deprived' and of course the opening, anti-authority anthem of 'Fuck Authority'. Actually the only bitter aspect of *Reagan's In* is 'Uni-High Beefrag', with its ridiculously sexist lyrics. Other than that, it's a mandatory record of that scene, up there with *Adolescents*, *Group Sex* or *Fear of Life*. And did I mention that it also includes one of the most iconic record covers, that happens to be Pushead'a first record cover offering, here credited as Pushead Lamort and that the back cover of the album features Edward Colver's photograph of an upside-down stage diver in midair?

(Wasted Youth, Red Cross, Social Distortion, Overkill LA and the Disposals at Bards Apollo, Santa Monica, California, 03/07/1981)

The initial recording lineup of Wasted Youth included Danny Spira (vocals), Chett Lehrer (guitar), Allen Stiritz (drums) and Jeff Long (bass), but things changed radically. It took Wasted Youth five years to release their second LP due to them being inactive from 1983 to 1985; the 1986 *Get Out of My Yard*, was released on their own, on vocalist's Paolo Rossi indie label, Open Circle Records. By now, Jeff Dahlgren, frontman after Allah Akhbar (1983–1985), left the band, Paolo Rossi took his place with Joey Castillo as the new drummer and Bryen was the new bassist. The result, sounded exactly like the sophomore LPs of Adolescents (*Brats In Battalions*) or Circle Jerks (*Wild in the Streets*), albeit slightly more metal. Still in the hardcore punk vein, only this time not as inspired or as classic as *Reagan's In*, *Get Out of My Yard* contained some terrific songs such as the frantic 'Blind Nuns' or 'Missionary Imposition' next to some mediocre such as 'Happy Birthday'. *Get Out of My Yard* is still a very good record, however, somewhat uneven.

(Wasted Youth, Slam, The Dehumanizers, Token Entry and Vampire Lesbos at Knights of Columbus Hall, 04/08/1986)

Wasted Youth continued to be a seminal band in the Los Angeles hardcore scene, appearing in 1986 and 1987 alongside other contemporaries like Nip Drivers, Descendents, T.S.O.L. and Bl'ast!. However they went on hiatus in 1987, only to come back a few months later with Bryen leaving and being replaced by Dave Kushner, with Rick Seccombe joining on second guitar. This is where the story of crossover Wasted Youth starts: "The band had been trying out guitarists for about a year through a recycler ad and me and two friends tried out at Chet's dad's warehouse in Canoga Park in '87. I jammed my riffs with their drummer Joey Castillo and they asked me to join. I used those riffs and some new stuff for 90 percent of the music for the *Black Daze* record, which we recorded at Prairie Sun studios north of San Francisco" Rick narrates.

"For me crossover was because I wanted to hear better musicianship, tonality, longer, harder, faster songs" Rick adds. "The culture changed in that it got wider to include metal and they fit right in… D.R.I. is the first I remember using the term and making a deliberate change. It seemed both sides welcomed it. I don't remember anything negative. There was rarely any violence, if caused by a culture clash. Some metalheads and old timers didn't understand slamming and resisted it but caught on in time".

Rick also offers the band's (and his) influences at the time of *Black Daze*; "Regarding punk, these include Black Flag, Bad Brains, Agression, GBH, TSOL, CH3, Anti-Pasti, first Wasted Youth LP, Social Distortion, Redd Cross. As for metal, it's Motörhead, Metallica, Black Sabbath, early Raven, Slayer,

Exodus... My clothing style though was influenced by cholos and dads: button down collared shirts, vintage or used slacks - full break with cuffs, used black hard sole dress shoes, flannels".

So, in 1988 Wasted Youth released on Medusa Records, a subsidiary of Enigma Records, their final LP, *Black Daze*. I can recall the day and the place that I got this record, about in 1996. I was already heavily into crossover, and it didn't leave me a great taste initially; however, this changed the subsequent years. *Black Daze* is definitely a brilliant crossover LP minus the Van Halen cover, and the lyrics of 'Ordinary Woman', that reminds me of the direction that Leeway took. Actually, it sounds like something in between the first and second Leeway records. Technically challenging, weird and catchy crossover thrash, with great songs like the instrumental 'Bucket Head', the powerhouse of 'Gang Violence', and of course 'Good Day For A Hanging' (that went on to become the band's first and only videoclip, depicting a motorcycle spinning amongst concert-goers in a mud-pit). "Troy Gregory wrote some and arranged most of the song 'Black Daze' and my old drummer Marc Neville wrote the main riff for 'Any Gun Can Play' and 'Gang Violence'. Chet had some riffs in various songs as well" Rick adds.

(Wasted Youth with Manowar at the Country Club, 11/02/1989)

Post the release of *Black Daze*, Wasted Youth went to perform with hardcore acts such as D.I. and Last Round Up as well as with metal bands like Manowar (!), Exodus or Death Angel. Rick mentions that "I loved playing at clubs mostly... Dancing Waters, Cuckoo's Nest, Country Club, Palace, Palladium, Whiskey...some of the craziest things I've seen in my life happened there: John Macias from Circle One dominating the pit in L.A. in the very early 80s at least. Riots and pits at the Palladium, giant pit at Motörhead and Venom, three days ear ringing after Motörhead at the Palladium, cops hitting on punk girls at Suicidal show near Venice and punks telling them they might have a chance if they shaved their moustaches! Watching Motörhead, Venom, Metallica, Bad Brains, all in their prime, fantastic times".

Wasted Youth called it quits later in 1989 with Rick mentioning that "we played until 1989 and were burned out a week away from a national tour when we had a falling out with our manager and quit", and never reformed since then; only as Wasted Ones with members of Wasted Youth and Circle One performing early Wasted Youth songs. As most of you know, Joey Castillo later played for countless bands, including Social Distortion, Danzig, The Bronx, Bloodclot, Queens of the Stone Age. Dave Kushner played in Danzig, Velvet Revolver, and Electric Love Hogs among many others. Regarding other earlier members, Jeff Dahlgren is an actor in the London-based film-mini-series *Kosmos*, and the French thriller film *Giorgino*. As a studio guitarist he has played on the highest-selling albums in French history and as lead guitarist performed in the largest grossing tours in Europe. Jeff Long on the other hand, played for several years on Savage Republic. You can read their story in the book, *We Can Be The New Wind*.

"Crossover now seems to be diluted maybe by the addition of so many other mixed styles" Rick concludes. "It appears to have expanded to larger genres, industrial, hip hop, etc. Excellent examples throughout".

At a glance: Hardcore punks reading this book of course know and love *Reagan's In*. It's one of the most classic L.A. hardcore records, in a time that the quality bar in that scene was way above high. I'm a completist, that's why I have all their records; however *Black Daze* is wholeheartedly recommended to everyone into the late-1980s riffing crossover thrash like Leeway but also get *Get Out of My Yard!* too. It contains some great songs. Did I mention that Wasted Youth appeared on the soundtrack of *Leatherface: The Texas Chainsaw Massacre III* with their song 'The Gift of Death'?

RESISTANT MILITIA

(Resistant Militia band picture 1989, courtesy unknown)

Since 1986 one of the loudest, political and uncompromising crossover acts, and still active in 2026, Resistant Militia from El Monte and Los Angeles, California were rooted in the hardcore punk scene, only to add metal leanings into their sound. "Initially I was a lone wolf looking to form or join a pack, and while going to punk shows at the Olympic Auditorium in L.A., I met Russel (Russ, who played drums) and Donald who played bass" vocalist Anthony Rezhawk narrates. "Not long after that, I met Hector at school. He was a metal guitar player who'd never been into punk. He didn't really know the culture or the music; he was a 100 percent metalhead. At that point, we had all the elements we needed, and our pack was complete. Donald was a talented fingerpicking bass player, one of his main influences was Steve Harris [Iron Maiden]. Russel was a natural for what today people call D-beat. He would mix D-beat with thrash, this would give us a good and solid crossover rhythm section. And Hector was influenced by Black Sabbath, Slayer, Metallica, Hendrix, Iron Maiden, etc. My influences vocal-wise were Motörhead, Possessed, Celtic Frost, Hellhammer, etc. So, between three punk rockers and a metalhead, we created what was a natural alchemical blend of metal and punk. When it came time to writing music, we all agreed that we would break the punk rock establishment rules and mix in metal elements, such as playing guitar leads, using growl vocals, using effects on the bass and guitars. We were pretty much a crusty metal band playing d-beat thrash punk…"

"Discharge hands down, and Suicidal Tendencies right after" Anthony mentions when asked about the first crossover band. "Most well-known punk rock magazines and zines totally disregarded both bands, saying they were metal, not punk. But their opinion didn't matter much, because the punks eventually gravitated to these bands, as their music was a breath of fresh air for a stagnant and dying scene at that time in my opinion. This crossover took place because some of us liked the aggression of punk rock in the lyrics and attitude and the sonic heaviness of metal. It wasn't just a musical crossover, it was also a crossover of the youth. I came from a very purist form of punk rock philosophically where metal was discriminated against. Mostly because metal, at that time, was associated with the big hair glam metal bands of the 80s in Hollywood, and in the eyes of the punks, glam metal was based on shallow and self-absorbed ideals and attitudes. And bottom line, it wasn't music to mosh to. But it was seeing and/or listening to bands like Motörhead, Hellhammer, Celtic Frost, Possessed, etc., that gave us a different perspective on what metal and its sub-genres could be, which in turn gave us that much needed variety of sounds, tones, and attitude in the musical universe to create with. I'm sure it was the same for the youth that came from metal into the crossover movement".

In 1987, Resistant Militia went on to release their first record, with a contract from Wild Rags Records. Anthony remembers that "while playing one of our first few shows, a man approached us and said he was a producer, he went by the name Mastermind, aka Jim Faroni. He said he wanted to produce a vinyl EP and release it on Wild Rags Records. Wild Rags gave us a $300 budget to record the EP". Ironically, the title of that 12" EP was *Crossover or Die*, but unfortunately, the title didn't make it to the cover, as it was a generic black cover with an imprint that read *Hardcore Demo Series* and a sticker that read 'Resistant Militia produced by Mastermind'. The result was an ultra-harsh sounding piece of vinyl, that sounded like a cross between GISM, early Cryptic Slaughter and Celtic Frost! There are some absolutely crazy moments, such as the opening 'Rotten Power' and 'Don't let it be', manic crossover of the highest order, alongside vicious powerhouses such as the Celtic Frost/Slayer influenced 'Slaves' or 'Life Process' that has a resemblance of Amebix. Not only very unique sounding especially for a West Coast crossover band, but Resistant Militia also had a massive political stance, as evident in their songs, with lyrics on anarchism or Native American rights.

(Resistant Militia, Dr. Know, Cryptic Slaughter, Insted and Headstrong at the Balboa Theater, L.A.. 28/03/1988)

Resistant Militia offered a vibe of politics and music in the crossover scene, something that actually shocked metalheads: "For the metal folks it was a culture shock to come into this crossover musical ecosystem where there were established traditions like the DIY culture, zines, cassette tape trading, silkscreen printing, record labels, tours, etc" Anthony adds. "For the punks, the crossover infrastructure was our natural environment, the slam mosh pit was part of our ritual at shows, and the philosophy was that if someone falls in the pit, you'd pick them up. When metalheads came into the picture, a good number of them misinterpreted the slam mosh pit. They would go in the pit and act erratic and even violent, not understanding the mosh pit code of conduct. They would intentionally hit people, and so the punks would gang up on them and jump them. Slowly the metalheads learned the ways of the pit".

A raging crossover beast, Resistant Militia took their cues out of "our musical diet of Discharge, Suicidal Tendencies, D.R.I., Possessed, Destruction, Hellhammer, Celtic Frost…those were the bands we loved back then", and headed to record their second 12-inch *Living By Law* (1989) on Metal Storm Records. On a funny side note, Resistant Militia might have been the only crossover band having released their records on two of the most questionable labels of California, since I know quite a few people and bands being dissatisfied both with Wild Rags and Metal Storm Records. *Living By Law* was a step forward in terms of extremity, compared to their earlier release, and this time the band sounded like it added some influences from the UK Britcore scene of that era, especially Extreme Noise Terror. Another stellar release even though with a very low budget recording is not for the faint-hearted, with crazy songs like the eponymous or 'The Way It Is'. Get it because it is nasty, venomous, and political as it should be.

"Over time the aesthetics of this crossover movement had a metamorphosis, it went from your typical punk or metal fashion to no fashion at all" Anthony mentions, when asked about the aesthetics of crossover. "Bands would be wearing (jogging outfits) sweats onstage. Then when Suicidal Tendencies exploded, their "cholo gangster" look took over the scene by storm. Resistant Militia, however, held down the punk rock fort within the crossover scene by sticking to our mohawks, liberty spikes, combat boots, studded jackets, etc. Eventually we gave in and grew our hair long for a good while, and then went back to mohawks, etc. Later, we picked up the black clad style, which to me had its roots in black metal. So, from the beginning there has been a blending of the two back and forth, music and fashion".

(Resistant Militia, Lethal Gene, Darkness and Terrorizer DIY show, 1988)

Resistant Militia through their existence appeared in almost exclusively alongside hardcore or crossover billings, with shows with bands like M.D.C, Civil Defense, Bulimia Banquet, Youth Of Today, and Insted. "Some of my best memories are from the Olympic Auditorium when Golden Voice, the production company would host the best in UK, American punk, and metal bands of that time" Anthony admits. "There we saw GBH, Bad Brains, Subhumans, Slayer, No Mercy, etc. However, one of my best memories is being at the Vernon Theatre in L.A. for a PR and Triple MMM Productions show featuring Possessed, D.R.I., and Exodus. I actually volunteered to work at that show, so I could see the show for free since I worked the stage. It was a fun show! Good times!".

Resistant Militia kept it up until the early 1990s, then changing name to Resistant Culture in 1990. They appeared on the 1991 *Los Angeles Death Coalition* compilation alongside Fear Factory, Demolition and F.C.D.N. Tormentor and the 1995 *Resistant Militia* demo. They went more metal in these releases, dropping the crazy crossover of the early days in favour of a more death metal-meets-crust-grind approach. This is something that continues to this day (2026) with *Ancient Future* (2000), *Innate Rebellion* split (with Contravene, Resist and Exist and Fallas Del Sistema), *Welcome to Reality* LP (2006) which featured the late Jesse Pintado (RIP) of Napalm Death and Terrorizer on rhythm guitar, *All One Struggle* (2010) LP and the single *Shadowed Man* 2018, all great death metal meets d-beat punk releases.

(Resistant Militia, Fear Factory, Sarcastic, Harsh, Silent Scream, Hardcore 918V, WarDance at Coconut Teaszer. 12/01/1991)

With many stories under his belt, Anthony offers some final words: "At one point Resistant Militia decided to add a second guitarist, so our friend Jesse Pintado joined us for a little while. Unfortunately, he was a teenager without wheels. He depended on his dad for a ride to practice, which was at least an hour each way, and eventually Jesse's dad told him he couldn't bring him to practice anymore. That's when Jesse put together Terrorizer in his local neighbourhood. Another story to share would be that at the beginning of this crossover movement in L.A., the clubs would frown upon the scene and wanted nothing to do with it, especially for bands coming from the east side of the city. So, it was up to the youth and community to make it happen. Most of the shows took place at people's backyards, where it was Better Youth Organization and/or they would have keg beer, etc. Sometimes the shows would take place in halls, gyms like Hoover Park, etc. One of many crazy stories is the time we were playing at the 'dust bowl' (someone's backyard) in East L.A. I was going in and out of the pit, and while I was standing, watching the pit and the band at the same time, a butterfly knife came flying out of the pit and it almost hit my head. LOL... As a matter of fact, that was the night Jesse introduced me to Commando Pete, Terrorizer was playing that night too. More good times! That said, I miss so much those clubs: Hoover Park in L.A., California, Anti Club in East Hollywood, California, and Fender's Ballroom in Long Beach, California".

Anthony also appeared in the comeback LP from Terrorizer, *Darker Days Ahead* (2006) and *Hordes of Zombies* (2012) alongside Katina Culture. Resistant Culture are keeping the flag high till today (2026), playing alongside mostly anarcho-punk and hardcore bands.

"Absolutely, it's always going to be relevant" Anthony discusses about crossover. "The only thing is that the people playing the music sometimes don't understand or know the origins and roots. Today the parents of all 'extreme' music are either punk, metal, or goth in my opinion. Crossover is alive and well. In the case of Resistant Militia's crossover style, it became what today is crust metal-crust punk".

"If it's possible I'd like to acknowledge the musicians who played in Resistant Militia over the years who were not mentioned in this interview: Eric Ross (guitar), Jimmy Sotelo (drums), Tom Montez (bass), Carlos (guitar). Also, I'd like to shout out to some of the awesome bands we played with regularly; F.C.D.N. Tormentor, Latchkey Kids, Darkness, Bloodcum, Necrophagia, No Ones Ally, Yapo, Dissension, Civil Defense, Apocalypse, 918-V, and last but not least Terrorizer".

At a glance: Resistant Militia will surely make happy those ones into the most extreme side of crossover; I believe that fans of e.g. early Cryptic Slaughter, Impulse Manslaughter or darker sounding stuff such as Lobotomia or early Ratos De Porao, will definitely enjoy both their releases, without excluding though fans of British crustcore such as Deviated Instinct or Hellbastard. The Resistant Culture stuff will appeal to fans of Napalm Death, post-2000's stuff. Bands like Resistant Militia were a sheer joy for me to introduce and review, not only because of their music, but their always relevant politics.

MIDWEST AND MIDDLE AMERICA

Like many places, there was a massive division in Chicago between the metal and punk communities back then. While metalheads were always looking for something heavier, the punks were always ahead of the curve in terms of speed and aggression. It was the narrow mindset of the metal scene versus the judgemental views of the punks that caused this.

Something had to change for better or worse, there were far too many younger people growing up into both sides. I think that here, when a new breed of metal band like Zoetrope started playing gigs with bands like the great Articles of Faith, it was fuckin' amazing. It put everyone in the same room and made you acknowledge each other. It inspired creativity, shared with the same passion. I'd like to think that it was for the best though sometimes it really wasn't. Progression isn't always good or bad, is it? Haha! --Karl Patton, vocalist of Impulse Manslaughter, Nam Land, Alehammer, Gutterhead and Warfilth

WHOPPERS TASTE GOOD (W.T.G.)

(Whoppers Taste Good live 1987. Courtesy of Gary Philips)

I've been on the hunt for Whoppers Taste Good since the release of *Crossover The Edge*, and instead, they found me first! Vocalist Gary Philips got *Crossover The Edge* and made a post on Facebook telling 'find this guy!' Truth is, that I really wanted to find W.T.G., since they are the first and the best crossover band that was ever out of St. Louis, Missouri. Formed in 1986, I can recall the U.K.'s Vinyl Solution Records distro leaflet selling their *Don't They?* 1987 EP, calling it 'foodcore-wild and fast fun' or something like that, and I knew that I had to find it somehow!

But let's Gary narrate their story: "I kept seeing Rick Ulrich (guitar) and Tim Goggins, aka 'Whitey' (bass) behind Mississippi Nights concert venue drinking before shows. I was already an alcoholic and so were they, and back when we were underage, the goal was to get as fucked up as possible and wait until the last second before we went into the show. I saw then for like the fifth show, after Accept, Exciter, Mercyful Fate and Slayer in a row when I went to see Battalion of Saints in 1985. I was drinking a beer and smoking a joint out back like usual and decided to go up and say hi and in see if they wanted a hit off the joint which neither of them did. But it was our first punk rock show, and I think we were a little scared, but we traded numbers and went in, and it was great. For a first show, it was an experience of a lifetime, locals White Suburban Youth and Drunks With Guns opened.

After that I hung out and drank with Tim and found out they could play instruments. Rick and Mark Deniszuk (drums) had a metal band called Merciless Sin and Whitey and our mutual friend Bill Berblinger (guitar, vocals) had a band called Undead and both bands did 4-track demos. I was just hanging around drinking with them and Bill flaked out on jamming and I happened to have some really stupid lyrics [to] 'I Like Eating' that I had written, and we put them to some of Whitey's new songs. I never dreamed anybody would let me front their band, but they had no one else ahaha! Once we got a few songs thrown together, we recorded our first demo on a Tascam 4-tracker which I did the vocals for in Whitey's apartment where he still lived with his mom, which is why my vocals are so 'whispered' and not 'yelled' on the first demo.

We never, ever took ourselves seriously. The drinking always came first, and band practice was just something to do while we drank. Some of our shows were great, some were train wrecks, but people loved it regardless because we were always funny and entertaining".

Their first demo, the 1986 *Sarcastic Anal Tracks* is as immature, funny and raging as you can imagine; under the layers of lo-fi production noise there are eight tracks of superfast crossover hardcore, with great riffs. 'You're A Termite' has a Suicidal Tendencies guitar riff, that progresses into a speedcore chaos, while 'Rent A Guard' kicks of like Discharge gone metal speedcore! 'Patio Burrito' exceeds all speed limits, and obviously, I'm a fan! Too bad though that I couldn't find anywhere their second demo *Ride the Spike* (1986) to review.

(Whoppers Taste Good, Ultraman, Jetsons and Laffin Stok gig flyer, 17/02/1988)

Regarding their influences, Gary narrates that "we got turned on to punk rock through Suicidal Tendencies. That was the first punk album that leaked to us metalheads because Slayer's singer was in the video for 'Institutionalized'. Alongside A.O.D.- *The Wacky Hi-Jinx Of...* LP; Dayglo Abortions- *Feed Us A Fetus* LP; and G.B.H.- *City Baby Attacked By Rats* LP were the three albums that we loved. Still to this day I put that A.O.D. record in my top 10 punk albums. But that opened the floodgates to everything fast and heavy. COC, Dr. Know, Verbal Abuse, Broken Bones, etc... But then D.R.I.- *Dealing With It* came out and it's basically so great it influenced Slayer's drummer and is the blueprint for punk crossover thrash metal. You can hear bits of ripped off pieces everywhere in the early stuff haha!"

St. Louis metal and hardcore scene included in the 1980s some more known bands like Anacrusis, Ultraman, Terror To Society, Big Fuckin' Deal, The Skitzos, Justified Violence or Drunks with Guns, Conquest and Deeler, alongside more obscure ones like e.g. Dunwich, Axe Minister, Heaven's Flame but overall, it was a very condense scene-and even though St. Louis has a reputation of being one of the most violent cities in the USA, this wasn't the case with the metal hardcore scene; "St. Louis was too small to have any of that skinhead violence or anti-longhair stuff" Garry adds. "Our first show was opening for the Rhythm Pigs at a rented hall. We didn't know what to expect, but everybody was cool, and everybody we opened for always immediately noticed that Rick is an exceptional player. We stuck out though for sure looking like a stereotypical 1980s metalheads bringing in a huge drum set with double-kick drums and Marshall amps".

(Whoppers Taste Good and Beer Frogs gig flyer, 10/04/1988)

W.T.G.'s first release on vinyl was the 1987 *Don't They?* 7-inch on their own label, Papa Whopper Records; sounding now more mature than their demos, *Don't They?* simply shreds. I'm not a fan of the goofy humorous lyrics. In their case not only this works, but it sounds so mental! Fast and fun crossover hardcore with some slight metal influence creeping in. Songs like 'Corinthian Leather Warrior', the ripping 'Bugs For Beer' and 'Beaver's a Wino' are just examples of their genius! Mind that, they sound very fearsome and rough. This contrast with their lyrics is an oxymoron that makes them even more special.

Continuing with the issue of scene violence, Gary narrates that "nobody ever messed with us and in retrospect I think it's pretty cool that the punks were so open minded to us. But when we started getting some shows, they were downtown at Turner's which was in a racially charged neighbourhood that was switching white to African American, but the altercations were also between the whites in the neighbourhood and the punks. They didn't like punk rockers coming into their neighbourhood. It seemed every show there was some scuffling going on outside after it, but the great thing about being longhairs, was that the punks knew who we were, and the neighbourhood locals thought we were one of them, so nobody fucked with us. We're the Whoppers, we're not tough!"

In the 1980s Whoppers Taste Good had the chance of playing many shows alongside both local, and touring bands too; Garry recalling some of his favourite shows mentions that "we got to open for 7 Seconds, Verbal Abuse, The Accüsed, Dayglo Abortions and the Adolescents to name a few but I think just seeing D.R.I. for the first time blew my mind. There was a circle pit that had like 100 kids in it. We never got big, packaged crossover tours in St. Louis, so it was just one good band at a time."

With more fuzzy-sounding guitars, the 1989 *Haunting White Castle* not only spawned a hilarious cover art (taking the piss out of Slayer's *Haunting The Chapel*), but also exhibited great songwriting too, for one more time! 'Prove A Point' is a rager, while 'Lopsided' even reminded me somehow of Dayglo Abortions! The closing 'Sleepin' on the Green Thang' sounds like a car crash between Gang Green and Murphy's Law and Ludichrist, crazy! Another one hilarious info for this release is that the band members were given themselves some nicknames like Whitey Araya, Burger King, Big Boy Lombardo and HawkMan Hanneman!

(Whoppers Taste Good 1990 gig flyer)

W.T.G. kept the flag high in the 1990s too, but sadly, I couldn't find the *Detroit, MI* (1992) demo to review it; however, I found the 2006 *Four Year Debacle* compilation CD, that included two lineup changes with Phil taking over the vocals and Pat now on drums; this is their most metal recording. I firmly believe that metalheads with a love on crossover will definitely enjoy this one, that in terms of recording it reminds me of D.R.I.'s *Full Speed Ahead*. Obviously, I like it, but I miss the snot and rough energy of their 1980s stuff-still though, songs like 'Ride the Spike' and 'John Green' are major thrashers!

Regarding his favourite release, Gary smiles, "this probably is the first 7-inch just because we did it! And we did it ourselves, the recording, the art, the pressing. I can't really listen to it without cringing on my vocals, I didn't know what I was doing, but it didn't matter because it was so cool getting your own music put on vinyl and then holding the finished product in your hands. Just like the excitement of getting a book or zine back from the printer..."

On the same style, the 2007 *Whoppers Taste Good* CD was released on their own Papa Whooper Records; with the exception of the horrible cover (come on guys, you could do far better than that…), this is another one wild thrasher, that included many re-recorded songs from the 1980s such as 'Lopsided', 'Prove A Point' or 'Pissin', alongside new ones like 'Smugglers Blues', 'In Gut We Trust'. Heavy and fast stuff again, and slightly more into the hardcore side of crossover, ace!

Regarding the other bands that Whoppers Taste Good members played before or later, it has to be mentioned that Mark Deniszuk played before in the speed-thrash metal combo Merciless Sin; post-WTG he went on with the excellent punks Ultraman (check 'em out too, many great records of hard-hittin' punk) and Bent. Rick Ulrich was also a member of Merciless Sin, as well as the death-thrashers Vacant Grave and later in Bent. Tim Goggins played in the death-thrashers Undead.

"I think it has seeped into everything as far as being influential, yet every generation seems to have to take it to another level of extremity, so you'd have to ask a kid that one" Garry adds, regarding the legacy of crossover today. "They're doing that karate metal shit now and I'm the old man saying, 'That's not MUSIC!', but most of the metal crossover punk bands are touring still are just playing those classic records and not putting out new stuff. No one wants to hear the new songs. I firmly believe the 1980s was the best time for music. I'm old and I still listen to those old records because they have so many good drinking memories attached to them".

Whoppers Taste Good are (2026) active and offering shows in St. Louis quite frequently.

At a glance: WTG are one of the craziest 1980s crossover bands, with a wild sense of humour, alongside fuzzy, crazy-fast paced speedcore! I have a very soft spot for their first 7-inch, the 1987 *Don't They?*, because it has that rough, underproduced DIY feeling, a very raw, meat n' potatoes speedcore style, where everything crashes and bangs in less than 90 seconds! Crossover kids though more into metal sounds, will also enjoy the *Four Year Debacle* compilation too! Check also the Archive of St. Louis Punk, on https://stlpunkarchive.omeka.net/. Now, somebody get me the two 1980s 7-inchers of W.T.G.! (Last minute add: Gary sent me a package with all W.T.G. stuff as a gift and I'm so thankful for that!)

HYPER AS HELL

(Hyper as Hell various pictures, taken by their Primer At This End – Rock And Roll Liberation Front – Mr. Fixit – Demos 1987 DLP compilation. Courtesy of Hyper As Hell)

A truly blasting combo, Hyper As Hell formed in early 1986 in Kent, Ohio by Donny Vision (vocals), Boom (drums, ex-member of Boom and the Legion of Doom and the excellent hardcore Plasma Alliance-be sure to check out their 1985 *We Can't Wait* 7-inch), Jeff 'Howard' Hutchings (ex-Kien Krieg) and Rich 'Dicky' Gambert (ex-Plasma Alliance), before recruiting guitarist Ron E. Banner in September, solidifying the original lineup. Ron E. Banner alongside narrates that "then came a string of drummers: Jay Lucarrelli, Diane Globbe, Aaron from Mannequin Odd, and Nick Remis. Finally, someone was crazy enough to stick it out for a while. Matt Apanius joined the band and Hyper as Hell started to really jell and started playing with national touring bands like SNFU, COC, D.R.I., Dayglo Abortions, Life Sentence and Dr Know".

Hyper as Hell had a definite hardcore background, and this was evident in their crazy approach of crossover. I couldn't find anywhere their demos that were released from 1987 up to 1993, a total of four. Matt Lindsay, the band's drummer since 1993, was super-kind enough to send me their 2018 double LP compilation of their demos titled *Primer At This End – Rock And Roll Liberation Front – Mr. Fixit – Demos 1987*. Literally, this is hard to review their stuff, without one thinking that I'm exaggerating, but it's just fierce, crazy, underpolished and lo-fi crossover that reminded me of a rawer Dissension, and on their speediest they even sounded like Lethal Aggression. A definite collection for all fans of crossover.

"Early D.R.I., Slayer, MDC, The Crucifucks, Metallica, COC, Decry, Christ On Parade, Die Kreutzen, Celtic Frost, Voivod and lots and lots of acid" Matt adds, regarding their influences, and I can't disagree because their sound was definitely very diverse-Hyper as Hell followed a difficult crossover route.

(Hyper as Hell, COC, False Hope and Sacred Hate Concert at Stambaugh Ballroom, Youngstown, OH. 12/08/1987)

In the 1980s, Hyper as Hell gigged prolifically with dozens of Cleveland bands such as Blood of Christ, Domestic Crisis, False Hope, Sin-Eater, Civil Disobedience, Decimation, Blatant Disregard, Verrucose, Schnauzer and many others. Through their existence they comprised of Donny Vision (vocals), Howard Hutchings (guitar), Richy Ringworm (bass), Ron E. Banner (guitar), Matt Aponius (drums, 1986-1989) and Matt Lindsey (drums, 1993-1994). In their first two periods, 1986 to 1990 and 1993 to 1994, they released four demos; as aforementioned, all included in the double LP compilation. The initial 1990s demos were brutal speedcore, the reformation of Hyper as Hell in 1993 with new drummer (Verrucose's Matt Lindsey) with the demo called *Mr. Fixit* went to incorporate a new approach. Before *Mr. Fixit*, the band mostly did hardcore metal while *Mr. Fixit* was a lot slower and more compared to the likes of late 1980s and early 1990s Bad Brains. The band fizzled within a year of getting back together before disbanding for good in 1994.

Most members lost contact over the years, until the death of Jeff 'Howard' in 2014 in a surfing accident, leading the members to get back in touch. "Also notable in our bio is that Howard Hutchings got sober after twenty years of heroin and numerous near-death ODs, moved to Hawaii and died surfing, unbelievable." Ron narrates. "The band reunited in 2018, and we reissued their last three recordings on double vinyl with bonus 4-track songs never previously released. Matt Lindsey took Howard's spot on 2nd guitar and Matt Apanius rejoined the band for some reunion shows. We are currently (2024) working on some new material".

(Hyper as Hell, The Plague, The Floyd Band, Basket Case and Dick Head gig flyer at Cleveland Public Theatre, 1988)

Matt Lindsey alongside offers that "it is interesting to think about how music influenced other music back in those days before the Internet and when underground music was informing the mainstream music of what was cool. People from different communities would develop different styles of their own, and the bands would tour, and that's how the other towns would learn about your style. Some of us would maintain life-long friendships with the people and bands from other towns that we networked with. Also trading tapes and buying peoples demos in fanzines was a big deal back then…I also had a lot of friends who taped records for each other. Making mixtapes for your friends and getting mixtapes in return was probably the way I learned the most about music in my teenage years. There were no CDs, there were only records and tapes".

Hyper As Hell are active since 2018, and are offering local shows, as well as working on new songs.

At a glance: I'm a sucker for the mental, more hardcore-oriented speedcore of 1980s Hyper as Hell. They kind of remind me California bands like Dissension or Attitude Adjustment-you know the deal, simple riffs, ultra-catchy stuff. So, getting the double LP compilation of *Primer At This End – Rock And Roll Liberation Front – Mr. Fixit – Demos* (1987) will be a treat for fans of this style. *Mr. Fixit* demo on the other hand, is more complex, weirder, but still great crossover!

TRANSGRESSION

(Trangression band picture. Courtesy unknown)

Shane Dabinett's Manic Ears Records was a force to be reckoned with if you were into some of the fiercest hardcore punk stuff around with bands such as Extreme Noise Terror, Ripcord, Concrete Sox etc; as well as if you were an afficionado of worldwide hardcore punk such as Spermbirds, Vicious Circle, Stikky or Sons of Ismael. There was actually a time in the late 1990s when I wanted to collect all the records by my favourite labels: Manic Ears, Better Youth Organisation, Clay, Rough Justice, Toxic Shock, SST etc. This is explained because of the high quality of those labels' releases. So, this is how Transgression's 1988 *Cold World* LP came into my collection when I traded Napalm Death's *From Enslavement* LP for this and Raw Power's *Scream from the Gutter*.

Formed in Indianapolis, Indiana in 1985, by three punk rock kids and joined soon thereafter by two metal heads, with this initial lineup opening for Impulse Manslaughter in Marion, Indiana. A true crossover was born in Transgression, and the bands members were Dino Codalata (guitar), Doug Ketchem (bass), John Zeps (guitar), Matt Van Kersen (drums) and Paul Linhart (vocals). "We were heavily influenced by bands like Cryptic Slaughter, Lethal Aggression, Napalm Death, Extreme Noise Terror, Heresy, Septic Death, Slayer, Larm, COC, The Accüsed, Adrenaline O.D. etc...on the metal side of the fence I loved bands like Sodom, Destruction, Celtic Frost" John Zeps narrates.

"D.R.I., Suicidal Tendencies, Black Flag then S.O.D. perfected crossover in my opinion" John admits. "I think it was the sign of the times when metalheads started attending punk shows. I was one of them haha! I used to get a bunch of weird looks as I was the only longhair at early punk shows especially from skinheads. There was a division then…"

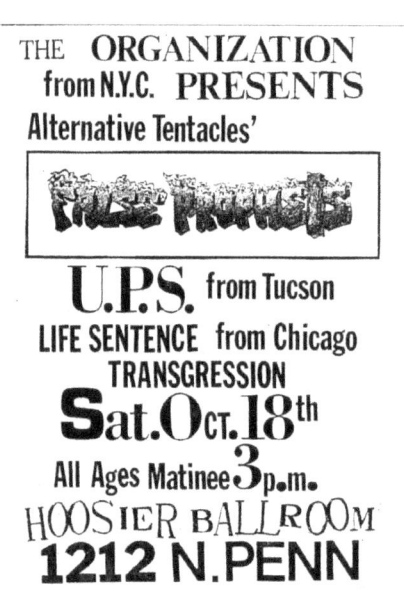

(Transgression, False Prophets, U.P.S., Life Sentence gig at Hoosier Ballroom, Indianapolis, IN. 18/10/1986)

Transgression appeared in their career in both metal and hardcore punk billings, with the likes of Death Angel, Rigor Mortis, D.R.I., Holy Terror, MDC, Toxic Reasons or False Prophets and Life Sentence. This didn't happen out of nowhere; it was that Transgression were just in-between metal and hardcore punk since their early beginning. The frantic 1986 *Transgression* demo sounded like a cross between early Attitude Adjustment, Cryptic Slaughter, Lethal Aggression and Impulse Manslaughter. One can understand that Transgression were fierce and crazy since day one. Songs like 'Mass Hysteria' sound like a galloping thunderstorm coming your way. 'Working Class Dick' even brings in mind the early bombastic styles of D.R.I. and Capitalist Alienation. 'Busted Up' is my favourite tune off this demo, an absolutely rough and mental recording.

"I really loved playing at the Arlington Theater here in town" John adds about his favourite place to play. "That's where we played our most memorable and biggest shows. Also Exit Inn in Chicago…as for my all-time favourite shows in the days of crossover, these must have been shows of Cro-Mags, Raw Power, D.R.I., Napalm Death and A.C."

Pushead offered a raving review of Transgression first demo on *Thrasher* magazine actually calling it as 'this twelve song cassette shows brute strength and packs a mean punch that continues without hesitation track after track'. Transgression's next offering was the 1987 demo of *Better Days*. This time a little more on the D.R.I. style of *Dealing with It* and *Crossover*. *Better Days* is another winner with songs like 'Better Days', or the manic 'Final Conflict'- but I kind of miss the raw energy of the first demo.

Transgression also had an absolute political stance again fascism and Nazis, something that led to quite a few incidents: "We use to call out the racist skins from the stage and remember getting chased by them after our gigs" John recalls. "We narrowly escaped on several occasions. I would be slammed to the ground for headbanging in the pit but didn't let it bother me. Took my lumps early".

(Transgression, Holy Terror and D.R.I. gig at The Arlington Theatre, Indianapolis, IN. 11/11/1988)

It was 1988 and it was time for Transgression's first LP to be released. John narrates that "Pushead's reviews secured a record deal with Manic Ears Records out of Bristol, England which was recorded and produced by Paul Mahern of the Zero Boys". Shane Dabinett of Manic Ears was a fan of the band and offered them a deal. Transgression's only full-LP, 1988's *Cold World* has many old songs re-recorded, as well as new ones in the same style. Transgression released a great record, full of with blasting sixteen songs. It still remains sadly an unknown classic of crossover hardcore. Verging more on the hardcore edge, with metal leanings, songs like 'Go To Hell' or 'Head in the Smoke' are reminiscent of D.R.I.'s crossover period, while 'It's here to stay' and 'Prejudice Kills' are more into the Lethal Aggression and Cryptic Slaughter tradition. Great lyrics too, with 'Won't Bent My Knees' being my favourite tune!

"We even did Anal Cunt's very first tour with them" John recalls. "I remember playing in Chicago at Club Dreamers the night after GG Allin played. There was still shit on the stage and the back wall had GG's last stand spray painted with the date he was supposed to kill himself on!"

Transgression's final stand was the 1989 split 7-inch with the Walnut, California hardcore/crust greats Apocalypse, and this time they went back in their early harsh sound, going for a more extreme approach. Three songs by Transgression, with 'Last Goodbye' being my favourite. Now sounding more like a Larm-influenced crossover hardcore band, this split was a great way to end. Transgression called it a day later in 1990.

John Zeps is still an active musician to this day (2023), playing post-Transgression in Soulpaint (grunge), Ice Nine (hardcore), Burn it Down (hardcore), Majhas (hardcore), Fax Arcana (emo/hardcore), Amongst The Swarm (hardcore), Action Strasse (rock) and Machine Guns and Motorcycles (rock).

"It definitely is still relevant today but not as cool when it was brand new and only a hand full of bands around that you had to seek out pre-internet" John concludes about crossover. "I still wear my early crossover days as a badge of honour growing up in the best of times. It's kept me young all these years and have always played in bands since the 1980s. I'm playing guitar in Drunks With Guns and we are playing NYC and Philly this weekend. Fuck yeah man!"

At a glance: I guess that only a few of you are familiar with Transgression-and this is sad. If you like your crossover political, loud, and heading for an all-out-attack approach (so many UK82 hints here…), you should get *Cold World* LP. I wish though a label would re-release their first demo, it's just A-class crossover blast bomb, for everyone into the sweet sounds of Lethal Aggression, early D.R.I. and early Cryptic Slaughter!

ENVIRONMENTAL HAZZARD

Originating from Cleveland, Ohio's heavy metal scene, Environmental Hazzard had their own story of crossing over from metal to hardcore since their formation in 1988. Guitarist Chris Faiken tells the story: "Environmental Hazzard formed in the late eighties while I was in junior high (8th grade). Two other players were in high school at the time. We got together and played cover songs like Metallica's 'Four Horsemen', Celtic Frost's 'Return to the Eve' and D.R.I.'s 'Five Year Plan'. That version of the band would dissolve, and I took the reins, the name and the spark to start something new. We had found a new drummer who was just in high school also. The band slowly morphed into the band that recorded the first self-titled EP in 1989. That EP contained ¾ of the band that would record our breakout album *One Stands Alone*. The EP was played tirelessly on college and some mainstream radio. It was a hit with the local metal community with the fan favourite being the cut 'Blatant Disorder'. That EP is impossible to find these days!"

Following the typical party metal attitude of the day, Environmental Hazzard initially were formed out of pure fun. "We wanted to play hard-edged music, especially since thrash was really starting to get huge" Chris adds. "We wanted to be like the Big 4. We also were young and wanted to be rock stars. We grew up with the hair bands and those parties looked amazing! We loved to drink beer and play music! Our biggest influences were the Big 4 (Metallica, Slayer, Anthrax, Megadeth) along with Testament and bands like Crumbsuckers, Dayglo Abortions, The Accüsed, D.R.I., Celtic Frost, Queensryche, Dokken, Motley Crue's first two albums, the list goes on. It's hard to give one album that left the greatest impression. I would say Metallica's *Ride the Lightning* and both Crumbsuckers albums were ones that really stand out today. The other guys would say the Crumbs as well".

(Environmental Hazzard, Hatrix, Craw and Screwtractor gig flyer. December 18, 1988)

Environmental Hazzard released on 1989 their cassette EP containing twenty-five minutes of technical thrash metal blended with some hardcore influences; still, this is a bit too typical metal for my ears, however when crossover hits the break, there is a definite charming Crumbsuckers influence 'Rebirth' and 'Gone but Not Forgotten' are really interesting, but I guess that metalheads would be much more interested in this release. "The scene where we lived was insane" Chris recalls. "Cleveland, the city we are based out of is about twelve miles from where we were so the east and west sides had their own thing, but everyone was amazing. We shared the stage with bands like The Spudmonsters, Integrity, Hatrix which became Mushroomhead, Face Value, Winters Bane with Tim 'Ripper' Owens, Hostile Omish, Mutant Soldier. I can go on and on. It was very competitive. The locals treated us like rock stars. It was an amazing time. We played to huge crowds had radio airplay on college and mainstream radio. We had a rabid fanbase which followed us in other bands that we did on our off time".

Time to release a proper full-length CD came, and Chris narrates the story behind *One Stands Alone*: "we went into the studio in 1990 to record the first full length album, *One Stands Alone*. We were self-financed, how we did that I have no idea, but we did it. We were kids, two of us were still in high school. We were approached by a couple of guys who were forming SinKlub Entertainment. They wanted to package and distribute the album, so we said yes. The details are foggy, but I do know that we were the first release on their label. We recorded the scratch tracks with new drummer Dave Zales. We took a few months to add vocals, bass and guitars... a lot of guitars! We did this at famed MARS Recording studios with Bill Korecky engineering and co-producing. We recorded there along with side projects for many years since we were sixteen years old. Bill is the greatest, what a great guy. It was a great time of creativity and learning the way to build a great sounding album, no pro tools back then. It all went straight to two-inch tape. The release took another year or so to come out. It charted on the Loud Rock 100 above Metallica in 1991. An accomplishment I still cherish today. It didn't chart higher than them for long, they are Metallica of course..."

(Environmental Hazzard, Mushroomhead, Embalmer and Hatrix gig flyer. 23/10/1991)

One Stands Alone mixed several and different styles, ranging from the thrash metal of Metallica to Sacred Reich and then to later Excel; by no means an 'easy listening' record. The album shows the progress of the band towards a darker sound, that borders with some crossover elements. It is apparent on tracks like

'What Evil Brings' and 'End of Bickering'. Not my cup of tea (maybe mostly due to the modern metal approach), but still a release that fans of the aforementioned bands will enjoy.

Environmental Hazzard called in quits in 1995 and Chris adds that "our most memorable/favourite show was February 25, 1995. We played the final show at our favourite home concert venue named Flash's. We did a co-headlining gig with The Spudmonsters. What a blast. We run across people still that say they were there, how awesome is that? There were a lot of bands who released their own albums from Cleveland. The Spudmonsters are the most memorable, Breaker, Hatrix, Severe Warning, Mutant Soldier, Mystik, Hostile Omish and a bunch more…all great memories of an era".

The band was revived in early 2000 as 'Environmental' this time, and released one independent CD in 2001, this time into a full-modern metal sound with a hardcore touch, you know, the kind of sound that Pantera was doing at the time, that sadly leaves me pretty cold.

"I think the resurgence of crossover is great" Chris adds. "It's good that younger people can carry on the tradition and the history of all these albums. Cleveland was a hot bed for hard rock and metal. There were a lot of bands breaking out in the very early 1990s. To see them still get their due is a heartfelt thank you to new fans. A lot of these early bands, including us laid the groundwork for what was to come. I am extremely proud that the album *One Stands Alone* has become so sought after. The prices people are asking are ridiculous! It reminds me of our collective accomplishments when we were very young. I hope it continues to be something people want to hear!".

At a glance: If you fancy your crossover more metal, dark, with an edge of later Excel, go for Environmental Hazzard's *One Stands Alone*. Not something groundbreaking, but I guess that fans of this sound mixed with late 1980s Metallica, Sacred Reich etc will dig it.

SIK MENTALITY

(Sik Mentality band picture. Courtesy unknown)

Formed in Houston, TX, in 1984, Sik Mentality were a band formed by childhood friends. "The original members were four friends in grade school, 7th or 8th grade, I can't remember exactly" lead vocalist and guitarist Mark Montalbano narrates. "We discovered punk, mainly from hanging out in the 'hood and going to the local record store, and there was no turning back. Our primary influence was punk and hardcore. Originally, we were trying to sound like some of the hardcore bands that we discovered such as JFA, MDC, early punk D.R.I., and Black Flag and other bands like Sick Pleasure, Verbal Abuse, Cro-Mags, and Agnostic Front that were also huge influences for us. But this was a time when you'd go to the record store and see these wild new metal bands as well, so we were also being influenced by some of the thrash metal bands like Slayer, early Metallica, Exodus, and Anthrax, or at least, I was. It was considered underground at the time as well. I had a friend that was in a punk band and also in another band that was metal, so I'd go to a punk show and a metal show to see him play. They hadn't merged yet. So, I was exposed very early to a sound that was coming where metal was getting faster, and punk was getting heavier. That guy later joined Verbal Abuse as their guitarist. So, Sik naturally just naturally had a sound that incorporated both worlds. We had some friendships with some of the before mentioned bands such as Verbal Abuse, D.R.I. who were both Houston, Texas-based bands as well and loved what they were doing, as well as the sounds coming from bands like Corrosion of Conformity and Dr. Know, emerging out of different areas regionally. These bands, and a few others, were slowly edging toward a new sound, coined the 'crossover' sound. All of that said, I would still describe Sik Mentality as more of a hardcore punk band than a metal one... but I guess we ended up appealing to a lot of metalheads!".

(Sik Mentality and the Fuck-Ups gig at Cabaret Voltaire, 20/09/1985)

Sik Mentality's lineup consisted of Mark Montalbano (lead guitar, vocals), Joe 'Dead' Bonaparte (guitars), Sean Riley (drums) and Bill Mackey (bass). The band started playing shows with local bands like Deadhorse, and touring with bands Scream and The Fuck-Ups. "I personally was influenced by Minor Threat, Bad Brains, Adolescents, early Black Flag, D.R.I., Verbal Abuse, and Cro-Mags, to name a few" Mark admits. "That was, of course, the punk side. Slayer, Exodus, and early Metallica (*Kill 'Em All* and *Ride the Lightning*), and a few others were influences over on that side. But let's not forget, we were also listening to other genres like post-punk, New Wave, noise rock, Oi!, ska, reggae, and early hip-hop. It's really hard to define what happened when there were so many things happening at once".

(Sik Mentality, Raw Power, Decry and Morally Bankrupt gig at Cabaret Voltaire, 30/11/1985)

Asked about which band Mark considered the first one to pursue the crossover between metal and hardcore punk, he offers his point of view: "This is a tough one. It was so long ago! I mean, to me, the obvious answer is D.R.I. but there were actually a lot of bands racing to that line at the same time and just sort of riding a wave together, with hearing each other's music and all. But it was like the Hundredth Monkey. It was happening in different places at the same time. Some of the others I mentioned in the previous answer were there as well, and I'm sure I'm leaving some bands out. Bands like Bad Brains, a personal all-time favourite band, and others like Verbal Abuse were starting to sound more hard rock, with a tinge of metal. This was a little before D.R.I.'s. ultimate descriptive album *Crossover* was released. Suicidal Tendencies was also one of the first. So, there were a few bands sort of doing it all at once. Also, somewhere around this same period of time, Scott Ian from Anthrax would also co-create S.O.D. I sort of credit their *Speak English or Die* album as possibly the most important album that made a lot of metalheads see the hardcore scene. But, in my experience, most metalheads, or headbangers that I knew were mostly NOT at all into punk. Whereas there already were a lot of us punks into some metal. Look... I mean, many of us were listening to Iron Maiden before getting into punk! Some of us were simply into both sounds at the same time. Like I said, many of us were previously listening to bands like Black Sabbath, AC/DC, and Iron Maiden before we got into punk. Again, I personally lean more toward punk but there was just a strong momentum with various factors that were making the two musical styles merge at the time. It certainly wasn't the radio! So, it's hard to place. Going to a Slayer show gave the same, or similar, feeling and level of adrenaline and a sort out-of-control feeling that one also got at a hardcore show. I guess you could say independently owned record stores and show promoters had a play in it, as shows started getting booked at the same places".

Regarding the reaction of metalheads and punks to this new crossover sound, Marks states that "there seemed to be much more punks embracing the faster, heavier sound which ultimately led to the crossover sound, than there were metalheads embracing punk. Again, from my point of view. In fact, I'll go farther. It didn't seem like diehard metalheads cared much for punks at all. We'd go see bands like Slayer, Anthrax, and Celtic Frost and start a pit and just run around in a circle bumping into each other at these shows, having fun but pissing off the headbangers. I have very vivid memories of these perfectly groomed longhaired headbangers giving us pissed off looks like they had never seen anything like it. They'd sometimes even start throwing actual punches at us and really trying to hurt us. Because, you have to understand, it was all foreign to them. For the record, punk wasn't really violent. Or, it was at times, but mostly it was just people having fun. 'Slam-dancing', the term we used before 'moshing' became the word to use, was fun and there was a feeling of comradery out in the 'pit'. So, I sort of see that when the two concepts merged and the music got even faster, it became more violent… But, again, I only have the perspective of a teenager in the Houston scene. It might have been different in places like L.A. because California, in general, was ahead of everyone else, in this regard at least. Yes, I saw violence at shows but, again, mostly I saw metalheads annoyed with the punks. Then, one day, suddenly, in the blink of an eye, it all started to merge. And right around the time that happened, BOOM, suddenly, 'grunge' was here too".

After three years of existence, Sik Mentality released their first-and only-record, the 12-inch *Bad World* EP out on their own, Mr. Yuk Records, *Bad World* sounded like a cross between Venom, Verbal Abuse, D.R.I. (*Crossover* LP era) and Dr. Know. Heavy, menacing and brutal, *Bad World* contains six songs, with 'Terminally Sik' and 'Society Disease' being my favourites. I think that they have a Beyond Possession vibe in, only that Sik Mentality are way less complex, and more typically punk, still though *Bad World* will please all crossover fans.

Sik Mentality in their heyday shared the stage with bands like Suicidal Tendencies, Adolescents, M.D.C., Agnostic Front, and Dr. Know among many others, and Mark adds that "my favourite shows were D.R.I. in both the *Dealing With It* and *Crossover* tours but the show that was my biggest highlight was when Sik Mentality opened for Suicidal Tendencies at Fitzgerald's in Houston. That show was madness! To see the biggest pit going around in a circle at insane speeds right below us while we were performing was just so memorable. In general, I enjoyed punk shows best. But I also don't see things in such a drastic clear and cut way. We'd go see Black Flag, D.R.I., some funky punk music, Slayer, some art punk shows, and then I'd personally go see Santana or Stevie Ray Vaughn, or a reggae show, on some other night. The 1980s was the best blend of so many styles happening all at once".

"I know that everybody mentions that era to be totally wacky" Mark adds, "but truth is, that it wasn't that crazy. There was some violence at shows such as guys pulling out knives outside of the Slayer show and making others give them their leather jackets. The crazier shows were usually punk such as Butthole Surfers and their trippy vibe or tripping on LSD and watching Bill Stevenson of the Descendents drumming in his underwear. The metal shows felt satanic, heh! Other than that, the only other thing I'd say is that it was truly a DIY, underground scene during those days. Nobody was signing us; we were figuring it all out by trial and error and doing it all ourselves.... and not getting paid a dime! Well, the top metal bands were getting paid. Also, historically speaking, you could say Houston was a big part of the crossover scene as some of these early bands were in L.A., in San Francisco and Houston. As well as New York City too (Anthrax/SOD... Cro-Mags). The metal bands such as Slayer and Metallica were of course L.A. and SF bands and some of the bands that started the crossover scene, such as D.R.I., Verbal Abuse, while known as being SF bands, were originally from Houston.... they were part of our family of musicians. Suicidal Tendencies was from L.A. and the band Dr. Know was from the Ventura-Oxnard scene called 'Nardcore'. But one of the odd ones, in regards to location and sort of being out in a different area, geographically-speaking, was Corrosion of Conformity, who came out of Raleigh, North Carolina. They were definitely a huge influence!".

(Sik Mentality, Deadhorse, Blind Ignorents, Bay of Pigs, Mass Crematorium Complete and Sister Moon at the D+I Colonial. Date unknown)

Sik Mentality called it a day in late 1980s, with members later playing in other Houston hardcore punk bands. Sean Riley performed in Dixie Waste (hardcore-thrash), Humungus (punk rock, with a record alongside Dead Boys' Cheetah Chrome) and Bastard Cult (hardcore punk), while Joe Bonaparte played also in Humungus and in Any Three Initials with Will Shatter of Flipper and Negative Trend and Rogue Nation (punk rock). "In Houston, for me at the time, it was a place called Cabaret Voltaire" Mark continues. "That place gave us our start, and I saw so many shows there. The third location eventually became the famous (Houston famous) Axiom, where many bands such as Nirvana played. We were scheduled to open for Verbal Abuse on the club's opening night but the police shut the club down! I also shared the stage there with Dave Grohl when he was in a band called Scream. The most exciting show we played was, again, opening up for Suicidal at Fitzgerald's and a personal favourite for me was playing with the Adolescents".

"Are you kidding me? It's immeasurably relevant!" Mark concludes when asked about crossover's relevance today. "So many of the sounds we listen to today, and throughout the last twenty years, all came from that merging of punk and metal into crossover and grunge, etc. I think stoner rock was part of it too, which is, in my opinion, what played into creating the grunge sound. Also, the fact that you can 'mosh' and stage dive at a mainstream pop or country show, shows just how influential that era was. It had been only punks doing it in the 1970s and early-mid 1980s. In fact, a little lesson here... many people don't know that it was HR from Bad Brains who coined the term 'mosh'. He was telling the crowds to 'mash it up' out on the dance floor, but his accent sounded like he was saying 'mosh'. So, in this regard, punk, in general, was a huge influence on the current culture that we have".

At a glance: I think that Sik Mentality's *Bad World* 12-inch isn't just for crossover completists, but I believe that more than a few people would enjoy its sheer power. Not a milestone or a classic, but definitely enjoyable, good and honest crossover with vicious sound and vocals!

UGLY BUT PROUD

(Ugly But Proud band in action. Courtesy unknown)

Detroit, MI in the 1980s had a massive hardcore punk scene with Negative Approach, Necros, The Meatmen, Bored Youth, L-Seven, not to be confused with the 1990s group L7, and The Fix from Lansing, not the UK group The Fixx. among others. Detroit also had an extensive heavy metal scene with Madam X, Red Machete, David Neil Cline, Halloween, Wages of Sin, Messiah, etc. Both music scenes had a common denominator in most cases, a rough sound that characterized the city's aura. However, I managed to identify only two crossover bands: Scruffy Tearways and Ugly and Proud.

"Ugly But Proud was formed in 1985 by me - 'Ugly' Mike McCabe (guitar), brother 'Proud Mark' McCabe (drums), and 'Hideous' George Wright (bass). Home base was Pontiac, Michigan" Michael McCabe narrates. "After a brief search for a lead vocalist it was decided that I would be the lead vocalist, mainly because I wrote the lyrics. Previously, I had played drums for Detroit hardcore punk pioneers Negative Approach on their 1983 *Tied Down* tour. Mark and George were in hardcore punk band Plain Truth. From 1985 until 1990 this lineup played at many venues, including the legendary Graystone Hall and Blondie's, as well as performances in Cleveland, Indianapolis, and San Francisco. Ugly But Proud would play on bills with all the big shots including Bad Brains, Suicidal Tendencies, The Mentors, The Meatmen, D.R.I., Bad Brains, Agnostic Front, Corrosion of Conformity, Death, Sacred Reich, M.O.D., GWAR, The Accüsed and many more".

(Ugly But Proud, Angry Red Planet and Inside Out at Mr. N's Mystery Lounge, 30/11/1985)

What was the case of Ugly But Proud's crossover is that they sounded more like a speed metal band with a huge Motörhead influence gone hardcore, very close to what early Excel or Beowülf did in Venice, L.A., albeit with a rough Detroit sound. "Two bands come to mind with the punk metal crossover thing; Motörhead and The Plasmatics" Michael admits. "Both had short three-minute tunes that were speedy and aggressive, and both bands were popular with punks and metalheads without being specifically marketed to either demographic. D.R.I. is generally regarded as the first 'crossover' band, but naming an album *Crossover* seemed a bit…much. Locally, I would say Ugly But Proud were pretty much the first crossover band. Negative Approach had started playing slightly longer songs as opposed to the thirty-seconds of rage that was the trademark of most hardcore. But Negative Approach had yet to really garner a metal following. UBP did mainly because we had all been in the hardcore scene for a while and our first shows were with punk bands at hole in the wall punk venues. And a lot of people on the metal fringe were getting curious about the hardcore scene. They would come to our house parties and make friends, or fight, sometimes both. But I think a lotta hardcore 'punks' were just metalheads who were tired of million-dollar spectacle shows and were hankering for something more aggressive and less concerned with image and stage shows. You didn't have to be a virtuoso with endless guitar-drum solos, four chords and you're on your way!"

In 1985 Ugly But Proud released their first demo *Kim Never Forgets* that I managed only to get a handful of songs in my personal collection; however, the quality of the band is evident from day one. Nasty, superspeed but complex and melodic crossover, with a huge dose of Motörhead and GBH. With great songwriting in songs like 'Ugly and Proud' as maybe one of their best songs ever and 'No Free Ride'.

What is actually very interesting is that the sonic assault is blended with Michael's more melodic voice- just ace stuff!

(Ugly But Proud, Damage and Aspirin Damage at the Graystone. Date unknown)

"Our main influences as far as Ugly songs go would be Motörhead, Judas Priest, Black Sabbath, classic metal stuff like that, and Negative Approach, Black Flag, Minor Threat, stuff like that on the hardcore side" Michael offers, adding that 'We didn't call it 'punk', it was 'hardcore'. Punk was stuff like the Sex Pistols, the Clash, we had gone beyond that kind of thing. Visually we could have cared less about costumes or shit. We just ran around, did the headbanger thing. A lotta places had just a bare bulb hanging from the ceiling. But later on, when we started playing more metal-type shows we did like a decent light show. But hair bands with all their makeup and colourful leotards, that was anathema to bands like us'.

Crazy and unique band Ugly But Proud were, they sometimes also credited among their band members are a dog named Thor that had his own song, 'Thor War', and Kim McCool, a fan of the band nicknamed as 'King Zeus' who sat onstage at some of their shows and provided 'psychic uplift'! "We had a lot of crazy stories" Michael laughs, adding that "there are too many to recount or remember. You'll have to wait for the movie! But violence? Nah not really. When I first started going to shows at the Freezer Theatre in 1981 we called it 'slamming' or 'thrashing'. I don't know where 'moshing'' came from. But it wasn't about targeting people for getting hit. Well maybe sometimes, haha, but generally it was about going crazy and randomly bashing into people. If someone fell, you would help them up. Nowadays it's all about football killers trying to hurt each other. No thanks. Hell, I'm too old for that shit anyway!".

Ugly But Proud's first vinyl release was the 1987 *Knuckles From Nowhere* 7-inch on the small hardcore punk label Depression Records, from Detroit. Fast, raw, crazy but always with a rock 'n' roll feel good style. *Knuckles From Nowhere* includes four songs of wild speed metal-hardcore crossover, not too dissimilar from the likes of Beowülf or early Excel from Venice, the whole 'Motörhead meets GBH' style that's always a great fun to listen! As for my favourite songs off this 7-inch? 'Split Personality' is just amazing, while 'King Zeus' sounds like a thousand bombs dropped! But overall, this is one of the most frantic 7-inch EPs that was released in the crossover style, period.

(Ugly But Proud, COC, Straw Dogs and Sacrifice at Traxx. 09/08/1986)

Two more demos followed in 1987 and 1988 respectively, in their usual great style; too bad that songs like 'Friend or Enemy' never saw a vinyl or CD release. Ugly But Proud kept on playing alongside bands like Agnostic Front, Lethal Militia, Death Corp. However they went under the radar, especially from big and medium sized labels; that's a pity, because their musical output was just phenomenal.

So, it took them six long years from 1988 until 1994 to release their first CD, *Bein' Ugly Is Alright*, self-released on their Proud Productions label. This CD is more like a recollection of their career, with a new sound, and obviously all songs are just ripping crossover of the highest order, with the new editions of the melodic stomper of 'Lights are Always On', the banger 'No Hope For Redemption' or the styling of Motörhead and GBH heard on 'Bein' Ugly is Alright' pleasing every fan of metal punk crossover. Amazing release, however coming out in a time when even bands like D.R.I. found it hard to get a contract to release their music.

"I don't listen to a lot of new music, so I couldn't make an informed argument about the state of it today" Michael offers. I do think that what passes for 'punk' today is pretty much mainstream pop, like Green Day or Blink-182, stuff like that. It's too family friendly to be called 'punk'. There are still some bands flying the flag of old school hardcore, so more power to them. Metal has gotten so genre-fied it's hard to keep track anymore. Ya got death metal, Norwegian black metal, black metal, melodic metal, nu metal, rap metal. Most of it I call Cookie Monster metal because the vocals remind me of the Sesame Street guy. But I do enjoy the shows, some of the costumes those bands wear are incredible! I will always enjoy music that is heavy and original sounding. As long as there are people in need of an aggression outlet, there will be metal and hardcore, and the two are quite intertwined".

Other bands that Ugly but Proud members were involved are the thrashers Somethin' Awful (Jake Speed and Sean Awful played there), as well as Deathcorp, The Black, Vampirella, The Exposers, Thicke Hawkins and Voyeur (for Jake Speed) and The Black, Subject to Change and Voyeur (for Hideous George).

Ugly but Proud disbanded in 1995 but came back in 2015 and are still (2025) active offering local shows, and hopefully for a lot more years to come! A new release someday maybe?

At a glance: I really go apeshit over the sound of Ugly but Proud. As aforementioned, they remind me of what was taking place at the same time in Venice, California and bands like Beowülf and early Excel, that is mental crossover with a huge Motörhead/GBH dose, only that Ugly But Proud have a rougher sound, taking their cues from the Detroit hardcore scene. All their output is recommended but check *Knuckles from Nowhere* 1987 EP as a starter, brilliant stuff!

SCRUFFY TEARAWAYS

(Scruffy Tearaways band picture. Courtesy unknown)

Another crossover band from Detroit, Scruffy Tearaways had their own story to share in the hardcore and metal history. "Starting in high school while living in Ortonville, Michigan I became fascinating with punk rock and metal the point of wanting to be in my own band. My head was whirling with the inspirations of Sex Pistols, Frank Zappa, the Ramones, Twisted Sister, and more. I did not have the stick-to-itiveness to learn an instrument, so I fell into offering yelling and screaming as ersatz singing in various groups. One coalesced into parties and gigs as Generation Gap and this became The Misdirected. However, the story of Scruffy Tearaways started out in August 1988 formed by members of various metal & punk bands in the Detroit area. The name Scruffy Tearaways was derived from an old episode of the British comedy show 'The Young Ones'. The band existed from 1988 until about 1994 when the Scruffys finally died out. The original lineup consisted of Tom 'Tommy Tearaway' Schulte on vocals, Sean 'Smitty' Smith on guitar, Mike Hasty on guitar, Matt 'Mr. Soggy' Carlington on bass and Jason 'Jay' Clifton on drums. Early on Justin Jackson took over on drums and played on the first demo entitled *Demolition by Neglect* recorded by Dave Feeney at the Tempermill (his basement in Livonia, Michigan)", Tom 'Tommy Tearaway' Schulte offers, and this story is taken under his permission, from his forthcoming book.

(Scruffy Tearaways with Go, Bad Trip, FFS and more, 14/07/1990)

"What got our attention at the time in Detroit was NYC crossover: Cro-Mags, Crumbsuckers. We were also paying attention to Ludichrist, Lime Spiders and more. But if I had to offer some bands that influenced us, these must have been C.O.C, Dayglo Abortions, Crumbsuckers, Minor Threat, Celtic Frost, D.R.I. and The Misfits" Tom admits.

Scruffy Tearaways' first offering was the near perfect *Demo '88* cassette containing a track titled 'Ozymandias'; the track is named from a sonnet written by English romantic poet Percy Bysshe Shelley. Shelley's sonnet, 'Ozymandias' was first published in the 11th January 1818 issue of *The Examiner* in London, a leading intellectual journal expounding radical principles during this time. The sonnet was included in Palgrave's Golden Treasury in 1861 and most English verse anthologies since. *Demo '88* contains four songs, blast after blast of excellently executed speedcore, and at least two cuts are real scorchers- that is 'Crawling Through Tunnels' and 'Ozymandias'. Sounding like a cross between Lethal Aggression, D.R.I. and some elements from bands like Doomwatch or Celtic Frost as evident in 'The March', Scruffy Tearaways' introduction was impressive.

Scruffy Tearaways initially appeared in shows alongside other Detroit local bands such as Bomb, Forced Anger, Feisty Cadavers, Almighty Lumberjacks of Death, Blasphemous and touring acts like Empathy, False Prophets, Mallet-Head or Post-Mortem. Almost all their shows being held at Blondie's, maybe the most legendary showroom for hardcore, punk and metal in Detroit.

(Scruffy Tearaways, Disgust, Antfarm and Intact flyer, 10/02/1989)

"Fusions are inevitable. For us at the time we just liked the sound of it" Tom admits, regarding crossover. "But there was no cultural crossover; we were too punk for the metalheads and too metal for the punks. Punks are generally politically aware in a progressive away. Metalheads are often apolitical and when they are political it can be adverse".

Next release was the 1988 demo *Demolition by Neglect*. It that was a step forward towards a sound more into Celtic Frost, with hardcore outbursts of energy of course. On this demo Scruffy Tearways remind me of a cross between Dream Death, Doomwatch and Ludichrist. The demo included hard and heavy crossover thrash, with songs like 'Party at the Morgue' and 'Premature Burial'. I kind of miss the energy and frantic speed of the first demo though…but I guess that people into this sound will dig it. "The title *Demolition by Neglect* came from seeing the phrase stencilled on an abandoned building in Detroit. I was told at the time a photographer hired to do come-visit-Detroit pics turned in ruin porn instead and then flipped out and did all these stencils. The ruins of Detroit were a great part of its charm, at the time" Tom offers.

"The guys in the band just dressed like the wanted. I overtly mixed the styles, such as punk patches on burnout denim and a head half shaved, half long hair" Tom admits. "

More shows followed, supporting bands as diverse as GG Allin (and of course there's a story to mention later!), Victims Family, The Stain (from Toledo), Funeral Nation, The Uknown, Slaughterhouse, Slapshot and Ugly But Proud (to name a few), and the band recorded one more demo on 1991, named as *Big "D"*

Binge; some older songs revisited, as well as new stuff, now with a less (yes!) Celtic Frost influence, back to speedcore, and I really enjoyed 'Generation Gap' (very Ludichrist, second LP-era) or 'Fragments'.

"The Slapshot show was supposed to be great, but we played first out of like three acts, ahead of Full Circle. There was no audience for us, so over time so few people remembered us on the bill I started to think we never did it. David Nick recalled that: 'That Slapshot show was one of my favourite shows ever… I always think of how nonviolent the pit was, as compared to the pits of today. No one tried to take anyone's head off back then. It was one of the best, most fun moshes I was ever in'" Tom offers, while adding the story about the GG Allin show mentioning that "I recall laying out the lefthand flyer including using a translucent green template for lettering. GG Allin had a real stage persona that he turned on to get to the bile shouting and poo-flinging. I and others he knew stood close by stage right and despite how animalistic he may have acted; he had the presence of mine not to throw shit or fists at us. By this time, Muskegon's the love affair with Muskegon's Disappointments was fading and GG asked us to go on the road with him. I was game, which speaks to what I had going on in life at the time, but the Scruffy Tearaways democracy offered no consensus toward this artistic change".

"However, my favourite shows in the crossover era must have been the Dayglo Abortions at Blondie's in Detroit in the late 1980s, and Boston bands Post-Mortem and Mallet-Head. All in Blondie's- I do miss the original club on Seven Mile as run by Rosie…"

(Scruffy Tearaways, Means To End and The Ice Pic. Date unknown)

Scruffy Tearaways lasted up to 1994, when they called it quits. Jef Sanguis later played in Sanguis, Rebel Spies! and J-Men Forever, Tom played in Generation Gap, Jeff Shankin played with Ruthless Horde and

Universal Stomp, Jason Clifton played with Earthmover, Humanity's End, Effigy, Chaosmongers, U.I.F. (Uninspired Fuckheads) and Graverape, while Mike Hasty played with Apathemy, Earthmover, It's All Gone To Hell, Tank (the Detroit metalcore band) and Walls Of Jericho, while also owning and operating his own recording studio, Cloud City Studio.

Tom ends our conversation with a thought if crossover is relevant today, mentioning that "I am sure it is in some ways, to people that care about the chain of inspiration into the past....".

At a glance: Scruffy Tearaways were more than a decent speedcore act, that musically they went for a heavier and slower approach, while lyrically they were on the 'have a good time camp', using metaphors, but always being anti-government and anti-racist. An honest band with a background on the hardcore scene of Detroit, with three good demos that hopefully will see the light of day again, re-issued for the new generation of crossover maniacs.

EAST COAST

"As far as New York was concerned, D.R.I.'s 1983 debut EP-LP served as the new blueprint for many fledgling bands wearing the badge of HC or what was blossoming as thrash metal. It was anthemic, faster than fast and reckless. Up the BPMs or hit the highway as long as you didn't forget the occasional NY style mosh part. Tape-trading circles were going nuts at a million miles per hour.

NYC was already home to outfits such as Urban Waste and a young Agnostic Front; both of which boasted fast songs. Other parts of the East Coast had bands like Void (DC) and Siege (Boston), each presenting like a bullet train going off the rails. Throw in that first Dirty Rotten release and you start to get the picture. The world already had line-straddlers the likes of Venom and Motörhead, and let's not forget that Metallica and Slayer dropped their debuts in '83 as well - featuring higher tempos than any previous metal records. Queens' Anthrax followed suit.

By 1985, the crossover cake was largely finished baking, in large part due to D.R.I.'s sophomore album Dealing With It, as well as Corrosion of Conformity's second long-player Animosity. Hardcore was becoming heavily metal, and metal was speedier and less self-conscious. In the Big Apple, long-haired kids were flocking to CBGB's Sunday matinees and skinheads were trooping out to L'Amour's in Brooklyn. The small pockets of speed-addicted youth sprinkled throughout the Tri-state area were quickly becoming a force, and a more combined scene was coming together.

New York boasted bands like NYC Mayhem, Nuclear Assault, Cro-Mags, S.O.D., Leeway, Crumbsuckers, Carnivore, Ludichrist and Agnostic Front. These bands became NY's leading purveyors of metal-hardcore and helped carry the movement across the globe with their "controversial" second offering, Cause for Alarm featuring songwriting contributions by Carnivore's Pete Steele. I say controversial because of the band's drastic change in sound from AF's classic debut, Victim in Pain. Nearby in New Jersey, you had Adrenalin O.D., Lethal Aggression and Whiplash.

It all progressed (fell apart?) from there.

--

H.J.I.C. since 1968!"

(Howie Abrams of In-Effect Records as well as co-author of *The ABCs of Metallica* and *Finding Joseph I: An Oral History of H.R. from Bad Brains*. Abrams is the author of *The Merciless Book of Metal Lists*, *Misfit Summer Camp: 20 Years on the Road with the Vans Warped Tour*, *Hip-Hop Alphabet*, *Hip-Hop Alphabet 2*, *The ABCs of the Grateful Dead* and *Vinnie Stigma's The Most Interesting Man in the World* biography)

KILLING TIME

(Killing Time band picture. Courtesy of BJ Papas)

What can you say about such an iconic band like Killing Time? Formed in 1988 as Raw Deal in New York City, they managed to push the boundaries of NYHC becoming one of the most influential bands for the 1990s NYHC style. Their significance is massive, and even if you find it an overstatement, Killing Time and Sick Of It All were for the third wave of NYHC what Cro-Mags and Leeway were for the second, and what Kraut and Agnostic Front were for the first wave.

Their history starts as Raw Deal on the early 1988, with the initial lineup being Carl Porcaro (guitars), Rich McLoughlin (bass, RIP 2020) and Anthony Drago (drums), who were former members of Breakdown. The Raw Deal lineup was grounded then, after the inclusion of Anthony Comunale (of Token Entry, vocals) and Mike Sentkiewitz (ex-Sick of It All, guitar).

(Raw Deal with Sick Of It All, The Icemen and Maximum Penalty at CBGB's, 22/07/1989)

"I don't write music. That was Carl and Rich" Anthony narrates. "To me, this was the second wave of hardcore. 1985 and before had a strict hardcore punk sound but as the older bands disappeared or progressed, everything changed. The new crop of kids came from a Metallica and Slayer background and incorporated it into the newer sound. I was lucky to meet Carl, Drago and Rich after leaving Token Entry and given the opportunity to sing for Raw Deal".

Raw Deal in 1988 went to release their first and only demo named appropriately as *1988 Demo*, that still to this day, stands as one of the best demos ever in hardcore. They took the hard and gritty sound of the Breakdown *87 Demo*, and transformed it into something catchier. I think that this is partly to Anthony's very characteristic voice. Seven absolutely great sing-a-long tunes with an overall negative outlook on life, ha!. While the Youth Crew bands had a positive message, Raw Deal and later Judge, headed for a darker, negative approach, and they did it with gusto and style. The recording of Raw Deal is in line with the classic NYHC tradition of its day, rough, brutal and only slightly metal. As for my favourite songs of this demo, well, I can't pick; it's just an ace release.

"I came from a punk and original hardcore background" Anthony adds. "I was in a band called Gilligan's Revenge. We were a skate band. I had a straightforward style which sucked because unfortunately, I can't sing. I couldn't hit a note with a Mack truck so when I joined Raw Deal, I was able to go for a more aggressive growl type which fit the music we were doing".

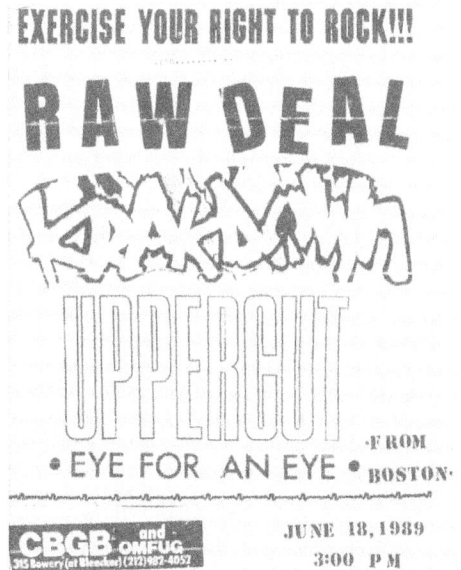

(Raw Deal, Krakdown, Uppercut and Eye For An Eye at CBGB's, 18/06/1989)

Right after the release of Raw Deal's demo, Mike Sentkiewitz left the band. Even worse, Raw Deal from UK, a heavy metal band threatened to press charges against the use of the name 'Raw Deal', so the band decided to change name to Killing Time. Anthony narrates that "when we signed to Relativity and tried to copyright the name Raw Deal, we were sent a letter from a group in Europe who had the rights. I think Drago came up with Killing Time. It was a smooth transition as we were playing a lot of shows and NYHC was popular at the time, so it wasn't really a detriment".

A newly founded label from Queens, NY named as In-Effect, and an imprint of Relativity Records, offered a deal to Killing Time for one record. This resulted in the release of one of the best NYHC records ever made, the 1989 *Brightside* LP that was co-produced by the band and Tom Soares. *Brightside* took the energy and streetwise mentality of NYHC and blended it with a slight metal sound. While not crossover in the traditional sense of the word, it surely contained characteristics that could appeal to metalheads too. With a surgical precision, every second of *Brightside* rips; the songs of the Raw Deal demo now sound more powerful than ever, and the new ones are as inspired as before. *Brightside* is a record that kept me company in very difficult times, when I was struggling with myself, battling depression. It was also one of those records that kept me company during my boxing sessions, making me unstoppable, hard as a nail. So, how can you review your life? Is it possible?

Killing Time's reputation as a live band gave a full boost to them, but problems arose; not because of the band, but because the NYHC scene. According to people that witnessed it first-hand, the scene went to become ridiculously brutal, with violence escalating. I won't refer to rumours, but truth is that it must have been pretty problematic back then, and I guess that this fact somehow held back many bands as well as Killing Time of making it bigger.

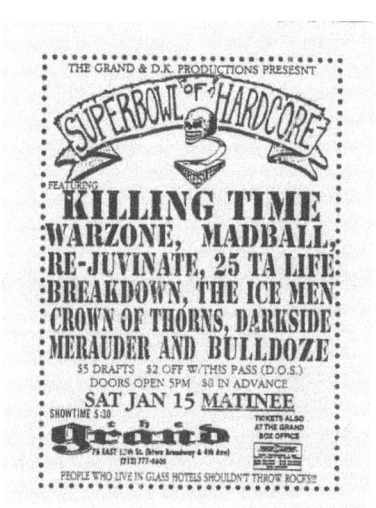

(Superbowl of Hardcore fest at the Grand NYC, 15/01/1994)

In 1992 Blackout! Records from the Netherlands released the *Happy Hour* LP that was actually one side of new songs, and one side of Raw Deal stuff and a new version of a Killing Time song. I can only recall one more NYHC record that got released in Europe and not in the USA, and that is Leeway's *Desperate Measures* LP, that was released via Profile (boooo....). Anyway, sadly *Happy Hour* didn't get much love initially. It's definitely calmer and more melodic than *Brightside*, but this doesn't mean that it's not great! Now with a more hardcore-oriented sound, the new songs are just fantastic! I love the melodic leads of 'Happy Hour' as well as the nutty saxophone of 'Whole Lotta Nuthin' Pt. II' and the beautiful guitarwork of 'Going Nowhere'. Yes, *Happy Hour* is another classic, albeit different!

The band went on a small hiatus (maybe because *Happy Hour* was a disaster in terms of acceptance...). They returned in 1995 with *Unavoidable* 7-inch, that was a comeback to a fiercer hardcore sound. The band hit the studio now under the production matters of Dean Rispler, the bassist of The Voluptuous Horror Of Karen Black and countless others, as well as a producer. The result was the excellent *The Method* LP (1996), again on Blackout! Records that at least had a US version for it!

The Method is a comeback to a more traditional NYHC style, dropping off the metal elements of *Brightside*, in favour of a more straightforward approach. The band now sound totally pissed off, comparing it to *Brightside* it also dropped the hopeless sentiment in favour of 'I'm going to rip your head off', haha! Songs like 'Can't Get Around It' or 'Symptom' and the frantic 'Personal Hardcore' are some of my favourites off another one exceptional record.

"My personal favourite is *The Method* LP" Anthony admits. "I really loved the sound. The recording was rawer and more live. My vocals were coming into a good place for me. Much better than *Brightside*. *Brightside* had that over polished 1980s quality that was big at the time. I wish people appreciated *The Method* more. I think the songs are superior, but all people want to hear is the first album. It's fine. Give the people what they want. After shows fans come up and chat. Tell us what an influence or help *Brightside* was to them. Got them through rough times. Even kids in their late teens at shows tell me how much it means. In the end that's what really matters. To know something we did has had a positive effect or inspired others to pursue music. Wouldn't trade that for anything. I'm so honoured and humbled that people appreciate what we did and continue to do".

(Killing Time, Sheer Terror, The Icemen, American Standard and Eye For An Eye at the Marquee NYC, 26/07/1991)

The Method LP was a success, and the NYHC scene was reviving with great comebacks like Agnostic Front, Cro-Mags or with successful bands that were carrying the torch such as Madball and Sick Of It All. Killing Time were laid to rest in 1998, but only for a while; they revived though in 2005. In 2010 they released *Three Steps Back* LP, that is another one hit! Sounding like a tribute to their punk and hardcore roots, it sounds more traditional than ever. Songs like 'Spaceheater', 'Rope A Dope' and 'Half Empty', are some of my most favourite Killing Time anthems! What can I say, I really love all their releases!

"I don't really have any crazy experience but cherished memories of all the bands and friends and fans we made since late 1987 and on. Every show is different, but the folks remain the same. Very supportive and welcoming. It's so great to see so many young folks up front. Singing along, dancing. So many young women as well fronting bands and upfront dancing. I'm happy that at almost 59 to still be able to play and meet so many diverse and friendly people!" Anthony concludes.

Members of Killing Time have a huge history in playing before or after Killing Time when in other bands; Alex Gopoian in Inside Out and Justice System; Anthony Comunale in Gilligan's Revenge and Token Entry; Anthony Drago in Breakdown; Carl Porcaro in Alone In A Crowd, Breakdown, Electric Frankenstein, Kings Destroy, Mind's Eye, The Arch Rivals, The Monumentals; Chris Skowronski plays in Kings Destroy and Mind's Eye, and Mike Sentkewitz in Crawlpappy and Terminal Confusion. Rich McLoughlin in Breakdown, Ironbound NYC, Unholy Swill and Maximum Penalty. Sean O'Brien in Giving Tree, Ironbound NYC and Everyday Dollars.

Killing Time are still strong in 2025 offering shows in USA and Europe, and I hope that they will release a new record someday soon!

At a glance: OK, every record by Killing Time is mandatory if you are into NYHC, simple as that. The same applies to the Raw Deal 1988 demo. However, crossover kids should start with *Brightside*. This is one of the few life changing records that you can come across in your existence, an unmissable manifesto of hardcore apotheosis with the precision of metal. It's up there with the best NYHC records, end of story. And be sure to catch Killing Time live when they play in your city!

EXECUTIONER

(Executioner band picture. Courtesy unknown)

Formed in 1984 in Boston as Last Generation, Executioner were a trio with Marc Johnson on vocals and guitars, Dan Scannell behind the drums, and Ari Vianio on bass. They went on to become one of the heaviest crossover bands to come out of Boston to date.

Initially, Executioner were a total heavy-speed metal band. This is evident in their 1984 demo; a definite Iron Maiden influence is here in songs like 'Final Destruction'. While 'Battlelands' or 'Hell and Back' even remind me of bands like Steel Assassin, you know, the type of US heavy metal that was hot in the underground back then. "It was Slayer that was the game changer in the whole crossover movement' Marc admits. "I think the raw speed and aggression of hardcore punk appealed to metal fans and bands even though I don't think the two cultures ever really blended".

New Renaissance Records took notice of Executioner early on, and this resulted in their inclusion in the *Speed Metal Hell* 1985 compilation with 'Victims of Evil'-now this time Executioner started sounding more punk-fused, like a cross between Motörhead, Exciter with some early Boston hardcore, a really punishing song. "We also mixed our image between the two" Marc adds. "Initially, we wore spikes and bandanas; but as we blended with hardcore bands, we stripped the look down to just jeans and T-shirts. It was more gritty and real".

(Executioner, Gang Green and Ghoul Squad at Rockit Records. 25/05/1986)

Local shows followed alongside The F.U.'s and Gang Green. The band entered Le Studio in Boston and proceeded to record its debut album *In The Name Of Metal*. Johnson and Vainio shared lead vocals on this album, with songs such as 'Stand Up And Fight' and 'Death By The Blade'. This is hands down their best release with full on hardcore punk-metal thrash that punches hard, with every song being a winner! Now, Executioner sounded more raging, faster and menacing than ever, like a cross between the Venice GBH and Motörhead crossover and Boston Hardcore, with a heavy dose of melody too. What is actually great in their case is that their crossover sounds like no one else, they definitely have their own style, and while songs like 'Nuclear Nightmare', 'In a silent way' and 'Cyanide' are short blasts of energy, you have great anthemic stuff too such as 'Your life is over' or the re-editions of 'Hell and Back' and 'Victims of Evil'. Excellent stuff!

The fierce power of *In The Name of Metal* offered Executioner local recognition, and their popularity spread with a national tour that followed. The *In The Name Of Metal* tour took Executioner through dozens of cities including: Trenton, New Jersey; Miami Florida; Enfield, Connecticut; Atlanta, Georgia; and one of the band's favourite cities, Pittsburgh, Pennsylvania. Unfortunately, while in San Antonio, Texas, Vainio broke his hand and the remainder of the national tour had to be cancelled.

"Thankfully, there was no violence at any of our shows" Marc smiles, adding that "Initially, I think both groups were wary of the other, but over time each embraced the other. Metal fans took to moshing and punk fans began stage diving and crowd surfing at metal shows".

Back in Boston, Executioner and Vainio parted company. The band quickly regrouped, and after a brief stint with then-hair-stylist Greg Dellaria on bass, Seth Putnam (who later went on to greater fame as the founder behind the A.C. a.k.a. Anal Cunt) was recruited to fill the bass slot on a permanent basis. With Putnam holding down the bottom end, Executioner launched back into the recording studio to record the follow-up *Break The Silence LP*.

"Slayer, Metallica, D.R.I. and Anthrax-these were my favourite crossover bands in those days" Marc mentions. "Slayer concerts were always the best. We also saw some amazing Anthrax concerts, but we also liked seeing live Iron Maiden, The Cro-Mags and GBH".

(Executioner, D.R.I., COC and No System at Enfield Roller Word, 12/06/1986)

In 1987 Executioner released again on New Renaissance Records, their second LP, *Break The Silence*. Even though I don't rate it as much as its predecessor, it's still a very good record. What Executioner lost in terms of songwriting, they gained it in ultra-power, incorporating more crossover riffs, blast beats and weird structures! Come on, songs like 'Eye on the needle' or 'Hatred' and the excellent 'Stand up and Fight' are massive winners! I just find *Break The Silence* a bit more polished compared *to In The Name Of Metal*, which of course isn't a bad thing!

The release of *Break The Silence* was followed by a US national US tour which saw the band perform throughout the country with such acts as: Megadeth, Voivod, Kreator, Nuclear Assault, D.R.I., D.R. Know and The Accüsed. But back in Boston, it was not long before Executioner and Putnam parted ways and a third bassist, Tommy Flynn was brought on board. With Flynn on bass, the band returned to the studio for a third time to record the album *In Cold Blood*. Unfortunately, shortly after the recording of *In Cold Blood*, Executioner disbanded, in 1989.

"Our best show was at Fender's Ballroom in Long Beach, California. Gary Tovar was an incredible promoter. We all miss the Rat and the Channel--two iconic Boston clubs" Marc sighs, adding a story: "In 1985, we were opening for The F.U.'s in Cambridge and punk fans started to stage dive. I think that was a first in Boston. Also in 1985, we opened for COC in Cambridge and when we came out onstage our fig machine set off the smoke alarm, and the show was stopped until the fire department came to kill the alarm!"

(Executioner, Dream Death and Dr. Know at Electric Banana, 12/10/1986)

Ten years after their split-up, Executioner briefly reformed and released what it was supposed to be *In Cold Blood*, now re-named as *The Storm After The Calm*; more complex, more extreme and weirder than before, this was their offering of pure hardcore-thrash, with a good Slayer influence. I like it (and most people that have heard it prefer it to their two previous records) but allow me to have a sentiment for their earlier, sloppy punk metal approach. Still, songs like 'Devastation' or 'Time after Time' will please all those ones into most extreme forms of crossover (such as fans of Cryptic Slaughter).

Executioner folded in the early 2000s, and Marc admits that the lines now are blurred; "I think the two genres have been blended for so long now that it's basically just ingrained in each style".

At a glance: I'm a sucker for Executioner's sonic approach on *In The Name Of Metal*, this sloppy, fast and catchy Motörhead-GBH styles mixed with Boston Hardcore, that I can't recommend enough this record! Their subsequent releases were at least good, and I believe that fans of most extreme crossover style will enjoy.

ANTIDOTE

(Antidote in their metal rock days live picture. Courtesy of Drew Stone/Ed Esposito)

I have to admit that I was very harsh on my review of Antidote's *Return 2 Burn* LP on *Crossover The Edge* book. I gave it many chances later, and tried to somehow 'disconnect' it from the fact that their *Thou Shalt Not Kill* 7-inch was one of the greatest NYHC 7-inchs, and actually *Return 2 Burn* is enjoyable for what it is. So, I had a chat with Drew Stone, vocalist of *Return 2 Burn* and steady member of Antidote since their reformation in 2008.

Antidote formed in New York City in 1982 and were active until 1986, being one of the first-wave era bands of NYHC alongside Urban Waste, The Abused, Kraut, Heart Attack, The Nihilistics, Reagan Youth and Agnostic Front, to name a few. Drew narrates that "they put out the iconic 7" *Thou Shalt Not Kill* and at the time was one of my favourite bands. After singing in The High & The Mighty, I joined in 1984 replacing the original singer. Initially we played from 1984 to 1992 before breaking up. Sixteen years later we got back together in 2008. In 2020 we split with the original guitar player and rebranded the band 'Antidote NYHC'. At that time the original guitarist got back together with the original singer and did some 'Antidote' shows. At that point we wanted to make a new start, and we renamed the band 'Incendiary Device' which still plays to this day".

The initial lineup of Antidote included Louie Rivera (vocals), Robb Nunzio (guitar), Brian Caufield, aka Tommy Victor on bass and Arthur McGuckin (on drums). With this lineup they released the *Thou Shalt Not Kill* 7-inch on their own label, Antidote Records. A heavyweight classic of NYHC. Fierce and rough, *Thou Shalt Not Kill* includes eight bombastic tracks, the backing vocals of John Joseph in 'Real Deal', and if you exclude the moronic lyrics of 'Foreign Job-Lot', this is one of the most raging hardcore records ever released, up there with the Negative Approach same titled 7-inch, Poison Idea's *Pick Your King* or Urban Waste's same titled 7-inch. It certainly has a slight heavy metal edge guitar-wise, like the one that The Abused also had in their *Loud and Clear* 7-inch. This is pure hardcore attack and a must-have record for anyone into American hardcore. Ridiculously limited on its first pressing, it now fetches big bucks, but you can find it for a decent price as a re-issue both on 12-inch on Radio Raheem label and as a 7-inch on Bridge Nine Records label.

(Antidote, Murphy's Law, Gilligan's Revenge, Cavity Creeps CBGB's 09/10/1983)

However, a few years after its release, there were huge changes on Antidote's lineup; Drew Stone took up the vocals, Robbi Conti went on bass, Chris Praz was now on drums, Jimmy Garcia on the guitar, with only Robb Nunzio remaining from the original lineup. And the change towards a more metal style was about to take place. "D.R.I., Agnostic Front, Suicidal Tendencies and later Cro-Mags were some of the first bands I heard that successfully combined the two genres" Drew narrates. "Later on, Biohazard really brought it to the next level. It can't be understated what a huge influence they were on many people. It was just the natural progression of things. Both genres were loud and aggressive music. Personally, being a hardcore kid, I didn't care for heavy metal when it first showed up. Not everyone liked the infiltration of metal into the scene back then. Eventually I warmed up to it. However, my musical background like many other kids growing up in New York City in the 1970s was what we now know as classic rock was what I listened to. Eventually in 1981 I got into hardcore and punk".

(Drew Stone 1989, photo by Ed Esposito)

Antidote's new style in the late 1980s drifted towards a more metal rock sound; as aforementioned, I was initially harsh when reviewing it, however, *Return 2 Burn* 1990 LP on their own label, Metropolis Records, is a good rocking rockin' metal-hardcore record. A decent dose of AC/DC influence is blended with some mid-1980s Adolescents and Circle Jerks as well as glam metal (e.g. on 'Positively Negative' or 'I Threw It All Away'), a re-edition of 'Something Must Be Done' and songs like 'Return 2 Burn' and 'Be True To Yourself' that sound like Gang Green at their rockiest possible. *Return 2 Burn* is an enjoyable record. "*Return To Burn* was a shock in music terms" Drew admits. "And it has a long and complicated story. Yes, many people were taken aback and not happy when the *Return 2 Burn* record was released since they were expecting a hardcore record much like the *Thou Shalt Not Kill* 7". Soon after I joined the band in 1984, we became bored with the hardcore thing and changed musical direction leaning more toward rock and metal. As young people at that point we were more influenced by Guns N' Roses, Judas Priest and KISS than the same old hardcore stuff. It's hard to say in retrospect if the *Return 2 Burn* record should have been released under the Antidote name but on the other hand it brought a whole new audience to our shows. We played some great shows in that era".

(Antidote and Blitzspeer at the Limelight, 20/05/1990)

"There wasn't any violence specifically at our shows" Drew adds, "but certainly at some of the CBGB's matinees at the time. It could get very ugly from time to time down on the Bowery.

Antidote in their early days were part of the A7 hardcore bands, playing alongside Murphy's Law or The High and Mighty, and later at CBGB's alongside Agnostic Front, Crumbsuckers etc. During their rock-metal days they started having shows alongside bands like Blitzspeer, Hell's Kitchen or Warzone in their rock era at Limelight. "The Limelight was our home during the Antidote rockin' metal era" Drew adds. "From 1989 to 1992 we played some incredible shows there before going on hiatus until 2008".

In the early 1990s Zum was added to the band as their new bassist, and Frank Cruz took over the drums, with Antidote releasing in 1992 the compilation CD *Viva Los Pendejos* that also included some new songs on the same metal style; 'Caught Up' went even for a funk metal style, while 'The Choice' was a fantastic song, not too dissimilar of early Faith No More! 'Don't Care' is my favourite of those new songs, with a total SoCal punk feeling into their sound.

"That's a tough question" Drew smiles. "But I have to say that Cro-Mags - *Best Wishes*, Leeway - *Born To Expire* and *Desperate Measures*, Suicidal Tendencies - *How Will I Laugh Tomorrow* are my favourites from the early crossover era. Later on, I'd say Biohazard's *Urban Discipline*."

Antidote called it quits in the 1990s, but they were back in 2008, now with Drew Stone (vocals), Robb Nunzio (guitar), Zum (bass) and Rea (Aryeh Lemberger, on drums). Firstly, *Thou Shalt Not Kill* got an official re-press in 2010, on Bridge Nine Records. I still remember the day I got it in a huge mail order from Ebullition Records-and my lousy 1991 German bootleg could be laid to rest finally! And then, a new record was out, the excellent *No Peace In Our Time* (2012, Bridge Nine Records) with nine new blasting hardcore outbursts, plus a Black Flag cover of 'Rise Above'. Antidote were back for good! No metal here, just simple and brutal hardcore with punishing songs like 'No Peace In Our Time' or 'Don't Blame Me'. NYHC enthusiasts don't let this one go under your radar!

"Any early Cro-Mags shows in New York City and a little bit later Biohazard at L'Amour in Brooklyn were incredible" Drew adds. "But I certainly don't miss the violence that permitted that era especially at places like L'Amour in Brooklyn. Any time you went out to a show there you felt like you were putting your safety in jeopardy. It was stupid and ugly. but it was part of what made it exciting".

In 2020 Antidote split with the original guitar player Robb Nunzio and rebranded the band as 'Antidote NYHC' while Robb continued on with his own version of Antidote. Antidote NYHC released in 2021 the *Scarred* 7-inch on Unity Worldwide Records. The band lineup being now comprised of Drew Stone (vocals), Tom Capone (guitar), Tristan D' Graves (bass) and Matt Gray (drums). *Scarred* is even better than *No Peace In Our Time*! Top-notch NYHC, frantic, simple and catchy as hell, and *Scarred* includes four songs, with 'Divided State' being my favourite! Alongside, in the *Scarred* sessions, Antidote NYHC recorded two Minor Threat covers 'Filler' and 'I Don't Wanna Hear It' as an homage to the seminal band from DC.

Antidote NYHC went on to make a new start and new name to Incendiary Device, and are still (2025) active to this day, offering shows, plus having a self-titled record out (2023) that includes some of the catchiest NYHC the old-school way you can check out! Not to be missed, because tunes like 'Incendiary Device' or 'Accelerate' and 'Living In The Past' have a melodic catchiness reminiscent of even Orange County punk bands-oops!

The history of Antidote is connected with many bands that its members played or play with. Drew Stone played in The Mighty CO's and The High And The Mighty, but also is a film director, producer, film editor and author and musician. His works include music videos, commercials, documentary films and television. Check *The New York Hardcore Chronicles Film* that went into transforming into a YouTube show named as *The New York Hardcore Chronicles LIVE!*. Drew also appeared in records by Biohazard, Dog Eat Dog, Nucleus, Sick Of It All, and has a massive background in producing music videos including Madball's 'Pride'. Arthur McGuckin was the drummer of Misfits, and also played with Modern Clix, The Noise and Upnrunin. Tommy Victor of course founded Prong, and also played with Co-Conspirators, Danzig, Ministry and Primitive Race. Chris Praz played in YDI. Matt Gray played also in Bigwig and Label The Traitor. Aryeh Lemberger played in The Disenchanted. Tom Capone played in Beyond, Bloodclot, Bold, Crippled Youth, Handsome, Instruction, Quicksand, Shelter and Nympho. Tristan D' Graves in Pawnshop

Kings, Sunchild, The Undead and now in Incendiary Device with Mat Gray, Shaun Brennan and of course Drew Stone.

"Crossover of hardcore and metal is absolutely relevant today" Drew concludes. "Like any primarily youth driven musical movement the wave goes in, and the wave goes out. New people come into the scene that discover the genre, are influenced by it and add new life into it".

At a glance: Those not familiar with Antidote, start with *Thou Shalt Not Kill,* there's a LP compilation re-issue of it on Radio Raheem. Unbelievable classic of NYHC. Crossover lovers, check out *Return 2 Burn*; it's enjoyable, and I think that people into late 1980s Gang Green will dig many songs. However, you should also seek for the Antidote/Antidote NYHC records of 2010s, and also Incendiary Device's LP. And subscribe to Drew's *The New York Hardcore Chronicles LIVE!* Channel on YouTube, because it's awesome and always full of surprise guests!

SAM BLACK CHURCH

(Sam Black Church band picture, courtesy unknown)

I wanted so much to write about Sam Black Church in *Crossover The Edge*, however it too me a while to have them interviewed and obviously I missed the deadlines. However, justice is served, and the story of one of the most unique sounding crossover bands is now included. What is phenomenal in their case is that they were much more metal than other crossover bands but still sounded more hardcore! Formed in 1988 in Boston, MA, Sam Black Church (also known as SBC) were named after the West Virginia community of Sam Black Church, the hometown of drummer, J.R. Roach. Jesse 'Jet' Crandall took over the vocals, his brother Ben Crandall was the guitarist and Richard G. Lewis handled the bass duties.

"Without a doubt, the first metal and punk crossover was Bad Brains. Their first releases were definitely punk, but over time their sound grew increasing metal" J.R. narrates. "I think that crossover grew organically in both ways. Bad Brains and Cro-Mags expanded the range of the music to include elements of both metal and punk, becoming what came to be known as 'hardcore'. Fans of metal and punk naturally liked elements of both styles of music for different reasons, and the two different styles no longer needed to be mutually exclusive. It happened naturally".

(Slapshot, Leeway, Sam Black Church and Only Living Witness at Boston's The Channel. 29/09/1991)

After a first demo (1988), Sam Black Church went on to release their first 7-inch named as *Unincorporated*. Quite a shock for me when I first got it (actually, the first release that I got off them). You could hear a band that had a definite Bad Brains influence, but blended with blast beats, crazy metal riffs, slow parts...not an easy listening record, but highly enjoyable! Four songs, and I think that 'Disjustice' is my favourite tune.

"Well, most of us grew up in rural West Virginia, so our early influences were pretty mainstream, like Iron Maiden, Motörhead, Van Halen, Judas Priest, and Metallica" J.R. smiles. "But as we started to go to college in Boston, we discovered bands like Bad Brains, Cro-Mags, Hüsker Dü, Voivod, etc. We came from more of a metal background... Although we grew up on metal, none of us were into any kind of glam aspect of it. We were strictly about the music, so it was natural that we would look more hardcore than anything else. We weren't very punk, either".

After one more demo, and their inclusion on Al Quint's *Suburban Voice* compilation with their track of the sheer craziness named 'Formaldahead', Sam Black Church entered the new decade with the same-titled 12'-inch on Boston's Taang Records. Again, four tracks of their own ilk, now more controlled though, without the frenzied speed of their earlier stuff, but with a chunkier, more powerful style. Songs like 'Infernal Machine' you can almost sing along to them! Very heavy, powerful and nasty crossover metal hardcore, but not typical of the speedcore era, really genuine stuff.

"Well, I think there were small factions of fans who remained loyal to their base for a time, but as bands started to play mixed bills, like Motörhead playing shows with Cro-Mags for instance. By the time the 1990s rolled around, those mixed bills were pretty commonplace" J.R. adds. "And none of the violence that occasionally happened at our shows appeared to be between any factions based on music taste!"

(Sam Black Church, Straw Dogs, Slaughter Shack and Jerry's Kids at the Green Street Station, Boston. 22/04/1989)

Playing endlessly alongside other Boston greats such as Slapshot or Straw Dogs or Jerry's Kids as well as out of town bands like Leeway, Bad Brains and Ringworm. Sam Black Church pretty much established their name in the 1990s as a great hardcore combo, with a sonic approach that was not heard before. On Taang Records again, Sam Black Church released their first full length LP, *Let In Life* in 1993; more melodic than before even though songs had outbursts of ferocity, this is maybe their finest effort. Songs like 'Re-Alive' or 'The Right Fuel' have a definitive alternative metal hardcore style, while 'Guardian Of Hopes And Dreams' is maybe the best song they ever written. However, *Let in Life* strays away from the vicious hardcore metal crossover sound, heading into a different route, and as much as I like it, I think that hardline crossover people will find it difficult to identify with.

"Motörhead, Cro-Mags, Bad Brains, Slayer. Those were the bands I loved seeing back then" J.R. admits. "I remember that Bad Brains played Bunratty's in Boston, and the day of the show it was changed from all-ages to 18+. Dozens of kids couldn't get into the show, so Dr. Know and H.R. kept taking a kick drum case out the back door, putting kids inside of it, and smuggling them into the show".

Superchrist CD followed (1995) as well as *That Which Does Not Kill Us...Makes Us Stronger* CD (1999) and *The Black Comedy* CD (1998), all with a far better production than before, and a return to a more vicious sound, that fans of modern hardcore will definitely enjoy. They sound more refined and controlled, and I kind of miss the spark of earlier days, but still, Sam Black Church deliver with style!

"We always loved playing The Channel and Bunratty's" J.R. mentions with a huge smile on his face. "Our first headlining show was at Bunratty's, and we still remember it as one of favourite shows ever. It's also the place where we were able to make the leap from all-ages, day shows to 18+ and 21+ night shows. The Channel was the first large venue we played, and it's really where we got an education playing with bands like Dark Angel, Bad Brains, Murphy's Law, and Slapshot".

(Sam Black Church, Bad Trip, Jawbreaker and Only Living Witness at the Wetlands, 30/08/1992)

Sam Black Church initially split up in 2000, with brothers Ben and Jesse 'Jet' Crandall forming Jetfuel (heavy hardcore), J.R. Roach forming C60 (hard rock) and Richard Lewis playing with alternative country rockers Memphis 59. They returned back several times in the 00s, and then back for good since 2016, and they still (2024) remain active, while J.R. also plays in heavy/stoner Blood Lightning.

"You hear the influence of both styles in so many variations that classifications of styles keep becoming more and more diverse. It happened organically, and it's still happening organically. So, crossover is absolutely relevant today" J.R. concludes.

At a glance: I love the spark, authenticity and manic ferocity of early Sam Black Church-they sound like a more metal Bad Brains on helium, so I'm perfectly happy with that! Not an easy-listening band by any stretch of imagination, you should dive into their sound if you love the whole of 1980s Bad Brains mixed with some (early?) Slayer. Start with *Unincorporated* EP.

SLAUGHTER SHACK

(Slaughter Shack band picture. Courtesy of Mim Michelove)

Crossover's history includes bands that were totally innovative, however they didn't enjoy success in their heyday. One case of such a unique sounding band was Slaughter Shack from Boston, Massachusetts. Formed in 1986, their approach in crossover was heavy, crunchy, angular with the gruff vocals of Colin Burns. Guitarist Dana Ong narrates that "I have to go into the backstory a bit. My cousin, Tim Lee, was touring with Let's Active in the 1980s when I was living in Boston. During their stint through the East Coast, he invited me to go to their show at Maxwell's in Hoboken, New Jersey. Tim knew I wanted to play bass in a band, so he introduced me to a few of his friends looking for a bass player. I ended up taking the bus to New York City to rehearse with the Wygals but ultimately, I wasn't ready to commit to New York City or the style of music they were playing. I loved listening to them, but the teenage punk rocker in me started was screaming for more. I was going to shows in Boston every chance I could, the first one was the Proletariat and the long-gone Chet's Last Call. But I was also going to see bands like The Neats, Black Cat Bone. I went to everything I could from punk to new genres that had evolved out of punk. My first friends in Boston were a band called the FIVE, still one of my favourite bands of that era. They were a bit like the band The Birthday Party mixed with American blues. They were heavy, dark, passionate, and wildly energetic. From the outset, they were one of the Slaughter Shack's most important influences and allies. More on that later.

(Slaughter Shack early lineup. Courtesy unknown)

I started looking around for people I wanted to create something new with. I didn't want to start a full-on punk rock band, and I didn't completely relate to the newly emerging indie-rock bands. In came Colin Burns, we had adjacent studios at the Museum School of Fine Arts where my work as a little too edgy for some, and I'm sure Colin's was too. We blasted Black Flag, he smoked cigarettes, I was covered in tar and other materials like a lunatic; we quickly became friends. During some drunken party, I managed to convince him to start a band with me".

And this is where the story of Slaughter Shack starts, with Dana mentioning that "the first iteration of Slaughter Shack was myself, Colin Burns, Ellen M, Deb Scott, and George. With the help of the FIVE we started to find our path. Their drummer's wife was our first drummer. They invited us to open for them for our first gig. On some Sunday trip to who-knows-where with Tom from the FIVE, we saw the newly opened entrance to one of Boston's subway lines. It was a silver, unadorned dome that led downstairs. In our collective imagination we thought it looked like an entrance to a human slaughterhouse. Tom, with his keen sense of humour said 'slaughter shack', and that was it! Perfect band name for us".

Slaughter Shack went on to record (1988) their first demo that contained two songs, 'Transformer' and 'Dreaming Ape'. If you can imagine a mix of The Stooges with Birthday Party, Sonic Youth and all filtered through a metal sound of heavy and rough metal hardcore, you can get the point. Another one song of this session ('Damaged Shelter') was added with the raging 'Dreaming Ape' on the 1988 *Suffer This... A Compilation Of Boston's Backwash* compilation LP, mind-shattering stuff all over.

"We were messy, heavy, artsy, with a touch of Sonic Youth" Dana adds. "We recorded a demo in a friend's basement. I think that's when we recorded 'Transformer' and 'Dreaming Ape'. I still think 'Transformer' was one of the best things we ever recorded. For brevity's sake, I'll skip the messy part and get right to the time me and my friend Tracy found the *SPIN* [magazine] story about Metallica, I think they mentioned the Misfits, and Kirk Hammett was wearing a Pushead T-shirt, I was hooked! We tried to figure out how to play the riff from 'Master of Puppets'. I was barely skilled on guitar and could only get through 10 seconds of it with my hands, but that riff probably drove the direction of Slaughter Shack more than any other single thing".

(Slaughter Shack, Hullabaloo and Pelvic Thrust at Museum School, 28/10/1988)

"Our main influences in no real order were" Dana adds, "Black Flag, Metallica, Wargasm, Meliah Rage, Temporary Insanity, The Birthday Party, Gun Club, The Stooges, Rites of Spring, Einsturzende Neubaten, the FIVE and all of Boston rock from punk to country punk and all of the great bands in between, the Misfits, Danzig, Die Kreuzen, a bit of Sonic Youth, and so many more".

Changes took place in the lineup of the band, and this led to musical changes too: "we split ways with Deb and George" Dana adds. "We gained John Queenan from the local metal band Maelstrom. We played as a 4 piece for a while until Andy Strachan, formerly from Boston's straight edge band, DYS joined. He brought that incredible Les Paul gold top sound and also some metal skills. Barry Hite joined, his musical resume is longer than I can recount. He had some heavy hitting mixed with a taste of groove. We started consolidating into a metal band but heavily influenced by punk and its offshoots".

The new lineup recorded and released the 1989 *Slaughter Shack* demo, that contained four songs of vicious, punishing metal thrash-hardcore, with elements of noise rock; mid-tempo and very heavy, songs like 'Grievous Angel', later covered by the Boston thrashers Wargasm. The excellent 'Vampire' had a definite Metallica influence, but it was all filtered through their diverse elements.

"I don't remember the reaction to crossover punk so much" Dana admits, "except I think DYS caught shit for jumping from the album *Wolfpack* to *Fire & Ice*. I know there was blow back, I heard the criticism and condescending remarks when Slaughter Shack evolved. But as usual, I didn't care. And as for my favourite shows from that era, these would include Black Flag in 1984-not crossover, but I wouldn't have wanted to play live if it weren't for that show. Bands from favourite shows we played while in Slaughter Shack: Hullabaloo, Wargasm, Cardinal Sin, Gay Bikers on Acid, Bla'st! (cross-over adjacent), White Zombie, Lunachicks".

Dana admits that meeting the thrashers Wargasm was a turning point for the band: "Then we met Wargasm, total game changer. They supported us with full passion. Rich Spillberg, the guitar player helped mentor me and even came to the recording studio in 1990 to help me record leads. Most of them including crew, were front and centre at the Rumble in 1990!".

Another one demo was out in 1991, with three new songs ('Drive By', 'A.T.F.' and 'Sleeve'), showcasing their most metal effort; heavy and haunting. 'Sleeve' actually is just mental, while 'A.T.F.' is their fastest song, a pulverizing speedcore killer. 'Drive By' and 'A.T.F.' were later re-released in the 1992 *Fuck You / Fuck You Too* split 7-inch alongside Stompbox (stoner-hardcore or something like that!). "My favourite recordings include the songs 'Transformer', '100', 'A.T.F.', and 'Fuck Yeah' Dana mentions.

(Slaughter Shack and Wiseblood at the Rat, Boston, 12/02/1990)

The story of Slaughter Shack ended in 1993 with no reunion in the later years. "I moved to New York City in 1993, Slaughter Shack didn't officially disband till later" Dana narrates. "I think crossover has been an important bridge to music but I'm not actively listening to new bands in that genre or going to shows much. I played in a band called T.Y.T.L. here in Hawaii in 2009, mostly punk with skateboarders Jay Adams, Mark Alva, and Lange Sheppard. Jay had recorded one of his songs with Suicidal Tendencies and lived with Black Flag so we definitely had a crossover influence. Due to family things, that was the last time I was actively involved".

Members of Slaughter Shack appeared also in other bands. John Queenan played in the metal band Maelstrom, while Barry Hite played in Slapshot who I saw on November 11, 2025 for the last time ever in Greece. Dana later played as mentioned in T.Y.T.L. (Thirty Years Too Late), while Ellen Mieczkowski played in the doom sludge 13 and in The Concussion Ensemble. Andy Strachan played in the Boston hardcore pioneers DYS, while Darryl Shepard played in The Scimitar, Deslok, Hackman, Blackwolfgoat, Iron Fisted (Motörhead tribute), Kind, Test Meat, Black Pyramid, Drug War, Fighter Captured, Headcleaner, Milligram, Necrosapien, Roadsaw, Slapshot, Supahead, The Chair.

At a glance: If you like your crossover to be challenging and out of any typical form, you should give Slaughter Shack a chance, because their eclectic musical mix is very enticing. My favourite release off them is the 1989 *Slaughter Shack* demo, that kind of bridges the early, art damaged approach with their later, more metal style.

METHEDRINE

I was searching endlessly to find some info on Methedrine, as well as a member to interview, since the days I was writing *Crossover The Edge*, but no chance. Luckily, I came across guitarist Lee Stefanko, and he connected me via email with Methedrine's founding member, vocalist Jim Murray.

"Methedrine was really a natural development in the friendship the four original members had at the time" Jim narrates. "Me (vocals), Britt Nixon (drums), Mike Heaton (bass), and Dan Hamilton (guitar) became close through our love of the growing underground metal and punk bands we were discovering on what seemed like a daily basis. The early Metallica, Slayer, D.R.I., Corrosion, Misfits, etc had such an impact on us, such a rallying and subcultural call to us, that we inevitably picked up instruments in the attempt to be a real part of the movement. It wasn't simply music to us: it was the bond between us. It was infectious, and it spoke to us in the same way it spoke to millions of other teens in the mid to late 1980s".

(Methedrine's demo Meth Til Death, 1988)

Lee Stefanko was soon enough added on the second guitar, and Methedrine's lineup was set and ready to go. "The first band to crossover? Hmm" Jim wonders. "This has always been a bone of contention in the crossover world. Some say Black Flag, Corrosion of Conformity, some even say Motörhead. But to me, to be a crossover band you have to cross over from something into another. Those bands were hardcore, but not crossover. In my opinion D.R.I. was the first true crossover band. I understand the Suicidal [Tendencies] argument, but I don't think Suicidal got as metal as early as D.R.I. D.R.I. struck the right balance, at least in the mid-1980s. You could hear it on *Dealing With It*, and the albums *Crossover* and *Four of a Kind* solidified it for me".

Originating from Scullville, New Jersey, I think that Methedrine was one of the very few bands to ever come out from this place. "We had a pretty good metal and punk scene in the New Jersey and Philly area though" Jim adds. "What was funny though is that sometimes we would get booked at clubs that didn't know where to put us. There weren't many crossover bands around at the time, so many times we would have to play with hair bands, punk bands, death metal bands, etc. I don't think we ever played a show with only crossover bands. Maybe once or twice when we rented out a hall, but ninety-nine percent of the time we were out of our element. There was this one gig where we were booked to play this VFW BBQ near our rehearsal space. We loaded our gear on the flatbed and started playing. It didn't take long to notice that no one was really watching us or even facing us, except for the few with confused looks on their faces. Finally, one of the older grey-haired guys yelled out, 'know any Skynyrd?' 'Or at least any Judas Priest?'. That gig ended early, needless to say".

Methedrine hit the studio, and this resulted in their first demo, the 1988 *Meth 'til Deth*. More metal than other crossover contemporaries, Methedrine exposed great technical skills. Even from the very start including some crazy bass lines, and their sonic approach was somewhere in between Nuclear Assault blended with Suicidal Tendencies, with a vocal style reminiscent of Kurt Brecht of D.R.I. Songs like

'Hunger' or 'You've Changed' are just ace, top stuff. 'Porno Stars' is just frantic, and the lyrics are not sexist crap, just condemning the life in the porn industry.

"The first band that influenced me was Metallica" Jim admits, when asked about his influences and overall, Methedrine's influences. "I still remember when I first heard them in 1985 with *Ride the Lightning* album. Life was never the same. I went from listening to Rush and Zeppelin and Motley Crue and WASP to Metallica. Those other bands faded into the rear view. The other band was D.R.I. Same year. I heard *Dealing with It* and couldn't believe my ears. The speed, those riffs, the brazen words that seemed to be speaking directly to me. Again, it changed everything. Others were Celtic Frost, Voivod, Suicidal Tendencies, Minor Threat, The Misfits. The list goes on".

(Methedrine's Differences Rather than Similarities 1988 demo)

"Despite the conscious attempts to keep the genres apart and hostile toward one another, metal and punk found common ground in crossover for two reasons" Jim narrates. "One, the musical styles: those were both hell-bent on speed and heaviness, aggression and volume. Combining the two was inevitable. It really was organic in the truest sense. No one had to force that. Two, and maybe more importantly, the two also shared a worldview. At least in the broad sense. Whether it was politics, social change, horror movies, history, or current events, thrash metal and punk were subcultures that did not buy into the stories or messaging being thrown at them daily. They were the antithesis of the glossy 1980s happening around them. These groups of people were wise to the system, and through this new and bold music they united in the expression of that wisdom. I always used to say that my friends in the thrash world were some of the smartest people I've ever known".

Next release for Methedrine was the 1989 demo *Crawl...Before You Walk* that was on the same musical mentality like *Meth 'til Deth*. Now with more of their own character, plus many mosh parts like on the opener 'Crawl Before You Walk', it's another one winner. Balancing between riff-laden thrash metal and hardcore, songs like 'Lullaby' and 'Image Wise' are just sheer shredders!

"Yeah, we saw some fights, but nothing too crazy" Jim recalls about the days of crossover, and mixed shows. "By the time we came out the animosity between thrash and punk had died down a little. This was 1987-88. It was still there, but subdued… I remember seeing quite a few fights between metalheads and punk at concerts. And I knew people who couldn't tolerate the mixing of the two, whether in songs or at shows. It always seemed stupid. I could understand the distaste for hair metal. That was something thrash and punk could agree on. But the exclusivity of each subculture, the almost possessive stance toward the other was just dumb. As if the whole genre would get ruined by the influence. Small minds I guess".

Methedrine in 1990 released one more demo, their final one, *Differences Rather than Similarities*. Sadly, I couldn't find it anywhere to review it, however I'm pretty sure about the definite quality of this release too.

"We saw so many shows back then" Jim recalls with nostalgia. "Slayer in 1986, D.R.I. on the *Four of a Kind* tour, Kreator multiple times, Suicidal [Tendencies] on the *Join the Army* tour, Metallica on *Justice*. There are so many. Believe it or not, to this day the best band I saw between 1986-1990 was Voivod at City Gardens in Trenton, New Jersey. They headlined on the *Nothingface* tour. The openers were Soundgarden and Faith No More, right after Patton joined the band. Voivod was incredible…In terms of Methedrine favourite places to play, I would say Gwillikers in Pennsauken, New Jersey. Loved that club. Every time we played there, we would get a great crowd and sell out of our demo tapes. And it didn't matter who we played with. The people that went to that club were great".

Methedrine called it quits on early 1990s, never to reform. While there's no info regarding other bands that its members played with later, I'm sure there were a few. Jim adds on a final note that "I do not think crossover is still relevant because it is a subgenre that defines a certain time. It is not a timeless style of music. Unlike regular metal or even punk, crossover expresses something that was momentary and just can't be recaptured. Music changes over time, influences inspire different sounds for different generations. And though music might not always 'progress' it nonetheless changes with time. I mean, sure, you could write some crossover songs, but it wouldn't be crossover anymore. It would just be a facsimile. Thrash metal suffers from a similar fate. There are thrash bands out now, but nothing can recapture those golden years between 1982-1990. Different time. Different spirit".

At a glance: I hope some re-issue label (F.O.A.D. maybe?) would pull off some kind of a collection of everything Methedrine ever recorded. It was surely a good band, that fans of the most riff-approached crossover would enjoy. Sometimes they get a bit too metal for me, but the next second they come back with a frenetic hardcore tempo and riff, I'm in!

WRECKING CREW

(Wrecking Crew band picture. Courtesy of Hawker Records)

Boston, Massachusetts Wrecking Crew are cited as the band that put Boston hardcore on the map alongside Slapshot during the second wave of Boston hardcore. This was post-1984, after all the original X-Claim bands disbanded or changed their sound e.g. Gang Green; though bands like The Freeze were always active offering excellent hardcore punk. However, Wrecking Crew had a definite metal edge into their sound, and this was the reason of their inclusion in this book.

Formed in 1986 by Glenn Dudley (vocals), John Darga (guitar), Ralph DiNunzio (guitar), Keith Bennett (bass) and Taras Hrabec (drums) and Keith Bennet narrates that "Wrecking Crew was a band born from a group of friends who loved punk, hardcore and metal. We had most of our dreams come true, played with so many of our heroes, made A LOT of mistakes along the way but in the end it was worth it. Grateful for the adventure!"

(Wrecking Crew with Eye For An Eye, S.T.P. and Quicksand at the Bunratty's, Boston. 04/11/1990)

(Wrecking Crew, Victim's Family and Corrosion of Conformity, 23/05/1987)

Wrecking Crew with their all-out-attack approach on the first (1988) demo, had already a definite metal edge, however not alike their oldest Boston peers such as SSD, DYS or Gang Green and those bands' sophomore records during the mid to late 1980s. Brutal and hard-hitting, they sounded like a blend between Negative Approach and Cro-Mags. All eight songs shred, especially 'Balance of Terror', the brutal moshcore of 'Guts and Glory' and the homage to Negative Approach, of 'Tied Down'. Four songs off the demo were later released as a 7-inch in 1988 through their own label, Vortex Records, and of course, it's a classic.

"Both in equal measure" Keith replies when asked who influenced who, punk or metal. "Musically I think it was both scenes being drawn to the power of each other sound. Culturally it was two groups of youth finding a bond over the world and society that was looking down on us all, but the first one was Motörhead. No doubt about it. They were the great equalizer for all of us. There are only two kinds of people: Motörheadbangers or assholes".

Their explosive sonic and visual live assault, playing alongside bands like Seka or NYHC bands like Sick of it All offered great publicity to Wrecking Crew, and Hawker Records, a Roadrunner Records' short-lived hardcore imprint, that included also the great Token Entry, Pagan Babies, No For An Answer and Jones Very. Hawker Records offered them a contract for one record with the 1989 release of *Balance of Terror* LP. *Balance of Terror* dropped like a bomb; heavier than before, more technical but more vicious. Wrecking Crew offered a masterpiece of Boston hardcore with a metal edge; re-recording the demo tracks alongside new ones like the skull-crushing 'Old Enough' or 'Right Or Wrong / Nothing For Me', this is just top-notch, brutal attack to all senses, and the secret here is the songwriting. Wrecking Crew don't play fast for the sake of playing fast, they prefer writing bloody tunes!

(Wrecking Crew, Sick Of It All, Raw Deal, Rest in Pieces at Green St. Station 13/08/1987)

"There definitely was suspicion and scepticism from both sides" Keith adds, regarding the reaction of metalheads and hardcore punks towards crossover. "But the truth and power of the music was undeniable. Punks saw that not all metalheads were foolish Van Halen types and metalheads saw that there was something deeper and sincere in hardcore punk".

Wrecking Crew in 1990 released the *1990 Demo*, and it's a damn pity that this thing never got a proper vinyl release. Now more clean sounding, it contained four songs in their usual style, but then again why change the winning formula? 'Blank Mind' is the winning song here, alongside the very Cro-Mags styled 'Thousand Yard Stare'. "By early 1990s both worlds, hardcore and metal were colliding totally" Keith adds. "Any growing process can be painful; in this case it was literally…some shows were a total bloodshed".

Regarding the sonic approach of Wrecking Crew, Keith acknowledges that "personally it will always begin and end with Motörhead. Discharge, Cro-Mags, Venom, GBH, SSD, Hellhammer/Celtic Frost, The F.U.'s, Agnostic Front, Misfits, Negative Approach all shaped the sound of Wrecking Crew". However, one has also to refer to the visual approach of the band. They looked like a blend of metalheads, hardcore kids and skins! "Absolutely!" Keith agrees. "Doc Martens, bullet belt, studded leather and cut-off denim. Mandatory!".

Lineup changes in Wrecking Crew took place in 1992 with Nick Clancy of Subjugator and Bloodlust joining in as a guitarist, and Elgin Nathan James of The Law and later in 454 Big Clock, Righteous Jams and The World Is My Fuse. as a vocalist. This resulted in the release of the 1993 *Wrecking Crew* 7-inch; now sounding even cleaner and more professional. This release contains four typical and great Wrecking Crew songs, with 'Passing Time' being my favourite-a complex and hard-hitting hardcore anthem with a crazy bassline! Dean Baltulonis later joined on guitar in early 1994 but the band folded, only for its members to follow another music paths.

Wrecking Crew reformed on various occasions through the next decades to perform live. In 2005 Wrecking Crew on Bridge Nine Records released the *Why Must They / Live At CBGB's* 7-inch. Keith Bennett alongside Chris Lauria (Deslok and Slapshot), John Bean (Deslok and Headcleaner) and Rich Spillberg (Wargasm and Maniac) formed Bitter in 1995, who released the excellent *Bitter* CD and the 1995 *No Miracle* 7-inch that sounded like a continuation of the sound of Wrecking Crew, albeit much darker and heavier.

(Wrecking Crew, Warzone, Converge, Arise at The Baptist Church, Boston, 13/03/1991)

"It honestly would take a book on its own to really go into detail about Boston during that era. Believe everything you've heard!" Keith laughs, adding that "my favourite places to play were The Rat, The Channel, The Anthrax, CBGB's were always beautiful chaos. I miss them all very much indeed….as for my favourite shows in the crossover era? So many, but I would say Motörhead with Cro-Mags at The Ritz, GBH with Agnostic Front, Anthrax with The F.U.'s, Trouble with Kilslug come to mind immediately but there were hundreds besides those".

Post-Wrecking Crew Dean Baltulonis played with 454 Big Block, Eye For An Eye, Foreign Islands, the excellent melodic hardcore Supertouch, No Warning and Scarlet Heaven among countless others. John Darga played with Fast Actin' Fuses, Hellcats From Outer Space, Kilslug, X-15, while Ralph DiNunzio played in 454 Big Clock. Taras Hrabec played in the hardcore STP, and Glenn Dudley performed with Diecast. Keith Bennett alongside Bitter played in Cold Northern Vengeance (black metal!), Death Ray Vision, Ramallah, Vein, Conclave (doom metal!) and still performs with the Motörhead-fueled hardcore of PanzerBastard. Prolific, talented and with a wide love for various music genres!

"Of course, crossover is relevant today my friend!" Keith smiles and finalizes our discussion about such a great band like Wrecking Crew.

At a glance: Every Wrecking Crew release is just top class. I would though recommend *Balance of Terror* LP for a starter, because it's pretty easy to find for a decent price! Wrecking Crew weren't crossover per se; however, I believe that they had something for everybody, from straight edge hardcore kids to thrashers.

PLASMATICS

(Plasmatics band picture. Courtesy of Richie Stotts)

Obviously, this is mostly a reminder chapter of what a significant band were the Plasmatics for the evolution of the punk metal crossover. One of the most controversial, self-destructive, and wild bands in the history of rock 'n' roll. Plasmatics formed by manager Rod Swenson and his on and off partner in life

Wendy O. Williams in New York City in 1977. The band was always centred around Wendy and guitarist Wes Beech, who was the only steady member of everything that Wendy did through her career.

Appearing for the first time in CBGB's in July 1978, as a three-piece, Plasmatics established their fame as one of the wildest live bands ever. And the only way to release their music was through their own label, Vice Squad records, because US labels were reluctant of offering them a contract. This resulted to three in a row ultra classic EPs: *Butcher Baby* (1978), *Dream Lover* (1979), and *Meet The Plasmatics* (1979), before signing to the UK label Stiff Records. Already home of The Damned, DEVO and other lunatics of the time, Stiff didn't miss the chance.

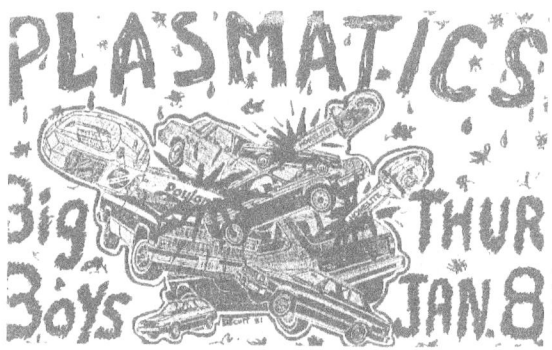

(Plasmatics and the Big Boys at Club Foot, 08/01/1981)

Guitarist Jean Beauvoir was added in the ever-changing lineup, and the first seeds of the new Plasmatics were *Monkey Suit* 7-inch (1980), *Butcher Baby* 7-inch (1980) and the classic *New Hope For The Wretched* LP (1980). "It was the craziest childhood someone could have imagined!" Jean smiles. "Fuelled with rebellion, angst, *New Hope For The Wretched* and incredible fans!".

Jean was just eighteen years old when he joined Plasmatics, and he was already an accomplished bass and keyboard player. 'The Plasmatics were the first ones to crossover metal with punk, that's my opinion... When the Plasmatics were wreaking havoc on Sunset Boulevard, no metal bands were playing yet. As a matter of fact, because of all the dismay that we imposed on the Sunset Strip, it allowed metal to become 'a la mode' in those clubs, because they'd had enough of punk and what it was bringing".

New Hope For The Wretched was a shocking LP, not only in musical, but as well as in lyrical terms. Still on the punk side of things, with a slight metal edge, it contained tunes that were basic yet brutal, and catchy as hell. Anthems like 'Monkey Suit', 'Want You Baby', 'Butcher Baby' or my favourite 'Won't You' are simply timeless. I remember myself jumping up and down to the sounds of 'Monkey Suit' in my parents' house. I used to blast the original version as well as the Didjits lunatic cover!

(Plasmatics with The Rattlers and Mitch Ryder, at the Palladium 16/11/1979)

"It was a wide range for me" Jean discusses regarding his influences. "Led Zeppelin, KISS, Eric Clapton, Rush. At the same time, Motown and even classical music. I think it comes from the roots of the musicians who get together in a band. A metal guitarist starts to dig punk and merges his style with that of the punk band, or vice versa. This also applies to the other musicians and singers. I believe this happens in many types of music, but it comes from the people who create the music".

Countless arrests, chaos in live shows, being banned, destruction, drugs and booze, lineup changes, and inner fights. Plasmatics seemed unstoppable. Their second LP, *Beyond The Valley of 1984* (1981) was another classic. Now heading for a more metal direction than before, but still with many punk elements, songs like 'Nothing', 'Masterplan', 'Fast Food Service' (a frantic punker) and 'Living Dead' make me go apeshit. Plasmatics released another record in 1981, the *Metal Priestess* 12-inch that exposed a turn to a more heavy metal sound, with the exception of the excellent 'Doom Song' that blended punk and metal equally, and still a good record.

"We always had head banging and slam dancing. People would just from the stage and get hurt sometimes, but the metalheads and punks always co-habituated well at our shows" Jean adds, and it's no lie that in the 1980s Plasmatics appeared as headliners in both punk, hardcore, or metal shows. Or, even mixed together, with bands as diverse as Cro-Mags, Vardis, Big Boys, The Rattlers with band member, guitarist Mickey Leigh, Joey Ramone's younger brother, or KISS! "I believe that people are influenced by many things that surround them. Knowingly and unknowingly and I think that's always been the case with me" Jean adds. "However, my favourite places to play were always in London! Wembley Stadium, and the Marquee in London".

(Plasmatics with Vardis in Hammersmith Odeon, London. 08/08/1980)

Capitol Records offered a contract for one LP, and this resulted in the 1982 *Coup D'Etat*, that was another step forward for the band. Wendy sounded like an absolute menace now, it is definitely her wildest vocal performance on any Plasmatics or WOW recordings. In musical terms, *Coup D'Etat* kept the metal-punk blend, only this time slightly more metal than before. It also though includes some of the best songs the band ever written, 'Mistress of Taboo', 'Stop' and of course 'The Damned' which is one of the best songs ever.

Their relationship with Capitol Records went down the drain though, and this led to the Plasmatics' hiatus. To avoid legal trouble, now the band renamed to WOW (Wendy O. Williams). Wendy O. Williams first LP *WOW* (1984) included a new lineup with Eric Carr of KISS behind the drum kit. *WOW* was a massive commercial hit, which led Williams receiving a Grammy nomination for 'Best Female Rock Vocal' in 1985! However, now Wendy headed for an all-out heavy metal party and hard rock party approach that I'm not so fond of. Fans of this style love this record, however I only like one song, the amazing 'It's My Life'. The frantic metal punk style came back in the great *Kommander Of Kaos* LP (1986)! Reminiscent of the earlier days of the band, this one's a winner, and how else could it be since 'Goin Wild', 'Party' and 'Pedal to the Metal' are in.

With Beech back in the band, Plasmatics were together for one more time, and this time they went on to release their most challenging record; the 1987 *Maggots: The Record* LP. This record blends speed metal with punk and operatic vocals, while lyrically it focusses on the environmental abuse of planet Earth. It kind of reminds of what Warfare did later on *Hammer Horror* LP or The Blood's *Se Parare Nex*, not in strict musical terms, but on the artistic tendencies of presenting something completely different from the past. I find that the only drawback of *Maggots: The Record* are the spoken word passages, but when the music is on, we are talking about a classic Plasmatics record, with anthems like 'Destroyers' or 'You're a Zombie'.

(Plasmatics at the Ritz, 13/01/1983)

Wendy O. Williams went on to release a rap-rock LP later in 1988. Under the moniker of Wendy O. Williams' Ultrafly And The Hometown Girls. It's largely forgettable. She later went on to move to Storrs, Connecticut in 1991, where she lived with her long-time companion and former manager, Rod Swenson. She worked as an animal rehabilitator and at a food co-op in Willimantic. She sadly ended her life on 6 April 1998, when she was forty-eight years old.

Other members of Plasmatics also pursued a musical career post-Plasmatics. Chris Romanelli played with Richie Stotts, Shotgun Rationale and Ziggy Marley And The Melody Makers while he also played with Phantom and Savoy Brown. Jean Beauvoir has a very successful career to this day, not only as a guitarist, but also as a bassist, singer, and composer, playing with bands like Crown Of Thorns, Hand In Hand For Children e.V., Little Steven himself and with his band, Voodoo X, KISS, the Ramones. Jean has a solo music career, plus he also produced music for movies such as *Pet Sematary*, penned by Dee Dee Ramone and sung by the Ramones. Did you know that Jean also produced and co-wrote the Ramones song 'My Brain Is Hanging Upside Down', originally titled 'Bonzo Goes To Bitburg'? Richie Stotts has his own solo career, while T.C. Oliver played with T.M. Stevens, The Hounds Of Hasselvander, Terry Burrus, Angela Bofill and Symba. Wes Beech also performed with Shock Therapy.

"I think there's more of the crossover between punk and metal now than before. I believe music will continue to evolve as time goes on".

At a glance: Everyone into Motörhead should at least have one Plasmatics record, *Beyond The Valley Of 1984*. And everyone with a taste in all things punk metal, should at least have three Plasmatics records: *New Hope For The Wretched*, *Beyond The Valley Of 1984* and *Coup D'Etat*. I have a very soft spot for *New Hope For The Wretched* and the early singles, but I would also recommend *Maggots: The Record*, this is a very diverse and unique record. Plasmatics were maybe the last most dangerous band in rock 'n' roll alongside GG Allin. Their records are celebration of what rock 'n' roll is about: wild fun!

THE MOB

(The Mob band picture. Courtesy unknown)

A pioneering band of the first wave of New York Hardcore, The Mob formed in 1980 after Jack Flanagan's (bass, later guitar) departure from another classic (now) NYHC band, Heart Attack. Based in Queens, The Mob's original lineup included Ralph Gebbia, John Frawley, and Nicko, and while initially they were a punk rock band, they went into an all-out attack approach after seeing Bad Brains perform in CBGB's. By 1981, Jose Gonzalez (bass) officially joined the group, following John Frawley's departure to join Heart Attack, and Jamie Shanahan replaced Nicko on drums. This lineup recorded their first two, highly sought-after and beyond any doubt classic 7-inchs, the 1982 *Upset the System* and the 1983 *Step Forward*, both released on their own label Mob-Style Records.

Alongside, The Mob were included in *The Big Apple - Rotten To The Core* LP compilation (1982). They were one of the founding household name bands of A7, as well as regulars in CBGB's, either as headliners, or supporting touring bands such as Minor Threat. So, what has led me to include The Mob in this book? The answer is on the 1986 *We Come To Crush* LP.

(The Mob with Mourning Noise, Chronic Disorder and Vatican Commandos at CBGB's, 25/02/1982)

Christopher Hackett, who replaced Jose Gonzalez on bass duties, played in *We Come To Crush;* and he's still in 2026 a member of the band, offering us the story: "When I got involved with The Mob in the early 1980s, hardcore punk was very small scene. Very intense and as soon as I saw it, I was addicted. I remember sitting in my car with Jack Flanagan. He was three years older than me, and I was playing him demos of songs I was writing. He said to me you have to listen to something hard, and he played me the Bad Brains *ROIR* tape and I was never the same... when Jack gave me the first The Mob 7-inchs, I had never heard anything that fast. It was incredible. That a band could release their own music complete do-it-yourself situation. And Jack was a genius marketing guy, as he used for the rest of his career in music... For us, as far as influence, it was 1970s hard rock and heavy metal; those were the influences of The Mob. The early influences. We were listening to Aerosmith, Queen, and Motörhead. As Jose from The Mob says you can answer all these questions with Motörhead. Motörhead is the missing link to all of this as far as we are concerned. And of course, there were Dickies and there were the Bad Brains, and the Ramones. Jose and I used to put old hard rock records like Van Halen on 45 rpm to hear how intense they sounded sped up to double the speed. I specifically remember us liking listening to 'On Fire' by Van Halen on 45. Van Halen was way better on 45!".

(The Mob live at A7, 19/12/1982)

The Mob were one of the groundbreaking A7 club bands alongside Agnostic Front, Cause For Alarm, Warzone, Reagan Youth and many others. Their initial musical approach was obviously hardcore. The kind of hardcore that only New York produced at the time, nasty, dirty, that reflected the lifestyle of NYC. "For me MC5, Iggy and The Stooges, Patti Smith... those are the root punk rock for me. The New York Dolls, the Ramones" Christopher admits. "But The Mob wouldn't exist if not for the Bad Brains. That's a fact. The Bad Brains were the prototype. The fastest. The most intense. That is why Jose left The Mob to join H.R. solo band in 1984".

And funny thing is that The Mob began in Jackson Heights, Queens as a Van Halen- style cover band, but that all changed when they saw Bad Brains. Their first gig was actually opening for Bad Brains on 5 June 1981 at the BC club. "What made The Mob different from a lot of the hardcore bands of the time, was that The Mob never pretended to be anything other than what it was" Christopher adds. "The Mob never got heavy into the fashion or style side of things. Period. We just try to get up and play harder and faster than anybody. Kicking ass from Queens".

The Mob set up their own label, Mob-Style Records. In 1982 they released their first 7-inch, the classic (now) *Upset the System* with rapid fire hardcore punk, blast after blast, setting the blueprint for countless to come, nine songs in nine minutes, so you get it! This is just outrageous hardcore from an era that USA produced one classic after another, and I can't get enough of tracks like 'NY Slam' and even in this early release, the heavy metal guitar licks are there already.

(The Mob with Big Boys, Major Conflict and Agnostic Front at CBGB's. 17/09/1983)

"Early on, 1981 or even early 1982 we didn't see speed metal coming up at the same time. I grew up in Queens, and I remember seeing Anthrax play the Battle of the Bands at Bayside High School, and I became friends with Danny Lilker (later in Nuclear Assault). He used to come down to The Mob shows and I'll come down at Nuclear Assault shows and we hang out in Bayside smoking. I remember once in particular; I wasn't yet playing with The Mob but I was roading for Jack and hanging out. I think we were down in Virginia and he played 'Ace of Spades' with one of the bands there I think they were called Amazing Grace. So that hard rock and punk connection was always there".

On 1983 The Mob again self-released a 7-inch EP, and this time they went all the way creating a massive classic. Even better than *Upset the System*, The Mob sounded on fire on *Step Forward* 7-inch. A definite Bad Brains influence was there especially in guitar riffs. The production was tighter, heavier, and the three ripping songs presented The Mob in their wildest, most inspired days. Songs like 'Step Forward' are just hardcore classics, and no one can beat the frenetic 'Unity Lives On', amazing stuff.

"As forgetting along it shows, I don't remember any clash between the metal kids and the punk kids. That really wasn't any issue that I remember" Christopher recalls. "What we were against was racism and Nazi bullshit. Rock against racism, Nazi punks fuck off. Period. The scene that I knew was much more about inclusion than exclusion. The only thing we excluded is violence and discrimination. That's my memory".

Bronx small indie label Big City Records was the one that released the first full-length album by The Mob, *We Come To Crush* in 1986. Big City Records had other releases such as the excellent speed metal hardcore of The Unjust, or Armed Citizens and Bitter Uproar among the others. Truth is, that on this LP, The Mob really crush. Now with Christopher Hackett on bass (replacing Jack Flanagan), *We Come To Crush* sadly did not get the love it deserved. Like a blend of early Bad Brains until *Rock for Light* with the production of Agnostic Front's *Cause for Alarm*, the band sounds totally raging. We *Come to Crush* offers some new recordings of old songs such as 'Upset the System', however the new songs too are totally wild. 'Spinal Tap' reminds the approach Warzone took in their early recordings, while the guitar licks of '101/F.A.S.T.' are simply addictive. A flawless record here, and a shame that tracks like 'New Metal' never got the recognition they should.

(The Mob with Agnostic Front, Antidote, Crumbsuckers and Krakdown at Jim's Country Inn. 22/06/1985)

"Our songs have progressed from one and a half minutes to three and a half minutes with lots of intense changes and skanks. During the *We Come To Crush* era, Jack's playing was at its all-time best. And he was really channelling hard rock and intense right hand muting technique, ala Dr Know." Christopher adds regarding the new approach of *We Come to Crush*. "As far as *We Come to Crush* goes, Ralphie always says that was the closest we ever got to metal and was really pivotal at that point. Way ahead of its time. Unfortunately, it was poorly recorded, and we didn't have much funding, so it sloppier than it should be. But some of the songs really rip and Jack was just playing really great guitar at that time. But even at our most metal, we were a total hardcore punk band. We did not play speed metal or thrash metal. That was our style, lyrically or musically".

The Mob called it a day in the late 1980s, with reformations to come over the next decades, and right now (2026) are active, still offering shows. They also released in 2012 the *Back to Queens* 7-inch, now playing more anthemic hardcore punk, more relaxed, but still great, the eponymous song is just an anthem!

"I want to add also one of my favourite memories of that era. I was playing onstage at Danceteria. Dr. Know of Bad Brains came by to see us. He is standing on the side of the stage and Jack calls 'Right Brigade', and we go into it, and Jack puts his guitar strap over Dr. Know for the guitar solo. Dr. Know looks down at the guitar, he's like Jimmy Page, the guitar is way down at his knees because Jack is so much bigger. And then he just rips the most intense lead ever. A great moment!".

Christopher finally adds that "I don't know if crossover is relevant right now. The only thing I know is that if I was going to summarize like Jose Gonzalez always said, it was Motörhead and Bad Brains. Period. Those are the foundations!".

At a glance: I'm a sucker for both eras of The Mob. Hardcore kids already know how crucial the first two EPs are, however, everyone, including metalheads that enjoy Agnostic Front's *Cause for Alarm*, should check out *We Come To Crush*. It's maybe one of the most underrated crossover records. While it's not as crossover as you can think of! The Mob piece is dedicated to the late Jack Flanagan.

DRESDEN

(Dresden band photo 1986. Photo courtesy of Robert Kenney)

Dresden were one of the bands that I was constantly chasing to get an interview, while working *Crossover The Edge*. They remain to this day, one of my favourite crossover bands that only a few people have a clue about, and mostly those ones with a hardcore punk background. The reason for this is simple, as guitarist Frank Buzan narrates: "Dresden was only a side project band. It was a culmination and collaboration between several friends coming from punk, hardcore, rock and metal backgrounds...I, being from a prog metal background, enjoyed this project because we were able to easily write songs and riffs in our sessions together and tailor each song into a new sonic adventure. Everyone really put their best efforts forward on the 2 records, and I'm very proud of the results".

Dresden formed in 1985 in Bridgeport, Connecticut, by members of some of the best hardcore bands to ever come out of Connecticut, such as C.I.A., Lost Generation and Vatican Commandos. The initial lineup included E.J. Marquardt (bass, of C.I.A.), Glenn Sanders (drummer, of Lost Generation and No Music), Ginger Boe. Hammond (guitars, of Lost Generation and Bad Attitude), Frank Buzan (guitars), Joe Dias (vocals, of Lost Generation) and James Spadaccini (of Vatican Commandos) and Frank mentions that "It was a perfect storm of sorts to marry those 2 styles into a hybrid genre...the creativity was off the charts and it presented a new niche in music on the scene. A new beast, if you can describe it as such!".

(Dresden with Corrosion of Conformity and D.R.I. at the Anthrax, CT. 20/11/1985)

Frank adds that, in terms of musical influences, he was always a fan of "Black Sabbath, Zep, Deep Purple, Uriah Heep and later morphed into prog influences like Dream Theater, Periphery, Symphony X...still though appreciate the power of hardcore punk, it was a musical revelation for everybody that came across it in Connecticut, those days... sonically, speaking what influenced my style, I have to say that I was mesmerized by Malmsteen and that changed my style of playing, even early on in my career".

"There were many bands that crossed-over different sounds that I love, but I will offer you an answer that might surprise you: Red Hot Chilli Peppers, mainstream-wise, they were on top of the game of crossing different sounds in rock music" Frank confesses. "And the fans, from both backgrounds, either metal or hardcore punk, they embraced the new crossover sounds. The fans were great and receptive to the crossover, they appreciated the different dynamics in the music...and as for the violence? There was no violence because of the music, maybe only drunk assholes who couldn't be cool and handle their liquor".

Dresden hit the Downstairs Studio (notorious for having mainstays many CT hardcore bands, with Youth Of Today, Bold and Seizure being among them) in Bridgeport in late 1985, and released in early 1986 their masterpiece, *Too Many Skeletons* LP, released on vocalist's Joe Dias label, Incas Records. "The reaction of friends, and overall, in the CT scene regarding *Too Many Skeletons*, was positive and it was very well received...everybody found something to appeal to them in this record I suppose" Frank adds.

(Dresden and Crumbsuckers at the Danceteria, NY. 08/05/1986)

Too Many Skeletons is a tremendous monster of crossover power; wild and punchy, Dresden managed to combine some of the most ferocious sounds of that era, from both camps, but was actually struck a chord to me, was that they were one of the few US crossover bands that exposed a huge Discharge influence in some songs! Kicking off with 'Too Many Skeletons' everything is crystal clear that it's a record of high quality. "In Fear of God" blends Discharge with Motörhead, all flavoured through an American East Coast style, and so does the frenetic "Black Riders", while the cover of "Sounds of Silence" blows away every cover of this song, The Dickies included! 'Starvation' sounds like Savage Grace (the metal band) gone crossover, while 'It's your Funeral' has a huge Misfits dose in-ace!

With The Anthrax (the club) being the Mecca of Connecticut hardcore, Dresden found easy a place in that club; "By far, the best place was The Anthrax, when they moved it into a giant warehouse in Norwalk, CT. Massive venue to bring known and unknown acts to the eye of the public. Many great shows there...our own hidden gem" Frank admits.

Dresden kept it up until 1990 (with a reunion show in Fall 2002), with some lineup changes (such as Carl "Meego" Grinnan as a session guitarist and Edward Bullen in drums), and recorded on 1987 their sophomore LP, *Reign Of Terror The Dark Lords*; a sad fact that it was never originally released (only included on an anthology double CD in 2015), that was in the same style of the first LP, sounding though a bit more on the Raw Power side, especially in excellent tracks such as 'Fight to Unite' or 'Till Death'- again, this is a total winner, while it also includes short hardcore blasts such as 'Libya' or 'Ripped in Half'. It was their grande finale.

"Crossover stood on its own merits as it does today, and there is always room for more creativity" Frank concludes. "And how lucky is the youth today; digital platforms are godsend for those new artists getting their material heard, so they won't have to strive like us".

Post-Dresden, Joe Dias (now 2023 in Hairforce 1) and Ginger Hammond kept it up with Lost Generation for a while, Ginger also performing with Dead City, and Frank (Franco) Buzan performs to this day (2026) with Shamemix Shenanigans.

At a glance: Dresden's *Too Many Skeletons* is a huge crossover classic, for everyone into the rough sounds of Discharge, East Coast hardcore, Motörhead and early Venom-it's simply ripping! I would get the Anthology DCD that contains *Reign Of Terror The Dark Lords*, that is ace too, however, let this Dresden feature be a guide for some people not familiar with some of the best bands ever to come out of East Coast hardcore, and I'm talking about C.I.A. and their *God, Guts, Guns* 7-inch EP, 76% Uncertain (all their records), Lost Generation and the great *Return from Incas* LP, as well as *Never Work* 7-inch and Seizure. I'll stop ranting, check the Incas Records back catalogue, it contains great and underrated stuff!

THE CATATONICS

(The Catatonics band picture. Courtesy of Bob Cat)

The Catatonics are a band that I looked forward in interviewing them in *Crossover The Edge*, because their 1984 *Hunted Down* 7-inch is such a classic! "The Catatonics were Syracuse and Upstate New York's first hardcore punk band" Belvy Klein, drummer, adds. "We were 4 bored, pissed-off high school kids stuck in the middle of bum fuck NY state (5 hours north of NYC). We were just trying to play the fastest and heaviest music we could. We pretty much pioneered the original 1981-1982 Syracuse and Central New York Hardcore scene and our debut 7-inch EP *Hunted Down* is now considered one of the first hardcore thrash metal releases. Or so they tell me!"

Formed in 1981, The Catatonics lineup included Farmer Brown (guitar), Jeff Jacques (bass, vocals), Belvy Klein (drums, vocals) and Joseph D. Miller (guitar, vocals). "The first band to really be doing punk through a metal aesthetic has gotta be Motörhead but they were really their own fucking awesome unicorn" Belvy smiles". "That first Discharge full length was a game changer for sure...still the heaviest, most powerful shit to this day. For American hardcore, I guess it's like Suicidal, COC, Crucifix, D.R.I., Catatonics, SSD. Early Slayer definitely, early Metallica not so much. The first MDC album had some insanely fast songs with these crazy metal guitar parts that were just all over the place".

When asked about the crossover between hardcore punk with metal, Belvy mentions that "when we were doing it there really was almost zero crossover. The two scenes were basically completely separate and didn't really want anything to do with each other. At the time we all thought metal bands were corny, especially the vocalists. We did like some of the guitar parts and me personally the double kick drummers. We also liked the power and better production of metal albums. I mean bands like say, Raven and Anthrax were ridiculous, but they sounded huge on record..."

(The Catatonics with S.F.B at the Club Soda, Buffalo NY. 19/07/1984)

The Catatonics in 1984 released their first cassette on their own label, Anorexic Nympho Music, that included four frenzied hardcore tracks. Under the rough production, you could definitely hear the metal guitar licks; e.g. on 'I Can't Take You Anywhere', that reminds of what COC were doing also at the time.t I would go even that far adding that there was a Septic Death vibe that was of course, accidental, but I guess that it was due to some influences that both bands shared on songs like 'Don't Call Me Honey' and 'Drink More Brew'. Overall, this is the kind of stuff that will make anybody into early 1980s East Coast hardcore go apeshit-just passionate and lunatic to the max!

"There wasn't much crossover in terms of the crowds blending then" Belvy adds about those early 1980s days, "but you'd see the odd metal guys at punk shows here and there. They were usually harmless. I mean in Syracuse and Upstate New York if you were a punk or a metal head you basically stood out and were looked at as a loser or a dirtbag so it was kind of kindred spirits in that respect I guess you could say...And as for the violence, it was more like between punks versus rednecks or punks versus normies".

The Catatonics performed a good number of shows in Syracuse's The Carousel Club, alongside other local acts (such as The Fems), and later in other upstate NY clubs (such as The Club Soda), spreading the word in fellow punks about their nutty sound. "In those days most clubs in upstate N.Y. wouldn't book punk and hardcore bands and definitely not all ages either, so we would mostly just rent out halls like Knights of Columbus or just do illegal warehouse parties" Belvy narrates. "Unfortunately, The Catatonics never made it down to NYC, so we never got to play CBGB's. It wasn't until I joined 7 Seconds that I actually got to start playing big clubs and theatres".

(The Catatonics with 7 Seconds, Stillborn and B-Solution at the Ukrainian National Home. 11/10/1984)

In later 1984 The Catatonics released their masterpiece, *Hunted Down* 7-inch, on their own label Anorexic Nympho Music. This time with a more metal sound, and more metal guitar licks, *Hunted Down* was still hardcore to the max. However, it sounded like a beefed-up version of The Worst or early Gang Green, the kind of stuff that sounds like a blast after blast, leaving you speechless! Five songs, all winners, and even I find it very hard to pick some highlights, these would have been the vitriolic eponymous 'Hunted Down', the heavyweight of 'Obstinate' or the blazing speed of 'Bet I Can' that is the musical equivalent of several slaps to the face. *Hunted Down* is an endless classic of brutal and wild music.

Regarding what was the inspiration behind The Catatonics and the bands that influenced them, Belvy replies that "For me at first it was the classic '77 bands like The Clash, Pistols, Stiff Little Fingers,

Ramones, Buzzcocks but it was a little hard to relate to because those bands were much older than we were. As teenagers we needed something that was more on our wavelength and relatable, and for us that was American hardcore. For Catatonics influences I'd say Gang Green, Minor Threat, SSD, Circle Jerks, Crucifix, *Rise Above*-era Black Flag. I was also big time into the UK82 bands, especially Discharge and GBH. At the time we were just pulling influences from everywhere. We liked the power and a lot of the guitar parts of metal. I think another thing that's important to remember here is that this was the heyday of MTV and the only stuff they played with heavy guitars was like Iron Maiden, Priest, Motörhead, Motley Crue. No punk, no hardcore. So, pre-internet, if we weren't practising or playing shows, or listening to whatever the latest punk and hardcore records you were getting through mail order, you'd sit around and have MTV on. I'm sure some of that drifted in. For a song like 'Never Again', we kind of nicked Judas Priest for the opening riff. The verses of 'What You See & What You Say' are like 'Looks That Kill' on speed. 'Can't Take You Anywhere' was us basically doing Motörhead".

The Catatonics appeared in the 1985 *Flipside Vinyl Fanzine Vol 2* compilation with another absolutely lunatic track, 'Descending In "E", reminding of what P.T.L. Klub from Boston were doing at the same time too, albeit with a more metal edge. What is actually so rad regarding The Catatonics was that they were actually young kids. Belvy was thirteen years old when *Hunted Down* was released! However, they sounded so proficient in their instruments, and unbelievably confident.

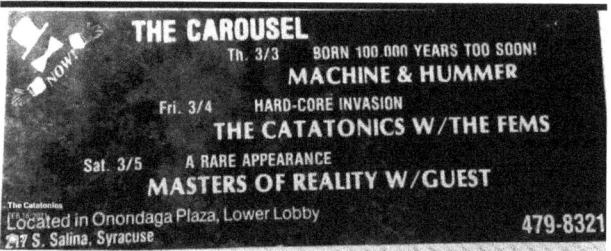

(The Catatonics and The Fems at The Carousel, Syracuse NY. 04/03/1982)

"We were punks, absolutely" Belvy adds. "Leather jackets. I had liberty spikes for a while. I would throw on Nikki Sixx camo eye paint from time to time but that was just to piss punks off!", Belvy smiles while adding that "our favourite shows from that era, were the ones that they wouldn't shut down by the police! And I can recollect, when we played a bar in Rochester and had the owner come out and pull a gun on us. Happened at a biker bar in Syracuse once too. Fun times!".

By 1985 The Catatonics called it quits, and Belvy found himself playing in 7 Seconds and the brilliant *New Wind* LP. In later years Belvy played in bands like the top NYC punks D Generation, in UK Subs, in Libertine (punk), Lindy (pop), Tuuli (power pop- punk) and in Brit-pop styled Madison Strays, while Joe Miller performed briefly with Fang and also appeared in in Bobby Osborne's bluegrass band!

On April 23, 2022 (Record Store Day) Southern Lord released the *Hunted Down* compilation LP, that includes *Hunted Down* 7-inch, compilation tracks, early demos and live recordings remastered from original tapes, making it a mandatory collection for everyone into hardcore, or the most hardcore-flavoured crossover types.

Belvy concludes that "I think the term crossover really picks up steam a tad later when you have the NYHC bands like Cro-Mags and Agnostic Front and classic era D.R.I. bring in a more obvious metal influence on their sound. And at the same time, you start to hear more pronounced hardcore punk influences on metal bands like Venom, Slayer, Exodus, Megadeth, Anthrax, early Metallica, etc. I personally never thought most of the metal bands, aside from Slayer and Venom, pulled it off very well. Wearing GBH and Discharge T-shirts doesn't magically make you punk. I think the two genres - metal and hardcore punk - are generally way, way more open minded and have a lot more in common now than back then. There are so many sub genres and cross pollination now compared to then, so that's a good thing".

The Catatonics are not active today (2025), but you never know if some revival shows or some new recordings happen in the future!

At a glance: Fancy a mix of the F.U.'s, with GBH, Discharge and metal guitar licks akin to NWOBHM? Well, you should hunt down the discography LP of The Catatonics, because it's one of the most vicious stuff ever to come out from early US hardcore. A sheer delirium of pure manic attack, this is not to be missed!

McRAD

(McRad band picture. Courtesy unknown)

The ultimate skate-rock band, McRad from Philadelphia, Pennsylvania are one of the best kept secrets, when we are talking about crossover. Formed in 1983 by professional skateboarder Chuck Treece (guitar, who moved from Newark, Delaware) alongside fellow skaters Ethan Jarvis (vocals), Tristan Reignier (drums) and Zeke Zegar (bass), After their inclusion with two songs on the *1983 Philly Hardcore Compilation - Get Off My Back (We're Doing It Ourselves)* LP, alongside Ruin and heavyweights YDI among others, McRad released on 1984 the rabid hardcore *Dominant Force* 12-inch EP. The recording wasn't far off the legacy of J.F.A or Minor Threat, with a dose of Bad Brains, especially on the reggae songs of 'No Guns' and 'Forget Those Years', all played in frantic speed and power. My favourite tunes here are 'Dominant Force' and 'Sundial'. Rumours also mention that Greg Norton of Hüsker Dü offered McRad their name!

McRad's appearance on *Thrasher* magazine's 1984 compilation *Blazing Wheels And Barking Trucks - Skate Rock Vol. 2* had put them in the forefront of skaters' preferences, and through all the 1980s they appeared alongside classic hardcore bands such as A.O.D., Crucifix, Heart Attack and Suicidal Tendencies. However, they were actually slow in terms of releasing new music; this happened in 1987, and lineup changes brought Rob DiJoseph (bass) and John Wagner (drums).

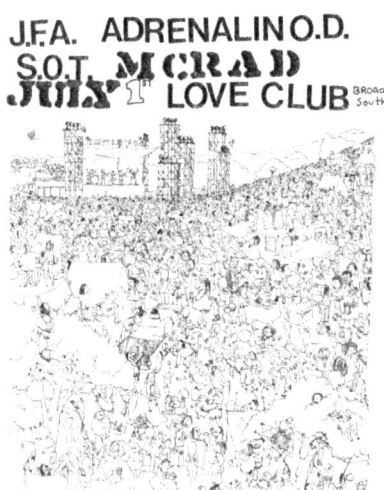

(McRad with J.F.A, Adrenalin O.D. S.O.T. at The Love Hall, Philadelphia, PA. 01/07/1983)

"I joined the Philadelphia hardcore scene in early 1982 when I was fourteen years old playing bass with a band called Little Gentlemen" Rob narrates. "We would ultimately put out a 7-inch and two LPs as a band and played with every important punk band that you can think of; the Damned, the Angelic Upstarts, Black Flag, Sonic Youth, Scream, the Replacements, just to name a few. About a year later McRad started playing gigs and I quickly became friends with the guys in the band; they were my age and maybe even younger. Little Gentlemen and McRad played a lot of the same bills and venues. You have to realize there was only about ten punk bands back then in the city of Philadelphia and only a handful of venues to play. Fast-forward to 1986 and I have quit Little Gentlemen and start becoming good friends with Ethan Jarvis (may he rest RIP), the original singer for McRad. I went to a rehearsal and was pretty blown away with how Chuck Treece's musicianship had advanced. One thing led to another, and I joined the band in mid-1986. We quickly got to work on writing the *Absence of Sanity* LP and played gigs locally. *Thrasher* magazine had a vanity label at the time called Beware Records so a West Coast trip to play gigs and record the album followed in the summer of 1986. I was in the band from 86-90 and then again from 1999-2003".

(McRad with Heart Attack, Ruin and AWOL at the LCD. 29/05/1984)

"I know that Chuck Treece and I were pretty obsessed with both the Bad Brains and Slayer going into recording the *Absence of Sanity* LP. We had both been huge fans of the Bad Brains going way back to around 1982 and Chuck in particular developed a close relationship with them. They were game changers. I was a Slayer fan from the jump but after *Reign in Blood* came out it was just an incredible mind-blowing experience. We wanted our hardcore and speed stuff to be as intense as Slayer and our reggae and midtempo rock to be as in the pocket and soulful as the Bad Brains. Obviously scores of other bands we loved and were influenced by, but if you want a simple answer that's as easy as I can boil it down" Rob adds, mentioning also that "the first band to crossover hardcore and metal gotta be Corrosion of Conformity. I think COC laid the groundwork for crossover with *Eye for an Eye* and later Animosity. LG played a gig with them in early '84 and I was blown away by what they were doing. Reed Mullin (RIP) was a great guy and was a true trailblazer. However, the first band that was cool to like for both punks and metalheads was definitely Motörhead. I just never thought of them as a metal band though, just an amazing combination hard rock, blues and methamphetamine".

(McRad with J.F.A., Void, Dove and Sun City Girls at The Newton Theatre, Washington, DC. 13/07/1984)

Beware Records, the skate punk sub-label of San Francisco's Deluxe, offered McRad the chance to release their first full-length, the 1987 masterpiece *Absence of Sanity*. "Even though it can be considered a crossover record, I have always considered myself to be 'a punk rock guy', since my roots will always be in punk and hardcore. Chuck and I had an extensive and eclectic musical taste that extended to The Police, Elvis Costello, Gang of Four to punk and metal. As far as how we presented ourselves visually, we were part of the skate scene, and we were pretty much about a no frills look; army pants, skate shirts, shorts, Vans etc".

Absence of Sanity is hands-down, the best record McRad ever recorded, a top 10 skate-rock LP and flawless from start to finish. I had a very hard time tracking down this LP for a decent price, and it seems that everybody is holding on to their original copies-no wonder why they are nearly extinct! From the opening 'McShred' to the crazy 'Dead by Dawn', *Absence of Malice* is a manifesto of wild fun-let alone tracks like 'This Indecision' or the closing 'Brain'. It will make you jump up and down in your room, blasting everything in the way! But what is spectacular about this record, is both the musicianship and the recording, that offers more power and punch, with a crystal-clear sound. Not to be missed, one of the highlights of 1980s, *Absence of Malice* is definitely hardcore, however the crunchy metal guitars and solos are more than enough to file it under crossover.

"I think some liked the whole crossover style and others didn't, but most people in Philly seem to embrace it as inevitable" Rob adds. "I don't remember there being any sort of aggression or clashes between the two factions. In like mid-1985 it just sort of happened in the scene that I was in. Bands like COC, the Crumbsuckers and others were playing on bills at punk venues. So, I think it just kind of happen organically at least in the circles I rolled in…honestly for me I hate the idea of factions or cliques. I remember vividly in the early 80s as a high school kid and not caring that I would piss off my high school metalhead friends by wearing Sex Pistols and Stiff Little Fingers T-shirts and piss off my punk rock friends by wearing Maiden, Priest and Motörhead shirts. I have pictures of me wearing Maiden T-shirts onstage in the early 80s and the punk rockers were none too happy. To me though I think it was natural the two styles would sort of coalesce. The best metal was always on the faster side and obviously hardcore was an accelerated tempo as well so a natural fit as far as I was concerned".

Chuck Treece later went on 1989 went to provide backing vocals for the Bad Brains on the *Quickness* LP, as well as being the vocalist and guitarist on Underdog's classic *Vanishing Point*, while later he became the drummer of Bad Brains for three tours, touring with Urge Overkill, and pursuing his new and/or solo projects for the years to come. McRad went on and off for the subsequent decades, releasing some stuff that is very good including: the Bad Brains-inspired *FDR* CD (named after the skatepark) in 2007 and the split CD with the melodic punks Frontside Five. In 2013 the excellent *The Begin* CD was released, as Chuck Treece & McRad, a total Bad Brains-fuelled record!

"There were so many shows that left memories that lasted forever!" Rob smiled. "Ones that come to mind quickly were with D.R.I. and Testament in Long Beach, California. Also, at Trenton City Gardens with Agnostic Front was also very memorable. Probably the most memorable show was with Suicidal Tendencies at Trenton city Gardens. I'll get to that in your next question. We played a lot of other great shows but more so with punk bands like Scream, Circle Jerks, Bad Brains etc…but I have a crazy story to share about Trenton City Gardens. It was a legendary club from the early 1980s to the early 1990s in central New Jersey that was a great venue but in a not-so-great neighbourhood and also unfortunately had a pretty aggro group of skinheads that would come there and start fights and trouble. We played with Suicidal Tendencies in like 1987 I think it was. We played right before Suicidal and we're given a bit of a cold shoulder due to the fact that Chuck is African-American and we mixed in reggae with our crossover stuff. When Suicidals came on the first song it's totally packed up front but then the place totally clears out during the second song. Turns out the skinheads were out trashing Suicidal tour bus, I mean they were really doing a number on it. Somebody must've gotten into the ear of Mike Muir, and before you know it, he was out the door with all of his band and crew in tow. It degenerated into a wild melee out in the parking lot, and let's just say that Mike Muir is one of the toughest dudes I've ever seen in my life. There's a chapter about this gig in the Trenton City Gardens memoir that came out a few years back".

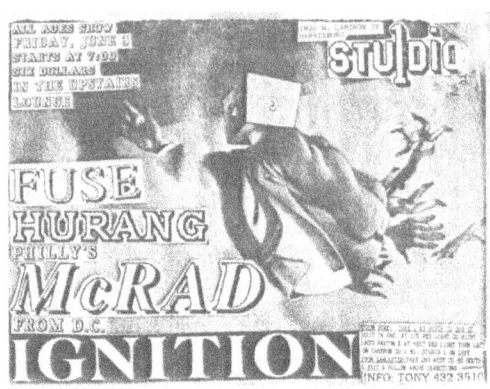

(McRad with Fuse, Hurang and Ignition. 03/06/1987)

Beyond Treece, other members of McRad also performed with other bands. Avery Coffee played in Stay Down and Up the Chain, Branden King in Leiana, John Ilisco in Go! For The Throat and Officer Roseland, John Langsford III on the prog rockers (!) Witch Fist, Zeke Zagar on the roots reggae group Eezeeqeel & Bloody Blood Stone, and Tristan Reignier in the dub rockers Crazy Pink Revolvers.

"A lot of great clubs I think my favourites were CBGB's, we played a bunch of the hardcore matinees on Sundays there" Rob admits. "Definitely a bucket list venue. Maxwell's in Hoboken was also great. In Philadelphia my friend Chuck Meehan booked a place called Club Pizzaz that had some great shows that McRad played. Fender's in Long Beach California was also pretty badass also. All those clubs are gone now and I miss them all…"

The status of McRad is unknown, but I have checked out that their last live appearance was on 2015, and I believe that they are going on/off active status for quite a while.

Finally, Rob mentions that "I'm pretty sure that crossover is still relevant today. I mean you still see it everywhere. My band that I'm in now, Anthrophobia absolutely has crossover aspects, and the bands I see at the gigs we play definitely still see crossover as a genre with relevance today".

At a glance: *Absence of Malice* is just a blinding LP, totally recommended for everyone into e.g. the metal punk days of Gang Green, or even the Bad Brains (post-1983). However, I would suggest getting *Lion Pure* DLP that contains both *Dominant Force* and *Absence Of Sanity*, along with the tracks from *Thrasher's Skate Rock Vol 2 Comp Blazing Wheels And Barking Trucks - Skate Rock Vol. 2* and other bonus tracks. I would also add Underdog's *Vanishing Point* though to the list of greatness, alongside the post-1990s McRad stuff. All ace!

ABSOLUTION

(Absolution band picture. Courtesy of B.J. Papas)

Formed in early 1987 in New York City, Absolution's first lineup included people from different backgrounds; guitarist Gavin Van Vlack had previously played in Side by Side, although he left before they recorded their 7", and in N.Y. Hoods. Bassist Alan Peters had played on Agnostic Front's raging classic *Liberty and Justice For...* LP, Bronx-born vocalist Djinji Brown was the son of jazz alto-saxophonist Marion Brown, while drummer Greg Johnston was originally from the Midwest. Absolution were part of the third wave of NYHC scene if we could consider first wave bands being Antidote, Urban Waste, A.F., and second wave being Cro-Mags, Leeway, Ludichrist. Third wave included the ones of Youth Of Today, Gorilla Biscuits, Bold etc.

"Absolution was started by myself and Djinji Brown. We were to young hardcore kids that were looking to take music we loved in a different direction blending a lot of different musical and cultural influences" Gavin narrates, adding that "in my personal opinion The Stooges were the first to really do both styles of those genres, metal and punk, although totally unintentionally".

(Absolution with Sick Of It All, Raw Deal and Krakdown at CBGB's. 24/01/1988)

Absolution were a part of the then current straight edge hardcore scene, however their sound wasn't as strictly hardcore as it was of e.g. Youth Of Today, Bold or Beyond. Moreover, they played regularly at CBGB's with their first appearance taking place on Sunday, 2 January 1988 alongside Sick of it All, Krakdown and Raw Deal. What was magical about them was that they appealed both to the tough guy scene of CBGB's, the peace-punks of ABC No Rio, as well as the punks of Squat or Rot.

"It's always been a matter of vibe and emotion for me" Gavin admits "I get the same feeling from 'Lonesome, Ornery, and Mean' by Waylon Jennings that I do from 'Another Perfect Day' by Motörhead. That's a hard question to answer, but indeed, it's all about what makes your heart pump faster".

Absolution's first appearance was in the now classic *New Breed!* cassette was released by Freddy Alva. Alva, writer of the book *Urban Styles: Graffiti in New York Hardcore* book and zines *NYHC Black Book, American Hardcore Black Book;* he also ran the hardcore label Wardance and was a booker at art collective ABC No Rio and countless others. Along with Chaka Malik (later of Burn), they released a compilation that featured thirty-five exclusive tracks from twenty New York City bands, with Absolution's contribution being the absolute smasher of 'Never Ending Game', that took the Bad Brains/early Cro-Mags formula to the next level of straight edge extremity.

(New Breed Tape Compilation ad)

"Visually I am a hardcore kid but in my own musicality there is some very metal influences!" Gavin smiles. "Hardcore and metal, they are two musical genres that speak to kids. There is a haven in the frequencies of those styles that frustrated, bored kids can find refuge and solace in. I know this is a very heady, high-minded statement but I believe these styles of music have saved lives from the communities built around them. They have more in common than in difference… even though a lot of hardcore punk purists reviled at it. I believe the metal scene was much more open to the idea. And then damn violence, yes it was there, and it was pretty stupid".

From Albany, New York, Dave Stein, a show promoter and entertainment lawyer for punk and hardcore acts, had established his label Combined Effort Records. In 1989 Absolution released their first and now classic 7-inch on Combined Effort Records. The same-titled record included four blasts of NYHC. With a slight metal edge, and while many of their peers headed for an all-out attack approach, Absolution built upon power. They sounded like a gradual fight, where blast after blast was rolling in, not with ultimate speed, but with massive power. Of course, the Cro-Mags and Bad Brains especially in the vocal style of Djinji was evident, however Absolution sounded like a more complex version of both of them, with an added straight edge flavour. The tremendous force of 'Armed with Anger' or the heavyweight energy of 'Revealing the Prey' are examples of Absolution's greatness, and while you can't file them under the 'crossover' tag, the metal sound of this release can definitely appeal to metalheads too. Yes, it is way rough sounding in terms of production, but this adds more to the magic!

(Absolution with Underdog, Krakdown, SFA, The Radicts, Public Nuisance, Hammer Brain and Ed Gein's Car at Rapp Arts Center. 23/05/1989)

"Hands down D.R.I.!" Gavin replies when asked who his favourite crossover band was. "I believe that D.R.I and in particular their drummer Felix Griffin was massively responsible for a lot of punk's influence on metal. Slayer in particular".

Absolution called it quits initially in 1990, but many of the members that were in the band's existence, went on to other bands and projects; Alan Peters (RIP 2020) went on to the great hardcore/rockers Crawlpappy, and later in Savage Amused, Gavin Van Vlack went to Big Collapse, the excellent Burn, Canonized, Die 116, Pry, and While We Wait, Sergio Vega went to Quicksand and Deftones among others. John Kriksciun played in Project Kate and Collapse, Andy Guida to My Rifle and Running Like Thieves among others, while Djinji Brown pursued a career in electronic music.

A complete discography double LP was released in 1997, containing all their tracks, plus demo and live recordings, and the resurgence of Absolution took place twice, once with the re-recording of the first 7-inch on 2013 released on Lush Life, and the excellent *Juxtaposition* 7-inch (2017), on Freddy Alva's Wardance label. Actually, *Juxtaposition* included some old songs, re-recorded, and the result is just over the top-fantastic, frantic and ultra-powerful stuff, kind of reminds me of what Fireburn did later!

"Heh, got so many stories to share" Gavin smiles. "But you take me so far back and I don't want to incriminate anyone, haha! If you ever run into me on the street, I would be happy to tell anyone face to face about some 'incidents'. Just tell me I sent you. However, I shall say that my favourite club would always be CBGB's. So much love for what Hilly let us do".

Finally, Gavin when asked about the relevance of crossover today, adds that "Today's music has the potential to pull from such a rich library of influences from all over. Look at what bands like Sepultura have down, Meshugah, Gojira, and even going back to the early nineties with bands like Barkmarket who were pushing sonic boundaries at that point".

At a glance: While not a crossover band per se, Absolution included the spirit of crossover's blending in influences, just like the e.g. Cro-Mags did, albeit in their own, unique and straight edge way! Focussing on building tremendous power rather than speed itself, every Absolution release is mandatory, even though I have a soft spot for the *Juxtaposition* 7-inch. Metalheads check also Onslaught from Stamford, Connecticut, the first band of Gavin and their great melodic power-thrash metal 1984 demo *The Slaughter*, that Mike Catricola brought me in touch with in his show!

DEADSPOT

(Deadspot band picture. Courtesy unknown)

Formed in 1981, Deadspot from Philadelphia, Pennsylvania are one of the most hard-hitting bands included. The band's recording lineup was comprised of Mike Illes (vocals, guitars), Paul Juestrich (guitars), Larry Horn, aka "The Kid" (drums), and Larry Leifheit (bass). Illes offers his side of the band's story: "Deadspot was formed at Tyler School of Art in Philly in 1981-82. Paul and Joe lived down the hall and had some gear. They were into Queen and Van Halen, I grew up on Sabbath, KISS until I saw Motörhead open for Ozzy in 1981. Seeing Motörhead was a revelation. All of the local bars to see music were very conservative, covers only, even Twisted Sister was a cover band for two sets. If you could make it 'til 2 am you heard the originals on their first EP. Inspiring. Then came the Ramones, for fifteen times in one year playing to 100 people in New Jersey. Our art school had at least four bands out of 800 students, nobody did homework. One night this new guy comes in with his longhaired silent brother to play in the student centre. Just a Marshall and a drumkit, they kicked our ass, shook our world. We looked at each other and said, 'yeah, we can do this'. Then we didn't think we needed a bass player, so we padded up my bedroom over Dirty Frank's and wrote not knowing we going to get evicted because we lost the key to the mailbox. Anyway, Joe finds us a place to make a demo. This after he made Sigma Sound (!) give us a lecture: "This is for real professionals, $300 an hour". Ended up doin' it all sweaty with Richard Birch from Decontrol and his partner in a day. Now we had a bass player better than the lead guitarist. Played a gig in a church basement with Phantom Tollbooth, earned the long-hair guy's interest who then turned me onto Discharge and became obsessed over The Saints, The Stooges etc. The best part of the early years was that were too dumb to be disillusioned. We needed Motörhead style double kick, found The Kid and fired Joe (at a phone booth in a crack hood)…however, we were old for the hardcore kids, too punk for the metalheads, so we ended up in a different limbo. Example, first show at CBGB's was with Prong and Sick of It All, GG Allin, Pantera, Circle Jerks, Soundgarden, Faith No More, Gwar, UK Subs, Rollins, Foetus, Urge Overkill, L7, Lunachicks, 7 Year Bitch Biohazard...we took any gig that would have us. So sometimes it got testy".

(Deadspot with M.O.V., Stepping Razor, Mikey Wild and the Mess, Ashtray, Still Stupid, Destroy All Bands, Doctor Bombay and Decontrol. 09/12/1987)

Michael, literally unstoppable, continues about who he regards that was the first one to pursue the crossover between punk and metal: "First crossover band? Tricky question, in college we were exposed to a bunch of stuff more eclectic than mall metal. The Sonics appealed with their rawness, as did Heartbreakers and Fear. It all tied into Motörhead, because it was raw, apolitical and unapologetic. Around 1981-82 we were going to Jonny Zazula's little shop in a flea market. I remember one afternoon Manowar were doing an in-store signing. Going through the small punk section, I picked up the GBH single *Catch 23*. Ross the Boss looks at the cover and says, 'Buncha faggots!'. I bought that right then. The thing was Jon was working with Metallica before *Kill 'em All*, but he had all of this punk stuff that screamed no bullshit, we were all hungry for noises we craved. COC, Hellhammer, Slayer's 'Chemical Warfare' all shared space with The Stooges, Hüsker Dü and Replacements".

Regarding why crossover took place, Michael narrates that "in my experience the suburbs where I grew up were too conservative, even though I was able to score *Damaged* and *Let Them eat Jelly Beans* (Bad Brains, Circle Jerks etc.). So, we all meet up in the dorms and go into the city. The city had original bands, great record stores, and people with Venom and Anti Nowhere patches on their leather jackets. We liked the danger. The suburban mall metal dudes lived differently, they had girlfriends and jobs. But...they eventually came around, because of that punk attitude got translated into a tough guy middle finger. So, Lemmy again!'".

Deadspot in their career found themselves in billings with touring bands coming to Philadelphia such as A.O.D., Gang Green or Toxic Reasons, as well as local ones such as Phantom Tolbooth (actually, their first show was with them), McRad, YDI and Executive Slacks, a proof that Deadspot were first and foremost part of the hardcore scene.

(Deadspot with The Accüsed and Brotherhood at The New Arch Street Empire, Philadelphia, 21/05/1989)

Their first release was the 1985 demo, containing nine songs of frenzied, wild and great hardcore-no metal licks, with terrific songs such as 'Friday Night In Hell', 'Another Day' or the closing raging menacing

'Paris is Burning'. I wish someone would re-release this demo on LP, because it's just dark, evil hardcore punk, that will make fans of Void, YDI or even Septic Death go crazy.

"First time I heard 'Whole Lotta Love' on AM radio I went WHADDAFUGGIZZAT?" Michael smiles. "Before it was just Beatles and everything that followed beside old school country. Top 40 radio taught me 2.5-minute songs that had a hook. The sound in my head was heavy, sought it out, KISS wasn't enough, Deep Purple neither. Judas Priest was too shiny. Sabbath, but I was angsty. Angry Samoans, Black Flag, Bad Brains, anything that said 'fuck you' was the real deal. Weirdos, GBH, Discharge, Venom. If it had a hook that could beat the shit outta you, I liked it".

Deadspot then appeared on the classic now *Discpan Hands: A Philadelphia Compilation* LP, alongside other great Philly bands such as McRad, Pagan Babies and Legitimate Reason, with the re-recording of their 'Suicide City', now with more metal overtones than before; "it was crossover on its heyday" Michael adds. "There was violence, not between the scenes, because metal dudes were all about staying pretty then. But we did have a gig when racist and anti-racist skins started a brawl and security got onstage with a shotgun, 'click-click, CLEAR THE ROOM!', and riot ensued outside. But there was violence, it was there, like in City Gardens, New Jersey (check the book *No Slam Dancing, No Stage Diving, No Spikes*). Plus, the wonderful GG Allin gig, beside the shit there was a stabbing. Between the scenes there was a sceptical stand-off; punks were supposed to be skinny kids, metal dudes, wannabe bikers, all cos play. When serious people came everybody shut up. Checked out Minor Threat in Camden, New Jersey, Wheels of Soul bikers showed up, and Ian had to mollify them. If you wanted violence, it could be found. Always be aware of your surroundings, not everybody loves you".

It was about time that Deadspot released their first LP, *Adios Dude*; initially out on Los Angeles Genius Records, this LP got also released by Heavy Metal Records in UK, as well as BMG Records in Germany. Kicking off with 'Addiction', it's pretty obvious that Deadspot are now in the crossover territory-albeit they were still a hardcore band. Sounding like a more menacing Slapshot, or a darker Cro-Mags, *Adios Dudes* had class written all over it. Songs like 'Inside' sound so haunting, like a cross between Dr Know with Septic Death, with a definite Motörhead vibe in, while 'Another Day' even reminds me of mid-1980s GBH, top stuff!

"There were many favourite shows, and many favourite places that we played in those days" Michael admits. "Regarding favourite shows, Colin's birthday party was a good one; Biohazard singer guy comes up and says, 'Where you from?' then points at his Brooklyn tattoo, and says 'Uh I'm from here, don't have to write it down'. Played on a flatbed in his backyard until the cops came and we hid in the van. Spent three days playing pool and beer. The first time we played after sixteen years made me weep; I loved it so much! As for my favourite place? The best thing about playing somewhere else is that you may not need to come back. Our jam spot where Big L and his brother lived was awesome. Spider from Pure Hell's spot. Hit happy hour at 4 on Thursday, crawl out Monday. Play the set, write, watch *Goodfellas* again, play until you can't hear. My other favourite place was by accident. In 1992 *No Clue* tour, we ended up in Madison Wisconsin at O'cayz Corral, a reimagined Old West bar by twenty-year-olds. Quaint as fuck. But it's a college town in June, so there was nobody. We play to the staff and two attendees that are probably on the guest list, they loved us. 'Can't pay you but we'll give you free beer', so we played three or four nights. Even making a demo before our manager destroyed it because he wanted to rip us off first. There was a wolf named Fred in the cellar, found out he got put down at two from some strangers on my trip here. I heard this place was burned down, and there is a Slint video on YouTube of this place!"

Out on their own Letterbomb Records, co-released with Genius records, followed their next release, which was *Built in Pain* 7-inch; produced by Jack Endino. It was the first release that exposed the tremendous power of the band to the fullest! Containing two new songs ('Razors' and 'Built in Pain') and a The Stooges cover of 'T.V. Eye', Deadspot were in full form; their own, original songs were now slightly more metal, with 'Razors' being maybe my favourite Deadspot song, like Poison Idea gone crossover. Wild and venomous stuff!

(Deadspot with Faith No More at City Gardens, NJ. 24/11/1989)

"I have so many funny stories to share" Michael chuckles. "One night, we were playing with... Nitro, the glam metal band! Singer asking for a tanning bed, no shit. Fuckin' two-neck guitar guy! Unfortunately, I had to say sorry to too many well-intentioned people. Although, there are times you must be a dick. We played this gig with Murphy's Law and Wargasm in Philly. Load out, where's our money? 'Um, we didn't make any' says the coke head manager, so I went into the bar area and put as many stools I could fit in my truck. 'Tell the guys that own this place I have their seats!' So, here you are, $125".

"And another one" Michael smiles, and I had no intention to stop him! "We had a gig in New York, CMJ [College Music Journal] Showcase. The Kid has a buddy with a van cheap. Our boy Graf (of Shemales, Mama Volume and should have been in Soungargden 'cuz he wrote the *Rusty Cage* bass riff when he auditioned, but I digress). We get loaded in and head out onto the interstate, and every twenty minutes we must stop and put oil in this thing. Graf and I were in the back; 'Uh, do you feel weird? YES! We're being gassed!' The van dies outside of New Brunswick, New Jersey, and I call Rock 'n' roll Bob from Genocide showing up with a van twenty minutes later. So, it's a Friday, everyone is driving into Manhattan. Halfway through the Holland Tunnel we get a flat tire. Now, seven of us get out to fix it, the jack won't work so we believe it's the weight of the gear. Unload everything into traffic like that Pink Floyd picture, nothing, the Kid is waving traffic by…Suddenly a Port Authority unit squawks, 'MOVE YOUR VEHICLE NOW!'. We threw everything back in with no regard bumping out to the exit. Tow truck is repairing the flat when six cop cars run into the tunnel we just left. There was a riot inside. We proceed to the Pyramid Club, where we got maced during line check. Bassist and drummer never noticed".

Out on C/Z Records (the Seattle label that released some of the very first recorded output from some of the region's most significant bands such as Nirvana, Soundgarden, Skin Yard, Melvins, Built To Spill, 7 Year Bitch etc), and again under the production matters of Jack Endino, Deadspot released on 1991 their final LP, *Built-In Pain*. Crushing stuff again here, even heavier than before, with wild songs such as the instrumental 'God Machine', 'Hit the Wall', the frantic cover of 'New Rose' by The Damned, or the heavyweight powerhouse of 'Wrong Time', this actually sounds like a beef between Cro-Mags, Poison Idea, Sheer Terror. Class.

Another inclusion in a collection this time the 1992 *Something's Gone Wrong Again: The Buzzcocks Covers Compilation* LP, where Deadspot covered 'Orgasm Addict', and later in 1992 Deadspot called it quits. Guitarist Paul Juestrich formed in 2014 The End A.D. including members of Anvil Bitch and Dominance among others, keeping the spirit of Deadspot, albeit in a modern way-even covering 'Addiction'.

Michael ends up our interview with these words: "My guess that as long as humans go, the desire to yell and scream about their disillusion about the world, the loss, the indignities of mere existence and the underlying need for communication will always be. People like to fuck and eat and love, but when a system is put in the way, the river always finds a way around".

At a glance: Sadly, still under the radar of many people, Deadspot haven't gained their place in history as they deserved. What's more annoying, is that you can still find their brilliant records for a nice price! So go get all their output, everything they released is top notch stuff, and I would start with *Adios Dude*. However, as aforementioned, somebody should re-release their first 1985 demo on vinyl; I wish I had the time and money to do it myself, but you never know!

STILLBORN

(Stillborn band picture. Courtesy unknown)

You already know that I'm a sucker for a slight metal 1980s NYHC sound, and this is the case with Stillborn! Formed in 1985 in Brooklyn, they were one of the second wave NYHC bands, that sadly never received anything more than a cult status. Bassist Mike Catricola narrates their story: "In the fall of 1985 is when our story started. Terry was doing an internship at Brooklyn college in the radio station for a student DJ named Don Kaye who hosted a heavy metal program. He would ask me to come down to the school and hang out and help and to meet Don. After a few weeks the program director told us we should meet his brother Dave who played drums and was in a band with a guitarist named Andy Guida [Stillborn's original guitarist]. His exact words were 'My brother is into that loud noisy music that you guys like'. I was in high school and I believe Dave was in junior high school. He said they needed a bass player and a singer. Terry and I did not play instruments or sing but wanted to just be in a band. I said I would sing, and Terry would play bass if I remember correctly. After a few days Terry said he could not get the money to buy a bass guitar. I asked my father if he would get me one and I became the bassist and Terry the singer. At the first rehearsal Andy would have to show me where to place my fingers for each song to teach me to play. It took a long time to figure it out enough to be able to play. Andy and Dave had nine songs written for the first demo *Dying for Progress*. I wrote my first song that January after the Space Shuttle [Challenger] exploded called 'Dying for progress'. Right after we recorded the demo Andy decided to leave the band to start playing industrial music. He was also a great drummer who later went on to play with Absolution, Altercation and Supertouch. Not long after he left, we found Mike Fringo and that's when Stillborn became Stillborn".

(Stillborn with Token Entry, Side By Side and Krakdown at CBGB's. 17/05/1987)

Stillborn were a part of NYHC scene since their beginning, offering shows at CBGB's alongside local shows in Brooklyn (and Long Island), and were there, when crossover started exploding. "I think what happened at least for me was by the mid-1980s most metalheads were looking for something faster, rawer and more intense" Mike admits. "Hair metal was rising, and we were looking for the next thing to progress to… The old school punks though were not happy metalheads coming to their clubs and hijacking what they felt was their culture. However, I must mention that the bands that started the whole crossover trip for me were Cro-Mags and Agnostic Front".

Stillborn's first offering, the 1986 *Dying for Progress* demo was an unbelievably rough and nasty NYHC blast, reminiscent of a blend between NYC Mayhem and first wave NY-NJ hardcore, like Mental Abuse and The Abused. Terrific stuff obviously, and songs like 'Unspoken Majority' and 'Dying for Progress' with drive you crazy. "On the metal side I was influenced by Mercyful Fate and Venom for sure" Mike admits. "On the hardcore side, it was Cro-Mags, Agnostic Front and Bad Brains… I grew up a metalhead and still am until today. Our first demo was pure hardcore punk. After Andy Guida left, I became the sole songwriter and being a metalhead that sound and style became apparent in our newer songs".

As mentioned, Andy Guida left when Stillborn were already recording their second demo, the 1986 *Answers Left Unquestioned*; again, this was a mental NYHC release, and the band sounded even more tight and crazy. Some slight metal guitar licks were creeping in, and D.R.I. (*Dealing With It*-era) were added to the influences; something that is very apparent in the excellent 'Open Your Eyes'. 'Far from the middle' or 'Personnel Trauma' might be my favourite blasts, again a superb demo.

(Stillborn with Affirmative Action, Sheer Terror and Rest In Pieces at the Grunge Club, 28/02/1988)

"There was never any violences at our shows, not at all" Mike adds. "After all, we played for mostly a hardcore crowd and everyone was out to have a good time…as for me, I always loved to see the Bad Brains live, the energy was insane! Loved also seeing Crumbsuckers, Leeway and above them all, it was Sheer Terror".

Stillborn through their existence shared the stage with bands like Sheer Terror, Hogan's Heroes, Rest In Pieces, Life's Blood, Leeway, Token Entry, Nuclear Assault…the list is endless. They were unlucky though not having any of their stuff released on vinyl.

Their next release was the 1987 *There for the Taking* demo; more metal than before. Still this was NYHC of the highest order: rough, angry, bitter, and heavy, with lots of mosh parts but with the speed of crossover. 'Need to Release' is a banger and so is 'Once too Often'. There is a definite Youth Crew influence here, however this is total, authentic, NYHC with a metal edge demo.

"New York had an amazing scene" Mike narrates. "From Albany down to New York City it lived and thrived. The whole East Coast of America was great. Best show we never played was in Washington DC with our friends in Sheer Terror opening for Warzone. It was a large venue packed to the rafters, the biggest show we ever would have played. Our singer Terry took the van, because he had family in the area and wanted to go visit them before the show. We were about to go on and no Terry to be found anywhere. The other three bands on the bill kept swapping start times with us while we waited for Terry. Warzone went on and the show was over. Still no Terry. He got lost coming back and could not find the venue. This was the mid-1980s, no GPS or cell phones. We missed playing that gig. I laugh at the story now. But the van ride back to New York City was not a fun ride that night..."

In 1989 Stillborn released their swan song with the demo *Scorn of Absence*. Perfectly executed, melodic, due to the vocals of Terry Rosenzweig, but very powerful NYHC with a metal edge, an ace release. Songs like 'Echoes' or 'Little Ceasar' send shivers down my spine! This is their most crossover moment, and you need to hear this, as well as all their stuff released.

(Stillborn with Sheer Terror, Mental Abuse and Life's Blood at CBGB's. 24/04/1988)

"The Grunge Club in Middletown, New York had the greatest vibe. I loved it" Mike smiles. "But when we headlined CBGB's in January 1988 and drew a good crowd on our own, that was the best we ever achieved!"

Stillborn split in 1989 and Mike Catricola went on to play with Iron Tyrant, Requiem, and Savage Damage, while Andy Guida played with Absolution, Altercation, My Rifle, One Sided War, Real, Running Like Thieves, Supertouch, The Press, While We Wait, and The Mistaken.

"Not really. I don't believe crossover is relevant now, in 2025. It was new and different back then. Today there are so many genres of metal and punk and everything else mixed together. I think the relevance has been lost".

At a glance: I can't get enough of bands like Stillborn-it's true. Raw and wild stuff from an era that the NY bands were amazing, Stillborn sound great even aften all these years. There's no way to find their demos one-by-one, so pick up the *Answer's Left Unquestioned* 2009 LP compilation, and check also The Heavy Metal Mayhem Radio Show, because Mike Catricola is the host and he's doing a tremendous work!

AT ALL COST

(At All Cost band picture 1988. Courtesy unknown)

Formed as Violent Youth in 1987, At All Cost were a band comprised of High School friends from Rockland County, New York, and guitarist Wade Babcock narrates their story: "Well to start with At All Cost, it really was such great times. All we did was listen and play music. We played some covers, got some shows and kept building and getting tighter. We started writing our own songs, practiced and went in and recorded our first demo; then bigger and better shows started happening and the added members came in, and we did the second demo. We played more shows and had great memories. We really never broke up or anything; I will always feel together with those guys, so I thank them all very much".

Formed with the lineup being Wade Babcock (guitar), Charlie Oberle (bass), Darin Galgano (drums), Chris Scott (guitar) and Jeff Guzman (vocals), At All Cost went on to release their first demo (the so-called *Demo 88*) that contained 6 songs (plus an intro and an outro) of sharp, vicious and ultra-powerful hardcore (with a slight metal edge, mostly conveyed through its production), that was in-line with what was happening right then in the third wave of NYHC scene (Youth Crew that is); At All Cost had a definite Token Entry influence, alongside with added early 7 Seconds and the mosh part style of Youth Of Today. Every song is a ripper, and you should just check 'Decisions', the brutal 'Walls Around Me' and 'Shallow Feelings'.

(At All Cost with Token Entry, Yuppicide, Capital Punishment and Vision at CBGB's. 15/10/1989)

Wade regarding his influences narrates that "I was influenced by tons of music; there is outlaw country that was in my home and HeeHaw on TV with some great guitar players like Roy Clarke. Then I heard Steve Miller Band and loved it. Then I got Aerosmith *Rocks*, then KISS but when Black Sabbath came into my world it certainly changed everything. I loved a lot of punk and thrash too; it really built things in terms of making music".

Darin Galgano on his interview for NoEcho.net adds that in terms of At All Cost influences were "Agnostic Front, Token Entry, Black Sabbath, Slayer, Excel, 7 Seconds, Minor Threat, Suicidal Tendencies, Metallica, all '80s-era stuff, of course".

Quickly gaining fame in the NYHC and the NJHC scene, All All Cost found themselves supporting Destruction and Cro-Mags, or Token Entry, Vision and Maximum Penalty and Biohazard, they had a song ('Decisions') included on the *Metal Disorder* Tape (1989), as well as two live tapes, one recorded in CBGB's in 1989 and one in WNYU in 1990. "The place that was special to plays for me was CBGB's; it was such a show with Token Entry and Vision" Wade adds. "And my favourite crazy story is when we e played with Biohazard in Yonkers I think; when we went on, people started moshing and slamming. This bar never expected this type of crowd or music, but the owner ran onstage and yelled 'Get the fuck out'. The show was shut down, and Biohazard didn't even play which sucked, because I wanted to see them and spoke to them before the show- all cool and great guys!".

(At All Cost with Maximum Penalty, Destruction and Cro-Mags at Sundance. 21/04/1989)

Second-and final-release for At All Cost was the *Demo 90* in 1990, with lineup changes; Marc Calimbas on guitar duties (Chris Scott leaving), and Brian Getkin now on bass. *Demo 90* was a step forward to a more crossover style without losing the fierce hardcore edge. Six brutal songs, on a terrific style that was reminiscent of Youth Crew bands with a Leeway/Cro-Mags touch, the kind of stuff that drives me wild! 'Strength Within' will make you wanna demolish everything, while 'Enuff Said' is just a powerhouse. Two re-recorded songs from the debut demo are also included ('Hidden Lies' and 'Decisions'), while 'Roll With The Punches' is maybe the best song they ever wrote.

Shortly after the release of *Demo 90*, At All Cost split in early 1991, with members appearing in other bands; Darin Galgano played with Brian Getkin in Dahlia Seed (emo hardcore) and The Nolan Gate (mathcore) and Marc Calimbas played in Atlas Shrugged. A record compilation, including both demos, appeared in 2023, named as *Nothing Comes Easy* that was the actual title of a record that was supposed to have been released on 1990…better late than never!

"I believe that some bands still have the crossover sound" Wade admits. "Municipal Waste comes to mind. I also think Prong had crossover sound-also we never proved this, but we think that Tommy Victor from Prong recorded our live show at CBGB's in 1989!"

At a glance: You know the deal; into the NYHC style of late 1980s, mixed with metal riffs and guitar solos? You need At All Cost stuff like air and water! Get the *Nothing Comes Easy* compilation LP (2023), because it contains all their stuff. Time to slam!

CONFUSION NYC

(Confusion NYC band picture 1990. Courtesy unknown)

Just like in the case of Darkside NYC, Confusion from Brooklyn went for a different crossover between hardcore and metal, thus blending hardcore with death metal. Death metal in the early 1990s was in the peak of its popularity in the heavy metal scene. Confusion was formed in 1990 and bassist Michael Scondotto narrates their story: "Confusion started in the summer of 1990. I was brought into the band by original guitarist Frank Collins (RIP, 2002) after their first bassist was beaten up by our drummer Ralph Canovic after the band's very first show haha! I was at that show, which was September 1, 1990. It was memorable because it was held in the backyard of a girl named Jennifer in Colt's Neck, New Jersey and the lineup was Confusion, Social Decay, Patterns, Merauder, Dmize and Lament, my brother Jon's band, which was formed out of the ashes of Maximum Penalty. Confusion was initially playing standard NYHC with thrash influences but progressed into a more death metal hardcore hybrid sound, especially after the 7-inch came out in 1992. We recorded our first demo in November of 1990 and a second one in February of 1991. We were a band until our final show in December of 1994, opening for death metal legends Deicide for the second time (since the first was in 1993) at the legendary club L'Amour in Brooklyn".

(Confusion NYC with Carnivore at L'Amour. 04/06/1988)

Confusion's lineup through the years included Michael Scondotto (bass), Ralph Canovic (drums), Mike Fried (vocals), Mike Price (guitar) and Frank D. Collins (RIP 2002), a guitarist who was later replaced in 1993 by Pete Melucci. They quickly went on to release their first demo in 1990 titled *Four the Force* that showcased a new kind of crossover between hardcore and metal. This crossover was much slower, heavier and based on the mosh parts of NYHC, however it still wasn't an outright death metal hardcore blend, but more of a Celtic Frost-Sheer Terror mix with late 1980s NYHC like Killing Time. 'Taste of Hate' or 'Selfishness' are unbelievably brutal and rough yet still controlled, even though the ultra lo-fi production doesn't help!

"It may be Suicidal Tendencies with their 1983 debut" Michael discusses while asked about what band he considers to be the first one to crossover hardcore and metal. "But the word 'crossover' wasn't being used in 1983 to my knowledge. If you jump to say 1985, D.R.I., COC, SOD, and Agnostic Front all dropped hugely important crossover LPs in that same year. D.R.I. with *Dealing With It*, COC with *Animosity* and SOD with *Speak English or Die*, Agnostic Front dropping *Cause For Alarm*. By then that word is definitely a 'thing'. Also, I think it was probably just a natural progression at the time. I have always felt that hardcore was a reaction to punk. Punk was becoming too 'fashion', too uniform, and too stale. Hell, many of the OG punks went New Wave or New Romantic. Hardcore was a way of saying, fuck all of that. We are also taking it back to jeans and T-shirts, no more leather, no more fashion, and we are going to be faster and harder. Crossover was probably a similar reaction to first wave hardcore, the next level of extremity, but it was short lived as the more straight up hardcore sound was exploding by 87-88, here in New York City at least. By the time I came in the scene, early 1988, people were calling as 'crossover' D.R.I., COC and Suicidal metal bands, or thrash metal bands. As a matter of fact, I had to find some of those bands on my own as the kids that got me into hardcore were all about the New York City bands of the day like the Cro-Mags, Sick Of It All, Youth Of Today, Breakdown, Token Entry, Gorilla Biscuits and Rest In Pieces. I wasn't there in 85-86 for that crossover explosion".

(Confusion NYC with Deicide, Dismember and Vader at L'Amour. 14/05/1993)

Their second demo *Distorted Visions* was released in 1991, containing three songs, including a re-edition of 'Confusion' plus two new ones. As a far better effort than the first demo in terms of production, now Confusion captured their blazing firestorm style! 'Confusion' sounds out of this world, while the moody 'Without Hope' includes some Cro-Mags influences, and 'Distorted Visions' is their heaviest anthem by then. A ripping demo!

By 1992 Confusion started appearing both in hardcore billings alongside Sheer Terror, Warzone, Carnivore etc as well as death metal shows alongside Deicide, Unleashed, Cannibal Corpse. Michael narrates that "we were influenced by a mix of the NYHC bands of the late 80s, the thrash metal of the late 80s and the exploding death metal scene of the day. The second wave CBGB's scene ended the year we began, 1990, so we didn't get to play there until 1992. We were received pretty well initially for a band with a quadriplegic lead singer who sang with crutches onstage and used a wheelchair off stage. I think many didn't know what to think of us, until the set began and our maniac friends started killing everyone in the pit haha! By late 1992, we were getting on lots of death metal bills, and bringing our hardcore fands to those shows. All through 1993 and 1994, we gained a lot of local death metal fans from being on bills with Deicide, Dismember, Cancer, Disincarnate, Morpheus Descends, Cannibal Corpse, Unleashed. etc. Hardcore was getting heavier in the early 90s, but the scene was way smaller than the late 80s. We were a bit ahead of our time with our sound and should have never stopped when we did, but such is life".

"As far as my look" Michael adds, "I had very long hair from 91-95, and so did some of the people in our crew. In 88-90, I had a haircut like Porcell from Youth Of Today. I loved death metal, but I still loved the hardcore of my era too. I also loved the industrial, grunge and hip-hop of the early 90s too. It was a great time to be into music, period. Confusion was not an image conscious band, but I wanted us to wear all black and wear death metal shirts more haha!". Regarding cases of violence in their shows, Michael mentions that "there were some for sure in the early 1990s. But by then, the shows in New York City were filled with what were called hardcore kids, most of whom had short hair and looked neither punk nor metal. Many were straight edge and had a youth crew look, which I had for a time. But a lot looked almost preppy in their style or just very 'normal'. Hardcore was very come as you are then. There were skinheads, straight edge kids, hardcore kids, some with long hair and a very few actual punks at these shows. There was a separation of hardcore, punk and metal for sure in the late 80s New York City scene".

The only vinyl release that Confusion had in their existence as a band, the *Taste Of Hate* 7-inch was released in 1992. Now with a professional recording at Fastlane Studios, with a sound more akin to death metal, Confusion reached their peak with this record. Crushing metal hardcore with a twist, mosh to the max NYHC death metal blend of the highest order, that sounded innovative back then and set up a blueprint for countless imitators. The new recording of 'Confusion' and 'Distorted Visions' are ace, while 'A Fatal Infection' and 'Early Frost' are vicious crushers, especially 'Early Frost' with its shocking changes of pace and style. A classic release.

(Confusion NYC with Life Of Agony and Warzone at L'Amour. 25/12/1993)

"Although I was a bit late to the party in 1988, I will say it was amazing to come up in the New York City scene when I did. I got to play and see some amazing shows" Michael adds. "The two clubs that I miss the most are CBGB's in Manhattan and L'Amour in Brooklyn. L'Amour was the best room for Confusion for sure. Brooklyn also had a spot called the Crazy Country Club from 90-93 which was fun. Two other great Manhattan spots for Confusion were the Wetlands and Bond Street Café".

Confusion disbanded in 1994, while their final song written ('Storming The Walls') was released on the compilation *A Call for Unity: East Coast Hardcore Compilation* (1995), another hot mosher! Post-Confusion Michael played in The Last Stand, Hiroshima 22, Close Call and Direct Approach, while now he is the frontman for the hardcore thrashers Inhuman. Pete Melucci played in Allegiance and Skism, as well as Toximia. The late Frank Collins after Confusion played with the hardcore band Out Of Line.

"Seeing the Cro-Mags for the first time in 1989 on the *Best Wishes* tour. Seeing Slayer in 1990 at L'Amour for *Seasons In The Abyss* was wild, with tons of violence inside and outside the club. There was my first time seeing Carnivore, fall of 1990 at one of their reunion shows at L'Amour. Pete threw fake blood out onto the crowd and said 'here's some AIDS blood for ya!'. There was another show in November of 1990 at L'Amour with Leeway and Suicidal Tendencies which was insane. A huge all day long show for Roger from Agnostic Front in January of 1989 at CBGB's" Michael adds regarding his favourite crossover shows, while concluding that "I believe that crossover is relevant today; I just think it has taken on new forms and new terminology".

Confusion have played in various reunion shows since their disbandment. They played a reunion show in January 2003 at CBGB's as part of a memorial show for their former guitarist Frank Collins, who died in June 2002. They also played two shows in 2007, one in New Jersey and another in Peekskill, New York. In 2023, they played two reunion shows at The Brooklyn Monarch, Brooklyn. So, let's hope for some new recordings too?

At a glance: Not for the faint-hearted, Confusion are one of the innovators of the crossover between hardcore and death metal, and you can hear echoes of their legacy in bands like All Out War (even though they were just a few years later), Earth Crisis etc. I'm not a fan of the later metalcore style that took its cues from those bands; however, Confusion's crossover is raw, unpolished and highly original. If you can afford to get the excellent *Taste Of Hate* 7-inch, you'll get one piece of excellent hardcore metal in your record collection, however I totally recommend getting the 2023 *Storm the Walls: 1990-1994* LP compilation that includes all their recordings!

DARKSIDE NYC

(Darkside NYC band picture. Courtesy unknown)

Darkside NYC are another one example of a different crossover, between thrash, death metal, and hardcore. Their roots can be traced back to the early 1990s, when former Sheer Terror guitarist Alan Blake formed the band shortly after his departure from said band. Over the years, singer Rich O'Brien and guitarist Matt Melnick have been the driving force holding it all together, despite periods of inactivity.

Formed as Darkside in 1991, the band's core and best-known lineup consisted of Blake, with Rich O'Brien (vocals) and Joe Branciforte (drums). The bass slot was, at times, a revolving door, but Jeff Morlos, Scott Helland, Joe Heller, and Baron "Thorn" Misuraca appeared on recordings. The band officially added "NYC" to its name in early 1993.

"The correct answer is Motörhead" Rich replies, when asked about the first band to pursue the crossover. "I think it was destiny. The jump from Motörhead to *Welcome To Hell* to *Kill 'Em All* took a certain amount of time" Rich adds, when asked why and how he believes the crossover took place. "But all the shit that came next was a lot more rapid succession. Hellhammer demos were mixing Discharge and Venom. It was already in the pot cooking before anyone else in the mid-80s 'crossover' years had the idea to mix things."

(Darkside NYC with Confusion, Starkweather, Merauder and Sheer Terror at CBGB's. 02/08/1992)

Darkside NYC took on a much heavier approach that other NYHC or crossover bands from day one. As apparent on their *Demo 1991*, cross Carnivore with Sheer Terror, add some Celtic Frost or even death metal, and you get the point—nihilistic, negative NYHC with mosh parts. Songs like 'The Final Fall' or 'Under Your Skin' are jaw-dropping, heavy and dirge-y sounding, but still with the feeling of NYHC being everywhere.

"Well, the older punks and hardcore guys didn't like it much" Rich responds regarding the initial influx of metalheads coming to hardcore shows. "The crossover was my era so I'm part of that hated wave that came along and 'ruined' things, haha!"

"In the late 1980s there were lots of metal shows with hardcore bands opening. L'Amour, The Ritz, etc. There'd be brawls and beatdowns inside and even outside on the street. It was a bloodbath when certain bands played (Slayer and Carnivore specifically) because it attracted the most maniacs".

Darkside NYC's second demo, *Suffer In Silence!* (1992) went for an even heavier approach, a more mean, nasty sound, and rough as hell. It is evident in songs like 'Impending Extinction' or 'Forgiven Not Forgotten'. Yes, the Celtic Frost-meets-Carvivore-meets-Sheer Terror is still here, however, this time a good dose of death metal elements is added in, plus even wilder NYHC mosh parts. *Suffer In Silence!* is another excellent release.

(Striving For Togetherness fest. Unknown year, unbelievable lineup!)

"Speaking from personal experience, I started out rock 'n' roll, and moved into hard rock, then early metal. By the time thrash and death appeared I was well entrenched in all of it and already knew punk. I found lots of things in common but was particularly drawn to nihilism and aggression as a maladjusted kid".

As aforementioned, Darkside NYC took a different route in their crossover, adding death metal influences too. Rich explains that "It was intentional, and I enjoyed that it seemed to piss off a lot of the audience. We were always the band to zig when everyone else zagged. Mixing hardcore and thrash was already being done for years but death metal was relatively uncharted territory at hardcore shows in New York. I came out swinging and growling and it was a different kind of energy. Blake and myself were obviously super into Celtic Frost and Hellhammer so we just took what we were already into further into darker heavier and more sinister realms.

The 1994 demo *Ambitions Make Way for Dread* included three ultra-brutal songs, with 'Parasitic Worm Contraction' being blatantly death metal, and 'Bearing the Brunt' being one of the most punishing songs they ever wrote. This demo finds Darkside NYC into their most mature style before sadly disbanding in 1996.

"We were more of a hardcore band that played metal. Back when hardcore meant something entirely different to what it is now. I am totally removed from whatever hardcore is today. Fifty-year-old guys trying to fit in with a scene of 20-25-year-olds is laughable. Just stop" Rich adds.

In 1998, a collection of tracks named as *Ambitions Make Way For Dread* were finally released for the first time on CD and vinyl, while the band remained inactive. *Ambitions Make Way for Dread* LP was their best recording production-wise so far, and maybe the best release of the band in the 1990s era. I kind of miss the dirge of the early demos, but the ferocity is still here! Shit, 'Casualties Of A Fleeting Existence' even includes powerviolence breaks!

"As for my favourite crossover shows" Rich adds, "Bad Brains and Leeway comes to mind. 1989. But also, any show I've seen with D.R.I., Suicidal Tendencies, Carnivore, Nuclear Assault, Prong, Cro-Mags. All of that. COC, SOD, Crumbsuckers…Too many to list regarding our influences. But all the classic shit and the obscure as well. Very little if any of the trendy bands everyone called their 'guilty pleasures' found their way onto my boombox".

After a one-time reunion in 2003, Darkside NYC came back for good in 2006 and remain active in 2025 in terms of recording but have retired from performing live. And of course, you won't think of them becoming more mellow on the 2014 *Optimism Is Self-Deception: Vol. 1 & 2* CD; kicking off with the unbelievably crazy 'Kill All The New Jacks' that even incorporates noise. Songs like 'Universal Conviction On A False Pretense' keep up the legacy of their earliest days, but then you have the absolutely mental noise of 'Astral Projection On DMT' that is reminiscent of Whitehouse or the anthemic 'Stroll Through A Falling Rock Zone In My Subconscious' that starts with acoustic guitar and features timbales and violins! *Optimism Is Self-Deception: Vol. 1 & 2* is their most diverse work.

(Darkside NYC with Killing Time, Warzone and Snapcase at The Wetlands, NY 29/08/1993)

"Wetlands was my favourite club to play, hands down. I loved the circular stage they used to have. CBGB's was my second." Rich admits. "I would also add The Unisound in Reading, Pennsylvania and Sea Sea's in Moosic, Pennsylvania were both always great. The Rat in Boston. QE2 in Albany, New York… I drank a lot back then. Three or four 40-oz malt liquors and things tended to get interesting. Live shows could be great or fail spectacularly!"

Past and post-Darkside NYC, there were many bands that Darkside NYC members were a part of: Rich O'Brien (1992-1996, 2006-present) and Matt Melnick (1995-1996, 2006-present) are currently working on Diminished Capacity, their new project that ranges from rock 'n' roll to metal to crust punk. Rich also played drums in Everyday Dollars, Mad Mulligans and Ultra Violence. Matt Melnick played in Blood of a Zombie, Downlow NYHC, Z.Z.Z.Z., Disassociate, School of Violence, Dank Sinatra and Jesus Chrust. Mark Sokoll (bass, 2013-2022) in Chaka, Terminal Confusion, Realm and Hypoxia. Rick Beenders (drums 2013-2022) played in The Skullies and Mad Mulligans. Jeff Morlos (bass 1992, 1993, 1994) played in Without A Cause and Downlow NYHC. Matt Fleming (2006-2008) played in the Functional Idiots and Deep In Vein. Baron "Thorn" Misuraca (1991, 1993) in Sabinas Rex, Vasaria, Desecrator, Baron Misuraca, Baron Misuraca's Retro Lounge, Carnivore A.D., Sex & Violence and Sheer Terror. Jason Martin (1991) in Sheer Terror. Alan Blake (1991-1995) in No Control and Sheer Terror. Joe Heller (1992-1993, 1995) in Amid Pain, Revoltage and Awful Truth. Joe Branciforte (1992-1996, 2006-2008) in High Strange, The Communion, All Out War, Archon, Disassociate, Merauder, Sun Descends, Die Pigeon Die, Carnivore A.D. and The Voluptuous Horror of Karen Black, Awful Truth and Deep In Vein. Scott Helland (1993-1994) in Outpatients, School of Violence, and Deep Wound, Guitarmy of One and Frenchy and the Punk. Joe V. Vitale (1994-1995, 1996) in Profound Effect, The Third Kind, Downlow NYHC, and New Faith, Son of the Soil. Tomoyuko Také (2008-2012) in Cryptic Revelation, Dyingrace, Deathtortion, Burden of Despair, Cease2Exist, Everyday Dollars and Hell Brigade.

Finally, Rich adds that "there's not much left to crossover but I'm doing a new band that is mixing black metal and blues and D-beat and blues. I am very confident we will be the pioneers of that haha! Diminished Capacity is the band Matt and myself have been doing for over a decade behind the scenes, and exclusively since 2022. Our new project that is crossing metal with crust punk, extreme metal with old school hardcore-punk, black metal and Oi! Our ratio is like one-third thrash death black and hardcore metal, one-third punk (d-beat, traditional and Oi!) and one-third rock 'n' roll and blues".

At a glance: You must give it to bands like Darkside NYC (as well as Confusion NYC) for going on a very different and diverse route in NYHC. Darkside NYC's approach is simply revolutionary, adding and blending so many different sounds together, even from their very start. Metalheads into Celtic Frost and Obituary, you will love them. And hardcore kids with a taste in those brutal sounds, as well as bands like Deviated Instinct and Hellbastard, Darkside NYC is an excellent treat. I would love to see their first two demos re-issued on vinyl!

UNITED KINGDOM

"There was a time when 'Metal' – as in the 'Heavy' variety – was a dirty word in the UK punk scene. Sure, everyone cut Motörhead some slack, but even the likes of Iron Maiden and Judas Priest were frowned upon back then, because of their air raid siren vocals and spandex strides although most people secretly loved 'The Number of the Beast' regardless!

At some point though, the tides started to turn. Discharge started playing solos, albeit of the atonal variety, so there was clearly some wriggle room when it came to battle lines - but when 'Grave New World' came along, it was still definitely the wrong side of every line ever drawn. Perhaps they should have changed their name like The Rejects did when they released 'Quiet Storm', out of some modicum of respect for their back catalogue. What no one realised though was how thin the veil between the two scenes really was.

But whilst the punk scene wasn't ready for Heavy Metal in one fell swoop, it was more than susceptible to it creeping in riff by riff, US thrash bands drip-feeding a stagnating scene with a youthful energy and intensity. Tape trading was rife, and demos by the likes of Metallica and Possessed were making their way across the pond (themselves heavily influenced by Venom, of course, so what goes round...), and after several years of subtle infiltration, 1984 was probably Ground Zero, when the call was too damn loud to ignore and was enthusiastically answered by UK punk bands such as English Dogs, Sacrilege and Onslaught, who all got faster, tighter and more intense as a result. And once the floodgates were opened, it was hard not to be swept away by the metal surge, as everybody from The Exploited, Broken Bones and GBH to Antisect, Concrete Sox and Hellbastard embraced the power of the riff.

For some it was a breath of fresh air, a much-needed creative shot in the arm and a chance to promote positive punk ideals to a whole new audience, but for others it was a dilution of those punk ethics and an erosion of the DIY stance. And sure enough, soon dyed-in-the-wool hardcore punk labels like Peaceville, Earache and Vinyl Solution were cultivating full-on metal rosters. Of course, the truth as regards 'selling out' was somewhere between, and it was neither the salvation of our scene, or the death of it; in fact, it was just another step change, and your take on it very much depended upon your tolerance for double kick pedals, but growth is always painful, and sometimes you take two steps forward, one step back and the occasional side step into the unknown. Either way, you evolve or die." -- Ian Glasper- Decadence Within, Stampin' Ground, Warwound, Zero Again, Suicide Watch, Sun of the Endless Night, Ammonia 77, Burnside, Thirty Six Strategies, and your favourite punk author!

DRIVEN TO DISTRACTION/DEATH WARMED UP

Birmingham's unsung heroes Driven To Distraction, have a long story in the hardcore punk and crossover scene. Formed in 1985 as Death Warmed Up, they are active with a few pauses in-between, making them as one of the most long-standing UK crossover acts. Guitarist/vocalist Clive Hetherington narrates their story: "We were initially a three-piece band – Andy Quinn – bass, Rob Wheldall – drums and me on guitar/vocals, formed in late 1987. We'd all previously been in the punk thrash band Death Warmed Up which fell apart in early 1987. We'd played loads of gigs quite a few of which were a little violent, and had a suspect reputation through association (ok - some of that reputation was deserved!) and so it made sense to split up while we were all still in one piece...As Driven To Distraction we recorded the four track demo *No Pain...No Gain* in 1987 and the following year added a mate of GBH and sometime punk roadie Tomo (Richard Thompson) on vocals. Tomo added a new punkier dynamic to the band. We recorded a couple of tracks for an aborted EP in 1988; the guy who paid for the studio time got the master tapes but then we heard he'd had a nervous breakdown so that was that! One of those tracks did appear on a UK thrash compilation tape though. We then self-financed the *Never Forgive...Never Forget* 7-inch EP in 1989, which was played on Radio 1 by John Peel no less, but by 1990 we'd started to run out of steam, money and beer. Tomo was on the road abroad a fair bit with The Exploited and GBH doing their tours and the punk metal scene seemed to be slowly fragmenting so we decided to call it a day".

(Death Warmed Up with D.R.I. at The Mermaid, Birmingham, UK. 03/10/1987)

As Death Warmed Up, their first release was the 1986 *Death Head* demo, that included two songs ('Death Head' and 'King's Devil') of rough and catchy thrash-punk, like English Dogs and GBH gone Venom, with 'King's Devil' clocking over nine minutes and there's a definite Amebix feeling to it! I'm a sucker for those underproduced stuff, and Death Warmed Up sound so brutal on this recording, while the same applies to the 1987 *The Battle Rages* demo, only this time it's slightly more complex, and with even faster songs like 'Dead Time Stories' or 'Stormbringer' (that has an intro riff reminding me of Crumbsuckers, before going on a full scale metal punk assault like English Dogs), terrific stuff!

"I think the 'crossover' tag is open to interpretation – how is it defined?" Clive argues. "For us we were too punk for the metallers and too metal for the punks, so I guess we qualified in that way strangely enough. I would say that we never set out to be any specific type of band really and if anyone asked what sort of band I was in, I'd say you tell me! At the time though we were quite a mash up musical wise whereas all the other bands in Birmingham were either one thing or the other. Rob the Drums always said all the other bands had a consistent opinion about us that never changed: they admired our music, came to our gigs but still hated us! First crossover band? I see it as more of a progression that led to that genre. I was a metalhead but used to buy singles by the likes of The Stranglers, Skids, Damned and The Ruts and then the UK Subs and Exploited. Metal wise it was the NWOBHM, Venom and Motörhead of course. I was introduced by a punk mate to Discharge, English Dogs, Broken Bones, Conflict and GBH - we played with all of them! So all the elements were there…and then thrash and hardcore popped up".

(Death Warmed Up with Toxic Waste and Exit-Stance at the Crypt, South London. 31/03/1986)

The final release of Death Warmed Up was the 1987 *We Go To War* demo, that headed for an ultra-fast thrash punk sound, like in the opening 'Winter of Our Discontent'. While 'Incinerator' follows a more anthemic style; still rough and tough as nails sound that would please even fans of crustcore bands like e.g. Doom or Deviated Instinct (even though Death Warmed Up don't belong in this scene).

"Regarding why crossover took place" Clive narrates, "I think the lazy answer would be that the punk bands became better musicians and incorporated metal into their songs. Personally, I always played rock-metal guitar and were invited into punk bands for that reason – to beef them up and add some lead work. I don't think crossover was a cultural thing really, just a collision between different musical styles that complimented each other. I gravitated towards the punk metal scene because I liked the eclectic nature of it, but it wasn't the safest way to have fun!"

Death Warmed Up renamed to Driven To Distraction with the lineup being Clive on guitar/vocals, Rob on drums, Andy on bass and in 1988 Tomo joining in on vocals. In 1988 they released a series of three demos: *Demo 2*, *Demo 3* and *No Pain...No Gain*. While they retained the heaviness of the early days, now their thrash punk was more controlled, and less crusty; more in line with the American crossover. All three demos are absolutely great, and songs like 'No Pain, No Gain' (with its 'GBH gone thrash metal') or 'Friend? No Liar!' from the first two demos (I'm going to refer to *No Pain...No Gain* later) are just great examples of their own brand of crossover.

(Death Warmed Up with GBH and Depth Charge at the Mermaid, 27/06/1987)

"To be honest that period (mid-late 1980s) in Birmingham, I didn't even know there was such a thing as crossover. It was more the mixing of the punk, hardcore and thrash crews that happened gig wise that caught my attention" Clive admits. "It was global thrash and hardcore bands, not just American bands that were popular at the time though and that seemed to be having an influence on where things were heading UK wise. Death Warmed Up did gigs supporting D.R.I. and the Circle Jerks and they were fantastic experiences; those gigs were rammed! The metallers started wearing punk T-shirts; not so much the punks the other way round but we went to the same gigs mostly. Another thing was that the punks and metallers I knew in Brum shared a common dislike of the skinheads, and the Hells Angels; it made sense to forge some form of alliance. I crossed the Angels once or twice and on one occasion ended up with a knife at my throat for being too 'cocky'. A bit of trivia - GBH released *Live In Los Angeles/Live At Victoria Hall* video at the time and on it was Jock wearing a Driven To Distraction T-shirt onstage; that was a very proud moment for us! We'd played gigs with lots of the UK bands that are mentioned as crossover, but to my ears they didn't sound similar enough for a categorisation that I could relate to. I think the requirements for 'crossover' as it's become known for me would have been fast, varied, heavy and unvarnished, and a lot of the UK bands we played with certainly met those criteria. Venues wise we had 'The Mermaid', The Barrel Organ', 'The Pen & Wig' and 'Edwards No. 8' where medium-sized punk bands and metal bands could play on the same bill but it could be a tense affair. I think we were quite lucky in the number of venues we had, but at the time I don't think we realised it".

Driven to Distraction were already an established name in the Birmingham scene (even though they didn't have the chance to release something on a vinyl record up to 1990), and this made them appear in billings with various hardcore, punk or thrash bands of the era. "We got to play with loads of UK bands that were instrumental in forging crossover" Clive smiles. "UK Subs, Exploited, Broken Bones, English Dogs GBH, etc. I suppose one of the most unusual gigs we did though was supporting all female Scandinavian thrash band Ice Age – I don't think they were too sure about us, but we thought they were great! The Birmingham thrash crust bands started to make a serious impact at that time, so we got to know them of course, the likes of Doom, Bolt Thrower, and Cerebral Fix. I think we got to play with one or two of them, but they kept us at a distance as a rule. I should mention all the international bands that played in Birmingham like Sepultura, Sacred Reich, Slayer (I got thrown out for fighting) The Hard-Ons, Gwar, etc. Great times, we were spoiled for choice. Most of Driven To Distraction's gigs were loony for one reason or another; probably because me and Tomo were in the band and we all liked the odd beer. I'm sure Tomo would agree that he could be a bit confrontational at times, he roadied for GBH so it wasn't a big surprise! He's mentioned in Ross Lomas's autobiography. A gig supporting Exploited at Edwards No. 8 nearly went up because the skins turned up and Tomo was not a fan to say the least. His berating of them from the stage was proper. Luckily the majority of the crowd agreed with him (for once) so the boneheads kept quiet. We supported Exploited at the Apollo in London I think - the biggest venue we'd played but by the time we got onstage we were wasted and played on auto pilot. The crew who went with us from Birmingham said it were like watching the punk version of Spinal Tap. We supported the UK Subs at Edwards No 8; for once we were almost sober and played pretty well. I bumped into Subs singer Charlie Harper after – his only comment was, 'If you're going to play that hardcore stuff you need to jump around a lot more…'. We supported GBH at the Academy in Birmingham and the crowd were really pumped and volatile. The first support was a thrash band who lasted ten minutes. Tomo tore into the crowd from the very start, we lasted twenty minutes and were lucky to get out alive. Andy the bassist got us a slot onstage at the end of year party for the local university; I thought they were mad to put us on! It was obviously full of uni indie students in their finery, and we ambled through the crowd and onto the stage in our punk metal finery. We ripped through our set – Tomo insulting the crowd as usual and finished to total silence. We ambled back out and went to the nearest pub. And that's how most of our gigs went, they were such fun! I got a lot of our gig's audio recorded from the PA for posterity and put them on YouTube. We weren't the most professional band, but we had a real dynamism, and I think you can hear that".

While Clive mentions that 'we weren't the most professional band', I tend to disagree, because in terms of recording and songwriting, the 1988 *No Pain...No Gain* demo is just excellent; nearly fifteen minutes of crossover brilliance, this time Driven To Distraction sounded more inspired and ferocious than ever before-and even though their sound went for a total US approach (think Ludichrist, Crumbsuckers), all four songs are just ripping; 'Mercenary' is just a crossover anthem. Try to listen to 'Driven to Distraction' while seated, you can't! A damn shame this demo wasn't released on a 7-inch.

"Our influences were as you'd expect, Motörhead, GBH, thrash, Crumbsuckers, Beyond Possession and a bit of 70`s hard rock in my case" Clive admits. "With Driven To Distraction I think because we all had different influences that drove our sound we never came across as being really focussed in one direction hence the crossover tag we've been given. It surprises but pleases me that anyone is that interested in us at all to be honest, especially as we never even brought an album out! There was one review of us that said we sounded like One Way System; I'd never heard of 'em! I eventually did hear them and saw the connection they were making. There was one review of the EP in a metal mag as well where it started with "a band that'll only ever play to a bunch of pissed-up punks in the back room of a pub" and ended with "a metal racket" – correct on both counts! We did get good reviews though especially for our live stuff, we were a pretty tight outfit onstage. Style wise during that period we were all picking stuff off each other. GBH (that band again) had it perfect with the hard looking don't mess with me punk metal uniform. Lots of thrashers in Birmingham looked more like them than say Anthrax. That might have been down partly to the culture in the UK at that time, plenty of violence whether in the pub, at the football or being in the wrong place at ANY time. We played a gig in Coventry in 1986 supporting some old school anarchist punk bands, I was wearing a biker jacket and an AC/DC T-shirt ha! The animal liberation punks started heckling us – probably bored with the guitar solos and our singer said something like "eat your dogs" - they went mental. They were shouting stuff like "the wankers in the leather jackets" not realising at the back of the venue were a GBH looking crew wearing...leather jackets, we left before the fighting started. There was a bit of a shift in the late 80s though where more people were adopting that straight edge skateboard style thing. We didn`t: we couldn`t afford it and it might have looked good in California, but it looked rubbish in the rainy UK. I'd argue that slight style shift started to fracture the crossover scene, most of the punks and metallers in my sphere didn`t think much of it. Too clean, too safe and too corporate".

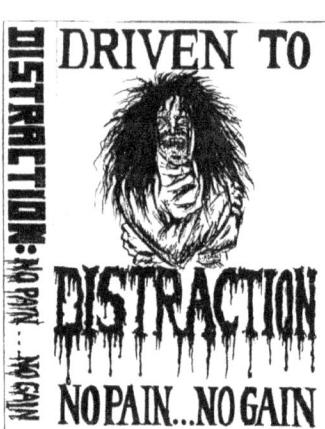

(Driven To Distraction No Pain...No Gain cassette cover)

Driven To Distraction's final effort was the 1990 *Never forgive, Never forget* 7-inch EP, that was self-released by the band-and what a great release it was. Tomo's vocals always deliver that GBH-style, however the sound was more reminiscent of Lethal Aggression, Ludichrist and Crumbsuckers, aka New York and New Jersey heavyweight crossover acts. All three songs are just ace, with my favourites being 'I Don't Care (No More)' and 'Terrorisation', with its rap part. Definitely a winner, however Driven To Distraction called it a day later in 1990.

"Favourite venues of that era? Obviously, The Mermaid was the best venue by far for countless reasons but Driven To Distraction never actually played there! I always missed playing the Barrel Organ after it closed and another fave Edwards no 8 mysteriously burnt down. I liked the George Robey in London; it had a good vibe. Tiffany's in Rochdale which had a galleon with seating on one side of the stage and all the other venues we played where we managed to get out of without getting battered".

Driven To Distraction got back together in 2017 as a trio (Rob, Clive and Pen and Wig's Steve Longstaff on bass), and are still (2025) active, offering shows in Birmingham area. So, I guess we should expect someday a record or a release of their demos on record? Who knows! The story behind this interview with Clive is fascinating, since *Crossover The Edge* was discussed in a Facebook post, and Clive commented that "that guy at least did justice to Driven To Distraction", so I approached him and he was more than happy to offer me an interview.

"The original crossover is relevant in hindsight I expect. We never knew we were a crossover band but we've been told we were so we must have been. I suppose crossover could only genuinely exist in a period when the musical conjunctions were right; we were fortunate to be there at that time. I suppose crossover of a sort did carry on with bands that incorporated hip hop and rap but ended when it became the godawful nu-metal movement. To me most bands now have fallen into the trap of being one dimensional, maybe it's easier to get a gig or an album out that way, maybe we should have tried it - ha! Rob the Drums and I still play our mash ups for fun and put YouTube videos out there…that's our nostalgia trip! Andy Q the bassist plays with MC16, a punk band who regularly gigs around and releases CDs. Tomo's part of a stage lighting company I believe".

At a glance: If a mix between GBH and early English Dogs with New York City-styled crossover such as Ludichrist and Crumbsuckers is your thing, you're going to love Driven To Distraction. If you add to this mix a crustier sound, you will love Death Warmed Up! Hopefully we'll see a re-issue of their stuff, because demos like *No Pain...No Gain* and the 7-inch EP *Never Forgive, Never Forget* are just sheer enjoyment for any metalpunk or punk metalhead!

(Death Warmed Up supporting Circle Jerks and Gang Green at The Mermaid, Birmingham. 20/11/1987)

CANADA

FRATRICIDE

(Fratricide band picture 1986. Courtesy of Fiona Harris)

One of the two bands, the other being Neuroot from Belgium that were part of one of the greatest mysteries of unreleased hardcore crossover records ever. When talking about the test press that never became a proper release, Pusmort's *The Neuroot/Fratricide* split LP comes to mind. Fratricide formed in 1986 in Vancouver, British Columbia, and even though their existence lasted only for two years, their imprint was left in the worldwide crossover scene.

"Fratricide happened after the remains of a goofy punk band called Abortions On Toast" bassist Dan Walters narrates. "Eric (Thorkelsson) switched up to guitar and brought some songs over to my place, Eugene (Buthot III) followed on drums then a few months later Jonzo (John Tsolinas, vocals) showed up, and we all started jamming together. 5 months later we went into the studio, then played our first live show a month after that".

Fratricide's first release was the 1986 *Blind Faith* demo, and to be honest, this one's one of the best crossover demos ever; not only it's professionally recorded, but the band sounds like it's on fire. Crossing The Accüsed with Septic Death, one can also spot a definite D.R.I. influence *(Dealing With It*! era) with some Raw Power thrown in, Blind Faith is a definitive winner with bomb-blasts like 'Blind Faith', 'Going Under' and 'Blood Red Dream'.

(Fratricide band gig picture. Date and courtesy unknown)

"I remember Motörhead brought a lot of the metal and punk kids together, at least the ones I knew" Dan believes. "A lot of the music was being heard by both crowds. As some of the punks learned to play their instruments better and the metalheads woke up to more serious and realistic song subjects, the crossover all felt like a natural progression to me…we all just kind of started showing up at each other's gigs. I remember a metal girl in my high school in the locker next to me asking me about the artwork on some of the gig flyers I had taped up in my locker. We started trading tapes, then showing up at gigs. She liked Dave Gregg D.O.A.'s long hair and Death Sentence's first album, haha!".

Pushead was impressed by their sheer power, and Fratricide were included in the 1987 *Pusmort Sampler* 7-inch with 'Going Under', while Fratricide recorded a split LP with Neuroot, that was supposed to come out on Pushmort, but was never released back then (only a few test-pressings exist), with the reason of its non-release being that there was a problem with the artwork not being able to be reproduced up to Pushead's standards (something to do with the colour separations), alongside problems with the pressing plant in France. It's a story that has left both Neuroot and Fratricide being downhearted towards Pushead, even though the tracks of both bands have been re-released a few decades later as separate releases.

(Fratricide with Subverse, Witches Hammer and Adversity at the Kennedy Hall, 03/07/1987)

Fratricide were also skaters, a fact that made them big towards *Thrasher* magazine readers, and Dan mentions that "visually we all just wore what was comfortable skating in- Eric and myself grew our hair long because we were lazy...so much so that my hair ended up dreading, lol. I was the only one wearing a leather jacket and studs for a while, haha!". And regarding Fratricide's influences, Dan mentions that "for me personally I really liked old hardcore, but we all listened to Discharge, Crucifix, old Metallica, 7 Seconds, Minor Threat, and got into a lot of early German thrash metal".

By 1987 Brad MacDonald (drums) and Ray LaChance (vocals) joined in, and the *Mission of Christ / Fratricide* split 7-inch EP was released on Final Notice Records, and while Mission of Christ's side was good thrash metal, Fratricide on the flipside offered two ragers, 'Razor Piss' and 'Circled Adventure', and Fratricide were lucky and good enough to play shows alongside bands like D.R.I., Corrosion of Conformity, The Accüsed, Suicidal Tendencies, Beyond Possession and Subverse. "Some of our (or at least my) favourite shows back then that were in the crossover realm were a big GBH show, D.R.I. and Beyond Possession's first time here in a small club in 1985 and a Verbal Abuse show with Vancouver's first speed-thrash metal band Witches Hammer was totally rad" Dan offers. "Witches Hammer played a lot of hardcore shows here with DOA and Death Sentence and were responsible for getting the crossover scene happening. There's a great write up that Marco Banco wrote in an insert in the new Witches Hammer 7-inch reissue put out by Supreme Echo- you should check it out if you haven't already…accordingly, most of the violence at shows back then was from the idiot skinheads fighting with both the punks and the metalheads. We all kind of bonded against a common enemy, so to speak".

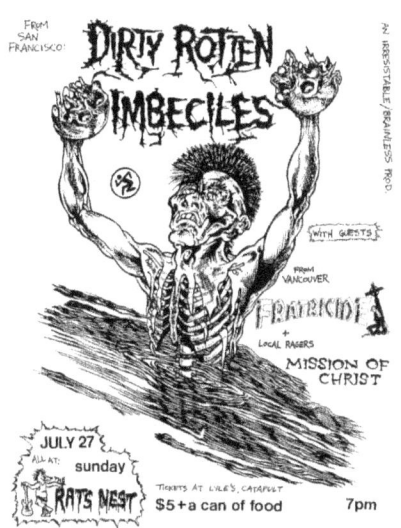

(Fratricide with Mission of Christ and D.R.I. at the Rat's Nest, 27/07/1986)

Sadly, in 1988 Fratricide called it quits, with members moving to other bands; Dan Walters played in Headfirst/Headstart and now is in Christ Air (alongside John Tsolinas), John Tsolinas played in the late 1990s-early 2000s in the crossover Hong Kong Blonde, Eric Thorkellson played in the hardcore Strain. Two years after their break-up, Germany's HeartFirst Records released the 1990 *Scream Bloody Vengeance* 7-inch, that included the eponymous song that is one of the best they ever wrote, alongside three old songs that were recorded live on CFRO Co-op Radio, January 2, 1987. Again, a hit!

"I remember hearing about a lot of punks showing the metal kids how to stage dive at an early Metallica show here at the York Theatre" Dan smiles. "I didn't make it inside because I was broke and couldn't afford the ticket…bummer! As Fratricide, our favourite places to play were the wickedly cool York Theatre, where most of the big all-ages punk rock shows happened and a little basement house in Victoria called The Rat's Nest. One of the shows we played there with D.R.I. was totally nuts".

Fast forward 2010 and Schizophrenic Records alongside Ugly Pop Records released on a single LP, the side of Fratricide that was supposed to be released as the split with Neuroot; such a shame this phenomenal frenzied attack of nasty speedcore took twenty-four years to be released, it's just Fratricide top recordings and songs like 'Grave' and 'Beaten Senseles' will drive you wild, a total holocaust of The Accüsed meets early Gang Green meets Septic Death meets Beyond Possession!

"Is crossover still relevant today? Totally!" Dan smiles. "I missed out on the whole bro-core/metalcore stuff in the late 1990s/2000s though, but the old school throw-back (including Jonzo and my new skatethrash band Christ Air) is where my heart is…"

At a glance: Under the radar of most people, Fratricide released some of the wildest crossover ever! If you are a fan of the most hardcore crossover, with a taste in the Splatter Rock of The Accüsed played at maximum speed and ferocity, Fratricide is for you. All their releases are of great quality but be sure to pick up the 2010 release of the side in the split with Neuroot. Mind-shattering stuff!

SLAUGHTER

(Slaughter band picture, 1986. Courtesy unknown)

There are more than few good reasons that Slaughter from Ontario, Canada are included in this book - so calm down metalheads! Obviously, they were one of the first bands to bridge thrash with death metal. The hardcore influences were evident in their music since the beginning, creating some of the most extreme sounds that derived from the metal scene in the first half of 1980s.

Slaughter's inclusion in the book was way beyond any deadline, and I asked from Terry with the help of Dave Hewson to provide me short and sweet answers in just a few days, and so they did!

Formed in 1984 by Dave Hewson (vocals, guitar), Terry Sadler (vocals, bass) and Ron Summers (bass), Terry narrates that "we started in 1984 and we went on initially to learn play our instruments, haha! Then, we released a few demos (with the best one in my opinion being *Surrender or Die*), and Fringe Records offered us a contract for our first LP. That is the early story of Slaughter".

Slaughter's first demo was the 1984 *Meatcleaver*, a frantic and vicious underproduced effort that resembled more of the noisy hardcore punk contemporaries, rather than anything that had to do with metal;

OK, in terms of lyrics they were metal. However the music especially in songs like 'Eve Of Darkness', 'Slaughter-House' and 'Strappado' sounded like Discharge on 78 RPM! The follow-up demo, the 1984 *Bloody Karnage* headed for a more metal style, even though songs like 'One Foot In The Grave' sounded like a cross between Discharge and early D.R.I., while 'Disintegrator' was a definite metal punk noisemonger. *Bloody Karnage* was a by far better effort.

"Motörhead and Venom were the first ones to merge punk with metal, it's non-negotiable" Terry smiles. "And the crossover took place because both musicians and fans wanted to discover new territories. Rock music was getting stagnant, and punk came along and gave rock a very good kick in the ass, making it wild and interesting again".

(Slaughter with Exodus at Larry's Hideaway, 15/08/1985)

In 1985 Slaughter released on cassette their first ever live show they played on March 25, 1985 with Sacrifice. The cassette was named *Live Karnage*, that showcased their chaotic firepower onstage. Their best demo though was about to be released later the same year, and in was the classic *Surrender or Die*; rough thrash metal that took its cues from Celtic Frost and Venom, with the speed of crossover and hardcore like Cryptic Slaughter and D.R.I. This demo pre-dated their later classic releases. Songs like 'Tyrant of Hell', 'Maim to Please' and 'Strappado' have this definite hardcore crossover edge, while they are still metal!

"Our influences then varied" Terry adds. "We loved everything from KISS, Black Sabbath and Alice Cooper to Celtic Frost, Judas Priest, Venom, Motörhead to Plasmatics, GBH, Discharge, Sex Pistols and Direct Action".

In 1986 Chuck Schuldiner of Mantas and Death was asked to join in, and he was added for a few months as a second guitarist, moving to Canada in January of that year. However, shortly after he found himself not happy of following Slaughter's vision and decided to move back to Florida to bring in life his own vision through Death. Schuldiner was only for two weeks in Slaughter!

The first official release from Slaughter landed in 1986 on Fringe Product's sublabel Diabolic Force Records. The much sought-after nowadays in its original form *Nocturnal Hell* 7-inch, found Slaughter on beast mode. It was produced by Brian Taylor, the vocalist of the hardcore punk band Youth Youth Youth- who also produced records by Sacrifice, Razor and Sudden Impact. Slaughter achieved to sound heavier and crazier than ever before, and even though this can be filed under 'thrash-death metal', the hardcore explosions of 'One Foot In Grave' and 'Tortured Souls' can definitely apply to crossover and hardcore fans too. The sound here is almost as rough as Repulsion's *Horrified*!

(Slaughter with Nuclear Assault and NYC Mayhem at Starwood, Toronto. 17/01/1986)

Ron Summers was then replaced by Brian Lourie (RIP 2008) on drums, of the crossover hardcore Guerrilla Warfare, and Slaughter headed on recording again under the production matters of Brian Taylor and releasing again on Fringe Product's sublabel Diabolic Force Records. The LP recorded stands among one of the most classic and influential metal records of 1980s. It's actually funny, since this record sounds so mean and having a total influence of hardcore punk. Yes, I'm talking about the 1987 *Strappado* LP. Now Slaughter incorporated a heavy metal production, and contained some more complex new songs. *Strappado* is considered as a masterpiece of extreme metal, taking its cues from Celtic Frost and early Slayer in songs like 'Fuck of Death', 'Parasites' and 'Tales of the Macabre'. But when things speed up such as in the excellent 'Maim to Please' that wasn't included in the LP version, only in the cassette, 'One

Foot in the Grave', 'Death Dealer' or 'Tyrant of Hell', thus the re-recordings of the old songs, the hardcore crossover spirit is there!

"We went to play shows with so many bands then" Terry adds "however, in terms of crossover, I believe that when we played a show with Corrosion of Conformity, it really stands out. They were a fuckin' impressive act, and we were fans of them since very early".

Slaughter in 1988 went on to change their sound and release two demos of technical thrash metal that sounded very Bay Area-influenced, with *Paranormal* and *The Dark-Demo IV.* While those demos are good for what they are, they are far away from the scope of this book. This led to the break-up of Slaughter, and Dave Hewson founding Strappado in 1989, accompanied by Mike Dalton (bass), Brian Lourie (drums), and Bobby Sadzak (guitar). Strappado focussed on straight-forward Bay Area thrash, with releasing the 1991 *Not Dead Yet* LP, and the 1992 *Fatal Judgement* EP. More than good records for metalheads, sounding like a cross between Testament and Metallica, with a techno-thrash vibe added in.

In December 1994, Bobby Sadzak, Dave Hewson, and Brian Lourie had a short reunion as Slaughter and recorded a cover version of Celtic Frost's 'Dethroned Emperor' (that can be found on the tribute compilation CD *In Memory of... Celtic Frost*, released by Dwell Records in 1996. Slaughter disbanded in 1995 and never re-formed since then.

"The craziest memory of Slaughter includes the very first time I watched Dave Hewson rolling around on the floor out of his damn mind playing 'Bloody Karnage' onstage, hahah! And I really miss playing Larry's Hideaway (RIP) in Toronto…" Terry adds.

Slaughter maintained though their cult status in the underground metal scene in the following years since bands like e.g. Napalm Death were always referring to them as influences (plus, covering songs off them), and many releases/re-releases saw the light of day, with the 2021 *Live - The Starwood, Toronto - Nov 24, 1985* LP being the most recent one.

"Crossover is and will always be relevant" Terry concludes.

At a glance: While not strictly a crossover band, Slaughter would appeal to the crossover crowd that fancies the brutal sounds of Cryptic Slaughter, NYC Mayhem or Wehrmacht. Their *Surrender or Die* demo, as well as *Nocturnal Hell* 7-inch and *Strappado* LP are just classics of extreme metal, with a hardcore flavour-their hardcore influences are more than obvious in most songs. Metalheads will enjoy their releases as Strappado too. I wasn't impressed though since they miss all the raw power and frenetic hardcore energy of early Slaughter.

DISTORTED INFLUENCE

(Distorted Influence, 2023. Photo courtesy unknown)

A crossover hidden gem, Distorted Influence from Victoria, British Columbia, didn't have the luck to have a proper release in their first incarnation, other than their *Afford To Be Honest* 1990 demo, even though they existed from 1989 to 1993 and were very active in the local scene. This was about to change though with their 2023 revival being active today too, in 2025. Vocalist Andy Beaveridge narrates their story: "Distorted Influence basically came about while I was still in high school. Chris Locker (vox/guitar) and Pete Locker (drums) lived down the street from me. We ended up talking and becoming friends because Chris heard Luke (original drummer) and me jamming in my parents' garage. Luke and I met through a mutual friend. I was nervous when we first started playing because Luke was a few years older than me. Chris and I hit it off immediately because we both were really into bands like Mission of Christ, Poison Idea, and Accused, and a lot of the Pacific Northwest punk and hardcore bands. We kind of evolved from like a '82 hardcore style and incorporated a little more speed, and double kick drumming when Pete joined. The band was basically a way to hang out and just have fun. Most of our stuff was deeply rooted in humour and inside jokes. We spent a lot of time at the beach just drinking terrible wine with a huge fire. It's funny because the punk scene always thought we were a bit too metal, but the metal scene never really took us seriously because we weren't as professional, not quite as technically perfect, and always assing around. We still wore punk and hardcore on our sleeves".

"I can't answer for the other guys" Andy continues, "but to me crossover was just sort a natural progression of bands trying to be faster and bringing something different. But back in those days, crossover didn't really exist as a 'thing' though. Bands were just taking their punk and hardcore roots to the next level. I think it was a natural progression of bands writing new stuff and trying to out-do what they did before. I also think that crossover allowed both punk and metal bands to become more interesting. But also, there's a lot of mutual interest in punk and metal scenes. I don't think anyone really set out to do it on purpose though. There lots of crossover ancestors - bands like Discharge, even G.B.H. to an extent. All the d-beat style bands were incorporating a bit of metal. The '83 Suicidal Tendencies self-titled album while it leaned more punk, was definitely heading into some crossover territory. Listen to the guitar work on that album. And it's so fast. But when I first heard Accused, man that changed everything. 'Wrong Side of the Grave', 'Martha's Revenge'. THAT is the real deal. *The Silence in Grave* demo from Mission of Christ was such an eye opener".

(Distorted Influence with Forced Entry, Malevolence and The Accüsed at Sanscha Hall, Sidney, BC, Canada. 06/12/1991)

In 1990 Distorted Influence released their first demo, named as *Afford to Be Honest*; that demo blended the sounds of The Accüsed, alongside Beyond Possession (albeit in a harsher way). Good stuff, but the best was yet to come! However, the quality is already here, with songs like 'Debourge' and 'You Must Learn'.

"Oh man so many musical influences" Andy smiles. "For crossover bands, Suicidal Tendencies - *Self titled* and *Join the Army,* Accused - *The Return of Martha Splatterhead* and *Maddest Stories*, Poison Idea - *Feel the Darkness*, Werhmacht - *Beermacht*, Spazztic Blurr, Mission of Christ - *Silence in Grave* demo, Cryptic Slaughter - *Money Talks* and *Convicted* LPs, Dayglo Abortions - *Here Today, Guano Tomorrow*, AMQA, Dehumanizers, Corrosion of Conformity - *Eye for an Eye* and *Technocracy*, D.R.I. - *Dealing With It* and *4 Of A Kind*, Sudden Impact - *Split Personality.* There's SO MANY! I can't even list them all hahaha! I also love old school death metal (Death-*Scream Bloody Gore*, Entombed) and Napalm Death. KISS, Black Sabbath, Van Halen, the list goes on and on".

"The Pacific Northwest punk and metal scene was very special to me as a kid in the late 80s" Andy admits. "In Victoria and Vancouver, we seemed to be very symbiotic with the Seattle scene. I grew up listening to Accused and Dehumanizers long before I was ever introduced to the 'larger bands'. But the house parties and basement gigs were crazy and very cool to be a part of - even when the doors would get kicked down by the police and we'd have to run for it. And I don't really remember a specific reaction towards crossover other than kids were just listening to what they liked. There was animosity (see what I did there?), between the scenes for sure earlier on, but places like the Rat's Nest (basement gigs), had punk and metal shows back in '85ish. I always grew up liking what I liked. Whether that was COC or Death, or MOC, or Accused or the Dayglos. If it was interesting and heavy, I dug it. I didn't care if it was punk or metal. Mission of Christ certainly attracted hardcore kids and metalheads alike. C.O.C, I mean everyone loved *Animosity* - punks, metal heads, hardcore kids, whatever".

In 1992, Distorted Influence recorded their *Cold* LP, that sadly remained unreleased for years to come until recently. Supreme Echo Records and Jason Flower released it in 2023 direct from the original tapes, and remastered by Brad Boatright. What a pity that *Cold* remained unavailable all those years…now we're talking about top-class crossover thrash, that take its cues from The Accüsed, with a slight Poison Idea influence, and totally raging songs like 'Old Bros In The Hood', 'Rituals Of Abuse' and 'Life Of A Misfit'. Ace, raw and wild stuff!

Through their first period Distorted Influence appeared in many local billings, and Andy recalls some of his favourite: "I loved playing at the Fernwood Community Hall, the Rat's Nest, and we did that amazing show with Accused, Forced Entry and Malevolence at Sancha Hall in Sidney British Columbia. Most recently we got to play at Centennial Square right in Downtown Victoria. That may be my favourite gig of all time. But I do miss the shows at the old Union Hall, and Fernwood. I really miss the old Starfish Room in Vancouver too. Also, The Cobalt when W13 was running it. Plus, we never experienced and violence at our shows; we opened for Accused in 1991 at an all-ages gig and the pit was absolutely nuts - one of the most insane I had seen, but it wasn't violent per se. Other gigs in previous years had more violence between the punk and metal crowds, but those gigs were earlier on (1986-87)".

(Distorted Influence band logo)

Sadly, Distorted Influence disbanded in 1993, before even releasing *Cold*. They are back though since 2023, playing in Victoria area, as well as writing new songs.

"Absolutely I do believe that crossover is relevant today- but not specifically because it's what we now call 'crossover'. To me, it's bands that are just pushing it, going faster, being interesting, not holding back. Getting a little unhinged. I love that stuff. I think that the best, most interesting metal bands are those with punk in their DNA and vice versa. There's some cool crossover now still! Listen to the latest Fully Crazed album. It's great. It's punk at heart but it's got some metal in it veins for sure. I find standard, run of the mill metal a bit boring to be honest. I need that edge - that's what crossover brings. It's not about technical prowess for me. It's about bringing a punk edge to de-sanitize metal".

At a glance: Distorted Influence and their metal hardcore-thrash will please everybody into The Accüsed, as well as those ones into the more metal phase such as *War All The Time* from Poison Idea; *Cold* is a great LP, and you should get it by Supreme Echo Records!

SCHIZOID

(Schizoid band picture. Courtesy unknown)

I'm pretty sure that you haven't heard of many 1980s hardcore, crossover and metal bands originating from Newfoundland, other than maybe Kaos or Festered Corpse. Well, Schizoid were the first crossover band to ever come from St. John's, Newfoundland. Bob 'Average' Armstrong narrates their story: "I was in a band called Public. We only did one demo but never circulated it much. Everyone moved to Toronto, so we broke up. I was left behind. I wanted to play again as I was really excited by COC and… well mostly COC. One day I was leaving my parents' place, and I ran into an old friend from junior high. I had the *Animosity* with me and my friend Rod had an Onslaught record…we started talking and found out we could kind of lent each other records and stuff; him Slayer, me D.R.I, that kind of thing. We decided we need a band. We recruited some friends, I wrote 'Purpotrator' and we jammed! First jam was with John (Pastore) from Rise's mom's place, John on bass, me on guitar, Rod Wills on drums and Chris Jerrett on vocals. Also, Ken from the Watchman was there too, he played in a band called WAFUT, aka What a Fuckin Ugly Truck".

"I think it was the aggression of the music that led to crossover. Metalheads and punks were still way different. I believe we taught the metalheads emotion and politics… the metalheads got us heavier. Me and Rod used to make jokes about the dipshit metalheads way to the mall and the way the punk would go. It was funny-I think we used Tesco Vee and Slayer as examples…it was in fun. However, once crossover exploded, metalheads, were all for it. I think they finally realized that there was too much cock in their rock!".

Changes in lineup, and in March 1986 Phil Winters went on guitar duties and Danny Thomas on bass joined the band. Danny was from another band in town called Tough Justice and Phil was just a friend who hung around. This lineup stayed together until August 1986. From the very first day Schizoid had a fair share metal approach into their crossover sound, like a blend of COC's *Animosity* with Slayer and Possessed. And as you can imagine they were very brutal on their 1986 *Total Fuckin' Mayhem* demo; now with Don Ellis on bass, Schizoid sounded like a menacing, out of control crossover combo. With tracks as raging as 'Possessed', 'Death Deliverer' or 'Haunted House' they even remind me of Repulsion is some cases! Absolute bangers!

"KISS got me into music" Bob adds. "Cheap Trick got me into melody, Sex Pistols opened my eyes, D.O.A. made everything possible and COC made me form my band that I lived the most and pushed me into getting the St. John's scene rolling. But regarding crossover? Let me think…it was a punk band that started it. COC or D.R.I. come to mind but Beyond Possession and Personality Crisis were doing it. Genetic Control were too! Not sure though, this is a tough one! Maybe Rattus too or even Raw Power!".

St. John's had a vibrant punk and hardcore scene, with bands like WAFUT, The Asmathix, Malpratice, Bottom Dogs, Red Scare, The Crypt, Inferno, NRK and The Riot, of whom the common point was Dead Upturned Puppy Productions, the promoter that used to book their shows, as well as Schizoid's of course. Time has come for their second release though, the 1987 *Datin' Satan* cassette demo; still mental as anything, still catchy. Schizoid offered another piece of metal crossover, with songs like 'Grief' or 'Death Deliverer' will make you bounce on the wall! 'Gun in Hand' though is maybe one of their best songs ever, brutal and chaotic!

(Schizoid with Tough Justice at the Retired Citizens Club. 11/05/1987)

In mid-1987 Schizoid all moved to Toronto to make a go of the band. They decided that they should take some tracks from *Datin' Satan* and release them as a 7-inch. So, they took off to Toronto to record with Brian Taylor for the Diabolic Force label (home of Slaughter, Razor, Sacrifice, Sudden Impact and Lethal Presence). To their surprise, Diabolic Force wanted a certain amount of money upfront to cover recording cost and in return they would handle printing the album cover, marketing and distribution. Schizoid went on to re-record four songs, and this resulted in the now classic *Beer Thief* 7-inch. Schizoid sound crazier than ever on these recordings, with a sound akin to early Slaughter due to Diabolic Force studio treatment, but with a massive hardcore influence, reminiscent of early The Accüsed and their utter chaos. *Beer Thief* is their best release, and all four songs sound now massively brutal and venomous, top-notch crossover. I'd like though to pick 'Possessed to Golf', this is just out of control! *Beer Thief* is a classic, full stop.

"When we moved to Toronto, we got to see COC, D.R.I., Beyond Possession with their 15-year-old bass player, and also Sacrifice. These were all separate shows…living in Toronto and Montreal in those times was a smart move. We saw everyone! Government Issue, D.O.A., GG Allin, Verbal Assault, The Accüsed, Voivod, Cro-Mags, Big Drill Car, All, Doughboys (who are one of my all-time favourites). The list goes on and on … 7 Seconds…I'm sorry most of this isn't crossover. I forgot about The Accüsed! They were equally as influential as COC We were supposed to play with them but of course we were a bunch of pussyfooters and broke up!"

(Schizoid with Tough Justice and WAFUT at the Maxines. 15/03/1987)

"I will always love The 301 Club, Maxine's" Bob admits. "This was the first place Schizoid played; I did all the shows there. It was one of those bars that was insanely huge and had so much potential, but there were four regulars everyday... that's it. How did they survive? She let us use the area downstairs as all ages. Upstairs you could drink with the regulars. She was so nice and understanding...until some asshat mother ratted us out on the afternoon before SNFU were to play. So fucked! Alongside, there was another bar called Bounders. All booze shows but the owner was an absolute sweetheart! Jack did soooooo much for the local bands!"

Schizoid called it quits later in 1989, and Bob moved away and joined Rise, a great band that you could read about them on *We Can Be The New Wind,* from Montreal for a while. Chris took over the pipes for Sudden Impact for a tour. Rob ended up joining other bands, one with Johnny and Rod from Tough Justice and with Don from Schizoid, as well as Privateers. Rob also got involved in a thrash metal band called Sacrament and Danny from that band formed Sheavy. Don Ellis played with Tough Justice, Rise, Hardship Post and Potatobug. And last but not least Phil started a very well-known band in St John's called Bung, also played in Astroglossa, Sea Dogs and Jigger.

"Crossover is more relevant than ever!" Bob adds with enthusiasm "Municipal Waste and Power Trip have the sounds we were trying to get. Out of Boss distortion pedals and Traynor amps... we never had any money in Newfoundland... but these bands are flying the flag. So heavy so tight! I'm pretty sure they listen to punk. When we started that metal kids came straight out of Rock 'n' roll Heaven listening to Skid Row cover bands, then we played them Black Flag, D.R.I., COC and The Accüsed and that was it!".

At a glance: I just wish a label would re-release everything that Schizoid ever recorded! Brutal crossover for fans of The Accüsed, COC, but I would also add Slaughter (Can) to the mix. Be sure to listen to everything they released and then pick up *Beer Thief* 7-inch-it's pricy but it's awesome!

B.A.R.F.

(B.A.R.F. band picture, courtesy unknown)

Definitely a historic band, B.A.R.F. are one the longest running Canadian bands since their formation in 1986. Guitarist Denis LePage (formerly of Groovy Aardvark) narrates their story: "B.A.R.F. came together really during a Halloween party in 1986 when a mutual friend brought Marc Vaillancourt, our singer, to try out with us. The rest of the band had been together for about a year before that under the name Cataclysm during which time I was attempting to sing and play guitar; the other guys thought my voice was too low at the time (which is also very funny seeing as a few years later the growler style just exploded) After a few unimpressive trials, Marc just blew us away and after jamming 'Milk' from S.O.D. with us, he was in! It only took one song to convince us. In those days, we mostly played Slayer, S.O.D. and D.R.I. covers and Marc suggested to change the name to B.A.R.F. (Blasting All Rotten Fuckers) which seemed more fitting for the type of crossover we wanted to do. And so B.A.R.F. was born. We started writing our own stuff, recorded a first demo and started playing small shows around Montreal. After quite a few changes in the rhythm section throughout the years (four different bass players and drummers) we have managed to keep the same (also the best) lineup since 2004 with Carlos Araya on drums, Dominic "Forest" Lapointe on bass, Marc and myself. Sort of B.A.R.F. 2.0!".

(B.A.R.F with Massive Confusion and Revelation Zero at Bar La Terrase, 24/03/1988)

The initial lineup of B.A.R.F. included alongside Denis and Marc, Stéphane Arsenault on bass and Martin Séguin on drums. Their first release was the 1988 *Social Disorder* demo cassette; fast, wild, underproduced and crude. *Social Disorder* included ten short hardcore blasts that have a definite early D.R.I. influence and obviously I love this kind of stuff, even though B.A.R.F. are not as revolutionary as their influences! "I personally discovered crossover with S.O.D." Denis admits, "although I don't think they were the first. D.R.I. and Suicidal Tendencies where there before...I think a lot of kids where into both metal and punk at that time and just started to mix both together to create a fusion style that was fresh and took a life of its own. I think a lot of bands preferred addressing social issues than Satanism in their lyrics while keeping a rather metal approach musically. That was certainly the case for myself and still is".

"We tried a bunch of different things in the 1980s in stylistic terms" Denis adds. "Marc had spikes, I shaved half my head, we wore ripped jeans, patches, sleeveless jeans, vests and leather coats and the occasional bullet belt, but in the end, I think we always looked more like metal heads than anything else".

The second release by B.A.R.F., the 1990 *Blasting All Rotten Fuckers* demo, was a move towards a more crossover sound; it's still hardcore, albeit with many Slayer influences. Again, this is a vicious and harsh recording, and I find myself enjoying the more hardcore songs like 'Wo Wo Tabarnak' or 'Artificial Peace' that has a definite Cryptic Slaughter-meets-Extreme Noise Terror edge. "You are right" Denis agrees. "Musically I think Slayer and D.R.I. are probably our strongest root influences but bands like Cryptic Slaughter, Septic Death and Extreme Noise Terror certainly helped shape our crossover style. With a pinch of American hardcore like M.D.C., Minor Threat and Circle Jerks".

"What I mostly remember from that time is the reaction of the skinheads in the shows While they did not get along with punks, they loathed metalheads. Apart from that, I feel that crossover rather happened naturally. I never really considered myself a punk but I certainly do have a lot of friends that consider themselves punks. But yes, most of the time the serious violence came from the skinheads. Of course, at the beginning punks felt that bangers knew nothing about slamming or trashing but that quickly changed!".

Another release by B.A.R.F. on 1992, the *Tumulte* CD, and this time there's a change of style; even though the production now is crystal clear, the band abandoned the frantic hardcore thrash of their earlier years, and headed for a punk metal approach, with twenty-nine songs (!), that had a definite fun element (crossover pathetique maybe?) and a very weird edge. Songs like 'Intoxicated' or 'Anytime, Anywhere' are just hilarious, and *Tumulte* reminds me of a crazier Mucky Pup with a semi-Extreme Noise Terror style of vocals.

(B.A.R.F. with Les Bons A Rien at Au Bar Le Jet, 15/11/1994)

"My all-time favourite show was D.R.I. at the Montreal Spectrum during the *Dealing With It* years. By far, the most intense mosh pit I had ever seen. Like going to war!" Denis smiles, adding that "I also remember a specific show back in the late 1980s called Week-end Trash that took place in Quebec City in some weird underground local space. Two busloads of crazy freaks came down from Montreal. They were coming off the bus already stumbling on PCP. With the old Quebec guard Yog-Sototh, Soothsayer, and Damnation among other ones. A crazy weekend. Little red fishes got splattered!"

B.A.R.F.'s next record, the 1993 *Ignorance Chaos Suicide* qualifies as my favourite one off their first period; written in French language almost exclusively, *Ignorance Chaos Suicide* blends their crossover hardcore with some grindcore, and songs like 'Ma Corde' or 'Empty' are definite winners, plus the bands sounds more technical than before.

When asked about his favourite place to play or see bands, Denis mentions that "as far as Montreal goes, I think the Rising Sun was probably the one bar that would bill crazy American crossover bands. It closed before we had a chance to play there. Also, the Montreal Spectrum which is now a condo tower! The Palladium, an old roller-skating rink on Berri where shows like the Banzai Festival and World War 3 took place. Of course, Foufounes Electriques on Ste-Catherine remains an all-time favourite even after forty years!".

B.A.R.F. keep it up until today, releasing loads of records since the mid-1990s that I won't review here due to lack of space. However, things went through a mix of grindcore, hardcore punk and crossover thrash metal, but with crazy technical abilities, and I must admit that their *Brûle Consume Torture* CD is maybe their best. B.A.R.F. remain active, playing shows in 2025.

Denis concludes our interview mentioning that "while many people might think crossover is old and irrelevant given all the different sub-genres that are now out there, I would argue that most modern alternative rock bands integrate punk and metal elements without even realizing it. While the crossover genre may have been transcended, it remains a major influence in the stuff coming out today!"

At a glance: B.A.R.F. are another band from Canada that owns its own style and it's a pretty weird and unique one! While their sonic approach isn't my cup of tea, I still like their early demos, and some songs off *Ignorance Chaos Suicide*.

CAPITALIST ALIENATION

(Capitalist Alienation band picture. Courtesy unknown)

Regarded as Montreal's response to D.R.I., Capitalist Alienation were much more than that! Capitalist Alienation were metalheads that went on to a full hardcore attack. Capitalist Alienation formed in 1985 with the lineup being Eric Bourque (drums), Joel Tremblay (bass), Tamiko Watanabe (vocals) and Carl

Bouchard (guitar). "At the beginning, I listened to metal then I started to listen to more underground metal" Joel confesses. "One day I don't remember when, a guy arrived with a tape with two groups: The Exploited and GBH. And from that moment, I really felt challenged by this kind of music, I cut my long hair and sported a mohawk! When we, Carl the guitarist and I arrived in Montreal was new for us to see the hardcore punk scene. We came from the metal world, our friends were in Voivod, and the musicians were very efficient. But watching punk shows we thought we could play that; I bought a bass, and we started playing and composing".

"Quite possibly D.R.I. were the first ones to pursue the crossover" Joel admits. "It was both a musical and cultural crossover, many people like me, were metal before they became punk (and vice versa) and listened to both styles. However, the metalheads didn't really understand the punk scene and the mix was not that easy; punks were jumping everywhere and the metalheads looked surprised and thought it was violent! Even though there was a little violence, but it wasn't the rule. The people in the shows were open minded".

Capitalist Alienation hit the studio in early (February) 1986 and recorded/released one of the craziest speedcore demos ever, the *Makes Me Shit !!...* cassette, that included ten short blasts of early D.R.I.-inspired ferocity, blended with that early chaotic Voivod style. Ridiculously fast, relentlessly powerful but most of all, so inspired, this is one of speedcore's highlights. This is no 'normal' crossover by any kind of means. It's mostly hardcore with a metal edge that sounds totally out of control!

(Capitalist Alienation with Ludichrist and Cancerous Growth at the Spectrum, 12/04/1987)

"Believe it or not" Joel adds, "we were mostly influenced by Venom, D.R.I., Discharge, and The Exploited, even though we didn't sound like them! And in visual terms, we kind of blended metal with hardcore too".

As written in *Crossover The Edge*, the band were friends of Michel Langevin, aka 'Away' from Voivod. This led to his design of the sleeve art for both their releases too, the demo and the LP. But the craziest story here is that during Voivod's 1987 European tour with Kreator, Away brought copies of Capitalist

Alienation's album with him and handed them out for free to anyone who was interested! A limited to one thousand copies when released, now it's a huge collector's item, fetching big bucks!

And regarding their first LP, the 1987 *Capitalist Alienation*? Now better recorded, but still wild and raw, one could also hear echoes of Beyond Possession and Cryptic Slaughter into their sound, alongside D.R.I. of course. Songs like 'Braindead' and 'Drugs Saved My Life' are just mental, while short blasts like 'Make me Shit' or 'Nuclear Trash' carry a slight early Voivod influence, mostly in terms of chaotic raw sound. *Capitalist Alienation* LP isn't for the faint hearted, but those daring for wilder stuff, they will love it.

(Capitalist Alienation with Beefeater and Alternative Insults at the Rising Sun, 02/07/1986)

Capitalist Alienation through their short-lived existence played alongside touring bands like Beefeater or in festivals alongside Ludichrist. "At the beginning, in our first show the audience was frozen, but then a lot of people came in our shows even though our co-existence with other groups was difficult (in music terms) but all went well. From what I remember, there was a lot of drugs and a lot of alcohol. Then it seems to me that metalheads and punks weren't so bad together. On the other hand, there were skinheads in our shows, and they provoked a lot of violence, and we didn't like it at all. Anyway, skinheads were causing problems for everyone. We tried to play as much as possible, but it was difficult to rent rooms for punk shows".

Capitalist Alienation faded by the late 1980s, and Carl Bouchard played afterwards with A Perfect Murder (metalcore), Damaged (crossover thrash), Final Word (hardcore). Carl Bouchard, Eric Bourque and Joel Tremblay formed Overbass, with a good local following, and released four records of metal-punk-hard rock through the 1990s.

"My favourite club was the Rising Sun in Montreal, because I saw a lot of bands there and I was always dreaming to play to on this stage…" Joel smiles. "And yes, all the mixes of styles are interesting, I mixed a lot of styles with my other bands too (Overbass, Colectivo). I always listen to bands that mix punk with hardcore, with metal, with reggae or whatever!".

At a glance: Capitalist Alienation's self-titled LP will please the souls of everybody into early D.R.I., Neos, Beyond Possession, Cryptic Slaughter, with a little chaotic early Voivod touch. This is totally recommended for people that love their speedcore as wild as it gets! Be sure to get the 2021 *Discography* LP on Fox Records and I Owe You Nothing Records, because they carry all their mayhemic releases!

CORRUPTED REPUTATION

(Corrupted Reputation band picture 1988. Courtesy unknown)

Corrupted Reputation was founded in spring 1988 in Repentigny on Montreal's North Shore. The formation was composed of Karol Lafond on guitar, Ghislain Fleury on drums, and two other members on vocals and bass. The real version of Corrupted Reputation was composed then by Karol and Ghislain, and the addition of Guylain Meilleur on vocals/guitar and Pierre "Piggy" Martin on bass. With this formation, Corrupted Reputation recorded their demo *E.T. Is Back*! in the fall of 1988.

Corrupted Reputation started off as a pure hardcore act, later heading for a more crossover approach; "I would say that D.R.I., S.O.D, Agnostic Front and many others were the game-changers for our sound" Karol Lafond offers. "I think it was inevitable that the two genres would meet and end up merging together. There are always metalheads who liked the aggressiveness of punk and punks who liked the speed of metal".

Corrupted Reputation's first demo, the 1988 *E.T. is Back!* Reminded more of a crude attempt towards the early Negative Approach and Agnostic Front sound, that is primal, basic, fast and brutal East Coast hardcore (of course Corrupted Reputation weren't as crucial though…). The lyrics were mostly socio-political (with the sad exemptions of 'Fucking Whore' and 'Sally Fool', come on guys now…), and I really liked songs like 'Acid Rain' or 'New Generation'. "When crossover came in" Karol adds "it was like a punch in the face haha! When I arrived on the scene with Corrupted Reputation in 1988, the coexistence was already established between metalheads and punk, so for violence it almost didn't exist anymore. This was not the case two or three years ago. 1985 or 1986".

(Corrupted Reputation's first show. With B.A.R.F. at Le Grand Café. 25/11/1988)

Corrupted Reputation went on to change their sound in the 1992 *Demo 2* release, now heading for a heavier, meatier crossover sound. It was an excellent release, heavy and fast and brutal, still more into hardcore, but with some metal influences creeping in, plus some crazy changes in pace like in 'La Marche des gros Baveux'. Funny as it might sound, their approach reminds me more of Brazilian bands like Lobotomia or Ratos De Porao, rather than the US style of crossover, so it was a pleasant surprise! "C.R. has always influenced by both styles" Karol admits. "Ghis and I being more punk and hardcore and Guylain and Pierre were more metal. We have always been open to a mix of the two".

"I was a metalhead from the age of twelve to sixteen with bands like Venom, Voivod, Slayer, Celtic Frost, Metallica, Possessed, etc… but when I discovered hardcore punk, the bands I listened to (and still listen to) were Agnostic Front, D.R.I. Suicidal Tendencies, Attitude Adjustment, Septic Death, Death Sentence,

Dayglo Abortions and also Montreal hardcore bands like Fair Warning, S.C.U.M. and Genetic Control", Karol offers.

(Corrupted Reputation with Obvious Problems and Genetic Error at the Jailhouse Café. 27/03/1989)

The 1994 *Corrupted Reputation* demo was in accordance with their previous sound, albeit slightly more hardcore-and reminiscent of the Brazil rough hardcore acts such as Ratos De Porao, that is primal, raw, but very catchy crossover hardcore. 'No War, No Peace' and 'Mickey Mouse for President' are among the highlights. While I'm very fond of their sonic approach; only a handful of bands outside of Brazil played this kind of stuff. "There have been several, but the most striking without a doubt was the No Speed Limit Weekend" Karol recalls with nostalgia, regarding his favourite crossover shows. "Two nights with Voivod and their guests for the two nights were Agnostic Front, Aggression, Nuclear Assault, Possessed, D.R.I. Sacrifice and Countdown Zero".

After folding in 1994, Corrupted Reputation released their final demo, the 1995 *Qui sème la stupidité...Récolte le chaos!* cassette that Karol so generously sent me; and I was so happy, because this is their brightest moment. This final demo holds the best production they ever had, and the band sounds just brutal total crossover craziness. Only this time their sound has progressed with some weird melodic parts added here in there (like in 'Halloween'), but you also get the straightforward, beefed-up punk of UK82 mixed with the Latin American sounds, a US-crossover flavour as apparent in blast beats and gang vocals, this is just an excellent release. "My memory play so many tricks on me right now" Karol laughs. "But surely, there was a great number of hysterical moments!".

(Corrupted Reputation 1993 live picture. Courtesy unknown)

Post-Corrupted Reputation Guylain Meilleur (who sadly passed away in 2024) played in Wasted Souls (heavy metal), Skullmace (death metal) and Voor (thrash-death metal). Vincent Laplaca (RIP 2016) played in B.A.R.F. (it was like a brother band, with the same crossover sonic approach) and Moral Minority (crossover, and another good one) alongside drummer Peter Jackson. Finally, band's last drummer, Stéphane Corbin played also with the thrashers Majester.

"I would have liked to know the Montreal scene from 1982 to 1986 with the Rising Sun, the Cargo" Karol sighs. "They were mythical places with all the shows produced with bands such as DK, Corrosion of Conformity, Suicidal Tendencies, D.R.I., GBH, Cro-Mags, Agnostic Front, etc…today, there is still the Foufounes Electriques which is the Mecca of the Underground scene. Otherwise, the places that I liked to play apart from the Foufounes Electriques, there are the Katacombes, Jailhouse Rock Café, Café Chaos all these places no longer exist today, too bad".

Corrupted Reputation never reformed, and it's always a product of the crazy youth of some Montreal kids that were into the great hardcore and crossover scene of their days!

At a glance: Fans of Canadian bands like B.A.R.F. as well as Brazilian ultras of Lobotomia and Ratos De Porao take notice, because you're going to love the pissed off, brutal sound of Corrupted Reputation. I enjoyed all their demos and releases. However I think that their best moment is the 1995 *Qui Sème La Stupidité... Récolte Le Chaos*! On a final word, check also Union Made, which was a short-lived band that Denis Bélanger formed alongside Peter Jackson when he left Voivod in 1994 and recorded a full-length CD in 1999 and a 7-inch single; total alternative punk metal, like 1990s Voivod to their punkiest possible!

BRAZIL

"Back to those years in the beginning of 1980s, I was very into bands like Discharge, Disorder, GBH and so. But suddenly Discharge released the Warning 12", in the same period I was also attacked by Onslaught's Power from Hell LP and the amazing To The End of Earth 12" EP from English Dogs. I knew that at the same time, Slayer and Metallica were releasing their first albums. But sincerely, at least for me, these albums from Discharge, Onslaught and English Dogs started this transformation into the crossover definition!

In Brasil, some bands decided in a way or another to follow this path around 1985. Ruídos Absurdos (during the period that João Gordo joined them), Ratos de Porão (Descanse em Paz LP), Armagedom and Lobotomia kind of decided to add some metal into their hardcore punk music. We all had similar influences at the same time. It was a period that these Brazilian bands had such influence from UK crossover, of course something also from US. But for me, UK influence was much stronger!" (Javier Montecinos, Armagedom)

EXTREME VIOLENCE

(Extreme Violence band picture, 1988. Courtesy unknown)

From the ashes of the proto-death metal band Skullfucker that lasted from 1986 to 1988, Extreme Violence formed in Macaé, Rio de Janeiro. Their crossover approach was as raw and primitive as you can imagine. "Initially Extreme Violence was a trio playing an uninspired death metal with some influences of European hardcore" vocalist Carlos Fred Bastos who was also a member of one of the earliest thrash bands, Agressor, narrates. "After our first gig in 1989, the lineup was reformulated and our music changed to the style of bands we've heard the most since then, such as Cryptic Slaughter, Heresy, GBH, Concrete Sox and others. And this was the style we played until the end of the activities in 1992".

The initial lineup of Extreme Violence included Carlos Fred Bastos (vocals, drums), Alex (guitar, vocals) and Irland (bass). Their first release was the 1988 *Endless Psychosis* demo. I tend to disagree with Carlos, since I don't hear any death metal influences here, however this is one of the most brutal-sounding, venomous and nasty crossover hardcore-thrash ever recorded. Guttural and crazy, *Endless Psychosis* sounds like an exercise to extremity. While songs like 'Antidrugs' and 'Marching To War' sound like a mix between the frenzied sounds of Ataque Frontal, Olho Seco, and even Brigada Do Ódio, with some metal influence in, and as you can imagine, this is as harsh sounding as possible.

"I believe that in the USA and UK the things were happening in a very natural way and for me it was something beyond just a musical crossover, there was rather a crossover between both cultures and their ideologies" Fred believes. "In my opinion bands like Corrosion of Conformity, Septic Death, Cryptic Slaughter, Sacrilege (UK), Agnostic Front, Onslaught, Attitude Adjustment and certainly D.R.I., with their classic album *Crossover*, were fundamental to the definition of the musical style…however, in musical terms, I really think that Motörhead was the first one to crossover. But the first stuff I heard from a genuinely punk band playing a music strongly combining both styles I believe was the EP *To The Ends Of The Earth* by English Dogs".

(Extreme Violence live picture, 1989. Courtesy unknown)

Their second release included Jair (ex-Skullfucker) on drums, so now Fred would be only the vocalist of the band, and this resulted in a live split cassette alongside D.O.H. Now the crossover tendencies of Extreme Violence were more evident than before. The cassette includes one cover each from Nuclear Assault ('My America') and Attitude Adjustment ('Fuck Chuck'). Fred when asked about the initial reactions of the Brazilian metal and punk scenes in this crossover he mentions that "here in Brazil it was not an easy thing to be assimilated by most punks and metalheads in those times because there was a very strong musical and ideological barrier between both, as well as problems with gangs. We grew up in a small town on the coast of the state of Rio de Janeiro and for us there was no problem in that sense, because we were kids interested only in music, skateboarding and surfing. But in big cities, like São Paulo and Rio, things were not at all quiet and we always heard stories about fights in gigs. In 1986 we already had Brazilian bands mixing both styles, such as Armagedom and Lobotomia. In my opinion the first Brazilian album to explicitly assume the union between styles was *Descanse em Paz* by Ratos de Porão".

(Extreme Violence with D.O.H. at Colegio Luiz Reid, 28/01/1989)

Americo (ex-Skullfucker) took over the bass duties. Their next release, the 1989 *Living a Neurotic Life* demo is maybe my favourite off them. Buzzsaw crossover, like a cross between early Ratos De Porao with Cryptic Slaughter and Attitude Adjustment, *Living a Neurotic Life* rips. Songs like 'High Society', 'Dead' and 'Last Visions' are just ace, but my favourite is 'Bugbear', wild punk metal! Did I mention that there's also a Ramones cover of 'She's the One'?

"When I was a kid (1982-1983) I started to listen to KISS, Black Sabbath, Motörhead, Venom, Slayer, Metallica, Devo, New Model Army and soon after, bands like Corrosion of Conformity, Dorsal Atlântica, Grinders, Cryptic Slaughter, Rattus, Ratos de Porão, Sacrilege (UK)" Fred admits. "These were some of the many bands that became my favourites and exerted direct influence on everything I did in musical terms from that point on… Initially we were all metalhead kids in our area, because punk and hardcore only arrived here when we got the punk compilations *Grito Suburbano* and *SUB*. From then on it was normal to see I and my longhair friends wearing shirts of hardcore bands like D.R.I., RDP, Olho Seco,

Heresy etc. Then, I have to say that Brazilian labels Punk Rock Discos and New Face Records were very important for us in the beginning of the crossover era".

Back in the frenzied, guttural style, Extreme Violence on their 1990 *Break Your Neck* cassette demo went on to sound like a cross between Celtic Frost, Electro Hippies and Extreme Noise Terror; I think that's too extreme for my taste, but still, this is just primal and unbelievably menacing. Songs like 'No Way Back' and 'I Won't Breathe' are sheer craziness!

"In our area everything was fun and the gigs were in peace and with lots of fun" Fred smiles. "But in big cities, violence was usual. So today I see that we were lucky to grow away from the big centres... I really don't remember what my first crossover show was, but I saw very good shows of Dorsal Atlântica and Phuneral playing a strong mix of metal and hardcore, but they were not classified as crossover bands".

The final offering of Extreme Violence was in-line with *Break Your Neck*. The 1991 *Primitive Society* demo kept the route of 1000 mph hardcore blended with crunchy metal parts, leading to a sound bordering on the logical extreme of crossover. 'Ciclo Da Vida' and 'Strike Breaker' are my favourites off this release.

(Extreme Violence with Gasoza, Gangrena and others at Agio Silk, 22/06/1991)

Extreme Violence called it quits later in 1992. Fred played with the hardcore Nao Conformismo, while Alex played with the hardcore punk Protesto Suburbano. Fred remains in 2025 a great fan of hardcore, punk and crossover. I was unbelievably happy when he sent me a message via social media, just a few weeks after the release of *Crossover The Edge*. And he was unbelievably kind enough to send me the 2021 3 x box set compilation of Extreme Violence named as *Another Day To Go Nowhere*!

Speaking of *Another Day To Go Nowhere*, as you can imagine is a collection of everything Extreme Violence ever recorded or released, plus a DVD that includes a live appearance, a studio rehearsal and an interview of the band. Totally recommended if you ask me!

"I have some good stories from those times, but I have to share one that occurred in 1990 when Extreme Violence played for the first time away from our area in a festival in the metropolitan area of Rio" Fred recollects. "The place of the gig was a club normally used for Brazilian funk fans and their parties were famous mainly for gang violence. They were upset when 'their' club was leased to make a metal-punk festival. Extreme Violence was the last band to play on that night and soon after we finished our set, they invaded the club starting a real battle where punks and metalheads united against the 'funkeiros'. I remember the police arrived a little later.... In the end, everyone came out alive and with an unforgettable story to tell! Other than that, I have to admit that I miss Garage Art Cult in Rio. Great place and great gigs".

On a final note, Fred adds that "for me, crossover is still relevant, because what has been done in the past will forever be marked in history. But I miss the old energy, today I see many bands very concerned with technical issues leaving the passion and feeling in the background".

At a glance: If you are into Extreme Noise Terror (1980s), Electro Hippies, first two Concrete Sox LPs mixed with Olho Seco, Ratos De Porao and some US crossover like Cryptic Slaughter, look no further. Because you're going to love the raw, unpolished sound of Extreme Violence. My favourite release off them is *Living A Neurotic Life* demo, but you should get the triple-CD *Another Day To Go Nowhere* collection, because it rules!

EUROPE

EXTREMITY

(Extremity onstage, 1987. Courtesy unknown)

I must admit that on *Crossover The Edge* I was a bit rough, regarding my review (that you can read it in the Belgium section in the end of the book). I spoke with vocalist Enzo Izzi, and decided to pull out a piece on Extremity, for various reasons, historical, and musical of course.

Extremity were from Seraing, Liège in south of Belgium, a place that literally had no hardcore or crossover scene whatsoever. Extremity was formed at the very beginning of 1986 and lasted a little bit more than three years. The band began to rehearse very quickly by covering their favourites like Slaughter (Canada) and Messiah (Switzerland) and then began to write their own songs and gig everywhere they can with local bands and confirmed ones like Tankard or The Accüsed and toured the Benelux. Vocalist Enzo Izzi narrated that "at the very beginning the band was strictly a metal band attracted by thrash metal, especially bands like Slayer, Metallica, Megadeth or avant-garde thrash bands like Voivod, until a friend of ours came to us with several records to listen like D.R.I.'s *Dealing with it*, (*Crossover* was not released yet), the Bad Brains, S.N.F.U etc…and was blown away so the decision was made to do shorter songs, faster tempos and mix both styles which is crazy because we didn't took notice that other bands in the US or so were doing the same, at the same time!".

Extremity included through their existence many members: Sandro (guitars), Marc (guitars), Rikou (drums), Jack (bass), Plouck (drums), Lol (guitars) with the late Willy Nollomont (bass) (RIP). Willy Nollomont was later with Hiatus as a vocalist. "Like I said before" Enzo adds "everything changed when we discovered hardcore it pushed the boundaries a little bit further for a new genre". This resulted in the first demo of Extremity, the 1987 *Thrashin' Unity* cassette, a collection of rehearsal and live recordings.

Extremity were a vicious and venomous act, with a rough, guttural sound that reminded me of G.I.S.M., albeit with a thrashier approach.

Regarding the Belgian scene of the time, Enzo adds that "the crazy thing about Belgium is that we always had great bands and great labels even at the very beginning of the eighties like Killer, Ostrogoth or Acid who still nowadays have an impact on the music scene, we had Cyclone a pure thrash-metal band who was the first to play with hardcore bands here in Belgium. And as concerning the crossover movement we had the chance to have great promoters like Metallisee or Hageland hardcore which gave us the chance to see bands like Suicidal Tendencies, Nuclear Assault and D.R.I. (which was the one that had both equal metalheads and hardcore kids and the craziest gig I saw on their first European tour). Tons of great bands emerged too; like Sixty-Nine who did a great record *Just For The Fun* and then became Channel Zero and Deviate, Damaged Corpse, etc…tons of zines too. To put it simply even people from France came to Belgium to see those gigs (you have to remember than none other than Slayer chose a picture done at the Heavy Sound Festival here in Belgium on the back of *Reign In Blood* because it was their first European date ever)".

Another one cassette release by Extremity, this time a live recording from 1988 titled *Live in Verviers* demo (1988). Enzo recalls of the final days of Extremity: "around 1989 the band decided to enter a studio to record a demo which was released and sold well for a demo and was called *Blind by…?* but was not happy with the result as it was not as much as aggressive compared to our live shows. We then split up after a little tour in France and one last gig with Excel and became cult in Belgium. Some members went on to form Hiatus, a crust band who did several releases and tour and became cult too even if they still doing some gigs occasionally".

Blind by…? was Extremity's swansong, and included six songs of their own brand of rough thrash-hardcore. Again, I still believe that Extremity had many musical similarities with G.I.S.M., and I think that fans of this dark and moody metal-punk stuff will definitely enjoy tracks such as 'Computers Control' that oddly enough starts with a solo bass, just like BGK's 'Computer Control'! or 'Living 'till the end', that definitely has a Celtic Frost influence too.

Enzo concludes adding that "the biggest memories I have is all the great times we had and the friends we made along the way from all over the country and still friends to this day, the sing-along to our song 'Extremity', the first time we played with a bigger band like Tankard in front of 300 maniacs and the fact that thirty five years later still people are talking about Extremity when they see me!".

At a glance: Fan of rougher, darker and moodier metal-punk like G.I.S.M., with a dose of Celtic Frost/Venom-or even some Brazilian hardcore influences like early Ratos De Porao added in? I think that you will enjoy Extremity's final demo, *Blind by…?*

NEUROOT

(Neuroot band picture, 1982. Courtesy unknown)

One of the bands I wanted so much to include in *Crossover The Edge*, Neuroot from Doesburg, Holland (later in Arnhem) have a massive history in European hardcore, and their own share in the crossover game for one record. Formed in 1980 by Marcel Stol, who narrates that "I became a punk in 1977 at the age of 13 and always wanted to start a band. The first one was called Radiation, and we rehearsed in my room in the attic at home. We lived in a small town near Arnhem called Doesburg. We only had a bass guitar and a guitar, but no drums. After a while I decided to rename the band Neuroot and soon a drummer joined. At that time, I played bass, Wouter played guitar, HP was our drummer, and Leon Schaar was our singer. We had a few songs that later appeared on the *Macht kaput* cassette and played a few concerts in Arnhem and the surrounding area. Schaar was a really good and cool singer, but somehow, he couldn't learn lyrics by heart. So unfortunately, we had to kick him out and Wouter switched to the microphone. Instead, Edwin came in, who played guitar in a New Wave band but really wanted to play in Neuroot because of the hardcore concept and sound. With this lineup we then got a complete setlist, as Edwin also contributed songs. In 1982 our first tape, *Macht Kaput Wass Euch Kaput Macht*, was recorded in the studio of and released by the Limbabwe label in Venlo. From then on, we started playing a lot of concerts in Holland, Belgium, and Germany".

"Being a punk since 1977 I have been able to witness first-hand the developments in my own subculture" Marcel adds, regarding the evolution of crossover. "The first band really was Motörhead and right behind them Discharge. You must understand that metal at first didn't exist. There was hard rock and there was punk; hard rockers hated punk(s) and actively sought to beat them up (as did the disco's) so we hated them too. The hard rock subculture basically and originally was known for its quite conservative, straight and right-wing outlook on the world. Visiting record stores often I can remember finding Motörhead LPs in the punk section more often than I cared for back in the day. Motörhead was too coarse, raw and sometimes too fast to be able to be labelled hard rock presumably and sounded more punk than hard rock. Besides that, Lemmy of Motörhead was in the Damned (The Doomed) for a short while and fraternised a lot with the 1977 London punk scene. We punks ignored all that at first until the moment 'our' bands like Discharge, GBH and a lot more of the UK82 bands began citing and fronting Motörhead shirts and stuff. Truckloads of punks started listening to Motörhead and liking it. So first off it was Motörhead and the UK82 scene with Discharge and GBH and the likes of The Varukers, Anti Sect, The Skeptix, English Dogs, Sacrilege etc., and Napalm Death as well".

(Neuroot with Chaos Front, Br. Fozzy, Pandemonium and Inferno, 27/05/1984)

Neuroot kicked off their discography appearance with a live recording, the 1982 *Live Stokvishal 1982*. It was a soundboard recording of their performance during Anti Fascism Festival at Stokvishal Arnhem on 18 December 1982. This tape included seven excellent hardcore blasts that appeared later in their studio releases too. They took their cues from the UK anarcho and UK82 scene mostly. There's a definite Disorder flavour, while 'Ignorant' and 'G.B.O. Gestapo' are hands down my favourites. "Discharge, GBH, Amebix, English Dogs, Varukers, Antisect, all the D-beat bands from the UK basically and later it was Metallica, the Melvins, Bad Brains, Poison Idea and Cro-Mags from the US" Marcel adds, regarding the bands that influenced Neuroot.

"We still are a punk band, but we did have a stab at the spray paint cover (on *Plead Insanity*; the re-release has a very different cover by the way) a lot of the metal and crossover bands were sporting back in the day. A lot of the punk bands were doing this but was a bad idea. We never did long hair (pleeeease, go away!) but did do bullet belts style and that's it" Marcel laughs.

Next was the 1983 *Macht Kaput Wass Euch Kaput Macht* demo, that is one of my favourite ever European hardcore demos. It is a total barrage of adrenaline, fueled by a highly political band, raw, spastic and catchy hardcore that to my ears sounds like a blend between UK82 and Scandi-punk of that era (yes, it's so noisy, still so catchy). Songs like 'Conservative' or 'State Brain' will drive you wild if you're into that stuff, while 'Democracy' is one of my favourite Neuroot songs. I was so happy when *Macht Kaput Wass Euch Kaput Macht* was re-released on LP in 2009, because I consider it one of the best Netherland releases, up there with records from Pandemonium, B.G.K. and Agent Orange (NL).

In 1986 a split LP with Neuroot and Fratricide was supposed to be released on Pusmort, a release that you can read the story on the Fratricide chapter. Neuroot started adding a little more of a metal element into their sound albeit not something wild, just to spice it up a little bit. "I think hard rock had a much-needed blood transfusion through the directness, brutality and aggression of punk and developed a strand called thrash-speed metal which in its turn influenced punk again to become crossover. Punk never took over the narrowmindedness and straightness and bigotry of metal-hard rock in Europe, although I think it did in the US with NY Hardcore (yes, the Cro-Mags too…) starting with S.O.D. with *Speak English or Die*. Since then, this strand of US punk has influenced a whole mass of European bands whom I don't recognise as punk anymore".

While I'm not sharing Marcel's feelings towards Cro-Mags (in terms of bigotry), since I managed to meet Parris in NYC and discussed over those things for hours, it's true that certain aspects of the crossover in NYC were highly questionable, even problematic, just like in the case of S.O.D. Back to Neuroot, their music took a slight different approach on the 1986 *Right is Might* 7-inch, heading for a more metal-hardcore style; more complex, more guitar-driven, and even more controlled. *Right is Might* is an unbelievable classic; and if you think that I'm exaggerating, you'd better listen to all four songs of the 7-inch that was released through their own Smeul Productions and recorded at Joke's Koeienverhuur in the basement of Emma Squat Amsterdam. 'Politicians and Businessmen' still send shivers down my spine!

In terms of the reaction of punks and metalheads to crossover, and how this was perceived in Netherlands, Marcel narrates that "punk was open to influences and we liked the aggressiveness of thrash and speed metal. Don't know what it was like for the metalheads, but they seemed to like it alright. There was no real bonding of the subcultures though other than through the music and visiting gigs and stuff".

(Neuroot with MDC, SNFU, Disabuse, R.O. Conspiracy and Idiots. 13/11/1988)

Just slightly more metal but still hardcore, at least 80 percent was Neuroot's final offering for the 1980s. On the 1988 *Plead Insanity* LP; this is top stuff once again. One can spot influences ranging from Kafka Prosess to Cro-Mags, and from Metallica to Poison Idea. With fifteen songs in thirty-five minutes, *Plead Insanity* carries brilliant stuff such as 'The End', the raging 'Spark of Hate' and the complex metal-hardcore of 'Heavy Metals'. Neuroot did it again with gusto and style.

"In those days of crossover, I didn't notice any violence in the shows" Marcel adds. "The metalheads were outnumbered and held their head down at punk/crossover shows so they were no bother and they seemed a bit shy at first, being on other turf and stuff…as for my favourite crossover shows from back in the day, these have to do with every time I saw Accüsed, God (Amsterdam), Gore (Holland), Metallica and Raw Power (Italy)".

After an extensive break for about thirty years, Neuroot re-formed, and they began releasing new music! First it was the 2018 LP *Obuy and Die*, and Neuroot were still hardcore, still political and always relevant. Their sound now took a shift towards Black Flag from Rollins era, blended in with some Melvins. Songs like the great 'Fuckoshima' is just so melodic, bordering with stoner rock! However, they were back in hardcore on the *Nazi-Frei* 7-inch that was released with *Artcore Fanzine* #38, another slab of vinyl containing politically charged fast hardcore albeit not that fast as before!

Even better, is their last release, the 2024 *False Profit* LP; very Poison Idea-influenced, especially songs like 'The Punk Wars', this record is a brilliant introduction for newcomers. Slightly metal, always hardcore, and another top release for a band that has quality written all over all their output.

(Marcel Stol onstage, 1987. Courtesy of punkfoto.de)

"The Goudvishal in Arnhem, Holland will always be my favourite place to play, and I think that the blend between punk and metal is here to stay" Marcel concludes. Neuroot have been touring the world the last couple of years with shows in Malaysia, Indonesia, Cambodia, Thailand, China, Taiwan, Japan, Hong Kong, Singapore, USA, Europe, Iceland. On 2025 Neuroot concluded a South America tour, and they are planning for a South Africa tour in 2026. If this takes place, they will have achieved playing in all continents through their existence!

At a glance: One of the best European hardcore bands ever, Neuroot, had also some slight metal overtones in their late 1980s records. While all their back catalogue is mandatory for any hardcore fan, I would recommend *Right is Might* 7-inch and *Plead Insanity* LP to those ones into more crossover sound, even though both records are not crossover, but raging metal-hardcore punk. A top-class act, they remain under the radar of most people, Neuroot offered some of the wildest and most political output in days when the hardcore bands were blooming all over the world!

NEW INTERVIEWS FROM BANDS INCLUDED IN CROSSOVER THE EDGE

AGNOSTIC FRONT

(Agnostic Front 1986 touring lineup. Courtesy unknown)

You already know from *Crossover The Edge* how much I love Agnostic Front. The ultra-classic, long-standing NYHC stalwarts that formed in NYC in 1980, are still strong in 2026, with a consistent back catalogue of excellent releases. While we all have our (different) favourite records by AF, there are two records off them that have a special place in my heart: *Victim In Pain* LP (1984) and *Cause For Alarm* LP (1986). The former is one of the best hardcore records ever, while the latter is one of the best crossover albums ever. I have seen live AF sixteen times and looking forward for even more! As a recommendation for someone not familiar with them (is there any?), go check them live, it's a life's experience. Be sure to get all their records up to *Dead Yuppies* for a start, and then you can proceed to the post-2001 stuff. I'm a huge fanboy as you can imagine, so there can't be an objective review in their case!

(Agnostic Front with The Fuck-Ups and Verbal Abuse at The Sound Of Music, San Francisco. 04/05/1985)

(Agnostic Front with Exodus at L'Amour, 20/12/1985)

In *Crossover The Edge* I had interviewed Rob Kabula. Now it was time for Roger Miret, vocalist of AF [as well as Roger Miret and The Disasters, The Psychos, Alligators, Lady Luck (emo/indie!) and bassist for post-punks Aura!]. Roger, alongside Vinnie Stigma, will always be the heart of AF, and I was so happy that he offered me this interview regarding *Cause For Alarm*, a record that everybody with even a slight interest in crossover shall have in his collection.

Q: *Cause for Alarm* marked a major shift for Agnostic Front, bringing a strong metal influence into your hardcore roots. How did that transition come about, and what were the main reasons behind embracing a crossover direction at that point in time?

Roger: To be honest it was just an organic type of crossover for us. Rob (Kabula) and Alex (Kinon) were really liking the newer metal bands and it kind of just came across on the writing. At the same time a lot of either metal or hardcore bands were embracing each other's fury and talent, so it was just a time and a place... not some sort of plan.

Q: If you had to choose your top 3 hardcore records and your top 3 metal records of all time, which ones would they be, and how did they shape you as a musician?

(Roger AF on the 1986 tour. Photo by B.J. Pappas)

Roger: I would say The Misfits - *Bullet* 7-inch and Black Flag - *Nervous Breakdown* 7-inch and Negative Approach's self-titled 7-inch, those three are incredible to me! For metal, it's a little harder because I generally do not listen to metal and never really dove into it as much as hardcore punk but to name some would be Metallica - *Kill 'Em All* and Exodus - *Bonded By Blood* and Slayer - *Reign In Blood*.

Q: When *Cause for Alarm* first came out, the NYHC scene was known for being very protective of its hardcore identity. How do you remember the reaction from the scene to the heavy metal influence on that record?

Roger: Well, it was a shock if I remember correctly only pre-*Cause for Alarm* because we had recorded it. Then played a show in December and wanted to showcase the songs with the recording lineup that featured Lou Beatto from Carnivore fame at the time. So, people were confused yet still receptive. I think once it was released it was easier. Though some of the hardcore purists at first despised it but funny, later started crossing over too!

(Agnostic Front with Violent Children, Gilligan's Revenge and Blood at the CBGB's, 28/04/1984)

Q: Looking back at Agnostic Front's first era, from *United Blood* 7-inch to *One Voice* LP, which of those records is your personal favourite and why?

Roger: Those are two different animals and way different to compare! *United Blood* being very primitive sounding in every aspect still holding that flag. Almost ten years later came *One Voice* and by then the band had already released two studio records and the infamous *Live At CBGB's* record. There was a lot of growth again in every aspect.

Q: Agnostic Front has remained one of the most enduring bands in hardcore, still gaining younger fans today. What do you think is the key reason behind that lasting impact and relevance across generations?

Roger: I think it's that we are a genuine band and it shows. Specially at our live shows and if you get to meet us. We keep it real. I mean who wants to be a part of something fake right? We also love the newer bands and playing live with them. It keeps us fresh and alive!

Agnostic Front are (of course…) active in 2026, and have already out a new LP, *Echoes In Eternity*. They've been touring the world endlessly, and I won't even mention the various projects each member has/had! The legacy of Agnostic Front has left the footprint on many scenes: they were the ones that put NYHC on the map in terms of popularity worldwide. They were the ones that spearheaded alongside D.R.I., Cro-Mags, Suicidal Tendencies in the crossover's explosion, tearing down barriers between different scenes. AF re-invented the NYHC sound on *One Voice*, and passing the torch to the newer generation, and many more.

On a final note, I remember myself in my late teens, spending endless hours observing the crazy artwork of *Cause For Alarm*, reading all the lyrics, and having objections on 'Public Assistance' and 'Shoot His Load', trying to get hold of every record by everyone band that was mentioned on the special thanks (except for one, you can guess which band was that…), and blasting the music on my stereo for endless days and nights. It remains one of my all-time favourite crossover LPs, and a mandatory record for everyone with even a slight interest in crossover. I would add *Liberty And Justice…* LP in the crossover equation too. It always sounded to me like a cross of *Victim In Pain* with *Cause For Alarm*, and the term 'war hardcore' is downright appropriate to describe it!

CRUMBSUCKERS

(Crumbsuckers 1987 band picture. Courtesy of Metal Forces)

If life was fair, Crumbsuckers would have been getting major references for both being one of the best, as well as one of the first bands to even mix hardcore with metal. They were not New York City natives since they originated from Baldwin, Nassau County, Long Island. Crumbsuckers though could be considered as a first-wave NYHC combo, even though they weren't an A7 band, since they formed in 1982. They first lineup included Kevin Caroll (drums), Dave Brady (vocals), Gary Meskil (bass), David Wynn (guitar), and I had a chat with Chuck Lenihan regarding his musical influences, the story of Crumbsuckers, as well as things related to crossover.

"I grew up with older cousins who shared records with me at a young age. *Goodbye Yellow Brick Road* was a big album early on and then I found out about other groups like KISS, Nugent, Boston, Hendrix. I got a guitar on my fourteenth birthday, and everything expanded from there. Eventually I would hear Sabbath, and of course Van Halen", Chuck narrates about his musical upbringing.

Crumbsuckers kicked off with the 1983 *The Crumbsucker Cave* demo (that included a hilarious cover of Chubby Checker's 'The Twist'). It was a release that even though it is rough and underproduced, contained some excellent hardcore songs like 'A-OK' and the superfast 'Kids In My School', pure teenage fun! Things were about to explode soon, with Crumbsuckers being regulars at CBGB's hardcore matinees, and the recordings of two more demos.

(Crumbsuckers onstage. Date and courtesy unknown)

The 1985 *Charge Of The Light Brigade* demo included some musical and lineup changes; Chuck Lenihan joined in with his special guitar style, and Carroll was replaced by Dan Richardson, a sixteen-year-old drummer. The musical style shifted towards a slightly more metal approach, a perfect blend of hardcore-metal. *Charge Of The Light Brigade* demo included songs that were later re-recorded on their first LP, and it exposed the brilliance of Crumbsuckers: fast, heavy, catchy and highly unique! If only they re-recorded the 'Charge Of The Light Brigade' in their LPs...

"I'm not sure who started the crossover, it but I remember when the Cro-Mags and Agnostic Front got second guitar players and added more guitar solos" Chuck adds. "Crossover was probably just a natural progression - the intensity of hardcore and the skill of being able to play metal appealed to both genres so naturally as bands became more known the cultures would blend a bit ".

(Crumbsuckers with Insanity Defense, Cro-Mags and Krakdown at the February's. 27/05/1985)

"It was an exciting time for music and people from different surrounding areas were coming out to be a part of it" Chuck adds. "The metalheads had a tough time at first and some shit did go down at shows but not always".

Dave Brady left the band, and Krakdown's Chris Notaro was recruited. Chris' voice had a definite rough edge. He sounded like a more metal John Brannon in his Negative Approach days, while offering a more extreme style to Crumbsuckers. The new lineup entered the studio, and under the production of Norman Dunn (Flipper, Raven, Anthrax, Carnivore and later producer of Agnostic Front, Ed Gein's Car), and the visuals of Sean Taggart, they went on to record and release the masterpiece of *Life Of Dreams* LP (1986).

Released in US by Combat Core and in Europe by Rough Justice Records, *Life Of Dreams* is one of the best crossover records ever. The band balances between hardcore and metal, sounding like a cross of NYHC, Negative Approach, Metallica and early Iron Maiden. Sixteen songs, every one is a classic. It's not a coincidence that the Crumbsuckers weren't imitated later by anyone. It was because they could not be imitated! From the iconic 'Trapped' to the bullet-speed of 'Shot Down', and from the Eastern melodies of 'Face Of Death' to the all-out-attack of 'Live To Work', this is just one of 1980s highlights.

"My favourite crossover records? *Age Of Quarrel* was big for me, and *Retaliation* by Carnivore, too!" Chuck smiles. "Carnivore is a great example of a metal-based band who got influenced by the hardcore scene and brilliantly captured that crossover energy. In terms of crossover shows, I saw many, but the ultimate show for me was the *Age Of Quarrel* record release party at CBGB's. One of my top five all-time shows ever".

After the release of *Life Of Dreams*, Crumbsuckers played many shows in New York City and on the East Coast. Their first time on the West Coast was in Long Beach, California opening for Bad Brains and included also travelling to Canada, supporting Dark Angel. "CBGB's had the best sound for me always, but I also liked bigger rooms like Webster Hall and L'Amour" Chuck adds.

(Crumbsuckers with Sacred Reich and Deadly Blessing at L'Amour. 17/06/1988)

More lineup changes, and in 1987 Dave Wynn left the band and Robbie Koebler stepped in, to record the follow-up of *Life Of Dreams*. The result was the **1988** *Beast On My Back* LP on Combat Records. The LP showcased a new direction, even from the first seconds of the opening track, 'Breakout'. I remember being disappointed when I first got it, partly because I missed the frenzied energy of *Life Of Dreams*, however, over the years, it became a grower that I love today. More controlled, yet more diverse and melodic, with a huge progressive rock influence, it includes songs like 'Breakout', 'Jimmie's Dream' or the mental 'Initial Shock' instrumental, that sounded like a progressive jazz gone hardcore metal combo, and 'Rejuvenate'. While initially *Beast On My Back* didn't get as much love as *Life Of Dreams*, I'm happy that the last years finally gets the recognition it deserves!

"I like both albums for different reasons" Chuck admits. "For me personally I think the *Life Of Dreams* album captured the band in an exciting time where things were less structured and there was a bit of that unexplained phenom in the air. *Beast On My Back* had more navigating to it and looking back probably captured the band in its ability to preserver for the time".

After the release of *Beast On My Back* Crumbsuckers hit the road again, and this time the US tour was extended and followed by a small UK tour with Onslaught and Slammer. "One of the most fascinating stories took place when we went to the UK in 1988" Chuck recalls. "We were in Birmingham, and I went for a walk and when I returned to the bus there was this kid from Worcester apparently, who was playing my guitar. He just made himself at home lol. We became friends and he dreamed of coming to the USA, so I told him he was welcome to visit anytime. When I got home there was a letter waiting from him saying he bought his ticket already - we are still friends today!"

The story of Crumbsuckers ends here though, because they disbanded in 1989 due to musical differences; a new vocalist came in (Craig Allen), and the name of the band changed to Heavy Rain, with a new musical style, more into progressive metal-rock. Did I mention that in the special thanks of *Beast On My Back*, a small band named Majesty and its members are included? Yep, the ones that became Dream Theater, and they owe big time to the Crumbsuckers, because they were the ones that promoted their music to NY's Mechanic Records and the release of *When Dream And Day Unite* took place!

Heavy Rain didn't last long, they broke up in 1990. Gary Meskil with Dan Richardson later formed Pro-Pain (that you all know of), gaining popularity worldwide with excellent records like *The Truth Hurts*. I won't refer to the countless bands that Crumbsuckers members played in (all these can be found on *Crossover The Edge*). But I have to mention that Chuck Lenihan is currently a member of the Vasaria, and the excellent The Aggros, as well as Carnivore AD, and he played with Parris Mayhew in Psychic Orgy.

Crumbsuckers re-united in 2006 and in 2014 to 2015 offering shows, while F.O.A.D. Records released the fantastic *Turn Back Time: The Early Years 1983-1985* DLP compilation (2014). They are no longer active though.

"Of course, I believe that crossover is relevant today" Chuck concludes. "With a lot of the Carnivore AD shows we are seeing a new generation of young kids coming out. They know the songs, the lyrics; and the energy is the same exciting energy we had in the early days".

LUDICHRIST

(Ludichrist band picture. Courtesy of Bonnie Graham)

Unbelievably raging, but on the same time technically proficient and unique crossover bands is Ludichrist from Long Island, New York. Formed in 1984, they went on to become a very beloved band both in the NYHC scene, as well as the thrash crossover worldwide. Founding member drummer Alan Bazin, aka Al Batross narrates their story, in one of the best interviews included in this book!

(Ludichrist with Nuclear Assault and Bloodlust at L' Amour, 18/04/1986)

"Ludichrist grew out of myself and Mark Kanabrocki, aka Durnex starting to jam together in our mid-teens. We met through school and became best friends as we shared similar interests, such as a love for horror movies and Monty Python. Plus, we both liked beer and marijuana. We lived in a boring suburban town called Syosset, so finding someone like-minded was a stroke of good luck for both of us. Mark had never listened to punk or hardcore before we met. He was into bands like Iron Maiden and Judas Priest, that kind of stuff, which I was never into. However, I had amassed a pretty impressive collection of punk and hardcore LPs and EPs by ordering them through the mail and he willingly converted when I shared them with him, embracing punk and hardcore as fervently as I did. I got into that music initially by first being a fan of the Ramones, which led to a friend, several years older than me, turning me on to the Sex Pistols and The Clash. That friend, however, was insistent that the UK punk scene was the only authentic one and the only music worth listening to. Some time later, a high school buddy of mine who was a music nut leant me the Dead Kennedys LP, *Fresh Fruit for Rotting Vegetables* and I was like 'Whoa - what is this? This is weird and fucking amazing' and I decided my UK obsessed friend didn't know what he was talking about.

The moment that sucked me fully into the hardcore and punk scene, worldwide, was in the early eighties, when I dialled in a radio station on the family radio console at home on Long Island and discovered a show broadcast from New York University called 'Noise', hosted by an enthusiastic guy named Hal. The very first show I heard, and thankfully I had an audio cassette to tape it, was an hour-long broadcast playing only songs that were less than a minute long. I can't overstate the effect that broadcast had on me. This was a world I immediately wanted to be a part of. I was hooked and started collecting records by the bands I most liked that had been played during the show. The band that stood out the most to me at the time was Rudimentary Peni. Their tracks 'B Ward' and 'Media Person' had made my brain light up like a Christmas tree. That was it. That was the moment I decided I wanted to be in a band that played that kind of music. I started teaching myself drums by listening to tracks repeatedly, wearing headphones and using cardboard tubes, removed from old clothes hangers, to bang along on a set of books I laid out on my bed. When Rudimentary Peni's next EP *Farce* was released, Mark and I absolutely devoured it. The lyrics spoke directly to us about everything we didn't like about the world, society and how we were expected to be and act and said it all so damn brilliantly. I still think RP's lyrics are some of the best ever written. Our first jam sessions together often involved playing their songs. For example, the song 'Government Kids' came from us playing songs like 'Farce', 'Cosmetic Plague', and 'Sacrifice' over and over. That was the soil that Ludichrist eventually grew from.

First, we called ourselves Intestinal Militia, a laughably humourless and desperate sounding name that came from me trying way too hard. Mark had a knack, right away, for coming up with good, simple hardcore riffs. We found a vocalist named Chuck, who was more of a 'singer' than a typical punk band would have, but he was several years older than us and both charming and willing, so away we went.

Without a bassist, we played at CBGB's, back when it had a dedicated 'audition showcase' night on Monday evenings. In the crowd that night was a guy named Chuck Valle who had answered an ad we placed in the *Village Voice*, looking for a bass player. He'd later confessed that he'd been coked out of his mind, was playing pool the whole time we performed and barely listened to us, but he decided to join anyway. (Chuck, not long after that night, quit doing any drugs or drinking alcohol and remained that way for as long as I knew him). So, now we had a bassist. Around this same time, I had started playing with another group called Live Murder, which was much different musically, much slower and more in the vein of groups like The Cramps. Tommy Franco, aka Christ was the vocalist, and he had a great, powerful, extremely raw voice. I forget exactly how it happened, but it clearly dawned on us that he would be a much more appropriate front man for Intestinal Militia.

Around this time, I had been sent to a Catholic school by my parents for acting up and being a more than typically delinquent teenager, and I picked up Rudimentary Peni's first LP *Death Church*. Mark and I had been particularly annoyed by the Catholicism that had been forced on us, and not believing a word of it ourselves, RP's lyrics on religion felt like they spoke directly to us. I remember having two experiences at that school, almost immediately, that shone a light on how hypocritical and destructive it all was. First, our teachers, who were referred to as 'Brothers' and akin to priests, spent an inordinate amount of time bad mouthing another Catholic School in a neighbouring town for some odd reason. The second was witnessing a student quietly vomit into his book bag, rather than raise his hand and ask to be excused, because he was terrified of the teacher. It was all just so ridiculous. Stifling, hypocritical and tribal. One morning, while sitting in a homeroom at school, I started thinking up and writing down potential band names and landed on the word 'ludicrous'. I thought… ridiculous Christ... what about Ludichrist? That became the new name. We rehearsed once or twice weekly, working on new songs that Mark wrote, along with songs we had already been playing as Intestinal Militia, and before long we had enough for a full set. We started playing any gigs we could get, which weren't many, and paid to go into a studio and record a demo tape, which resulted in the first recordings we sent out to promote the band, and also sold through the mail. I think we placed an ad in *Maximum Rocknroll*.

Some time later, I believe through Tommy, we came to know another New York-based group called Horror Planet, a really cool, unique band that put on a great show and had a very talented guitarist named Glen Cummings. We got Glen to come along to one of our rehearsals with his guitar and once he started playing with us, the music suddenly had a far greater dimension than it ever had before - more layers, more harmony, more musicality in general. Mark was great at writing songs for the band and was skilled enough to play rhythm guitar, but Glen was exceptional, far and away the most talented of all of us, musically. I still remember being blown away by both his playing and his humble nature. We immediately asked Glen to join, and he smiled and said something along the lines of 'Great. I got away with faking it'. Charming self-effacement. To me, it was an instant transformation and Ludichrist immediately had its own musical identity. The songs we had recorded for the demo prior suddenly sounded empty to me, almost barren, so we went back into a recording studio to redo four tracks with Glen on board.

There was a *Maximum Rocknroll* compilation album called *Welcome to 1984* and on it was a unique track called 'Chicken Farm' by the Japanese band The Stalin. I absolutely loved it. There was nothing else like it on any of the many compilation LPs I picked up. It was a very simple, powerful punk tune, exceptionally well recorded, that had an extra guitar track on top where the guitarist went apeshit with leads and harmonies etc, making it instantly unforgettable. Take that guitar layer away and you would have had something close to what our first demo recording sounded like, only much slower. Years later, a friend in another band I played in leant me several releases by The Stalin and I was disappointed to find that guitar was not anywhere to be found, so to this day I don't know if that was a one-off done just for that compilation track, or what. To me, our simple hardcore songs suddenly had that magic layer 'Chicken Farm' had, laid on top of them, and I was thrilled. In the years since those days, I've met some people who preferred Ludichrist before Glen joined, not liking the added guitar layer he brought, thinking it somehow stopped being real hardcore at that point, but I completely disagree. The band wasn't in a finished form before Glen joined. That's the way I'll always feel about it.

We started playing gigs in our new form and on the day, we played a really successful matinee at CBGB's, Mark announced that he felt the band had become too much work, too much of a 'job' and not solely fun, so he wanted to quit, now that we had 'made it' with the CBGB's show. I was deeply hurt and really didn't understand him - to me this was what we'd been working for, to be in this music scene we had wanted so much to be a part of. His decision just seemed lazy to me. I was also concerned because he had been so instrumental in writing our material. I'd say the *Immaculate Deception* LP is 80 percent made up of songs and riffs written by Mark, but there was no question the band was going to continue. We looked for a new guitarist and found Joe Butcher, who was better guitarist overall than Mark was, and though a bizarre coincidence was also someone I had hung out with many times, years ago on Long Island. Joe fit in well and we continued to play shows and tour. Probably through our friendship with Crumbsuckers, we somehow got on Relativity-Combat Core's radar and were signed to the label.

(Ludichrist with Murphy's Law and Good Humor at CBGB's, 19/07/1986)

We all had our first 'professional' studio recording experience with Randy Burns and *Immaculate Deception* was released. Not too long after, Tommy and I started to have a falling out, which came to a head when he drunkenly tried to start a physical fight with me after a gig, which Glen broke up. During a tour not long after, I think it became clear our friendship had dissolved, and he'd come to dislike me. Some of it was his fault, not helped by alcohol, but it was also mine as well. I was several years younger, and a bit of an immature, smacked ass kid who took things too seriously and could be quite moody. I think he got tired of me. I also think Tommy resented whenever I spoke for the band, feeling it was his place to do that and not mine. Some time after that tour, we were booked to go play a gig with Voivod in Canada and prior to the show I was in a car accident as a passenger. Although I was fine, mostly was just picking tiny glass shards out of my forehead for days afterward, my parents forbade me to travel, so I had to back out of the show. The band decided to do the gig anyway and I think Voivod's drummer sat in with them. After they returned, I got a call (I believe from Chuck) telling me I was no longer in the band. I took it very hard, but if they didn't want me, there was nothing I could do about it. I've never been comfortable forcing myself into places where I'm not wanted, but that didn't mean I wasn't depressed about it for quite a while.

Around six months later, while rehearsing with another band (I think it was a short-lived project with Eddie from Leeway) I heard from Tommy that he and Glen wanted to talk to me. They drove over and picked me up and told me the drum auditions had not gone well. Admittedly, that felt really good because Tommy seemed to have a newfound appreciation for what I did. I remember him telling me about one drummer they tried out, who when asked what song he'd like to play, said 'You pick it' and when Tommy said 'Most People are Dicks' the drummer exploded saying 'That's the most difficult one!' (it wasn't, at all). Things had apparently gone like that. They played some new material for me on an audio cassette, and we parted with a promise that I would make a decision, but I decided not to rejoin. The bad feeling I had when I was kicked out was gone, and I didn't really feel like it was my band anymore anyway. It turned out for the best as the material they were working on was much more metal influenced and that really wasn't my thing. Plus, they eventually pulled in Dave Miranda from The Six and Violence, who was one of the most highly skilled drummers I've ever met. Dave was, and probably still is, a force of nature, a guy who could play anything exceptionally well, crisply and with overflowing energy. He was a pro, whereas I was self-taught and merely competent in playing my own style within a comparatively narrow subset of music. A couple of years later, Dave and I became good friends, and I even took drum lessons from him for a while. However, I was a lazy student so I didn't benefit from it as I should have. Technically, practically everything I did when I was in Ludichrist was single stroke rolls. To develop my speed for double time beats, I would play just the first three out of four hits on the hi-hat or ride with my right hand, skipping the fourth where the second snare hit would fall, to raise my stick and emphasize the next one, out of the next set of three out of four. It's hard to describe but you can hear it in our recordings of the fastest songs. While this was certainly a questionable technique, it did have the benefit of helping make the tempo extra clear, which turned out to be very helpful a decade later when I played with MDC, as the singer Dave had a habit of getting ahead of, or behind, the beat. Anyway, when I finally heard Ludichrist's second LP, *Powertrip*, I knew it was for the best that I did not return, both for me and for the band, plus Dave's drum tracks are fucking stellar.

(Ludichrist with Abombanation, First Order and Headstrong at CBGB's. 19/02/1989)

That's pretty much my full history with the band. Obviously, I'm unable to speak knowledgeably about anything that happened after I left. Sometime later after *Powertrip*, Ludichrist placed an ad in a New York area music-focused paper, inviting people to submit possible names for the band that they would next turn into, which I thought was rather sad. It felt like the band completely gave up on meaning anything. They chose the submitted name Scatterbrain. I think *Powertrip* is a good record, even if I don't really think of it as Ludichrist. As far as Scatterbrain goes, I'll just leave it as I don't have anything positive to say.

Ludichrist and Scatterbrain did some reunion shows in 2007 and Tommy asked if I wanted to participate and play a few songs, but it would have involved travelling to Long Island from NYC for rehearsals with a band that now only contained one person I'd ever met. Plus, they already had Dave Miranda onboard for the songs I wouldn't have played, so they really didn't need me at all. At the time, I was playing in two or three other bands and didn't have the need to be part of a reunion, so I declined and went to the show at BB King's instead as a paying customer. It was gratifying to see the crowd there, and I bumped into Glen, who I hadn't seen in ages and who had also declined the reunion offer. It was great to see him again, but musically it was a strange and surreal show to watch. It didn't feel like Ludichrist to me, it felt more like 'Tommy Christ sings the songs of Ludichrist and Scatterbrain'. At one point, I think they played a Kid Rock cover, and I stopped listening altogether and instead talked to Glen and a few other people I bumped into for the rest of the show.

The final thing I need to talk about is the one true tragedy of Ludichrist, the murder of Chuck Valle, our bassist. Chuck also left the band sometime after *Immaculate Deception* and was working successfully as an audio engineer. He had also joined Murphy's Law. In 1994, while in California touring with a band as their sound man, he got into an altercation with some dirtbag while getting lunch at a hot dog stand. The dirtbag left, but unbeknown to Chuck or the guy he was with, he lay in wait nearby with a knife and later attacked Chuck, stabbing him to death. It was senseless, stupid and cruelly unfair. Chuck once told me he had a poster in his bedroom, I believe from a guitar manufacturer, that had a picture showing a musician, seen from behind, walking out onstage to perform for a huge crowd. It had a motivational message on it, something along the lines of 'you worked hard to get to this moment, now it's your time to step out there'. He shared with me that it was what he believed and was dedicated to, working hard to deserve it when that day came. He was a man set on a mission. Chuck did indeed work hard, and he was a really good guy. He had a reserved, serious demeanour, and could appear to be a bit tough from a distance, but he wasn't. He was kind and gentle, and when he laughed it came out in a high-pitched titter, like a joyous little kid. There is no other word but tragic to describe what happened to him, how he had that future he worked so hard for stolen from him by some random dirtbag. Sometimes, life just doesn't make any sense at all. God, most definitely, is not everywhere. He's glaringly absent".

The lineup that released the 1985 demo included Al Batross on drums, Chuck Valle on bass, Mark Durnex on guitar, Glen Cummings on (lead) guitar and Tommy Christ on vocals, and the furious style of Ludichrist was evident from day one; the 1985 demo is one of my favourite demos of this era, fast and wild stuff here, with a surprisingly good production! The metal element here is just slight, to spice things up, and this is a sheer hardcore assault, 15 catchy tunes of smashing (sub)urban style. And while Ludichrist sound pissed off and venomous, below there lies the aspect of fun. Plus, I wish they would later re-record two songs off this demo, 'Corpse' and 'FSSBS'.

Regarding Ludichrist's main influences in that early period, Al narrates that "speaking only for myself, I don't think Ludichrist, during the demo through *Immaculate Deception* period, had much to do with metal. Maybe my perception is wrong, but I saw the music as being a kind of hardcore that was open to incorporating, or even satirizing, other types of music. I suppose it was a risk, more so back then, and in a scene as hard as New York, but I really liked that we had the freedom to play songs that varied - some purely raw, some more melodic, some where we deliberately incorporated different music genres - we weren't as locked into that thing that happens to bands where they become slaves to the idea that 'our songs have to sound like this or it doesn't fit the band'. Having that humorous aspect to the band, and our name, gave us room. By *Immaculate Deception*, we had at least two songs that could fairly be described as having overtly metal parts, but I didn't view it as anything more than another type of music we dipped into. I never would have adopted double bass drums for a song, for example, as I thought it was something of a cliche at that point in time that I didn't need to add to.

(Ludichrist 1985 demo)

I used to sometimes listen to the Discharge LP *Hear Nothing See Nothing Say Nothing* on 45 RPM instead of at regular speed in the early days of Ludichrist, and when I was teaching myself how to play. To a degree, that's what some early Ludichrist songs on the original demo sound like, minus the guitar solos. That Discharge album came out in 1982. Some people may disagree, but I didn't hear that music as metal at all. To me, it was a particular style of punk. I think the crossover perception of Ludichrist came mostly from what Glen added when he came on as second guitar. He wasn't a metal guitarist, it was more that he brought in playing fifths and the kind of musical language that had been missing from the songs prior, and he could play blistering leads and not shy about shredding in a way that was more common to metal and rock than it was punk. As I mentioned prior, the track 'Chicken Farm' from The Stalin was an exception to that generalization, and I think Glen's guitar was closer to that than it was to something overtly metal. It was melodic and very musical. By the time 'crossover' became a common term to describe that style of music, truth be told, I really didn't have much interest in it. Thrash I understood, to me it meant fast and with heavier guitar. Crossover felt like too much of a deliberate attempt to cater to two different crowds, too on the nose. Despite wearing a D.R.I. shirt on the back of the Ludichrist LP, it was just the D.R.I. debut LP and *Violent Pacification* EP that I loved. I mostly stopped listening to them after that. By that point I was more interested in bands that did their own thing or brought in other styles of music to punk and hardcore, besides metal. While there are bands in the various subgroups of metal since that I definitely respect and like. Overall, metal just wasn't a genre of music that ever resonated with me, beyond early Black Sabbath, that kind stuff.

I'd say the drummers who most influenced me back then were Jon Greville from Rudimentary Peni, Ted from the Dead Kennedys, Al Schvitz from MDC and Eric Brecht from D.R.I. - with further influences (far beyond my ability but inspiring nonetheless) coming from the drummers who played with Frank Zappa, especially Vinny Colaiuta and Terry Bozzio. That was in part due to the fact that my dad (who divorced from my mom when I was very young) had exposed me to Zappa's music at a very young age. My dad was also a keyboardist for a Boston area group called Jinx when I was in my early teens, which exposed me to the band life for the first time. In addition, Ian Underwood was an uncle of mine in my family when I was very young. I went to the premiere of *Close Encounters of the Third Kind* in New York City with both Ian and Ruth Underwood. For example, Zappa fans will recognize how unbelievable that is, Ian was supposed to be the guy in the film who plays the keyboard to the aliens during the climax, but allegedly Spielberg didn't think he had the right face for the role. He was doing synthesizer programming around that time. One regret I have in retrospect is I was too young to really understand who these people were. If I knew then what I knew about Ruth a decade later, I would have chained myself to her immediately and begged her daily to instruct me in percussion. Unfortunately, by then I was a who-gives-a-shit teenager and not a cute little kid anymore, so I lost my chance. Also, Ian was no longer an uncle by then and had pretty much cut off from my family, and Ruth had virtually disappeared from public life.

Some other favourite bands of both myself and Mark in the days before the band, and in the early days of Ludichrist, were MDC, the Dead Kennedys, Discharge, The Freeze, The F.U.'s, Void and D.R.I., with the biggest influence on the earliest form of the band being Rudimentary Peni, as I mentioned. As can happen with musical influences, the music you write and how you wind up performing it may not resemble those influences when it comes out, or be discernible to listeners, but the influences are there, just the same".

Even from their very beginning, Ludichrist appeared in billings with the cream of the crop of the New York scene, playing shows alongside bands like Nuclear Assault, Cro-Mags, Leeway, Murphy's Law or

Crumbsuckers. Their 15 May 1986 live at CBGB's went on to be recorded live and released by Hilly Kristal (owner of CBGB's) on cassette, and Al provided me of a good-sounding rip of it. What is fascinating in the case of this live recording is that the band sounds really tight, performing onstage so challenging songs with quite an ease! Wish again that they would later re-record 'Excommunicated', what a blazing thrasher that is!

While the NYHC scene in the mid-1980s was known for its diversity but also for its strong identity, I wanted to know how the scene initially reacted to Ludichrist's more technical, crossover direction, so Al mentions that "I think we were lucky in that we seemed to come along at the right time. Naturally it took a little time to grow an audience that came out to see us, specifically, and no other bands playing the same show, but I don't remember any frosty receptions or hostile crowds. We played a venue or two on Long Island that we were ill-suited to and were sparsely attended, a place called February's comes to mind. The sound guy hated us and trod on one of my cymbals when it was lying on the stage, bending it backwards and destroying it, but overall, I think we were lucky to be more or less accepted fairly quickly. I think it helped that we were fast and well-rehearsed, and that we had enough of a musical identity not to sound like every other band on the bill. Being young and not exactly city smart at that time, I was a bit worried initially that some of the rougher New York crowd might hate us, but it didn't happen. It was a relief to see guys who could eat me for breakfast seemingly dig what we were doing, and even look out for us during the shows, protecting people from banging into our equipment when they came onstage to dive off. I can't recall any of the established New York bands giving us a hard time or being unfriendly to us.

When Mark and I first started going to punk shows, we found a lot of the bands were very friendly to us, probably in part because we radiated that smiling, wide-eyed 'we're fans of your music' thing. One of the first shows we went to was out on Long Island at a club called My Father's Place, where we saw the Nihilistics and another band called Satan's Cheerleaders. To two naive suburban kids, the Nihilistics seemed a bit scary to approach, but we did it anyway after their set ended and to our surprise Ron, the vocalist, invited us backstage. Ron and the band couldn't have been nicer to us and patiently answered our dumb questions. When we told them we were starting a band they were nothing but encouraging. Experiences like that made it all seem possible, like we COULD actually form a band and become a part of the scene. When we saw Scream at CBGB's, we were standing in front of the stage as they set up to play, grinning from ear to ear, and the drummer Kent spotted us. He pointed to a pitcher of some beverage he had and motioned to us in a way that said 'Do you want some?'. We were a bit shocked but nodded yes, and he brought over two cups and poured us both a drink. We expected it was beer, but it was, in fact, soda. We looked at each other, rather confused, wondering why he did that. Then it hit us. It was just an act of pure kindness. They were about to play, and Kent probably knew by our age and enthusiasm that we were going to go nuts during their set, which we did. He was being friendly and making sure we were hydrated, which was just a lovely gesture. Either that or he did it as a welcoming gesture to two kids who probably looked a bit out of their element. Despite the sometimes-scary reputation the New York scene had, both the bands and the clubs, there were these wonderful acts of kindness. I think without them, we may not have had the confidence to form Ludichrist.

I did have an experience at one of our first gigs at CBGB's that served as a sort of 'welcome to the big city, suburb boy' moment. After we finished playing, Chuck and I put our equipment in his car and went back into CBGB's to hang out for a while. When we returned to the car, we found our equipment had been stolen. About a half hour later, we hung out in front of CBGB's, talking to friends about what had happened, and a homeless guy came walking down the street carrying one of my drums. He walked right up to us and asked if we wanted to buy it. We eventually learned he had traded something with the thieves who stole it in the hope he could make a dollar or two by selling the drum on the street. It was sheer luck that he happened to have poor enough judgement to walk right up to a music venue only three blocks from where it had been stolen. Incredibly, Chuck did get his bass back. Apparently, the guy who had bought it from the thieves also bought Chuck's backpack, and he had a girlfriend who noticed Chuck's info in his bag and then called him at home. She had felt guilty, knowing who it had been stolen from and had gotten the impression from the stuff in his bag that Chuck was a dedicated, and not at all wealthy, musician, which he was. Chuck wound up meeting them that night and got everything that was stolen from him back, paying I think two hundred dollars or so to make up for what the guy had purchased it for. Presumably, my drum equipment was split up amongst several buyers, probably all walking around the city with a piece of it in hand, hoping to sell it to someone on the street. I never saw any of it again, except for that single drum.

Despite that experience, I wound up moving to New York City about two years later and I continued to live there for twenty-five years, until finally moving to Connecticut. By the time I left the city, CBGB's was long gone, as were all my other favourite venues and places like Kim's Video Underground. The city had morphed over the years into something much different, more gentrified and homogeneous, and something I no longer felt any attachment to. I don't miss it, because the Manhattan I loved only exists in the past".

Their masterpiece, *Immaculate Deception* LP, was then released in 1986 (it was supposed to be released on late 1985) in US by Combat Core and in Europe by We Bite Records; with a cover by Ed Repka that I sadly couldn't find to get an interview, and the production treatment of Randy Burns, *Immaculate Deception* simply smokes. There's a good reason why I have two copies of it in both US and Euro versions, this LP reminds me so much of my youth, being belligerent. When I first got it, it struck me really hard. It contained some of the most blazingly furious music I ever heard, but on the same time it was well-played and fun. This record is one of speedcore's crowning moments, and songs like 'Murder Bloody Murder', 'Tylenol' and 'Green Eggs and Ham' (that appropriates the riff of Run DMC's 'Rock Box' and has a great background story that you will read below) make my blood boil up to this day! Again, the power of visuals,

I bought the Ludichrist LP while not knowing anything about the band; it was pre-Internet days and I was sixteen years old, and got it just because of the back cover pictures of Al wearing a D.R.I. T-shirt and Chuck wearing a Beastie Boys T-shirt!

Al narrates the story behind the guest appearances in *Immaculate Deception* mentioning that "the guest vocals on 'You Can't Have Fun' (Roger from Agnostic Front, Chris from Crumbsuckers, John from Nuclear Assault and Eddie from Leeway) came about because Tommy asked them if they wanted to do it and they all said yes. It was really that simple. They were all nice guys, and their bands were quite welcoming to us when we came on the scene, I think at least in part because we were doing our own thing and weren't clearly derivative of another band. We could play with any of them and not feel like an extension of what they were doing but could be also appreciated by much of the same crowd. We had played gigs with each of them, most often with Crumbsuckers. They were sort of a big brother band to us, in that they played in the same Long Island-New York scene, were established well before us, were in the same ballpark music wise and were generally a bit more accomplished as a band than we were when we first started playing with them. Plus, we got along well. Agnostic Front was obviously well established in New York, and we did a short US tour together, which I'll refer to later. Leeway, I'm pretty sure, we had played with at CBGB's and Nuclear Assault we had played with at some more metal-oriented venues like L'Amour in Brooklyn. Everyone got along great at the recording session for that song. There was an easy-going camaraderie there, a fun, laid back, non-competitive, no ego atmosphere. We were lucky to be with a group of supportive bands in New York, and to have had friendly encounters with local and out of state bands, early on. I'm sure there were a lot of bands out there around the same time that struggled far more than we ever did. So again, we were lucky".

Ludichrist after the release of *Immaculate Deception* toured the US, and in some cases they opened for Nuclear Assault and Agnostic Front, however several lineup changes took place prior to the release of their second LP, *Powertrip*; the new lineup included Tommy Christ (vocals), Paul Nieder (guitar), Glen Cummings (guitar), Mike Walters (bass) and Dave Miranda (drums). The new musical direction that the band was about to follow was already evident in the 1987 *Basement Demo*.

"I'd have to pick the *CBGB's Off the Board* recording, released by Hilly of CBGB's, as the personal favourite" Al admits regarding his favourite Ludichrist recording, "because it was so unlikely that the owner of such a justifiably legendary venue took an interest in us, to the extent that he asked us to do it. We played a set as part of a hardcore show, which they recorded, and then came back the following day when CBGB's was closed for the afternoon. We then played another set for an empty house, except for the guy running the sound board and a few employees, and someone later edited it so there was some of the stage banter from the previous day's show, but once a song started it was the recording we did that day. You can barely hear the crowd at a few points following a song, and that's because it was all being recorded through the sound board, so none of the mics were picking that up. At the very end of the release, the same guy spliced in a 'Thanks a lot for coming' type goodbye and a crowd applauding, but hilariously that's not even us, it's some other band. I think that recording is the best record that remains of what we actually sounded like, and overall, I think it's pretty good. I was in contact with Hilly not long before CBGB's closed, because I had some inside information about the Bowery Residents Community trying to get CBGB's shut down, and all those years later he still had some cassettes of our *Off the Board* release and he gave me one. I wish the master tape for the recording could be found and remastered, as any surviving version of it that I've heard has a lot of flaws, many of which no doubt stem from the source being very old cassette tapes, but I'm glad it survives at all. So, for several reasons, it's my favourite recording that Ludichrist did.

The recording of the *Immaculate Deception* LP was also memorable, as it was the first 'professional' studio recording for all of us, at a modern studio with equipment rented from SIR (Studio Equipment Rentals), an established producer, and an executive from Combat popping in to watch us record the drum tracks (which were done first) with scratch guitar, bass and vocal tracks. I know that when I was done, I definitely had a feeling of pride. I'm certain of this because the producer, Randy Burns, cracked up when he saw me out in the hall of the studio afterward and said something like 'You seem pretty pleased with yourself'. I was eighteen at the time, and I guess I was, I was probably strutting about like a scrawny Yul Brynner, which is both funny and embarrassing to recall now. It was definitely an amazing experience to hear our songs so well recorded, but in the years since I've wondered if it might have been better had we gone down a different path. It was mixed afterwards out in California, with only Tommy, Glen and Chuck being allowed to go, which was disappointing. I learned later that Randy, Tommy and Glen had a little TOO much fun partying while out there, which explains why some mistakes were made, such as Joe's rhythm guitar track for 'Young White and Well Behaved' being overlooked and left out of the mix entirely. I don't really have any complaints about the handling of my drum tracks, but there are elements of the mixing, and guitar and bass sound in places, that I would have liked to have been done differently. I think it's too clean, a bit sterile in places, which robs it of some energy. The other unfortunate aspect of that release was the album cover, which we all disliked. We had no say in it. Combat used an artist they had been using for their releases, and he came up with it on his own. Glen had drawn art for Ludichrist flyers in the past and had used Alfred E. Neuman from *Mad* magazine as the image for Christ, which was miles away from the serious looking, angry, grimacing figure on the cover. I guess Combat knew what they wanted in order to market the record, and using a *Mad* magazine Christ would have certainly gotten us sued, but it's unfortunate that cover art was what was used to represent us. It did not fit at all, in my opinion, but there was nothing we could do about it. To give Combat credit, they definitely knew how to promote it as, incredibly, *Immaculate Deception* was reviewed in an issue of *People* magazine, right underneath a review of a Bryan Adams record. It is frankly unbelievable that we got that kind of coverage in a mainstream, mass produced (and vacuous) pop culture magazine. That kind of thing just didn't happen back then, especially given the type of band we were and it being our first commercially available release.

It was practically a miracle. However, it might have been a better path for us had we not signed with Combat and kept things more under our control and aesthetically closer to what we actually were as a band".

Powertrip LP was released on Combat Records (US) and We Bite Records (Germany/Europe) in 1988 and was a departure from the band's earlier barbaric sound; now more metal than before, and more controlled. It showcased great technical competencies in all aspects, incorporating funk rhythms, constant changes in pace, even classic music (e.g. on 'T.B.O.S.'). Even though I love *Immaculate Deception*, I have to admit that I also have a soft spot for *Powertrip* too; however initially I didn't like it! It worked as a grower all these years, and now I enjoy songs like 'Powertrip', 'The Tip Of My Mind' (maybe the best song on this record), or 'Yesterday For You'. The hardcore element is still here, but if I was to offer a definition for *Powertrip*, I would file it under the 'progressive crossover' tag! This is so technically challenging that would even put most progressive rock bands in shame!

(Ludichrist with Forced Anger and False Hope at the Sabers, Cleveland, OH. 04/02/1989)

Ludichrist as aforementioned, played countless shows during the 1980s, so Al offers the gigs and tours that he remembers as defining moments for the band: "Certainly, playing at CBGB's, especially having been there many times prior to being in a band to attend hardcore and punk matinees, was a dream come true. I played there close to a hundred times in various bands during my life and there was no more enjoyable or comfortable place for me to play. On tour with Agnostic Front, I still remember that at one out of state gig we had been booked to do two shows at the same venue but didn't know that until we arrived. We played a hardcore matinee and then the place cleared out, and the crowd filled back in with locals, many probably bar regulars, and we were expected to play another show for them, a decidedly non-hardcore crowd. For that show, we combined forces as 'Agnostic Christ' and played a mix of our own material and a bunch of rock cover songs, swapping between band members. I think we even slowed down a few of our own songs to make them a bit easier for them to digest. We won the crowd over, which didn't seem likely to happen at all, so that was a fun and memorable show.

I think for us as a band, the most pivotal show we ever had was when we first played out of state, at a club called The Anthrax in Connecticut. We didn't have any idea what to expect and the crowd was just astonishing - super energetic, fully engaged, enthusiastic and warmly positive, immediately making us feel like we were a success as a band. I'd say it became a favourite place to play, in that we had the same awesome experience every time we went. They made us feel like whatever the punk equivalent of rock stars is, which was something I had not expected or experienced before, and I doubt anyone else in the band had either.

On the negative side, we did a tour with a UK band called The Stupids and played the famous 9:30 Club in Washington DC. It was a big deal for me at the time, as the DC bands were a huge part of my early punk and hardcore education. I owned most of the Discord EPs back then, and thought very highly of that scene, including Minor Threat. On the day of the gig, however, almost nobody showed up. I remember being absolutely crushed, depressed as hell. After the gig, we got to talking to one of the few who had attended, and he told us the local scene had deliberately not come because a bunch of shit had been flung about over us being a band from New York. He went on to say that Ian McKaye from Minor Threat had said 'Oh they're from New York? They're all probably smoking crack'. It was a really shitty thing to do to us, and to The Stupids, who had come all the way from England. From that point on I couldn't listen to any of Ian's music, but it didn't ruin my impression of any of the other DC bands. There was a strange dynamic like that in several areas, their local scenes, that was hostile towards bands from other states, or bands that didn't play a certain type of music, which we thankfully didn't encounter too often. New York had some of that, too, which I'll speak more about shortly.

(Ludichrist with Mental Abuse, Sick of it All, Stillborn and Rest In Pieces at Right Track Inn. 05/07/1986)

(Ludichrist with The Stupids at The V.F.W., Kansas City, MO. 06/01/1987)

We definitely had a few out of state shows where the crowds just sort of stood there and watched, which we were not used to. They didn't boo or walk out, anything like that, but they were quiet and passive. New York and our general luck had spoiled us. We were looking for crowd energy, for moving and slamming bodies, and I think we saw it as a failure when we didn't get that reaction. In fairness, I think in some cases that's just what that local scene was like, where people just listened intently. I remember that at one of those gigs, between songs, Tommy asked the crowd, in frustration, 'Are we really that bad?'. Looking back, I think it was just that we were spoiled by the energy we got from crowds early in our gigging history, at places like The Anthrax, and didn't know what to make of a quieter crowd focused on taking in the music.

Honestly, we weren't a very dynamic stage band to watch. We were no Bad Brains, that's for sure. The bass and guitars didn't move much as they were so focused on playing, and while Tommy was a terrific frontman, part of his persona was to be fairly subdued onstage, as opposed to many other bands where the vocalists were very acrobatic or so physical it verged on self-destruction. Tommy wasn't like that, and it fit. He didn't so much work the crowd as he did joke with them. It wouldn't do for the illegitimate Son of God to be flailing about like a madman. So, I think it felt particularly awkward to us if we didn't get energy from the crowd in response, and to be able to feed on it. When we did get that explosive energy, there was no better feeling than to be onstage, playing the best set we could. It made all the work and rehearsing, the thankless traveling, the sweat and frustrations, the expense of equipment and the rehearsal spaces - all that stuff, the starving artist lifestyle in general, all worth it".

Ludichrist after the release of *Powertrip* played in Europe for the first time, in Holland, Germany, Denmark, Austria, Italy, Switzerland and Belgium alongside Erosion, and in some cases with SNFU, and M.D.C. On their 1989 tour they played in the US and Canada too, and in early 1990 they recorded their third album. However, the In-Effect records didn't like the band name's religious connotations, so it was changed to Scatterbrain. Under this name they released two full-length albums (and several EPs) up until 1995. Even if I own and like both *Here Comes Trouble* LP and *Scamboogery* LP, these were by far inferior to the Ludichrist material; Scatterbrain went for a thrash metal-funk hybrid that was good, but not brilliant.

Recalling a memorable story from the Ludichrist days that still sticks with him after all these years, Al remembers that "truthfully, I wasn't all that focused on the music scene in New York at that time. I was listening to bands from all over the US and the world, aided by a bunch of compilation records. I would mostly pay attention to those bands who supplied the tracks I liked most. Other than the Nihilistics and a few others, including the bands we'd eventually play gigs with, I wasn't really following bands like the Cro-Mags and Kraut etc. So, I don't really have a good sense or overview of the New York scene in particular. I think I knew more about the bands happening in California, and in Boston and DC. It was a much wider scene for me, back then. I didn't have any particular preference for hometown bands. That being said, the New York scene was quite good to Ludichrist, and I had some incredibly fun times going to see bands at New York venues, but the memories of them are now a bit of a blur, sort of all run together. I know I had a good time, but details escape me.

I'm not sure if others you have interviewed mentioned this about the punk and hardcore scene in the US in the eighties, but there was this weird 'Locals Only' attitude that cropped up in certain areas - an irrational hostility toward bands from certain states, or bands that didn't play a particular style of music. I absolutely hated it, as to me that was the idiotic, tribal, hometown sports team mentality that should have no place in a punk scene, the realm of the 'jocks' who I thought of as being our polar opposites. It was sometimes a thing in New York City, too. I remember going to see Hüsker Dü and Articles of Faith, an amazing show, and there being barely anyone there, despite both bands being well known and the gig being well advertised. The New York City scene also had its boneheaded, close-minded crowds as well. I saw the Dead Kennedys play with the Meat Puppets (at the Rock Hotel, I believe) and the crowd booed the Meat Puppets off the stage after only a few songs, because they had moved in to their later style and weren't playing the type of music on their first two releases, and because the bassist was wearing a tie-dye style T-shirt with the word 'peace' or 'love' written on it, possibly both. The crowd chanted 'Woodstock shit!' at them and a divider came down, ending their set as they flipped off the crowd. I also remember some people in the crowd being mad that Jello Biafra was being 'too preachy' and complaining about his onstage theatrics. I could only shake my head in disgust at these dolts. So, among all the unforgettably wild and inspiring shows, there were also experiences I had that made me embarrassed as to how the New York City crowds could behave. I developed a lifelong dislike for the whole aggro-tough guy thing, the guys who stood around scowling with their arms folded, intimidating people, starting fights and acting like thugs. To me, the punk scene overall had wonderful communities, but also a number of unfortunate cliques, including straight edge, which I found both silly and tiresome. Individuality was what I thought punk was all about. If there was a uniform or a set of rules required to be in a club, who wants to be a member? Fuck that".

Since 2012 Ludichrist are back, performing shows from time to time, with the current lineup being comprised of Tommy Christ (vocals), Guy Brogna (bass), Paul Niederauer (guitar), Dave Miranda (drums) and Pete Testa (guitar). Post-Ludichrist Al played in The Spunks and Big Sniff, both punk rock, and in MDC of course.

"I think a legacy is probably something best decided by others, rather than anyone who was potentially part of it" Al concludes, regarding his thoughts on the legacy of Ludichrist. "I do think we were one of the first bands to incorporate a flat-out rap section in an otherwise hardcore song, but that was all due to Chuck Valle being a fan of that music (I wasn't). I think we managed to get in more musical diversity than was typical for that time in general, but other than that I can really only speak about what Ludichrist meant for me, and to some others I met later in life. For example, having been in Ludichrist helped me get in to audition for MDC. As a result, I got to play with them for two years, which was a dream come true, considering how much they meant to me in my early hardcore days. There have been many times over the years were mentioning that Ludichrist was my band gave me considerable clout, led to friendships or at least resulted in a warm welcome or a shocked 'No Way!' reaction. Even when touring with The Spunks in Japan, decades later, I was invited to spend an evening at the home of the lead singer for a highly respected OG Japanese punk band, based purely on Ludichrist, and I had an absolute blast. Being made to feel that welcome when you are so far from home is a pretty great experience to have.

While doing some digging into the past, through old boxes of band stuff, and double-checking things like dates etc to prepare to answer your questions, I discovered that pretty much everything we ever recorded, including our demos, has been released by different labels and distributors over the past decade or so. Even the *CBGB's Off the Board* record is on iTunes. I had no idea any of this was the case until now. To learn that there was still sufficient interest to warrant that is something everyone who was a part of Ludichrist can be proud of, I think. Can't really ask for more than that, especially now that there is so much music readily available for people to find online, and musical tastes have changed so much. I'm glad that Ludichrist is remembered at all. I want to thank everyone out there who made that happen, and you too, Alexandros, for caring enough to contact me all these years later".

You know what to do; grab *Immaculate Deception* at any cost. I wholeheartedly recommend the God Is Everywhere - *Demos 1985 / Live At CBGB's 1986* double LP collection that was released on FOAD Records in 2014 but seems to be a rarity nowadays (a re-issue maybe?). Fans of more 'progressive' style will definitely enjoy *Powertrip* too. A one-of-a-kind band!

N.Y.C. MAYHEM

(N.Y.C. Mayhem band picture. Courtesy unknown)

One of the craziest, absolutely extreme crossover bands, was born in Long Island, New York in 1984. Initially as a thrash metal combo on their 1985 *Mayhemic Destruction* demo, N.Y.C. Mayhem went on to crossover with hardcore on the 1985 demo *Violence*, that went for an explosive musical blend, with blast beats heard on 'Necropolis-City Of The Dead', 'Ripped To Shreds', ultracore frenzy on 'Adrenalin' and 'Taken By Storm', or short blasts of energy with 'Body Bags', you can imagine why bands like Napalm Death referred to them as an influence.

N.Y.C. Mayhem formed with Tommy Carroll on drums and vocals, Gordon Ancis on guitars, and Tony Marc on bass, who was replaced in 1985 by Craig Setari. In 1986 the changed name to Straight Ahead, following a more hardcore style that was equally great too! Plus, members of N.Y.C. Mayhem went on to play and many wide known bands later on: Tommy Carroll played in Corrupt and Youth Of Today, Gordon Ancis played in Zero Hour, Leeway and Agnostic Front, and Craig Setari plays in Sick Of It All, while having also played in Rest in Pieces, Cro-Mags, Agnostic Front, Axe Attack, Bloodclot!, Crab Society, Creep Division, Cro-Mags JM, Smegma, Straight Ahead and Youth Of Today.

(N.Y.C. Mayhem with The Psychos, Token Entry and The Num Skulls at CBGB's. 06/10/1985)

I found Thomas Carroll and he was super-kind enough to answer my questions regarding N.Y.C. Mayhem. Fact is that not many people nowadays refer to their name as one of the most extreme bands of 1980s, and for justice done, there needed to be a piece on them in this book!

Q: In the mid-1980s, N.Y.C. Mayhem were among the first (if not THE first) in New York to push hardcore into a more metal direction. How did this crossover shift happen within the band - was it a natural progression, or a conscious decision to mix punk and thrash metal?

Thomas: It was the opposite. We were a thrash metal band going into a hardcore direction. I guess it was a natural direction. It seemed to be something we wanted to project. A more opened style of music and not locked into a particular style.

Q: At that time, much of the NYHC scene wasn't very receptive to 'metal' sounds. How was N.Y.C. Mayhem received by the NYHC scene, and your heavier crossover style?

Thomas: Well, we came with our own group of kids. And the people who were still around in the hardcore, especially the ones in bands seemed to be growing musically and opened to a change. You have to be open-minded to grow in anything you do.

Q: Looking back, which hardcore and metal bands (US or international) were your favourites or influenced you most during the early days?

Thomas: Black Sabbath, Iron Maiden, Metallica, Motörhead, Slayer, Venom, Agnostic Front, Bad Brains, Cro-Mags, Minor Threat, D.R.I. So many that the list may not end.

(N.Y.C. Mayhem with Agnostic Front and Mental Abuse at The Showplace. 02/08/1985)

Q: N.Y.C. Mayhem are often credited in retrospect as pioneers who were ahead of their time. Do you feel you've received recognition in later years for the revolutionary role the band played in shaping crossover?

Thomas: Never thought about that. Just played and loved playing what we were playing. Glad to be a part of that music scene at the time. It was a lot of fun. I'm glad people still remember it and when people message me like yourself. It makes me feel good about what we did all those years ago.

Q: From your perspective today, what do you see as the lasting legacy of N.Y.C. Mayhem within both NYHC and the wider crossover-thrash movement?

Thomas: Well, I view N.Y.C. Mayhem as a start to what was to become Straight Ahead, Rest In Pieces and Sick Of It All. A small group of kids who happened to find each other and create music that stood the test of time and had a great time doing it!

Do yourself a favour and purchase Radio Raheem's 2014 *For Real!* LP compilation, because it includes all the stuff that N.Y.C. Mayhem recorded and released. And don't forget, there's only two true Mayhem(s); N.Y.C. Mayhem and Portland's Mayhem, ha!

LEEWAY

(Leeway band photo. Courtesy unknown)

Drummer Tony Fontao offered a small interview regarding his entrance in Leeway in 1987. The Leeway sub-chapter is dedicated to the late Mike Gibbons, an incredible human being, that I was about to meet in NYC two years ago, but he was already sick and Eddie Sutton; both no longer with us.

"Well back in 1987 I had a friend who knew Gordon (Ancis), and I found from him that Leeway was looking for a drummer to replace Mackie, so we set a date and Gordon took me to the rehearsal to meet the other guys there; if I am not wrong Eddie gave me a cassette tape with the live songs for me to learn in a week, and I did. After that we got together in the studio and after the first rehearsal I joined Leeway a few months later. Gordon was replaced by Mike Gibbons our dear brother who recently passed away and started gigging all around New York State. At the same year we sign with Profile Records, and they took us to Rhode Island in a small town called Warren (not sure) with Tom Soares being the sound engineer. There we recorded the classic album *Born to Expire*. I believe took us a week or so to do it, but then we had problems with the band's management and took us two years to release the album (in 1989). After that I had personal problems that separated me with the band, I guess my last gig was at CBGB's. I still have good memories about those early days. With the guys we were more than a band - we were friends, and I'm sure no Leeway album reached even close to *Born to Expire*. That was a quick review of my time as a part of the original Leeway lineup".

(Leeway with Murphy's Law, Gilligan's Revenge, Major Conflict and Sacrilege at The Coventry Club. 16/11/1984)

Tony regarding *Born to Expire* adds that "in my opinion is a great album with great songs in it, I gave my best to record those songs at the time, I remember killing each track in no more than two takes, that was very tiring, but very pleasant. If you hear closely the drum tracks of the album you feel the precision of the double bass tracks matching up perfectly with those two guitars and the bass, we were unbelievably tight. Another thing Mike and Zowie used to joke around with me and call me 'Bonzo' because of my aggressive a tight way play of drums. If you watch in YouTube *Leeway live CBGB's 88* you see Eddie introducing the band and joke with me, call me John Bonham lol..."

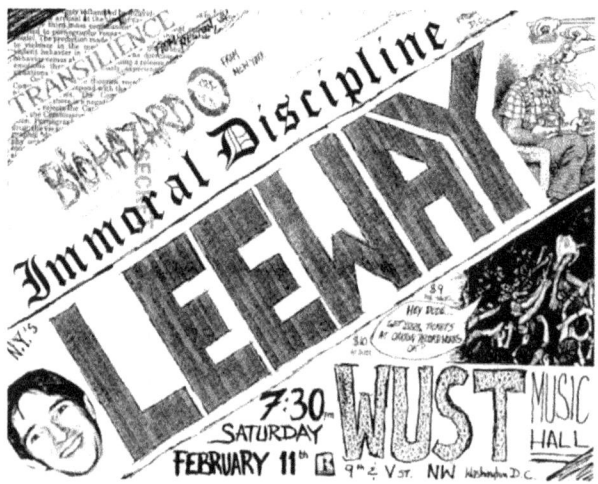

(Leeway with Immoral Discipline and Biohazard at WUST Hall, Washington, DC. 11/02/1989)

(Mike Gibbons, RIP. Photo courtesy of Ed Esposito)

Adding, Tony mentions that "back in the early days the band were very influenced both by hardcore, as well as metal. AJ and Eddie were into hardcore, while Zowie, Mike and I were more into metal, 1970s rock and progressive, all that were mixed together in *Born To Expire*. As aforementioned, I was and still very influenced by Bonzo, you can clear hear that in the drum tracks of *Born To Expire*. And as for the bands that I loved and influenced me, these must have been (and still are!) Led Zeppelin, Genesis, Rush and Cream".

(Leeway with Slapshot and Only Living Witness at The Channel, Boston. 29/09/1991)

(Leeway with Bad Brains, SFA, In Your Face and Situated Chaos at the Sundance. 22/04/1989)

Leeway were hands-down one of the best crossover bands ever. *Born To Expire* LP (1989) and *Desperate Measures* LP (1991) are just mandatory for everyone, either in hardcore or thrash. I also love their first demo *Enforcer* (1985) re-released on LP on Generation Records, because it sounds so raw and out of control. But I also have a special place in my heart for *Adult Crash* LP (1994) and *Open Mouth Kiss* LP (1995) for the more experimental route that they took. There's also a great live LP on Generation Records named as *Live At CBGB March 22, 1987*, but if I was to pick one record for a starter, right now, this would have been *Desperate Measures.* This record has helped me so much through difficult times, and its gloomy style is just very rare to find it in most crossover records. Check also the Leeway documentary - I also participate in the extras! Leeway will be sorely missed.

GANG GREEN

(Gang Green band picture, 1986. Courtesy unknown)

As you already know from *Crossover The Edge*, Gang Green are one of my all-time favourite bands, both in hardcore as well as in crossover. Chuck Stilphen (guitar), alongside with his brother Glen Stilphen (bass) and Walter Gustafson (drums), were the members that Chris Doherty (guitar/vocals) gathered in the first re-formation in 1983 of Gang Green, and that headed from the ultra-frantic hardcore of 1980 to 1983 to the rock-metal crossover of *Skate To Hell* 7-inch (1985), *P.M.R.C. Sucks* 12-inch (1985) and the major classic of *Another Wasted Night* LP (1986).

Chuck Stilphen had already been a member of The Freeze, the classic Boston hardcore band as well as Smegma And The Nunz. While post-Gang Green, Chuck formed Mallet-Head with his brother Glen and Walter Gustafson, pursuing a more metal-hard rock style. Mallet-Head released two records in the mid to late 1980s. Glen and Chuck were also members in Scratch, a metal-alternative hard rock combo in the early 1990s. I wanted to have a small chat with Chuck regarding his background, and how things evolved in Gang Green, with some answers including surprises. Here we go!

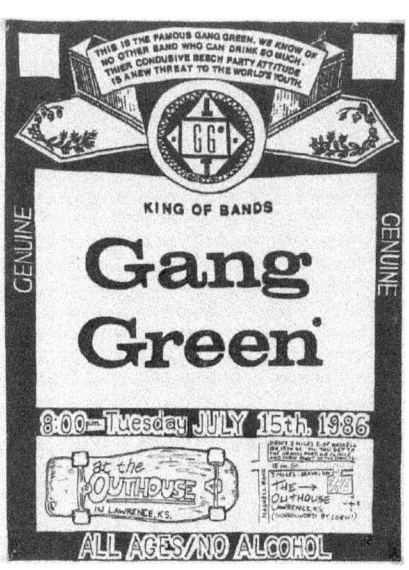

(Gang Green gig flyer for a show at the Outhouse, KS. 15/07/1986)

Q: You came into hardcore punk at a time when it was total underground. Can you tell us about your earliest punk influences and how they shaped your approach to guitar playing?

GS: I was mainly (oddly) just into Pink Floyd in the late 1970s, then *Heaven and Hell* by Black Sabbath came out and changed everything for me. I guess my early punk influences were the usual suspects, Minor Threat, [Sex] Pistols, Bad Brains, DK's. Bands with standout guitar players.

Q: If you had to pick the three punk records and the three metal records that had the greatest impact on you as a musician, which would they be, and what exactly did you take from each-riffs, attitude, or overall energy?

GS: Sex Pistols-*Never Mind The Bollocks*, Minor Threat- *Out Of Step*, Bad Brains -*ROAR*, Black Sabbath-*Heaven and Hell*, Motörhead- *No Sleep 'til Hammersmith* and Motley Crue- *Too Fast For Love* (it's so fucking stripped down!).

Q: Gang Green-*Another Wasted Night*; that album is often seen as a turning point in American hardcore: fast, aggressive, but with clear crossover tendencies. From your perspective, what pushed Gang Green in that heavier, more metal direction while still staying rooted in punk?

(Gang Green with Blank Shots and Militant Neighbors at The I.P. Lounge, Columbus, OH. 12/08/1985)

GS: Gang Green prior to *Another Wasted Night* had just Chris playing guitar, I tend to play heavier and I have to credit myself with the direction that was going in.

Q: Was the shift toward a more crossover style something you consciously discussed as a band influenced by what was happening in the scene around you, or did it evolve naturally out of the music you were writing and the records you were listening to?

GS: There was never a plan to go in any particular direction, it just happened as songs were written. With Chris writing the majority of the songs, he was going in some other direction that continued after I left the band.

Q: You also played with Mallet-Head, Scratch, The Freeze, and Smegma And The Nunz. How did your experiences in those projects differ from Gang Green, and did they allow you to explore different balances of punk and metal in your guitar work?

GS: Smegma was my first band experience, great fun but no releases till years later. Playing with The Freeze was fun for a few months, great songs but not mine. Also, my first US touring experience. Mallet-Head and Scratch were definitely more rock than punk, again good songs and good fun but couldn't make any traction. The last band I ever played out with was Bitter. I really liked playing them, great songs but I moved out of Boston after just one show.

Q: With the benefit of hindsight, how do you view *Another Wasted Night* today? Do you see it as primarily a punk record with metal creeping in, or as one of the early true crossover statements that helped bridge those two worlds?

GS: *Another Wasted Night* was mixed by different people in different studios. Some of the production I just can't listen to. The two songs from the 7-inch, *Skate To Hell* and *Alcohol* are by far the best songs and honest production. That should have been the direction and sound Gang Green went toward as far as bridging the punk metal worlds. Oh well.

(Gang Green with Dayglo Abortions and Problem Children at The Bridge. 09/07/1986)

Having a slight interest in crossover? Do you love hard-rocking, party hardcore punk ? Gang Green are your band! Get everything you can off them, but in terms of crossover *Another Wasted Night* LP (1986), *You Got It* LP (1987) and *Older...Budweiser* LP (1989) will blow your mind! I have a soft spot for all their records, all their phases, because every time a Gang Green record plays on my turntable, magic happens: I'm eighteen again!

MANIMALS

(Manimals band picture, 1983. Courtesy unknown)

I consider Manimals as a band that should have achieved a way bigger career, and that should have gained much more popularity. The phenomenal combo from Cleveland, Ohio, formed in 1982 and remain active today in 2026, were the first that incorporated the horror element in crossover. An element evident in punk with bands like Misfits, The Undead and Mourning Noise and in metal-rock such as Alice Cooper, Mercyful Fate, but not in crossover. And in music terms, Manimals had a very special approach too. So, before discussing and reviewing their discography, a small chat (again) with Larry Cahill, aka Larry the Wolf (vocalist and bassist) follows. Larry is the only founding member of the Manimals that keeps the legacy of the band alive.

Q: Manimals were the first theatrical punk-metal crossover band, incorporating horror rock attributes into their image, visuals, lyrics and sound. Can you please further expand on that - why you chose it, who were you influenced by, how the local scene reacted to this?

(Manimals Larry Cahill onstage. Courtesy unknown)

Larry: Growing up, I played sports in school – no music. I collected comic books and anything to do with the Universal monsters: Frankenstein, the Wolfman, etc. My father and uncles were all athletes and had served in the military – no musicians among them. However, one uncle loved music and played Elvis Presley for me, who remains my all-time favourite artist. When I was very young, I saw Paul Revere & the Raiders playing garage rock on TV and noticed that they wore unusual revolutionary soldier uniforms, while most other bands were wearing trendy 'mod' or hippy outfits. The bass player and guitarist did synchronized moves, sometimes while standing on top of their amps. They looked and sounded different from everyone else, and I really liked it. At age of ten, I moved to Ohio when the original Alice Cooper band was about to explode. Aside from the radio hits 'Schools Out' and 'I'm Eighteen', they had darker tracks like 'Billion Dollar Babies' and 'The Ballad of Dwight Frye' which appealed to me. Plus, I saw pictures of their wild stage show with the electrocution, the guillotine, etc. I was young, with no thought of ever playing music myself. Everything started to change when I saw the *KISS Alive* and *Destroyer* records in 1975/76. It's like they had thrown rock & roll, comic books, and horror movies into a blender. I saw KISS on the *Spirit of '76* tour – my first concert - and it was life changing. I bought a used Gibson EB-3 bass and taught myself how to play by dropping and lifting the needle on *Alive* repeatedly, to learn Gene Simmons' bass lines. The music wasn't complicated, and I thought that maybe someday, I could do something like this.

Q: Do you recall any other bands from either punk or metal having a similar approach then?

Larry: After KISS, the early Plasmatics influenced me a lot, as did The Cramps. I saw both bands perform in 1981 and 82 and each of them were very unique. The Cramps blended horror movie themes with dark music, but they didn't do any kind of staging. The Plasmatics had a wild stage show – smashing TVs, blowing up cars, chainsaw, bombs – but the music was secondary to the gimmicks. I consider them to be among the very first crossover bands because the rhythm section was tight like a metal band, but the vocals by Wendy O. Williams were much closer to hardcore.

The Cramps were campy, the Plasmatics were gimmicky, and KISS had stopped being dangerous. Early Iron Maiden played metal with some horror themes, while Misfits played hardcore with horror themes. It seemed like there was a need for a band to merge metal with punk, add classic horror themes, add flash pots staging, and play it very seriously. I liked to draw and had sketched several pages of a proposed comic book around a character called 'MANIMAL'. He was a combination of Wolverine and Dirty Harry, with a name based loosely on the 1932 movie adaptation of H.G. Wells book 'The Island of Dr. Moreau'. The idea hit me to turn that character into a band.

Our earliest shows (1982-83) were with punk bands. The audience didn't really understand what we were doing, and my bandmates did not want to wear the half-man/ half-beast outfits or makeup. To finish our set, we would play a KISS cover – usually 'C'mon and Love Me' or 'Strutter' - and blow-up flash pots with confetti bombs. The kids would go nuts! We kept doing this and more metal kids started showing up. I knew that we could draw fans from metal as well as punk, who just wanted to see something wild and didn't care about labels. In 1984 we shifted to playing predominantly heavy metal shows but continued to draw punk fans as well. We made an impact on other bands in both scenes as the punk bands started adding longer songs with leads, while the metal bands started playing faster. One thing that separated us from other bands who had an image or who had horror themes is that we were serious. We sang about classic monster themes and not campy, B-movie horror. We took the music and beast-metal personas seriously, like early KISS and Alice Cooper.

(Manimals with Fate Unknown, Suburban Blight and Wrong Verdict at the Clubhouse. 12/02/1983)

Q: I know that you played with Misfits in some cases – tell us a bit more about their reaction towards Manimals!

Larry: Manimals played just one show with the original Misfits. It was 1 September 1983 in Toledo, Ohio, with the Necros added later. In a 1982 issue of the magazine *Forced Exposure* Glenn Danzig mentions their upcoming Misfits tour and a band called Manimals who '…play a KISS cover and blow shit up onstage'.

My drummer and I went up to see them play Dearborn that Friday and met Jerry. He was very friendly, gave me an envelope full of promo stuff and said that they were excited to play the show on Sunday. They were heading out to play Chicago on Saturday and then circling back to play Toledo on Sunday. We mentioned that we were going to see KISS on the *Creatures of the Night* tour on Saturday, and he said that they were big KISS fans. At that time, KISS cast a very big shadow and influenced virtually all bands. In fact, some hardcore fans used to refer to the Misfits as the 'KISSfits' because they wore stage costumes. The night of the Toledo show, I remember the Misfits standing off to my side of the stage watching. I was playing an 8-string Kramer bass with an aluminium neck. The drop ceiling was too low for me and in the very first song, I swung my bass up and bent the metal ceiling frame above me. I played out of tune for the entire set. We blew off extra powerful bombs early in the show and I was standing too close when they exploded. I had trouble hearing anything for several days. I remember Glenn watching very intently with no expression, but Jerry and Robo had big smiles, encouraging us to keep it going. Doyle was cool and offered to help me move some amps that night, saying that he wished he could have gone to the KISS show that we attended the night before. The Misfits and Necros had toured together and had a lot of stage experience. We did not. I knew that we weren't very good, that our outfits were lacking, and the music needed to improve. Nonetheless, we always made an impression. About eighteen months later, I played with Glenn again on the first night of Samhain's 1984 *Season of the Dead* tour. By that time, I had replaced my guitarist and drummer with two guys who were from a metal background and who agreed to my vision of makeup, costumes and stage effects. I had written longer, better songs and our look was dialled in. I remember Glenn saying something along the lines of us looking much better. I recall that they had someone with them who sat the door. A guy named Joe who may have been a cousin – who said afterward that we sounded like what Glenn was trying to head towards a more metal sound.

Many years later, when Jerry reformed the Misfits, we talked about me possibly being the new singer and I made a guest appearance with them in 1997. However, no one can replace Glenn. He is a great singer-songwriter and the only person who should be singing those songs. They had an influence on me when I first saw them in January 1983, but I'm certain that Manimals had an influence on them when they came back as a crossover band in 1996.

Manimals never achieved the success that we hoped for. Some have told me that our timing was off. We were one of the very first crossover bands but needed to follow up the *Blood Is The Harvest* EP with more releases and more shows. This was supposed to be my creative outlet, and I didn't like having to handle the business side of it. In 1999 I reformed the band, brought in a new guitarist, wrote new songs and designed new staging for the *Horrorcore* album. We started to build momentum again, but other band members were having medical issues that derailed us.

My friend Tanner Rawleigh, an artist who is currently working on packaging for a 40th Anniversary *Blood Is The Harvest* vinyl reissue, told me that this is how he describes Manimals to people who are unfamiliar with us: 'The Manimals are your favourite band's, favourite band'. It's a very generous compliment, but I'm sure that there's some truth to it.

Manimals' first appearance on a record was on the 1983 *We Got Power (Party or Go Home)* Mystic Records compilation, with their 'Things Under My Bed'; a one-minute blast, sounding like a deranged Cramps! Their first release was on their own label House Of Pain Records, and *Blood Is The Harvest* 12-inch EP (1985) is one of the greatest records ever to come out from the 1980s 'crossover' scene. It's a definite blend of punk with metal, but not in the speedcore way. This is tuneful, catchy, sing-along metalpunk with elements of Misfits, Plasmatics and Alice Cooper. Songs like 'Blood Is The Harvest' and 'White Zombie' (guess that the eponymous band took their name after this tune?) or 'Island Of Lost Souls' will stick in your mind for years!

After a long hiatus from 1990 to 1998, Manimals came back with a 1998 demo, and the excellent *Horrorcore* CD (1999), then another huge break in 2012 to 2024. They are back for good, with a new single out, the 2024 'I Hate Me', that has a total Motörhead-meets-horrorcore style! *Get their Studies in Scarlet* (1982-2018) compilation CD, you're going to love it.

CRYPTIC SLAUGHTER

(Cryptic Slaughter band picture 1986. Courtesy unknown)

Cryptic Slaughter formed in Santa Monica, California in 1984. They were one of my favourite crossover bands while I was growing up. Their lightning-fast speedcore power was what it made me fall in love with them initially, especially on their first two LPs, *Convicted* (1986) and *Money Talks* (1988); I got *Convicted* off a heavy metal fan in 1998 who told me that 'I guess you will like it...I thought that it was speed metal, but it's way too chaotic and hardcore'. And he was right! *Convicted* is one of the most brutal speedcore records, it's an all-out-attack with short blazing songs like 'M.A.D.', 'Lowlife' or 'Nation Of Hate'- a true crossover classic! The sophomore *Money Talks* is more controlled, yet no less brutal (just a little bit more complex), and 'Could Be Worse', 'Money Talks', and 'American Heroes' are some of the best songs they ever written.

What always intrigued me in Cryptic Slaughter was both their visuals and covers, as well as their politically charged lyrics. They had more in common with the hardcore scene, rather with the metal one, and even though they went on to be highly influential for both scenes, their core is always rooted in hardcore.

(Cryptic Slaughter with Wehrmacht, 5150 and Righteous Pigs at The Club, Las Vegas. 20/06/1987)

Their 1988 *Stream Of Consciousness* LP was a slight disappointment initially for me, but it went to become a grower! Very lo-fi and underproduced, this is maybe their most extreme-sounding record. While the songwriting here is not as great as in their previous two efforts, you can still find gems like 'Aggravated' or 'Addiction'. Their final LP, the 1990 *Speak Your Peace* found the band with a totally different lineup, as well as a different sonic approach. I was very happy when Marco Sannino of Radiation Records asked me if I could write the liner notes for its re-release. I always thought that *Speak Your Peace* was very underrated. On this record Cryptic Slaughter headed for technical crossover-thrash metal combo, like a wild mix of late 1980s Voivod with Die Kreuzen and D.R.I. 'Deathstyles of the Poor and Lowly' and 'Still Born, Again' contain the hardcore edge, while overall this is a good - not a classic, but very enjoyable record.

Cryptic Slaughter disbanded and came back to life several of times also as Lowlife. They are currently active under the name Manifest Chaos. Les Evans, guitarist and founding member of Cryptic Slaughter alongside Scott Peterson (drums), Bill Crooks (vocals), and Rob Nicholson (bass) is just a real gentleman, and one of the kindest people to interview, and he offered me some replies to questions regarding Cryptic Slaughter. Enjoy!

Q: Cryptic Slaughter were often considered far more extreme than many of your contemporaries, pushing hardcore into almost uncharted speed and intensity. Looking back, what drove that extremity in sound, and did you feel like you were deliberately trying to outpace what was happening in punk and thrash at the time?

Les Evans: It's so funny to look back now on how everything evolved from the outset in the summer of 1984. There was no "grand plan" in the beginning. We were just kids obsessed with making fast music, and we immersed ourselves in discovering new underground bands. It was still so exciting and new back then. All we really knew was that we wanted to be a part of it.

Scott remembers a story that I don't, when I was first trying to put the Cryptic lineup together. Before I even met Scott, I asked him over the phone if he could play fast. He responded that he could. Then I asked him, "But can you play Slayer fast?". So that was our jump-off point. We were covering Slayer, Venom, Motörhead, GBH, and RKL in the early days. Scott started really practising playing faster and faster, and as his pace developed, I started writing riffs to accommodate that additional speed.

The demo was fast, but obviously we hit another gear on *Convicted*. Even after we got signed to Metal Blade (in September 1985) our sound was still evolving. It didn't really hit me at the time that we were developing something unique. It was really more about making music that got our blood pumping, but it evolved very organically.

When our producer, Bill Metoyer, played the *Convicted* rough mixes for Metal Blade president, Brian Slagel, Brian asked Bill if he had artificially sped up the tape!

Q: By the time of *Speak Your Peace* (1990), Cryptic Slaughter took a sharp turn toward a more progressive, thrash hardcore hybrid style. What inspired that shift in direction, and how do you personally view that record today compared to your earlier, rawer works?

Les Evans: Every Cryptic record sounds different to me. Even with the original lineup, we never tried to replicate what we had recorded previously or adhere to any sort of formula. After moving to Portland and putting together a completely new lineup, I had no desire to mimic the original band. Not only would that have felt disingenuous, but music was evolving, and my tastes were changing.

Brian Lehfeldt (drummer for *Speak Your Peace*, and more famously the drummer for Wehrmacht) and I were roommates at the time, and we were completely enamoured with Voivod, and their bizarre brand of sci-fi thrash. They were our primary influence at the time. It was all very experimental, too. We wanted to push into new territory. Also, bear in mind that the *Speak Your Peace* album came together incredibly quickly. I moved to Portland in May of 1989, and that record was released in June 1990. Written, recorded, and released within a year is pretty unusual.

And yes, I do like that record. I understand why many fans don't, and that's totally cool. My advice to anyone who hasn't heard it is to just pretend it's a band you've never heard of before. You might like it if you forego the inevitable comparisons.

Q: The Santa Monica and wider Southern California scene in the 1980s was incredibly fertile, with punk, hardcore, and thrash constantly intersecting. What do you remember most vividly about that scene, and how did it shape Cryptic Slaughter's sound and attitude?

Les Evans: It's important to remember there was a time when the punk and metal scenes did not mix at all, except for the occasional brawl! Crossover, however, helped to change all that, and here's how it started for me, specifically...I was wearing my Slayer *Show No Mercy* shirt at my high school in 1984, and a punk kid I didn't know at all approached me and said, "Hey, I've been wanting to check those guys out. I heard they're really radical." We started talking, and we became friendly after that. It was all about discovering that common ground. Not long afterwards, I started bringing Slayer, Venom, and Metallica records to school to let my punk friends borrow, and they brought Minor Threat, Bad Brains, and GBH records for my education. It was an entire musical universe that I didn't know existed. That's how it started for me, and I'm sure for others, too.

Additionally, I had reached a point when I realized that the lyrics in punk and hardcore aligned with my own political beliefs very closely, whereas most metal lyrics didn't hold much substance for me.

So, with both scenes starting to come together, it was incredibly freeing from a songwriting perspective. It was an exciting time, and none of it was motivated by profit. There was still no real money to be made because it was all still very underground. Everyone involved did it because we loved it, and we wanted to nurture it to make it grow.

(Cryptic Slaughter with Excel, Violent Coercion, Clown Alley and Chronic Plague at Ruthie's Inn, San Francisco, CA. 20/12/1985)

Q: Do you feel that being from Santa Monica, slightly outside of the central L.A. and Orange County hardcore hubs, gave Cryptic Slaughter a unique perspective or freedom in developing your sound?

Les Evans: I feel so lucky to have grown up in Santa Monica in the 1970s and 80s. It was such a different place then. Now it's the perfect example of how gentrification can gut the soul of a city.

There was so much talent in Southern California, but at the same time Los Angeles is so vast and spread out. That's why there were so many different local scenes within the greater LA basin. And we were totally insulated from all of it on a musical level. In that regard, we never felt like we were a part of any local scene. I think that because we felt so disconnected, it gave us a real sense of musical freedom. We weren't living up to anyone's expectations but our own, so our musical development went totally unchecked, haha!

We weren't even part of the Santa Monica/Venice scene, even though we became great friends with the Excel guys and played several gigs with them. Excel vocalist Dan Clements was a big help to us in the early days when it came to getting gigs, obtaining merch, and providing general information about how things worked, because we were totally ignorant. I'm proud that he's still a close friend today.

(Cryptic Slaughter with Excel, Stikky, Psycho, Indifference, Against The Grain and Necropolis at the Fender's. 08/11/1986)

Q: Cryptic Slaughter's influence is still heard in grindcore, powerviolence, and modern crossover. At the time, did you feel like you were laying down something new, or was it more just about playing as fast and intense as possible?

Les Evans: It definitely started out with the idea of playing as fast we could until the wheels fell off. But by the time we were getting ready to record *Convicted*, we felt like we were on to something new. Not that we were the only ones playing extremely fast. You had Siege, Wehrmacht, Repulsion (who weren't even Repulsion yet, they were still Genocide), and others who were all working towards that same goal.

I definitely wanted Cryptic to stand out, and I didn't want us to sound like anyone else. The incorporation of hardcore into our music was also a big part of that. At the time when we started recording *Convicted*, I was listening to mostly hardcore and punk, and our direction had changed pretty dramatically from the demo.

Another distinction that I believe helped to set us apart was our sense of melody. As fast and extreme as we were, my goal was to write catchy songs with great hooks and sing-along choruses. I think that has a lot to do with the staying-power of those songs as well.

It's important to remember that, especially in the beginning, Cryptic was very polarizing. There was no middle ground. People either loved us or they hated us, but those who loved us REALLY loved us. That's when we knew we were onto something. When you can illicit that kind of emotional reaction, good or bad, you know you've made an artistic statement that, if nothing else, can't be ignored.

Q: Fans always love hearing the wild stories behind the music. Do you have a crazy or unforgettable memory from Cryptic Slaughter's active years that really captures the chaos and spirit of that era?

Les Evans: It was never easy for us to find gigs. There were very few venues, and a ton of bands, so we were happy whenever we got the opportunity to play out. We scored a great gig in April of 1987, opening for Dark Angel and Possessed at Fender's Ballroom in Long Beach, which was the biggest and most consistent venue at that time. We were supposed to play second on the bill, but the band who was slated to open the show argued to the promoter that they should play second, and Cryptic should be the openers.

The promoter reached out and asked if we minded playing first. I told him we were just happy to be a part of it, and we'd play whenever they wanted us to play. For context, *Convicted* was released in July 1986, and even though it was selling well, we really had no way to know how we'd be received as the opening act for a couple of really big bands. And as most people know, many fans don't even arrive until the opener has already played. Much to our surprise, the entire place was packed when we stepped on the stage. 1,200 people! And as soon as we started playing, the place erupted! They even knew our songs! That's the first time I remember hearing the roar of a large crowd, just for us. Right after the set, I rushed back to the merch table, and I sold every one of our shirts. About eight dozen, which is not bad considering we were the opener! Also, that same night, D.R.I.'s manager (at the time), Ron Peterson, offered to manage Cryptic. I turned him down, which was probably stupid, but at the time Bill's dad was managing us.

Lastly, one my favourite memories from that night was when we were packing up our gear. Scott's mom drove out to the show in her station wagon to pick up his drums, and the legend, Gene Hoglan, from Dark Angel was helping Scott carry his drums out to her car. It's important to note that Scott's mom was very tiny, for sure less than five feet tall. And Gene was a mountain of a man. The entire time Gene was conversing with Scott's mom in the most respectful manner you can imagine, saying "Your son Scott is going to be a great drummer, Mrs. Peterson". It was exactly how you're supposed to behave around someone's mom, and he was just great. By the way, this was the same Gene Hoglan I watched throw diapers at Jeff Hanneman, while he was performing onstage, about three months earlier at a Slayer-Dark Angel show in Orange County. I said, "Gene, why are throwing diapers at Jeff". And he responded, "Because that fucker passed out on my couch last night, and he pissed all over it!".

Pick up Cryptic Slaughter's *Convicted* if you're not familiar with them; it's a real speedcore-crossover classic. If you like it, proceed to *Money Talks*, and then to all their recordings!

LETHAL AGGRESSION

(Lethal Aggression band picture. Courtesy unknown)

I still recall the day I first saw Lethal Aggression's *Life Is Hard... but That's No Excuse at All!* LP. I was sixteen years old, and I found it while I was flipping through used records in a record store in Greece. I was excited with the front cover, and when I found out that it contained twenty-one songs was enough for me to pay the price; around 3 euros/dollars/pounds back then! Hailing from Asbury Park, New Jersey (1985), Lethal Aggression were quite easily one of the most schizophrenic crossover acts, both on and off stage, as well as on their records. They were notorious for being wild party animals. They even went on a European tour with Youth Of Today who must have freaked out with the band's alcohol and drugs heavy consumption every night! Anyway, Lethal Aggression kicked off 1985 with their demo *From the Cunt of the Fucking Whore* that is rough, messy, awfully titled but absolutely crushing! 'Spooge' was always my favourite anthem, just to piss off my metalhead buddy Apostolis and 'Vodda Vodka' is one of the first blast-beat songs too! One more demo (1986) followed, as well as their inclusion in a cassette compilation named as *Piss Shit Puke & Rotting Thrash* (1986) alongside D.R.I., Mental Abuse, and Minor Threat, where Lethal Aggression covered two Slayer songs! Their first LP, the 1988 *Life Is Hard...But That's No Excuse At All!* got released by the now defunct German label Funhouse Records. As you can imagine is a crossover-speedcore classic. Songs like 'No Scene' or 'I'll Fight' will make you bounce on the walls, while 'No More Wasted Time' or 'Cuntry Pig' are absolute moshers! Loose and fun, this is just a damn brutal crossover crown! Their 1990 *Subliminal Erosion* 7-inch is even more extreme and more diverse, songs like 'Ineluctable' are just evidence of this great 7-inch. *Just Killed Rock n' Roll II* 7-inch (1991) was an absolutely lo-fi recording, still on the mental speedcore style-'Regret' is such a vicious tune! They split after that and returned in 2001, releasing one more record *Ad Nauseum* (2009) or being included in split EPs. Now with a more modern production and style, and songs as good as 'That Piece' and 'Stupidity', but I kind of miss their early frantic energy. Check also Dave Gutierrez's current band, Despairadisio, as well as Rob Hultz's The Disease Concept and Michael Sica's Solace, out of the countless bands that they have played or playing. Ah, check also the thrash metal Oblivion, good 1980s band. And now, pick up Generation Records *From The Cunt* LP re-issue (2025), *and Life Is Hard...But That's No Excuse At All!*, my favourite releases of Lethal Aggression.

(Lethal Aggression-total drugcore flyer!)

"Everyone in the band had a wide range of musical tastes besides metal and punk, John (Saltz, vocals, RIP 2016) listened to the Grateful Dead and Radiohead, Dave (Gutierrez, guitar) listened to rap and some ska, and we all were into progressive rock like Pink Floyd or Rush. Myself, I didn't listen to a ton of punk and hardcore, mostly just not to subconsciously sound like other bands in the genre. We always strived to sound a little different than what everyone else was doing at the time. Led Zeppelin, Rush were the first ones to have a big influence on my playing along with Motörhead, Black Sabbath and *Kill 'em All* by Metallica. On the punk side The Accüsed, Bad Brains, The Offenders and D.R.I. all made a big impact with me. We never said 'we want to sound like this or that band or style', we just did what we did. Looking back on it now, I guess you could say Lethal was prog/punk/thrash? From 1988 on, the arrangements got more untraditional, more parts in short songs and odd time sigs started creeping in but we never intentionally thought, 'this song needs a section in 9/4 or this part should go five times instead of four'; usually the weirdest stuff we came up with is what stuck". (Kenny Lund)

(The notorious Euro-tour with Youth Of Today)

"The very early stuff was hardcore and some punk oriented. The metal stuck its nose in. I was cool with that, I love metal from The Rods, Exciter, Mercyful Fate to Slayer. So, when side 2 of COC's *Animosity* came calling alongside of Agnostic Front's *Cause For Alarm*, I knew I found my voice. I wrote 95 percent of the songs so off we went to hardcore thrash and I never looked back. My favourite bands were Adrenalin O.D., Mental Abuse, Agnostic Front, Battalion of Saints, COC, B.G.K., Ill Repute, Exodus, Circle Jerks, MDC, shit like that….My favourite Lethal Aggression release was *Subliminal Erosion* 7" for sure. It was all new stuff, and we were partying so hard. Taking a lot of acid, smoking dust. The stuff was new ground for us. We spent a lot of time working it out and it was sorta more complex. I was so into it at that time. Close second is *Ad Nauseum*. More hardcore punk that I was into at the time and many years after *Subliminal Erosion*, the songs were a lot of fun to play and skank to, so those were good times. We did a lot of cool touring behind that with Gang Green and Discharge. We were at our top of our game after 10+ years I'm guessing. Probably more… hmm…1989 to 2001? My guess was pretty good haha!" (Dave Gutierrez, guitarist of Lethal Aggression as well as of Social Decay, T.F.N. and Oblivion)

(Lethal Aggression with D.R.I., Death Tripper and C.B.S. at Cameo Theatre, 23/05/1986)

"As for some wild stories of Lethal Aggression…Damn, how many hours do you have? Haha! A few of the early ones are detailed in the vinyl re-release booklet of the demo (a car accident jump starting the band, the first demo recording) but here's a fun one: September 27, 1985 - Lethal had been playing together for three weeks when the four of us, Saltz, Rob De Froscia, George and myself went up to the city to see Slayer, Megadeth and Bad Brains at the Ritz. Our first time going to a show together as a band. George is driving and we're all downing beers on the ride up. When we get to the city, John tells him to stop at 7th & Varick and gets out. We drive around the block a few times and then pick him back up. He copped a bunch of 10mg Valium. We get to the show and are in the bathroom, John's handing out the goods to us - I had never taken Valium before and ask John how many do you usually do? He says, 'four should get you high'", so I down four 10mg V's with a beer. A random dude in the bathroom is looking at me like wtf are you doing - should have been a hint! We go in and work our way up to the front for the show to start. Bad Brains come on, and the place goes OFF! I stagedive on the second song and fall right into a hole and go straight to my back on the floor and get knocked out. I wake up halfway through the Bad Brains set on a pinball machine that someone is playing, or so I was told. What I missed was: John diving and doing a flip and going face first into the floor busting his face open to the tune of five stitches, Rob getting clocked in the face in the pit and breaking his nose, and George dislocating his ankle when someone fell into him. So, by about five songs into the show, all four of us are fucked up (in more ways than one). We scraped ourselves back to the car somehow and John drove to the ER. He got his face stitched up, George got his ankle reset and Rob got his nose straightened out while I was passed out in the car. I woke up the next day in George's basement where we practised barely able to move wondering what happened. George hobbles down on crutches to fill me in on what went down over breakfast beers. We hadn't even played a show together yet but we both had a pretty good idea of what the future was going to hold, and we were right - it was going to be a lot of fun!" as told by Kenny Lund drummer of Lethal Aggression and Solace and visual artist for Northwinds' *Sleep With Evil*.

HOGAN'S HEROES

(Hogan's Heroes band picture. Courtesy unknown)

I've been in contact with founding member, lead guitarist of Hogan's Heroes, George Barberio and it's always a pleasure talking with him. He's a great, level-headed and kind guy. I was so bummed that his copy of *Crossover The Edge* book was stolen, but we've done better as I've asked him for an interview and George provided me audio clips with his answers.

"I don't necessarily feel who was a first band to pursue the crossover; I think that there were a bunch of bands that had a piece of metal in them, and that they leaned toward classic rock, and I don't think that the first crossover thrash happened until when people used bands like Metallica, Iron Maiden, Accept and Judas Priest mixed with hardcore punk, that would be the beginning. I believe that it takes guitar techniques, which are the main proponents, that led to the crossover between metal and hardcore punk techniques such as divebombing, whammy bar, metal solos, metal riffing, crunch distortion etc."

"In music terms, KISS showed me before anyone the power of rock chords, and the excitement of the crowd with albums *Alive!* and *Alive II*, after that Black Sabbath, Judas Priest, Metallica, Iron Maiden, alongside all my favourite hardcore scene bands such as Charged GBH, the Ramones, The Dickies, Minor Threat, Generation X, the Bad Brains, The Nip Drivers, Fear, T.S.O.L., the Misfits, Samhain, Toxic Reasons, Battalion of Saints. Then when I felt forced out of my second metal band....'because I was required to wear metal spiked wristbands and clothes I didn't usually wear. I was a metalhead-metal band playing-skateboarder and friends Matt and Scott were asking me to be in a hardcore band with them again, instead of the metal band and there was no dress code required. When I first played hardcore, it was heavier, but I was leaving all the metal attributes behind"

(George Barberio flying with his skateboard. Courtesy unknown)

George narrates regarding his influences. Playing along with metal albums and then playing along with hardcore albums made me wonder why hardcore music which is based in power and being powerful in musical expression wasn't employing this supremely more powerful guitar sound.

"And for me it was so many influences, such as Black Flag - *Everything went Black,* T.S.O.L - *Weathered Statues* and *Beneath The Shadows,* the distorted guitar of Government Issue's *Joyride,* Toxic Reasons' *Kill by Remote Control* had me wanting to make musical hardcore. Battalion of Saints' *Second Coming* wah-wah I took my wah-wah pedal out of the basement I wasn't going to use it in hardcore and Laney amplification (that no one was using); the Bad Brains, the solos on guitar that meant something, that it was OK to solo with substance. I wasn't going to play guitar solos in hardcore…not full-on metal solos. Later on, things like Boogie Down Productions, *By All Means Necessary* often mentioning about producing made me feel like when there was no other choice that if I thought about it that I could produce too. Eric B's and Rakim's *Follow The Leader* taught me a lot regarding being a competitive musician. The sleigh bells in 'Spiderbite' are because of 'Microphone Fiend'. Back also in my musical influences, it was also D.R.I. in terms of speed, and an early hardcore fave is Agnostic Front's *Victim in Pain*, a classic, seminal hardcore record that I learned about in the backseat of a friend's car a few times and needed to know who we were listening to".

(Hogan's Heroes with Uniform Choice, 7 Seconds, Justice League and Token Entry at City Gardens, NJ. No info on the date)

"Some of my favourite shows back in the early days of crossover" George smiles, "were Biohazard, Hogan's Heroes, Ludichrist and Prong, 1989 at CBGB's. Destruction, Hogan's Heroes, 7 Seconds, and Circle Jerks at the Sundance in Long Island. And a show with Hogan's Heroes, Destruction, and Death Angel, a weekend after they hosted in MTV Headbanger's Ball, which was also at the Sundance in 1990".

"Some of the great things about fans and about the band of course was that they would ask you what bands you like and if you had any live concerts to trade" George recalls, about the relationship of Hogan's Heroes with the fans. "And sometimes, you wouldn't have any show to trade, but the fans would still send you bootlegs, live shows that you never heard before-I did get a few! And all these bootleg shows, of old bands, was a great way to find out what was happening before our scene happened. Regarding though the acceptance of metal in hardcore, maybe the first motto I learned in late 1984 was that 'metal wasn't welcome in hardcore'. You could see a couple of metalheads, longhairs, at the shows getting harassed, followed…even people talking shit to them. If they didn't respond, they might have been given a free pass so to speak to participate in the enjoyment and the pit. If they responded back, they might have got punched and tossed out. In conclusion, the reaction of metal and hardcore people towards crossover (after the D.R.I.'s release of *Crossover* LP) was the same as before, for us, as Hogan's Heroes we had metal in our music prior to 1986 *Crossover* LP and we had metal solos from day one. I don't think it really became a thing until many doors were opened by others- did metal and hardcore start to creep in as the 1990s dawned and beyond as far as a noticeable effect after *Crossover* album. You would have had to have metal in your group to see more of them headbang up front, wearing a Metallica shirts or some punks and metalheads stage dive, slam and mosh in circles together in the same building and show...it all came out pretty naturally to be honest".

(Hogan's Heroes with Warzone and The Uprise. 19/08/1988)

"The first two demos of 1985, the third demo of 1986 and all the albums it's one sound for nine years 1984-1992 including the Hogan's Heroes self-titled LP are all my favourites, I gotta admit that!" George confesses. "*Built to Last* was recorded in Henry Hirsch Waterfront studios where artists such as Madonna and Slash recorded ('Justify my love'), while also other talented and famous musicians recorded tracks there too (like blues legend BB King, and Lenny Kravitz who recorded most if not all his hits there), and we were there, producing it...so there was a magic behind this record, because of that, producing it ourselves.

As for the second LP, *Hogan's Heroes*, this was recorded at Sonic Edge Studio NYC, 15th floor studios in Saatchi & Saatchi's ad firm recording facilities The engineer mentioned we had some mere minutes left on the reel. And then the label asked us to include one more song if we had one, to complete the space on the recording reel. Our vocals were late to practice almost all summer, John started playing this bass part and not knowing what else I wanted to do with I started doing my sort of what would be a Bad Brains influence on guitar we had so much material to one take, because it was written out of boredom from waiting to jam over weeks. After the album was out. I remembered no one was ever supposed to hear that instrumental to complete the reel. A pretty fun experience too!"

In terms of 'magic', I would like also to add that *Built To Last* was initially self-pressed by the band, through their label Straight-On, while it was later next year re-released on New Red Archives. Now can somebody send me a copy of the original pressing? Heh!

3 Fists & A Mouthful was produced by George Barberio at Ocean Recording studios summer 1991 in Ocean County, New Jersey. "Basically, whole reason *3 Fists* was recorded, was because in there were three of us in the group, and one member going to school over 1,000 miles away for two years and we currently had no drums. After about a year I initially suggested we record an EP so that it would afford us time we would need to start supporting it, so no one would think we broke up. During the process I started to scour recordings of us for a few unfinished ideas and find stuff plus some sections I didn't want for the Atlantic records (The Drifters/Led Zeppelin etc etc) label stuff and demos and turned it into a full album. John added to the tracks with a new song and lyrics and suggested recording The Beatles 'Something'. Skip was given a copy of the instrumental tracks and went to work writing lyrics for everything that didn't have vocals. At that time Alice Cooper and Nelson (the band) were demoing there. "It was local and a friend of mine, Jack Ponti was doing work there, with both Alice and Nelson. He was Bon Jovi's guitar player, and so much more. I met him a few years earlier, in 1988, and didn't have a clue who he was! I wanted us to record there, because I was new to driving and was falling asleep at the wheel, plus the level of artists demoing I knew I could make a good record there, and I wanted Jack to hear our music. I have seen him quite a few times in there and one time right before the record was completed, I saw him by the coffee machines and invited him in. He stood there motionless and left. Damian and I went back to mixing. The doors burst open about a half hour later! It was Vic Pepe and Jack Ponti. He liked it so much that he came back into the session told the engineer he wanted make sure I had enough money to get a good mix in case the label wanted me to wrap it up and he said 'were going to give George ten hours on the session and paid for extra ten hours and during the recording process'. He also helped the engineer co-producer Damian Kain to dial in a bass head, and so much more…it was such a fun time!".

I still don't know why Hogan's Heroes remain under the radar of fans of hardcore and crossover. It's a band that literally had everything: the hooks, the style, the attitude and even when they altered their sound, it was done with class.

There are at least a few high-quality YouTube channels keeping the legacy alive, current and accessible through the sharing of every demo, live recording available and official release, in the best quality available, with newly created masters and newly discovered masters.

George played with other groups with members from Dragpipe, Monster Magnet, and others. KISS Konvention founder Gary Danko paid and contributed for some recording sessions of his Atlantic Records demos. He is featured on front cover of the 1990 international compilation album *Hardcore Breakout USA*. In the 2010s he scrapped a video interview at the Paramount Theatre in Asbury Park, New Jersey for *Riot on the Dance Floor* documentary, but is seen briefly along with some live Hogan's Heroes' crowd and is used in at least one movie trailer used across the film festival circuit to promote the 2014 movie. In the July 2013 issue of *Guitar Player* magazine's article 'Court of Opinion' he is quoted "it's all how you turn the knobs" Los Angeles based Cleopatra Records re-released 1990s *Hogan's Heroes* on limited edition green vinyl with George on the albums cover and centre labels and along with their 1988 debut *Built To Last* on limited edition pink vinyl. He also played guitar with NucleuS, a stoner rock-hard rock combo. NucleuS was formed by bassist-vocalist-composer Carmine Vincent, who plays lead guitar on Biohazard's *Kill or Be Killed* LP. Check out their *Touch* EP and *So Far Gone Demo*, sheer power. Now, pick up some Hogan's Heroes records for your crossover musical pleasure!

OVERKILL L.A.

(Overkill L.A. band picture 1982. Courtesy unknown)

One of the very first bands that managed to blend punk with heavy metal, Overkill L.A., formed as early as 1980 in Los Angeles. The initial lineup included guitar player Kurt Markham and bass player Ron Cordy, later accompanied with Geoff Dimmick on guitar (with Kurt switching to drums), and John Joe Gurule on vocals. Soon enough though, Gurule was out of the band, and Merrill Ward was in. One amazing trivia is that Black Flag's Greg Ginn wanted Merrill to be the new vocalist of the band, but Merrill rejected his offer for Overkill! So, here goes their story according to Merrill:

"Everything happened quite organically but unexpectedly. I had known Kurt Markham, one of the most amazingly talented drummers I've ever encountered several years before I found out anything about Overkill. After turning Greg Ginn and Chuck Dukowski's offer to sing for Black Flag, before they had approached Dez Cadena to step in, Greg and Chuck seemed to be looking for a project for me to step into. They played me the original tracks recorded for the *Hell Keeps Getting Hotter* EP. When I found out that Kurt was the drummer and they were looking for a singer, I stepped up and met the rest of the band including bassist Ron Cordy and guitarist Jeff Dimmick who was fourteen years old at the time. I liked them all immediately and learned the songs, which were already in place, pretty quickly. They liked my approach and so I agreed to be their frontman. With respect to my brothers and those tracks, I referred to these songs as 'Kiddie Punk'. With songs like 'Burn the School', 'Urban Cowboy' and the title track, 'Hell Keeps Getting Hotter', I felt the songs were a bit juvenile delinquentish. But having a strong sense of humour, I recognized that I could play this angle up and it just seemed to work for our earliest shows. After several months, if memory serves, Jeff was having some issue with school, and his dad pulled him out of the band which I was really sad about and thought we were done. However, in steps Felice LeCoco, who I didn't realize had played with Ron and Kurt before and had an entire array of songs that I was completely unaware of and were really quite amazing. The only band that these songs sounded like was Motörhead. Dez Cadena had previously turned me on to the music of Hawkwind and I fell in love with Motörhead learning that this was where Ron and Kurt had gotten the name for Overkill, which was one of their songs. Felice was an amazing metal guitar player and he, Ron & Kurt sounded like they had already been playing these songs, which became the tracks for *Triumph of the Will* but none of them had lyrics or even concepts. SST wanted to release this music so I had to put the hammer down and write lyrics that would do justice to those amazing tracks that were a clear merging of the punk and metal sounds. I then had to meet the ferocity of the music with equal intensity. All this was happening as Black Flag was getting into their legal disputes with Unicorn Records and we were recording at the Unicorn studio (formerly the Beach Boys studio) and the pressure was really on me to pen those lyrics and record before the whole shit show went up in flames".

(Merrill Ward onstage. Photo courtesy of Edward Colver)

On SST Records, Overkill released their first 7-inch in 1982, named as *Hell's Getting Hotter*; produced by Spot, this is the punkiest effort of Overkill, with a slight metal influence, and I disagree with Merrill's opinion over it. It's just fast, snotty and classic L.A. punk, catchy and infectious-all its 4 songs are classics! The influence of early Black Flag is obvious and evident, with 'Our War' and 'Hell's Getting Hotter' being my favourite songs.

Overkill L.A. started in 1982 writing the songs for their first LP, *Triumph Of The Will*, that was supposed to be released the same year, but this never happened due to the legal problems that SST Records had with Unicorn Records. However, Metal Blade Records offered a slot to Overkill in the *Metal Massacre II* compilation LP with 'No Holds Barred', alongside bands like Armored Saint, Warlord, Hyksos or Savage Grace, heavy metal bands that were actually way less rough and hard than Overkill!

(Overkill L.A. gig flyer-check out the 'Balls Out Metal' tag)

Merrill narrates the story behind the recording and release of *Triumph Of The Will*: "I think I wrote all the lyrics in about week and then jumped into the studio and laid them all down in about three days, maybe less. I ad-libbed the lyrics 'No Holds Barred' and then forensically wrote the lyrics to match whatever the ad-lib sounded like after the fact. The result was *Triumph of the Will*. Again, my off-beat humour was always on display. To a degree I felt that a punk rock-heavy metal crossover band was a novel (and kind of funny) idea. Songs like 'Ladies in Leather' and 'Head On' are good example of this. Personally, I was always a big Alice Cooper and KISS fan, and many of these songs were more inspired by these artists. Each song on that album, lyrically, was an homage to some aspect of my life. We got a lot of flak for the title of the album and the SS Skull artwork, which I found hysterical, considering that I was bar mitzvah'd through a Chassidic lineage of Judaism. That song was never about fascism, it was about the exhalation of the True Will of the individual and overcoming life's many challenges and was more inspired by the religious spiritual philosophy of Thelema, generally attributed to Aleister Crowley. The only other bands I had heard in L.A. at that time which were remotely similar were Saint Vitus, also on SST, which sounded more like Black Sabbath and perhaps The Stains, also on SST which had a distinctly more punk edge but that merged into punk. Maybe Suicidal Tendencies, which came out later, but again, much more hardcore punk influenced".

Triumph Of The Will is the definite crossover record that Overkill L.A. released (on 1985); like a blend of Black Flag with Motörhead and Black Sabbath, this was crossover the pre-dated the hardcore/speedcore style, where songwriting was focused on mixing the different styles, and not following any kind of 'speed-for-speed's sake' formula. The cover artwork is hilarious and way too provocative (a Totenkopf ffs!), while in musical terms, songs like the excellent anthemic 'Victimized', 'No Holds Barred' and 'Lost Life' are among the highlights of a classic LP.

"In terms of favourite release, it would have to be *Triumph of the Will* (the album), as that was really are only full LP and likely my favourite song on that album is 'Victimized' with a close second being 'Addict'".

And the crossover didn't stop here, because Overkill were playing shows with both punk and metal bands, in an era and place that this was a big no-no.

"One cool thing to note was that we were able to easily fit into many punk bills, playing with other L.A. and O.C. outfits like Social Distortion, Circle Jerks, Fear, Bad Religion, the Adolescents and TSOL in addition to frequently playing with other SST favourites like the Minutemen, Saccharine Trust, Hüsker Dü and, of course, Black Flag" Merrill offers. "And, we were also doing metal shows with the likes of WASP, (early) Metallica, and a number of other exclusively metal bands at the Troubadour and Gazzarri's, etc., so that was pretty unique at the time as you really didn't a band playing in both of those milieus and this was prior to 'Hair Metal' taking off which came several years later with the predominance of bands like Guns n' Roses, Poison, Motley Crue, etc. Perhaps my favourite and most notorious gig with Overkill was when we opened for Spinal Tap at a benefit concert for an after-hours club I managed and worked the door at called the Zero One, Harry Shearer and Christopher Guest used to frequent the club and the owner was able to get them to agree to do a local show at the Music Machine in West L.A. and I was able to get us added as the opener. Pretty fucking fun".

(Overkill L.A. with Social Distortion, Adolescents and TSOL at The Vex. 02/08/1981)

It must be mentioned that Overkill never added the 'L.A.' in their name, this was added later by Greg Ginn when he re-released the Overkill material on SST in 1992 to differentiate them from the New Jersey Overkill, the thrash metal band. And truth is that they didn't need to add it, since they were formed earlier than the New Jersey outfit; plus, in my opinion, they were far better than the long-haired thrashers who released only one record that I really like-*Feel The Fire,* but that's a different story. Overkill L.A.'s first period ended in 1983. They came back in 2005 under the name SST Overkill and finally folded in 2007.

Post-Overkill, Felix LoCoco formed Crackhead Killer. Kurt Markham played in D.C. 3 and Twisted Roots. Merrill Ward played in SWA, Ron Cordy played in the metal band Bitch and Scott Kidd played in the glam metal Slumlord. Steve Jones also played in Stepmothers, The Poorboys and The Unforgiven.

On a final note, I read an article many years ago (that sadly I couldn't find it now), that Metallica's Lars Ulrich once saw Overkill L.A., and he went afterwards backstage to congratulate them for being such a daring band to mix punk with metal; alongside, he mentioned that 'we [Metallica] belong to a crop of bands that are willing to bring the new style in heavy metal, mixing punk in. Only a few bands right now are doing it, and Overkill from Los Angeles are one of those bands' (or something like that!).

Overkill are not just a band with historic significance, but also a great one too. They are one of the very first to mix heavy metal with punk alongside China White from Huntington Beach, if we want to add the geographic location factor too. I love both their records, however crossover afficionados, people that like Side A of Black Flag's *My War*, early Saint Vitus fans, and Motörhead freaks should get *Triumph Of The Will* LP.

SACRILEGE B.C.

(Sacrilege B.C. band picture. Courtesy unknown)

I wish more people knew Sacrilege B.C., especially from the thrash metal scene. Overstatement or not, I rate their first full-length LP, *Party With God* (1986) as high as the classic crossover releases, and higher than most of the thrash metal classics of their day. Their story though was problematic even from the beginning. They were supposed to release *Party With God* on Pushead's Pusmort Records, and Pushead decided to release the UK Sacrilege's *Behind The Realm Of Madness*, so the Berkeley band had to add the 'B.C.' to avoid any confusion!

Formed in 1984, Sacrilege enjoyed the luck of playing both in hardcore crossover as well as in thrash metal billings, with all the (then) cream of the crop: from Metal Church, Possessed, Death Angel and Death, to D.R.I., Nomeansno, Christ On Parade, G.B.H., The Boneless Ones, R.K.L. From 1984 to 1991 Sacrilege B.C. participated in amazing billings, plus they did a small UK tour in 1989. Their initial lineup included Gary Wendt (guitar), Strephon Taylor (vocals), Matt Fillmore (drums), Sean Smithson (drums) and Tim Howell (guitar). Members later have formed or appeared in bands which included: Skinlab, Neurosis, and The Ghost Next Door among many others.

In *Crossover The Edge* I interviewed Strephon Taylor (vocalist), who was more into the hardcore stuff. In this book I decided to have a chat with Gary Wendt (guitarist), another founding member of the band, who was then a metalhead, more into the metal scene.

(Day On The Farm III fest. 27/12/1986)

Q: Looking back at the 1980s, which crossover bands, both U.S. and international stood out as your personal favourites or biggest inspirations, and why?

Gary Wendt: I didn't really have any favourites. The band's big influences starting out were Exodus, Metallica and to a lesser extent, Slayer. We thrived on a steady diet of those bands at first. Then we started to get into more hardcore bands moving forward. I do think that though, being from Berkeley, the whole punk thing was ingrained in our music from the start. When I first joined Sacrilege B.C., I listened to pretty much only metal bands. During the 1980s I kind of split off and started to listen to alternative music more. I pretty much never looked back. To this day, I only listen to a handful of metal bands. None of which would be considered crossover. I did love *Dealing With It* by D.R.I. though.

Q: *Party With God* is often considered a cult-classic in crossover history. Can you walk us through the process of writing and recording the album-what was the atmosphere like in the band at that time?

Gary Wendt: Some of those songs were, straight up written from top to bottom. Some were pieced together and arranged by the band (as a whole). Recording was done in a weekend, as we didn't have much of a budget. We set up, tracked and overdubbed in two days. I'm not sure how long the mix took. I'd imagine that it took them just a couple of days to do that as well. I think there were drugs involved during the tracking. Don't know if I did any or not. Probably.

Q: How was *Party With God* received within the punk-thrash crossover community back then? Did you feel embraced more by punks, metalheads, or equally by both sides of the scene?

Gary Wendt: I thought it was received well. The line between some punks and some metalheads was so blurred, that you couldn't tell the difference actually. I would say we were embraced pretty equally by both sides though. Maybe not at first with the hardcore crowd. They came around eventually.

Q: Sacrilege B.C. had the intensity, songwriting, and energy that could have made you much bigger in the 1980s crossover explosion. In your opinion, what were the reasons the band didn't 'make it big' despite having the qualities?

Gary Wendt: Poor decision making, poor management, lack of focus and/or discipline. All the things it takes to make anything a success, we were lacking. We were super tight at the end too, and were writing, in my opinion, our best stuff. Also, some folks' hearts just weren't into it anymore. To this day, most of the surviving band members aren't in bands or even playing music at all.

Q: Looking back now, how do you see the legacy of Sacrilege B.C. in the wider crossover thrash history? Do you think younger generations of fans and bands have started to rediscover your work in recent years?

Gary Wendt: I don't really think about it much. I do get a kick out of the fact that the band still has some traction to this day though. The first album has been re-released multiple times. I think I have made more money off the band in recent years than I did the whole time we were active! But yeah, folks bring up Sacrilege B.C. to me often. As far as the youngsters, yeah, they listen to us. I get approached all the time by young bands and fans who dig the tunes (Gary Wendt, guitarist of Sacrilege B.C. as well as The Ghost Next Door, Sumerian Crown, Skinlab and Release).

(Sacrilege B.C. with Sadus and Uncalled For at the Stone, SF. 23/12/1989)

Sacrilege B.C. can boast that they have at least two classic releases; kicking off with the excellent *Sacrilege* 1985 demo, that contained four blazing speedcore anthems, unbelievably raw and powerful, like a blend between Slayer, Exodus, Attitude Adjustment and D.R.I., taking the metal cues of the former and transforming it to the sheer power of the latter! The first three songs were also re-recorded and included in *Party With God* LP, while 'Heed No Warning' is a personal favourite.

Party With God LP on Alchemy Records is a whole different story. I like to refer it as 'Slayer and Dark Angel gone crossover', and (sacrilege or not), I prefer *Party With God* over both *Reign In Blood* and *Darkness Descends*. Fast and wild as hell, a non-stop barrage of endless slamming, with thirteen songs that are damn catchy. The production by Alchemy guys Mark and Victor sounds fresh even today, and the songs shine through it. Like a whirlwind, *Party With God* just rips. Songs like 'Crucified', 'Time To Die' or 'Slaughterhouse' are eternal crossover classics.

Medusa Records offered Sacrilege a contract for one LP, and this resulted in the 1988 *Too Cool To Pray*; more relaxed and metal now. It's a good thrash crossover record, however I miss their early energy. Still, some good songs like 'Where Are We Going', 'Revenge' and 'Silence Screams', but nothing to flip over about. The same applies to their final recording, the 1990 demo that headed for a darker, more metal style, and even though songs like 'Dark Carnival' and 'No Promises' are good, well, they couldn't hold a chance against *Party With God*.

So, yes, pick *Party With God*. It has been re-released too on Southern Lord Records as a double LP, with the 1985 demo included, and get ready to fuck shit up!

IMPULSE MANSLAUGHTER

(Impulse Manslaughter band picture. Courtesy of Vin Newman)

Karl Patton's (vocalist and founding member of Impulse Manslaughter) offering and interview on *Crossover The Edge* was stunning and one of the highlights. Moreover, it was the only interview that was conducted via snail mail, so how cool was that? I kept contact with both Karl and his partner Natasha, kind and beautiful human beings too! Even though Karl's words are also included in this book, this time, with his permission, I got an interview from another super-kind person of Impulse Manslaughter, drummer (1990-1993) Daniel DuChaine.

(Impulse Manslaughter rehearsal photo 1987. Courtesy of Karl Patton)

(Daniel DuChaine, smashing it up. Courtesy unknown)

Formed in 1985 in Chicago, Illinois, Impulse Manslaughter took crossover to a different level of extremity. They combined the ultra-speed of US hardcore with UK82 punk ferocity, blending Die Kreuzen with Discharge, Wretched with Motörhead, Voivod with early D.R.I. and Cryptic Slaughter. "We were blessed that we were all into music early on, and we found out that it was defining us" Daniel offers. "For us, it was always music and finding people in your neighborhood that also shared the same interest. This quickly evolved into a love for everything from the Ramones, Motörhead, and the work ethic of Black Flag. We put all those things together and decided that this is what we wanted to do in our spare time-make music".

Accordingly, Daniel narrates regarding his musical career, starting from his first band, Speedfreaks: "So, we had the Speedfreaks from the summer of 1984 that was ultimately a garage band (we were fourteen-year old kids) and their music wasn't categorized or marginalized by any genre, with thrash or speed metal existing in a musical form, but not getting known to the public yet. We experimented in our basement, learning to play, with a shared interest of religiously reading the pages of *Maximum Rocknroll*, *Thrasher*'s PusZone and tape and zine-trading. The Speedfreaks had their little thing going, and we were fortunate enough to have things rollin', and from the backyards and basements we started playing in clubs, supporting bands".

Daniel continues the story of how he met Impulse Manslaughter: ""I met the Impulse guys-I remember reading about them in the PusZone initially. I had an interest in them, their music was traded around, and if I can recall they were on a Peel Session with Extreme Noise Terror. Speedfreaks had the chance to play a show with Impulse Manslaughter in a nearby city (and it was a fun night), and since that day I kept in contact with Karl (Patton). They were about to play a show with Poison Idea, and my friend Grant Kasten from the band Demise, the hardcore band from Germantown. Wisconsin. We went to go to that Impulse

Manslaughter show, that took place in Chicago, with Poison Idea, Impulse Manslaughter and Sloppy Seconds. Turned out that Impulse Manslaughter wouldn't be playing because they just split with their drummer. So, we scheduled a jam session in 1990, and I relocated to Chicago, joining Impulse Manslaughter, and becoming fast friends with them. We loved the same movies, the same music, same stuff!".

(Impulse Manslaughter with The Accüsed and Brotherhood at the Stars Inn, Chicago. 10/05/1989)

"That's a question I can answer differently in every single day!" Daniel smiles, regarding who does he thing that was the first band to crossover metal and punk. "So, today, I'm going to mention that you can't deny the influence of Venom. Yesterday was the anniversary of *Black Metal* LP, and I remember initially how it blew my mind. I immediately heard punk when I heard it, I was more attracted to its ramshackle approach just like the Ramones, that offered the perception that anyone can play music and have some fun with music. Also, at that time, the metal sound of Broken Bones, even though they were right off Discharge, they went to incorporate both styles. I don't know if people mention the Amebix anymore due to their strange last years and their story. However Amebix took the Killing Joke approach to a whole different level, it was a mental state of mind, provocative. So yes, Venom, Broken Bones and Amebix for today!".

Impulse Manslaughter's first 7-inch *Burn One Naked, And Nuke It* (1986) was released on their own, Freak Accident Music, and it was a devastating mix of early D.R.I. with Die Kreuzen, with some of the most maniac vocals you could ever witness. Karl Patton puts in shame all 'extreme' metal vocalists, even today! Totally frantic hardcore with only slight hints of metal e.g. on 'Nothing'. Songs like 'Sedation', 'Slithis' and 'Oatmeal' bring me in mind some of the craziest Italian hardcore bands such as early Negazione or Wretched, unbelievable stuff here!

"I recall D.R.I. galvanizing the term crossover with their eponymous LP", Daniel adds. "Suddenly there was an influx of hardcore punk audience reaching into the metal one, while the metal audience did the same towards the punk and hardcore genres. This came out necessity of wanting to explore music and play exciting music. They both found qualities in each other, so for me crossover was a natural progression. Plus, we didn't sign up to any 'title' to any of those scenes. It was just music that we liked, and we wanted to play at the time. Crossover then was all new and all exciting. Sex Pistols weren't even ten years old, and it seemed that the fuse was lit in the mid-1970s and was still going. It was the time and place that made crossover happen".

(Impulse Manslaughter and Pain at the Fotch's, Chicago. 16/09/1989)

On Chicago's Underdog Records, and on the newly formed European Nuclear Blast Records, Impulse Manslaughter went on to release their classic *He Who Laughs Last... Laughs Alone* LP in 1987. Obviously, they didn't mellow up, however some metal influence was added in their speedcore fury; fast as hell and frantic as much as you can imagine. It contains songs like 'Vomitheads', the belligerent 'Walls' or 'Pills', that sounds if Doom (the UK band) had relocated to Chicago. Head-crushing and ear-splitting stuff here, that will please the souls of all noisemongers in the crossover and hardcore.

"I was fortunate enough to have a friend that relocated from England" Daniel mentions, adding that "so, Nick got regular packages from England, containing magazines such as *NME*, *Sounds*, *Kerrang!* ... that was our passport to a lot of music. So, as you can imagine, Motörhead was huge for us. Karl Patton and I had a mutual love for Motörhead, while I'm not sure where he stood with the Ramones, but their musical ability gave us the confidence that we can play music and have fun. The work ethic of Greg Ginn (both in SST Records as well as in Black Flag) was also fundamental to me: that period of *My War* and *Slip It In*… seeing them playing in my town, bringing their own PA equipment and being so self-contained. I just saw the new version of Black Flag a few days ago and again, Greg's playing still blows my mind. Bad Brains, that made me want to try harder, to be better, the best I could be. Later in the mid-1980s it was the exploration of the California and Nardcore scenes. I also remember the Death Records lineup roster of Dr. Know, Beyond Possession, the Ugly Americans (such a unique band), and COC and their early works, that I also loved…Impulse Manslaughter were also in *Complete Death II* compilation with their song 'Pills'!".

Impulse Manslaughter went on to release their sophomore LP in 1988 on Walkthrufyre Records (a label that Screeching Weasel had a song later against for named as 'Professional Distribution'), titled *Logical End*. Now more mature, more controlled, and focussing on the great songwriting. This is another excellent record. Each and every song rips here, with my favourite ones being 'Crimson Dreams', 'Not Quite Sure' (check out the awesome, so nostalgic official videoclip on YouTube), and 'Face It'-plus it contained two covers by Motörhead ('Stone Dead Forever') and Rolling Stones ('Gimme Shelter').

"I was lucky to have seen so many shows through the years" Daniel offers. "Music is more needed now than ever. We need to have a positive political message, to inform. I remember seeing the transition of Circle Jerks, D.O.A., D.R.I., Dr Know and COC but still carrying on the strong message of awareness. Two favourite shows from back then include Dr. Know and COC. They both brought 'different vibe' to town. Punks and Metalheads - one and the same. Living in the Midwest, we didn't have the opportunity to see the Bay Area bands. Even though Karl and Impulse Manslaughter was lucky enough to play with many of them like, Christ On Parade. It was wild, since you have the East Coast and the West Coast, while Milwaukee was devoid of the hardcore and punk bands in the early years. Punk here was mostly aligned with the New Wave sound. We had Die Kreuzen here, and they took us on a rollercoaster of musical exploration, plus we had a very strong underground, even though the Milwaukee bands often didn't have longevity and poor documentation. There is a label called Unlawful Assembly that my friend Leo runs. He's always releasing interesting stuff; plus, his band Necron 9, are always pushing things forward. Leo introduced me to a band named Hologram a few years back. It was like a rebirth of Void forty years later! That said, the festival that Leo hosts every year, it contains some of the best modern punk and hardcore bands from all over".

In 1992, with Daniel added on drums, Impulse Manslaughter went on to release *Sometimes* 7-inch, that was back to their all-out extreme approach, now adding elements of crust in their speedcore. Very heavy, very rough, very political, and always great. Songs like 'Mighty Harness' are on a total new level of ferocity, and 'Sometimes' is an epic crusher.

"Every day in being in Impulse Manslaughter was an adventure" Daniel smiles, offering that "sometimes it bordered with total insanity, haha!". "I immediately recall playing a show in an automotive garage where it had quite a good turn-out, around 100 people, and there was a car there that they could…well, get out their frustrations! There wasn't a big dancing area, but they had the ability to take sledgehammers and destroy this car while we did our set. We had a rapid circular tornado of people dancing, while others were smashing the car. I wish there were cell phones at that time to capture this! It ended with the car on fire, and I believe that Wendy O would have been proud of us! However, it was always rewarding for us to go a great distance and whether it was in ABC No Rio in New York City or playing in Montreal or Corpus Christi in Texas; having people waiting for us to play, that got in touch with our music either via tape-trading of via the small network of pen pals. Sometimes though, you could drive for fourteen hours to find out that the show was a day before, or that it was cancelled! Another day that I will never forget though was when we played in NYC in 1993, when the World Trade Center got attacked".

Impulse Manslaughter's final release when they were active was the 1993 split 7-inch with the German death-grind act Provocation. In this 7-inch one of the best songs they ever released is in-I'm talking of course about 'Blanket Of Fear'. 'Givin' is another ace burst of energy, while the bombastic 'Gutterhead' almost borders with grindcore. They split shortly after this release. In 2004 the *Live At WFMU* CD was released on Beer City Records, including a live radio broadcast on WFMU, East Orange, New Jersey February 25, 1993, as well as songs from their records, and the unreleased 'Deceived'.

"There's room for everything" Daniel concludes. "I think that people see music as a mirror, they see themselves in it. It's always great to have your 'go-to' place in music, it's always there for you. However, I also want to go to musical places that I haven't been to before. So, through crossover, one can discover so much other music along the way also. I see a lot of bills that are cross-pollinated right now with hardcore punk and metal bands. My band Speedfreaks re-ignited in 2007 for what was to be one show, and that turned into two and a half years of shows. As well as doing a new recording of old material, the process now is so much faster than in the 1980s.

The sad thing today is that everything is SO fast that people cannot ingest and digest the things thoroughly they are exposed to, they're inundated. However, it's good that people are still revisiting crossover and still finding ways to approach it"".

(Impulse Manslaughter with Rights of The Accused and Samhain at the Cabaret Metro. 13/04/1986)

Impulse Manslaughter have not been active since 1993. However its members went to appear in many bands since then. Dan Duchaine played in Sreedfreaks, and in Burning Sons and Feck. Karl Patton in Alehammer Warfilth, Gutterhead and Nam Land. Chris Hanley in Nam Land and No Class. Glen Herman in Leng Ick'e and Vermicious Kuids.

John Tolczyk in Eyegouger Nam Land, The Satanic Overlords Of Rock 'n' Roll, and Vermicious Knid. Mike Schafer in Abomination. Nick Stevens in Terminal Death and Sindrome. Ted Domurat in Gear, Generation Waste, Terminal Death and Poison. Vince Vogel in Screeching Weasel, Vermicious Knid, Severed. Rob Lanam in Bottles Flying. Rick McKelvy in Dead Drunk.

Trivia: Karl Patton is the brother of Bill Patton, vocalist of Death Squad and half-brother of Bryant Patton, guitarist of Nam Land! Mike Schafer is the brother of Dan Schafer, aka Dan Vapid, guitarist of Dan Vapid And The Cheats. Dan Vapid is also in Generation Waste, Noise By Numbers, Screeching Weasel, Sludgeworth, The Methadones, The Mopes, The Queers, Riverdales and the one that offered the foreword for my next book!

Fans of the most extreme-sounding imaginable crossover, Impulse Manslaughter will become one of your favourite bands ever. All their output is totally recommended, so start with the first 7-inch (*Burn One Naked, And Nuke It*), and proceed to all their recordings.

AMAZING GRACE

Vocalist Steve Lambert offered an interview regarding Amazing Grace-something I always wanted to include in Crossover The Edge, since the band was an exceptional combo of punk-meets-metal-meets-TSOL, minus some awful lyrics. He narrates their story as such: "Amazing Grace was a combination of two bands ending and a new one rising in the wake. I had recently returned to Miami from New York City after the dissolution of the band that I was in up there (which was from Miami as well). I received a phone call from Ronnie Norton, drummer extraordinaire, that I had known from his stint in a local band. He told me that he was working with the guitarist that he knew well (Billy La Volpe), and they had several songs that they were working on. I am at the guys' rehearsal studio to take a listen. And I believe that we all felt and saw a future with this lineup. My brother Gary was brought in shortly after on bass guitar".

(Amazing Grace with Die Kreuzen and The Drills at the Cameo Theatre. 14/09/1985)

"The edges were beginning to thin making room for a musical and cultural explosion uniting both fronts" Steve regards about crossover. "There will always be the naysayers and the new directions. Perhaps you may call them purists. But of course, there are those who are welcoming to new ideas". Regarding violence at Amazing Grace shows, Steve mentions that "there was hardly ever…we didn't seem to draw any metalheads per se. Or that much of a diverse crowd. The only violence was the expected amongst those that clashed with the skinheads when someone invaded their turf i.e. the mosh pit. The diversity that did exist was probably measured in years… Plenty of young girls and guys and gals well into their thirties".

Regarding the musical influences of Amazing Grace, Steve mentions that "we were looking to find a blend somewhere between the musical sound of Killing Joke and the in-your-face power of GBH. Some years later we were greatly honoured to be able to open up for Killing Joke when they came to Miami…I would have to say that those ones were our influences, well at least for me personally. But I know that Ron was a Jon Bonham style drummer. And some people have said they hear a type of Pantera feel in guitarist Billy's arrangements. My job was basically to interpret the messages that were coming from them in a musical format".

(Amazing Grace with Belching Penguins and Gang Green at the Cameo Theater. 24/01/1987)

The stories of that era have been recorded by many people, and Steve offers his one: "The only real story might be when Suicidal Tendencies came to Miami, and we were the opening act. They came into the small backstage area trying to be very intimidating just by their very presence I presume...add threats of violence. But we were like… Bring it on! This is Miami and we are in no way intimidated by your West Coast attitude. There was a very tense standoff for a while. But both vans were able to make it through the show unscathed!".

And what about Steve's favourite places to play? "It would be Flynn's and the Cameo Theater, both on Miami Beach. As far as a club goes Flynn's wins hands-down".

Lastly, Steve smiles and says 'crossover it will always be relevant to me!"

Only one LP for Amazing Grace, the 1986 *Entities* on their own label Amazing Grace Records, and if you fancy your crossover to have a dark edge, more metal-punk than hardcore-thrash, this is your choice; just avoid 'Boat People'.

BEYOND POSSESSION

(Beyond Possession band picture, 1985. Courtesy of Phil Pobran)

One of the most unique, diverse and challenging crossover bands, Beyond Possession were included already in *Crossover The Edge*. Drummer Phil Pobran approached me and offered an extensive and excellent interview. I'd like though to apologise to Phil for forgetting continuously to send him my second book, *We Can Be The New Wind* until I finally sent it one day, so, Phil, please accept my apologies!

Initially, I asked Phil about his version of events regarding the tour with Melvins, and he narrated that "we were heading down the West Coast to do some shows by ourselves. Our plan was to have the Melvins join us in San Francisco and take them with us to about eight to ten shows once the Melvins got there. We gave them the address of where we were staying in Concord, California. We were a bit wild, when we weren't playing shows, and had been partying it up at the house in Concord. When they showed up in Concord, Buzz wasn't comfortable and said they would meet us in El Paso, Texas. We were to finish up our California shows with one in San Francisco and then drive to Fresno for our last show in California, before heading to Texas. The Melvins had left, and we headed to Fresno. Our van broke down, and we got stuck in Gustine, California. It was a small town, and we had to leave our van there because the garage had to order in parts and rebuild the motor. It was cheaper to leave the van there, rather than have it towed back to San Francisco. San Francisco was like our home base in California because we had friends that would help us with places to stay.

(Phil Pobran onstage 1986. Courtesy of Phil Pobran)

So, Bomber from RKL, drove to Gustine with their van and brought us back to San Francisco. We stayed there in San Francisco for about two weeks waiting for our van to get repaired. Meanwhile, the Melvins had already left California to go meet us in El Paso. Once we knew about our van, we told them when they contacted us where we were staying. No cell phones back then. We hooked them up with RKL because the Texas and Louisiana shows were to be with BP, RKL, and the Melvins. We just figured the Melvins and RKL could continue on together without us. Apparently, there were problems with the shows they were to play together. Then, the Melvins also had a van breakdown, although not as severe as ours. After they got that straightened out, the Melvins just went home to Washington state.

We ended up hanging out with friends in San Francisco while we waited for our van. We had played a show with Verbal Abuse, and they were our friends. So, we hung out with them and had other friends as well. At one point we were all split apart staying at different houses with different people we had met there. It was pretty crazy times as we had little money, no van, and were in a different country other than our own.

I remember buying some bread and eggs and living off French toast for about a week lol. It was a stressful time for us but luckily, we had made friends that helped us with places to stay. Once our van was fixed, and a couple of weeks had passed, the next show we could have played was in Georgia. It was too far to drive to resume the tour, and we had run out of money. Our label wouldn't help us, so we said fuck it, cancelled the rest of the tour, and made the 28-hour drive back to Calgary from San Francisco. That was the end of that tour lol. We went back to the states another time. It was after that, when we brought the Melvins up to Canada for some shows. We also played some shows in Washington state with the Melvins when we went back to the States another time.

The Melvins had no vinyl out at that time. Only a demo on cassette tape. They were great guys, and we were all very close and became very good friends. We had a lot of fun together in Canada. Just really humble guys. I would say that those are some of my fondest memories from those days back then".

(Beyond Possession and The Melvins at the Monastery, Salt Lake City. 27/05/1986)

When asked about a crazy story while in Beyond Possession, Phil offered the time when they met Metallica: "The first time we were in California, we played a show at Ruthie's Inn in Berkeley. We were opening for D.R.I., March 1985. After we were done our sound check, we noticed James Hetfield and Cliff Burton sitting at the bar, drinking beers and watching some sports on TV. So, we went up and talked to them. They were both very nice to us. That was the first time we met.

The next time was at the Skate Rock Show at the Farm in San Francisco. Pushead's band Septic Death was playing, and James Hetfield was the master of ceremony for the show, meaning he would introduce each band. So, we hung out with him. He really liked BP!

Now we get to December 1986. Metallica is doing their *Master of Puppets* tour. They are playing Max Bell Arena in Calgary, the large venue. Probably 16,000 people there. I asked the other guys in the band if they wanted to go to the concert. They all said no. I liked the *Master of Puppets* album and wanted to check them out. So, I bought a ticket and went by myself. When I got there, I went down to the stage area. You couldn't get anywhere near the band because of the security. So, I walked up to some huge security guy.

I said to him 'my name is Phil. I play drums in a band called Beyond Possession. I was wondering if you could ask James Hetfield if I can come back and visit'.

He says 'Really? Here in Calgary, you know James Hetfield?'

I said 'Yes, you should go ask him because he might get mad if he finds out I was here and you didn't tell him'. Lol. I wasn't sure what would happen.

So, he says 'OK, wait here' and walks away.

About ten minutes later, he comes back with a backstage pass. He says 'this is for after the show, but we don't have any before show passes, but you can use this and go back'.

I said 'Thanks'.

So, I was allowed back. Hung out with James for a bit and met the rest of the band (Jason Newsted was playing bass, from Flotsam and Jetsam, as Cliff had passed away in Europe earlier that year). Lars was a bit stuck up. I felt like telling him I could kick his ass on a drum set but didn't lol.

When Metallica was getting ready to play, James says 'hey Phil, you can hang out at the side of the stage. Just make sure you stay back from the curtain so people out front don't see you onstage'. So, I got to watch that show from the side of the stage when they were at their best. Just stage monitor sound. It was like being in a rehearsal with a good practice PA. It was killer. They were very tight. Great show. That was the last time I crossed paths with James".

Phil was also asked if he could recall other bands having a similar style with BP, and in terms of personal preferences, which were the crossover bands that he enjoyed the most, and the most overrated bands: "That's a very interesting question. I don't really remember hearing or seeing any bands that were similar to BP. As a Led Zeppelin song said: 'We come from the land of the ice and snow'...meaning that we were really in the middle of nowhere in the Canadian prairies. Long cold winters. Not many bands coming up. We were always behind in hearing many new releases because we were in Canada and it seemed we would get new releases months after they came out in the States. So as far as bands from that metal-hardcore vein, I don't think we really sounded like any of them. We were just lost in our own frozen tundra, hiding in a basement and putting songs together. As a drummer, I don't really pay much attention to a lot of bands that were coming out because I was too busy with the band I was in.

Once we started touring, we were lucky to play with some really cool bands.

I really liked D.R.I., COC, Tales of Terror, Dr. Know, the Melvins, Crumbsuckers, Agnostic Front, Poison Idea, Voivod, The Accüsed and a few others. I didn't care for many of the 'California punk bands'. I thought that many had similar styles and a lot of them just didn't stick out to me. Many of them just weren't intense enough for me. At the risk of sounding arrogant, I thought there were a lot of 'overrated' bands back then as it seemed like everyone was starting up a label and releasing whatever they could get their hands on.

I'm sure some found us overrated as well. That's their right.

Our whole purpose was to go onstage and play the best we could. We were always in the moment when we played. We took pride in our live show and made it our mission to try and blow away any band we played with. Not to say we did. But we tried! We had enough confidence in our live show to never be intimidated by so-called 'big bands'. You can add in that I thought the punk bands from the UK, were very overrated.

(Beyond Possession with COC and Zero Hour at Macewan Hall Ballroom, Calgary. 16/09/1987)

Alongside, Phil was asked why BP disbanded even though their LP and last demo showed that they could go even further, becoming a long-lasting crossover band. He offered that: "for me, BP was a juggernaut. For BP to continue forward, the motivation to rhythmically drive that band had to be there. We had been around as Beyond Possession from 1984-1989. During those five years, we had a great time playing shows with many really good bands. It was an amazing experience that I'll never regret…I was not a fan of the music industry itself. I loved the art of playing but hated the industry. Our experience with Metal Blade Records was not a positive one. It took its toll on us. By the time 1989 rolled around, I was losing my motivation to stay in the band. There were many outside influences that also affected the band that I'm not going to get into. We had some labels that were interested in the band but there was always some condition or issue that made it hard for us to find another label.

For me, it got to the point where I just felt my contribution to the band had run its course and it was time for me to move on. I left the band, and James Yauk, the guitarist, followed. We both moved to Vancouver and got involved with other bands.

The BP demo that was recorded, and released on the *Repossessed* CD, featured a different drummer and guitar player, so I can't speak to that, only to say that one of the songs 'Reappearing Images', I had recorded drum tracks for previously on another demo. I'm not sure why the band faded away after I left as I had moved on..."

Finally, Phil was asked about his musical influences; this question took place because his drumming style was very unique and extraordinary. "My influences were definitely 70s and early 80s rock bands. In my high school years, I tended to practise to music that had more technical drummers. As I was really getting into my drumming, I would practice any where's from three to six hours per day depending on weeknights or weekends. Probably, the most influential drummers for me would be: Stewart Copeland (The Police, first three albums), Neil Peart from Rush, John Bonham from Led Zeppelin, Ian Paice from Deep Purple. I always liked listening to, and trying to play, songs by those bands. Then around the age of 18-19, I saw DOA. Chuck Biscuits was great! Then I started getting into punk rock with a preference to bands with good drummers".

Beyond Possession's two recorded and released output, the 1985 *Tell Tale Heart* 7-inch and the 1986 *Is Beyond Possession* LP are just pioneering crossover records. While *Tell Tale Heart* is quirkier, skatecore driven and slightly metal, *Is Beyond Possession* is pure crossover. Both are excellent, not just in terms of songwriting, but also in terms of musicianship. Just check 'Vengeance', 'Life Force' or 'Final Daze'. Only a few bands can match their technical proficiency, and sometimes they even sound like if the fastest Rush song is played at 78 RPM! I'd love to see a full discography triple LP with all their demos included someday.

D.R.I. (DIRTY ROTTEN IMBECILES)

(D.R.I. band picture, 1987. Courtesy of Metal Forces)

Sadly, no longer with us, since he passed away on 31 January 2020, Josh Pappé was an incredible human being. We used to chat a lot regarding bands, and he was always friendly and kind. Josh played bass in *Crossover* and *4 Of A Kind* LPs, moving later to Gang Green. I always loved his heavyweight playing style. This was the last interview he offered, just a few days Josh before leaving this world. RIP Josh.

"Both Gang Green and D.R.I. were fun bands to play in. I'd say we were more punk at first in D.R.I., then we grew our hair and got more into metal. However, I ended up joining Gang Green after a European tour when I was in D.R.I. I had grown tired of our management ripping us off and wanted to play different music…Gang Green was more my style at that point. It was just less stressful and I'm very proud of the live album we did in 1990 in London".

(Josh Pappe. Courtesy of Alison Braun)

As for his initial influences as a musician, Josh offers that "I'd say Black flag, the whole L.A. scene, some Black Sabbath, the Rolling Stones. I grew up listening to a lot of different stuff. Then a friend played me the Ramones and I was hooked…regarding though which band I believe that was the first one to cross over, there was a band called China White from Huntington Beach California. They were doing this type of music long before we (D.R.I.) did or Slayer or any other band you can name. Great band but never get any recognition".

Regarding the uprise of crossover, Josh mentions that "it was maybe music first, then the cultures, as both became more tolerant of each other. It was all kind of a blur really. I think the metalheads did more stage diving and slam dancing, and altogether with the punks started to listen to more bands like Cro-Mags, Slayer, all that stuff that included influences from both camps…and even though I think there was some violence, but that may have depended on where the show was-there were places in the USA that were really scary anyway, and violence was all over".

"There are no stories from that era that I can out in the book without getting arrested, ahahah!" Josh laughs, adding that "Felix (Griffin, D.R.I. drummer) remembers more than I do. But I have to say this: We played a show with Slayer in L.A. and there was like five pits going at once. It was on 7 November 1986 at The Olympic Auditorium, alongside Bl'ast! and Metal Church. It was a real mayhem that day, with gangs fighting all over the place. One of my favourite shows though was when I saw the original Cro-Mags, early on. They were on fire, incredible band".

(D.R.I. with Slayer at the Salinas Community Center. 21/02/1986)

Josh says that his favourite clubs were "the Mabuhay Gardens in San Francisco. It was intimate, hot and the beer never stayed cold. CBGB's in New York was fun as well…but I would also add the Marquee Club in London, UK, just because I have so many great memories of the live record we released with Gang Green in that show, it was just pure fun to the max".

Regarding of where crossover led to today, Josh concludes our conversation mentioning that "crossover is still maybe relevant for a few bands, but it's just all rock 'n' roll to me. I mean really, the lines have been wiped out. Look at all the festival lineups. It's all mixed".

What else can you say about D.R.I. that hasn't been already written? They are the longest-standing crossover band, they still in 2026 offer crazy shows since 1982, and their records are pure gold for fans of this style. I have a very special place in my heart for their first three LPs and first two 7-inchs, so here it goes: newcomers from the metal side of things, *Crossover* 1987 LP and *4 Of A Kind* 1988 LP will blow your mind! Hardcore kids, you rarely will find something as frenzied and outrageous like *Dirty Rotten* 1983 EP and *Dealing With It!* 1985 LP. But then again, once you are into D.R.I. for good, get their whole discography. That said, the song 'The Five Year Plan' will always be my life's soundtrack. Revenge!

A.M.Q.A.

(A.M.Q.A. band picture, courtesy of Medusa Records)

A last-minute inclusion, A.M.Q.A. from Seattle, Washington always had a special place in my heart because of their good sense of humour. While other crossover bands failed miserably in this, A.M.Q.A. had their fair share of politics and humour, keeping up the coolness tradition of bands like A.O.D. Drummer/bassist Kevin Johnson narrates their story: "A.M.Q.A. hailed from the small suburb of Tacoma, Washington called Puyallup. It is nestled in the foothills of Mount Rainer. The original formation of A.M.Q.A. was a five-piece band with Corey Ladas on bass, Bob Bulgrien on drums, Dirk Bennet on guitar, Flash on guitar and Paul Kimball on vocals. This version of A.M.Q.A. was more of a raw, young punk rock style with a lot of humour in the songs. If I remember correctly, Dirk moved out of state and that configuration of the band fell apart. The second version of A.M.Q.A. was initially a three piece with Corey Ladas moving over to drums, me (Kevin Johnson) on bass and Mike Crum on guitar. The vocal duties were originally shared between me and Corey. Later, we added Corey's younger brother, Kevin Ladas, on as the main singer. This version of the band was more of a thrash metal punk crossover band. The songs changed to more serious topics. The band split up as we all graduated high school and started to either move on to college or full-time work".

Kevin continues, regarding why and how crossover happened: "For kids like me, we were loving both the metal that was happening at the time as well as the punk music. There weren't many places to play nor was the scene big enough for each one of those genres to stand on their own. So often, shows would have both metal and punk bands on the same bill. There were similar energies shared between both styles of music. Similar intensity... For me, D.R.I. and Corrosion of Conformity were the first bands I noticed that were crossing over. Then S.O.D. came out with their record that blew our minds".

"I don't think it bothered most people, whether a punk or metal head. I think the music took precedence. For the most part, both sides coexisted together fine until the scenes sort of meshed into one" Kevin adds. "At first it was just a musical crossover. But the cultures eventually melded together. At least that was the case up here in the Pacific Northwest. Punkers and metalheads both kept their look and style, but culturally speaking, the lines started blurring. Some of the old school punkers grew their hair out as an example. I don't recall much violence between punks and metalheads. There definitely was violence between the skinheads and everyone else, punk or metalhead. It seemed they attended the shows specifically to stir up violence. But in the end were extremely outnumbered.".

"Among many others" Kevin admits "the bands that influenced A.M.Q.A. were COC, Dr. Know, The Accüsed, Poison Idea, Cro-Mags, Agnostic Front, Blast, Slayer, Exodus, D.R.I., Agent Orange, G.B.H., No Means No, Dayglo Abortions, the Dehumanizers, Septic Death, Metallica, Exploited, S.N.F.U., Anthrax, Destruction, etc. The list is huge. Far too many to name here".

And what about any specific story regarding the scene in Tacoma, WA? Kevin mentions that "before there were any venues to play at, we used to have shows at the 56th and M Street house in Tacoma. The bands would play in the kitchen. Everyone would be packed in like sardines. Since there was no stage, we would stage dive off, of the couch. Those were the great times".

(A.M.Q.A. with The Dehumanizers, Danger-Mouse, Muck and Wankster Flu at Community Word. 09/05/1987)

"I believe that it played an important role in what we know as the aggressive music culture that exists today" Kevin concludes. "Many of the current metal bands would definitely lay claim to being a fan of several of the bands I mentioned earlier. In places like Indonesia, an entire scene was created when our old record label shipped all the unsold records over there which included A.M.Q.A., the Dehumanizers, Neurosis, Sacrilege BC, Poison Idea, Clown Alley and several others. This was the first anyone over there had ever heard of music like that. Take a look at Indonesia now. It has a thriving culture of aggressive music of many styes that stemmed from early crossover. And I am thankful to have been able to contribute and be a part of that scene".

It's a very difficult task to inject humour and fun into your music, without getting ridiculous. In the case of A.M.Q.A., that stands for 'Apple Maggot Quarantine Area', they managed to pull this style in a great manner! Their 1986 *Cats Are Neat* 7-inch is just amazing, pumpin' hardcore punk, fast and furious, yet on the same time funny, with songs that make me smile and make me mosh at the same time. Songs like 'Rick' or 'Stiff N Blue' and 'Cats Are Neat' are brilliant stuff! 'Cats are neat, meow meow meow meow' must be the best lyrics ever written!

(Thrashfest vol. 1 at Carpenters Hall, San Diego. 03/01/1987)

Their 1988 full-LP *Mutant Cats from Hell* is still in the hardcore punk tradition, only this time it's more pissed-off, with slight metal elements such as solos and double-bass drumming that are often heard in metal. 'Faceplant' alongside 'Red Streak and Fever' are my favourite songs. It's very enjoyable, fast hardcore with a minor metal influence.

Go get both their records if you fancy your crossover to be more hardcore punk-influenced, with a good dose of humour!

ONSLAUGHT

(Onslaught at their first gig at The Summit Youth Club, Bristol. 28/10/1983. Courtesy unknown)

I can never get enough of Onslaught. In my humble opinion, early Onslaught up to *Power From Hell* LP were one of the first and best dis-core bands that went to include those creeping metal influences into their approach, creating a wall of sound that is unbeatable in terms of power, even nowadays. Onslaught from Bristol, UK, the motherland of the craziest punk of that era, aka Disorder and Chaos U.K. were initially a total GBH-clone, as I was informed by British punks that had seen their early shows, before incorporating the Discharge influence. Vocalist (and later bassist) Paul 'Mo' Mahoney is still a 100 percent punk. Check out his YouTube channel of @UKPUNKLIVEAUDIO-uk82 with daily uploads of unbelievable rare punk stuff from 1970s and 1980s. He was more than happy to reply to some questions that were targeted in the early era of Onslaught, explaining how things transformed later.

Q: In the very early days, Onslaught were closer to a punk band than a metal act. Can you take us back to that period - what drew you into punk in the first place, and how did bands like GBH shape your earliest sound and energy? Which were the punk influences of Onslaught in the very beginning?

A: I was drawn into punk but the LPs of Sex Pistols and The Clash. My older brother played them to me, and I immediately picked up on the energy of what became punk. By the time I caught up with Onslaught in mid-1983 they already had the Discharge sound, I'm not sure any other band mattered to them at that point!

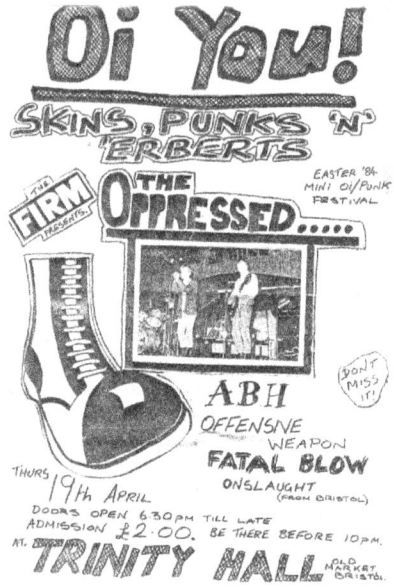

(Onslaught gig at Trinity Hall, Bristol with The Oppressed, A.B.H., Fatal Blow and Offensive Weapon. 19/04/1984)

Q: You've often mentioned Discharge as a huge influence. What was it about their style or attitude that really resonated with you and pushed Onslaught toward something heavier and more extreme?

A: The basic raw energy of Discharge was a major attraction along with basic short lyrics, it was an easy sound to copy and, to sound good doing it. Onslaught always had decent equipment from the start so even the practise sessions were loud and powerful.

Q: At some point, your sound started crossing the line from hardcore punk into a thrashier, metal-driven direction. Can you pinpoint which three metal records had the biggest impact on that transition, ultimately paving the way for *Power From Hell*?

A: Nige (Rockett, guitar) was pretty much the main songwriter and I think he was drawing influences from Motörhead, Iron Maiden, AC/DC before we heard any Metallica or Slayer, so I guess he was always going to take the band in that direction but we were still learning our instruments at that point so *Power From Hell* was the best we could do at the time.

(Onslaught gig flyer with Bloodlust, Firefox, Sic Boy Federation at The Station, Gateshead. 07/09/1985)

Q: When you first mixed punk aggression with metal riffing, did you see yourselves as part of a wider movement, or was it simply a natural evolution happening in your rehearsal room at the time? Do you remember other bands from Bristol area pursuing this style too?

A: I think just a natural progression; after *Power From Hell* was released we got heavily into Metallica, Slayer, Exciter etc which obviously influenced the playing and writing. Not sure there were any bands locally playing this style, indeed, not too sure that the UK had yet woken up to it, so by the time of our second album *The Force* we were pretty much alone as a major concern in the metal world, in the UK anyway.

Q: Looking back on *Power From Hell*, do you consider it more of a punk record with metal elements, or a true hybrid of both worlds? And how did punk fans react compared to metal fans when they first heard it?

A: It's kind of punk metal I reckon. This was before such tags as thrash or black metal were banded around. I think quite a lot of punks were turned on by the new metal sound coming in from America so we kind of turned up at the right time though I'm surprised that the album still sells well, and many older punks remember it well!

All their early demos of Onslaught, from 1983 to the 1984 *Hatred Towards The System* demo are some of my favourite stuff regarding UK82 punk; fast and furious dis-core, political and minimalistic, brutal and catchy stuff. You can find songs off these demos on *The Shadow Of Death* 2008 compilation and just enjoy the genuine power of 'Overthrow of the System' or 'The Black Horse of Famine', top-notch D-beat. Onslaught's first LP *Power From Hell* (1985) remains to this day one of the most influential punk metal albums ever; they took Discharge and GBH and mixed it with Venom and Slayer, and the result was just phenomenal-songs like 'Steel Meets Steel', 'Power From Hell' and 'Thermonuclear Devastation' make all the classic thrash metal bands blush with their sheer power. The 1986 *The Force* LP was a total turn into thrash metal, and while it's OK, I surely miss the monstrous power of the earlier releases. Onslaught keep it up today of course (2025) and have released since many LPs. But no LP can much the intensity and the influence of *Power From Hell*; nearly all the metal punk bands, from Toxic Holocaust to Midnight and from Inepsy to Tiger Junkies, everybody loves *Power From Hell*.

SACRILEGE

(Sacrilege band picture with Mitch Dickinson of Heresy and Unseen Terror. 1986, courtesy of Metal Forces)

I always wanted to offer some exposure to Andy Baker, since I consider him one of the best drummers of his time in punk and metal. Andy had a punk background, and from the 1980s up until late 2010s he played in bands Warwound, The Varukers, Sacrilege, Arbitrater, Cerebral Fix, Disgust and a very early incarnation of Cathedral. Andy played in the first two (and best) Sacrilege LPs *Behind the Realms of Madness* and *Within The Prophecy*, The Varukers' *Led To The Slaughter* 7-inch, *Another Religion Another War* 12-inch and *Massacred Millions* 12-inch (absolute classics, offering his very characteristic tempos), Cerebral Fix's *Tower Of Spite* LP and the split 7-inch with Selfless, and in Warwound's early 1980s demos. He still hasn't gained the recognition he should have as a prolific, creative, and absolutely crushing drummer. So, I got in touch with him, asking a few questions on his past, as well as about Sacrilege and Warwound.

Q: You started out in the heart of the UK punk explosion. Can you tell us about your very first punk influences? I know GBH and then Discharge were big for you. How their sound or ethos pushed you towards picking up the drums?

A: I was first influenced by early punk bands, my favourite being 999; it was Pablo Labritain who inspired me to learn to play the drums, but I have had many favourite drummers over the years including Garry Maloney (Discharge, The Varukers), Paul Ferguson (Killing Joke) and Pinch (Andrew Pinching) from English Dogs.

(Andy Baker early 1980s picture. Courtesy unknown)

Q: If you had to name the three punk records and the three metal records that had the most impact on shaping your style, energy, and direction, which would they be, and why?

A: Punk records would be first 999 album, Bad Brains-*I Against I* and Killing Joke's first album. Metal records would be Exodus-*Bonded by Blood*, Candlemass- *Epicus Doomicus Metallicus* and Nuclear Assault- *Game Over*.

Q: Warwound's early material was pure raw punk. How do you see Warwound's place in the crossover story, and did your metal influences seep into the way you approached drumming for them?

Warwound was on the verge of signing a record deal when I left and joined The Varukers, so didn't really have any influence in crossover bands. None of the band members from the original lineup (not the later Thompson/Martin version) were into metal, they were just heavily influenced by Discharge and GBH only.

Q: Sacrilege-*Behind the Realms of Madness* is now seen as a landmark in UK crossover history. Looking back, what do you remember about the creative process- the atmosphere in the studio, and the intention behind pushing Sacrilege into that thrash-infused, metal direction while still rooted in punk?

A: I joined the band at a stage where they were writing new material which ended up on the record. More of a metal influence rather than the early demos that the band produced. But Damian being a very talented song writer was combining metal riffs with large punk influence which made the record quite unique.

Q: Having played with Sacrilege, Arbitrater, Warwound, and The Varukers, you've been part of bands that straddled both punk and metal scenes. How do you see your own drumming and musical identity: as a punk who absorbed metal, a metal drummer with punk roots, or simply someone who blurred those boundaries naturally?

A: I think a mixture of all really, I have been lucky in my lifetime to see many excellent bands over the years and have taken influence from all really ranging from the early punk days up until today!

(Sacrilege with Hellbastard at the Riverside, 09/11/1986)

Go for Sacrilege's *Behind The Realms Of Madness* 1985 mini-LP, as well as their demos released on the *Ambulance Station Squat, London, 1985 Plus the First & Second Demos* LP. These are great ways to start with Sacrilege, enormous and powerful hardcore-thrash the UK way, rough and sounding like a cross between Varukers, Discharge, Venom and Slayer-or like one million demons coming out of hell! Having seen Warwound performing 'The Closing Irony' and 'Out Of Sight, Out Of Mind' with Rat Varukers on vocals, Ian Glasper in bass and Danny Thompson on guitar in New Cross Inn, just blew me away!

THE NEW BARBARIANS (Post-2000's Crossover Bands)

AGGROS

(Aggros band picture, 2023 touring lineup. Photo courtesy of Barblin Mayhew)

I didn't want the Aggros sub-chapter to be structured as the other ones, since Aggros are Parris Mayhew's newest project, that has a unique, exclusively characteristic style. Aggros are the first ever instrumental crossover band! So, instead of doing they typical thing, I would like to narrate their story in a different way and add my personal experience with Aggros and Parris; this kind of style will also take place in my next book, *Teenage Freakshow,* so watch out!

For those ones who don't know, Parris played the guitar at the age of 15 years old in the seminal art-mad NYC punk band The Mad, then formed Cro-Mags and was the co-writer of their songs in their best LPs. He played also in White Devil and Psychic Orgy. Alongside, he is a director of several music videos that you all know, among them being Biohazard's *Shades of Grey*, Nuclear Assault's *Trail Of Tears*, Onyx's *Slam* or Type O Negative's *Black No. 1*. A New York City native, I think that Parris lived in all five boroughs of New York, with his early life being in Bronx, and I believe that he is one of the most characteristic and representative figures when we are talking about musicians from New York City, regardless of genre.

Regarding Cro-Mags, I won't go into many details (since you can find my reviews and the band chapter on *Crossover The Edge*), but I must mention that *Age of Quarrel*, *Best Wishes* and *Revenge*, are three of my all-time favourite records, regardless of genre. *Age of Quarrel* is the first hardcore LP I ever got, and to this day, thirty years later, when I put it on the turntable, it still sounds like the first time: it's kind of magical, that only few records can do this in your lifetime. As for *Best Wishes*, initially I was disappointed when I first got it. But it has become the biggest grower ever over the years, when I finally 'got it', it was infectious! Plus, every modern hardcore band owes *Best Wishes* big time for sure! *Revenge* has also a special place in my heart, it's maybe the most diverse Cro-Mags LP. Musically it ranges from punk, to hardcore, to crossover and sadly remains so underrated.

In 2017 Parris formed his new band, Aggros, to pursue his artistic dream: a hardcore crossover band that would be instrumental and would push the genres limits towards many styles. When I first heard and saw the videoclips directed by Parris of the first two singles, 'Chaos Magic' and 'City Kids' I was floored. I couldn't believe my eyes and ears, Aggros had taken crossover to a totally different level, adding elements from heavy metal, progressive rock, guitar shred, sounding so fresh and genuine! But I think that the appropriate way prior of reviewing their work, is to read what Parris narrates while interviewed.

(Aggros promotional flyer for their first LP, 2023)

"Hardcore is what I do. The Aggros and the Cro-Mags are the same thing, just a continuation" Parris replies when asked about Aggros. "They are both just vehicles for my music. I write music, I can't help it. When I was fifteen years old, I wrote a batch of songs after hearing Motörhead and Sex Pistols and decided I was going to start a band to play my music. That band was Cro-Mags and those songs were 'World Peace', 'Show You No Mercy', 'Life Of My Own' and what became 'Seekers Of The Truth'. The music was in place, and I had to assemble some people to play it, that's how Cro-Mags came about, simple as that. When the Mags ended, I made a lateral move into the film business. I've been a film maker for many years, but I never stopped writing music. When the Pandemic happened, I found myself with time and a lot of music ready to go again, just like when I formed the Cro-Mags and found myself in an era where you can make records easily and cheaply on a computer, and I didn't have to wait for a 'record deal" or a band to do it. So, this time instead of looking to other people to play my music, I just did it myself. The fire that made Cro-Mags never went out and Aggros is just a continuation, a new vehicle for my songs".

When asked about the early days of Cro-Mags and the NYHC and crossover scene, and the core ethos or energy that still resonates in the heavier underground scenes today, Parris replied that "I'm not sure I'm connected to the early days of the NYHC and crossover scene anymore. That time has passed. Our little scene was just a resource for me to begin with. That's where the action was. So that's where I took my music, and as a byproduct I also found an extraordinary community, a very small group of musicians who were tight and all friends. It was a dream for me. How could we have known how lucky we be to have found each other? If I could go back to that place where I could run into Jimmy Drescher [Jimmy Gestapo] any night of the week or have a beer with Tommy Victor at the Village Idiot bar or hang out in the ladies room lounge of Irving Plaza Adam Yauch [Beastie Boys], Dr. Know, Michael Diamond and Gabby [Glaser] from Lucious Jackson or see HR reading the Bible aloud in the park or shoot pool with Earl Hudson at Blanche's bar any day of the week or talk music with Pete Steele while I DJ'd at the Wah Wah Hut or stand on a street corner with Roger Miret. I would go there right now if I could. But I can't. It doesn't exist. But I bring that extraordinary life I had as a kid on the streets of New York with me, and it's always a part of my music and who I am. I'm forged. I heard a lot about ethos back then, everyone said they stood for something or other, be it straight edge, skinhead, peace punks, stupid religions, drugs, anarchy but none of that passing identity rang true to me. I never understood the need to attach those things to our scene in order to justify the time put in? For me it was altogether different, as a musician, that was the beginning and the end of my motivation. But our scene was more important than ethos, it was something extraordinary, it was all very personal, like loyalty to friends and the family we chose. That was the only real ethos I came away with, the music provided the gravity. We saw each other every day for years. We spent all our time together, making music and dreaming of making it our lives. It's hard to apply that now in an anonymous scene where I don't know at least half the people in the room. So, even though I'm not surrounded by a scene, today, I still make my music exactly the same as I did back in 1982, alone in a room with my guitar, I bring no ethos into that room. The music is ultimately the important attribute of the scene, wherever it is. And the music and the passion to make it will never go away. No philosophy required".

(Cro-Mags with Angelic Upstarts at the Rock Hotel, 09/03/1985)

"But when I write songs, I imagine myself on the dance floor looking up at the band, they've been on for thirty minutes and I say to myself, 'what do I want them to do next?' Parris continues. "They already check the boxes, heavy, hard, fast, fun, but now thirty minutes in, what can they do that will make my adrenaline surge and want to continue to expend every ounce of power here on the dance floor. 'What could they do surprise to me, blow me away, inspire me, what will make me lose my mind?' Then I do that. I play and play for hours until I find one riff that makes me happy and then I play it a thousand times until I find the rest of the song. You must blow yourself away first! You must love it. That's the best method".

Me and my partner visited New York City in 2023, and I had the opportunity of meeting special people such as Freddy Alva (Wardance Records, ABC No Rio and Urban Styles book among others), and of course Parris. We had set up an appointment at 21:00 pm at Broadway Bar in Brooklyn located in-between Bushwick and Bedford-Stuyvesant. When we exited the underground, my partner told me 'Alex, are you sure that it's not dangerous here?' as she heard some screams from the background. I said it's all going to be OK and headed for Broadway Bar. At 21:00 sharp Parris was there too, but we weren't allowed to get in, since me and my partner didn't have our ID's. Duh. Parris then took us a ride to another bar, and we started chatting about all things Cro-Mags and Aggros for about three hours. He also had a copy of *Rise*

Of The Aggros LP, an Aggros T-shirt, and Aggros stickers that I gave one to my friend Apostolis when back home in Greece.

What struck me initially with Parris when I had previously him in Athens, Greece, at the first Cro-Mags show in An Club, was how kind, level-headed and knowledgeable he was regarding music. He has a wide taste in music, with strong loves (Cockney Rejects, Yes, Black Flag, Rush, Bad Brains), and strong dislikes (Iron Maiden, ha!). And no matter what people say, the greatness of Cro-Mags must be attributed firstly and foremostly to Parris; he was the most reasonable of all (and obviously the smartest), to be followed by Mackie, Pete and Doug. And from the musical output, he was the most talented of all. Later on, he dropped us to Gates Avenue subway station, offered us two big hugs, and we said, 'we'll see each other soon'. And hopefully we will go back to New York City, yes!

Back in Greece, I was sleepless with massive jetlag, but the only thing that mattered was to hit the turntable with *Rise Of The Aggros*, the first LP of Aggros. I already knew two songs, but I wasn't prepared for this! 'Best Destiny' is one of the best instrumental songs ever written, even adding a progressive rock keyboard edge, and man, it's damn difficult to write a seven-minute instrumental crossover song without sounding boring. Overall, *Rise Of The Aggros* includes five songs that are just unbelievable. The closing nine-minute *City Kids / Ghosts of New York / Haunted* sounds like if Eloy or Yes (*Close To The Edge* era) were locked in a cell for two years, listening exclusively to Cro-Mags and Bad Brains. And as you can imagine, the musicianship here is top-notch; I can think of many progressive metal bands that would kill for some riffs!

"What's changed is the definition of the word crossover, or its parameters" Parris adds. "Because crossover is now so normal that it's impossible to say what's what. Many bands today call themselves 'hardcore' and that isn't what I would have called them, never in my wildest dreams. I think most 'hardcore bands' today are metal bands and really don't even sound remotely like historical hardcore. So, what is hardcore now? With social media the fans now define what hardcore is. That's really no different than it was in 1982 but back then, there were only 100 people voting. Today's voting machine is Facebook. Combine that with what the popular bands say they are. So, as a result, 'hardcore' is what Knocked Loose and Turnstile say it is. The truth, in this case, is democratic. And the votes are for the popular bands. That's evolution. Anyone who wants to be stubborn and argue with a million thirteen-year-olds on Facebook about what 'hardcore is?' You have my sympathies. Why bother? It only matters if it matters. And a thing you cannot change doesn't matter. And I remember a time before there was a genre called hardcore. I wrote many of the *Age of Quarrel* songs before that word was in use. So, it's no skin off my nose if that word gets appropriated. 'Hardcore' came way after my musical mission began. I'm not precious about it. I make music, period. You call it whatever you like! Crossover seems to fit Aggros best".

For the live appearances of Aggros, Parris is accompanied with a band comprised of drummer Denis Cobz Cedeño (ex-Torturous Inception), the great guitarist Chuck Lenihan (Vasaria, Crumbsuckers, Carnivore

AD, Heavy Rain, Psychic Orgy) and Dierk Peters on keyboards. Now, could please a promoter bring them to Europe?

"I'm proud to be part of this second book" Parris smiles. "I guess I will always be a part of crossover historically but I'm more satisfied with continuing to be included because of the boundaries I continue to cross. Aggros takes all my musical influences to the next level, Aggros is much more than Cro-Mags musically. So, I'm happy to leave the past where it is and should be and thrive in the present! But I'm glad to see that my former bandmates have been able to make a living playing the songs that I wrote in high school".

Finally, concluding our discussion, Parris adds that "I would tell a young musician of today that crossover is freedom. I'm a fan of heavy music so my music will always be heavy and I'm influenced and drawn to much of the same music from my past, but influence is continuous and never ends, so I have also been changed by the music of all the years since Cro-Mags ended, by bands like Slipknot, Depeche Mode, Dead Can Dance, Slayer, Metallica and even Turnstile. They all show me what music should be and could be, and that is something I learn every day and with that I just add, I don't abandon the past, it all just becomes part of the stew. So, I say take it all in, love music and let it teach you what it should be".

Aggros are of course going strong in 2026 and a new LP is on the works!

At a glance: As you can imagine, I'm a sucker for the Aggros, not only because I love Cro-Mags or because I major respect for Parris. Aggros are THE non-typical, non-conformist, out of any boundaries crossover band of today, and more to that, they have bloody tunes, they can write actual songs that stick to your mind, not guitar exercises. Is this progressive hardcore? Instrumental crossover? I don't know. All I know is that *Rise Of The Aggros* rules, and you should check www.aggros.nyc and YouTube.com/theaggros, and join the Aggros Army! Plus, Aggros music is only available through Bandcamp on www.theaggros.bandcamp.com. Damn, I need to get some more T-shirts, and I feel such an idiot for not getting the skateboard!

COMBUST

(Combust 2018 live picture. Courtesy of Steven J. Messina)

One of the best bands of the current crop of crossover, Combust, was born in the NYHC scene. Kicking off in 2017 as a hardcore band, they incorporated crossover style in their most recent (2025) LP named as *Belly Of The Beast.* Vocalist Andrew Vacante narrates their story: "We're a bunch of friends from Staten Island who started writing tracks together in 2016 and 2017. We were all playing in bands together and around our scene for a long time and we just fell into place with what we wanted to do for this bands. The initial lineup is me, Andrew, on vocals, Peter Martingano on the guitar, Alex Basovskiy on the guitar too, Dave Sarnes on drums and Manny Muniz on bass who was later replaced by Eric Hoyt".

"Unfortunately, I feel like I'm not the best person to answer that question since I wasn't around then hahaha" Andrew smiles, when asked about why he thinks the crossover took place initially. "I'd like to say from my extensive research and obsession that hardcore punk and metal just started colliding due to the era and rise of that kind of music within the same time frame and it just naturally coincided with each other. Extreme music in both versions. They go hand in hand in influence if you ask me…and as for the first band, I'd say the Cro-Mags".

Combust in 2017 released their *Demo*, a crushing recording with five songs plus, a Breakdown cover of 'Dissed and Dismissed'. It's a release that oozed with the quality that the band holds from day one. It was re-released in 2018 on a 7-inch on Firepower. Combust is NYHC in the tradition of Killing Time, Raw Deal, Outburst, with a slight metal touch especially in the excellent 'My Fire'. Not to be missed!

"There are so many bands that influenced us, and me personally" Andrew adds "Sick Of It All and Cro-Mags were always two big ones. Killing Time and Dynamo, Iron Maiden was huge for me as well. A lot of metal stuff when I was young and then straight up hardcore once I found it".

A small tour with the hardcore monsters Downfall followed in 2018 named as 'NYC Meets RVA'. Combust released on 2019 *The Void* 12-inch EP; a huge leap forward to their early sound, now with a more professional recording, and some Cro-Mags influences added, *The Void* includes six brutal NYHC powercore dynamites, and I bet that songs like 'Last Wish' or 'Force My Hand' will leave you speechless. Unbelievable guitar power, from a band that knows how to write catchy hooks. Plus, 'The Void' reminds me of a more modern 'Seekers Of The Truth'!

"I was influenced both by metal and hardcore, 100 percent. They both play such a huge role I feel for me especially. I love the imagery and sound in both. When they come together it's perfect. Combust's two biggest influences, Killing Time and Dynamo I feel are a big mix of both of those things done in such an incredible original way" Andrew adds.

COVID-19 stood in their way in terms of touring, however Combust returned back with a US tour in 2022 named 'Play The Big Game In The USA', with supporting bands being Exhibition and Future Shock. In that same year, Combust released their first full-length LP *Another Life* on Cash Only Records. It's another ripping release, sounding more mature than before, but by no means less punching. And what is more fascinating is that now, their influences are not so distinct. Combust have created their own character and style. Technically challenging musicianship, you can hear it on the guitars in 'The Knife' or 'Another Life', as well as catchy, gang-styled vocals, created the perfect mix for a band that explodes! Yes, talking about 'Set To Explode' and 'Another Fool'.

"Seeing Cro-Mags in New York City the number of times I got to when I was younger was always amazing" Andrew discusses about his favourite shows. "Like a life-changing experience almost every time. Leeway as well. Power Trip in a basement in Chicago when I was on tour was sick!... And man, I have too many stories come to mind I'd say regarding touring with Combust…I have a lifetime of stories at this point which is something I cherish about what this music gave to me. Big shout out to Japan and Southeast Asia though because those scenes, fans, and regions are some of the most amazing kind-hearted individuals I have ever met through playing in a band".

(Combust Northeast Hardcore tour flyer, 2023)

A 2023 US tour with Drain, Gel, Restraining Order, Magnitude, Gumm, Outta Pocket, Drug Church, MSPaint and Torena followed; spreading the hardcore excellence of Combust. In 2025 they released their masterpiece: on Triple-B Records, the modern classic of *Belly Of The Beast*. I was instantly hooked when I first heard it, and knew that I had to find this record sooner or later. Luckily, I found it in All Ages Records, Camden, London, UK. When I dived into it, I was left jaw dropped. Now with even more hooks, a slightly more metal edge with some Slayer riffs here and there. Their blend of Killing Time and Cro-Mags here hits its peak, with every song being a major blaster. You can't imagine the energy and the power oozing from songs like 'Belly Of The Beast' or 'Swallowing Swords', the ferocity of 'N.Y.H.C.' or the manic ride of 'Distorted Dreams'. *Belly Of The Beast* also includes guest appearances by Jay Peta (Mindforce), Danny Diablo (Skarhead), Rory O'Neill (Imposter), Chiqui Rodriguez (Dmize) and Scott Vogel (Terror). You need this LP, like air and water, classic hardcore with crossover tendencies, their most metal so far in their catalogue.

"I have to say that I love playing in Gold Sounds of Brooklyn, New York" Andrew adds, while mentioning that "crossover is relevant right now, without a doubt. Now more than ever especially with the huge metal edge that has peaked through more and more. But I mean the best records of all time that are still cited today in my opinion are ones that were influenced by metal".

Check also Andrew's past bands (Don't Trust A Soul, Vice, Impact), Dave Sarnes (Vice and Impact too), and Eric Hoyt's Mutually Assured Destruction and Holy Land.

At a glance: Combust are one of the bands that in my opinion will make a breakthrough sooner or later. Their quality is evident, and what is most striking in their case is the fact that they can write songs, actual songs that you can remember and sing along too. Totally recommended for all fans of the late 1980s NYHC bands like Killing Time, Raw Deal, Outburst, as well as the ones into Cro-Mags and Leeway. Get their discography, and play *Belly Of The Beast* really loud. A Euro tour soon maybe?

STAMPIN' GROUND

(Stampin' Ground band picture, late 1990s. Courtesy unknown)

This is one of the cases that I don't know where to start from! Stampin' Ground are one of UK's most significant bands, because in the 1990s they managed to spearhead and spread the new wave of UK hardcore, bridging the 1980s sounds of hardcore crossover with the then new hardcore metalcore style. Everything started with Decadence Within, the band that Ian Glasper and his cousin Antony Mowbray played from 1984 to 1994, before heading to form Stampin' Ground. Decadence Within from Ledbury, Herefordshire have been extensively covered in *Crossover The Edge*, however, they should get a mention here too.

Decadence Within kicked off as a melodic but fast anarcho-punk combo on their excellent *Speed Hippy* 7-inch (1986), with anthems like 'Atrocity' and 'When You Stop Buying, They'll Stop Dying'. In their lyrics one can spot the influences of Omega Tribe, Subhumans and Flux Of Pink Indians. They took a drastic music change on their 1989 *This Lunacy* LP released on Peaceville Records, heading towards a hardcore-thrash crossover, albeit more metal than other contemporaries. I always found this record like a cross of H.D.Q. with some East Coast thrash metal, and it sounds so unique, compared to other crossover bands. Each song shreds, and I have a soft spot for 'Take It Or Leave It' and 'Fading Memory'. Their 1990

Soulwound was a step forward, incorporating in their sound elements from bands like Verbal Assault, and some of the then early post-hardcore, albeit more metal. *Soulwound* sadly never gained the recognition it deserved, and I believe that this was partially due to the uninteresting record cover. However, this is another one ace record and most significant, it was way different than their previous efforts. Songs like 'Investment Sex' or 'Inner Blindness' (that clocks over seven minutes!) are brilliant exercises of this new style. Their 1991 *Pay-Off Time* 7-inch includes one of the best songs they ever written, the melodic post-hardcore of 'Pay Off Time'. You should get it just for this song (the other two rule too, no worries!). Their grande finale was the 1993 *Reality Wake-Up Call* CD, went towards a fully post-hardcore direction, weird, angular, non-commercial and still top-notch stuff. It's like listening to Three (the Washington DC band), with a slightly more metal and early 1990s Bad Brains style and some metal rock riffs here and there! 'Get a Life' and 'In Pain We Trust' are some of the highlights of this record.

(Decadence Within with Negazione, Civilised Society?, Deviated Instinct at the Boardwalk in Manchester. 26/04/1987)

Bassist, author and overall, a beloved human being, Ian Glasper, narrates what lead to from Decadence Within to the formation of Stampin' Ground: "It was 1995, and myself and Antony Mowbray (my cousin – 'Mobs') had just finished with our previous band, Decadence Within, and wanted to do something much heavier and more direct and brutal. Mobs had drummed in Decadence Within, but he wanted to play guitar in Stampin' Ground, as he had a very clear vision of how he wanted the guitars to sound... massive, basically! I was going to stay on bass, because that was and is all I can play.

We recruited some local musicians – Paul Catten, from Medulla Nocte, on vocals, a guy called Martin Spencer on second guitar, and Rid, the singer from Decadence Within, on drums. Martin was soon replaced by Scott Atkins from a local thrash metal band, Cambodian Holiday, who we press-ganged into joining the band because he had an insane guitar tone, and we did our first demo. It was so disgustingly slow and heavy, it was virtually unlistenable, haha!

Rid was then replaced by Adrian Stokes on drums, also from Cambodian Holiday, and we recorded another demo, which saw us starting to really craft our sound and style. Paul then left to concentrate on Medulla Nocte, and we got Heath Crosby from Nailbomb and No Way Out on vocals. He had a ferocious voice, and that was the first proper lineup of Stampin' Ground, I suppose, who released the first two 7"-inchs in 1996 and then signed to We Bite Records for our first LP, *Demons Run Amok'*.

Stampin' Ground was from Cheltenham, Gloucestershire and formed in 1995, and alongside bands like Medulla Nocte, Withdrawn, Canvas, Knuckledust, Above All, Ninebar and 50 Caliber were the purveyors of the new generation of UK hardcore, that were different in musical terms than the past; however the elements of DIY of 1980s hardcore and the strong political stance were there. You can read more about this (so underrated) scene on Ian's *Armed with Anger: How UK Punk Survived the Nineties* book, that draws the picture of the whole scene in his own, always informative way.

(Stampin' Ground with Area Effect at The Star & Garter in Manchester. 09/08/1996)

Stampin' Ground's first two releases in 1996, *Starved* 7-inch and *Dawn Of Night* 7-inch were heavy as hell, metal-hardcore, with a strong Earth Crisis influence, as well as some Snapcase in their early phase.

The element of metal was filtered through the hardcore, and was only evident in some riffs, while songs like 'Starved' and 'Undone' still sound fresh today, total crushers.

"Well, there was a definite Earth Crisis influence during the very early days, haha, and then Slayer really got their teeth into us from the second album onwards" Ian admits. "At the beginning of the band, we just wanted to be as crushingly heavy as possible, and we were listening to Crowbar, Entombed, Hatebreed, Biohazard, Integrity, Snapcase… all that Victory stuff that was coming out around that time… that Inside Out EP on Revelation was a massive record for us when we first heard it too. If you look at the bands that we covered over the years, there's an indication of our influences: Cro-Mags, Judge, Vio-lence, Agnostic Front, Knuckledust, Cockney Rejects, Blood for Blood, Sick of It All…".

Stampin' Ground's first full-length album, the 1997 *Demons Run Amok*, was released on We Bite Records, and it was a slight departure from their early sound. Now, Sick Of It All have been added in the blend, with songs having changes of tempo, such as the headcrushing 'Damnation' or 'Won't Be Denied', as well as their heavy, ultra-brutal ferocity of 'Fester In Isolation' and 'Idol Mysticism'. Absolute heavyweight moshers!

"After *Demons Run Amok*, we parted ways with Heath, who was replaced by Adam Frakes-Sime, from Blood Oath, and Adam was more of a 'frontman', if you know what I mean, winning crowds over with ease. Then we left We Bite and went with Century Media Records, for the next three albums: 1998's *An Expression of Repressed Violence*, 2000's *Carved From Empty Words* and 2003's *A New Darkness Upon Us*" Ian narrates. My first exposure to Stampin' Ground was with the 1998 *An Expression of Repressed Violence* CD. I have a childhood friend, Gregory living in Sunderland then, that used to bring me every Christmas and summer issues of Terrorizer, alongside records and CDs.

An Expression of Repressed Violence was a huge step forward for Stampin' Ground; this is where they formulated their own sound, blending so many different things, and adding Slayer and thrash metal too in their modern hardcore mix. Kicking off with 'Lesion', everything seems to sound even more crazy now, while 'My Will Be Done' sounds like crossing *South of Heaven* with Machine Head and Earth Crisis! The cover of One Way System's 'Jerusalem' is a great homage to the UK punk scene, while my favourite song off this record is 'Betrayed By Many', total modern NYHC style!

I asked Ian that I recalled reading in a magazine back then that he wanted to blend the heavy riffing of Heathen and Flotsam and Jetsam with modern hardcore, and if he considers that the Stampin' Ground approach was something that could be regarded as a new form of crossover. Ian replied that "I would never have said either Heathen or F&J [Flotsam and Jetsam] were an especial influence, although I loved both bands… but perhaps Scott or Ade might have said something like that, as they were very into their thrash metal. However, SG were definitely a crossover band in the purest sense of the term, as Mobs and I were punk rockers through and through, albeit loving a lot of hardcore, whilst Scott and Ade were total metalheads, and where those two sets of influences converged is what created the SG sound. We also had the socio-political lyrics and DIY approach of punk underneath all the metal guitars and double-kick drums".

With Century Media, Stampin' Ground gained more exposure, and started touring both in UK and Europe, as well as overseas, performing in the 00's with bands like Diecast, AFI, Biohazard, Blood For Blood or even Anthrax, The Haunted, Sick Of It All and Soulfy. "The most memorable gig was probably playing the mainstage of Castle Donnington, for the very first Download Festival, in front of 50,000 people" Ian recalls. "That was crazy on multiple levels, haha! Because the field was split by a walkway straight up the middle, for safety reasons I guess, we had two walls of death and two huge circle pits either side, and it was quite something to behold. The first time in America was special, especially playing CBGB's... we were one of the first hardcore bands to go to Iceland, and the kids were nuts... Greece was always good to us, with Athens especially being insane... but we did so many amazing gigs over the years, with everybody from Slayer to Sheer Terror, from Napalm Death to Refused, from Sepultura to AFI... actually, the tour with AFI was a highlight for me too - they were just on the verge of becoming huge, so the crowds were way too large for the venues, and we had no idea how we were going to go down, playing with this gothic-ish post-punk melodic hardcore band, but they were some of the craziest gigs we did. I got on great with Davey Havok, and at the end of the tour we swapped shirts – he gave me his Nerve Agents shirt, that I had coveted the whole tour, and I gave him a 'Vegan' shirt in the style of the Venom logo, which he had taken a shine to".

Their 2000 LP *Carved from Empty Words* is their pinnacle, a classic of this new hardcore style. It contains some of the best songs they ever written. On this LP, they have taken the metal influence into a whole different level. Fast and heavy, with a strong thrash metal fuse, songs like 'Officer Down' (a fan favourite), 'Outside Looking In' and 'Everybody Owes A Death', my personal favourite-a crazy crossover blast, this is not only their brightest moment, but one of 00's top moments, both in metal and hardcore.

Their final from the first phase of the band), *A New Darkness upon Us* LP (2003), was written in its majority by Ian, and this is their most diverse record! From Slayer-styled thrashers ('Don't Need A Reason To Hate', 'Betrayal Has A Face'), to NYHC moshers ('Killer Of Society'), to what was about to become later as metalcore ('Dead From The Neck Up', 'Ashes To Scatter'), this is their most multi-dimensional record. "*A New Darkness upon Us* saw Neil Hutton from Benediction replace Ade on drums, and I left before they started to tour properly on that record, with Ben Frost from Unite joining on bass. When Mobs left in 2005, he was replaced by Paul Fletcher from Unite, but no new material was being written and SG eventually split in 2006..." Ian adds.

A split-CD was then released in 2003 alongside Northside Kings, containing covers with Stampin' Ground's cover of 'Bringin' It Down' by Judge and Inside Out's 'By A Thread' being totally out of control. In 2006 they split, only to briefly reform in 2014.

However…they are back! On 2 December 2024, Stampin' Ground announced that they will be playing at Damnation Festival 2025, celebrating twenty years of Damnation Festival along with the twenty-fifth anniversary of *Carved From Empty Words*. Since then, they are back together, playing shows again, and I guess that I will see them again both in UK and Greece in 2026!

On a final note, I asked Ian if there's a 'bridge' from the Decadence Within days, to Stampin' Ground, and how this can be explained. Ian mentions that "I think there's a thread that runs through everything I've done musically. I've been involved in a lot of different bands, so it's an eclectic career (well, it would be a 'career' if I'd made any money at all!), but I can't see the point in trotting out the same thing your whole life. That's why I've gone from bands like Thirty Six Strategies to Warwound, and Suicide Watch to Flux of Pink Indians… and, bringing it back to your question, from Decadence Within to SG. Decadence got a bit indulgent towards the end. We were constantly pushing ourselves musically, to stop ourselves getting bored, and it took the music to some unexpected places, which was great, but was turning audiences off… SG was a conscious effort to boil everything down to primal basics again. So, we went from a very complex and melodic, often high-speed, hardcore punk band, who liked to confuse audiences, to this brutal, bludgeoning, slightly groovy metalcore band, who wanted audiences to be able to go off to their music. It was an evolution of sorts. There wouldn't have been a Stampin' Ground if we hadn't spent ten years honing our craft slogging around the European squat circuit in Decadence Within".

The number of bands that the members of Stampin' Ground have played before, in-between and after Stampin' Ground are way too numerous, but I will try mentioning them all. Ian Glasper (bass) in Decadence Within, Burnside, Flux Of Pink Indians, Suicide Watch, Human Error, Betrayed By Many, Freebase, Thirty Six Strategies, Sun Of The Endless Night, Ammonia 77, Zero Again and Warwound. Ade Stokes (drums) in Reverence for Nothing, Sun of the Endless Night, Anger Management, Freebase, Suicide Watch, Taliesin and Betrayed by Many. Adam Frakes-Sime (vocals) in Rome Must Die. Paul Fletcher (guitars) on Romeo Must Die and Fates Messenger. Jim Saunders (guitars) on Reverence for Nothing, Sun of the Endless Night, The Seventh Cross, Murder One, Betrayed by Many and Robot Knows Best. Antony Mowbray (guitars) on Decadence Within, Ammonia 77. Paul Catten (vocals) on Medulla Nocte, Murder One, The Sontaran Experiment, Khang, Barrabus, Dead Sheeran, Paul Catten, Stuntcock, Thicko, Lazarus Blackstar and The Dark Half. Neil Hutton (drums) on Danmaku, Warlord U.K., Benediction, Sons of Chaos and Frog. Ben Frost (bass) on Romeo Must Die. Scott Attkins (guitars) and Heath Crosby (vocals) played only in Stampin' Ground (as far as I searched).

As mentioned, Stampin' Ground are back again in 2025, and hopefully, some new recordings will be released, right Ian? Now, pick up all of Ian's books on Earth Island!

At a glance: I strongly believe that the Century Media releases of Stampin' Ground (*An Expression of Repressed Violence*, *Carved from Empty Words* and *A New Darkness upon Us*) will appeal both to thrashers and hardcore kids of today. This is just some of the most original and brutal music of the 00s. And even though they are not 'classic crossover' in terms of sound, the spirit of crossover runs through them. Don't miss to catch them live, I've seen Stampin' Ground twice, and man…they are a totally different level live. Crossover kids, check also Decadence Within's *This Lunacy* LP and bands Zero Again and Suicide Watch!

POWER TRIP

(Power Trip band picture. Courtesy of Hristo Shindov)

Hands down one of the most known and loved today's bands, Power Trip need no introduction. This is a small piece on the Dallas, Texas band, that took its cues from bands like Exodus, Slayer and blended them with Leeway and Nuclear Assault, releasing only top-quality crossover thrash that might be a little too metal for me, but this is just me you know!

Formed in 2008, Power Trip's guitarist Blake Ibanez narrates that "we came from the hardcore punk scene and played within that for years before ending up more in the metal realm after a few albums… I think people liked the bands we took inspiration from, the classic stuff and the fringe metal and crossover bands that captured a similar spirit. There were some bands before us that started introducing people to the style, like Iron Age from Austin, TX".

"A lot of New York Hardcore at the beginning, which contained a lot of crossover bands, and metal" Blake admits about their initial influences. "Leeway, Cro-Mags, Icemen, Sick Of It All, Nuclear Assault, Exodus, etc. Our generation was mid-late 00s, so bands like Iron Age and Municipal Waste were some of the only crossover bands at the time. Any show we played with Iron Age and bands from the hardcore punk scene was fun, like the festival Chaos In Tejas that was happening annually in the 2000s. It had a lot of bands from all over the spectrum of hardcore, punk and metal".

The initial lineup of Power Trip included the late Riley Gale on vocals (RIP 2020), Chris Wetzel (bass), Nick Stewart (guitar), Blake Ibanez (guitar) and Marcus Johnson (drums). With this lineup they released every recording up to 2011, including the *2008 Demo*, the *Questions* 2008 cassette and *Armageddon Blues* 7-inch (2009) which are some of my favourite recordings. This is because they maintain a pure hardcore energy and speed outbreaks into their metal crossover, they sound like a cross between Cro-Mags from *Best Wishes* era alongside the speedy parts of bands like early Sick Of It All. 'Acid' and 'Vultures' are maybe my all-time favourite songs by Power Trip!

"Both types of music, hardcore punk and metal share similarities in aggression, and a lot of metal came from punk roots like Metallica, Slayer, etc" Blake admits. Adding that "so, it came natural for crossover to take place. I think though that the first band to crossover might have been something among Corrosion of Conformity, Discharge or Cro-Mags".

Another excellent release by Power Trip followed on 2011 with the *Power Trip* 7-inch. Their career really took off in 2013, with the release of *Manifest Decimation* LP on Southern Lord. I still like it, but this time the metal element was a little more than before which means more mid-tempo, and guitar driven stuff. This style appeared to be a major success, especially among metalheads. This time some influences by bands like Kreator or even Vio-Lence were brought in, and thrashers worldwide loved it. How could it be else since songs like 'Crossbreaker' or 'The Hammer of Doubt' are just stomping?

"I really love playing in New York, L.A., and Dallas" Blake adds. "But I like also exotic places; we somehow have a decent fanbase in Indonesia. We've been there twice and played a large festival in Jakarta to a lot of people. Also, the scene in Texas is very strong, lots of bands doing cool things, it's very based in crossover to thrash, death metal, hardcore punk".

(Power Trip record release show of 'Nightmare Logic'. 24/03/2017)

Several split records, EPs and more, Power Trip released on 2017 their most metal effort to date, *Nightmare Logic* LP. This record always sounded to me like a cross between NYC's Judge and Slayer, with even some Sepultura or Demolition Hammer thrown in. Obviously, metalheads love this record. I kind of miss the hardcore energy and spark of early releases, but still, *Nightmare Logic* includes anthems such as 'Executioner's Tax' and 'Waiting around to die'…top quality stuff.

Riley Gale's fentanyl overdose in 2020 was a shock, not just for Power Trip, but also for all the fans of the band. I always admired Riley's wild taste in music, that can be actually seen on the Amoeba Records 'What's in My Bag' Power Trip episode, with Riley wearing a Wipers' *Youth of America* T-shirt. The future was uncertain for Power Trip, until they decided to keep it up, with Seth Gilmore (formerly of the crossover thrashers Skourge) joining in as their new vocalist, and they are still active (2024).

Members of Power Trip have been involved in various other bands with the most known ones being Mammoth Grinder, Hatred Surge, Iron Age and Eternal Champion. And what is funny in the case of Eternal Champion is that their epic metal approach is taking bands like Cro-Mags, Raw Deal-Killing Time and Icemen, and transforming their style! Guess this is why Eternal Champion made a major fuzz in the metal scene, since no one could spot their influences, ha!

"Crossover is more relevant than ever, or since the 1980s" Blake adds. "Genres have merged in many ways, and it seems like everyone that enjoys hardcore or punk also enjoys metal, so it's in full force and there are lots of bands from different subgenres of metal with roots in punk".

At a glance: I really like the early, more hardcore period of Power Trip with everything up to the 2011 *Power Trip* 7-inch is gold. I know though that many people prefer their later period, and who am I to disagree? Anyway, for a starter, pick up *Manifest Decimation* LP, since it's the transitional LP from the first period to the second. If you dig it, get everything they released!

TOE TAG/THE ACCÜSED AD

(Toe Tag band picture 2025. Courtesy of Rahel Cook)

Toe Tag was formed in 2005 in Seattle, Washington by former The Accüsed members Alex Sibbald, Blaine Cook and Steve Nelson, Toe Tag are keeping the tradition of splatter-core, a style that they innovated with The Accüsed. Toe Tag is unapologetically fierce, raw, fast, and feral and it's just crazy considering that the band members have been around since early 1980s! Vocalist Blaine Cook narrates the driving force behind their formation: "Feral. I like it! We started Toe Tag way back in August of 2005. Pretty much right after we stopped playing with Tommy Niemeyer in The Accüsed. Alex and I had talked about putting something together prior to the last accused reunion. By this time Alex Maggotbrain was mainly playing guitar. We had a half a dozen or songs dialled in before we even had a bass player. Basic kind of 4-4, short blasts, guitar driven. Nothing too crazy... we stand apart in so much as that Toe Tag kind of blends that rawness of hardcore with metal riffing. I'd say we carry on the crossover thrash tradition. We're not doing it in a deliberate fashion. Not following what the current blueprint is for what makes a band a crossover band".

Blaine sent me as a gift their 2017 *Throat To Scroat* 12-inch EP when *Crossover The Edge* was released, and I was instantly hooked. Four heavyweight splattercore anthems with massive hooks, recorded live in studio. Maybe not as frenetic as the 1980s and 1990s The Accüsed, however they still strike you hard, with precision! Toe Tag have been releasing though records since 2007 (*Machete Killah* 7-inch), and have under their belt three LPs, one mini-LP, several split 7-inchs and EPs with the one being with Bandanos being my favourite. Toe Tag were also included in many compilation records, offering their very own brand of crossover for the new generation. "Crossover, thrash, punk, and hardcore; we're seeing all kinds of music coming full circle. Look at D.R.I., they're going stronger than ever. The respect The Accüsed received by bands like Municipal Waste and Lamb of God, it's humbling. It really speaks to the lasting impact of a band that was just doing their thing; music for the moment with Toe Tag. Honestly, beyond the West Coast, we're kind of existing within the shadows. The biggest influence that we have on the younger bands? We're still doing it. Still in the trenches. We're approachable and not a bunch of pricks. It's a great thing to be welcome in the all-ages scene. Playing both Toe Tag and The Accüsed AD set. There's definitely more 'demand' for us to play the old songs out".

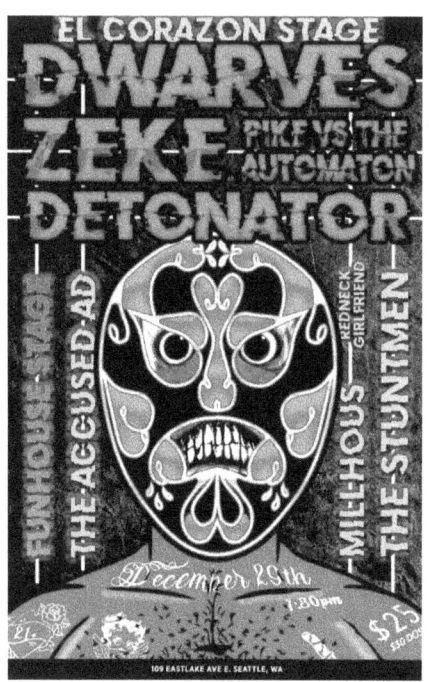

(The Accüsed AD with Dwarves, Zeke, Detonator etc 29/12/2023)

Toe Tag members formed in 2018 as The Accüsed A.D., crossing over (oops!) with Toe Tag, and releasing in 2019 *The Ghoul In The Mirror* LP, and a live LP honouring the memory of Steve Hanford, titled *Thee Slayer Hippy's Last Stand*. So, at the moment (2025) Toe Tag and The Accüsed A.D. are both active, but what is significant in their case is that they keep it up with the underground. "For sure it was a conscious decision" Blaine admits. "When we broke away from our former bandmate, we went back to the basics. Screen printing our own stickers and shirts. Developing relationships with smaller labels. Releasing singles, getting songs on comps. All of that really hands-on dedication. With so many bands on the landscape, it's difficult if not damn near impossible in some cases just to get a little push for your band. No aspirations of conquering the world. I would say that after almost twenty years of doing Toe Tag my biggest regret is not having all our releases available in the digital format. As far as what the 'underground' means to me in 2025: It's for the youth. The young people are driving the movement as they should. There's so much going on in Seattle with all-ages scene. The days of sticking up some flyers are over. The young crowd has their own way of getting the word out".

"I've had the opportunity to play music since 1980. I do what I can to embrace my youthful enthusiasm when we play out live" Blaine narrates. "I've also had the misfortune of rupturing each Achillies tendon. Unless I'm totally feeling it, I keep my jumping to a bare minimum. Lyrically, for the most part I stick to the same circle of topics. I'm by no means a lyrical genius. I'm sticking with the basic comic book horror themes of the past, the cruelty of the wars that never end. We go through creative spurts. Our most recent batch of new songs were released under The Accüsed AD banner. Currently we're focused on dealing in the splatterrock era songs".

So, if someone asked, 'Why should I check Toe Tag and The Accüsed A.D.?', what would Blaine say? "You got nothing lose. We got a little something for everyone. For the punks, for the hardcore kids, for the metalheads!".

Finally, Blaine offers some newer crossover bands that he totally recommends: "By having the opportunity to play different places around the world, I got turned on to Contrast Attitude, Summer of Death, Kandarivas, Rocky and the Sweden, and many others from Japan. Insecurity from Chile. There are so many good bands of every style and genre. Coming up from all over the world. West Coast crossover heroes Hirax are still killing it. The current lineup might be the best in years!".

At a glance: Come on guys and girls, if you are into The Accüsed you should already know that you will love Toe Tag and The Accüsed A.D.! Not familiar with their crazy speedcore holocaust? OK, start with *The Return Of Martha Splatterhead* LP. Seriously, this is a phenomenal release, like a blend of Discharge and Poison Idea with Slayer, all filtered through the horror of splatter movies. Like that record? Check everything The Accüsed, The Accüsed A.D. and Toe Tag have released!

HOLIER THAN THOU?

(Holier Than Thou? live picture, 2001. Courtesy unknown)

My favourite crossover band post-2000s was Holier Than Thou?. They had pretty tough competition regarding the bands that appeared in that era, from Bones Brigade to Municipal Waste and from Voetsek to What Happens Next?.

Holier Than Thou? hailed from Goleta and Santa Barbara, California where they were rooted in the hardcore scene. Guitarist Jeff Capra narrates their story: "I had the name for a few years before actually getting it together. The name came from the flier in COC's *Animosity* albums insert. DR (Douglas Robert Mawhinney, vocalist) and I had known each other for years; want to say 1990 is when we met but didn't really start hanging out till 1998 when he moved into an apartment I had. We would talk about current bands and the scene, and I told him the name and said 'you should sing'…because DR was a fucking talker! Plus, I knew he could actually sing. But mainly, dude had a lot to say and a way of saying things that I thought was funny. I met Noel (Sullivan, drums) while working at a music and video store in Goleta called Tempo. He and his family would come in to rent movies, but he bounced in one day and walked over to the N section of the CDs. As I watched him from behind the counter I thought 'this poor kid is probably looking at NOFX bullshit'. He's fumbling through the CDs looking a bit dejected and comes walking up with that typical Noel grin….'got any Naked Raygun?'…I was mind blown! I said 'no, that shit's not in print, but I can make you copies if you get some blank tapes'. That was the beginning of our friendship. He would come hang out at the store and I'd play him music. One day he followed me to my car, and I played him Bl'ast! and he said that he played drums. Now, he was like thirteen and I was twenty-one but there was something 'older' about the kid that I really related too as I had mainly older friends. I asked if he wanted to jam and that's when we started working stuff out. DR actually came later by a few months. We had a variety of song styles in the very beginning, before we had a bassist. One day Noel suggested he ask his old high school math teacher if he would want to 'come play some tunes'. Again, this dude was Noel's teacher the prior year….so after thinking about it for like thirty seconds, Kevin said 'sure!'. I think later that night we all got together, and we showed Kevin (Sheffield, bassist) the songs we had at the time, which was about five or six. There was one song where we always blew the fuse when we got to the middle breakdown, every fucking time we played that song we popped the fuse. So that tune got bailed. The song that stuck out as the strongest….and by strongest, I mean the song that sounded the most natural, powerful and where we all gelled was what became 'Infinity + 7 Divided By The Root Of All Evil'".

Jeff continues adding that "we had practiced a few times and after we finished that song that night I said 'this is our style…we're all clicking best on the crossover style'. I was stoked…I finally had found guys to play crossover with. It was a style I had gotten into in 1987 after getting Skate Rock *Wild Riders of Boards*. A few weeks after buying that, I got RKL's *Rock n' Roll Nightmare*, so there's the influence for Holier Than Thou. Purchased in the middle of those was Gang Green's *Another Wasted Night*, just to round out any questions as to influences. Both Kevin and DR loved this style as well as they had gotten to see many of those bands. I was too young to see them by like two years but had all the records. Noel took to it like a duck to water. We did a demo and then got asked my Jeff at Six Weeks Records to do a record, which turned into a 7" and two LPs. We also did a 7" with Flower Violence for a European Tour in 2003. We did another European tour in 2004 and did a US tour in 2003 with Annihilation Time and a lot of shows with Municipal Waste. Our first show was I believe 1 January 1999, and our last show was in 2005 at a fest".

I came across Holier Than Thou? via Darek at Scarecrow Records, in Greece, in 2002. Darek was running a distro that now is a physical and online store; and actually the best punk and hardcore and all in-between store in Greece, Scarecrow Records is located in Exarcheia, Athens. Darek had two crates of records in Biologica Squat, in Thessaloniki, for the Out Cold and Dead Stop show. I started flipping through the records, and got myself three Out Cold LPs, one Fuck on the Beach and a split-LP between Nausea and Disrupt. We had a small chat over music, and he gave me his distro catalogue (that obviously blew my mind, because back then you could get a Tragedy or From Ashes Rise LP for 8 euros). So, when I made my first order, he dropped in a Holier Than Thou? *The Hating Of The Guts* CD with a note 'I think you're going to like this'. You bet I did!

Holier Than Thou?'s first brutal offering was the 2001 *Holier Than Thou?* 7-inch (on Six Weeks Records), and what a blast it was! Mind you, crossover was totally out of style back then, and this release was a breath of fresh air. With a sound that was reminiscent of C.O.C's *Six Songs with Mike Singing*, blended with early Nuclear Assault, Excel, R.K.L. and even the Venice sound, *Holier Than Thou?* is just a harbinger of what would follow next. Four songs, all catchy, all winners, however my favourite is 'It's a Crime'. "We were definitely influenced by The Accüsed, RKL, Corrosion of Conformity, Gang Green, Aggression, Excel, Beyond Possession, No Mercy, Suicidal Tendencies, English Dogs and local bands like Threatened Hope and Section 8" Jeff admits. "R.K.L. had unbelievable riffs that I could never figure out. I tried to infuse some of their style as best I could, whatever licks I could figure out, I tried to copy. The other bands are all self-explanatory. That *Skate Rock Volume 3* comp was a huge influence too".

After an appearance on the 2001 *Wild In The Streets* 7-inch compilation with their awesome 'Dumb Motherfucker', Holier Than Thou? dropped the bomb with their first LP release, again on Six Weeks Records, with *The Hating Of The Guts*. Words can't describe how inspired, crazy and catchy this record is. Holier Than Thou? sound like they were on a manic ride, and every song slays. Here you can find everything from COC to Excel and from RKL to early Suicidal to Beyond Possession and The Accüsed and *Hating Of The Guts* is a modern crossover classic, that sadly remains under the radar of most into this sound. Featuring a great cover on Stalag 13's 'Conditioned'. If I was to pick just one song, that would have been 'Super Ego'; I mean, come on, this is just so out of control! And what can I say about 'Hopeless' or 'Rat Patrol'!

"Well for me, I had come from a metal background" Jeff narrates, regarding his musical influences and background. "As a young kid seven years old in 1982, I liked rock and heavy metal because that's what my neighbours all listened to and played. So, for me it was an easy concept and style to grasp being that I got crossover stuff right as I was exiting metal. I think for the early guys, they secretly or not-so-secretly liked metal at the same time as they were getting into punk. Most of those kids seemed to like early metal like Judas Priest, AC/DC, Iron Maiden, Black Sabbath, Deep Purple, Alice Cooper and Stooges and MC5. They already had rock or metal in their diets, but they also had Stooges and MC5 and New York Dolls. So, when they heard Sex Pistols, Damned, Ramones, etc, they had a palate for it. I think a lot of kids pretended to hate metal but listened to it at home or alone, because years later they ended up in metal bands. I think it was a combination of "letting-of-the-guard down, old interests resurfacing and an influx of new kids to the punk scene as years went by".

And what about crossover? Who was the one to dive into it first, and bring it to the world? "I'm of the opinion that The Accüsed were the first band to really fuse the two styles of music" Jeff admits. "Their first EP with Blaine was 1985 and I know those songs were written in 1984. I'd say the contender for the first one would be D.R.I. because *Dealing With It* was also 1985 and had moments of crossover. And I guess   one could also argue Septic Death, but the band that fused them where it was style fast but had speed-picking with palm mutes and harmonic pinch notes first was The Accüsed. At least in my opinion they did it first and the best in 1985 but weren't as noted until like late 1986 or 1987".

The Accüsed influence was apparent from day one in Holier Than Thou?. It was even stronger on their next release, the 2003 *We Come In Peace We Leave In Pieces* 7-inch, another top-class moment for the band. It kicks off with 'Get Snarly' and on the flipside of 'Grog', that sounds like a cross between C.O.C's 'Positive Outlook' with The Accüsed and R.K.L. Terrific stuff! Three songs to demolish your house.

(Holier Than Thou? with Annihilation Time, Reagan SS, Covered in Scars and Heavy Artillery at the Livery Theatre, 27/04/2003)

A European tour followed (sadly Holier Than Thou? didn't make it in Greece, however their brother band Annihilation Time did it, and I saw them alongside other fifty or sixty people), with Graham Clise joining in as a guitarist, replacing James M. Sanitate. "Most of our area was stoked" Jeff mentions. "It was not something you got to see or hear live for many years in our area, and I think the shithead tough guy element had been totally removed by 1999-2000. So many kids liked speed metal and black metal and death metal in that era that they ate it up, if they liked what we were doing. It was really just us, Municipal Waste and a few years later Destruction's End who really played crossover, with the speed picking and breakdowns. Most everyone else was fastcore and bandana thrash which was not the same thing".

Another inclusion into a compilation, this time the *Dark Thoughts - A Tribute To COC* 7-inch. Holier Than Thou? ripped it up with a medley cover of 'Citizen' and 'Not For Me'. Deranged Records released in 2003 another great release by HTT?, the *High On Barbeque* 12-inch. Now sounding more wicked, The Accüsed influence is on full effect here, and all five songs plus a Motörhead cover of 'Sex and Death' are in the usual high quality of the band. Kicking off with '50 Ways to Lose Your Liver', one of the best songs they ever written, on through the Ozzy mash-up of 'Metal Wounds' to 'Pacify', this is a record that if you like their previous stuff, you should get it.

"My favourite places to play were gone by the time Holier Than Thou was a band" Jeff sighs". "My spots were The Red Barn, Anaconda (upstairs) and The Mocando in Los Angeles. For Holier our spots were the Living Room in Goleta and I'd say The Smell when they first started doing shows. Those were good shows. We played Gilman Street a couple times, and it was cool, but I don't think that scene really cared…except for Sabado Gigante…that show was sick!"

A compilation (The Riviera Sessions) followed in 2003, and the band kept it up until June 2005, when they folded for good. If they could hold it for a few more years, they would have been huge today…oh well. Fast forward to 2013, Six Weeks released a record that was recorded in 2005 with *You Can't Have Slaughter Without Laughter* 12-inch as a great way to end a career. *You Can't Have Slaughter Without Laughter* sounds more mature and even a bit more bitter than their earlier stuff, containing great songs such as 'Twice As Bright' or 'Time to Go' and 'It's A Damn Good Thing I Don't Own A Gun'. Slightly more metal this time, but still speedcore at its finest!

I won't go into referencing in every band Holier Than Thou? members played with, before or after, because they are innumerable! I shall mention though that what is very significant in their case is that they played is such diverse and great bands such as Embassy (emocore), Uphill Battle, Annihilation Time (as aforementioned, a brother band, and if I can recall they shared a website together, named as holychurchofannihilation.com or something like that!), Possessor, Broken Needle, Become, Lecherous Gaze (hard rock!)…just so many bands. Alongside, Jeff Capra is one of US underground's heroes, playing in unbelievably many bands, different styles, since the late 1980s.

"I think crossover is relevant, even today, with bands like Dead Heat, Mindforce and that stuff; it's totally got that crossover vibe but maybe fused more with NYHC bands like Leeway and Crumbsuckers. I haven't heard a speedcore type crossover band in a while though, besides Municipal but they seem more metal now. I feel like there will always be an element of metal in hardcore now because it's been an element in some form since 1985. Some utilize it more and there are bands that have tried to stay away from it completely to great success. But I think there will always be some band that's riffing on metal licks and using it in their punk rock".

At a glance: As you can imagine, Holier Than Thou? are a favourite of mine. Be sure to pick up all their records, even if you like one of them. For a starter's recommendation, that will be *The Hating Of The Guts* LP. It's up there with all the 1980s classics that you love!

THE SHINING

(The Shining live band picture. Courtesy of Alex Almeida)

Amsterdam's The Shining are one of the most prolific and of great quality crossover hardcore bands since early 2000s, yet they sadly remain unknown. Maybe the fact that they remain loyal to the DIY hardcore scene can explain this, but it adds even more originality on what they do, that is fast and fierce crossover hardcore of the highest order! Bassist (and good friend), Rogier Heumakers narrates their story: "We started out around the year 2000 writing some hardcore punk songs. Most of us were always interested in both hardcore punk and metal. We all grew up in the nineties and started our respective musical journeys with bands like Sepultura, Madball, Machine Head, Agnostic Front, Warzone, Slayer. After a few years we got immersed deeper into the punk scene and its DIY ethics. That spoke deeply to us, and we started touring and putting out our own records in cooperation with other small DIY labels. That scene took us all over the world and gave us friendships that last to this very day. The band took us on quite a journey, and we played all over Europe and did tours of Brazil and Japan. It also introduced the nastier sides of punk, crust, crossover and metal to us, and these influences got more important in our sound. Hardcore punk was usually the basis of our sound, but it got mixed up with a lot of metal and some crust over the years. You know, write something loud and fast, add a little Slayer, some Cro-Mags, some Sacrilege, and you got a nasty little song".

Formed in 2001, The Shining through their existence released seven 7-inch EPs and split EPs, as well as three split LPs and two full length LPs. All of total class, starting with the split with Destructive in 2001, *The Amsterdam Connection*; nine songs under fifteen minutes, with a total B.G.K. worship in terms of bass-playing, and metal riffage here and there, reminiscent of Suicidal Tendencies from *Join the Army* era (just check 'Stupid Fuck'). Still more on the hardcore side, The Shining managed from day one to expose their excellent quality, as evident in ragers like 'Apocalyptic Genocide' or 'Punk for Politics'. Mandatory, if you're into the more hardcore side of crossover (like yours truly).

"Probably metal and punk were influenced both in terms of music and youth cultures mix" Rogier adds. "One always reads stories where the two would be at odds with one another but in the end, both had probably more in common than they thought. Especially thrash metal takes influence from punk in terms of ferocity and aggression. Both the music and youth culture were underground and, eventually they probably found each other and got along better. We were always fine with all! And I would add that they key band behind this crossover was Motörhead, even though I don't think they ever consciously tried to mix the two. They just appealed to both punks and metalheads. And for good reason! From there on the styles and subcultures probably started to mix slowly but surely. Later on, bands like D.R.I., The Accüsed, COC and such got very important but as usual everything starts with fucking' Motörhead".

After two 7-inch releases, The Shining released on 2008 their first split LP with the Dutch hardcore thrashers Waking The Dead, named aptly *Thrash Attack*, and what a blasting release was it! The Shining are in full form, ready to explode in six of their numbers, plus a mental cover of The Accüsed's 'Slow Death'. The influences range from hardcore to COC's crossover era, The Accüsed and even a healthy dose of Exodus and Slayer thrown in as well as Sacrilege B.C. Songs like 'Jehova's Tuig' are just crushing, while 'The Killing Point' is just another crazy anthem to slam dance to.

The Shining were playing endlessly especially in D.I.Y. shows, and appeared on billings alongside Fucked Up before they went on to become megastars, Love Potion, the oldschool-styled hardcore Citizens Patrol, Crippled Fox. They went on to perform not just in Holland, but also in other European countries e.g. Germany or Slovakia and Hungary, and overseas to Brazil and Japan! "In Amsterdam most of our peers found us to be a little too metal" Rogier admits. "But it was all good. We really got into the crossover thing around 2003 and started writing material to fit that. We often played hardcore bills and were a bit to metal for some but usually it was all good. We got along fine with everyone and would have a lot of fun playing our music. After a while there were some more bands would play stuff like us and that would be great.

Bands like Skull and Flames, Waking The Dead, Citizens Patrol, Crippled Fox, Violator, Crucial Section, Municipal Waste, Bones Brigade, Makiladoras and tons more would do stuff that we dug, and they were all more than supportive of us".

"We were influenced by a lot of punk, hardcore and metal" Rogier adds. "I think D.R.I., Slayer, BGK, Suicidal Tendencies, Black Sabbath, Sacrilege, Discharge, Gang Green, MDC, Crucifix, RKL, Skitsystem, Attitude Adjustment and many many more. We all listened to tons of different music but hardcore, punk and metal were always the main ingredients for our sound. Since we were all born around 1981 and 1982, obviously we didn't see the original bands in their prime. We did however share the stage with a lot of our biggest influences and other great bands like D.R.I., Napalm Death, The Accüsed, Wehrmacht, Armagedom, Violator, MDC, Life Sentence, Crucial Section, Citizens Patrol, Crippled Fox and tons more".

Another split release, this time a three-way alongside the great Verbal Abuse and Scheisse Minnelli was out in 2011 named as *Speed Kills, But Who's Dying?* and now The Shining went a little bit more metal (but by no means less fierce) in their five-song offering. Just fast and skull-crushing stuff such as 'Never Sign Up' or the RKL influenced 'Terminal Toothgrinder', another fine release! "Man, we had a lot of crazy shit happen in those seventeen years we have been around. I think some of the most memorable gigs where the shows on the Japan tour. Tokyo and Kochi were so cool. When we arrived in Kochi the drummer of Disclose and the guitar player of Forward invited us for dinner and took us out to a market to eat fuckin' whale. That was something. Brazil was great to. Goiana near Brasilia was crazy. A small leaking barn filled with die-hard thrashers, D.R.I. logo spray painted on the floor, directions for a circle pit next to it. Madness. Czech Republic, Slovakia, Hungary were always a party. The time four thrashers out of Belarus drove eight hours just to be able to see us play on a Monday in a squat in Warsaw ranks as a big honour too. I could go on for hours. Most of the good things that go on in my life I got through this music. My worldwide friends, my job as a history teacher and most of all my wife and my son."

And this is the essence of a DIY band that tours: meeting people with same mentality, meeting new friends, creating a worldwide family through their music and passion. Something that the big stars that are hiding behind their enormous scenes lost in the way. It's not bad to be a big act even becoming a 'hardcore crossover brand', and kudos to you if you financially made it, and you focus only on the music, rather than doing a shitty 9-5 job. But DIY has always its own charm.

(Thrashcore Fast VII gig flyer. 02/11/12)

Back in The Shining's crazy musical output, the 2013 *Rise of Degenerates* LP showcased a step forward towards a more complex, technically challenging crossover. The album is always full of explosive outbursts of manic speed rides with technical elements thrown here and there, just to spice things up! Obviously, another winner, with anthems like the COC-meets-R.K.L.' 'Degenerates', or the thrash metal fusion of 'Never Sign Up' and the excellent Attitude Adjustment-styled 'Drug Money'. Did I mention that 'Rules' is a B.G.K. cover?

"I think some of our favourite places to play would include the Sonic Ballroom in Cologne" Rogier admits. "Always good fun as well as our hometown turf The OCCII in Amsterdam. Thankfully they are still around. I would kill to play Earthdom in Tokyo, Hangar 110 in Sao Paolo or the abandoned military airbase in Czech where we played the 'Play Fast or Don't fest' again".

The Shining's last LP, the 2015 *The Infinite Reign of Madness* was just another stellar release. Now combining their earlier hardcore assaults with the thrash metal leanings of their early 2010s releases, this LP gets a rawer production treatment in favour of a more manic sound. And the songwriting? Wow…You can't imagine how infectious tracks like 'Come Crisis Comes Death' with its crazy guitar lead or 'Human Race Destroyed' are. Thrown in, an homage cover to the great Dutch hardcore band Gepopel with 'Ze Komen Ook Bij Jou'. Wild!

The Shining's final release as of 2025 was the split 7-inch with Brazilian hardcore thrashers Ameaça Cigana in 2016. Since then, there's silence in The Shining camp, while Rogier now plays with the Oi!-pub rockers Savage Beat, a terrific band. In terms of bands that The Shining members were involved prior or in-between The Shining, Rogier played with Armistice, Jerry A & The Kings Of Oblivion, Krigshetsare,

Open Wounds, Rinus Michels, Rupsband and The Works, Nils Feestra played also in Rinus Michels, Mark Binnenkamp in Rupsband (that I got their *8-Track Thrash Attack* on 2006 in Biologica Squat, Thessaloniki, Greece) and vocalist Robert Nijhout in Frightened Fiction.

On a final note, Rogier adds that "It's just that we're living in 2024 now and not 1986 so it's not really a comparison. People play what they like and some of the newer bands sound great. Foreseen, Powertrip, the last Municipal Waste album all sound cool; so I guess there is enough cool stuff going on. So, why not? Crossover is still a thing".

At a glance: Are you a sucker for a mix between R.K.L., Attitude Adjustment, some Slayer and Exodus riff style and The Accüsed? The Shining will be the perfect band for you. If I were to pick one release off them for a starter, this would have been the split with *Waking The Dead*, I love this record so much. Rogier was unbelievably kind when *Crossover The Edge* was out, and he sent me all The Shining records as a gift! Be sure to check out Savage Beat, it's an excellent band for all you skinhead rockers, and let's just hope Rogier's favourite football team Ajax won't ever meet again my team, P.A.O.K. because I'm sick of getting disqualified by them, ha!

DEATH IN YOUR YARD

(Death In Your Yard 2025 band picture. Courtesy of the band)

I guess that you didn't expect a band from Israel who later moved to Prague, Czechia in 2023, but here you are. Death In Your Yard from Tel Aviv-Yafo, with a definite anti-racist stance, rooted on the DIY punk scene of Israel. Vocalist and founding member Alon Hoffman narrates their story: "Death In Your Yard was formed in 2016 in Tel Aviv, Israel. I was in the middle of a shift in a pizza place I worked at the time.

I was listening to Municipal Waste and decided that I want to form a crossover thrash band. After two months, Death In Your Yard released their first EP. In 2019 the first full album of D.I.Y.Y was released. In the meantime, we were playing all over Israel. In October 2019, D.I.Y.Y we did our first tour in Europe. Since then, we've been performing in Israel and Europe. From the beginning of the band, D.I.Y.Y got a lot of support from the Israeli underground metal scene and the Israeli punk scene. In Israel both scenes share the same people, so we were welcomed from day one".

In 2018 Death In Your Yard released their first CD, *Make Crossover Attack Again* under the production treatment of Toxic Holocaust's Joel Grind. On this CD it was evident that they wanted to embrace the mid-1980s crossover style akin to The Accüsed, D.R.I., early M.O.D. or later heroes Municipal Waste. "The bands that influenced me the most are Suicidal Tendencies, D.R.I., Slayer, Municipal Waste and Wehrmacht" Alon admits. You can find their traces into songs like 'The Manson's Family' (my favourite off this CD) or 'D.I.Y. Till I Die'- good stuff!

"I think that the first bands to crossover metal and punk was Suicidal Tendencies, D.R.I and S.O.D." Alon Hoffman believes. "I think that crossover isn't just about music. It's a movement that unites two scenes together and brings together punks and metalheads because at the time these scenes were divided".

Death In Your Yard have released a good number of digital releases, but I will stick to their CD and vinyl record output. Their next offering was the 2022 *Bears Against Humanity* LP, that was a huge step forward (sonically speaking) in their crossover. Lyrically wise, the pizza thrash humour of like 'Beer Bear' that leaves me quite cold, but when they head on a serious mode, songs like 'We Are Sinners' or 'Shock Propaganda' Death In Your Yard are ripping. What is fascinating is that Alon reminds me of Italian vocalists of 1980s in his style and performance, which is a breath of fresh air.

Before departing for Czechia, Death In Your Yard were very active in the DIY punk scene of Israel, playing shows in squats, and Alon adds that "my favourite club to play at is Beit Alpha in Tel Aviv, it's a DIY place operated by punks. I miss the Rogatka club, a venue that operated since the 1990s under a different name. It was the place I saw my first punk show in 2009. It was shut down at around 2016…"

(Death In Your Yard with Allusion at the Tunel Bar, Prague. 14/10/2025)

"I wasn't there to catch the early days of crossover (I wasn't born yet), but I love to watch the D.R.I. show at the Ritz from 1987. The best crossover show I was at was a D.R.I. and Wehrmacht show in Italy I watched together with former D.I.Y.Y. band members" Alon adds, regarding crossover fantasies and realities.

"During COVID lockdown in 2020 we did an illegal secret show in a club in Tel Aviv. During the live set, policemen came into the club and stopped the shows. Some guy started arguing with them and they punched and choked him. While the officers were busy with that guy, everyone was jumping from the second floor to the ground to run from the police and avoid getting a fine or getting arrested. Shoshan our drummer just stayed onstage and casually took down his gear, when the officers started yelling at him and threatening with arrest, he just told them to wait, unless they wanted to buy him new cymbals. They let him take everything down and walk out the venue without even a warning. But I, like an idiot, forgot the band's merch at the club so I went to get it and got a fine!", Alon shares a Death in Your Yard story.

Death In Your Yard are active (2025) and performing through mainland Europe in DIY places, recording new music, etc. "I think that since Municipal Waste started bringing back the movement of crossover it became relevant again. Not just musically but also as a movement" Alon concludes.

At a glance: I can't stand bands with mindless humour; okay, there are obvious exceptions like Adrenalin O.D. or Descendents or Steve Stiletto and Stukas Over Bedrock, and pizza thrash is maybe the worst thing that can happen to me, but when Death In Your Yard are going for political lyrics, they are good. Their style is a mix of 1980s and today's crossover, and I think that newcomers to crossover will enjoy their shows in Europe.

TOXIC SHOCK

(Toxi Shock band picture. Courtesy of Guy Kokken)

Pieter Coolen (guitarist of Toxic Shock) was one of the first people that sent me a message when *Crossover The Edge* was released, and he expressed his enthusiasm mentioning that 'I looked forward for this book for years!". We started chatting immediately, only to discover soon enough that he is the guitarist of two of the most exciting current bands in Europe: Toxic Shock and Crime Scene (featuring members of Poison Idea). Years went by, we were always having a small chat regarding punk, hardcore and crossover, and time has come for a Toxic Shock feature.

Formed in 2010 in Antwerp, Belgium, Toxic Shock have been very prolific both in terms of live appearances and in terms of releasing music, and Pieter tells their story: "We started rehearsing in 2010. Four dudes that had been friends for a long time. We went to a lot of hardcore and metal shows together before we started Toxic Shock. We all had been in bands but never played in a band together. Wout, our drummer really wanted to be in the band, but we had two guitar players and a bass player already, so he just started drumming. He never played drums before so he kind of grew into the amazing drummer he is now. After trying a few dudes on vocals, we finally found Wally. He worked as stage manager sometimes in the venue where I used to work and wanted a band badly. I liked the dude, so we decided to give him a shot, and it worked out great. We're still the same five guys as when we started, and I love that. Sometimes a friend fills in on drums, bass or guitars, but most of the times Toxic Shock is Maarten, Wout, Wally, Danny and me. The four of us (except Wally) grew up in the same small town close to Antwerp. And we had a mutual love for Suicidal Tendencies, Slayer, Black Sabbath, early Metallica and a lot of hardcore and punk. That combined with my love for New York Hardcore and Danny's Venice adoration makes Toxic Shock what it is. Wally is a bit younger, so he brings in a whole newer batch of band influences. We shared the stage with a lot of bands we love: Poison Idea, Suicidal Tendencies, Power Trip, Gatecreeper, Agnostic Front, Cro-Mags, Municipal Waste, Iron Reagan, Slapshot, Disfear, Discharge, Negative Approach, D.R.I.

and many more. Special mention for Testament, we played a show with them, and they had a He-Man like backdrop that was also there during our show, ha-ha! I loved that".

In 2011 they released their first demo, and from the first song it was evident that Toxic Shock was special. Two songs of hardcore-thrash, reminiscent of a cross between Nuclear Assault and NYHC ('Mother of All Mothers') with Excel and early Suicidal Tendencies ('You Suck'), and the future was bright.

"Don't really know which band was the first real crossover band" Pieter argues. "I think some bands started mixing metal and hardcore around the same time, bands like D.R.I., Suicidal Tendencies, Corrosion of Conformity, Beowülf and a bit later New York followed with Agnostic Front, Cro-Mags, Crumbsuckers, Leeway. And maybe the first was Motörhead. Lemmy and company have their own special blend of punk and hard rock. Oh yeah, let's not forget Discharge. They took punk to another level with their ferocious mix of fast-paced hardcore punk and metal with great lyrics. As a young hardcore and metal kid I found out that all the early thrash metal bands that I liked were influenced by heavy metal and Discharge so I had to check them out…I think that crossover was an outcome that a lot of the hardcore bands got better at playing their instruments. And the hardcore kids brought some street and reality into metal. Now everything is mixed, but back then it must have been pretty crazy to see former hardcore bands with long hear and metal riffs".

Toxic Shock played both in DIY venues, as well as metal clubs, and they seemed to crossover even from their very beginning, not only musically, but in terms also of gigging. "It was difficult for some people to pinpoint us" Pieter narrates. "Was Toxic Shock a metal band or a hardcore band? For some people that was confusing. From the beginning we played metal shows, hardcore shows and punk shows. Some people found that confusing. A lot of metalheads liked the music but weren't used to a frontman who is really all over the place, doing backflips, climbing all over the stage, ending shows bleeding and in his underpants and sometimes even diving into the drum set. I love Wally for his craziness onstage. I think he's one of the greatest frontmen in Belgium".

Next release was the 2012 *Toxic Shock* 12-inch; I won't review all Toxic Shock stuff since there are so many 7-inchs, demos and split releases, so I'll stick to some that are fundamental for the band. *Toxic Shock* 12-inch that was a big step forward for the band. Their influences are still there in their three songs, plus an Uncle Slam cover. Now they sounded more confident forming their own sound. 'Ice Cold Black' and 'Hard Candy' are the best songs off this release, that was still on the boundaries of hardcore-thrash with a few more mosh parts thrown in.

"I have a few riff bibles and riff lords" Pieter admits, regarding his influences. "Exodus has fantastic riffs. I loved the Holt - Hunolt guitar team. Jeff Hanneman has always been a real inspiration. Cro-Mags, the first three albums are important to me riff-wise. Suicidal Tendencies from their debut up to *Lights, Camera, Revolution*. Agnostic Front *One Voice*. Love Matt Henderson's riffs (also the stuff he did with Madball).

AJ Novello and the first two Leeway albums are always an inspiration. Discharge *Hear Nothing, See Nothing, Say Nothing*. Black Sabbath, Judas Priest (the seventies stuff). And the past years Poison Idea is also a huge influence for me. Besides that, I get inspired by a lot of newer stuff, even soul music (breaks). NYHC up to 1992 or so is always an influence. I think what a lot of bands did there was totally original. When we recorded in Denmark with Flemming Rasmussen for our second album, I tried for months to only listen to stuff before 1984. I wanted to hear what the early thrash bands listened before they recorded their classis stuff. So, a lot of hardcore punk, Sabbath, Discharge and NWOBHM".

Their 2013 release, the *Daily Demons* LP released on Reflections Records finds Toxic Shock in full form. Some of their best songs are in this record. 'My Life' sounds like a cross between Slayer, Exodus and Poison Idea, 'Mr. T' goes for a Slayer-meets-Cro-Mags and Excel. While obviously 'I Shot Joe Biden' was an homage to 'I Shot Reagan' of Suicidal Tendencies (I would though prefer a song over Yves Leterme or Guy Verhofstadt, haha!).

"I was born in 1978, so when the first crossover bands started doing their thing, I was still a very young kid" Pieter adds. "My love for metal started when I was twelve years old and hardcore came a bit later. There was no internet to discover bands, and I had no older brother or sister (I'm the oldest) that paved the way for me. I thank *Aardschok* and *Metal Hammer* and some other well-known magazines for showing me many cool bands. Onno "Cro-Mag" [van Ravesteijn] (RIP) took care of the hardcore and punk stuff at *Aardschok* and *Metal Hammer*. Got to know many bands thanks to him. And there was a radio program called Metalopolis that introduced me to many bands. The local library had a lot of good CDs that I borrowed. And we made tapes for each other. One of the first hardcore shows I saw was Sick of it All when *Just Look Around* came out. They totally blew me away at that gig. I had a cassette with that album on and I liked it. But after seeing them live I knew this was the music needed to explore. I loved a lot of metal bands (Black Sabbath is still the best) and Suicidal and Slayer. And Cro-Mags - *Alpha Omega*, Agnostic Front - *One Voice* and Leeway - *Desperate Measures* were important albums for me".

Toxic Shock-Iron Reagan split 7-inch followed in 2015, with the artwork getting a treatment by amazing Ric Clayton of No Mercy and Suicidal Tendencies. Obviously, the first song named 'The Survivalist' kicks off with the shout 'I'm Back', just like ST's 'Suicidal Maniac'. A great song! 'Singalong Letdown' is just mental, maybe one of my favourite songs from Toxic Shock, fast, wild and to the point. Another fine release.

(Toxic Shock at the Surfing Eindhoven Dynamo fest, 12/06/2015)

Through their existence, Toxic Shock have appeared in big fests such as Venezia Hardcore Fest alongside The Exploited, Lion's Law, Mindforce, etc or Dynamo Fest, alongside Suicidal Tendencies; appearing live with bands such as Carnivore A.D. and Poison Idea, as well as smaller DIY shows e.g. Punk for the Refugees show in Belgium.

"A lot of our friends have the Toxic Shock logo tattooed" Pieter shares some stories from Toxic Shock. "We had a buddy doing flash tattoos at some of our release shows. And other people got a Toxic Shock tattoo after those shows. I thought that was crazy. We played at the Sonic Blast festival in Portugal twice. They love us over there (and we love Portugal). The crowd went nuts the three times we played there. We played after Nick Oliveri and Brant Bjork what would have never happened in Belgium. We sold all our merch at that gig after that show. There was a long line of people just waiting to get merch. Crazy! And we had a scooter in the pit once at a thing called Rampjam. There's a video of that somewhere on YouTube. We did a split with Iron Reagan with a cover by legend Ric Clayton. We had a crazy shirt drawn by T&C legend Steve Nazar. We recorded with Flemming Rasmussen in Denmark. Lots of great stories. There was talk of going to Japan when we did the split with Reproach. But unfortunately, it never happened (COVID was the main reason)".

Their next full-length release though, the 2017 *TwentyLastCentury* LP left me speechless; now bringin' into their sound some influences by modern crossover bands like Power Trip and Foreseen, all blended via the riffing styles of Nuclear Assault, Leeway, and Slayer. *TwentyLastCentury* is just a phenomenal release, a modern crossover classic. All songs are ripping with the Leeway-meets-Suicidal 'Immobilized and Paralyzed' being a crusher, and 'Great Great Gift' alongside 'Serpent's Tongue' being real hits. It's a damn shame that this LP hasn't got more recognition so far…

Toxic Shock's most recent offering was the 2023 *Reborn* 12-inch EP, that showed a progression through *TwentyLastCentury*'s sound, a bit darker, with some The Accüsed and Poison Idea influences thrown in, making it the most bitter and angry record they ever released. Songs like 'Quick to Forget' or 'Procrastination Frustration' are catchy as hell. Did I mention there is an Antidote cover of 'Real Deal' that shreds?

Other bands that members of Toxic Shock are playing (or having played with) include DK's and Wotte's Damaged Goods, and Pieter's Between The Lines and SYC. However, Pieter formed in 2020 the excellent Crime Scene, that is more based on the mid-tempo, traditional hardcore (with slight metal elements) sound of early 1990s Poison Idea, releasing one single, one demo, and one 12-inch EP, all crucial stuff for everyone into this sound-I love them. And how could it be different, since Poison Idea's Jerry Lang is the vocalist of Crime Scene!

"It's not as new or groundbreaking as when it started. Everything is already done" Pieter admits about the state of crossover today. "But there are always new bands that bring something great to the genre. I loved what Power Trip did. I'm glad they will be back (but I'm going to miss Riley for sure). But that band was on the way the be big, I guess. Enforced gets better and better with each release. I love Foreseen. So yes, if bands can get new kids enthusiastic about the music it's still relevant. There are many cool new bands in the UK that people should check out".

At a glance: Seconds ticking fast away on Earth's bio clock, and you have to get at least two Toxic Shock releases (I would recommend *TwentyLastCentury* LP and *Reborn* EP) if you are into the riff-laden, fast thrash hardcore of a musical mix that reminds of Leeway, Suicidal, Nuclear Assault, Power Trip, The Accüsed. Fans of Poison Idea: stay alert, because Crime Scene are a top-notch band, so be sure to pick up Crime Scene 12-inch EP. That said, Pieter was another one excellent guy that send me his band's records as a gift. Stay strong my brother--we will survive!

CLUSTERFUX

(Clusterfux band picture. Courtesy of Tracy Bailey)

One of the unsung modern heroes of crossover, Clusterfux from Denver, Colorado, formed in 1995 and are still active (and stronger!) today in 2025. Vocalist Josh Lent narrates their story: "Van (bass), Justin (Lent, guitar) and I all grew up in the same town together. In fact, Justin and I are brothers. Joe (McCumbee, drums) was from the next town over, and we met him in high school in the 1980s. Piker (Joe Mama, bass) was a bit younger and from the same town as Joe. Carbondale and Glenwood were small towns down valley from Aspen. We had bands and would try to keep a scene alive over there, but these were really small towns back then and some of us hungered for what the big city had to offer. Van, Justin and I all moved to Denver in the mid-1990s, and Justin put Clusterfux together. I joined shortly after, and we had our first gig only a week or two later in Boulder. Van joined us later but left the band for a few years and returned again after some time. Same with Piker, he was in, he was out, he's back! We recruited Joe (McCumbee) because we needed a new drummer and even though he lived a bit far we knew we wanted to play with him again. Earlier versions of the band had the dual male and female vocals, Jessica (1995-2000) and Celia (2000-2002). We took that idea from Nausea. After a while we settled on just me doing vocals, it was easier and there were too many people in the band! We always stood out from the pack, the classic 'too punk for the metalheads and too metal for the punks' issue. Rather than seeing it as a problem we saw the flexibility that gave us to play with grind bands, thrash bands, street punk, hardcore etc. I remember there was a time where we would intentionally wear metal shirts if we were playing with more punk styled bands and punk shirts if we were playing with more metal minded bands. Over the years we've been very fortunate to play with many of the bands we grew up listening to".

As aforementioned, in the first period of the band (1995-2002), Clusterfux had two secondary vocalists, Jessica and later Celia. Their first release was the 1997 *On Capitol Hill with Punks and Swill* split LP alongside the anarcho-punks Up Yours! Rooted in the DIY punk scene, Clusterfux's initial approach was in-line with the anarcho-hardcore and crust of the 1990s era, rough, very loud and political, with dual vocals, and songs as brutal as 'Committing Me' and 'Too Broke'. If you're into bands like Nausea, Brother Inferior or Civil Disobedience and Code 13 you will love Clusterfux in that era's releases. Still, no hints of metal; just a few double bass drumming here and there! Vicious stuff!

"Black Sabbath, they crossed over before there was punk or metal and it came forth in the song 'Paranoid'. Even Ozzy has referred to it as a punk song" Josh mentions, regarding the first crossover band. "Listen to how angry the *Sabotage* album is. It's punk as fuck. The way Sabbath wrote a protest song was shocking compared to the folk inspired protest songs of the era. John Fogerty is penning 'Fortunate Son' and Sabbath is talking about bodies burning in the field or the effects of drugs turning your body into a corpse and this was real, this was reality. And isn't that what punk being partly about, bringing some reality into music. I think that really shows how closely related the two genres are. From there it was likely Motörhead, they just took such a no bullshit approach to their brand of rock 'n' roll that it was punk and metal at the same time. It was crossover without intentionally being crossover. You could probably say the same about Discharge to some extent. There was a cross pollination taking place by the mid- 1980s for several reasons, after D.R.I. released *Crossover* it became much more intentional. But as far as being the first and it just emerging free of intent, it would have to be Motörhead if not Sabbath".

Clusterfux's first full-length is the 1999 self-titled LP, on Queen City Punks Records. Now things went a step ahead; fantastic anarcho-hardcore, tighter than before, reminiscent of a cross between Final Conflict, Detestation and Christ on Parade, with slight metal riffing. Absolutely brutal, with every song being a winner. 'Lying Here' is unbelievable, while 'Think It Over' and 'Air Raid' are simply powerhouses of brutality, plus a great cover of 'Amerikkka The Myth' by Christ on Parade. *Clusterfux* LP is among their best releases!

In terms of musical influences, Josh adds that "for me personally and as far as what I do in the band its Attitude Adjustment, Circle Jerks, Final Conflict, D.R.I., Agnostic Front, The Accüsed and the Cro-Mags. I know Justin has mentioned S.O.D., Exodus, Discharge and Overkill over the years. Joe speaks of Reed Mullen of COC. Septic Death, Nausea, The Exploited, D.R.I. and Broken Bones are on everyone's lists of influences. I think in visual terms we probably lean more towards metal influences. Skulls, gnarly shit. Not that punk bands don't use skulls but when I look at punk band art, our stuff is definitely more metal. I like shit that's cool, that's gnarly. A lot of punk art is goofy. I was just at a big 'punk' fest and it was just so obvious that much of what is considered punk these days does not resonate with me at all. I've always liked the more hardcore side of punk and in general that's true about the rest of the band. We are more likely to be found at a Napalm Death show than Rancid or something like that".

While Clusterfux where touring heavily on the US, playing mostly in DIY space, they were ready to unleash another one bomb; the 2003 *Thrash Mongrel* CD pre-dated their expansion towards a more crossover sound, even though their base was still into crust and anarcho-hardcore. From the opening shredder of 'Sign Of The Times' to 'Making Fuck' and the mental 'NeonChrist', Clusterfux sound on fire! More metal now, with some heavy breakdowns added mostly in the tradition of Cro-Mags, as well as a heavy bass sound reminiscent of the 2000s Varukers style. *Thrash Mongrel* is a record that would appeal to both camps of hardcore and crossover fans.

"There was metal or at least hard rock before punk started" Josh narrates. "So, these kids were listening to Black Sabbath and KISS as they were forming the first hardcore bands. It was inevitable, again the two genres are so closely related. I saw the Circle Jerks the other day and Keith Morris was wearing a Black Sabbath shirt. And then you hear the stories about how some bands were trying to distance themselves from the violence of the hardcore scene, or that they were getting bored with hardcore or even that they just learned to play better and it was the natural evolution. But then there were also the kids my age that came into things in the second half of the 1980s. We were metal heads, into Ozzy, Priest etc and we started to get into skateboarding and thrash. We were too young to be part of the early hardcore scene but were ready for this! When the 7-Eleven opened in our town and they had *Thrasher* in stands our world changed. *Thrasher* was far more influential on our scene than *Maximum RNR* ever was. Thrasher was half music back then, Pushead's 'PusZone' opened us up to a whole new world. Now we were being exposed to JFA, Excel, Suicidal Tendencies, GBH, The Exploited, The Accüsed etc. These new sounds were being added to our foundation of classic metal. I had a recorded tape with Black Flag on one side and Metallica on the other. It was all the same to us. It was all rebellious, fast, loud and aggressive. And so were skateboards. Growing up in a small town we took it all in, a separation of hardcore and metal scenes was something that maybe still existed in the cities but in the small town we were all hanging together, we had to for the numbers! So, it just all swirled together. The big band in our area was E.O.S. (End of Story). They were this crazy blend of D.R.I. and Dag Nasty. Even on the back of the album one dude is wearing a Dag Nasty shirt and another is wearing a Metallica shirt. Their drummer Joe is in Clusterfux now, has been for about ten years. It just made so much sense to us and then as you grow up, you're more punk or hardcore for a while, you get into a more crust-oriented groove for a while, ya' know you just go through the phases of life but there is always this foundation of Black Flag and Metallica".

Problem Reaction Solution CD was their next release (2009), another one exhibition of brutality: now heavier than before, Clusterfux on this release sound like Attitude Adjustment gone anarcho-hardcore! Surely one of their heaviest records, with songs as wild as 'Lies' and 'Bbaga' and 'You Suffer'; plus covers of 'Patriot Fight' by Dead Silence and 'Largactyl' by Amebix. The only thing that does not work well in *Problem Reaction Solution* is the trebly under-production.

(Clusterfux with Stalag 13 and Chew Thru at the HQ, Denver. 17/12/2021)

Regarding the clubs and spaces in Denver scene, Josh narrates that "Garageland was a rad venue in Denver that celebrated the larger punk and hardcore scene, and the lineups were always diverse. It brought a lot of people from all over the area together to take part in all things punk and hardcore, metal bands too. Blast-O-Mat was another favourite, it was the crust and grind epicentre of Denver for years. Sure, other bands would play there too but that was the main scene there".

Abandon Your Gods LP (2012) was the first release I got by Clusterfux. Josh was super-kind enough to send me a copy for free, when *Crossover The Edge* was released, telling me that 'I think that you will like our band'. And obviously, I did! The classic guitar acoustic intro is followed by the hardcore crossover explosion of 'Buy Or Die', and Clusterfux expose their crust roots too on songs like 'Ignorant and Arrogant' that sounds like a cross between Amebix and Sacrilege or the frenetic 'Everyone Dies'. Another cover here is also included, the 'Telling Me How To Die' by the excellent melodic hardcore E.O.S., getting the Clusterfux treatment! Ace!

Regarding his favourite crossover shows, Josh adds that "I only got to see Attitude Adjustment once, it was in L.A. They kicked ass so that show always stands out for me. When we brought The Accüsed AD to Denver that was really special too. Toxic Holocaust's first show in Denver was in Justin's living room! I remember Joe caught D.R.I. on the *Four of a Kind* tour with Kreator, what a killer lineup. I was always jealous of that one. Not really crossover but the first time I saw Youth Of Today it was just fucking insane from the first note, bodies flying everywhere. I had never seen so much stage diving ever, probably still haven't. One show that really stands out was a show in Denver in 1989 or so, it was all Colorado bands: the Violent Degenerates, Blistering Body Pus, Animosity and some others. It was a huge show, and it was long hair and mohawks everywhere with a few skinheads milling about. Even the dude I went with was more this Motley Crue type rocker and I was a skate punk in my Vans and mohawk. It was a total crossover melting pot. Justin caught the Agnostic Front-Cannibal Corpse tour back in the 1990s. There is this flyer for a show in California in the late 80s that I always thought exemplified crossover really well. It was Nuclear Assault with Dag Nasty and Youth Of Today. Amazing".

Clusterfux released many 7-inchs, demos and splits throughout their existence that I won't review, since they are too numerous to mention. However their 2020 split 7-inch with Paco Rivera's S.M.D. is wild! Their latest offering was the 2024 *Defy* LP; here, they went full-on crossover, with some anarcho-crust touches, and holy hell, this is just ripping! Fast and wild West Coast styled crossover, just imagine D.R.I. blended with Attitude Adjustment and The Accüsed, only with a rougher DIY approach! *Defy* sounds absolutely out of control, just check songs like 'Blood', the blasting 'Trained To Kill' and 'Bomb Blast, Anthrax, Gas Attack', this is just top-notch crossover!

Finally, Josh adds a few stories from Clusterfux, from over the years: "When we used to play L.A. a lot, we always saw the craziest shit at shows. One of the first times we played was like North L.A., Van Nuys. Some kid got stabbed next to our van, there were this really young punk rock kids smoking meth or crack behind the van. This kid got stomped out in the pit, everyone just beating the fuck out of him. And then the L.A. sheriff raided it. It was like an episode of *Cops* [American TV program]. They were coming over the walls of the backyard wearing those green windbreakers that say sheriff on the back and the helicopter was circling overhead. Another L.A. show was in this vacant lot and one of the dudes from one of the bands busted this dude in the face with a brick which bounced off his face into the SMD guys' van and still have enough force to bounce off there and hit Rito (from SMD) in the shoulder. There was a huge bonfire and sure enough LAPD, and the fire department raided the scene!".

And what about crossover's relevance today? What Josh things about it? "The crossover, the cross pollination is complete for the most part. There really isn't much of a difference anymore. There are some old die-hards that are heels dug into whatever camp they align with but for the most part its all the same now. Agnostic Front just toured with Obituary, that' s it ya' know? The big punk fest I was just at was an example of that, there were kids in black metal shirts, Cannibal Corpse shirts, there were a lot of Metallica shirts. One of the last big shows we played there were mohawks and long hairs all running around in the pit. Propaghandi took on a more metal sound on a recent album, The Casualties added some more crunch to their guitar tone. The dude from Rancid has his metal band now, Charger. Not all bands are crossover per se but as far as the fan base and people's interest in music, that part has completely crossed over. And again, I take it back to Black Sabbath. Everyone loves Black Sabbath, they started all of this. RIP OZZY!".

Clusterfux are active (2025) and going strong, while Justin and Josh also play on the crust ROÄC. Justin also played in Thaumaturgy (black metal) and Hirax, while Dan (RIP 2024) played in Apocalyptic Christ (death-grind), and Joe Piker plays in Bloodstrike (death metal) and played in the crossover thrash Doomed Youth. Josh and Justin operate the excellent Chain Reaction Records that is also a record label too which opened August 2014 in Lakewood Colorado. Chain Reaction Records is a destination for all things punk, hardcore, metal, etc and a skate shop, so if you are near the area, you know what to do!

At a glance: I would trade one hundred 'pizza thrash' goofy bands of today for just a 7-inch release by Clusterfux. They are heavy, dedicated, DIY, political and brutal as fuck. I believe that all their periods have something, either for hardcore kinds, crust punks or crossover types, however, in terms of crossover, their last LP, *Defy*, is just mandatory! But yes, visit www.chainreactionrecords.com and buy yourself some Clusterfux records!

INHUMAN NATURE

(Inhuman Nature band picture 2023. Courtesy of Issy R-L)

The new wave of UK crossover includes bands as good as Pest Control (Leeds), Rakshas (Bristol), Rad (Brighton), Grifter (London), Manic Aggression (Sheffield), Syncratic (Glasgow), Contract Killer (London), Implement (Leeds), Peacekeeper (London), Asidhara (Cardiff), Overpower (Bristol), Road Mutant (Norwich) and Freeze (Kent). Inhuman Nature from London belong to this current crop of bands, being formed in 2017. Their lineup now (2025) includes Simon Grubb (drums), Mack Stray (guitars),

Christopher Barling (vocals), Ben Taylor (guitars) and Daragh Markham (bass). The band members have been in or are currently in acclaimed bands such as Hang The Bastard, Dungeon or the excellent heavy metal of Amulet.

I'd like to than my friend Theodor Papargyris for bringing me in touch with Inhuman Nature; he's not only a huge fan of them, but also a friend of the band, that kindly responded to all my demanding questions!

"It's a little hard to pinpoint any one band, even harder to say if they mixed the two consciously, and there's valid arguments for numerous contenders, but my gut says Discharge were the first to mix punk and metal" Daragh narrates. "They were simply a game changer for the musical landscape. Without them, their apocalyptic heaviness, their speed, their D-beat, their nuclear themes, you wouldn't have the thrash that would later meet hardcore and become crossover. You wouldn't have this punk that was faster and heavier than most metal of the time, that metalheads could find palatable and exciting and inspiring. As we've been told, things were very tribal back then, a lot of parochial mentalities, metal and punk kept separate. And you can understand why - a lot of first wave punk must have sounded just crap to metalheads. And then by 1981, with all that '77 era punk stuff truly passé, Discharge dropped the *Why?* EP like an atomic bomb. Jesus, even their first couple singles before that inspired die-hard metal nerds like Tom G Warrior. Whether Discharge were intentionally working metal into their sound or not is another argument of course. (You could maybe also argue Amebix, who were influenced by Sabbath, Motörhead and Venom as much as they were by Killing Joke, Crass, etc. and were making very dark, heavy, metal punk early on. But their sphere of influence on metal was much, much smaller than Discharge's)".

Inhuman Nature's first release was the *Other Realms* 2017 demo was limited to fifty copies with excellent cover artwork. The demo has three songs of echoey, hard-hitting crossover thrash that is reminiscent of Power Trip, Cro-Mags, Exodus and The Accüsed, with my favourite being the 'Lowest Depths' that has a very Nuclear Assault vibe too! On the same style but with even better songwriting, came the two next singles, 'Taste The Steel' (2018) and 'Satan's Claw' (2019).

"Simon and I used to be in a band called Hang The Bastard which was very active in the UKHC scene from around 2008 to 2012 so that did make getting this band off the ground a little easier, and when we started out, we mostly played with hardcore bands" Christopher adds. "Our first show was with Burn and then before we'd hit the ten-show mark we had played with Judiciary, Sheer Terror, Turnstile and High-Vis so we seemed to slot in well to hardcore shows but soon found ourselves playing more and more metal shows. It wasn't an intentional shift; it just seemed to happen naturally. For us, mixed bills and playing with bands that are different from us has always been our preference and what we enjoy the most, and sometimes that's just because it can be more of a challenge live".

Time had come for their first, full-length release, the excellent *Inhuman Nature* 2019 LP; containing the two previous singles, *Inhuman Nature* included some new influences too. One can hear the Slayer-meets-

Exodus-meets-Leeway on 'Carnivorous Lunar Activities' or even Testament-gone-crossover-and-Sodom on 'Forgotten Tombs'. This LP was (then) their best effort, and things could have been way different if COVID-19 didn't show up…no gigs was a disaster for so many young and promising bands that years.

"Regarding crossover, I think it was political" Daragh continues. "Music and youth culture often inevitably cross over as music and youth culture go hand in hand together. But the 1980s, as with nowadays, were an incredibly politically charged time. Unemployment, stagnating and abandoned industries, mass strikes, the imperialism of the Cold War, the threat of nuclear annihilation, Apartheid, the rise of Neo-liberal policies and upwards concentration of wealth, the return of fascists and nazis in the streets, the police being wielded as a private army. All the social and political problems that festered from the mid-1970s onwards, now began to burst open, the poison seeping freely. Let's not misconstrue things - Black Sabbath had written about war and poverty and social issues since day one, but it wasn't in the same way that Crass, for example, depicted things. So, with Discharge taking Crass' thematic cues, but creating this monstrously heavy, fast, angry music, with the politics right in your face. It gave metalheads of the time permission to be more overt in writing about politics. It wasn't the wimpy 'I can't get a job, I'm just a yob' politics of the late 1970s punk. It was apocalyptic, doomsday, hellfire shit (the nineteen fucking eighties, baby). What metalhead doesn't love that stuff? The times were getting worse, darker, the end of the world seemingly drawing ever-nearer. Accordingly, the music and themes matched the anxieties of the time, resulting in heavier, faster, darker music, opening the doors for metal and punk to cross over back and forth more freely than ever before. Besides all that, metal and punk as genres were maturing. Walls were starting to come down, borders slowly being erased, and the fans were growing up too. It's only natural for creative people to experiment and mix different things together. If I stuck to listening to the same metal bands I enjoyed as a teenager and nothing else, I'd need my fucking head examined".

However, Inhuman Nature didn't stop being prolific in terms of releasing great music. In 2020 they released on cassette *Live At The Dev* recorded live in London at The Dev, Camden 18 January 2020. In 2021 they released the split 7-inch with Road Mutant, and their 'Master Of Souls' was a monster mosher. In the following year, 2022 they released the cassette EP *Under The Boot* with the eponymous song containing some of the best guitar work they ever had in a song. A split LP with Ninth Realm was released in 2023, with Inhuman Nature contributing two songs: the vicious 'Take Them By Force' (with some echoes of Obituary creeping in!) and 'Beyond The Realms Of Sanity'.

"I joined the band later on, but my all-time influences are Discharge, Poison Idea, Motörhead, The Clash, Judas Priest, Black Sabbath, Amebix, Wolfbrigade, Swordwielder, MC5, Stooges, Anti Cimex, Morne, Repulsion, Gauze, Extreme Noise Terror, Disrupt, Instinct of Survival, Antisect, Deviated Instinct, Nausea, Sacrilege, Bolt Thrower, Neurosis" Daragh admits. "I don't get much gig-envy, but Carnivore would have been a good crossover band to have caught live back in their heyday".

After the release of a live cassette in 2024, *Meltdown In Milton Keynes*, Inhuman Nature released on 2025 their best record to date; *Greater Than Death* LP. The album is their most post-apocalyptic release, yet it maintains the element of immediacy. Songs like 'Dawn Of Inhuman Man' have added Celtic Frost to the blend (actually this one sounds like a NYHC gone Celtic Frost anthem), 'Servants Of Annihilation' is like mixing Slayer with Accused and NYHC, while 'Possessed To Die' even brings Testament in mind!

(Day Of Wreckoning Fest at Patti Pavilion, Swansea, 21/06/2025)

Inhuman Nature have been very active the last years, touring all over Europe, so I asked Chris if there were any crazy stories on the road: "Damn, they are so many! Here we go. Us and High Command sharing a dressing room with Sigh and they called us something in Japanese that loosely translates to 'stupid white people that drink'. We had hot boxed the room and drank all the beers, so they were quite on the money to be fair.

Me and Simon tag teaming a Stockholm to London drive in one go. It took us around thirty-three hours.

Turning up to a last-minute show in Weimar, Germany and being greeted with an enormous loaf of bread with our logo baked into it. Sadly, for me, not vegan.

Touring with the heaviest band of all time, Crowbar, is still crazy to me.

Driving nine hours from Prague to Warsaw to play to approximately nine people, including the members of Dungeon. I used all my beer tokens to buy the five people that paid in a beer as a thank you.

Playing at Sonic Blast Festival in Portugal at 3am and inhaling a bucket's worth of dust due to all the circle pits.

Famous comedian Henning Wehn turning up to a gig in Birmingham back in 2022.

Playing a seated only show at the Black Heart in Camden when those were the only shows you could have during COVID.

After playing a very cool show at Antwerp Music City, a tire on the van exploded five hours into an eight- or nine-hour drive to Gorlitz, Germany. The van swaying side to side as we hurtled down the Autobahn was terrifying. After a stereotypically efficient German roadside repair man arrived to sort this out, we got to the show with just enough time for it to happen and it turned out to be the wildest show of the tour".

"Theres a few places that are very dear to me and hold a lot of cool memories" Chris narrates. Playing big festivals and supporting bigger bands is all super fun and I love it, but when I look back over the last eight years, it's some of the early shows that I'm most fond of. Here's a few:

The Dev, Camden UK – The Dev is THE ultimate metal bar in London and where we played some of our wildest shows. Its small, cramped, the toilets are disgusting and mostly so are the people who go there, but what's not to love about that! Chris who manages the place fills in on drums for us all the time, a true legend!

Gerber 3, Weimar Germany – Imagine The Dev but instead of being situated in the disgusting hellscape of Camden, it sits quietly in the quaint little town of Weimar in Germany. We played here three times, twice in 2019 and then once again back in 2022. Apparently, it's one of the oldest squats in Germany. All the shows were great and everyone putting on the shows treated us so well, the punk stews have never been rivalled! Shout out to our mates Luca and Felix, we miss them!

Café na půl cesty, Prague Czech Republic – We played here twice back in 2019 on our first two EU tours, and each time was great! The second time with Dungeon being the most fun as we were just starting to get to know each other better, this was the first time we met Daragh who has now been our bassist for three years now. What I like about this place is that it sits in the middle of a little park in Prague and is just a nice little café serving vegan food to families throughout the day, and then at night you can have awesome hardcore, metal and punk shows! The shows were always donation entry, and everyone attending made sure to throw in.

Dolans Warehouse, Limerick Ireland – Okay so going back on what I said earlier a little bit, Dolans is a massive venue and the first time we played there was supporting Crowbar, which is obviously cool as fuck. Dolans was the first show on the tour, our first time in Ireland and it couldn't have gone better. Amazing crowd, everyone super friendly and welcoming. Trying Beamish for the first time, which could be superior to a Guinness. We made friends there that we'll have for a long, long time. Please get us back there!".

Inhuman Nature are going strong (2025), and hopefully their time will come because they totally deserve it. I like to think of them as the 'next big thing' in commercial status in crossover thrash, and I believe that they will achieve this one with their next LP.

"I would argue that the term 'crossover' itself isn't so relevant as so many bands today are inspired and influenced by various types of music, that unless you're intentionally homing in on and trying to replicate Cro-Mags album *Best Wishes* or something, then it's redundant to call yourself crossover in 2025. Almost anything can be classified as crossover really anyway, if you wanna take it far enough" Daragh concludes. "But, as long as the energy, aggression and themes/ideologies of punk and metal are still relevant, then any merging or crossing over of the two will continue to be relevant as well. Especially the political aspects. The world is much, much worse than when crossover first emerged. It needs a fitting soundtrack".

At a glance: Fan of Power Trip, Cro-Mags *Best Wishes*, Leeway, Exodus, Slayer and even some Obituary and Celtic Frost blended in? You need to check Inhuman Nature. Start with *Inhuman Nature* LP and then proceed to *Greater Than Death*. If those two fits you, get all their releases.

THE ONES FOR ALL

G.B.H.

(G.B.H. early 1980s band picture. Courtesy unknown)

Ah, G.B.H.! One of my all-time favourites, the band that got me into UK82 punk, and one of the bands that I have seen most times (fourteen in total) in my life. Formed in Birmingham, UK in 1978 as Charged G.B.H., along with Discharge, Varukers and The Exploited are the 'big four' of UK82, influencing thousands of bands from all over the world for nearly fifty years. The first lineup of G.B.H. included vocalist Colin Abrahall, guitarist Colin 'Jock' Blyth (both the longest-standing members of the band), bassist Sean McCarthy (replaced by Ross Lomas after two years) and drummer Andy 'Wilf' Williams.

On a personal note, G.B.H. for me were always the most rock-ish band of the UK82 bunch. I always loved the fact that they weren't as extreme as Discharge, nor as noisy as The Varukers or as crazy as The Exploited, however, they managed to bridge the UK punk's first wave with second wave, all filtered through their love for pub rock and Motörhead. I still recall the day I got *No Survivors* 7-inch in my teens, and when the eponymous song intro blasted into an all-out-attack, that was it. I became a fan instantly and started collecting their discography and catching them live whenever I could.

Some of the craziest shows I've ever been to include G.B.H. shows. They always attracted a diverse and rowdy crowd that included punks, skins, metalheads, rockers, rockabillies, and sometimes that mix would explode. In any case, their shows contained the pure essence of rock 'n' roll, that is wild fun.

(G.B.H two night-gigs on Broadway, SF 11-12/08/1983)

Obviously, this chapter isn't going to narrate the story of G.B.H.; most of you are familiar with it. I'm going to review some records off their huge discography, write a few thoughts regarding their influence. But firstly, there is a small interview with Andy 'Wilf' Williams, the first drummer of the band, who played up until the *1986 Oh No It's G.B.H. Again!* 12-inch EP.

Q: You joined GBH during a truly formative time for UK punk. Could you tell us a bit about your early influences both punk and metal and how they shaped your drumming style within GBH's sound?

Andy: Early influences were obviously Sex Pistols, The Clash and The Damned. Also, The Ruts were a big favourite. On the metal front, I grew up listening to Led Zeppelin, Thin Lizzy, etc. John Bonham has always remained my favourite drummer to listen to. Then Motörhead and Iron Maiden came along, and "Philthy Animal" Taylor was a big influence. I should add that nowadays I wouldn't piss on Maiden if they were on fire! I love Metallica too.

Q: When GBH first started, how did the local Birmingham punk scene react to the band? Was there immediate support, or did it take time for people to understand what GBH was doing?

Andy: The local punk scene was great with us, as we knew almost everyone. As our sound evolved the crowd evolved with us and remained loyal and supportive.

Q: Looking back at the classic GBH discography, which LP stands out as your personal favourite and why? Was it the energy in the studio, the songwriting, or the reaction from the fans that made it special for you?

Andy: My personal favourite was *City Baby's Revenge*, although it's difficult to pick apart. I think our songwriting had developed quite well and it was enjoyable to write and record.

Q: GBH toured relentlessly in the 1980s. Are there particular shows or tours that stand out in your memory as truly defining moments for the band?

Andy: I think the first time we played The Olympic in L.A. was memorable as it was the largest crowd we had headlined in front of (around 6,000) and they were absolutely crazy. That whole North American tour of 1983 was amazing.

Q: Is there any wild or unforgettable story from those days that still makes you smile (or shake your head) when you think about it now?

Andy: That whole era of punk is full of wild memories, and I can't really pick any out. Just glad I lived through those times!

(G.B.H. with Verbal Abuse, Cro-Mags and Nation On Fire at Club X, Santa Clara, CA. 16/07/1986)

The influence and legacy of G.B.H. has been massive through their existence, and it is spread in various scenes and styles all over the world. This is evident in the bands that covered their songs: Slayer and their cover of 'Sick Boy', The Accüsed and their version of 'Sick Boy', Cerebral Fix and 'No Survivors', Beowülf and 'Diplomatic Immunity', Ratos De Porao and 'Big Women', Looking For An Answer and 'Give Me Fire', The Forgotten and 'Knife Edge', Destruction and 'City Baby Attacked By Rats', Disfear and 'No Survivors', Death Breath and 'Lycanthropy', Whipstriker and 'Dead On Arrival'....the list is endless.

There was a time in the 1980s when you could see members of thrash metal bands wearing G.B.H. T-shirts, from Metallica, Hallow's Eve, Détente, Abattoir, Slayer to Sepultura, Kreator, Megadeth, Exodus, Holy Terror…G.B.H. were huge among metalheads due to their motörpunk headbanging punk style.

If you're not familiar with them, you should check out all their early releases for a start: beginning with their 7-inch EPs, the 1982 *Sick Boy*, *Give Me Fire* and *No Survivors* contain just hits! 'Give Me Fire' still sends shivers down my spine after all these years, while it remains a crowd favourite at their gigs, everybody goes crazy with this one. As for their LPs, the 1981 *Leather, Bristles, Studs And Acne* 12 EP is a huge classic, that is still based on the 1977 punk rock sound with some extra boost, and songs as mental as 'Knife Edge' and 'State Executioner'. The 1982 *City Baby Attacked By Rats* LP is one of the best records ever in punk (if you avoid 'Slut'). The band sounds totally out of control on this one; way heavier and rougher style than before. This is just a sharp shock to all senses with songs like 'Time Bomb', 'Maniac', 'I'm The Hunted' or the frenetic 'Passenger On A Menu', a real masterpiece. The follow-up of *City Babys Revenge* (1984) LP was calmer, more melodic, but still catchy and great. The songwriting here is just top with tunes like 'Diplomatic Immunity', 'High Octane Fuel' or 'City Babys Revenge', and even though I considered it a letdown when I was young, it grew on me over the years. Finally, their 1986 *Midnight Madness And Beyond* LP was their most metal to date. One trivia for geeks here is that the UK press of Rough Justice includes a crackle on all copies on the first song, something that is missing on the Combat Core version! Again, this is a great LP (yet not legendary like their previous output), with songs like 'Limpwristed', 'Future Fugitives' and 'Chance For Living'.

If you do like the records above, try all their later stuff too. G.B.H. never put out a bad record and their most recent studio LP, the 2017 *Momentum* is good too. And don't forget to catch them live; on their good day G.B.H. are one of the best live bands you can ever witness, driving big crowds crazy!

ANTI-NOWHERE LEAGUE

(Anti-Nowhere League band picture, Sounds magazine 22/05/1982. Courtesy of Chris Walter)

There are very few bands that achieved the crossover appeal not only between metalheads and punks, but between various crowds and subcultures that were punk and metal adjacent. Saint Vitus could gather hardcore kids, classic metal fans, and bikers. G.B.H. would have metalheads, punks and hardcore kids in their shows. Discharge, same as G.B.H. and Motörhead of course, with psychobillies and rockabillies and biker rockers included too. Misfits, however, their diverse fandom came after their initial break-up. And Anti-Nowhere League, from Royal Tunbridge Wells, Kent, England, that formed in 1979, just on the verge between first wave and second wave UK punk. They officially started as a four-piece band, with original members: Animal, Magoo, Bones and Baggy.

I was lucky enough to witness Anti-Nowhere League many times, both in England (Luton twice, London three times, Manchester twice) and in Greece in 2002. What always struck me in the case of their England gigs was that they managed to gather a diverse crowd that was comprised of bikers and rockers, metalheads, punks, psychobillies, skinheads (the Bedford-area skinhead crew in one of their Luton gigs were a damn fearsome bunch of lads), hooligans - every outcast you could imagine of, you could find him in an Anti-Nowhere League show. Their biker rock image, their harsh and nasty music that is catchy as hell, their tongue-in-cheek humour (not for everyone of course, and even me I have my objections) was the perfect blend for a show to explode.

You already know that bands like Metallica ('So What'), Sodom ('Let's Break The Law'), Antiseen ('(We Will Not) Remember You'), Vader ('We Are The League'), Parabellum ('For You'), Vision ('Let's Break

The Law'), Dimple Minds ('For You'), Benediction ('We Are The League'), SFA ('Let's Break The Law'), Toxoplasma ('Streets Of London'), have covered Anti-Nowhere League songs, totally different bands, from diverse musical backgrounds, and this is a proof of how great Anti-Nowhere League are.

But before continuing on with the interview that Nick Culmer, aka 'Animal' offered me with the loving help of Sophie Culmer, I would like to mention that all early material of Anti-Nowhere League are as classic as you can imagine. From the *Streets Of London* 7-inch and *We Are...The League* LP, up to *Out On The Wasteland*, Anti-Nowhere League are a class of their own. I have a very soft spot for the 1987 *The Perfect Crime* LP, since it proposes a new approach, more melodic, that shocked people - and this is fine by me! I also like records such as *Scum* LP which was the first I got off them, the date it was released. Overall, you can't go wrong with Anti-Nowhere League, you either love them or hate them! I'm on the lover side as you can guess!

And even if I 'damage' the persona of Animal, he was super-kind enough to provide me a great interview, so here we go!

(Anti-Nowhere League with The Meteors and The Defects at the Lyceum, 29/08/1982)

Q: Your early work was rooted in the raw energy of punk, but Anti-Nowhere League also carried a certain heaviness compared to many of your peers. Which rock or metal bands had the biggest impact on shaping your sound and attitude?

A: When Magoo (guitarist and founder member) and I first got together in 1979 our music came mostly out of 'glam rock' in the early seventies I was into Wizard, Mud, Sweet, etc then progressed into Meatloaf, Black Sabbath, KISS and so on... Magoo was more into Screaming Lord Such, T-Rex and old rock 'n' roll like Jerry Lee Lewis and Little Richard, but we were both turned on by the new bands like The Stranglers, The Damned, X-Ray Spex, etc…..Seeing Magoo and I both came out of the 'Bike' scene we knew we wanted a heavy sound but with the attitude of 'fuck you' and lyrically we did not want to scream out inaudible...we wanted everyone to hear exactly what we were saying about them...We had already gone round the block being bikers so our attitude of not wanting any success was forefront, although, what we did not expect was that a lot of people felt how we did about the times....the rest is history.

Q: Songs like 'We Are...The League' radiate aggression that resonates beyond punk. Did you consciously incorporate elements from hard rock or early heavy metal when writing, or did that crossover happen naturally?

A: As said in question one...we were bikers so naturally leant towards the hard rock scene, by the time the ANWL started punk was underway by five years, in those five years we had been hardened by detention centres and prison so anger was always going to be in our lyrics...along with criticism of politics and the piss taking of people who we called 'nowheres'...sad fuckers who were scared of living to the full.

Q: Over the years, many metal fans and even bands from the thrash and extreme scenes have cited Anti-Nowhere League as an influence. Why do you think your music connected so strongly with audiences outside the punk scene?

A: I think the 'respect'?....came from the fact we did not want fame (we had more fame on the outlaw bike scene)...we did not seek adoration ...we wanted nothing in return for our noise, that gave us the strength to go into the lyrical world with defiance without worrying about consequences or the fallout...love us or hate us we did not honestly give a fuck, it was the time for us to have fun...with two fingers up!

(Anti-Nowhere League with Social Unrest at Perkin's Palace, Pasadena. 05/07/1983)

Q: Metallica famously covered 'So What?', introducing the League to an entirely new generation of fans. How did that feel at the time, and how do you view the song's legacy today within both punk and metal circles?

A: 'So What' was written by Magoo and I in five minutes while listening to two boring fuckers in the pub bragging while getting pissed, on what they had done or dreamed of doing…as the conversation went on it got more stupid and ridiculous and so, the song took it to another level…a stupid song for the stupid 'one up man ship' pissed conversation of two dimwits…I think because it caused so much trouble back in the eighties it gave it strength for the metal scene…when played, it certainly upset people so if you are strong enough to carry it off then…light the blue touch paper and stand well back!…I think Metallica get off on playing it live to enjoy the fact that the biggest metal band in the world can still piss people off!…bless 'em.

Q: Looking back, do you see Anti-Nowhere League as a bridge between punk and metal- not only musically, but also in terms of attitude and audience crossover?

A: It depends on why you want to be in a band? To me writing songs is good therapy …write horrible things about people instead of doing things! Keeps you out of prison! Now, if you are seeking fame and fortune then don't look to the ANWL for inspiration…you will be doomed from the start, but….if you start a band just for the reason of having a great time upsetting people then it's a good life…what's the old saying?…'you build it they will come'…if your audience likes what they see and hear, then you have succeeded ….you can bleat till the cows come home of how fucking wonderful your band is and how fucking brilliant you are.. but only people will tell you the truth about you and your band and if you are worth going to see live, or even listen to……back the early eighties Lemmy and I used to knock around a lot due to the fact we had the same mates in the London bike scene ….and as that wonderful wise man always said….there are two kinds of music…good and bad! (But I would correct that into …good and shit)…RIP Lemmy. Long Live Punk…long live the ANWL!

OFFENDERS

(Offenders band live, 1984. Courtesy of Bill Leissner)

Not a crossover band per se, Offenders from Killeen, Texas were one of the most adventurous bands connected with the Austin scene. Their musical approach starting with the punk rock of *Lost Causes* 1981 7-inch, then heading into the hardcore of *We Must Rebel* 1983 LP and *I Hate Myself* 1984 7-inch, and ending in the crazy slightly metal hardcore of *Endless Struggle* 1985 LP. What was always significant in their case was their unbelievable technical proficiency, that even a not-well trained ear can get. Anthony Johnson (RIP 2012) was an excellent guitarist, that also played in Scratch Acid; J.J. Jacobson (RIP 2018) was the vocalist that replaced Mick Buck, and he was a street kid with a characteristic voice, that could balance with such an ease in hard-to-sing songs. Mikey Donaldson (RIP 2007) was one of hardcore's best bassists ever, with a sound of his own, top musicianship; while his contributions in D.R.I., M.D.C. and Sister Double Happiness were more than crucial. Pat Doyle, the drummer, just imagine a drummer than can pull off with ease jazz, progressive rock, hardcore, rock, heavy metal styles, and still sounding recognisable! Currently playing in the heavy metal band Ignitor; Pat also played in Butterscotch Tuna, El Pathos, Go Juice, Pocket Fishermen, T.A.N.G. and Texas Metal Outlaws, while anybody that has heard him mentions that you could recognise it's Pat's playing style, even two blocks away.

All their musical output is just crucial for hardcore kids, but I think that *Endless Struggle*, their final LP, will have an appeal also on crossover and metal kids. It's one of the best records ever, a crescendo of top songs, and Offenders sound like a mix between D.R.I., M.D.C. and Uniform Choice, under a heavy metal production, with guitar licks reminiscent of metal too. The musicianship sounds innovative even to this day heard on 'Face Down In The Dirt' or 'On The Crooked Edge'. It's like a jazz band performing hardcore attacks, while the songwriting on songs like 'Endless Struggle' and 'Get Mad' is top.

(Jeff Martin onstage, 1996. Courtesy of Mizuchi Bellum)

I had an interview with Jeff Martin, guitarist of Offenders when Pat Doyle and JJ Jacobson reunited the group in the 2000s. Jeff is as a punk, as he is a metalhead. He loves his punk and his metal so much, plus he was also the guitarist in the punk band Buzzcrusher, as well as Laughin' Dogs; again, with drummer Pat Doyle. He has also played with Motörhead tribute act Alan Davey's Ace Of Spades, and overall, he's a figure that can only make you love him.

Q: The *Endless Struggle* LP is often remembered for its raw energy and metal edge, even if The Offenders weren't strictly a crossover band. Which hardcore, punk, and metal bands from the past were your biggest personal influences, both as a musician and as a fan?

Jeff Martin: Alexandros, thanks for the question as I absolutely love talking about music! I have so many influences from so many different genres. I will start with a memorable quote from one of my guitar heroes, Pig Champion. Over whiskey and cokes I asked him, 'So who are you into Pig?'. We all remember the *Record Collectors* album cover, but I wanted to see where his current taste was. He looked at me and said, 'PSSSHHH – everything that YOU are into man!'. Great answer and it is true! At this point we all know the good stuff and have grown up on it. Music for me is pretty much pick a city, region, country or continent and its scene – and I can rattle off so many great bands from that area.

Hardcore? So many greats – of course D.O.A. (*Hardcore '81* – a Bible), Black Flag, M.D.C., Bad Brains, Battalion Of Saints, Poison Idea, Kraut, Discharge, G.I.S.M., Raw Power, Dr. Know, all the East Coast Kings like Cro-Mags, Agnostic Front, Slap Shot, Reagan Youth, F, etc.

Punk? I absolutely love and worship the first and second wave of UK punk and hardcore. Sometimes it is a blur to me because my favourites are kind of a blur of the two – hardcore punk. Punk can be fast and furious, and hardcore can be brutal and slower. The Stranglers and The Pretenders are two that I absolutely worship. Shout out to Aerobitch who I love also! American punk is in my heart as well of course. D.F.F.D. and cheers brother Jeff Dahl!

I absolutely love all international and national punk and hardcore – well, a hell of a lot of it anyway hahahahaha!

Metal? Early Maiden no doubt, mid Priest, all N.W.O.B.H.M., the *Fire Down Under* album by Riot (incredible!), early Saxon, Agony Column, *Blizzard Of Ozz*, Sabbath, etc. So many!

Biggest personal influences as musician and a fan? There are many, but to pinpoint: Motörhead – I found my way backstage at the age of fifteen in 1981 and they treated me like a king. They were all so incredibly cool. My all-time favourite punk band!

All of the guitarists and musicians that were led by Jerry A. from Poison Idea. I have never in my life heard or felt lyrics the way that Jerry writes and sings them – and that band and different lineups? Absolutely fucking insane. Incredible. Their fire will burn bright forever. Hard-Ons for talent and versatility – they can do any genre or style while literally standing on their heads! As people and musicians, they really don't get any better and I admire them so much. They deserve it all! For the classic rock blender with punk attitude and glam elegance the mighty Turbonegro. Alice became super relevant again thanks to them, and I swear that Happy Tom influenced hundreds of bands in the way he writes songs. I absolutely love them also. Thin Lizzy is also in my heart and soul. Had the privilege of seeing them on the *Black Rose* tour front and centre with Gary Moore, opening for Nazareth with Zal Cleminson on guitar. Two guitar players that daily blow my mind.

Last but certainly not least – my bandmates and friends in the Offenders. I joined my dream band, my heroes. It was the time of my life, and I always hope that my spirit and playing was a contribution.

Q: Thinking back to your bandmates — J.J. Jacobson, Mikey Donaldson, and Pat Doyle — do you recall what kind of bands they were most into at the time? (Especially since J.J. and Mikey are sadly no longer with us, while Pat went on to play in the metal band Ignitor.)

Jeff Martin: J.J. loved everything and I really came to understand that when I oversaw the music played during his memorial. He was the kind of guy that collected every Iron Maiden picture disc but could rattle off funk jams by Parliament or Commodores. Alice Cooper, the Dicks, Motörhead (the last lyrics he wrote were form a song called 'Long Live Lemmy'!) were all in his toolbox. To be truthful I think that J.J.'s favourite band was The Offenders.

Tony WORSHIPPED Leslie West and Mountain. Without doubt his all-time favourites. He also had a soft spot for the Ramones and UFO. Also collected Iron Maiden bootlegs!

Mikey had a wide range of taste too. I even saw Journey's second album in his collection. Later in his life he became obsessed with Swedish hardcore and of course he loved MDC and was a very early member of the KISS Army.

Pat loves his Scorpions and Judas Priest! Also, Montrose and Budgie. Iron Maiden is another big one. I think that there is very little classic rock or metal that Pat DOESN'T like!

Q: Out of The Offenders' recorded output, which record stands as your personal favourite, and why? What memories or qualities make it stand out for you?

Jef Martin: That is a tough one because the output was all so influential and important to me, but I must say it would be the first that I heard – *We Must Rebel*. The floor toms, the drumming as a whole and songwriting structure is absolutely nuts! Somehow it sounds like it was baked in the Texas heat. It sounds like cheap speed and Lone Star…I fucking love it. Nothing sounded like that before, and nothing ever will. Tribal. A true cry and release of emotion.

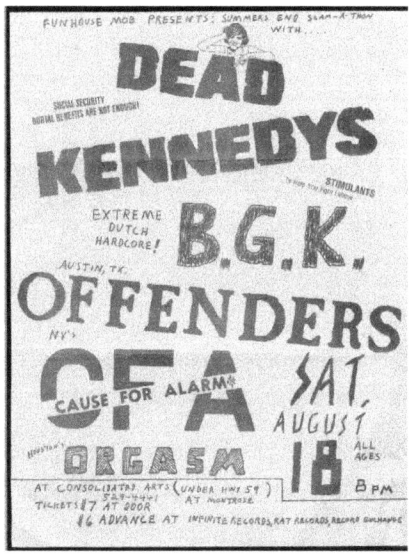

(Offenders with Dead Kennedys, B.G.K., C.F.A. and Orgasm at the Consolidated Arts, Houston, 18/08/1984)

Q: Looking back now, how do you see The Offenders' role in the Texas punk and hardcore scene of the 1980s, especially in terms of incorporating that metal edge that set you apart from many of your peers?

Jeff Martin: I can say this because I was a friend and fan first, before I joined on guitar – The Offenders were truly one of a kind. Just a kickass bunch of guys that had real belief in themselves and their band. Volume, integrity, a love for music, attitude, no giving a flying fuck about fashion…just laying it all on the table and playing it loud and furious. They had true musical chops, and I am so proud to hear about the influence they and we had worldwide. The albums and singles stand the test of time and are some of the greatest ever recorded. They were the real deal, and I miss that in life.

There were so many great bands from Texas…and I am proud when the Offenders are remembered and recognized. They without doubt have earned their place in time.

It may be an *Endless Struggle* but still, *We Must Rebel*. Stay young, stay free, and keep playing and supporting the good stuff!

Thank you, Alexandros, and thank you forever to Offenders believers everywhere!

(Offenders with D.O.A., Die Kreuzen and Shanghai Dog at Villa Fontana, San Antonio. 21/09/1984)

THE LABELS

GENERATION RECORDS

(Generation Records in NYC, courtesy unknown)

Not a strictly crossover label per se, Generation Records is a label that focuses on releasing either re-issues or demos of classic hardcore bands, since 2011. First and foremost a record store located in Greenwich Village. In operation since 1992, Generation Records have hosted many in-store performances, and I was unbelievably happy when I managed to visit the store in 2023.

When I visited the store, I didn't have the chance to meet the man behind it, Mark Yoshitomi. However I'd like to share a story of how I met him in London, later next year! I was in London for two shows: The Chisel and Cockney Rejects in December 2024. Me and my good friend Theo Papp hit initially All Ages Records in Camden where I got also the chance to meet the awesome Mike Fury. Blame Marginal Man and Wipers for that! Later we went down in Soho, at Sister Ray Records. So, there was a guy next to me, grate-digging in the 'hardcore' section, when he found a copy of Agnostic Front's *Victim In Pain* LP, the re-release by Generation Records, and took a photo of it. So, this is how it goes…

- Ahem, sorry, but you NEED to get this LP, you won't find it anywhere in Europe! It was released by Generation Records in NYC!
- Well…You know…Generation Records is my label…

I stood in owe, Theo freaked out. I mean what are the odds of meeting the Generation Records owner in London, while you haven't met him to his store! We laughed, sent a photo of us to Freddy Alva, and saw each other again at the Cockney Rejects and Infa-Riot show later.

(Generation Records crew with Roger Miret, 2024. Courtesy of Suzanne Tomatore)

Back at Generation Records label, I thought that it would have been a great idea to have a small chat with Mark, especially since he released three Leeway LPs the last years, so here it is. If you by any chance visit New York City, don't miss the chance to visit the store, you'll go nuts with the unbelievable amount of great records that are in. I'm a spoiled brat, so any friend that visited New York City also visited Generation Records to buy me stuff; thank you Stergios, George P., Giannis Konf. and Theo!

Q: Generation Records has long been a staple in New York's underground music scene. What motivated you to start reissuing hardcore and crossover classics, and how does that tie into your connection with the original '80s movement?

Mark: I just always wanted to put out records. I started buying punk and hardcore records when I was really young, so it's been a thing for me for a long time. I started going to shows in New York City when I was fifteen and Murphy's Law opening for The Beastie Boys was the first NYHC band I ever saw. I grew up in the second generation of New York hardcore going to matinee shows at CBGB's, The Pyramid Club, Lizmar Lounge, Anthrax Club in Connecticut, etc. I saw every band play that was on those classic NYHC comps from Revelation and Blackout! except maybe one (Norman Bates & The Showerheads).

Q: The NYC crossover scene of the 1980s was raw, political, and unapologetically aggressive. Which are your favourite records from that scene and era?

Mark: I didn't listen to a ton of crossover records back then. I liked more traditional hardcore, punk and Oi! music for the most part. The New York bands I liked back then were Cro-Mags-*Age of Quarrel*,

Crumbsuckers-*Life Of Dreams*, both Carnivore LPs and Sheer Terror-*Just Can't Hate Enough* (I consider that a more hardcore record, but it was influenced by a lot of metal). D.R.I. and The Accüsed and Cryptic Slaughter were some of the out of state more crossover type bands I liked. Everyone in the late 1980s were getting a bit more metal for the most part. Even that anarcho bands at that time in New York City. A band that played in straight early hardcore style like Life's Blood were seen as almost retro at the time only a few years after that first wave of NYHC.

Q: Reissuing hardcore and crossover records, especially from obscure or defunct bands must come with unique challenges. Can you share a specific story where tracking down masters or securing rights became a mission in itself?

Mark: Yeah, sometimes it's difficult to find members of those bands. Luckily, I know a lot of older people in the scene, and they were somehow able to get me in touch with a lot of the bands I've been dealing with. Most of the older crowd is very cool but once in a while you come across ones that expect an unrealistic pay cheque out of their old catalogue. I think only two of the bands we deal with had an actual reel tape that we had to get baked. Most of the sources are from either old records, cassette tapes or whatever a big parent company has as their source materials. Sometimes the band is like "just use the record, I didn't keep anything". If that's the case, we do get the sound tweaked on to give a bit better sound. My past licences have been fairly easy, but there's a bunch of titles I would love to do but either can't get in touch with the proper owners or have to deal with a huge corporation that can't be bothered to do a small project that they'll see very little on.

Q: Generation Records has played a key role in keeping Leeway's legacy alive. Leeway such a vital band within the crossover canon, and how has the response been to these reissues from both old-school fans and new listeners? One can see that Leeway's legacy is alive in bands like Combust or Mindforce and Drain for sure.

(Leeway's Enforcer demo re-issue)

Mark: I'm really honoured that we were able to do those titles. I saw them play a bunch in the late 1980s and AJ has been a good friend to me for like twenty or so years. For the most part, we got good receptions from the fans. I saw some people bitched about the lack of packaging in the demo reissue but that's the way AJ wanted it. No insert, like a no frills tape. Haha. They were definitely ahead of their time sound wise. It's kind of sad to me that bands that were clearly influenced by them are fucking huge and most of their fans have never even heard of Leeway. But I guess it always goes like that. I think AJ is pretty flattered that these newer bands are influenced by Leeway. Maybe that's the charm of a band like Leeway? They kept it too real for the masses.

Recommended Generation Records crossover records: Harley "Cro-Mags" Flanagan – *The Original Cro-Mags Demos* 1982/83 LP, Confusion – *Storm The Walls: 1990-1994* LP, Leeway – *Born To Expire* LP, Leeway – *Enforcer Demo* LP.

BEER CITY RECORDS

(Beer City Skateboards and Records logo. Courtesy of Beer City)

Beer City Skateboards & Records is an independent skateboard manufacturer and record label based in Milwaukee, Wisconsin, USA. Emerging from the underground in 1992 and becoming fully established in 1993, Beer City was built on a strong DIY ethic and a passion for both punk rock culture and skateboarding. From the very beginning, the label's mission was clear: to support and release music from quality punk and hardcore bands that were being overlooked by the mainstream and not receiving the exposure they deserved. As the years went on, Beer City grew steadily, gaining a reputation for authenticity, dedication, and consistency within the scene. While the label continued to push forward with new releases, it also began specializing in carefully curated reissues, bringing legendary and long out-of-print records back into circulation for new generations of fans to discover. This combination of championing fresh voices and preserving the legacy of classic punk and hardcore has solidified Beer City's place as an essential name in underground music culture. At the same time, Beer City has maintained its roots in skateboarding, crossing over on the two worlds of music and skate, just as they have always been in the fabric of DIY counterculture.

I've been following Beer City Records since the early 2000s, getting records by The Bristles, Disrupt Youth, Oppressed Logic and Very Metal (a great crossover hardcore band that released two CDs and it's still under the radar of most people). I was so happy that Beer City Records decided to re-issue some classic hardcore and crossover records on LP in the 2010s, like D.R.I.'s *Crossover*, Attitude Adjustment's *American Paranoia* or release new LPs by Clusterfux or Deathwish, motor-charged punk from Wisconsin.

Regarding Very Metal, their bass player Don Brazel, aka Vyvyan Mayall, aka Don 'Cunnilingus' aka 'Bastard' Brazel, adds that "the name Very Metal was a reference to The Young Ones, which we also used for the influence of the name of Bastard Squad (of St. Louis, Missouri). Our musical influences were the original punk bands like The Exploited, GBH, GG Allin, Broken Bones, Varukers, Peter And The Test Tube Babies and The Partisans, etc" (Don Brazel is currently playing in Bastard Squad, plus he's the owner of The Record Space record store in St. Louis).

I had a small interview with the mastermind behind Beer City Records, Mike Beer, and hopefully the Very Metal CDs will get a re-issue on LP some day!

Q: What motivated Beer City to reissue landmark crossover albums from bands like D.R.I., Verbal Abuse, Attitude Adjustment, and the Boneless Ones? Were these records chosen out of personal passion, fan demand, or a desire to preserve a vital era in underground music history? How do you balance staying true to the raw sound and aesthetics of the original releases while presenting them to a new generation of listeners? For example, what's your philosophy on remastering, artwork updates, or bonus materials?

A: For us it was making sure these classic releases once again were not only in print but also reissued properly. Not just some play, record, sloppy scan and we're done reissue. It must sound better and look better while staying true to the original. Bonus tracks and material is okay to if it adds to the release and isn't filler.

Q: Crossover has always existed at the intersection of punk and metal. From your perspective as a label, how do you see the legacy of those classic bands influencing today's punk, hardcore, and metal scenes?

A: You can hear the influence in the music. The really good bands are the ones that can take that influence and do their own thing with it.

Q: Beer City has deep roots in punk, skate culture, and underground music. How important is it for you to maintain that DIY spirit when working with iconic crossover releases, compared to larger labels who might approach them more commercially?

A: It's not really DIY spirit. It's making sure each record we put out sounds and looks its best.

Q: Looking forward, what role do you see Beer City playing in keeping crossover alive? Do you plan to continue focussing on reissues of cult classics, or are you also interested in supporting newer bands that carry on the crossover tradition?

A: We will definitely keep putting out reissues and putting out release by new bands that stoke us out.

Check Beer City Records on www.beercity.com and be sure to get Clusterfux - *Defy* LP and Deathwish- *The Fourth Horseman* LP, alongside some great re-issues!

Recommended Beer City Records crossover records: Very Metal- *Hit and Run* CD, Dirty Rotten Imbeciles – *Dealing With It* LP, Impulse Manslaughter – *Live At WFMU* CD, Deathwish – *Out For Blood*

LP, Attitude Adjustment – *American Paranoia* LP, The Boneless Ones – *Skate For The Devil* LP, Clusterfux – *Defy* LP.

F.O.A.D. RECORDS

(F.O.A.D. Records logo. Courtesy of F.O.A.D. Records)

A true powerhouse in reissuing hardcore, punk, and crossover records and demos, F.O.A.D. Records is an Italian thrash and hardcore label that traces its roots back to Turin in 1986, where it began as a fanzine and mail order service. Founded by Marco Garripoli (RIP), F.O.A.D. Records first emerged as a Xeroxed skate-hardcore-thrash fanzine, publishing seven issues between 1986 and 1990; each limited to just a few hundred copies. Over the years, the project organically evolved into a DIY label, with a strong focus on unearthing and releasing previously unheard recordings, initially through tape editions. What I always admired in the re-issues of F.O.A.D. Records is the great packaging that included flyers and posters or even OBI strips included in heavyweight records, that always managed to keep things as close as possible to the original recordings, always at decent prices. Their re-issues are so well-done, that I have found myself buying copies of records that I already have in their original pressings such as Raw Power, Indigesti, Wehrmacht, Lethal Aggression just because F.O.A.D. Records rules!

(The late Mario Garripoli, founder of F.O.A.D. zine and record label. Courtesy of Giulio Baldizzone)

I got in touch with Giulio Baldizzone, owner-manager of F.O.A.D. Records label and registered trademark, and we chatted a little bit regarding the label, so here we go!

Q: F.O.A.D. Records has become a go-to label for resurrecting long-lost 1980s crossover and thrashcore demos. What draws you to that specific era, and why do you think the '80s crossover scene still matters today?

A: It all started when F.O.A.D. was founded in 1986 as a fanzine, and if you look at the issues published in the second half of the 80s, the content was a perfect mix of the thrash of the time and hardcore punk. You could find bands like Coroner, Messiah, Wehrmacht, Necrodeath, Demolition Hammer, but also Negazione, Final Conflict, Attitude, Ludichrist, Youth Of Today, and so on. The person who created the fanzine, Marco (RIP), had this vision and was perfectly in tune with the attitude of the time, that is, the crossover between metal and hardcore and the union also in terms of human relationships that existed between the genres at that time. So, when we decided to join forces and start working on vinyl reissues in 2009, the pattern we set ourselves to follow was exactly that dictated by the spirit of the original 80s fanzine: a well-balanced mix of thrash metal and hardcore, which in the second half of the 80s was defined as crossover.

(Hard-Ons with F.O.A.D. zine. Courtesy of Mario Garripoli)

Q: You've reissued material from seminal and often overlooked eighties crossover bands; many of whom only released demos or EPs. What role do you think these 'demo-only' bands played in shaping the crossover movement, and how do you approach giving them the recognition they never received back then?

A: Honestly, we've never been ones to philosophize much about it; we've always been huge hardcore-thrash listeners and enjoyed digging into the most hidden and remote niches. From the beginning, we've always been aware that in the immense metal and punk scene, there are demo recordings that are sometimes better than more acclaimed bands who have released full-length albums. Take for example Jester Beast's demo tape *Destroy After Use*, a thrashcore gem that, if it had been released in New York or in the Bay Area would be considered a milestone of the genre. It's great in times like these to still have the opportunity to dig into rarities and exhume obscure recordings that have a level of intensity and songwriting that will leave you speechless. We have always enjoyed digging into these depths and making such rare material available in editions that do justice both in terms of sound quality and restoration and visual contents.

Q: The 1980s crossover scene was a melting pot of hardcore, thrash metal, and punk. How do you see F.O.A.D.'s work contributing to preserving the hybrid energy and rebellious ethos of that period?

A: I don't want to sound presumptuous, but I think we are the label still around today that has contributed most to keeping alive the spirit and magical melting pot of that period... we released some of the greatest crossover classics: Wehrmacht, Cryptic Slaughter, Ludichrist, Crumbsuckers, Attitude Adjustment, Broken Bones, S.O.D., Raw Power, Ratos de Porao and the list goes on and on. And in addition to these well-known legends, we did a myriad of more obscure and niche names that deserve to be recognized in the crossover panorama.

Q: Can you share a story behind one of your eighties crossover reissues; perhaps a release that was particularly challenging to put together, or one that felt especially meaningful in terms of preserving underground history?

A: Starting with the second point of your question: one of our most sensational discoveries in terms of saving underground history was the 1984 demo by Bulldozer, *The Exorcism*. Only three copies existed, one of which had been sent to Roadrunner at the time, one to King Diamond, and one remained with AC Wild and then miraculously passed on to us, who took care of restoring it and bring it back to light in the various editions you are familiar with. I also think that pressing S.O.D.'s demo *Crab Society North* on vinyl was another incredible rescue operation. On the 'challenging' side, however, the anecdotes are endless... There are works that took more than 10 years to see the light of day, such as Bloodcum, Fear Of God, and others. One of our most important prerogatives is consistency, perseverance, and stubbornness. As time passes, the members of those bands grow older and, between moves, divorces, life changes, and unfortunately even deaths, a lot of material risks being lost forever. Sometimes we keep projects open for years and years, hunting for the person who might have something, asking and requesting one person after another to keep looking, to make a minimal effort to help us... it's exhausting! Please keep in mind that what you find in our reissues is the result of meticulous research, hard work, and love for the preservation of extremely important musical content that, as the years go by, is increasingly at risk of being lost forever.

Recommended crossover F.O.A.D. Records: Lethal Aggression – *Life Is Hard, But That's No Excuse* LP, Raw Power – *Screams From The Gutter* LP, Crumbsuckers – *Turn Back Time: The Early Years 1983-1985*, Attitude Adjustment – *Dead Serious (Demo 1985 And Lost Session 1986)* LP, F.C.D.N. Tormentor – *Dungeon Days 1982-1985* LP, Mayhem – *As The World Burns - Complete Recordings 1984-1987* LP, Aftermath– *When Will You Die? - Demos 1986-1987* LP.

SUPREME ECHO RECORDS

(Supreme Echo Records logo. Courtesy of Supreme Echo Records)

Jason Flower (from Victoria, BC) has been one of the wildest enthusiasts of all things punk, hardcore and metal since the mid-1980s! An original 'crossover' kid, Jason still loves punk and metal with a passion. A passion that has been transformed into his two record labels, Break Even and Supreme Echo Records. Moreover, Jason played in as diverse bands as Black Kronstadt (anarcho punk-crust), Dementia (the first death-black metal band from Victoria), Enfa/lak (noise-industrial), Mexican Power Authority (hardcore-grind), Coconut Bulldozer (hardcore), Ruby Karinto (Experimental, No Wave, Post-Punk), Seat Belt (post-rock), Stick Farm (crossover-progressive metal, will refer to it later on more extensively), Third World Planet (powerviolence), Tomorrow's Hostility (hardcore punk).

(Jason Flower, 1989 picture. Photo courtesy of David Turner)

Supreme Echo Records was born in 2001, and has been archiving some of the most rare, unique and obscure punk, hardcore and heavy metal and hard rock bands, as well as niche scenes that were never documented.

A chat with Jason followed, and later there is a review of Stick Farm, as well as some favourite and recommended releases of Supreme Echo Records.

Q: Looking back at the formative years of the crossover explosion, which bands from the past whether American, European, or Canadian stand out as your personal favourites, and why do they still resonate with you today.

Jason Flowers: Corrosion of Conformity's *Animosity* combined the darkness of extreme metal bands with the fury of top-tier early US hardcore, channelled into exceptional song writing. To my ears, it's one of the absolute earliest and most unretrieved meldings of speed-thrash and hardcore; a catalyst that inspired both metalheads and hardcore kids to begin crossing over. Fave song: 'Mad World'.

Ludichrist

NYHC had already experienced crossover via *Cause For Alarm* (AF) and others, but *Immaculate Deception* showcased incredible dexterity, energy, eclecticism, intellect, and humour. I doubt everyone liked it, but it really exemplified a colourful new hybrid amidst a still developing sub-genre. For that reason, I revere it as an inspiration.

Negazione

I get excited just thinking about *...Lo Spirito Continua....*; 'Niente' is still to this day in my top five songs of the genre/era. European hardcore had such great diversity from country to country and Italian hardcore was some of the most frenetic output of the global hardcore scene. Negazione morphed metal influence into their sound naturally, the group weaved through their rhythms with vigour, and Zazzo raged hard on the microphone.

Beyond Possession

Is Beyond Possession is a crossover overdose! One of the tightest rhythm sections of the genre and the era. Jamie Kenney is quite literally the Steve Harris [Iron Maiden] of hardcore. Phil's drumming sounds like a precise polyrhythmic machine gun...And Ron Hadley scats and raps at such speed it sounds like his lips are going numb. Combine all this talent with the fact they were great songwriters, and you have one of the most original and impressive crossover albums of all time. A crown jewel.

The Accüsed

I still recall anticipating *The Return of Martha Splatterhead* arriving in the mail from David at Subcore. So heavy, so metal, so evil - and that voice. Blaine had one of, if not the, strongest razorblade screeching voices in hardcore, and when you added metal riffing, it only got better. This album combined the energy of PNW hardcore with tons of thrash/speed metal, resulting in a fluent hybrid that became a blueprint for success. 'Wrong Side of the Grave' is still my fave.

Cryptic Slaughter

I had the demo and debut, but for me *Money Talks* was the pinnacle. It took the elements of their debut and graduated to better song writing -- an album for young people beginning to question society and politics... an album for kids that grew up listening to both hardcore punk as well as metal - Cryptic Slaughter had the aesthetic of those two things balanced. As a kid, it was easy to like them, and I am glad to have seen them on the *Money Talks* tour.

Other bands and their albums that stood out to me at the time

The Dehumanizers - *End of Time*

Clown Alley - *Circus of Chaos*

Genoa - *What A Wonderful Life! Ha!!*

Brutal Obscenity - *It's Because...*

Wild Rags bands

AMQA - *Mutant Cats from Hell*

Extrem - *Terror Strikes Again* demo / *Voluntary Enslavement*

Agnostic Front - *Cause For Alarm*

Dayglo Abortions - *Feed US. A. Fetus*

S.O.D. - *Speak English or Die*

Spazztic Blurr – self titled

Fratricide - demos and unreleased Pusmort LP

Amebix - *Monolith*

Sacrilege UK - *Behind the Realms of Madness*

Q: Canada had a vibrant but often overlooked underground. Who were your favourite Canadian punk, metal, and crossover bands of the 1980s, and what do you think distinguished the Canadian sound from what was happening in the US or Europe?

Jason: I could go on and on!

Punk and hardcore
Neos, Infect, Fail-Safe, D.O.A., Youth Youth Youth, Nomeansno, Asexuals, Da Slyme, Sudden Impact, S.N.F.U., Section 46.

Metal
Voivod, Sacrifice, Slaughter, Witches Hammer, Arcfiend, Razor, Piledriver, Sacred Blade, Voor, Mal Havoc.

Crossover
Beyond Possession, Mission of Christ, Fratricide, Adversity, Corpus Vile, Sudden Impact, Soothsayer, Distorted Influence.

Undoubtedly, geographical isolation, relatively lower population numbers, and the size of Canada with vast distances between cities has made for a unique character as well as distinct regional character. From the West Coast to the Prairies, to Ontario with its massive population and endless cities, to Montreal's uniqueness and all the way to the Maritimes and Newfoundland. Our humour, our struggles, our stories -- a reflection of our society. Canadian arts are shaped by our environment and politics just as any country, its character is rich with complexity... and not 'American' (the USA has appropriated that word for themselves).

Q: Supreme Echo has built a reputation for digging up rare, lost, or underappreciated recordings. Are there any hidden gems from the Canadian crossover underground that you're considering re-releasing soon?

Jason: Yes, there's still more to be excavated! As for what is planned, there's plenty of labels who've discovered Canada's wealth of underground gems and published albums. It's best to hold my cards tight and not reveal/spoil future plans while likewise being a cheerleader for everyone else's archival output.

Q: What drives your work with Supreme Echo? Is it more about preserving history, giving unsung bands their due, or curating a certain aesthetic and sound that speaks to you personally?

Jason: All of the above, rather accurately. My first label Break Even (1989-98), was connected to playing in local bands plus live and studio recordings. Supreme Echo was initiated in 2001 to have a stronger mission and uniform aesthetic while still being broad in genre. Supreme Echo is focussed on long lost unreleased recordings, plus some reissues. Audio and visual material is sourced and professionally restored; the packaging is extra deluxe. The presentation is done from an anthropological perspective to document the history of global underground/counterculture. The booklets contain elaborate fact-checked details which contextualize the sociopolitical (and even geographical) environment which the music came from. I see a pattern of darkness in the majority of groups I'm attracted to.

Q: Crossover bridged punk and metal in radical ways, and you've been both a fan and an archivist of that movement. How do you see Supreme Echo's role in keeping that legacy alive, and where do you envision the label heading in the next few years?

Jason: Crossover was considered a relatively ugly term for a very long time. When we listen to a song we loved as kids, there is sentiment attached to it. When we discover a song or group from the past, being able to contextualize the environment in which it was created can bring an additional depth of appreciation to the art. Demystifying and uncovering the story of how something was created can be just as enjoyable as the music itself. Supreme Echo is a calling and a mission. My hope is that by including elaborate booklets with stories and information, there will be historical reference to these cultural movements and the network of global DIY underground music (punk, metal etc) thru tape-trading and self-financed publication.

In late 2025 we are living with massive inflation and great uncertainty about the future. Supreme Echo is first and foremost a passion project that occasionally turns a profit. With the cost of vinyl production skyrocketing, I could imagine reverting to smaller editions or eventually less output ... but for now, I continue to focus on rescuing as much great forgotten material as possible, the sea is never dry.

Supreme Echo Records recommended releases:

Northern Haze – ᓯᓇᒃᑐᖅ = *Sinnaktuq* LP
Aboriginal heavy metal/hard rock band from Igloolik, Qikiqtaaluk Region in Nunavut, Canada. Absolutely astonishing stuff.

The Stiffs – *The Stiffs* 7-inch
One of the first Vancouver punk bands that included later members of Subhumans and D.O.A.

Karrion – *Forsaken World* LP
Speed metal craze.

Neos – *Three Teens Hellbent On Speed* LP
Aye aye aye! The origins of superfast hardcore are here, in a compilation that includes all their 1980s stuff.

Distorted Influence – *Cold* LP
One of the greatest Canadian crossover LPs ever.

Mission Of Christ – *Silence In Grave + Realms Of Evil* LP
Ferocious crossover hardcore, vicious power and damn catchy.

Dayglow Abortions – *Wake Up, It's Time To Die* 7-inch
1982 recordings of the long-standing classic metal-punk band.

Sudden Impact – *Freaked Out* 7-inch
Their first demo, mandatory for everyone into slightly metal-hardcore punk.

Riot. 303 – *Riot. 303* 7-inch
Pre-Beyond Possession ace skatecore, slightly melodic and brilliant.

Sacred Blade – *Of The Sun + Moon* LP

Re-release of the 1980s classic ethereal/progressive metal LP.

A few more words though about one of the most special releases of Supreme Echo is regarding Stick Farm. Formed in 1989, Stick Farm was one of Jason's bands as a guitarist alongside Jeremy Turner who later went for a noise-electro style on Xipperstein. Stick Farm sounded like a blend between Voivod, Nomeansno and crossover. They released one cassette EP in 1990, one split 7-inch alongside *The Perfect Crime* in 1990, and the 1991 *Gut* 7-inch. No rules stuff here, way ahead its time blend of hardcore with progressive metal, with 'The Mission' and 'Scrum' being my favourite songs. No easy-listening stuff here, but once you get into it, you will be charmed. Try the 2022 *Reharvest* discography LP on Supreme Echo.

ALCHEMY RECORDS

(Alchemy Records logo. Courtesy of Mark Deutrom)

A very rare case for a label, Alchemy Records managed to release records that ranged from very good, to absolute classics, while the latter category refers to most of their releases! Founded in San Francisco by Victor Hayden (RIP 2018) and Clown Alley bassist Mark Deutrom. Alchemy Records was active from 1985 to approximately 1989. Amongst the crossover classics it released was Sacrilege B.C.'s *Party With God* LP. Alongside, what can you say about RKL's *Rock n' Roll Nightmare*? I got in touch with Mark Deutrom, and we had a small interview regarding Clown Alley that you can read on the band's section, as well as some questions about the fascinating history of Alchemy Records. Why it's fascinating? Well, read it below, and try to figure out how two people from so different musical backgrounds co-operated the label!

(Mark Deutrom, 2019 picture. Courtesy of Jennifer Deutrom)

Q: Beyond Clown Alley, your work with Alchemy Records was hugely important in the 1980s underground. Can you share how the label first started?

Mark Deutrom: My relationship with Victor Hayden was as exceptional as it was strange. It began on an odd note, stayed that way, and, remarkably, grew even stranger more than two decades after we first met. At the time, I was a musician (guitarist, composer, songwriter, producer) and, in the mid-1980s, a small record label owner in the Bay Area. The memory of those days resurfaced unexpectedly when, not long ago, I mistakenly called someone named Dan "Don". When I apologized, he replied, "No problem, I'm a huge Captain Beefheart fan." That instantly triggered a chain of memories.

For anyone familiar with Captain Beefheart, his real name was Don Van Vliet, and his cousin was none other than Victor Hayden, better known as "The Mascara Snake". And, as it happens, I ran a record label with The Mascara Snake back in the 1980s. The label was called Alchemy Records, founded in the heart of the Bay Area's underground scene. It existed only for a brief time, but it left a lasting mark. Alchemy became a home for some of the rawest, most adventurous bands of the era: The Melvins, Rich Kids on LSD (RKL), Neurosis, Sacrilege B.C., and Poison Idea.

(Victor Hayden, aka The Mascara Snake. Courtesy unknown)

My own band, Clown Alley, played regularly around the Bay Area. One night we were performing at New Method, a legendary underground venue in Emeryville. It was the kind of place where chaos and creativity coexisted. Bands like Christ on Parade, Violent Coercion, the Melvins, and Greg Anderson's False Liberty all played there. After our set, this intense, eccentric guy approached us-it was Victor. He was brimming with enthusiasm. "Wow, man," he said, "you guys were incredible! So high energy, just off the charts!". I handed him our demo tape, and right away he asked, "have you ever thought about making a record?". I laughed and told him that's all we ever thought about. He told us to keep in touch, and that was the beginning.

Over the next few months, Victor and I talked often about the local underground scene. We both felt that the Bay Area needed a label that could capture the power and creativity of its bands, something homegrown, but with real quality and ambition. That shared vision became Alchemy Records.

Victor had the resources; I had the experience. I handled the artistic and production side (organizing the bands, getting them into proper studios, and producing the records) while Victor financed the operation. Through a former *Maximum Rocknroll* contact, I secured a distribution deal in London with Southern Distribution, which gave our releases international reach almost immediately. Despite working on shoestring budgets, we refused to settle for the lo-fi, muddy sound typical of many punk records at the time. Instead, I scouted unused hours in top-tier 24-track studios around San Francisco, making professional recordings for next to nothing. That approach gave Alchemy's releases from the Melvins and Neurosis to RKL and Poison Idea, a power and clarity that stood out in the underground scene.

Soon, Alchemy began to generate buzz. Locally, it became synonymous with the Bay Area's new, aggressive underground sound. Internationally, word spread quickly through our London distributor. For a moment, it felt like we were building something that could truly connect the punk and metal worlds.

Victor and I even discussed opening a club in San Francisco dedicated to alternative bands; another of his visionary ideas. At the time, there were few proper venues for such acts. The few that existed, like The Farm, would host marathon shows featuring a dozen or more bands, from punk to metal. I did live sound at a couple of those events; exhausting but inspiring experiences that captured the unity and raw energy of that era.

The Bay Area underground of the mid-eighties was unlike anything else. Punk and metal bands shared stages, gear, and often audiences. The sense of community was strong, wild, unpredictable, but united by a shared passion for loud, uncompromising music. And in the middle of it all stood Victor Hayden: enigmatic, intense, and utterly unforgettable.

Q: Which Alchemy Records release you're most proud of?

Mark Deutrom: I can't say I have a favourite. They all seem to do different things and reflect the completely idiosyncratic circumstances involving the productions of all of them. I probably gained the most satisfaction from dragging them into reality. There are so many elements beyond your control operating on that level that you must more or less force the thing into existence. I might be partial to the Clown Alley record as it was my band at the time and it was gratifying to just accomplish that from writing the songs to hearing it finished in the studio.,

Q: How the experience of owning and running a DIY label shape your later life and perspective on music?

Mark Deutrom: Running the label was a challenge and a great learning experience. I learned how the entire process works and how you must be prepared for completely unpredictable situations that require immediate solutions without being reactive and emotional. At bigger labels there is a level of compartmentalization where a variety of people will be specializing in specific elements involving a release. I was involved all the way from first discussions with a band, to running sessions, to mastering and even PR and advertising, so it was a lot. It's been useful to have that knowledge to draw on since I am still very much in the underground and will probably remain so.

Things have changed so much in the decades since I had Alchemy for better and worse. Anyone who wants to release a project now can just upload it to Bandcamp or CD Baby and have it available worldwide in a second. For physical media, a label of some kind with a distribution network is probably ideal, but the revenues from that or streaming music are virtually non-existent at this point for 90 percent of people creating music. I have never received any revenue from any of the platforms my music has been on for years and probably never will. Music has been made valueless, and many younger people are growing up with the idea that music is just free.

Any artist with any kind of an audience now will be generating income mainly from touring and the merchandise associated with it. Not much of what I learned all those years ago has much relevance apart from touring to create income. Producing is its own thing and will possibly always have some kind of value, but AI developments may devalue that also eventually. This is somewhat of a bleak scenario, but I feel it's an accurate snapshot of the present.

Recommended crossover Alchemy Records:

Clown Alley – *Circus Of Chaos*

Sacrilege B.C. – *Party With God*

Sacrilege B.C. – *Too Cool To Pray*

Various – *Peace Through Chemistry*

Guillotine – *Bring Down The Curtain*

Virulence – *If This Isn't A Dream...*

Paranoia – *The Many Faces Of.*

Also recommended:

Rich Kids On LSD – *Rock N Roll Nightmare*

Melvins – *Gluey Porch Treatments*

Neurosis – *Pain Of Mind*

Poison Idea – *War All The Time*

The Grim – *Face Of Betrayal.*

THE VISUAL ARTISTS
SEAN TAGGART

(Sean Taggart in NYC, 2013. Courtesy of Dave Decat)

There are visual artists that changed your life via their work; in my case its Brian Walsby, Pushead and Sean Taggart. I can't even estimate the countless hours I spent as an adolescent, observing the crazy artwork of Agnostic Front's *Cause For Alarm*, or Crumbsuckers' *Life Of Dreams*. Sean's name was stuck instantly into my head in those pre-Internet days, and I was always searching for his art, while always wanting to find out who he is.

(Cro-Mags and the Mob flyer, 1985. Courtesy of Sean Taggart)

Sean Taggart, a New York City native, has been identified with the NYHC of second generation, if someone excludes Armed Citizens and Agnostic Front as first generation bands, as well as with the crossover of that place and era. You can see his art everywhere, from record covers to flyers. What is most significant in his style, is that it stands out, screaming 'Taggart!'. Alongside, he was also a member of the NYHC band Shok, that released one song in the 1985 compilation Big City's *One Big Crowd* LP, with the cover art being created by Brian Walsby. Sean offers what drew him in to the world of hardcore, first designing flyers for bands like Cro-Mags as their in-house designer, Murphy's Law, Agnostic Front and Crumbsuckers: "I was just a kid that liked punk rock. In New York, punk rock eventually e(de)volved into hardcore punk. The Stimulators were New York's bridge band between punk and hardcore. Much like the Germs were for L.A. I believe they were the ones that gave the Bad Brains their start in New York. So, of course, the Bad Brains changed everything. Like they had done in DC, kids gravitated towards the more aggressive, fast sound. Also, DC, L.A., and Boston had hardcore scenes before New York. So, there was a growing template of non-English sounding bands. USA! USA! We didn't like living under the shadow of England. So that's the long answer on how I got into hardcore…as for doing flyers and album covers, it started out as a friend thing. My good friend Parris (founding member of the Cro-Mags) and I went to high school together. When the Cro-Mags happened, he asked me to do flyers for the band. My work was a hit! Soon, I was doing art for bands like Agnostic Front, Crumbsuckers, Carnivore, and others. It didn't hurt that I knew the guys beforehand, either. I always tell aspiring artists to align themselves with something bigger than they are. Something that they love and are willing to devote their lives to".

Flyers were more than just promotional tools. They were part of the hardcore punk culture. So, how Sean approached creating them? "Well, my motivation first and foremost was to do something cool, that reflected what the scene was about" he adds. "Up until that point most flyers were of the punk rock cut-and-paste school of art. Which was cool but was definitely tired by that time. I wanted us to have our own 'thing', unique to us".

(Sean Taggart's first-and rejected-artwork for AF's Cause For Alarm, 1986. Courtesy of Sean Taggart)

Sean worked in some of the most iconic crossover LPs like e.g. Crumbsuckers' *Life Of Dreams*. Walking us through his process for that cover, and what the band meant to him at the time, Sean offers that "when I got the gigs, I was already a huge fan. I was really into it. I was fortunate to have already been friendly with the bands I eventually got to work for. They trusted me and let me do my thing. For the Crumbsuckers I listened closely to their songs, I got a feeling of a futuristic, dystopian world with a doped-up consumerist, fake reality society. Like the one we have today! I also thought crossover was the future of music, which influenced my interpretation".

In terms of how conscious he was of the cultural collision between was hardcore and metal while creating his work, Sean replies that "I was very conscious of it! It seemed like the logical next step. The speed and technically of the music and the in your face, socially relevant lyrics with straight up shouting vocals. Not that operatic bullshit metal singing style".

Looking back, what Sean feels was the lasting impact of the NYHC-crossover scene on underground art and DIY aesthetics? And how has that period influenced his later artistic path, if at all?

"Hmmm, I don't do much looking back. But I'd say it brought a much more professional opportunities for artists. Better quality overall. So, well-made work with the spirit of the scene made for a knockout combination. A one-two punch! For me personally, it built my self-esteem and allowed me to make a living being as an artist. I am eternally grateful to the NYHC scene for nurturing my talent. And for putting me on a righteous path".

(1986 Sheer Terror, Carnivore, Shok gig flyer. Courtesy of Sean Taggart)

Sean Taggart is still doing great covers and logos. Check out Agnostic Front's *Get Loud* cover, Aggros logo, Siberian Meat Grinder's *Metal Bear Stomp* LP and Sheer Terror's *No Ground For Pity* LP among many others. His fine art paintings have been exhibited in both group and one-man shows at Brooklyn's McCaig-Welles Gallery and at Exit Art in New York City. You can check out his work on his official site on seantaggart.com and follow him on Facebook/Instagram. Sean always has great stories and art to share!

Sean Taggart works from the 1980s era:

Armed Citizens – *Make Sense* 7-inch 1983

Carnivore – *Carnivore* (inner sleeve) LP 1985

Various – *Big City's One Big Crowd* LP 1985 (Shok Booklet Page Drawing)

Agnostic Front – *Cause For Alarm* LP 1986

Whiplash – *Power And Pain* LP 1986

Crumbsuckers – *Life Of Dreams* LP 1986

Underdog – *Underdog* 7-inch (record labels A and B side) 1986

Prong – *Primitive Origins* 12-inch EP 1987

Whiplash – *Ticket To Mayhem* LP 1987 (band logo)

P.M.S. – *Pre Metal Syndrome* LP 1987

Carnivore – *Retaliation* LP 1987

Loss For Words – *Prey* LP 1989

VINCENZIO PACKARD

(Vincenzio Packard, aka Vince Rancid. Courtesy unknown)

Vince Rancid, aka Vince Packard is an artist from Akron, Ohio, that is responsible for some of the most iconic hardcore and crossover cover artworks. Of course, I'm referring to Raw Power's *Screams From The Gutter* and *After Your Brain* record covers. With a background in the punk scene, Vince's first artwork was the iconic 1983 *Multi-Death Corporations* 7-inch by MDC, only to be followed by record covers that are now considered classic. His classic artwork appears on Vatican Commando's excellent *Hit Squad For God* 7-inch EP, and the neo-psychedelic masterpiece of Dimentia 13 self- titled LP (1985). Alongside in terms of crossover, Vince was the artist behind Dresden's *Too Many Skeletons* LP, False Hopes' *Cease To Exist* cassette and Plasma Alliance's *We Can't Wait* 7-inch (1985) (this one's hardcore, but it contains lots of metal riffing). Castle Blood and Travesty guitarist Charles Griffith brought me in touch with Vince, and he was happy to reply to some questions of mine.

Q: You created some striking and instantly recognizable artwork for bands like Raw Power and Dresden. How did you first get involved with these bands, and what drew you to the crossover and hardcore aesthetic of that era?

Vince: I was living in Akron, Ohio. I knew the DEVO guys and Chrissy Hynde of the Pretenders worked at my dad's art gallery, but all the punk bands wanted record contracts, so it was cool to have bands that wanted to take hard and edgy to the next level. I did a punk art zine named *SLaM* and started putting on shows at any available spaces.

(Raw Power record cover of Screams From The Gutter, 1985. Courtesy of Vince Packard)

Q: Your art often captured the intensity, chaos, and social tension reflected in the music. What kind of visual or thematic ideas inspired your work on those record covers? Were you influenced more by punk culture, underground comics, or something else entirely?

Vince: From Robert Crumb [R. Crumb] and Steve Clay Wilson [S. Clay Wilson] of the comix, the visuals just popped into my head when I cranked out the punk tunes. I also watched the frightening state of the world from my early teens, environmental and nuclear concerns, corruption and economic disparity, the horror of the techno-war machine.

Q: Raw Power's visual identity especially on their album art feels both confrontational and surreal. How much creative freedom did the bands give you, and how did you balance your own artistic vision with the message or sound of the music?

Vince: I had total freedom, maybe suggested by the title of the album and listening to the music. Also, to MDC, I suggested that it could stand for than Millions of Dead Cops, and we came up with Multi-Death Corporations.

Q: Did you also create gig flyers or other artwork for live shows back in the 1980s? If so, how did that process differ from working on record covers in terms of time, style, or purpose?

Vince: I did draw many show flyers, sent art to zines around the country and the world. I'd maybe though put a bit more effort into records; I usually had more time in order to draw a record cover.

(Dresden record cover of Too Many Skeletons LP, 1986. Courtesy of Vince Packard)

Q: Looking back, what do you think made the 1980s hardcore and crossover scene such a fertile ground for visual creativity? Do you see any parallels between that DIY energy and how underground art or music is being made today?

Vince: I'm sure it's different, as it was fresh back then and had nothing in the mainstream and no internet. The zines were the backbone of connecting bands and art. But who knows what all's going on being 'underground'. There's no way to follow everything, especially as I don't have a car and can't do the mosh pits like way back when, or even ten years ago. I'm into my sixties so I definitely feel it!

Vince Packard works from the 1980s era:

Dimentia 13 – *Dimentia 13* LP

Raw Power – *Screams From The Gutter* LP

Raw Power – *After Your Brain* LP

Dresden – *Too Many Skeletons* LP

Dimentia 13 – *Mirror Mind* LP

MDC – *Multi-Death Corporations* 7-inch

Vatican Commandos – *Hit Squad For God* 7-inch

Plasma Alliance – *We Can't Wait* 7-inch

Various – *The Master Tape Vol. 2* 2LP

Various – *Empty Skulls Vol.#2 - The Wound Deepens* LP

False Hope – *Cease To Exist* cassette

Check also Vince's art and support him on

https://www.deviantart.com/cannibol and

https://www.etsy.com/shop/WildMercantile

THE FANZINES

METAL CORE

(Chris Forbes on the right, with David Sanchez of Havok. Courtesy of Melissa Forbes)

Chris Forbes, the man behind *Metal Core* fanzine, has been issuing the printed version of the zine from 1986 up to 2001, when he decided to continue it as a webzine. An aficionado of all things metal, Chris also loved many hardcore and crossover bands since they first appeared on the map, offering exposure through his long-standing zine for four decades to bands that remained underground or went to become massive over the years. Chris was super-happy when I asked him for an interview, and his replies are evidence of his true passion of love for crossover and music in general, offering his own point of view regarding the zines and their future, crossover and the history of *Metal Core*.

(Metal Core zine #2. Courtesy of Chris Forbes)

Q: Can you tell us how *Metal Core* began, what motivated you to start it, what the early days were like, and how it grew into a respected voice in the underground?

CF: Sure. Now to backtrack a bit, my dad was a sportswriter for a newspaper called the *Philadelphia Inquirer* and he covered the professional football team the Philadelphia Eagles. This was in the seventies. He ended up becoming the sports editor for a national newspaper, *USA Today* and that was in the eighties. My dad has been to over forty Super Bowls and he even took me to a couple, and he is in the Pro Football Hall of Fame. I got the writing bug from him haha! I used to buy and collect metal fanzines and mags before *Metal Core* started. *Kerrang*, *Metal Forces*, *Creem*, *Circus* were just a few I collected back in the early eighties. The first underground metal fanzine I brought was called *Kick Ass Monthly*. It is also the greatest fanzine ever. Sadly, editor Bob [Muldowney] is no longer with us. He put out over thirty issues and a book with all his issues is long overdue. From there I started buying metal fanzines at shows and at any local stores that had them. One of the fanzines I picked up was called *Total Thrash* by editor Scott Helig. I have tried to find Scott with no luck over the years. He was looking for people to write and contribute to his zine, so I offered my services. Now this is before the internet mind you. Anyway, I started mailing him some interviews to use for his zine. I was sending him so many interviews to use, that at a show he said to me that since I am sending so many interviews, that I should start up my own fanzine. I took that up as a bit of challenge and told him I would and in December of 1986, I released my first issue.

I came up with the name *Metal Core* as S.O.D. (Stormtroopers of Death) was doing a mini seven-date East Coast tour with Overkill. I saw one of the shows at City Garden's in Trenton, New Jersey and they dubbed the tour the 'Metal Core' tour. When I saw the ad for the tour in the weekly *East Coast Rocker* mag, I loved it, so I decided to name my mag that as I loved both metal and hardcore. My first issue was half-size, thirty-five pages, with NO pictures or ads. Interviews were with South Jersey [New Jersey] bands (Machine Dog, Faith or Fear); and Philadelphia, Pennsylvania thrash band, Anvil Bitch. I also managed to get Combat Recording artists Nuclear Assault and crossover NJ bands Adrenalin O.D. and Lethal Aggression. The interviews were all done in person at shows I attended using my dad's mini recorder. I had my questions ready on a sheet of paper that I had written out prior to the show. The issue also included show reviews, some demo reviews, record reviews and also a page with other zines to buy. I printed up 150 copies and sold them for $1 at shows and managed to get rid of all of them. The issue was typed up on my dad's old typewriter as was my first couple of issues, until I moved up to a word processor. The next issue (#2) I moved up to regular size (8.5"x11") and had a cool cover with a metalhead and a hardcore person shaking hands. One of my favourite covers during the Metal Core run. I also started writing to bands and getting demos from them and this issue I branched out and had interviews with At War, Dream Death, Savage Death, Possessed, Dark Angel, and Hallows Eve. I also printed more than 150 copies and had a couple of local stores sell them. Each issue I ended up printing more copies than the previous one. When I got to issue #25, I went to newsprint and made the mag free! I made 10,000 copies and had no problem getting rid of them. A local printing plant did them for me and the ads in the mag paid for the zine and then some. As soon as I filled my car with the 10,000 copies, I went right up to Vintage Vinyl (New Jersey record store, sadly recently closed) and dropped off 1,000 copies. In three weeks, I would go up and drop a 1,000 more off. When going to shows, I could easily get rid of 500 or more, so doing 10,000 wasn't as stressful as you would think. I would make up little ads each time a new issue came out (thousands of them) and people would spread them throughout their mail, and I would do the same thing with their ads when I would send out my mail. It was a buddy system between the underground bands and other zine editors to help each other out. By like issue #5, tons of bands would be sending me their demos, and I was on all the record company promo lists. I got very friendly with the promo people at the labels and mail would get to be so much I ended up getting a PO Box for the zine. The days of writing and spreading ads, I will cherish for all my life. Those were the days, and it was a lot more personal and fun than doing the email thing. I stopped doing the print version of the zine in 2001 as the internet was starting to go strong, so I made a Metal Core website which is still up at: www.metalcorezine.com. Believe it or not, I am still doing reviews and interviews and that is for the [*Extreminal Extreme Metal Magazine*] site www.extreminal.com. I have complete 100 percent freedom with whom I interview and with my reviews and they put up everything I send them. I have been working with them for about six years now and it is a great relationship. Hails to Cenk and Soner over there".

(Metal Core Fanzine #6 cover. Courtesy of Chris Forbes)

Q: From your perspective running *Metal Core*, how did you first see the crossover movement emerging - what were the early signs that hardcore and metal were blending into something new and more aggressive?

CF: Now of course hardcore was around before the underground metal scene and when it broken open in 1983 with Metallica's *Kill Em All* thrash metal was born. I had never heard of The Misfits, but the Metallica guys were big fans. I would say by 1985, thrash has broken out big time with the whole Bay Area scene and labels such as Earache, Combat, Megaforce, Metal Blade, etc. and a lot of the thrash bands back then listened to punk and hardcore. I think privately some of the hardcore bands listened to some thrash and speed metal. It obviously exploded in 1986 with the release of S.O.D.'s *Speak English Or Die* release. It still amazes me that album was recorded in a mere three days. Lots of underground kids got into that album and it introduced many to the world of hardcore. Once they were, many became fans of hardcore music. With thrash also becoming big, I think some punk and hardcore bands started listening to thrash and when they did, it got influenced into their sound. It was an incredible time in the world of underground music as the sound was fresh and exciting, at least to my ears. I loved everything about it. Some of the indie metal labels even had their own crossover labels (Combat Core with Combat Records and Death Records with Metal Blade).

Q: Looking back at the 1980s, which crossover bands stood out to you the most as a fan and writer-and what about them in sound, lyrics, energy made them essential in your eyes?

CF: I loved the crossover era. I didn't mind that punk bands threw some metal sounds in their music (D.R.I., Agnostic Front, Black Flag, and many others). I went to a club up in Trenton, New Jersey called City Gardens and the promoter, not the owner, but promoter Randy Ellis booked a lot of punk and hardcore shows, and some underground metal shows there. I also went to clubs in Philadelphia, Pennsylvania to see hardcore shows. I had short hair, so I didn't get yelled at haha! Now as far as favorite crossover bands, my picks would be D.R.I., The Crumbsuckers, Agnostic Front, The Accüsed, etc. That VHS tape *D.R.I. Live At The Ritz* got played in my house so many times it's not even funny! Their *Crossover* release was the perfect blend of hardcore and metal. I also didn't mind when hardcore and punk bands played with metal bands. Randy once booked Venom, Black Flag and Overkill together. That was a wild show. Henry Rollins of Black Flag came out with a pentagram drawn on his hand and started chanting 'Satan…Satan…Satan'. OMG was that hilarious.

Q: Out of all the interviews you conducted, which crossover-related one remains your favourite or most memorable, either because of the conversation itself or the insight it gave into the band's mindset?

CF: I would say my interview with the band The Crumbsuckers. I think their *Life of Dreams* release is the best crossover release out there. The perfect blend of metal and hardcore. They were also an incredible live band. I was lucky back then as a band I was helping manage at the time (1986-1987) called Deadly Blessing, they opened for The Crumbsuckers in Long Island, New York in their hometown at a club called The Sundance. They played with them several times and it was my pleasure to get to hang out with them for hours and then watch them perform as well. Just a fantastic live band that blew me away every time I saw them live.

Q: Was there a crossover band you always hoped to interview for *Metal Core* but it never came together? Looking back, which "missed interview" do you wish you could have captured for the zine?

CF: Looking back, and I don't why I didn't, but I never got to interview S.O.D. I mean they went on to put out several more releases besides *Speak English Or Die* so the opportunity was there. I mean S.O.D.'s debut has sold over a million copies (that was as of 2001) and I saw them live on that seven-date tour, so getting or arranging an interview was certainly there and for some reason or another I never did. I mean their debut is easily a top 3 crossover release of all time. I didn't even try and get an interview and that is not like me at all. I mean I have interviewed Slayer and Metallica so it's not like I was like "oh they won't want to do an interview with a fanzine". Even though I didn't have issue #1 out, that would have been fantastic having an interview with them in my debut issue. Considering I named my zine after the name of their first ever tour, I wish I did interview them and at any point in their career, not just the debut release.

Q: Fanzines like *Metal Core* were essential to building the crossover network in the pre-internet era. How do you reflect on the importance of zines now, and what do you think they offered that online media today often struggles to replicate?

CF: Sometimes I go through my issues and will read some of my demo reviews and interviews and lots of times I would review demos and then a year later the band would be signed and have an album out. I was the first zine in the US to review the band Vio-lence demo back in the eighties. Soon after they signed to Mechanic Records and released *Eternal Nightmare*. I used to be pen pal buddies with guitar player Phil Demmel back in those days. Zines were the lifeblood of the underground back then. A great review in a fanzine would help a band in two ways: number 1: would help with sales of their demo tape and number 2: it would help with building a press kit to send to a label in the hopes of getting signed. I loved going to the post office all the time and going to my PO box, the semi-famous PO Box 622 Marlton, New Jersey lol, and seeing what had come for me in the mail. I had a small box, so usually when I went, which was like three times a week. I had a yellow slip in my box telling me I had too much mail in my box, so I had to go up to the counter to get my mail. One of the guys working there knew me by name and my box number and he would go get my mail for me. I would always have plenty of promos to review, whether it was from an unsigned band sending me a demo or a package from a record label. Not to mention zine orders, other zines sending me their latest issue which I fuckin' loved getting or pen pal letters from the various band members I had become friends with. It was a tight knit unit the underground back then. Now, yes, it is faster with emails as the person gets your letter as soon as you hit "send". To me it is just not as personal as it used to be. Back when I was doing my print zine, bands would love sending you their demo in the hopes of getting a review and a possible interview. Now to get a band to send you something for review is like pulling teeth. The underground is not the same, people go to shows and all they do is hold up their phones, bands, all they care about is how many likes they have on Facebook, etc. The closeness and togetherness are long gone. I still feel it at shows sometimes, but the days of yesteryear are long gone and it's a shame. Don't get me wrong, the internet is a great thing and a valuable tool, but sometimes I do miss the old days. I love seeing some zines having all their issues put into book form, that rules. The days of spreading bands and other zines ads throughout the mail was priceless. Also trading with other zine editors and getting their new issue in my mail was priceless as well. Getting interviews back from bands was great as well. I'm sorry you just don't have that these days. Back then we were all one big family, and it was priceless. Anybody reading this that was around back then will know exactly what I mean. I had my own desk set up down in my basement and had my *Metal Core* PO Box stamper; many envelopes, both regular size and 8 1/2 by 11 for zine orders; stack of white paper for letter writing, a box with all my mail to answer and another box filled with various ads from bands and zine editor ads that after I finished with my letter I would stuff it with various band and zine ads and they would go all over the world. Those were times I would never trade for anything.

xXx

(Mike Gitter, 2025. Courtesy of Ian McFarland)

One of the most classic US fanzines, *xXx Fanzine*, was based in Boston, MA and went up to cover not only the burgeoning hardcore scene of the city, but went to expand nationwide, and not limited just to hardcore, offering exposure to the then emerging metal and crossover scene. The mastermind behind *xXx Fanzine* was Mike Gitter, that later played in the excellent melodic hardcore bands Apology and Grin, both covered in *We Can Be The New Wind*, went to pursue a career as a journalist. He was later the A&R Director in Atlantic Records, Roadrunner Records and currently the Vice-President of A&R in Century Media Records. Mike run the fanzine from 1983 to 1988, and among the bands that appeared with an interview in *xXx Fanzine* were Circle Jerks, Suicidal Tendencies, Metallica, Corrosion of Conformity, Anthrax, Subhumans, Motörhead, Samhain, Agnostic Front, Cro-Mags and so many others. Mike was a crossover enthusiast even from its beginning, offering raving record and live reviews!

What is more awesome though about Mike Gitter is that to this day, he remains an extreme music aficionado, seeking out new bands, while being always humble and willing to offer his help in everything music related. So, he happily provided me a thorough interview regarding *xXx Fanzine*, and its connection with crossover. Here we go!

Q: Looking back, which crossover bands from the 1980s stand out as your personal favourites, either for their music, their live shows, or their overall impact on the scene?

Mike Gitter: Truthfully, with 'Crossover', where do you begin? It's a topic that can be debated. Do you start with Bad Brains and Dr. Know's steely rhythm playing? The Obsessed, who were playing alongside plenty of the DC hardcore elite? DYS, with the NWOBHM whispers on their second self-titled 'metal' record? Void, with their overtures to Venom and [Black] Sabbath on the unreleased *Potions For Bad Dream* album? Motörhead and Lemmy's associations with The Damned and Tank, with Algy Ward coming from The Damned? What came first? The chicken or the egg? The punk or the metal?

For my money, Amebix's *Arise!* is a grimy classic in its own right. It's an exercise in atmosphere and power that would later come to influence Voivod. And then, Voivod themselves are inherently 'Crossover' or Sepultura, who count Amebix as an influence are DEFINITELY 'Crossover'- particularly in the dirtiness of Max Cavalera's guitar playing. Amerbix's later LPs *Monolith* and *Sonic Mass* continue down that road in a massive way while echoing elements of early proto metal like Hawkwind.

My favourites? Naturally, Corrosion of Conformity, who are responsible for popularizing Crossover in so many ways. They had so many identities depending on the time and lineup. While *Eye for an Eye* directly reminds me of Void meets the Germs, there's an ungodly amount of Sabbath in that mix with Eric Eycke barking in a way that's as much Lemmy as it is Darby. By the time Corrosion moved on to *Animosity* or *Technocracy*, there's a technicality creeping in there, especially in the way Reed Mullins drumming and Mike Dean's bass playing was really adventurous, taking cues from the early thrash scene, but also, from the post-punk of Honor Role or the breathtaking dissonance of their neighbours in Confessor. That made the Simon Bob era their most divisive and occasionally uneven but also one of their most interesting career arcs.

One band that gets relatively overlooked is Dr. Know whose *This Island Earth* and *Wreckage in Flesh* LPs don't necessarily get the credit due. I've talked to Kyle Toucher (guitarist/vocalist) about this, and it really comes down to the fact that they didn't really put in the roadwork that COC did. Like their Death Records labelmates, they should have been much bigger if they stayed out there. Another favourite, coming from the metal side is Hirax. Katon wasn't afraid of straying away from his metal roots and upping the speed factor which is where you get a storming and influential record like *Raging Violence*.

Of course, there's other faves – particularly, almost everything released on Pushead's Pusmort label like Attitude Adjustment, Final Conflict and his own Septic Death who were beautifully and unexpectedly imaginative. Add to that UK metalpunks like Sacrilege and Onslaught. Onslaught's *Power from Hell* really did presage the rise of black metal in a lot of ways! We can't forget G.I.S.M, given Randy Uchida's dexterity as a guitarist. Jarring and awesome. Raw Power, who were just as metal informed as they were from punk.

Which, of course, brings us to the New York stuff. Cro-Mags did it best. *The Age of Quarrel* demo and album brought together the speed and intensity of the Bad Brains with the power and gritty tones of Motörhead and Venom. Cro-Mags were really the last of the first generation of US hardcore and the jumping off point for something new, *Best Wishes* is the sound of Harley and Parris imbibing a lot of

Metallica and alloying that to what Cro-Mags had already established. Their impact on the scene wasn't surprising given the touring they had already done tours with the likes of Destruction and Motörhead as well as infamous gigs with Venom and Voivod.

Then, you have Leeway. What a band! AJ Novello's riffing and songwriting combined with Eddie Sutton 's (RIP) Ozzy-as-an-MC vocals were totally groundbreaking at the time. Agnostic Front's *Liberty and Justice* era is quietly 'Crossover', in some ways more so than the *Cause for Alarm* album. I think you must give it to AF for always pushing their own boundaries and helping expand the reach of hardcore including initiating the modern hardcore sound with the *One Voice* album! And of course, I must top it off with Prong. Bringing together Tommy Victor's thrashy riffing with the scuzz of New York City and the art damage of Killing Joke, not to forget drummer Ted Parsons' schooling in Swans, made early records like *Force Fed* so relevant and set the stage for Tommy's still ongoing gigging and recording with Prong.

(xXx fanzine # 3 cover. Courtesy of Mike Gitter)

Q: As someone deeply embedded in the hardcore and punk underground, how early did you sense that crossover (the fusion of hardcore punk and metal) was starting to form, and what were the key signs for you that it was becoming its own movement?

Mike Gitter: The first and biggest sign of metal and hardcore's crossover was Bob Muldowney (RIP) writing about bands like COC and D.R.I. in the pages of his own zine, *Kick Ass Monthly*, which was a bible for the burgeoning metal underground. *Kick Ass* inspired so many metalheads to check those bands out and start going down the hardcore rabbit hole. I remember Keith Bennett eventually of Wrecking Crew, and myself taking a loooong subway ride to just get our copies of *Kick Ass*! Keep in mind that zines were the Facebook, Instagram, Reddit and Spotify of the day. For metal, *Kick Ass* was one of the best! But you also saw it on the punk and hardcore side with a lot of zines like *Suburban Punk* (later, *Suburban Voice*) having metal sections which I also did in *xXx* myself. Plus, seeing early Metallica and Slayer wearing COC shirts was a huge indicator that hardcore was on the move towards something heavier and that's to say nothing of Cliff Burton's omnipresent Misfits and Samhain shirts!

But even before that, being in Boston and in a scene that embraced metal and rock, was an indication that things weren't going to remain static. It wasn't uncommon to see someone like Jonathan Anastas from DYS at a Necros show in 1983 wearing a Venom shirt. Or, from Western Massachusetts, The Outpatients (basically members of Deep Wound that didn't migrate to Dinosaur Jr.) worshipping Motörhead as far back as '83. In the Bay State, the coming crossover was definitely in the water!

Q: Can you walk us through the origins of *xXx Fanzine*? Why you started it, what inspired you at the time, and what role you think the zine played in documenting and shaping that intense period in hardcore and crossover history?

Mike Gitter: *xXx* was very much a product of hardcore's second generation. Not the biggest or the best or the first zine out the there, but I think it's remembered and was eventually honoured in book form (*xXx Fanzine – Hardcore and Punk In the Eighties* from Bridge Nine) for sticking around for six years (1983-1988) and being part of a changing sonic landscape. It was an era of music in motion from bands like Black Flag slowing down and inspiring what would emerge as Sub Pop in Seattle to the rise of multiple movements including crossover, youth crew, indie rock, noise, and yes, even the rise of grunge. *xXx* hit all of it over that time, interviewing the likes of Minor Threat and SS Decontrol to Metallica and Anthrax early on, to Swans and Soul Asylum well before the 'Runaway Train' days. I started *xXx* for the same reason any of us got involved in the scene at the time. It was a matter of getting off the sidelines and taking control of your world in a way that only punk and DIY America afforded us. Plus, I wasn't musically gifted enough to start a band! To be honest, I'm still surprised at the zine's resonance people still remembering it!

Q: Out of all the bands you interviewed in *xXx Fanzine*, which crossover-related interview stands out the most to you, either because it revealed something unique about the band or because of the sheer energy of the conversation?

(xXx Fanzine #16 cover. Courtesy of Mike Gitter)

Mike Gitter: There were a few. Obviously, having Cliff Burton gush over his love for the Misfits and Samhain when I interviewed him and James [Hetfield] at the Channel in 1986 on what was supposed to be the first night of the *Ride the Lightning* tour was a key moment. Metallica had to cancel that gig as Lars had visa problems getting into the country in time. Then, interviewing Scott Ian at what was Anthrax's second gig ever with Joey Belladonna was great. Scott was and still is a friend. He spent a lot of time in Boston visiting his girlfriend who was going to school there at the time, so we got to know each other and obviously, he was down with 'the core' and the Boston scene. I also really liked Anthrax and that *Fistful of Metal* and *Spreading the Disease* era is still a favourite of mine! Realizing that Voivod were basically prog punks at the time just made me love them more. And, of course, how can you not come away from a conversation with Katon DePena on Hirax and not be buzzing? The guy is energized like few are! Still is. Also, at that time, Katon was very involved in the L.A. punk and hardcore scene and worked at Long Beach's infamous Zed Records with the likes of Big Frank Harrison [RIP] and Pat Dubar [Uniform Choice].

Q: Was there a crossover or hardcore metal band that you always wanted to interview but, for whatever reason, it never happened?

Mike Gitter: In retrospect, there have been a few. I would have loved to interview Tom G. Warrior at the time. Tom is not only a musical iconoclast but a true fan and lover of extreme sounds. It would have been amazing to get his perspective on the growing Crossover scene. Septic Death for sure. Final Conflict was one; though I certainly reviewed the *Ashes to Ashes* album and loved it! And I interviewed them for

Thrasher around that time. Ron is one of my favourite people to this very day and I did add Final Conflict to the *xXx* book in a 'those that got away' section. There were a few bands that I did interview for other magazines I was writing for at the time that didn't make it into *xXx* that I now wish I had them featured in my zine. Certainly Leeway! The Crumbsuckers. It would have been cool to have Jeff Hanneman talking about Slayer's punk predilections that eventually came to the forefront on the *Undisputed Attitude* punk covers record which is quietly one of Slayer's best.

Q: Looking back now, how do you see the importance of zines like *xXx* in documenting subcultural history, and what do you think they offered that today's digital media often misses when it comes to capturing the rawness of punk, hardcore, and crossover?

Mike Gitter: Like I said before, fanzines were the social media of the day but truthfully, I don't think one thing is better or worse. Sure, there's a tactile, hold-it-in-your-hands aspect to zine culture that you don't get with a world online. There's also the way the pictures in zines and magazines built a visual language and experience that can never happen again. You don't stare at a screen the same way you would read and re-read an issue of *Flipside* or even the early *Thrasher* mags but there is a level of access and immediacy that you can't discount nowadays. The biggest issue I have is one of curation and gatekeeping in a good way. You don't necessarily have those sources that you can trust and be excited about the way you did with certain labels and zines back then. But that was thirty-forty years ago! Times change and the way we get our music, and information has also changed. The good news is there's a lot of great music and a lot of great writers and photographers and scene makers out there. That's never changed.

Don't miss *xXx Fanzine (1983-1988) Hardcore & Punk In The Eighties* that is out on Bridge Nine Records for quite a while!

THE BLOGGER

NATE WILSON, True Punk & Metal blogspot

(Nate Wilson in his Das Oath days. Photo courtesy of Matt Average)

In the days of digital world, I was absolutely fascinated when I discovered Nate Wilson's *True Punk & Metal* on blogspot. I found it the year that Nate decided to launch it 2007 while his name was familiar to me, from the bands Das Oath and Devoid Of Faith that I had records of; I will later refer to Nate's massive discography and history in hardcore punk and metal. I have to mention that this blog opened my eyes and ears in many ways.

Nate used the term 'True' for the punk and metal bands that he presented not because of elitism; the term used to describe what was real for him, non-commercial, rough and pure. While I have tried to define the term of 'True Metal' in my *Heroes Of The Metal Underground* book, there are so many different dimensions that one should think of when offering the term 'True' to either a punk or a metal band. *True Punk & Metal* blog was a revelation to me in the 00s as there were a good number of blogs in that era. Some continue to be active such as the excellent *Wilfully Obscure*, before everything getting pushed aside by the (anti) social media, where there are countless 'experts' now, people that created a persona and drop down 'heretic' views on bands and music, just to impress and boost this persona. Most of the time, these people are nowhere to be seen.

True Punk & Metal remains online but has been put to rest since 2017 by Nate and still through his posts you can find excellent records and stories from the past, as well as some interviews such as the one with Eric Meade, a true metalpunk and bassist for Death. And you can imagine that a blogspot containing Crossfire and Infest, Intruder and Nausea, Subhumans (CAN) and Bitche's Sin is totally rad, right?

So, I found Nate and he was more than willing to reply to some of my questions

Q: Nate, you've always seemed to exist right at the crossroads of punk and metal, both as a musician and as a fan. What first drew you to each world, and how did you come to see the two as complementary rather than opposed?

Nate: I was a metal head from day one with my love of music: 1970s KISS, AC/DC etc. I loved the escape from the world that it gave me. The metal just kept getting heavier and faster for me until my little brother turned me onto the Suicidal Tendencies first LP and Black Flags *Damaged*. Soon after that I went to my first punk gig and was hooked. I loved that the music was even rawer and, in some cases, faster than metal, yet it had what seemed to me to be a real message behind it compared to 1980s metal at least. It blew my mind seeing bands like Youth Of Today or Bl'ast! with short hair looking like jocks and making music that was so angry sounding.

(Romper Room Rejects, Nate's first-and crossover-band gig)

Q: Through Gloom Records, you've released music that embodies that raw crossover energy - punk attitude with metal precision. What was your original vision for the label, and how do you choose which bands or reissues fit that hybrid spirit?

Nate: So originally *Gloom* started off as a fanzine in the early 1990s. Right away I was doing interviews with the likes of Dropdead and Mayhem, two totally different bands. I was dedicated to both genres even then. The label spawned out of the zine and only turned into a label out of the necessity to put out records by the band I was playing in, Devoid Of Faith. The first release was a split 7" we did with this Canadian sludge metal band called Seized. They had no guitars at all just three bass players playing slow heavy Sabbath inspired tunes. If I didn't put the record out, I wouldn't have seen anyone else ever doing it. Seized were just to out there for most punks and even metal heads. The 'no guitars' thing definitely kept the majority of people away.

After a while I just put out records by friends who needed help getting their music out there. Toxic Holocaust and Cut The Shit are bands that I became friends with and helped them release their music afterwords.

Q: Your *True Punk and Metal* blog became a goldmine for underground music fans. What inspired you to start documenting and sharing that history, and how and in what way do you believe these subcultures can and could co-exist?

Nate: I realized there was a ton of obscure old punk and metal music out there that wasn't available to people at the time. During that time period I started doing the blog some of us started ripping vinyl to digitalize it. Vinyl was in a lull and people weren't making certain things available. Most of the bands that I was sharing info and music about were bands that I had personal relationships with or memories about that impacted me into sharing the stories and music together.

Punk and metal have always been able to coexist. Maybe now more than ever. When I was going to punk shows in the eighties and I was a long hair I would be singled out sometimes by skinheads. Those days I think are gone. Metalheads today seem to be as politically minded as punks.

Q: As someone who's played in numerous hardcore and metal bands, do you feel the crossover between the two genres is stronger today, or has that boundary become more blurred and natural over

Nate: Extreme music is extreme music. I think there is more likely to be a crossover between the two genres more now than ever. There was some separation in the 1980s. Metal bands singing about cheesy things that punks maybe couldn't relate to…that seems to have changed.

(Das Oath live in action. Courtesy unknown)

Q: Looking back, what do you think defined the true essence of the punk metal crossover - was it purely musical, or more about a shared mindset, community, and rejection of mainstream norms? Do you have any wild stories of conflict between metalheads and hardcore kids from the past?

Nate: I think there was a shared rejected feeling or distrust of the mainstream that def brought freaky misfit people together. Again, I think it's more relevant and brought together today than it was back then. I don't think long hairs are judged by punks at shows in 2025. It's been forty years, so I guess things have just become more unified and accepted over the decades. In the mid-eighties elitist punks were fearful of metal infiltrating the punk and hardcore scene. Punks were afraid things would become commercialised and we're protecting it from being stolen. Metal almost seems welcomed now.

Like I said I definitely had been singled out when I first started going to shows at the Farm. The skinheads would look for us as the circle pit was in high gear. A longhair might likely get bashed by San Francisco skins and then if we fought back, it got even worse. Metalheads might be up front just enjoying the band and head banging. Potentially certain elitist punks and skinheads would create a wall of death to just smash you into the stage even more. We would turn around and just look at them as if they were laughing at us.

Q: On a final note, which are your favourite crossover records?

Nate: In no particular order (except for number one)

D.R.I. - *Dealing With It*

COC – *Animosity*

Agnostic Front - *Cause For Alarm*

Attitude Adjustment - *American Paranoia*

Clown Alley - *Circus Of Chaos*

Excel - *Split Image*

S.O.D. - *Speak English Or Die*

Suicidal Tendencies- Self-titled

Crumbsuckers - *Life Of Dreams*

Cryptic Slaughter – *Convicted*

Ludichrist -*Immaculate Deception.*

Nate Wilson is a multi-instrumentalist (bassist, vocalist, guitarist) and has played in many hardcore punk and metal bands. Those bands include: By The Throat, Das Oath, Deathsquad, Devoid Of Faith, Divine Malice, Fright, Green Dragon, Haxan, Intent, John Browns Army, Life Abuse, Monster X, Pariiah, Permanent Trip, Romper Room Rejects, To Hell And Back.

What began as a zine in 1992, Nate operates Gloom Records with a roster of releases by bands as great as Dead Ones, Last In Line, Devoid Of Faith, Toxic Holocaust, Fright. Nate was also a part of the Ebullition Records's HeartattaCk fanzine crew in the 1990s.

Selected discography of Nate's bands:

Romper Room Rejects- *Demo* (1987). Crazy crossover hardcore with a good Attitude Adjustment influence

Voorhees/Devoid Of Faith- Split LP (1999). Vicious hardcore with a Japcore influence

Das Oath- *The Oath* 7-inch (1999). Superfast thrashcore

Fright- Self-titled mini-LP (2021). Part dose of early Slayer riffs, part dose of Japanese hardcore like Deathside, and a good Poison Idea influence. Ace!

Monster X - *Attrition* 7-inch (1996). Absolutely mental mix of hardcore with grindcore, still catchy

Life Abuse – *Systematization* LP (2024). One of my favourite Nate's bands; melodic, yet rough and powerful neo-crust, and way better than the Tragedy/From Ashes Rise copycats

To Hell And Back – *Will We Be Torn Apart* LP (2011). Unbelievable hard rock-stoner mix with punk, so catchy and fun

Divine Malice - *Successor of Death* demo (1985). Classic heavy metal, fans of this style will flip over this!

(Romper Room Rejects with Nasel Sex, Happy World, Ribzy and Past Humous at Gilman St. Berkeley. 22/04/1988)

WHEN YOU LEAST EXPECT IT

Due to rights issues, I couldn't use any of the stuff written originally in *Crossover The Edge*, and it's a bummer, because there are so many great interviews, reviews and images in...so, what's the best way to tackle this situation? Obviously getting in touch with as many bands that their interview was included in *Crossover The Edge*, and ask one or two question(s), and add a new review!

THE FU's and STRAW DOGS

(The F.U.'s band picture, 1984. Courtesy of Bruce Rhodes)

"Reaction? I know a few people did get offended by it here but, for the most part, it really wasn't the case. Any controversy seemed to come from outside of Boston, for the most part. The whole "My America" thing was meant to be tongue-in-cheek. For one thing it was poking fun at people who accept what certain punk "icons" accept at face value instead of getting their own information. Looking for heroes. "What You Pay For" definitely expresses that. We're not handing out salvation, why's that make you so upset?" And, if you read the lyrics to the rest of the songs, they're pretty damned angry. Angry at people who constantly whine about things without doing anything to make their lives better. Angry at cops. Angry at jocks who rarely suffer consequences for their bullying actions. As for the title track, it's aimed at privileged people who rant about the state of the world but don't want to give up their comfortable lifestyle. Overall, it's a very anti-authoritarian, pissed-off sounding album and I think it's aged very well. I've never considered myself patriotic or been one to fly a flag and knew what was in their hearts. Also, the cover was from some company that had customized designs, and they picked that one. I always found the people in The F.U.'s to be stand-up guys. And they weren't jocks or Reagan supporters, either. Steve and John are both well-educated and have a sharp wit. Steve has a PhD, in fact. I find it funny that, forty years later, people are still asking me whether or not they were Nazis. They never had anti-welfare, homophobic or anti-immigrant songs, like some of the NYHC bands did. They were just being wise-asses. I haven't looked at the infamous MRR interview for a while, but I was once told it was late at night, they were tired and decided to really fuck with Tim [Yohannan] when he insisted on doing the interview right then and there. I think they were amused with his and other people's reactions" -- from John Sox, vocalist of The FU's and Straw Dogs.

(Straw Dogs 1986 band picture. Courtesy of Restless Records)

The F.U.'s loved stirring up some chaos for sure, but it was more of a 'when you are a real anarchist you have to bomb your own troops too' stance, and nothing else. There musical output was top-notch, both in their hardcore phase from *Kill For Christ* and *My America* LPs as well as in their more rocking hardcore of *Do We Really Want To Hurt You?* LP (1984). As for their more metal-rock continuation as Straw Dogs, it still held a high level in terms of songwriting, so go ahead and get *We Are Not Amused* LP (1986). The F.U.'s are (2025) active, and their latest record, *Death Squad Nostalgia* 12-inch (2022) is back on the hardcore track!

M.O.D. and S.O.D.

(M.O.D. band first show. Photo Courtesy of Steven Messina)

"Kenny Ballone (RIP) was the founder of Angry Corpses, which is the band that I am currently in once again due to a resurrection, which occurred about five years ago with Ken and I before he passed. Actually, *Resurrected* is the title of the EP that we put out. Angry Corpses was a full band with Kenny, myself, Keith Davis, and three other members before we met the singer of S.O.D. after they did their first record and went back to their perspective, bands. Angry Corpses was a crossover thrash band, a fusion of hard-core punk metal. And half of the first record, *USA for M.O.D.* was Angry Corpses material. In terms of influences for metal, it was Judas Priest; rock, it's AC/DC; hardcore, of course the Bad Brains; punk its gotta be Ramones; thrash metal, it's Slayer; and crossover, D.R.I." -- Tim McMurtrie, guitarist of Angry Corpses, Full Scale Riot, Self Destruct, M.O.D., ClassicTK, Rhythm Trip.

(M.O.D. first gig flyer at Rock Hotel, NYC, 21/02/1987)

Talking about provocative bands! M.O.D. were a high confrontational act, however no one can take off them that there are songs in their first (and best) record, *U.S.A. For M.O.D.* (1987) are built for destroying pits, wild fun of crossover hardcore like 'I Executioner', 'You're Beat' or 'Hate Tank'. Many records followed that also included many hits, however *U.S.A. For M.O.D.* is hysterical, even though the lyrics in some songs are WAY too provocative. Many records followed, all more than decent in musical style, with *Gross Misconduct* LP (1989) and *Rhythm Of Fear* LP (1992). The best songs on these ones include 'Get Up And Dance', 'True Colors', 'Satan's Cronies', pure fun. However, my personal preference will always be *U.S.A. For M.O.D.*, it's their hardest, fastest and roughest ever, because it contained many songs with the original lineup of Angry Corpses who are back since 2021.

(S.O.D. with Suicidal Tendencies at City Gardens, Trenton, NJ. 22/11/1985)

Regarding S.O.D., I admit that I was very harsh in the extensive review I did in *Crossover The Edge*. There are some pros and cons into their case, so I'll start with the former: they helped NYHC to gain more popularity with *Speak English Or Die* selling more than 1.000.000 copies which brought countless metalheads in touch with the hardcore scene, for better or for worse, I keep the better aspects of this. In musical terms, this was unbelievably well-played and well-recorded crossover hardcore, that offered another perspective to the NYHC bands that they could do it too. Danny Lilker's playing style is simply out of this world, and so is Charlie Benante, both of them sound totally on fire on this one. I wish though there were more songs like 'Kill Yourself', 'Chromatic Death', 'Fist Banging Mania', 'Milk', 'No Turning Back' and 'Douche Crew' (that is actually a diss song against Slayer).

Let's go for the cons: The lyrics, 'to kill the peace punks' from the song 'United Forces', really? Songs such as 'Speak English or Die', 'Fuck The Middle East' and 'Pussywhipped' were considered as jokes; pretty bad ones, if you ask my opinion. However ignorant people from either metal, hardcore or skinhead subcultures, took them literally. What's even worse is Billy Milano's views later expressed on M.O.D. too, which he continues to disgrace himself with them. Now the joke isn't funny at all. Also, I wish that bands that influenced S.O.D. such as Adrenalin O.D., and Nihilistics would even achieve one-tenth the levels of recognition worldwide that S.O.D. reached.

LOSS FOR WORDS

"Loss For Words, and my own part in how doing those background vocals, hanging out with Roger, Vinnie, and very young Madball and the AF guys while *Liberty and Justice For...* was being finished up is definitely an interesting story. Hearing the album pretty much almost done, as the mixing process had begun while finishing touches and a few overdubs besides the background vocals also happened while we were there was super fun and exciting for sixteen-year-old me. I think the band may have started to do the backgrounds by themselves but am not positive. I just remember Roger telling me that the wanted more impactful, powerful sing along BGV's like the live shows, but tight and not shouting per se. I remember his face lighting up listening to the playback after our first pass. He asked if we had time to stay and do the whole album, and I was like fuck yeah! We only played a tiny role in that album, but every time you hear the song along 'The Blood, The Honor, the Truth' that's us. I can definitely hear myself and Kevin out guitarist a bit when I listen closely. I seriously belted those lyrics out as loudly and in as close to a 'pitch' that complimented Roger's voice and emotion as I could. It was just cool that those guys put us sixteen- and seventeen-year-olds from a young Upstate New York on such a seminal album. I was a huge AF fan since I bought *Victim In Pain* on vinyl as a thirteen-year-old hardcore kid" -- Eric Fogelberg, vocalist of Loss For Words.

(Loss For Words Why? demo cover. Courtesy of Eric Fogelberg)

The world of hardcore and crossover has many great and interesting stories. Loss For Words were a crossover band from Elmira, New York. They happened to be in the studio at Pyramid Sound Studios, Ithaca, New York where and when Agnostic Front recorded *Liberty and Justice For...* in 1987. So, those young kids were asked by Roger to do the backing vocals on this classic NYHC record, and they did in perfect style. Loss For Words released four excellent, super-fuzzy and rough demos from 1986 to 1988, before releasing their only LP *Prey* in 1989; that is as vicious as you can imagine! Plus, Loss For Words is another band I managed to discover in the thanks lists of Agnostic Front because of *Liberty and Justice For....* In a very different time, you had to learn by heart each inner sleeve of records you love if you wanted to discover even more many bands!

PRE METAL SYNDROME

(PMS band picture, 1985. Courtesy of Yana Chupenko)

"Well, we were part of the scene from practically inception, so all the tough males were our friends lol. You protected your own back in day. We also held our own. You would be an idiot or an out-of-towner idiot to start shit with us. The fact that we had two Cuban sister firecrackers that would destroy you, helped (wink wink!). Now the only problem in that old scene which I had was from women who were green with envy and just toxic bitches. Not naming names. BUT if anyone ever thought of starting shit with me personally, I never shied away from a conflict, EVER. They just knew better than fuck with me. I had connections and some were told explicitly what would happen to them if they even tried. But those conflicts were practically non-existent. But while playing shows out of town opening for Bad Brains in Baltimore specifically, I think, there were a few dumb-assed skinheads who may have screamed something or other. HR stood in front of stage with folded arms and did not allow anyone to go near it lol! So, when the lemmings see the alpha protecting someone, the hyenas retreat. Now I did kick someone in head with my riding boots when we played at Ritz for Joey Ramone's birthday show in 1986, since they threw something onstage. But that was Wench!" -- Yana Chupenko, vocalist of Pre Metal Syndrome, Wench and Shiny Mama

(PMS with Reagan Youth, Wrecking Crew etc at Lupo's, 11/05/1987)

Imagine that: you are a band of sixteen and seventeen year old females, and your scene (NYHC) is one of the hardest, most male-dominated in the world. Now, you have to be really tough to not have anyone shit at you, and Pre Metal Syndrome were tough as hell! Moreover, their 1986 *Pre Metal Syndrome* LP, is pure fire! Wild metal punk, with crazy musicianship, and the jaw-dropping vocals of Yana Chupenko. Pre Metal Syndrome later went on to become slightly more metal style with Wench, again with excellent results; Wench were great both on their demos as well as in the *A Tidy Sized Chunk* LP (1991). P.M.S. songs like 'On The Run' or 'Rally Round' have to be heard to be believed. Cross Motörhead with Dead Boys and you are nearly there!

(P.M.S. with Cro-Mags and the Bad Brains at the Rock Hotel, Brooklyn. 20/07/1985)

ATTITUDE ADJUSTMENT

(Attitude Adjustment early band picture, 1985. Courtesy of Lisa Basso)

"I'm very happy that Attitude Adjustment is revered in the scene. It's very nice to know that we have a legacy in punk rock, hardcore and crossover history. Not really found any new crossover band that have captured my interest. To be honest there is no way to be crossover these days. For me crossover was a moment... not a music genre. It can't be replicated over and over. It's up to musicians to blend music together in a new way to make the new crossover happen... it's just not possible to play punk and metal as a formula and call it Crossover. It's hard to pick a favourite Attitude Adjustment record for me. Each record has aspects that I love. *Out Of Hand* is really cool. That record has some really great songs showing the bands musically. *No Way Back* is special to me as it was a great experience for the band recording in Denmark with Tue Madsen and Anders Ludemark. *American Paranoia* is the classic for sure. I guess in the end, I can't pick a favourite record" -- Chris Kontos, drummer of Attitude Adjustment and Forbidden, The Boneless Ones, Konkhra, Machine Head, Testament, The Alien Blakk, Verbal Abuse, Death Angel (live), Exodus (live), Hell's Kitchen, Anti-Trust, Custard Pie, Flange, Grinch, Sangre Eterna, The Servants.

(Attitude Adjustment with Uniform Choice, Corruption, Frontline and Necropolis in Philipino Hall, Wilmington, 13/12/1986)

Attitude Adjustment from San Francisco, California will always remain one of my most favourite crossover acts, period. Their insane style gives me goosebumps and makes me want to tear down walls, and I can't get enough of them! I just wished more current bands headed for their strict and direct hardcore style, that is flavoured with metal riffs. All their output is mandatory for everyone into crossover. I'd like to point out that *Dead Serious* 1985 demo is one of the best demos ever, and *American Paranoia* is a life-changing record! Like a crazy mix of Exodus, Discharge, Broken Bones and The Clay (JP). But then again, get all their records. I did it already and you know it. Also check Attitude, their follow-up and the excellent *Kein Schlaf Bis Deutschland* 12" (1987) and Condemned Attitude with members of Attitude Adjustment and Condemned To Death and the *Humanoid Or Biomechanoid?* LP.

(Attitude Adjustment with R.K.L. and Christ On Parade at The Rock On Broadway, San Francisco. 18/04/1986)

SNAKE NATION

(Snake Nation band picture, 1989. Courtesy unknown)

"Crossover the term meant nothing to me, really. This narrative that people hated each other and couldn't like punk rock or metal, has been totally blown out of proportion. At least, to my experience. I liked aggressive heavy music no matter what you called it. I think the term was invented after the fact, or at least when the D.R.I. album *Crossover* came out. It's an album I have never heard except for two songs. I stopped at *Dealing With It*, which I liked. I had nothing against anybody or anything I just don't know why people acted like it was impossible to like both punk rock AND metal before 1983. If I have to pick a top 5 'Crossover' list, it would be: Black Flag - *My War*, Void side of The Faith/Void split album, Corrosion Of Conformity- *Animosity*, Bl'ast! - *The Power Of Expression*, Die Kruezen - first self-titled LP. Those are five recordings that hold up and you still can't get tired of, even at my advance age. I will always love those records! Snake Nation formed only because Woody had a contract with Caroline Records at the time, they had re-released *Eye For An Eye* and put out that *Six Songs With Mike Singing* recording. I sang backup on it. The members of SNFU were in town at the same time I was, and they also sang on it. All of COC's partners at the time also sang on it. Anyways, Mike had already left COC, and it was during one of their down periods where they wasted a bunch of time doing nothing. This is before the *Blind* album lineup. I think Woody and Reed weren't getting along at the time…those guys did that sometimes. So, I think Woody asked me to play drums on some songs he had to which I said of course yes. Then he called Mike up and it was decided that he would be involved. I think Woody missed Mike and it was a no brainer. So, the Snake Nation project was the three of us and it was essentially half new songs that Woody and Mike had, and then the other half were old COC songs that Mike took with him when he quit. Some of those were some of the best songs COC had written, during the Simon Bob period. And I got to play on them! But it was also kind of weird…trying to replace Reed Mullin. And play like him, not an easy thing to do. But I did my best. Really, he should have been there but it was not to be. I wasn't going to say no though. It came out how it came out: rather poorly. I always enjoyed lousy sounding punk and metal recordings, now was my chance to be a part of one! When it came out, no one NO ONE cared. We played three shows in the area and that was it. Mike went back to wherever he came from and the *Blind* era COC was about to rev up. I always hear how much people liked the Snake Nation record, which is nice. It is certainly stylistically the last recording of the DNA of the old COC, or at least the magic between Mike and Woody and how they played Black Flag meeting Black Sabbath kind of stuff." -- from Brian Walsby, visual artist and drummer of Snake Nation, The Magpie, Davidians, Daddy, Double Negative, Polvo, Scared Straight, Shiny Beast, Siberian, The Patty Duke Syndrome, Willard, Wwax.

(Brian Walsby drumming for Snake Nation, 1989. Courtesy unknown)

Snake Nation from Raleigh, North Carolina were a one-record project of Woody and Mike (COC), alongside Brian Walsby. To this day, the record holds a very specific character in terms of crossover. Neither fast, nor thrashy, their self-titled LP is still one of the most innovative records that crossover ever offered. In-line with bands like Bl'ast! and Black Flag, but with a chunkier, jazzier and more angular approach, *Snake Nation* LP is just pounding metal-hardcore. Dark and bitter, it offers crushing stuff such as 'History', 'This Nation' or 'Beautiful Hills'. A hidden gem! And what can I say about Brian Walsby? People, if you want a great, friendly and kind artist to do your record and book covers, or to draw you great T-shirt designs, hit up Brian. He is the best.

METAL ONSLAUGHT

(Metal Onslaught with Aftermath, Macabre and Annihilation at the Thirsty Whale, 23/06/1988)

"I don't think the other guys really listened to a lot of punk stuff, mostly metal. All the standard metal stuff. When I joined the band, they were wearing spandex and playing Motley Crue covers, ahaha! I always thought we sort of sounded like a mix between Slayer and Megadeth. Another band we all liked a lot and is very underrated was Voivod. Always thought they should have been bigger. I liked a lot of different hardcore and punk stuff. The classic stuff like the Pistols, Black Flag, Fear etc. Then a lot of the newer hardcore. A lot of the East Coast stuff like the Crumbsuckers, the Cro-Mags, S.O.D., Bad Brains. Also, West Coast stuff like Excel, Suicidal Tendencies and humorous stuff like Ludichrist, Murphy's Law, Mentors. Also, local metal stuff like Zoetrope, Trouble, Macabre. As far as being ahead of our time I don't know. We were writing songs with a lot of guitar parts and tempo changes. So much so that we could have made three or four songs out of one song. I did start writing some more groove-oriented stuff similar to Pantera around the same time they came out with their classic albums. I'd say a lot of them were more of an inspiration rather than a direct influence. One story that comes to mind is when we were headlining The Vic Theater in Chicago. We went to hit the first big note of the intro into the set. Marty the bass player and singer jumped up and when he landed his wireless came undone and hit the floor, and the battery fell out which made a bad feedback noise. He went crazy, grabbed the microphone boom stand and threw himself on the stage floor and just started thrashing around with the mic stand. I didn't know what to do so I went up and started singing the song. The crowd was in shock. They didn't know what was happening. They weren't sure if it was part of the show. We got through the set somehow but after that the other guitar player quit, and Marty decided that he didn't want to sing anymore. So, after that we went to a 3-piece, and I started singing from then on. They had barrels of free beer for the bands. That may have contributed to problem. Another quick one: People used to do shows and have big parties in abandoned warehouses and lofts. We were playing a big loft party where there were big holes in the floor and the floors falling through. There was a group of punks that were really getting into us which caused a couple of fights. They were thrown out of the party. When we went to leave every car up and down the street had their windows broken out except our van. We were parked backed right up to the doors of the place. They saw us loading in and knew the van was ours and smashed every other car but our van. I thought that was sorta cool. Another night we were playing a show in a warehouse and GG Allin had played the night before and I swear there was what looked like poop on the ceiling above the stage. I believe that's one of the nights I threw up while playing. Again, alcohol playing a large factor. The poop didn't help! Now, I'm remembering all these stories. We didn't make any money, but we did have fun" -- Ken Vretfors, guitarist of Metal Onslaught, Lo$t $oul, Carnage, BarnYard Oddities.

(Metal Onslaught with Nuclear Assault and Trouble at Hemmens Auditorium, Elgin, IL. 10/04/1987)

Metal Onslaught were from Elgin, Illinois, an ultra-brutal thrash metal band, with crossover tendencies. They sounded crazy vicious on their twenty-minute LP *Cease To Exist* (1987). Songs like 'Waiting For Death' with its unbelievable mosh part in NYHC style, the punk metal attack of 'Redneck' and 'Death Do Us Part' with its infectious riff guitar work, will please both the fans of wild thrash metal as well as those that love the most extreme crossover bands like e.g. Wehrmacht or Cryptic Slaughter. Plus, I have a very beautiful story to share when *Crossover The Edge* was released. Doris Vretfors (RIP 2023), mother of Ken, found me on Facebook and sent me this message: 'thank you for making my son so happy, it really means so much to me'.

MAYHEM (Portland)

(Mayhem band picture, 1986. Courtesy of Matt McCourt)

"Oh dude! I was a punk rocker in 1977! Into Ramones, Pistols when they came out. I was sick of bands like Black Sabbath by then. That Ramones 'Beat On The Brat' was my heartbeat! Then I got asked to play with Mick Zane in a band in 1978; they played like Judas Priest and Budgie, bands I hadn't heard of. But they sold weed and cocaine at their band house and Tom Roberts (aka Pig Champion later in Poison Idea) came over there all the time, and we got to talk about this new punk music and became good friends. He was the band roadie, and I was a regular friend till he died. It was an honour of me producing the first Poison Idea 7-inch (*Pick Your King*). As for the late Steven Hanford, aka Thee Slayer Hippie, I knew him from the time he was eleven! He bought the first Wild Dogs T-shirt and always hung out at my house. By that time, I was a guy selling cocaine and weed, and I introduced them to Tom knowing that they would get on as friends, and that's how they all got into Poison Idea. As for the story of Mayhem, it started when I got a solo deal on Shrapnel, Roadrunner and CBS Japan for my projects called Dr. Mastermind at the time. Tom Roberts turned me onto the Mentors who I ended up doing seven albums with as a singer after El Duce died, and he turned me onto Motörhead which is really the only metal band I really like. Their bass sound it's just my sound, and they were punk rock before they were considered metal- they always reminded me the case of like Black Sabbath, that was an acid rock band before somebody said they were heavy metal band. So, that's how I got into Mayhem. In fact, this is the reason Wild Dogs got rid of me, it was because I was a punk rocker in a metal band. We were not on the same channel, so I joined Mayhem. So, the story goes that I found out that Wild Dogs were going to replace me, but they didn't have the guts to tell me. Boner, who was in Tom Roberts' first band (a drummer and a good friend) said 'dude you should show up and then leave as soon as the first song starts at your show'. So, I left them with a crowd of 700 people with no singer, walked out the door and took off, but what we did was we had twenty-four people involved in this little prank who are instructed to wait fifteen to twenty minutes and then go to amend their money back because I was not onstage! And it worked! We made like $200! Then, Steven thought that was pretty punk rock and asked me to join Mayhem the very next day. And this is where the deal with Black Dragon Records comes; Steve promised me that I would get money. I got the studio time, but those cheesy bastards went over the budget, so I got in trade with bringing bands to the studio. I never got paid, and Shrapnel put a cease-and-desist order, because we played a Dr. Mastermind song on the Mayhem record ('Domination'), so I was quite pissed because I ended up having to pay over $1000 and got nothing so it was basically a…fuck you (that's also my song!). *Burned Alive* was also re-issued on a German label three years ago, Diabolic Might Records. I had a stroke in 2022 and I'm kind of fucked up. I was blind for a year and a half, it popped the blood vessels in my eyes. Mayhem with me lasted less than a year, Steve, Eric and Craig later joined Poison Idea, actually right after we recorded *Burned Alive*. Steve later robbed a drugstore and sentenced to one year in prison. He did it again, this time with a gun, robbing for drugs with Dane Petersen from Blood Bath (who had the guitar player from Autopsy). Dane drove him to the drugstore, Steve went in robbed it, and the owner called the cops and described Dane as the robber. The cops beat the shit outta him causing him a bad brain damage, while Steve skipped out the beating, but got caught and got thirty years in prison" -- Matt McCourt, vocalist of Mayhem, Dr. Mastermind, Wild Dogs, Church of El Duce, The Ravers, The Violators.

(Mayhem with The Accused, Necrophile and N.M.E at the Rock Theatre, Seattle. 06/07/1985)

The outrageous lifestyle of the members of Mayhem is also reflected into their music; Mayhem from Portland, Oregon, included the young Steve Hanford who he was just sixteen years old when they released the 1985 *As The World Burns* demo. Their 1987 *Burned Alive* LP is now a classic of crossover, with lots of classic heavy metal and Motörhead influences. Get it, because songs like 'Defy Your Master', the frenzied 'Aerobic Genocide', the shredding 'Over The Top' are simply anthems for pure vagrants! And that Motörhead cover of 'Ace Of Spades' stands as one of the greatest one ever, just like the Battalion of Saints one. And do yourself a favour and pick up all 1980s LPs by Poison Idea. I miss so much Steve Hanford. We had so many great conversations…plus I can remember making me a video call while I was on the train to London to see Negative Approach, him telling me 'Alex, tell John [Brannon] that I said hi and that we should tour together'. Damn…

FINAL WARNING

(Final Warning band picture 1984. Courtesy of Maximum Rocknroll)

"When we were in our mid-teens we were all into heavy stuff like Black Sabbath, Judas Priest, and Led Zeppelin. Simon and Tim especially leaned that way, which gave Final Warning that riff-heavy, powerful sound. The political angle mostly came from me and Jeff, straight from the ethos of the punk and hardcore we were discovering. When we got together and mixed the metal power we loved with the intensity of bands like Germs, Discharge, and Disorder, it just clicked. We weren't trying to figure out some kind of 'crossover' sound, we were just throwing together what we liked and what each of us brought to the table. The punk side was huge. Records like Circle Jerks' *Group Sex*, Discharge's *Why?*, GBH's *Leather, Bristles, Studs and Acne*, and Portland band The Wipers' *Is This Real* were spinning nonstop. At the same time, we were into the heavier, faster metal coming out — Venom, Mercyful Fate, that kind of things. Later, Metallica's early records had an attitude we dug. I remember Cliff Burton wearing a Discharge shirt, and we thought that was cool as hell. It proved the worlds we were into weren't as far apart as some people thought. And of course, Motörhead was the ultimate blueprint. As for why it ended, honestly it was drugs creeping in and us not having the perspective to realize what a great thing we had going. We didn't have the experience or the work ethic to turn it into a career. In a word, we were clueless! It's a shame, but it's also part of the story" -- Dan Cunneen, drummer of Final Warning, Nightcaps, Obituaries, Zipgun.

(Final Warning with Poison Idea and Lockjaw at the Satyricon, Portland. 21/04/1985)

What I like to call as 'the US equivalent of Sacrilege UK', Final Warning, is a sinfully underappreciated band. Formed in 1982 in Portland, Oregon, their only 1980s releases were the 1983 Demo and the *Out Of Sight Out Of Mind* 7-inch (1984) on Pig Champion's Fatal Erection Records. Heavy as hell metal-hardcore, in the tradition of UK82 Punk, with a massive Venom influence. All four songs on the 7-inch are ripping, so if you like bands like Sacrilege, and Anti-System in their more mid-tempo, go for it. A classic release, but I would advise you to get the *PDX* CD compilation that was released in 2007 by Southern Lord Records that includes all their live and studio stuff. Plus, check their channel on YouTube for some live footage from the 1980s.

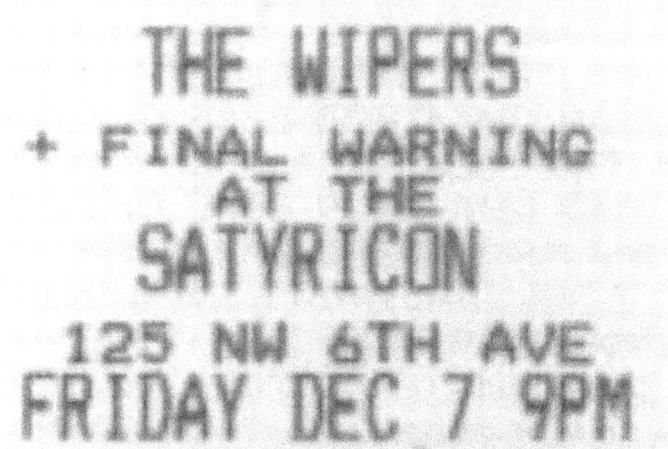

(Final Warning with the Wipers at the Satyricon, Portland. 07/12/1984)

THE BRAINDEAD

(The Braindead band, mid-1980s. Courtesy unknown)

"I grew about twenty miles east of Seattle in a little farm town called Issaquah. Issaquah was and is a metal town. It was mostly the commercial Top 40 metal such as Twisted Sister, Judas Priest, AC/DC, Motley Crue, you get the idea. There was the groups that were into the Top 40 pop stuff and then you get into the smaller groups for those who like the underground, alternative music like Bauhaus, Motörhead, Metallica, Venom and then there was a very small group of us who were into hardcore punk which I think there were only like four people in Issaquah in the early 80s that really lived. One that really stood out was my friend's sister, Wendy V. She dressed it and she modelled it with a great purple mohawk which at the time, you were touched by Satan. She was the nicest person, and I met her when I was fifteen. There were two other gals, Sid, and Sonia also and between Sonia and Wendy. I really dove into the deep end of the alternative lake when I was fourteen. I was already listening to Dead Kennedys, Black Flag, Suicidal Tendencies, and I still enjoyed metal, but I was bored with the long solos, lame ass tight pants, spandex, 125-pounds guys acting like they would murder you, etc. The scene in Seattle was great, very artistic but had a great hardcore scene with 10 Minute Warning, The Fartz, the Melvins, Soundgarden, Green River, DSML, False Liberty, Skank Puppies, Wicked Angel, Inverted Morals, BOT, The Dehumanizers and of course the kings of spatter rock, The Accüsed. Unfortunately, for being known for being such a liberal city, the city put in a lot of effort to shut down all age venues and shows, full-on attack to punk with this old fart, Lou Guzzo [local journalist]. There was one main venue called Gorilla Garden that had two rooms, and I think it was an old fish warehouse in the China District. There were so many great shows but the owner Tony never really got all the right permits or something so this place closed, he attempted to open in a couple areas, two riots I think finalized the city to put the Teen Dance Ordinance into place which pretty much made it impossible for small clubs to put on all-age shows. They closed dance clubs also. Now the two riots were legendary. One was the Circle Jerks riot in December 1985 and the Reagan Youth riot in 1986 at the UTC hall. In 1988 there was the infamous ferry boat riot that occurred on the way back from Bremerton to Seattle. All of them I am glad I had been there to experience them. But my little cow town scene grew with the crossover years, more mohawks showing up and we had a good time out there. Think of the movie *River's Edge*; to me, that movie was Issaquah. Small town but we existed as if it was a major city. Crossover brought all the outer city bands into Seattle which the scene just exploded. With Seattle shutdown basically, the music scene moved south to a little place called the Community World Theater on M Street. I would drive down almost every day for shows there and Legends. I believe there were a couple other spots down south also. Bands that really stand out for me are Subvert and AMQA, who later became the amazing Portrait of Poverty (check out all three). The Accüsed were an international band, Diddley Squat and the metal scene had Force Entry who were the most talented band in the scene, Bitter End, Coven, Sanctuary but the hardcore scene had Last Gasp, Aspirin Feast who were one of my favourites, The Derelicts, rest in peace Duane! There is more but what I can remember right now. It was a great time to be alive and in the underground Northwestern scene.

When we first started it with The Braindead, it was mostly just something we did with our other friends. Our first recording was just a live practice tape of covers. We were getting ready for our first show with a large audience which was playing a winter dance at our high school. The place was packed, we were so nervous, the first band was a great alternative band who was tight, well-rehearsed and professional while we were literally just a pack of punks who could somewhat play. It didn't matter because we opened the set with 'Six Pack' by Black Flag and when we all came in to start the verse, the place came unglued, which was a complete surprise to us. It was a rush; the nerves started to settle. We went into the second song then on the third song we were stopped by the staff. Lights came up because they could not control all these kids packed into the gym. Everything calmed down and we went into 'When The Shit Hits The Fan', and again, the place erupts. I get tackled by our principal because we would not stop playing, our singer Alan was yelling 'fuck you' to our friends, it was a party. They pulled the plug on us when we started again and that was it. We were banned from anything else at school. Which pissed me off. But then looking back, I wouldn't want it any other way. That's punk rock, right?

(The Braindead with Surrogate Brains, Breakaway, Paranoia and Post Humans at Gilman St. 05/08/1988)

After the original lineup broke up and the second generation of the band came together in late 1986 and this would be the core of the band to this day. I am currently working on new material for The Braindead. I was the one member of the band that was heavily involved with the scene in the Northwest, so I was known as one guy who had homemade stickers, handed out demos but the band never played. We had a hard time finding someone to be our drummer. We didn't have pro gear like other bands and honestly, we were trying to be this tight band but just have fun. We had one gig in the 1980s at the Community World Theater with a new band that transplanted from Colorado called The Derelicts, the band and scene just recently lost a great character Duane. I became friends with Duane after this show. It was another classic chaotic night with The Braindead. We pieced together a lineup with friends filling in on drums and vocals. In typical fashion, we partied like we always did, got completely messed up, went onstage, played sloppy with me eventually getting pissed, throwing my guitar and walking off stage to everyone screaming and shouting about it. The band finished the set with my guitar still feedbacking the entire time as I told them to fuck themselves from the side of the stage. But I was everywhere it seemed at that time.

I have a ton of stories as you can tell from the previous stuff. The riots were probably the most memorable moments for me in the scene. Ending up in footage on the news which was funny because one morning my dad and I are watching the news. He asked, 'let me guess, you were there, weren't you?'. I said, 'oh no, we left right away' and at the moment there is footage of me and the crew throwing snowballs and objects at the station wagon with the news crew in it, lol. Oh, I guess we were there, Dad, lol.

Issaquah was always crazy, honestly. From blood rituals to the brandings, our version of the Germs burns, constantly harassed by the cops and living life fast, so we could die young and leave an ugly corpse. We played as hard as the music we listened to and played. We were 'In League with Satan', hated authority, establishment, and were out to live life the way we wanted it. The scene was a mixing bowl of people, all very different but the music brought everyone together. In the centre of town was the Gull Station, where all the underground kids would go hang out. I was a late-comer to the Gull, but it is a great motley crew of extended family.

One memory I have during this time was at a Poison Idea and D.R.I. show in Tacoma and the one downside of crossover is that it drew in the jar heads and jocks to the scene which didn't blend well at times. During the show, some dude was fucking with Jerry, kept egging him on and eventually he found out after fucking around that Jerry will deliver if needed. The guy kept asking to be kicked in the face, not sure why but eventually his wish came true.

Christ on Parade played in Tacoma and handed out acid prior to the show starting. Great night with this new Bay Area band Neurosis and Subvert. It was a very colourful night.

I have a lot of great stories from this era. So many great bands, friends, and adventures. We lived life, we lived fast, and we left destruction behind us at times but had a great time doing it" -- Clark 'Chaos' Wheeler, guitarist and vocalist of The Braindead and Dogs In The Fight.

Chaotic and rough, this is the most fitting description for The Braindead from Kenmore, Washington. Formed in 1984, active still today (2025) The Braindead went on to release four demos in the 1980s of unbelievably lo-fi hardcore punk, in the vein of (very) early Accüsed. My favourite off those demos being the 1988 *Nightmares* with songs like 'Scum' or 'Skate' that are so demented! They went for a speedcore-crossover approach in the 1990s. Still crazy and out of control, and their two full-length CDs *Red* (1999) and *Born Defiant* (2003) are as wacky as you can imagine.

ACROPHET

(Acrophet band picture 1988. Courtesy of Eric Grett)

"Regarding my influences, from punk and hardcore it was Jeff Nelson [Minor Threat] and Felix [D.R.I.]. From metal, it was Dave Lombardo and Tommy Lee. Acrophet were way ahead of their time and place. There wasn't enough financial backing from the label, and we had limited press exposure and radio play. They'd only play us on the radio at 3AM. I wanted to move the band to L.A., but they refused because they absolutely hated Los Angeles, so after that, the label didn't pick up the option for a third album, so we disbanded. I moved to East L.A. at twenty years old and never left, and joined Killing Culture" -- Jason Mooney, drummer of Acrophet and Metal Militia, Killing Culture, Something Wicked..., MS2.

(Acrophet with Death and Sindrome at Eagles Club, Milwaukee. 22/01/1988)

Brookfield, Wisconsin wasn't the hottest place on earth for crossover bands, however, this doesn't remove any of the greatness of Acrophet. Acrophet were just kids with an average age of twelve when they formed in 1983! Their excellent 1987 *The Answer Within* demo didn't go unnoticed, and Roadrunner Records offered them a deal for two LPs. The first one, the 1988 *Corrupt Minds*, is a crossover classic, more metal than their peers, but still on the hardcore-thrash realm! Not even a weak song here. My favourites are 'Slaves Of Sin', 'Lifeless Image' and the hardcore attack of 'Victims Of The Holocaust'. Plus, the musicianship is just wild; they were just seventeen-year-old kids and sounded more confident and proficient than many of the 'bigger' thrash bands. I recall finding that record in 2000, in the 'special price bin'. While I was checking the back cover, I saw one member wearing a Minor Threat T-shirt and one other wearing an Agnostic Front one, so I had to pick it up! After a nationwide tour with hometown friends Realm, they went on to release their sophomore LP, the 1990 *Faded Glory*, that had a slightly more melancholic touch, still blending hardcore with thrash metal. It was another top release, and sadly their last. Just listen to 'When Time Stands Still'. And Jason Mooney, is just a beast of a drummer, still is and always will be!

N.M.E.

(NME with Mace and The Accüsed at Everett Masonic Temple, 17/04/1986)

"We liked the usual classics like Priest, Sabbath, AC/DC and that kind of stuff. As for our influences, Venom obviously! Also, Celtic Frost, Sodom, Destruction, and Onslaught. Loved all of them. For me, the ones that opened the doors for me were Judas Priest's *British Steel* and Motörhead's *Ace of Spades*. My cousin's boyfriend played those one day and I was hooked. The other three would be Raven's *All For One*, Celtic Frost *Morbid Tales*, and Metallica's *Kill 'em All*. It's hard for me figure out our legacy on new bands, and in general. I only know of a few bands that were maybe influenced a little by us, Sacrificial Blood and Midnight. Our legacy will forever be intertwined with the horrible event that happened with Kurt. You can't really separate the music from it. It will always be there. Hopefully people will take away the work ethic and the chaotic stage performance of the band. Kurt was the blueprint on how to promote and grow a band, as he put everything he had into it" -- Brian Llapitan, vocalist of NME.

(NME with Annihilation, Strychnine, Kil D' Kor, RPA, Malfunkshun and Max Planck at the Gorilla Gardens. 07/09/1985)

Some bands found themselves gaining recognition much later than their initial 1980s output-one of those bands is NME from Federal Way and Tacoma, Washington. Formed in 1983 as Night Prowler, NME released in 1985 one demo and in 1986 the *Unholy Death* LP that drive metalpunks worldwide crazy right now. Blame it for bands like Midnight or Children Of Technology, NME are currently enjoying their cult status, and their Motörhead-meets-Venom-meets Poison Idea. *Unholy Death* is an unstoppable barrage of punishing songs, check out: 'Louder Than Hell' or 'Speed Kilz'. They even went to incorporate noise rock elements on their 1990s records, and they are back since 2004 with their latest output being the 2024 *As Disgust* EP.

CORROSION OF CONFORMITY

(COC band, 1987. Photo courtesy of Naomi Petersen)

"It was a natural thing for the band as we were drawn to the rawness and sheer power of hardcore punk rock while also having a deep appreciation for heavy rock like Judas Priest, Black Sabbath, Deep Purple, etc. Part of our journey was unintentionally fusing it all together to create the band's sound at the time. I think the *Animosity* record captured it all very well" -- Woody Weatherman, guitarist/vocalist of Corrosion of Conformity and Snake Nation, Let 'Lones, No Labels.

(COC with Straw Dogs and Sacrifice at the Metro, Chicago. 08/08/1986)

Just a reminder; COC is one of the first, best, and most influential bands to pursue the crossover. From Raleigh, North Carolina, they formed in 1982 and is still active in 2025 and continue releasing records and touring the world. Their 1980s stuff is crucial: *Eye For An Eye* LP (1984), *Animosity* LP (1985), *Technocracy* EP (1987) and *Six Songs with Mike Singing* EP (1989). Those records are mandatory for anyone with a slight interested in crossover. I agree with Woody's opinion, *Animosity* is a monstrous record. Try Side A for pure banging frenzy, try Side B for some of the most hellish crossover ever. COC have been one of my musical guides since I started listening to crossover, and it was them that turned me into bands like Bl'ast! or Ugly Americans in the 1990s. See I was checking all their thanks lists!

AFTERMATH

(Aftermath band picture, 1989. Courtesy of Jim Katz)

"We formed on Halloween night 1985 not instantly thinking we wanted to be a crossover or speed metal band. We just wanted to write some heavy original music. Steve, Ray and I went to the same high school. Me and Steve had just graduated the year before and Ray was still in high school. Thrash was only a few years old at the time, but Ray and I loved it. As we started writing we wanted to be thrash but we added some hardcore elements. We wanted to make the fastest music ever but still make it catchy. We added Adam, he was a skinhead punk that had the attitude but not really the musical ability of Ray to Steve. By 1986, we were really writing crossover thrash songs that we eventually recorded in 1987. *Killing The Future* was our attempt to record the fastest thrash songs ever at that time, we think if they weren't the fastest, they came close. Don Kaye at *Kerrang!* called it too damn fast. He didn't mean it as a compliment, but he didn't realize that was the point. After we recorded *KTF*, I was done with the ultra-speed stuff and felt we needed to move on from it. We fired Adam in 1987, he couldn't play the songs we were writing. We knew he would never be able to and we wanted to really experiment with our music at that time. We needed a bass player that could really play. We added John Lovette on bass (he later moved to guitar; he wasn't a bass player). With the new line still a 4-piece, we really could expand the writing. We wanted to be a Pink Floyd of thrash. When John came clean and said he joined the band as a bass player because he really wanted to be in the band, but really wanted to play guitar, it was a simple decision. John switched to guitar and now we needed a bass player. With John and Steve on guitar we could really experiment. John was really into Sabbath and the slower riff, but he was also a shredder that played some extremely complex parts. His song writing was dark and slow. It all fell into place we wanted to be a progressive technical thrash band and with two guitarists that were both great writers and players it was natural to write really odd songs that were part of what would go on to become progressive technical thrash. That was 1987-88. It's funny we were at the beginning of two sub-genres within a few years apart. With Aftermath we have never written two demos or albums that sound like the one before it. I don't think any band in metal was an influence musically but more of an inspiration, if that makes sense. We loved metal and hardcore and wrote *Killing The Future,* but we didn't try and sound like any specific song or band. Bands that we loved back then 85-86 were Slayer, D.R.I., Suicidal Tendencies, Cro-Mags. As I said earlier, we wanted to be the Pink Floyd of thrash. Clearly, we didn't want to sound like Floyd we wanted to experiment like they did but be heavy. Voivod and Kreator were bands we really respected. Our very first show was at this club called Snobs. We started playing and the crowd went nuts, the pit was insane. We didn't expect this to be the reaction at the very first gig. My brother and manager were standing in front of the stage he gets hit his glasses go flying on to the stage I see him crawling on the stage looking for his glasses. We knew at that moment those songs would get crazy pits. That's just one story of many" -- Kyriakos Charlie Tsiolis, vocalist of Aftermath.

(Aftermath's first show. With Devastation and Terminal Death, 15/06/1986)

Chicago, Illinois's Aftermath are a sinfully underrated band that went on from crossover to progressive thrash with gusto and style. Their 1987 *Killing The Future* demo is one of the best demos ever in hardcore and metal, totally skull-crushing crossover thrash that sounds out of control and would put Slayer's *Reign In Blood* in shame! Okay, now that's a big statement, however songs like 'Chaos' or 'Meltdown' will drive you nuts, total crossover excellence. Re-released in 2011 on the *When Will You Die? - Demos 1986/1987* LP compilation, not to be missed. Check also all their recorded output, especially *Eyes Of Tomorrow* (1994), a brilliant tech-thrash LP. Still active too!

(Aftermath with Prong and Flotsam and Jetsam at Medusa's, Chicago. 29/07/1990)

THE BEAST (NJ)

(The Beast band picture. Courtesy of Kevin Hodapp/Megaforce Records)

"As for being received, we were welcomed because I was an elder scene guy who also worked in the local record store. Also, The Beast started out playing all Tyrant songs. Punk as fuck! The main club and bar was two blocks from the record store. I was bringing in all the hardcore L.A stuff, the punk and NWOBHM records. So, most of the local band leaders knew me. Damn you Alex! I struggled so much over my five favourite records ever! I left out my old faves as best I could. I could only narrow it down to six to include this century you can take one off for me as I can't…The eponymous White Witch 1972 LP, Hawkwind- *Space Ritual*, Alice Cooper- *Love It To Death*, the eponymous Wolftooth LP (2018), Dustsucker- *Jack Knife Rendezvous* LP, The Hellacopters- *High Visibility*. But also, Grand Funk Railroad, Black Sabbath, the Ramones and Dead Boys, plus the very first Roxy Music LP for me was the most important release ever. The very first King Crimson is right there also. So many influential groups and AM radio as a kid listening to soul music and British Invasion bands" -- Ronnie Acerra guitarist of The Beast and Tyrant, Glorion Blak.

(The Beast with Ronnie in the forefront. Courtesy of Kathy Bevacqua Campbell)

Just imagine blending early Circle Jerks with Motörhead and NWOBHM and you almost there regarding The Beast of Red Bank, New Jersey. Their 1983 *Power Metal* 7-inch EP on the classic hardcore Mutha Records can stand in both the KBD classic releases, as well as the underground metal ones, with 'Radical Man' being one of the most punk metal songs ever heard! Check also their contributions in *Born To Metalize*, their 1986 demo, and you don't need to break the piggy bank to find the money for the *Power Metal* 7-inch, go ahead and get the 2019 CD release of *Demos and Rarities*. The deluxe box has an hour-long live DVD, stickers and a poster; it's on Nervous Breakdown Records. Plus, find Ronnie Accera on FB and have many chats regarding awesome old and new music. He's a human database!

SEPTIC DEATH

(Septic Death live band picture. Courtesy of Septic Death)

"We were all skateboarders before starting the band...So, we were already into fast and aggressive stuff... punk scratched that itch for a while... but as punk morphed into hardcore, we were all in... the faster and harder, the better....We were influenced by the early Touch and Go releases, the early Dischord releases, the Neos, the Bad Brains, Discharge, Disorder, Chaos UK, Terveet Kadet, Agent Orange (Dutch), Shitlickers (Sweden), Rudimentary Peni, etc...In addition to that, Onj was a metalhead before we started the band....So, he brought a metal influence on what were into. And we wanted to be 'visual' too. Spiked hair and interesting clothes... and we wanted to be interesting to look at. We took all the things we were listening to and seeing in other bands and tried to push it even further... harder and faster, and I think that's what other bands did after hearing us. They picked up the ball and ran even further with it. It's interesting for me to see these bands that were influenced by us and grabbed a hold and pushed it even further. We never thought anything like that would happen... We were just kids playing the music that was inside us... and to influence other generations of music and genres is the highest compliment" -- Paulie Birnbaum, drummer of Septic Death.

(Septic Death promotional poster for West Coast tour and new record. 1984)

From Boise, Idaho, I need to add more about Paulie's words regarding Septic Death on how influential they were? Alongside Siege and Deep Wound, Septic Death set a new blueprint in terms of extremity in the hardcore scene, influencing not just hardcore or metal bands of their era, but subsequent musical genres as grindcore and powerviolence too. There's not a mediocre Septic Death release, and if you want to get into that band and stick with them forever, check *Now That I Have The Attention What Do I Do With It?* LP (1986). Songs like 'Thaw', 'Never Trust' or 'Terror Rain' will make you explode. Plus behind all their craziness that derives from Pushead's artwork too, there is always the catchy element! So, this is maximum rock 'n' roll in its entity, right? Paulie Birnbaum's drumming is phenomenal, check it out! A video of the final Septic Death live appearance re-surfaced on YouTube from a show in 1986 at The Farm in San Francisco showcasing Septic Death in their mental live shows.

VERBAL ABUSE

(Verbal Abuse live in Vancouver, 1985. Courtesy of Dan Walters)

"The whole crossover thing was seamless for us. Nobody was freaking out or banning this and that. In the Bay Area it was already happening. The metal kids and punk rock kids were at a bunch of shows and in the alleys sharing beers and such. And the same attitudes. Not sure where there would be a problem with the whole crossover thing. Half of all those Verbal Abuse songs on *Rocks Your Liver* LP were already there. I also don't think we gave a shit either. Some didn't get any push back at all on all our tours around the world. What I would like to add as a memory, is of my late buddy's Josh Pappe, of D.R.I. When they toured with Gang Green, they approached Josh and then he joined Gang Green. I miss him so much, he was my best friend" -- Scott Wilkins, vocalist of Verbal Abuse and of Electric Frankenstein.

(Verbal Abuse with Special Forces, The Boneless Ones, Defend The Keg and Industrial Hate at 770 Darina, Sacramento. 06/07/1985)

Relocating from Houston, Texas to California was something that many hardcore bands did in the 1980s. Bands such as D.R.I., MDC and of course Verbal Abuse, who went on to move to the East Bay. Formed in 1981 as a hardcore band, Verbal Abuse released one of the most classic US hardcore LPs: *Just An American Band* (1983) is an explosion of brutal energy blended with some of the most hateful lyrics ever heard. It was perfect! Their crossover era started in 1985 with their inclusion to the *Them Boners Be Poppin'* compilation and followed up with *Rocks Your Liver* LP (1986). Both LPs are on Boner Records. While initially I was slightly disappointed, I gave *Rocks Your Liver* many listens the next years, and it's a great record too, only different! A metal fest of guitar riffs mixed with hardcore's urgency, and a more party mood, songs like 'Metal Melissa The Pissa', 'Ratt Pakk' and 'Worth a Try' are awesome! Their recordings include: *Red, White and Violent* CD (1995), *Speed Kills, but Who's Dying?* LP-split with Schiesse Minnelli and The Shining (2011). More recently, their most current are *Hope is a Lack of Information* LP (2024) and Verbal Abuse keep the flag flying high in 2026.

AGONI/AGONY

(Agoni with Anti-Cimex, Heresy and Napalm Death at Mardi Gras, Nottingham. 07/07/1986)

"In terms of the bands that went on to blend punk and metal in Sweden, I think that the first ones were Asocial and Krixhjälters as well. I prefer Agoni when it was punk. I pretty much left, got kicked from the band because I am not a big metal fan. I like Motörhead, Venom and some crossover like Accüsed but I was never into virtuoso solos and *Lord of the Rings*-type lyrics!" -- Peter Hirseland, Agoni/Agony guitarist.

(Agony 1986 Execution of Mankind demo)

I first came across with Agoni via the UK crust punk band Doom when Agoni covered 'En Röst For Fred' which left me speechless. So, I had to find out more about Agoni. Formed in Solna, Stockholm, Sweden in 1984, they were some of the initial mangel punk bands, and as you can imagine they were as wild as their peers of Mob 47 and Crudity. Later they went on to be renamed as 'Agony' and adopted a more metal-thrash style. As Agony they signed a contract with the UK Active Records label, releasing in 1988 *The First Defiance* LP. The sound was more into the melodic thrash of bands like Testament, it's by no means a bad record; it's actually quite good and fans of this style will enjoy it. However, *The First Defiance* left me yearning for their earlier, prime rage and chaos!

METAL DUCK

(Metal Duck live picture. Courtesy of Nutley)

"We've not got any real crazy stories. Apart from the tour with Jailcell Recipes in London. They had a load of 2000DS crew get in free, cause a bit of trouble, a few gigs and good fun. Playing Nutley G8 with Jailcell Recipes and on tour. Wigan with Xentrix, they were very metal though! We had a laugh, and they were so serious! We had a huge laugh at Wigan. I had a sword onstage, taking piss like out of Manowar. All crowd loved us more lol! But Xentrix man, why they were so serious? Fun is always good always, you gotta be able to play. Our favourite release was probably the first demo *Quackcore* in 1987. I sent it to Don Kaye (*Deathzine* in Kerrap-ehm, sorry *Kerrang!*). Sent as a laugh and got a mega-good review. At that time no idea who Don Kaye was! It was so real times of tape trading, with the demo costing 50p, no Internet and digital world" --Dudester Burton, drummer of Metal Duck.

(Metal Duck with Deviated Instinct, Void of Sense, Active Minds and Brutal Assault at the Swinging Sporran, Manchester. 11/06/1988)

Hilarious, super-funny, and musically wild is the best description that one can offer for the Manchester, UK act of Metal Duck. When I first got the split LP alongside Lawnmower Deth titled *Mower Liberation Front / Quack 'Em All* I couldn't believe my ears! They were unbelievably brutal and raw, yet on the same time so funny! This split LP is my favourite off them, but yes, the 1987 *Quackcore* demo is even more nasty, a combination of the emerging Britcore sound with some thrash metal. To this day 'Bomb Bay Duck' makes me want to smash shit up while laughing! Good band.

DR. KNOW

(Dr. Know live picture 1982. Courtesy of Fer Youz)

"Dr. Know's main influences were Discharge, Motörhead and Black Sabbath. For me it was more Discharge than anything. Not the look so much, we were from a beach in Southern California, but the sound and lyrics were amazing, and it definitely showed how much they influenced early Dr. Know. I met those guys in Discharge early on, and Rainy and I are still really good friends to this day. I lived in Copenhagen with him for a while before COVID. Tezz and I exchange messages as well. He's funny. Rainy sends me music from all over the world. He's turned me on to so many amazing bands. As far as crazy stories of Dr. Know from back in the day, there are so many. Being in a scene like the Nardcore scene, and going to L.A. all the time, well, that was really an experience that I doubt kids will ever have the chance to be a part of again. We were young and free and able to express ourselves outside of many other influences, except what we loved and wanted to know more of. We surfed and we skated, and we went to gigs. That was daily life. No internet, no cameras everywhere, just crazy parties and gigs, and then there was the pen-pal connection that helped everyone learn about new bands, and set up shows, and trade tapes. My brother Blake, from Stalag 13, traded with Barry from the Necros who let us know about the scene there, and then we heard about the DC scene, and New York, and we went to L.A. to meet new bands from Texas, like MDC and The Dicks and the Big Boys. It was pretty cool to play with people you had never met, then drink all night with them and show them the ocean. We made a lot of lifelong friends that way, people we still see and talk to and even tour with. It was a magic and special time. Some of the best punk rock ever came out of that time frame from 1979 to 1984. I really think that was the best time for the really amazing punk rock that became hardcore punk. We got to see the change from X and the Weirdos and the Screamers and The Go Go's and the Bags, to the Germs, to Black Flag and the Circle

Jerks, the bands like Dead Kennedys, Flipper, The Lewd, Social Distortion, Bad Religion. Our bands from Oxnard, Wasted Youth, Social Unrest, Fang. Man, I could go on and on, and I'm sorry I didn't mention a ton of amazing bands. If you were there, you know who I mean. If you weren't, sorry. You missed it. It was the best." -- Brandon Jack Cruz, vocalist of Dr. Know.

(Dr. Know promotional flyer, 1982)

Alongside Crucifix, Diatribe and Battalion Of Saints, Dr. Know were one of the very first ones to pick up the UK82 punk influence and blend it with the catchiness of Californian punk. They formed in 1981 in Oxnard, CA, their demo recordings in 1981 with Brandon Cruz on vocals titled as *The Original Group... Featuring "Brandon Cruz".* This LP has some of the most crucial hardcore ever printed on vinyl, raw blast after blast of Discharge-type Cali punk. The tracks include political 'El Salvador', 'God Bless America' and very personal 'Waste Of Time' and 'Boy's Life'. Later on, Dr. Know went for a more metal direction, even though they were still hardcore. This can be heard on *Plug In Jesus* 12-inch (1984), *Burn* 7-inch (1985) and *This Island Earth* LP (1986). All excellent records of course; if you want one to pick up first, *Plug In Jesus* will be your choice. They went full-on metal on the excellent *Wreckage In Flesh* (1988) LP. It was a cross between Black Sabbath, Celtic Frost and hardcore. Check also their post-2000 releases. *Killing For God* LP 2008 is my favourite one, heading back for the total hardcore approach. After all these years they are still (2025) active! I consider myself so lucky that I found all early Dr. Know records at once, while purchasing from a US store in the late 1990s.

RAW POWER

(Raw Power band picture 1985. Courtesy unknown)

"Raw Power's live shows were the band's high point, just pure raw energy, aggression, and showmanship, but also with a touch of finesse and musical talent that was uncommon in those days. I wasn't really into heavy metal. I was more into Steve Jones, Cheap Trick, Dead Boys, Van Halen, The Beatles, and the old Scorpions. I was in love with The Jam. *This Is the Modern World* and *All Mod Cons* were on constant rotation. Mike Bloomfield was a big influence on my playing, though with Raw Power it was almost impossible to show that, hahaha! As for wild stories, once in the US I had guns pointed in my face by some guys, but I was totally reckless back then! Raw Power never used drugs or alcohol, and we were proud of that. It was just pure energy, aggression, and fun. In fact, none of the original lineup even smoked cigarettes. The only thing that kept us from being completely straight edge was sex!" -- Davide Devoti, guitarist of Raw Power and Chelsea Hotel, Animali Rari.

(Raw Power with Decry and 13 Key at the Graystone, Detroit. 25/10/1985)

The first Italian hardcore band to tour the USA. By statements of people that saw them back then, they left them jaw-dropped. Raw Power, need no introduction. Formed in Poviglio in the province Reggio Emilia in 1981 as 'Off Limit', and still active today (2025). They are one the most passionate live bands ever, and with a sequence of top releases since their first LP in 1984, *You Are The Victim*. Things took off for them with the next release, the ultra-classic *Screams From The Gutter* LP (1985) on Toxic Shock Records with production of Paul Mahern of Zero Boys. By no means 'crossover' per se, *Screams From The Gutter* incorporated metal guitar licks by Davide. Each and every song is an unbelievable winner, from the opening of 'State Oppression' to 'We're All Gonna Die' (that Davide initially recorded with Chelsea Hotel), to the frenetic 'Politicians' and 'No Card'. A record that every punk, hardcore kid and metalhead should have in their collection. The guy that traded it with me in 1999 gave me this and the Transgression LP for Carcass' first LP told me "I think you going to love it". You bet I did! I love the next one too, *After Your Brain* LP (1986). It might be tamer, but the songs are unbelievably catchy. Just check 'Nothing Better To Do', 'Dreamer' or 'No Place To Hide'. Raw Power released many records since then: *Mine To Kill* LP (1989), *Reptile House* LP (1998) and *Inferno* LP (2017). These are my favourites, all of great quality. Catch them live!

HELLBASTARD

(Hellbastard live in Manchester, 1988. Courtesy unknown)

"Hellbastard may be credited with coining the term 'crust', but our peers were way ahead of us: Antisect, Discharge, Amebix, Crucifix, it's a long list. The whole thing has meanings which some people just don't understand: Namely, the word 'ripper' is a term used by many Americans when describing music [as a great piece of work]. 'Man, have you heard this demo from this band? It's ripping! It RIPS'. describing the said demo as a great piece of work. In my opinion I used the word 'ripper' for this same reason but also to describe deforestation and the destruction of our natural environment and systematic destruction of nature. It's an environmental theme which Hellbastard always had, and the word 'crust' was probably inserted to describe the earth, the soil, etc. environmental issues pop up again. Aside from being influenced by bands we loved, the environmental themes were always at the forefront of our attention and lyrical direction. When we were just starting to play once we'd sorted a stable lineup, we couldn't afford any equipment. We just knew that we wanted to play heavier stuff than punk, but with intelligent lyrics. There's nothing 'cool' about poverty and wondering where your next meal will come from. This was the way it was back then you see. Our clothes were falling apart, not from trying to look 'hip and trendy' but because we couldn't afford to buy new clothes. So, we'd often fix and sew them so we could keep on wearing them. Simplistic and obvious really. We'd even go to the more affluent areas of where we lived and steal clothes from washing lines hanging in people's gardens. This was the reality of being from typical working-class families and neighbourhoods. As for the 'raw' era of the genre, and the more streamlined era of the crossover (metal-punk); well, both styles are just as valid as the other. It's all just opinion. It has to be said there is an honesty with the rawer and DIY produced music. But that's the beauty of doing it yourself and therefore not having anyone else influence your original creativity and decisions. Many years ago, I personally became less interested in the genre because most of the bands sounded the same, looked the same, said all the right things but I was always searching for something new, different and interesting and with more soul and substance. These days (2025) Hellbastard is still active, but lineup problems are present yet again, we basically are searching for a drummer, a good drummer. We've been writing new material and making demos and we may be forced to remotely add drums. Dennis the Menace from Chicago band Macabre is involved with Hellbastard and so is Larry [Paterson] from the bands Girlschool and Alcatrazz, so we'll see how it pans out". -- Malcolm 'Scruff' Lewty, vocalist/guitarist of Hellbastard as well as in Nero Circus, Feeble Minded, Headrot, Heavy Water, King Fuel, Moodhoover, Public Disturbance, Screamer, Sidewinder, Sons of Vengeance, The Apostles, The Dischargers.

(Hellbastard with Amebix, Deviated Instinct and Carcass at Planet X, Liverpool. 19/09/1987)

In their early years Hellbastard were from Newcastle upon Tyne, Tyne and Wear, England; later on Somerset, England. Even though Amebix are considered as the very first band to play in 'crust punk' style, Hellbastard were the first to coin that term in their first demo named as *Ripper Crust* (1986). As you can imagine it's a mandatory purchase; it has been re-released on LP record by Agipunk Records in 2009. Heavy and innovative, you can find here everything from Amebix and Discharge, to Venom, Celtic Frost and early Bathory, and overtly political, as it shall always be. 'Nazis Killed' and 'Deceiver' still send shivers down the spine. Even better, was 1988 *Heading for Internal Darkness* LP, that was heavy as hell and always political, with a slight touch of Metallica though added. Songs like 'Afrikkan Beggar' and 'The Pylons' include some of the best lyrics the band ever written, all in one of the most classic crust LPs ever. The metal transition of Hellbastard lasted for two records, the *Natural Order* (1990) LP, that was good and more focussed into thrash metal (however I really miss their early filthy sound) and the great 2009 comeback of *The Need to Kill*, that was rougher and more brutal than its predecessor. Their last full LP *Feral* was released in 2015 as their most diverse ever maybe. Their last release was *We Hate Everyone* EP (2022). Hellbastard remain active in 2025. The world needs bands like Hellbastard, because music without message is irrelevant. As for me, they will always have a fond place in my heart since the day I got *Heading for Internal Darkness* and I was blown away!

LOST CAUSE

(Lost Cause band picture 1987. Courtesy of Gene Ambo)

"Of course, the 1970s-80s rock legends, A-to-Z bands, all played a part in each member of Lost Cause. For Joe Kelly it was Alice Cooper and The Clash. Jimmy Kangles loved Exodus' first album (*Bonded By Blood*). Casey West was a big fan of Rush (still is) and Iron Maiden. And as for me, seeing the *Decline of the Western Civilization* and listening to college radio got me on track. Even though the band that we created wasn't really what we all wanted to sound like we did it anyway!

As for those shows that will last forever in our mind, the ones that we played with Bad Brains, Adolescents and Scab and the GBH and Cro-Mags show; both were at the Cabaret Metro in Chicago, and it was like a dream coming true" -- Gus Roman, drummer of Lost Cause and later of M.O.S.H.

(Lost Cause with Cro-Mags, Imminent Attack and Assault at The Cabaret Metro, Chicago. 08/03/1987)

Chicago will always remain one of my favourite scenes regarding hardcore punk, while its metal scene can boast that it had a specific quality in the 1980s. Lost Cause were one of those cases that excelled both as a hardcore punk band, and as a crossover one. Lost Cause formed in 1986, and had two releases, plus one demo. The 1987 *Lost Cause* LP being a fantastic hardcore record with some very slight metal leanings. It's a cross of early 7 Seconds with Naked Raygun with songs as catchy as 'Crazy', 'Where's Babylon' and the metal rager 'Bam'. This is a mandatory release for everyone into hardcore or even crossover. Their next-and final-release in 1989, *Chicks Go Wild* 12-inch headed for a definite crossover style with some rap thrown in! It still is ace, especially the second side with songs like 'Nothin', 'Justice' (hell, this is mental!) or 'Kill Or Be Killed'.

Members of Lost Cause after the release of the first LP formed M.O.S.H., while vocalist Joey Kelly recruited new members, with Louie Svitek (ex-Zoetrope and later of Ministry and Mindfunk among many others) being the most famous one. Jimi Kangles also played in Bonecrusher, Obyss and Rancid (not the CA band), while Danny Vega of Hammeron, Aftermath and Windows Rose joined in for live appearances. Lost Cause disbanded in 1989.

BAD YODELERS

(Bad Yodelers band picture, 1991. Courtesy of Jobst Eggert)

"Those days were different. Radio was terrible. You had to search out independent radio or college radio to hear something other than Foreigner and Bryan Adams. Luckily, we had KRCL in Salt Lake and I spent a lot of summers in Denver, and Boulder had a college radio that was okay. Generally, you depended on underground magazines and friends and going to the Indian Center to see bands traveling through to be exposed to hardcore and punk music. I really liked the early punk bands from England like the Sex Pistols, the Clash, the Buzzcocks. So much more energy than what was on the radio in the 1970s and 1980s. I saw the movie *Decline of Western Civilization* in 1981, and it introduced me to the L.A. punk scene and really sparked my interest in that genre of music. But I still had love for more melodic music and secretly listened to the early darker records from The Cure and I also was a fan of the darker records from Depeche Mode. In 1985 I saw Metallica and Exodus in San Francisco and that show blew me away. So, I feel like my influences were these...heavy from thrash metal and melodic from English punk and New Wave bands" -- Brent Peacock, drummer of Bad Yodelers.

Thanks for the help from Terrance Halterman-vocalist of Bad Yodelers and The Stench

(Bad Yodelers live at the Painted World, Salt Lake City 1990. Courtesy of Rick Egan)

There were cases of crossover between metal and hardcore punk that it wasn't all speed and over-the-top insanity. One of those cases was Bad Yodelers from Salt Lake City, Utah, a band that could easily fit in *We Can Be The New Wind* book too! Their blend of Metallica with Dag Nasty and some UK post-punk is imitated by none on their two LPs, the 1990 *I Wonder...* and 1991 *Window*. I wish there were more bands to pursue exciting, non-generic stuff, and I wish I can find all the records I want in the prices I got the two Bad Yodelers records!

DIRGE

(Dirge various band pictures, 1987. Courtesy of Maximum Rocknroll)

"We just kind of started that with a metal-hardcore sound. In the beginning, we had two guitarists, me and Eric Tucker. I kept trying to find us a bass player, but I wasn't having any luck. Then I ended up playing bass, since Eric was a far better player anyway. It turned out to be a good move. For some reason we liked colouring outside the lines and writing songs that were too complex for their own good. At the time though, we created some really cool stuff. We just had so many guitar riffs. Too many really, but Eric and I knew how to put the puzzle together and make some great songs. Dan Gollin's jazz style drumming was really tasty and really complimented the guitars. Jack Monahan's socio-political lyrics were a good fit for what we were doing too. Jack was bit older and a bit smarter than the rest of us. The crowds were always attentive, and we always had a good draw, so we could set-up our own shows here at the shore. Jack ended up booking just about every band touring through during the 1980s and 1990s. We were also lucky that there was a circuit we could work; the Anthrax in Connecticut, CBGB in New York, the Brighton Bar, the Pipeline, and City Gardens in New Jersey. Then there were a lot of other clubs and bars. As long as we didn't book the shows too close to one another, we were able to maintain a good draw. People liked us and we were all just part of one small scene, but it got bigger over time". -- Jim 'Rex' Hogan, bassist of Dirge and of Daisycutter, Scene Killer, Solarized.

(Dirge with Bedlam and Follow Fashion Monkeys at the Brighton Bar, NJ. 24/01/1987)

I love my crossover to be more punk driven, you know that already! Dirge were a wet dream for me when I discovered them. Originating in Holmdel, New Jersey, Dirge had a very rough sound on their good first two demos in 1986 and *Life Force* 1987, somebody re-issue them please? Their first full-length, the 1988 *Soulstorm* LP, follows the 'early Cro-Mags meets Motörhead' formula, with a good NYHC dose. So as you imagine, it's top class with songs like 'Negative Sanctions' or 'Superficial', sheer mosh-pit destroyers! Their two subsequent releases, *Fleshcrawler* 12-inch and *Dirge-Matrix* 7-inch EP both released in 1989 were of equal quality. *Fleshcrawler* includes my two favourite Dirge songs ever, 'Corrupted' and 'Small Scene' that incorporates some anarcho-hardcore elements!

LOBOTOMIA

(Lobotomia band picture, 1988. Courtesy unknown)

"The transition was natural, not premeditated. Back then, in the 1980s began a mix of trends, and we ended up in this mix as well. About festivals, no, I don't want to remember...lol. Yes, we had a lot of good memories. In the beginning, we listened to a lot of Nordic bands, mainly from Finland and Sweden, like Rattus, Terveet Kadet, Mellaka, Kaaos, Crude SS, and English punk, not to mention all the bands like Exploited, GBH, Discharge, Anti-System, and others, as well as bands from Germany, Spain, Italy, and America. In short, we had a lot of influences, and our sound is based on these types of music. Heavy metal is also included as an influence, it was Iron Maiden, Judas Priest, Black Sabbath and thrash metal like Metallica, Megadeth, Nuclear Assault and Testament". -- Paulo, guitarist of Lobotomia.

(Lobotomia with Acido Plastico. 10/11/1986)

Heavy, nasty, under-produced, vicious and rough crossover lover? You already know that you need to get some Lobotomia records soon! Formed in Sao Paolo in 1984, Lobotomia followed the same lines of heaviness like Ratos De Porao, Olho Seco, Armagedom, etc. They had a definite Finnish and Swedish hardcore influence, as well as UK82, and on their first record, the classic 1986 *Lobotomia*, they went on to release some of the heaviest and darkest crossover ever-just imagine if early Bathory abandoned all their metal influences and went for a Swedish hardcore style! Every song is a damn winner but allow me to get frantic with 'Politica Zionista', 'Faces Da Morte' and 'Distorção Policial'. Their 1989 *Nada É Como Parece* LP was still excellent, faster and wilder than before crossover, but I kind of miss the dark feeling of *Lobotomia*. There are more releases by Lobotomia since then, all great stuff, plus they are still (2025) active!

THE LEGION OF PARASITES

(The Legion of Parasites live at the 100 Club. Photo courtesy unknown)

"What inspired me and Wag to start playing this sort of music (ages fourteen and fifteen) was our love for bands like Discharge, GBH, the bands on Secret Records, early Exploited, Crass. It wasn't at the start so much the anarcho-punk scene but more hardcore in general. As we progressed and became a 'band' our lyrics took us over to that scene, but our music really stayed in the other part of the swamp to tell the truth. As we played so fast, and the metal crossover happened with Slayer, Anthrax, Metallica, etc we were already a thrash band you could suggest. Personally, I loved both sides of the fence, as long as it was powerful and full-on, that's what I liked. I never really got on with metal to tell the truth as it wasn't vicious enough, although I like early Venom as I think they were one of the first to gear it up a bit in metal. A funny story-when we were playing one of Dig's [Pearson, Earache Records] infamous gigs at the Vale Social Club in Nottingham, where he put on a million or so bands on a night for £1. We were doing an encore, Black Sabbath *Paranoid* at 100mph of course and Chumbawumba, an anarcho-socialist band pulled the plug on the PA saying pop stars do encores and slagging us off for it...Six months later they were signed to EMI and on the telly on *Top of the Pops* on BBC1...ahhaha!" -- Cian Houchin, guitarist of The Legion Of Parasites and bassist of Nephilim.

(Legion of Parasites with Exit-Stance, Karma sutra, Liberty and State Hate at the Bunker. 30/11/1985)

Formed in 1981, in Pavenham, Bedfordshire, The Legion Of Parasites kicked off as a band that mixed the UK82 sound with anarcho-punk lyrics, a deadly combination! Their first two LP releases, the *Undesirable Guests* (1984) and *The Prison Of Life!* (1985) should not be missed by anyone into the UK82 sound; even though there are hordes of punks around the world into the UK82 sound, The Legion Of Parasites get only a few references here and there. Get those records people, because they are flawless classic of UK82 style, albeit with a heavier sound! Check songs like 'Party Time' or 'Death In The City' and decide for yourselves. Their third LP from 1987 *Dawn To Dust* headed for a more metal-hardcore approach. It was by no means commercially driven, but rough and nasty as hell metal hardcore punk. It's an all-out attack that will please every noisemonger worldwide! The 1998 come-back CD of *Man Made Filth* signalled a return to the (slightly metal) hardcore punk of their early years, and it's ripping.

THE DEHUMANIZERS

(The Dehumanizers band picture. Courtesy unknown)

"There are many stories, and I really wouldn't know where to begin. It's hard to determine a single 'greatest show' - there were so many greatest experiences for different reasons. I can share a few that immediately come to mind including: The Mardi Gras festival New Orleans, Louisiana with SNFU, The Butthole Surfers at the Axiom in Atlanta, Georgia, Circle Jerks at Fender's Auditorium in Los Angeles, California, the pit was just unbelievably massive! At our show with Circle Jerks at Buffalo University, New York two interesting things happened: We found a wheelchair and our singer used it all day long, saying that he'd had a skateboarding accident. Everyone believed us including the Circle Jerk guys. When we began our performance, Joe was wheeled out to the microphone. This mystified the audience, and they were strangely, respectfully quiet. The band started to play and when time came for the vocal part, Joe jumped out of the wheelchair and launched into the pit. The place went crazy and we owned the stage that night. Later in the performance the sound system lost power, so I started to play some 'jungle drum rhythms' and Joe joined playing on my floor tom. People started to dance and instantly the stage was completely filled by people from the audience. Once the sound came back on then the band went right into the next song, and all the people were stage diving back to floor. At the end of the set we kicked over all the equipment, and the place went crazy. That was a pretty good show…I guess that another experience that stands out in my mind was when the Dehumanizers were playing with the Melvins in Seattle…I met their 'roadie' as he was sitting on our guitar players Marshall amplifier and had a brief conversation but he wasn't very talkative...His name was Kurt Cobain". -- Infra Ed Portnow, drummer of The Dehumanizers.

(The Dehumanizers with Cannibal, NME and J.B.H. at the Gorilla Gardens Rock Theatre. 17/08/1985)

Formed in 1984 in Seattle, Washington, The Dehumanizers are a frenetic combo that managed to bridge Frank Zappa with heavy metal and hardcore! Still active (2025), with a back catalogue full of enjoyable releases such as their 1986 *Kill Lou Guzzo* 7-inch, *End Of Time* LP (1987) and *Here's To You* LP (1988) LP, as well as more releases later in the 90s-00s-10s. Their combination of humour with mental musicianship is eclectic and unique. Songs like 'Grandma (I'm A Drug Fiend)', 'Chemical Death' or 'Television' are just frantic and wild! Not your typical crossover by any means, but I think that this is their biggest compliment: sounding like nobody else.

POST MORTEM

(Post Mortem band picture, 1986. Courtesy unknown)

"I loved D.R.I., Verbal Abuse, Raw Power, Crumbsuckers and COC when those bands went for a crossover direction. However, there were lots of disappointments too, so the crossover records I didn't like were everything released by the Straw Dogs, SSD's *Break It Up* LP and Gang Green. I'm sorry, I know you love 'em!" -- Eric Courtemanche, vocalist of Post Mortem as well as Jesus Chrust, The Scam.

(Post Mortem with Necropolis and Doomwatch at the Electric Banana. 11/01/1987)

Belmont, Massachusetts' Post Mortem formed as early as 1982, and after a few hardcore punk demos that were neat, they released their first LP. *Coroner's Office* was released on New Renaissance Records in 1986 blending hardcore punk with Slayer and Black Sabbath. Post Mortem were brutally heavy and crushing, with their sonic approach being reminiscent of what Carnivore did later on *Retaliation* LP, minus the awful lyrics. A huge gem, *Coroner's Office* includes crazy thrashers like 'Ready To Die' or 'Run Amok', along the punishing doomcore of 'No Time'. The same musical approach continued on *The Missing Link* EP (1987), while on *Festival of Fun* LP they headed for a more experimental approach. More records followed up to *Message From The Dead* LP (2009). I believe that fans of Dream Death, Doomwatch, Carnivore or even early Celtic Frost will enjoy them.

BL'AST!

(Bl'ast! band picture, 1986. Courtesy of Naomi Petersen)

"Our favourite record is always the new one we are working on! Tour stories is an array of life lessons and great times" (Mike Neider, guitarist of Bl'ast!, LAB and Blackout)

(Bl'ast! with skateboarder Rob Roskopp, 1985. Promotional flyer of Santa Cruz skateboards. Courtesy of Santa Cruz Skateboards)

The skate rock scene might be just a definition of bands comprised of skaters, and not a real 'scene' in terms of locality, but truth is that many of those bands had metal and rock elements into their hardcore such as The Faction, Suicidal Tendencies, McRad, etc. Bl'ast! from Santa Cruz, CA formed in 1983 and were a part of this so-called scene, offering their powerful and hard as nails hardcore, that was blended with metal and rock. Sounding like a cross between Black Flag and Black Sabbath, Bl'ast! released three terrific records in the 1980s: *The Power Of Expression* LP (1985), *It's In My Blood* LP (1987) and *Take The Manic Ride* LP (1989); with my favourite being the first two. The 2010s *Blood!* and *The Expression Of Power* LPs are remixed with different mix versions of the early records, while their first new offering was the 2016 split 7-inch with EyeHateGod. A mandatory band if you are into the heavy and angular hardcore stuff!

ZOETROPE

(Zoetrope band picture, 1986. Courtesy of Gene Ambo)

"Well, Zoetrope had ties and did shows with many hardcore bands. Lost Cause, Life Sentence, Naked Raygun and Sharon Tate's Baby to name a few. I did a handful of local shows and did dates across the country with Zoetrope with bands such as Heathen, Laaz Rockit and Exodus. The term 'Hardcore Street Metal' that was used in the back cover of *A Life Of Crime* LP was to describe Zoetrope's own brand of metal; it took its cues from hardcore, it was street-levelled, and it was metal, simple as that!" -- Louis J. Svitek Jr, guitarist of Zoetrope as well as M.O.D., Lost Cause, Mayhem Inc., MindFunk, The Beernuts, Ministry, Assaultt, Pigface and The Infamous.

(Zoetrope's promotional flyer 1980. Courtesy of Zoetrope)

Zoetrope were a band that deserved more recognition. Formed as early as 1976 (!) in Chicago, Illinois. They were maybe the first metal band to gain acceptance in the hardcore punk scene, besides Motörhead. While their first 7-inch, the 1980 *The Right Way* and the 1985 *Amnesty* LP were rough metal with some punk leanings. Their 1987 *A Life Of Crime* LP was a crossover masterpiece as fast and wild, with songs bordering on hardcore. Containing anthems like 'Detention' or 'Unbridled Energy', this record is so much fun to listen to whether you're a metalhead or a hardcore kid. Their 1993 *Mind Over Splatter* LP found Zoetrope with a different lineup, with on a more metal thrash style.

(Zoetrope with GBH and Toxic Reasons at The Cubby Bear, Chicago. 10/12/1989)

POWERTRIP

(Powertrip band picture. Courtesy of Robert Hill)

"With Powertrip we wanted to try to mix The Stooges with Motörhead. That was the idea, and it went pretty well with that first album. We had a lot of fun, and every show was over the top" -- Jeff Dahl, guitarist of Powertrip, Angry Samoans, Chemical Dolls, Jeff Dahl & The French Connection, Jeff Dahl Band, Jeff Dahl Group, Jeff Dahl Trio, Mentors, Motherfucker 666 and Vox Pop

(Powertrip with the Atoms, Anti and Naughty Women at Cathay De Grande, 06/04/1983)

Jeff Dahl is one of the greatest rock 'n' rollers alive, and active since 1976, while also being productive even to this day, releasing new music from time to time. After leaving the seminal punk band Angry Samoans, he formed Powertrip, one of the very first intentional crossover bands. *Lab Animal* 7-inch (1982) was their first release. Things took really off with the classic *When Cut We Bleed* LP (1983) on Public Records. It was rough and ready metal punk, with excellent songwriting with 'Into My Eyes', 'Iron Horse', and 'Powertrip'. This LP has a place in the record collection of every fan of Motörhead and their more punked-up songs. Take equal parts The Stooges, Motörhead and early Cali-punk, and here you go, you have Powetrip! Seek out also the numerous bands, projects and releases by Jeff Dahl; all highly enjoyable stuff that balance between punk, garage and rock 'n' roll.

THE WORST

(The Worst band picture, 1981. Courtesy of Julio Tellechea)

"I remember playing at Max's Kansas City doing a backflip off the tables, I went out into the crowd and landed into my drummer's kit, ahaah! Yeah, he was pissed but I think we opened up for the Bad Brains and they actually saw it. We talked later upstairs in our dressing rooms. It was in the late 1970s. Another one story, playing with Shrapnel at our high school cafeteria and Legs McNeil their manager and founding member of *Punk* magazine brought Joey Ramone and Glenn Buxton, aka Alice Cooper's lead guitarist. But shit, we got turned off in the middle of a song by the police who were there, because it was one minute after 10pm! Pandemonium occurred and a small riot that was the last time our rock 'n' roll high school ever had a punk concert ever. Third story: while we opened up for the Dictators at Fast Lane in Asbury Park, I made a couple of rude comments about Richard, aka Handsome Dick [Manitoba] (fit the name haha), something silly but in jest as we punks often did, and their manager (a fat little troll) threw a jelly doughnut at me and hit Sudz right in the face! We didn't even break playing and Sudz licked it off, it was epic and funny. I guess he thought we stop, but nope, this didn't happen, not for a second. But it wasn't the first time someone threw something at me…Another The Worst story was when I fell off a five-foot stage and face planted into the audience. I misjudged the end of the stage because I was distracted by a girl…So, why did I quit the Worst? It was always 'you're the singer and you shouldn't be playing guitar', but I did and it was good but everything was all Mike [Trezza, guitar] and it was his band, so it was a lot of drama for just too long, and I was tired of not experimenting with our sound and even tried to get a great lead guitarist who later became my guitarist for Insidious Behavior. Mike could sing worth a damn, and I tried to have Sudz (drummer) and Jerry (bass), but Mike said 'no'. So, after that and tired of making no money and being ripped off; I just went to our band rehearsal, aka Mike's parents' basement, took all my stuff and just ghosted the whole band for years and never talked about it. What type of music though did we like? For me it was Stooges, MC5, Sweet, Pink Fairies, Black Sabbath. Sudz was a huge Motörhead fan. Jerry wouldn't tell you the bands he loved. Mike was the album collector big time; he had great albums, but he was also a huge Stooges fan. Later on, Insidious Behavior was my punky metal band with major upscale music and writing.

I did leave out what happened at the Fast Lane show! You have the ticket picture above where our manager The Mutha was jumped in the mosh pit because he looked like a metal dude with his leather jacket and chains. They broke his leg, and we had to take him to the ER. It was a bunch of skinheads, trash kids who were throwing hands and elbows like idiots. I don't know if you have the flyer with Mutha we did for a benefit for his medical bills" -- Billy 'Lo' Lowe, vocalist of The Worst and Bad Guys.

(Mutha Records night at The Brighton Bar, NJ. 29/08/1983)

Though not a crossover band in the strict sense of the word, The Worst are one of hardcore's craziest, over-the-top bands, that included some metal leanings into their sound, as early as 1981! Their two releases on the seminal Mutha Records are rare as hell, but still mandatory for everyone into crossover or hardcore punk. The 1982 *The Worst* 7-inch is just shocking, belligerent hardcore with 'High Velocity' and 'Frustration' sounding totally out of control. Their final release, the 1984 *Expect The Worst* 12-inch is even wilder, with 'City Of Sin' and 'I Wanna Stop' setting the bar of playing crazy hardcore way too high! Get them both on Radio Raheem's *The Worst Of The Worst* 2021 LP compilation, and man, Billy 'Lo' Lowe is one of the most generous and kind human beings I ever came across. He even sent me a copy of *The Worst* 7-inch and Bad Guys' *No More / Ex-Cape* 7-inch (who were the power pop alter ego of The Worst) as a gift; so, now I have to find *Expect The Worst*!

SAVIOR

(Savior band picture 1988. Courtesy unknown)

"Wehrmacht for sure, those guys were Portland's crossover heroes! They mixed super-fast metal with hardcore and drew big crowds. But I would also add that Poison Idea, around *War All The Time* LP, started mixing metal into their hardcore punk sound. Both bands are legendary around here" -- Jeff Walter, guitarist of Savior as well as All Out, Beerzone, Chartbusters, Control, Dickfinger, Poison Idea, Secret Army and Shock Troops.

(Savior with Arachnid, Antagonist and Nihilism at the Pine Street Theatre. 12/01/1990)

Formed in Portland, Oregon, Savior were one of the first bands to blend thrash-death metal with hardcore; sadly releasing only demos from 1987 to 1993, and one cassette in 1995 titled *Exploitation* that is pure thrash-death metal. Savior never achieved anything more than a cult status. However, their first demo, the 1987 *Requiem For The Dead*, is a wild ultra-core tornado of thrash metal blended with hardcore. It also contains two S.O.D. covers and one Discharge, showcasing their influences.

SUBVERT

(Subvert band picture 1989. Courtesy unknown)

"Eric could give you a pretty good answer also relating to the political connection of Subvert. I know that we were all inspired by a lot of political punk rock including Crass, Discharge, Anti Cimex. Eric was really inspired by Conflict, Concrete Sox, Crass. John Grant who passed away wrote some lyrics and had very strong anti-fascist political views. Some bands we were in touch with and played shows with who had similar political views would be Final Conflict, Neurosis, and Christ On Parade. Our sound definitely developed out of love for so many types of hardcore bands. We weren't trying to be crossover, we just really loved everything from Slayer to Crass. Some of my favourites at the time would have been R.K.L., the Crumbsuckers, Voivod, Celtic Frost, D.R.I.- *Dealing With It* era, Melvins. My favourite recording we did was the very first which just recently was pressed to vinyl. It's called *A Simple Solution To A Complex Problem?*. It was our tape before we did the first 7-inch. I thought it captured our intensity and was recorded mostly live" -- John Purkey, drummer of Subvert as well as Machine, Noxious Fumes and The Load Levelers

(Subvert with Sad Boys, Christ on a Crutch and Aspirin Feas at the Legends, Tacoma. 23/03/1990)

Subvert, from Puyallup, Washington, were one of the most political crossover bands of 1980s. Their lyrics were rooted in the anarcho-punk scene, while their music was fierce and uncompromising crossover hardcore. *A Simple Solution To A Complex Problem?* demo is not that far from what Christ On Parade did at the same time, only with a slightly more metal approach, and as you can imagine, it's ace. *The Madness Must End!* 7-inch (1988), *Free Your Mind!* LP (1990) and the 1991 split with Antischism are all mandatory if you are into the more hardcore side of crossover. As a starter I would go with *A Simple Solution To A Complex Problem?* demo, that has been re-released on 7-inch-tracks like 'Psychopath', 'Madness' and 'What Does It Mean' are so raging! Did I mention that this demo was produced by Jack Endino?

ANGKOR WAT

(Angkor Wat band picture 1990. Courtesy unknown)

"One of my favourite Angkor Wat stories comes from a 1988 or 1989 tour with Cryptic Slaughter. We were a new band, with only one record out which was getting excellent reviews and actually selling as well. We set up this tour on our own and it was our first, so all the mistakes you could make in booking a tour were made in terms of payments, etc. Cryptic Slaughter were making all the money, and we didn't know about tour support so…we were basically eating lettuce sandwiches which, when you are hungry are like a feast. There was one guy in the band who was a rich kid and he was doing alright but most of were broke. Well, in spite of being skint on this tour we were tearing it up every night. We were killing it. So, one day when we were driving through North Carolina or Virginia, I don't remember. We stopped at this firework store, it was like a factory, they sold all kinds of explosives that burned full of colours. So, what do you do when you're a starving band on tour and you hit firework heaven? That's right. You spend $200 (nearly all the band funds) on fireworks. Yep. We had like four grocery bags full of black cats, cherry bombz, roman candles, and all kinds of poppers, bangers, boomers and spinning lotuses! Real responsible money management move on our part. So, after a brief roman candle fight in the parking lot, we loaded up in the van to continue the trip to the next city, the next venue, the next hardcore hootenanny! Now you gotta remember this was back in the 1980s when people still smoked cigs. I say that because I was the only smoker in the band, half the guys were health freaks and a couple of the guys were too young to buy cigs and then there was me. So, as we're driving down the highway, our singer Dave was driving, and I was riding shotgun and having a smoke. As I finished burning one down, I flipped the butt out the window and it got blown back inside the van through an open window in the back. And where do you think it went? Right straight into one of the bags of explosive fireworks. Suddenly as we're driving 70 mph down the highway, these things start going off, exploding and burning with amazingly bright light, little colourful fireballs shooting every direction, whizzing, banging burning. The van filled with smoke and Dave is swerving all over the highway. Finally, he pulls over and we all pile out as $200 worth of explosive fun goes off. The Cryptic Slaughter guys, who were following us pulled over too and laughed their asses off at the pyrotechnics happening in our van. Luckily the van did not catch on fire because then we would have really been fucked. It really was the most amazing pyrotechnic experience ever!" -- Adam Grossman, guitarist in Angkor Wat as well as in Skrew and Ministry

(Angkor Wat with Suicidal Tendencies and Fearless Iranians From Hell at the Ritz, Corpus Christi. 11/09/1987)

Angkor Wat formed in 1986 in Corpus Christi, Texas where they had a background in hardcore punk due to their affiliation with that scene of their city. They had a definite Voivod and Die Kreuzen influence into their thrash-hardcore. I loved the fact that their approach was angular, weird, not following specific patterns of crossover on their two eclectic LPs: *When Obscenity Becomes the Norm... Awake!* (1989) and *Corpus Christ* (1990). They are still active (2025) and in 2021 they released the highly enjoyable *Worst Enemy* EP-check. The video 'Something To Cry About' is on YouTube was filmed on Mexico's television show *ECO* in 1989!

EXCEL

(Excel band 1989. Photo courtesy of Julia Kwong)

"When I joined Excel, I spent a lot of time with Shaun and we would get stoned while he would play records by Candlemass, Saint Vitus, Trouble, Possessed, Crucifix, Discharge...when I hung out with Dan he would play me demos by Shower Of Smegma, False Liberty, and he, like Shaun, would also play Crucifix. By the time we recorded the *Jokes On You*, we had been listening to everything in Los Angeles: Red Hot Chili Peppers, Fishbone, Faith No More, the Cult, Janes Addiction...My favourite memory of those days was in Butte, Montana 1990. Excel was on tour as support for Overkill from New Jersey...Overkill cancelled their Butte performance after seeing the venue PA [sound] and lighting system, claiming it was not proper for their stage show. There was a decent crowd of small-town metalheads and punks hanging around the venue with disappointment on their faces. Excel's punk roots came in to play, and we all decided to stay and play the show without Overkill, or their approval. It was a mad show, as was the party afterwards. Overkill kicked us off the tour and it was well worth it as they hardly acknowledged us, nor were we fans of theirs in any way. Plus, another great memory was getting paid $50, then Dan asking for $10 back for a show in Oxnard with Exodus, Verbal Abuse, and NOFX. The $10 Dan asked for was each of us giving NOFX money for gas and food because they got stiffed by the promoter. We happily obliged Dan's wishes; that's the kind of guy he is" -- Greg Saenz, drummer of Excel as well as Cyco Miko, John Garcia and the Band of Gold, Vega, Yawning Man, My Head, The Dwarves

(Excel with The Exploited, R.K.L., Bl'ast! and Visual Discrimination at Fender's Ballroom. 18/03/1988)

Let's just keep it secret, between us, okay? I love Excel even more than Suicidal Tendencies. There, I said it! My twenty-year-old head was exploded when I first bought *Split Image* LP! Excel from Venice, California formed in 1983 as Chaotic Noise and are still active to this (2026) day, offering shows. After an inclusion in the classic Venice compilation, *Welcome To Venice* LP (1985) and a series of top-notch demos, Excel released *Split Image* LP on Suicidal Records. *Split Image* is an ultra-classic crossover hardcore LP that is excellent from start to finish. Check out 'Insecurity', 'Set Yourself Apart' and 'Looking For You'. Two 12-inch singles followed (again, brilliant stuff), and Excel then released the fantastic *The Joke's On You* LP (1989). This recording is more complex and technically challenging than before, Excel outdid themselves on this one. I even love their next LP, *Seeking Refuge* (1995), that went for a more alternative metal-meets-hardcore sonic approach. Their first two records as well as their demos are pure gold for anyone into crossover. On a sidenote, did you know that Excel did the backing vocals on Kreator's *Extreme Aggression* LP? Plus, just check the drumming of Greg Saenz; this man is just crazy!

CRUCIFIX

(Crucifix band picture 1984. Photo courtesy by Fer Youz)

"Crucifix started with Matt Borruso, Christopher Douglas, Sothira Pheng and Bryce Kanights. I believe they started as skater artist kids just having fun influenced by Flipper, The Germs and Joy Division meets Black Sabbath, etc.... The debut album was a collection of various subjects from the dislike of old hippies, the damage of religion and capitulation and becoming permanently damaged facing a brazen hell. When Bryce left, Matt went to bass, and I was asked to play guitar. I was a heavy classic rock guitarist into Judas Priest, Scorpions, Black Sabbath, Ozzy, Van Halen etc. I brought a heavy edge to the band, but I kept it subtle to not invade their new love of GBH, Discharge and the new wave of Studs, Leather and Spiky Hair! The band shifted, the songwriting changed, and I was starting to throw in lead guitar solos and using my Flying V guitar with the Floyd Rose tremolo. We made some demos and did pre-production for an album. My favourite is *Crucifix Exhibit A* or *Nineteen Eighty-Four* since I played on it. *Nineteen Eighty-Four* was our Germs meets GBH phase and a developmental stage as Matt, Chris and Sothira were discovering new music and ideas. Remember I was four or five years older than them, and they were just teenagers discovering themselves. The political edge of Crucifix came from Sothira being a Cambodian refugee and we were all part of the Reagan regime and Anti" -- Jaycee Frances Schmith, Crucifix and Proudflesh

(Crucifix with M.D.C. and Antisect at the Vale Social Club, Nottingham, UK. 09/03/1984)

One of my all-time favourite US hardcore bands, Crucifix from Berkeley, California, formed in 1980. They spearheaded the then-emerging UK second wave sound in the USA. Much more than that, they added the Californian punk flavour, as well as the political awareness of the UK anarcho-punk, making a combo that it's a force to reckon with. Their first two releases, *Crucifix* 12-inch EP (1981) and *Nineteen-Eighty Four* 7-inch (1982) are stripped-down hardcore classics, more than important for everyone into the styles mentioned above. My personal favourite though is the 1983 *Dehumanization* LP on Crass's Corpus Christi Records. It is slightly more metal than before, a wild mix of Discharge's brutality with G.B.H.'s catchiness, *Dehumanization* is one of the 1980s top releases, regardless of style. Just check the haunting opening 'Annihilation', the very metal 'Prejudice' or the blast of 'Rise And Fall'. Post-Crucifix, Sothira and Jaycee formed the good heavy metal punk of Proudflesh, releasing the 1988 *Powerbroker* EP and *Proudflesh* full-length CD in 2006. But start with *Dehumanization*, it's just a desert island record!

IMPALER

(Impaler band picture, 1985. Courtesy of Iron Planet fanzine)

"Well, that question you ask touches on the whole spirit of Impaler. You see, I think we connected all the dots so to speak. It's all rock and roll right!? If you think about it, you can draw a line from early blues and folk music straight through music history to metal, punk and beyond. We were inspired by it all and wanted to encompass all the great elements of rock music the best we could, at that point in time. We embraced all the past and present influences that were exciting to us and then pushed onto the future with our own mutated contribution…and we still do that. This has really stuck with me all my life. I'm considered a senior citizen now! And outside of my family and friends I love nothing more in this world than playing AND listening to rocking music! A funny story from our past was when we were working on *If We Had Brains…We'd Be Dangerous* LP with Bob Mould of Hüsker Dü fame. I came in the studio to do my vocal tracks one afternoon. We ran through a couple takes and Bob turned on the studio microphone and said 'Bill, I really want to capture your live energy with your adrenaline pumping…so, if you can go run around the block a couple times that will get you primed!'. So, I went outside and ran around the block, came back in and did just about every vocal track on the album. I have not used that method since, but I'll never forget it!" -- Bill Lindsey, vocalist of Impaler and Daddy Raw, Fear No Evil

(Tipper Gore on a war with 'obscene' songs, with Impaler's Rise Of The Mutants spotted. Courtesy of Dan Loftin for U.S. News & World Report, 1985)

Impaler from Saint Paul, Minnesota have a huge history in the heavy metal scene, and it's a damn pity that they didn't get more recognition. Formed in 1983, their approach was very diverse and unique. They included punk cover songs on every record, they had theatrical image in the tradition of Alice Cooper, their musical blend included Motörhead, Black Sabbath, The Stooges, Judas Priest and Dead Boys! After a number of demos, they released the fierce heavy/speed metal *Rise Of The Mutants* EP (1985), a great way of introducing their punk-infused heavy metal with songs like 'Impaler' and 'Shock Rock', short and sweet stuff! Their 1986 *If We Had Brains…We'd Be Dangerous* LP was produced by Bob Mould of Hüsker Du. It was a major shock to me when I first got it; absolutely out-of-control punkish heavy metal, 'Blood-Bath', 'Dancin' On The Edge' and a smashing cover of The Stooges classic 'Search and Destroy' make this record a must for every punk metal collection! Impaler kept it up through the next decades releasing great records in the same style, with their most recent being *The Great Hereafter* (2020).

NOT-US

(Not-Us as Natas various pictures, 1985. Courtesy of Maximum Rocknroll)

"It was August 1988, and we co-headlined a benefit with the Bhopal Stiffs at a place called Dirty Nellie's. It was the hottest show we ever played 104 degrees outside (40 Celsius). There was eight bands playing starting mid-afternoon. It was so humid that with a sold-out crowd packed in the club the air conditioning couldn't keep up. By the third or fourth band it was so hot and humid that between songs guys would run backstage puke in the garbage can and go back onstage! We played next to last a full 75-minute set. By like the fifth song I basically blacked out finished our set without remembering 90 percent of it! To this day I don't remember the Bhopal Stiffs playing, I was backstage lying on the floor in a pool of sweat! It took a few days to recover from this one..." -- Scott Natas, vocalist and guitarist of Not-Us and Snake Dance, Master

(Not-Us with MDC, Guilt Parade, Filth and Misled at McGregor's, Chicago. 17/06/1990)

Not-Us (earlier as Natas) from Chicago, IL, started off in 1984 as a very rough combination of Discharge and Venom, something that Scott Natas called as 'Deathcore' back then! You can imagine that their first three demos (*Demo Rehearsal* 1985, *Outcast Of Society* 1985 and *Internal Damnation* 1986) are just manic, absolutely deranged and punishing blend of death-thrash with hardcore, even reminding me of Repulsion in some cases! Their crossover turn took over in the *Think What You Want* demo (1987), and on their *Think What You Want* LP (1989) on Wild Rags Records, where their songs formulated short blasts of superspeed energy, with their LP gaining a cult status. Get their *Deathcore 1985-1992* compilation CD that includes all their stuff.

RANDOM CONFLICT

(Random Conflict 2017 band picture. Courtesy of Christen Barker)

"On a weekend in January of 2000, my band Random Conflict were set to play our first shows of the year, in Jackson, Tennessee and the following night in Memphis. We arrived at the venue which was the practise space of the band that booked the show. It was located in a small shopping centre near downtown Jackson. After waiting for an hour, no one was showing up, and we couldn't reach the booker. Then, a guy and girl showed up, and as it turned out the guy was in the band that practised at the venue that we were supposed to play with, and he informed us that the show had been cancelled earlier that day because of a family emergency, and we had already left to come over there before the guy that actually booked the show could reach us. The guy and girl that had showed up just happened to be driving by and saw us hanging around the practice room and were seeing what was going on. After a few minutes of trying to figure something out, the guy and the girl that was with him told us to just hang out for a few minutes and while we waited they started making calls to all their friends in the area, and within an hour or so over forty really cool people showed up, the guy opened up his practice room, turned on his band's practice sound system and while we set up to play the lady that had come with the guy, went around asking for donations for us. After we got set up, everyone crammed into the room, and we played an extended set to a very enthusiastic crowd who were very happy something was happening in their small town. After we were done playing, us and everyone at the show hung around for a couple of hours before we took off for Memphis (where we had an awesome show). We ended up making almost $200 dollars in donations, sold a lot of merch and met some very cool people. What was shaping up to be a lost cause ended up being a great experience, and all because by complete chance someone with a key to where the show was to take place drove by and saw us standing around outside the venue! Lesson to be learned: even a hopeless situation can turn out to be an awesome experience so get out in the world and live life! As for current crossover bands, Power Trip, Iron Reagan, Paralysis and of course Municipal Waste are a few great ones" -- Bill Reeves, vocalist and guitarist of Random Conflict and Miscarriage

(Random Conflict with Intruder and Excruciating Pain at the Huntsville National Guard Armory. 03/03/1990)

I can't get enough of highly political bands like Random Conflict from Huntsville, Alabama, who always respect their DIY and anarcho-punk roots. Formed in 1988, they remained true to the underground spirit of their own hardcore-thrash brand, releasing top records such as their 2013 *Tradition Is The Enemy* LP or the 2007 *Annihilation Generation* LP-which is my favourite from this band! Just imagine a huge mix of Poison Idea, Final Conflict, Discharge with Slayer and Motörhead, all filtered through the political anarcho-punk status, and you are nearly there. Random Conflict are still (2026) strong and active.

DISSENSION

(Dissension in action, 1987. Courtesy unknown)

"Growing up punkers in Long Beach, California, there were always influential hardcore records on our turntable: *Plug-In Jesus* and *The Burn* EP by Dr. Know were favourite records to listen to. We also loved the *Dirty Rotten* LP by D.R.I. Dissension loved so many bands like Discharge, Disorder, Suicidal Tendencies, along with local bands from Long Beach like Secret Hate, Target of Demand, The Crowd although not on the crossover metal side, but still influential to us. We strived to be as fast as D.R.I., Discharge and Suicidal Tendencies all mixed in one. Our first LP, *Why Work For Death?* (1986) had a wide range of topics from being bombarded by bullshit ('BBB') by the media to being the sole survivor of a nuclear war. Some of us struggled with addiction, which reflected on songs like 'Black Out' and 'Fate'. The lyrics from the latter rung out: 'Drugs kill, know your fate. Drugs destroy, it's not too late'. The song 'Why Work for Death', which was the title of Dissension's first record, reminded you that we all work, then we die. And if an average American kid was not going to work, he's no average American kid. We were punkers at heart, but we could not stop listening to Corrosion of Conformity's *Animosity* record, D.R.I.'s *Dealing With It*, S.O.D.'s *Speak English or Die*, Excel's *The Joke's On You*, and Hirax's *Raging Violence*. These are just a few bands that we looked up to as we progressed as a hardcore band. We have gone though some members for whom we are grateful, but with the current lineup, you are still going to hear what influenced us. *Amazing Disgrace* LP (2020) and *Bought The Pharma* CD (2023) are the band's favourite records to have recorded along with Paul Minor at Buzzbomb Studios. We also continue to remind our fans that drugs will destroy your life, and pharmaceutical companies and the government will leave you broke" -- Kelly Gilbert Vargas, drummer of Dissension as well as American Jihad, Slightly Stoopid and Sublime

(Dissension with Bitter End, Body Count, Final Conflict, Uniform Choice, Dissension and The Detonators at the Melody Dance Center. 31/01/1986)

Long Beach's hidden gem, Dissension formed in 1983 and are one of the most unsung heroes of that era, and it's a shame, because their musical output is just ace, hard-driving hardcore punk with some metal tendencies in terms of guitar work. Their LPs from the 1980s such as *Why Work For Death?* LP (1986) and *We The Fooled* LP (1988) were both released on Metal Storm Records, a division of Azra Records of David Thomas Richards. Check out its crazy story on YouTube on the video, 'Hollywood's Weirdest Record Label || WEIRD VINYL RECORDS | Documentary' on Aarol Films channel. Both records have a certain Crucifix-meets-Attitude Adjustment-meets SoCal punk, with excellent songs like 'False Promises', 'Hopeless', 'B.B.B' and 'Hypocrite', and both are mandatory for everyone into the more hardcore-oriented crossover or shall I say, slightly metal hardcore punk. I was so happy when I managed to find them both on a trip of mine in Rome, fifteen years back! Dissension went on to a hiatus for some years, only to come back releasing on 2013 *The Crude Wars* 7 inch, a split cassette with Out Of Tune (2014), *Amazing Disgrace* LP (2020) and the brilliant *Bought The Pharma* (2023) CD. They are still (2026) active and always raging!

THE SIX AND VIOLENCE

(The Six and Violence band picture in Manhattan, 1990. Courtesy unknown)

"The 'Jethro Tull' answer should probably come first in the order of those questions, because it was so influential to our sound...our history with Jethro Tull is something that really shaped our collective creativity. We all grew up together since we were little kids and we all got into Tull at a very young age, especially our lead singer, Kurt Stenzel who was absolutely obsessive about them, and he had a very unique relationship and situation with Jethro Tull; Kurt's dad was a head purser, steward, and lead flight attendant back in the days for PanAm Airlines and traveling internationally all the time. He was able to take Kurt with him on trips for free so over the course of years and I'm talking from the late 70s and early 80s even as a young kid, Kurt would turn up in a bunch of random cities in the UK & Europe and the States at Jethro Tull shows. The lead singer of Jethro Tull [Ian Anderson] would notice this young kid showing up at all of these random cities and shows all over the world and they developed a relationship.

The progressive styles of Jethro Tull, Yes, ELP and others were hugely influential on each of us and it definitely crept into our creative outputs. The different time signatures, voicings, unique vocal patterns as well as the heaviness that much of the progressive music at the time had was always on our mind when we were writing songs both individually and collectively...My guitar playing and style definitely had a 'Martin Barre' influence, Dave Miranda and Kenny Kim's combined drumming was a combo of Barriemore Barlow and Keith Moon influence...Kurt's writing style was definitely influenced by all that we listened to, and that was a huge contribution to it all.

Staying in touch for years, as we were forming the band and then starting with our first demos, into when we went to record our first album *Lettuce Prey*. Kurt put a cassette tape into Ian's hands and said 'you should hear my band'. Surprisingly Ian not only listened to it, but was very complimentary. He heard the humour, the style, the uniqueness and you could say he 'really got it' which was amazing because it was such a recognition that in our own way, we carried the mantle of progressive music along with our love of hardcore, punk, etc.

(The Six and Violence with Death Angel, Whiplash, Token Entry and Rest In Pieces at Animal Hall II, Brooklyn. 21/08/1987)

When we were going into the studio to record *Lettuce Prey*, Kurt saw Ian at a show here in the States and almost flippantly said 'we are recording our new album, would love if you would play on something' to which Ian said an absolute yes. We shipped the two- inch tapes of our recordings over to his studio in England, he recorded his parts on two songs and then literally carried them back to the States by hand on the plane. It was just mind-blowing that he did it! He was in the New York City area with Jethro Tull and came down to see us play at the Pyramid Club in the [East] Village which was another mind-blowing experience for all of us; to be playing right in front of one of our biggest influences, in a little club was fantastic and he again was super complimentary to us about it. We were his guests the next night at a Jethro Tull show in [New] Jersey at the Brendan Byrne Arena (back in the day that was what it was called).

Continuing over the years, Ian asked us to participate in a Jethro Tull anniversary album that had artists doing covers of Tull songs. In our own unique way we decided to do something 'different' and we made a medley of Tull songs from their first single, through all of our favourite tunes over all of those years and albums because as DEEP Tull fans, we knew every little inflection, nook and cranny of their songs and put our twisted take on them. It's called 'Sunshine Day' and it was included on Tull's anniversary release *20 Years Of Jethro Tull - The Definitive Collection* (1988); Ian Anderson was quoted in his auto-biography that 'he would rather here Six and Violence play Jethro Tull songs than any other band in the world' and is also quoted in an interview calling us 'one of the most underrated bands of all time'; yet again, super complimentary and that he got our twisted take on things.

Of all our influences and styles that helped make Six and Violence, Jethro Tull was a huge part; we paid a lot of attention to varied styles of music, and it made us try to do something that could hold a candle to those songs that we loved. To play fast, or heavy, or hard... to try to create songs that only the clumsiest of people could dance to, or for people that have the ability to discern the subtleties of those styles was always our goal..." -- Raymond Amico, guitarist of The Six And Violence and tour manager, production manager, engineer and producer

(The Six and Violence with Murphy's Law at Union Ballroom. 24/02/1989)

One of the most artistically challenging, wildest, and 'no-boundaries' crossover act ever, The Six And Violence, formed in 1984 in Queens, New York. Their story of connection with Jethro Tull and Ian Anderson is just one of those crazy rock 'n' roll stories, that happen so rarely! Their 1985 *Lettuce Prey* demo is funny without being ridiculous, mental without being insane, technically proficient without becoming boring; a real hidden gem of the demo's era, with seventeen songs that will drive you wild! The Six and Violence have outstanding musical skills. They sound like a hardcore punk band blended with progressive rock at 78 RPM! Songs like 'Surf Gospel' or 'Hamburger Hairdo' are just lunatic! Their next release, the *Lettuce Prey* (1990) LP included the songs off their demo, plus three more, now remixed/re-

recorded for added wackiness. *Lettuce Prey* LP includes Ian Anderson of Jethro Tull in 'Theological Guns' and 'Bursting Bladder' on flute, this is just way frenzied! I love this LP because it showcased that hardcore crossover had no limits, plus Raymond's drumming is one of the most delirious ever heard! A split 7-inch with No Redeeming Social Value was released in 1995, and their last offering, the 1997 *Petty Staycheck* included elements by styles so diverse as calypso, grindcore (!) or Eastern music! The Six And Violence were a class of their own, and so were their live shows.

ELECTRO HIPPIES

(Electro Hippies live in 1987. Courtesy of Reynard Toombs)

"Favourite bands? So different bands for different people, for example me and Simon liked Irish folk, defo not Andy's thing. Discharge though was the obvious choice for every one of us in Electro Hippies. I bumped at Jeff Janiak (Discharge's new/current vocalist) at a reggae gig in Manchester last summer. Discharge is still brilliant! As for stories of Electro Hippies, well, I'm full of them! One took place in Boardwalk in Manchester, where the bar was next to the stage; a very low stage. I'd bought a new long guitar lead. The intro was Simon and Andy, guitar and drums, so I decided to wander off and get a beer. With my bass still on me, I stood at the bar waiting to get served. I waited and waited and waited, studiously ignored by the bar staff, so I stood my ground. That intro went on for ever as you can imagine!" -- Dom Murphy, bassist of Electro Hippies as well as a member of Jailcell Recipes

(Electro Hippies with Chaos U.K., Deviated Instinct, Napalm Death, Ripcord and Extreme Noise Terror at the Mermaid, Birmingham. 13/09/1986)

One of the most metal acts of Britcore wasn't even metal! Baffled or not, the Electro Hippies from St Helens and Wigan, formed in 1985 and lasted for only four years until 1989. However, their musical output was highly influential, and sounds fresh even today. With fast as hell blast beats, their crusty metal hardcore includes influences ranging from Slayer to Chaos UK and Discharge, Siege, Deepwound and SSD to Celtic Frost. Their own brand of ferocity was evident in their very first demo from 1985, as well as their environmental and vegetarian stances. Jeff Walker (later of Carcass) was a member of Electro Hippies in their early days, while things went absolutely mental on their first release, the 1987 split with Generic on Flat Earth Records. You have to hear songs like 'Run Ronald', 'Wings of Death' or 'Am I Punk Yet?' that picks up the Slayer riff of 'Final Command' and transforms it to a crazy ultracore blast! The 1988 *The Only Good Punk... ...Is A Dead One* LP on Peaceville Records isn't as rough sounding, but it is heavier and more punishing and controlled. It contains excellent blasts like 'Scum', 'B.P.' or 'Profit', a total classic LP. The *Peel Sessions* LP (1987) was also released, as well as a *Live* (1989), and members of Electro Hippies later appeared in bands like Metal Duck, Carcass, Brujeria, Get the *Deception Of The Instigator Of Tomorrow... (Collected Works 1985-1987)* double LP collection on Boss Tunage, and prepare yourself for a Mega-Armageddon mosh!

ANIHILATED

(Anihilated band picture. Courtesy of Mark Ward, 1983)

"We got a fair bit of attention during the crossover phase; lots of gig offers, our 1989 album *Ultimate Desecration* was more metal than *Path To Destruction* and 1988's *Created In Hate* but got less attention due to very poor label support. We got much more attention for our comeback albums *Scorched Earth Policy*, *iDeviant* and *Anti Social Engineering*. I enjoyed the freedom of expression of the crossover days. We were gigging with young versions of Napalm Death, Extreme Noise Terror, Deviated Instinct, Doom, Bolt Thrower, Sacrilege, English Dogs and The Stupids. People were developing new sounds, and anything was possible. Once we went full-on metal it was restrictive, but we carved a niche and developed a style using hardcore anarcho-punk DIY storytelling on *iDeviant* so we always stuck to our principles and always tried to be individual.

Many great stories: one story of Anihilated is when we recorded the demo for *Path To Destruction* in a small shed in a friend's garden, and when we recorded the actual record it was our first time in a real recording studio, and we had no idea how it all worked! Shortly after releasing *Path To Destruction*, we played some dates with Concrete Sox and Sacrilege. At one gig in Leeds, Mark, our guitarist at the time, got food poisoning before we went on and had bags to vomit in onstage. During a few gigs with English Dogs, Nazi skinheads invaded the stage, and it was a full-on battle to get people safe. Me and Lee, bassist at the time, we're stuck in the bar area surrounded by skinheads thinking we were about to get hurt. The leader was a huge, tattooed guy with a moustache, Lee said to him 'you look like Freddy Mercury '; I'm thinking we are so dead! But the guy looks really happy and buys us beers! We were using stage pyrotechnics at one gig which malfunctioned and exploded as the girl helping operate the system put the cartridge in throwing her several feet" -- Simon Cobb, bassist and vocalist of Anihilated, as well as of Sun of the Endless Night, Nightbreed

(Anihilated with Instigators, Civilised Society?, Deviated Instinct, Disturbed and Autonomy and Queen's Hall, Bradford. 06/03/1987)

Formed in 1981 in Ipswich, Suffolk, England as Prospex began as a punk band in their first demos up to 1985. As Anihilated, their first release, the 1986 *Path To Destruction* 12-inch EP went for a rough-sounding hardcore-thrash crossover, with fast riffs, shouted hardcore vocals, and underproduced as hell! Great stuff, with 'Innocent Victims' and 'Thunderflash' being the highlights of this special record, and 'Shadows Of Fear' being one of the best they ever written. They later went more metal thrash releasing many LPs. Check also *Created In Hate* LP, as well as *The Ultimate Desecration*. They are active today (2026); metalhead fans of Anihilated consider their best LP to be their last one from 2015, *Anti Social Engineering*.

OUTPATIENTS

(Outpatients band picture, 1984. Courtesy of Lisa Foos)

"The one crazy thing I'll never forget happened after a show in Rhode Island in 1984. We stopped at a convenience store to grab some snacks for the trip back to Massachusetts. It was late at night, and we all got out of our rust bucket of a van to go into the store and some redneck guy yelled at us from the parking lot. We didn't think anything of it, but when leaving the store, he was waiting for us and calling us 'punk fags' and just being a total asshole. Our drummer at the time had a mohawk and we obviously didn't look like your regular downtown Joes. We basically avoided him and got back into the van. He ran up to us yelling and started to try and tear off our right-hand side mirror as we were backing up. It was one of those super sturdy over size mirrors used for trailers that was bolted on. He was basically clumsily jogging alongside the van yelling and spitting at us. We pulled out of the lot onto the main road. He then jumped up and started to cling on to the mirror! Our quick-thinking manager yelled from the back seat 'roll down the window' and as we're driving down the road with this fucking freak hanging off the mirror, she maced him. We weren't going fast luckily but he fell off onto the road screaming, holding his face. We drove off into the night, van mirror intact, headed home with that crazy story to tell. Perhaps he learned his lesson.

It's hard to comment on the legacy of an underground act like ours. But when I play shows now with my own projects people will come up and say how much they loved a live show that they saw Outpatients play back in the day, or that they still have our first demo from 1983. Little things like that are a reminder of the lasting impact the band had on people. Obviously having Painkiller Records release the full back catalogue on the *Readmitted* reissue LP helped keep the band alive and bring it to new hardcore fans.

As far as crossover music, styles are so mixed up these days it's hard to keep track of all the different genre amalgamations. I still see D.R.I. and bands of that ilk flying the flag for that sound, while newer bands like Mindforce seem to carry that tradition too. Suicidal Tendencies has played arenas with big headlining metal bands, so crossover definitely holds a place in music history" -- Scott Helland, bassist of Outpatients, Frenchy and the Punk, Deep Wound, School of Violence and Darkside NYC

(The Outpatients with The F.U.'s, Siege, Grey Matter and 6 Feet Under at the Orange, Greenfield MA. 18/02/1984)

Outpatients of Westfield, Massachusetts formed as early as 1980 as Mace, only to change their name. A few years later they released three excellent hardcore demos: *Basement Tape* (1983), *Basement Tape Second Version* (1983) and *Committed...* (1986). All those demos are just classic stuff of the first wave of US hardcore, rough and short blasts! Their first LP from 1987, *Free Association* is an amazing rocking and metal hardcore record released on Incas Records. It was given to me as a gift by my friend Elias Chatzialexis. This LP got mixed reviews from the punk community when it was released. However, I love it, because it sounds so diverse, with crazy guitar and bass work-songs like 'Ballon Head', 'Left Road' and 'Second Thought' are so evident of that! Not generic crossover, but rather a rock and metal hardcore LP, that fans of e.g. SSD's *How We Rock* will definitely enjoy. What Outpatients released afterwards was even more challenging! The *Test Of Time* (1993) CD sounded like a progressive crossover hardcore combo, obviously with unbelievable musicianship. I think that more daring fans of progressive will enjoy it, because songs like 'Jungle Of The Dead' or 'Escape Prisoner' contain the essence of this style. While I find myself absolutely in love with the early raging hardcore days of Outpatients that you can find re-issued on the *Readmitted* LP (2022) compilation, I have a soft spot for both their crossover days, as well as their final recordings!

CIVIL DISOBEDIENCE

"My favourite releases that I still revisit would be Attitude Adjustment - *American Paranoia*, Cro-Mags - *Age of Quarrel*, Corrosion of Conformity - *Animosity*. As for my fondest memory of the Civil Disobedience days is when I traded bass riffs with the bass player from Excel at a gig we opened up for. I was still developing and really dug that band!" -- Ed Stephens, bassist for Civil Disobedience, Harlot's Grip, Ringworm, Rip Ryde, Shed the Skin, Vadiat, Vanik, Vindicator, Sinister, Violent Night, Beyond Fear, Shok Paris, Gluttons, Byron Nemeth Group, Destructor, Abdullah and Pete

(Civil Disobedience Who's To Blame demo, 1989)

Cleveland, Ohio's Civil Disobedience formed as Concussion in 1987 and included members that went on to more famous bands later such as Spudmonsters, Blood Of Christ or Abdullah to name a few. Sadly, they only released six demos from 1988 to 1990. Their first demos were lo-fi, crude speedcore attacks that obviously have their charm! Their final one, *Civil Disobedience* (1990) was terrific hardcore-thrash in the Venice tradition of Excel meets Slayer, with songs as good as 'Fighting Stop' and 'Judgement Day'. A reissue maybe on vinyl of a collection of their demos?

DISCHARGE

(Discharge band picture, 1980. Courtesy of Mike Stone/Clay Records)

"From the earliest days of Discharge, whether they were an influence or not .... The Cortinas, Adverts, Magazine, early Clash, my favourite five records, that would have to be my favourite fifty-five records! My taste in music has always been very eclectic, from country and electric blues like Mance Lipscomb, Lightning Hopkins, Howling Wolf, Ten Years After and so on. Also, I always loved the 1960s psychedelic bands like Syn and Iron Butterfly! And early German progressive rock like Jane and Tangerine Dream etc. And obviously so many punk bands over the years, where does one start!? There are so many great bands from many countries. Other bands I love are Hawkwind, Chrome, Sonic Youth...and there's classical and world music, as it's sometimes referred to; I'm very open and varied in my taste for sound and music" -- Roy 'Rainy' Wainright, bassist and founding member of Discharge

(Discharge with D.R.I. at The Farm, SF. 07/09/1986)

You wouldn't ever expect to read so diverse bands influencing Rainy's crazy bass sound! Formed in 1977 in Stoke-on-Trent, Staffordshire, England, Discharge are not just the innovators of D-beat style in punk, but also the kings of extreme music in my opinion. There's no way for a band based in the 'rock' form to head into the maximum extreme territories without the influence of Discharge, whether this influence is direct or indirect. They kicked off as a Sex Pistols wannabe in their 1977 demo, only to turn up the noise and chaos level to the max on their first three 7-inchs, *Reality of War*, *Fight Back* and *Decontrol*, all released in 1980.

What Discharge did was taking off the blues influence from rock 'n' roll, stripping down the music to its bare minimum, presenting the most raw and basic form of rock ever released on vinyl; this was the ground zero for punk, the point of no return. Everything changed since *Reality Of War* was released, and even though Venom sounded extreme and nasty, even though Motörhead sounded like the wildest punk metal party, Discharge took things to a whole different level. The *Why?* 12-inch EP (1981) sounded like a million bomb raids, while the cover artwork went on to inspire thousands of bands all over the world; actually the black and white approach that Discharge got from the anarcho-punk is maybe one of the most rehashed in musical genres.

(Discharge with Battalion of Saints and Powertrip at Adams Ave. Theatre, San Diego. 16/12/1983)

Never Again 7-inch (1981) is another winner with full-on fast D-beat punk that still drives punks crazy all over the world. However, time had come for Discharge to hit their peak; I'm talking about *Hear Nothing, See Nothing, Say Nothing* 1982 LP, that spawned a mildly metal production. It went on to become one of the most influential records ever. This LP is just like watching a tsunami coming your way: you are jaw dropped, in horror, but on the same time shocked and fascinated. Fourteen songs that weren't as raw as before, but with unbelievable power and directness. There's no way to not be at least amused by songs like 'Final Bloodbath', 'A Hell On Earth' or 'Free Speech For The Dumb'. Another excellent 7-inch followed with *State Violence, State Control* (1982). By 1983, Discharge somehow slowed it down, and started adding more and more metal influences. In the mid-eighties they released *Warning* 12-inch (1983), *The Price Of Silence* 7-inch (1983), *The More I See* 7-inch (1984) are all good and catchy, but something appears to be missing.

And this brings us to the most disastrous record in the history of music, *Grave New World* 1986 LP (1986) or 'Discharge gone glam metal'. Avoid at any cost, this record could have been the final nail in the coffin, and it was followed by an equally catastrophic US tour. It took Discharge some years (and releases) to revive, since both *Massacre Divine* LP (1991) and *Shooting Up The World* LP (1993) are nothing special, however the *Discharge* LP (2002) was good. Things went way better initially with the inclusion of Rat Varukers on vocals on the great *Desensitize* LP (2009), and in later releases afterwards with Jeffrey Richard Janiak of Broken Bones, becoming a full-member of the band, releasing *End Of Days* LP (2016).

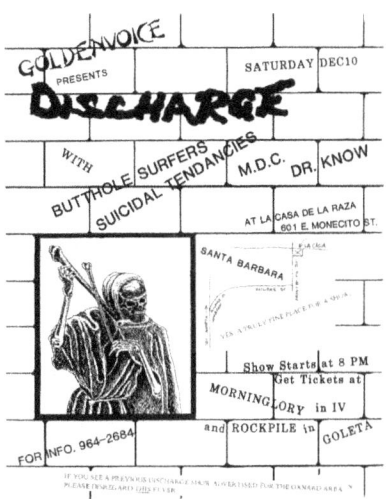

(Discharge with Suicidal Tendencies, Butthole Surfers, MDC & Dr. Know at Casa De, Santa Barbara, CA. 10/12/1983)

On a final note, everybody that picks up this book, should already acknowledge the influence of Discharge to various scenes and music subgenres: the Scandi-punk (from Anti-Cimex to Riistetyt and Rattus to Kuolema), death metal like Entombed or Dismember, grindcore of Napalm Death, thrash metal of Metallica and Anthrax, even the black metal scene. These genres and bands would never reach the levels of sonic extremity if it wasn't for Discharge. Their influence was of course massive in the US hardcore scene too. Bands like SSD or early Agnostic Front and Battalion of Saints loved Discharge. Also, with Discharge's metal sound, they paved the way for crossover to happen; Discharge had a massive appeal on punks and to weirdo metalheads that wanted to check out the most extreme band possible.

Discharge are active (2026), still offering shows, and they will last forever.

NUCLEAR ASSAULT

(Nuclear Assault band picture 1988. Courtesy of Alex Solca)

"Before joining forces with Nuclear Assault in 1985, I had been going to Jon Z's record store in the Route 18 flea market in New Jersey and buying up a lot of imports by Motörhead, Iron Maiden, Judas Priest, and bands of that nature. Jon Z had just started Megaforce Records and signed and released albums by Metallica, Anthrax, Exciter, Raven, and eventually, my band T.T. Quick. After getting thrown out of T.T. Quick in 1985, I needed a new band. I eventually found Nuclear Assault in their infant stage and joined forces. They were a crossover band of heavy metal, thrash metal, and hardcore music. I quickly became a fan of the new metal scene and swallowed up all the new material I could. My earlier influences being Metallica, mostly for the production on their records like *Ride the Lightning*, and then Megadeth (Garth was a great drummer). I never liked Anthrax, and even though I knew Dan Lilker was thrown out of that band, they did nothing for me. Neither did 90 percent of the new bands emerging at that time. I like groups with a solid sound, a solid drummer, and a singer I can tolerate. I would pass a band like King Diamond because the vocals got on my nerves like fingernails on a chalkboard. I really wasn't too crazy about John Connelly's vocals from Nuclear Assault either, and I sure wasn't alone in this opinion. That was actually the biggest complaint by fans about our albums. I've recently published my memoir book *The Final Assault* and I'm getting ready to publish the *Nuclear Assault Book of Song Lyrics* so fans can read along with the songs and understand what the FUCK John is saying.

(Nuclear Assault with Ludichrist and Cancerous Growth at CBGB's. 06/04/1986)

As for a wild story....so many of them. In 1985 we played a gig at some underground club in Detroit, and we all took acid. We tripped our asses off and afterwards I was supposed to drive our school bus to the hotel. It had been snowing throughout the day and into the night and by 3 am, it was several feet deep. This girl wouldn't get off the bus even after I told her several times that we needed to leave, and so while sitting in the driver's seat of the bus, I promptly kicked her, and she went flying backwards off the bus and landed in the snow like a snow angel. I then drove the gang to the hotel and called it a night" -- Glenn Evans, drummer of Nuclear Assault as well as of C.I.A., Steffan Rodd, Harter Attack, and T.T. Quick

(Nuclear Assault with Maximum Penalty and Mean Streak at Streets, New Rochelle, NY. 17/12/1988)

Now, let me exaggerate, because I'm a fanboy: Nuclear Assault (NYC) should have been on the Big Four of thrash, I prefer them over Anthrax or Megadeth anytime. That said, they were not your typical thrash band. They were one of the few metal bands that appeared in hardcore billings at CBGB's, plus, they bordered with hardcore on many occasions, sounding more extreme or hysterical than their metal peers. A credit for this to their bassist Danny Lilker, who was always into the most extreme stuff of his era. Metalheads don't like the use of 'crossover' as a description for their sound, but truth is that Nuclear Assault were crossover, only that they were originating from the metal side of things. Formed in 1984, they released one of the best metal demos ever: *Live, Suffer, Die* (1986). They headed from excellence from day one; all Nuclear Assault records from *Brain Death* EP (1986) to *Handle With Care* LP (1989) are pure perfection. Nuclear Assault was the most 'metal' band that I loved in my pure hardcore days, and this can be explained on the crazy mosh part of 'Brain Death', on the hardcore speed of 'Sin' (a song that would have been 100 percent hardcore with different vocals), on the bombastic nature of 'Cross Of Iron', on the frenzy of 'Equal Rights' or the blasting energy of 'Inherited Hell'. Their post-*Handle With Care* releases leave me cold; *Out Of Order* LP has some good songs, and so are the reunion records. Their 1980s stuff is gold. As a starter, pick up *Game Over* and get ready to go wild with 'Vengeance', 'Hang The Pope' or 'Stranded In Hell'.

ARDKORE

(Ardkore in live action, 1987. Courtesy unknown)

"I loved Venom, Slayer and loads of US hardcore and I am playing in a band with Abaddon from Venom. I love all sorts of stuff. Got a full-blown Voivod thing going on as one of our old fans is tour manager for them! There are so many stories, but here's a glamorous and unglamorous story around the old Ardkore days. Going right back to our first gig was in 1986 a place called Arches in Norton in England. It was just really friends and there was no family there, but surprise-surprise; friends come down to see what this buzz was about. It was like a posh pub and had a restaurant. But anyway, we did the Spinal Tap thing off getting lost trying to get in to find where the function room downstairs was and things are kind of never really improved from there.

We have many an escapade with us been a crossover band. We had a mix of skinheads, UK 82 punks, old school punks, the dog on a string, crusty brigade, remnants of the New Model Army looking lot. And then we had like, a big contingent of young thrashers because the scene was just really starting to grab all the public when we kicked off. One of our first gigs was playing with Warfare at Adam and Eve's in Leeds. That was highly entertaining. I think it was this one where the singer decided he would have a drive at the van and he did; you know had had a couple of shandies too many. Anyway, we got stopped by the police and he got arrested. We had to go back and pick him up from a nearby police station and when he turned up at the gig he decided to drink his blood sample, which was quite entertaining. But the Warfare gig was quite good, we started to build a good following from that gig. And there's quite a lot of people who went on to do noticeable things in the industry all were all lovely and nice, but we always had a chunk of people following. Whether it be in a back of a Luton box van or when we did Monster Mosh, in Birmingham at the Mosley Dance centre. Ace adventure that one in Birmingham! We had a coach load that went down. I mean it was a 52-seater coach, and it was virtually full. We had all our equipment on there and a couple of us went down in a couple of cars just early doors just in case the bus arrived late. We just signed to Metalworks when we did the gig, and I remember Virus headlining. And it was the first time I had seen Slammer live and they were good. But we ended up quite up, high up the bill and there was quite a lot of people like why they are so high up the bill. Anyway, when we came on, all the people who come in the bus ran down the front to give us their moral support down the front, as it were. I did get some test prints from the as there was a photographer there, he wanted loads of cash for the photos, so they never happened. I need to get them looked out and blowing up and pour out because it was a highly entertaining gig.

(Ardkore gig flyer. Arches Norton, 10/06/1986)

Another one of the most notable ones was I think it was after we played with the Exploited in Leeds. We came back and we stopped off for food, I think it was in Wetherby. Anyway, we were looking for somewhere around there Big Ernie was driving this one, one of our trusty roadies. We saw this Chinese restaurant and the lights on upstairs, so we went upstairs, and it was more like a casino! Can't remember whether it was a skinhead or punk or metalhead, or whatever but I remember seeing a table go flying. It appeared we had stumbled across some oriental-style gambling club ha ha! I thought 'right, best make a quick exit out of here' and we did. And I think Ernie had started driving the van. He must've heard the commotion, but remember jumping in the back of the van, turned around and all you could see was just like glinting of meat cleavers and whatever behind us. I rate Chinese or Japanese as unhappy people, but I mean, that's the, that's where, where we kind of 'yes, many an escapade" -- Steve Hoggart, Ardkore

Ardkore from Teesside, Middlesborough, England was formed in 1985 and lasted up to 1992. They had a definite very extreme approach in their hardcore-thrash crossover. This is evident in their three demos: *Demo* (1986), *Death Charge* (1986) and *Apocalypso* (1988), and their only LP, *Napalm Stix to Kidz!!* (1989) on Metalworks Records. Unpolished and very brutal, their sonic approach sounded like a cross between the UK Britcore of Ripcord with Cryptic Slaughter, Wehrmacht and the craziest moments of Nuclear Assault! Songs like 'Apocalypso' or 'Testament Of Lies' are just rough as hell, while 'Aggressor Of Pain' is simply amazing! They released also the excellent *Global Scream* digital single in 2025, that contained the eponymous songs; it seemed that nothing changed all these years in terms of brutality. *Napalm Stix to Kidz!!* LP can also have a crossover appeal to diverse listeners; crossover kids into the most extreme stuff will definitely dig it, as well as those ones into the rawer German thrash and the ones into the early crust stuff.

WHIPLASH/CEREBRAL HEMORRHAGE

(Whiplash band picture 1986. Courtesy unknown)

"1986 through 1988 were the prime years for the crossover sound, I think. We [Whiplash] started to play at CBGB's along with bands like Carnivore and Nuclear Assault. Then the hardcore bands such as Agnostic Front and the Cro-Mags began playing with metal bands at L' Amour in Brooklyn. I think all the bands influenced each other in many different ways. It was a rich and diverse music scene. Very creative people all around. The hardcore elements had a big effect on Whiplash. Tony Bono and I would go to CBGB's practically every weekend to the Sunday hardcore matinee shows. So much cool music!

(Whiplash with Caligula, Sheer Terror and N.Y. Hoods at CBGB's. 06/09/1987)

My personal favourite Whiplash album is *Thrashback*. Many aren't familiar with that one since the label was changing distribution companies and we got lost in the shuffle. With *Thrashback* we finally were able to record some great old songs the way we originally envisioned them and wrote some new songs as well. I think that album is really underrated" -- Tony Scaglione, drummer of Whiplash and Cerebral Hemorrhage, Ambush, Jackhammer, Zero Hour, Deathrash, Ludichrist, M.O.D., Slayer, 7 Licks, Cause For Alarm, Eightfold, Mantra, North Side Kings, Raging Slab and Sheer Terror

(Whiplash with Cerebral Hemmorage, Nihilistics, Dirge and Blatant Dissent at Club Hell, Dover, NJ. 16/08/1985)

OK, calm down! We all know that Whiplash of Passaic, New Jersey are one of the most classic thrash metal bands ever with three factors that led to their inclusion. Firstly, they were all aficionados of NYHC, and one of the few metal bands alongside Nuclear Assault and Carnivore that appeared regularly in hardcore billings at CBGB's. Whiplash members played also in hardcore bands: Cause For Alarm, Into Another, Sheer Terror, Mantra. And finally, the Cerebral Hemorrhage crossover hardcore project that included Tony Bono, Tony Scaglione, John Bongiovanni, and later, Joe Cangelosi. Believe it or not my dear metalheads, but also their *Power and Pain* LP has loads of hardcore elements, especially rhythm-wise; plus, Vinnie Stigma and Rob Kabula of Agnostic Front on backing vocals! Anyway, Whiplash is firstly and foremost a thrash metal band, with an impressive catalogue of great releases. I would recommend *Power and Pain* LP, as well as *Thrashback* LP (2008), whereas their more diverse records such as *Insult To Injury* are equally good. As for Cerebral Hemorrhage? Two wild demos only: the *Demo '86* (1986) and *Multiple Trauma* (1987). Both included crossover hardcore that took some metal riffs and transformed them into firepower speedcore ('Instigator', 'Bugs Bunny'), with hilarious yet very offensive lyrics.

DÉTENTE

(Détente band picture, 1985. Courtesy of Metal Forces)

"In 1985 we were added to a show that included Dark Angel and had Megadeth headlining. Even though there was bad blood between Dawn, Dennis, Dave and Jr; the Daves had flopped with Dawn and Dennis for a short period. We did see it as good show at a very good venue, the Chuck Landis Country Club in Reseda, California. Everyone promised to be on good behaviour, and we took the show.

While we expected tension with the Megadeth guys, we really did not know Dark Angel, but we got to know them quickly. Ross [Robinson, Détente guitarist] has a younger sister Roxanne, and she would take photos at our shows. We were in our dressing room, and she comes running into the room upset that someone in another dressing room had grabbed her. I asked her to show me who, and she takes me to the Dark Angel dressing room and points to this short guy, turns out it was Don Dotty. I called him out and we started having words and he lunges at me half running and throwing a swing or two, kind of sissy swings, if they connected there was no impact but at least the effort was there. We were in the hallway backstage at this point, and he was in real close, so I put him in a one arm headlock and started to bounce his head off the wall. Our respective bands pulled us apart and we returned to our respective dressing rooms.

(Détente with Legacy and Fuhrer at the Ruthies Inn. 15/02/1986)

While it was not exactly a brawl Dennis, Dawn, and I are a bit amped up now; Ross was always the quiet type, and who stops by with a sarcastic comment, the stain of course to throw some fuel on the fire. So, after playing we are in the audience drinking and after Dark Angel finishes their set Megadeth comes on and starts playing. After a few drinks and a few songs, Dennis decides it would be funny to pelt the Daves with a beer, and much like a food fight, others in the audience decide to join the fun. So, house management steps up to the mic and warns the audience to behave, of course the answer from the audience is a beer or two for house management. Megadeth leaves the stage, lights go on, and the audience is told to disperse. Of course, the chairs and tables start flying and the club is getting trashed. The beer fight led to a mini riot at the club and out on the street and metal was banned from the club for at least six months. It's only rock and roll but we like it!" -- Steve Hochheiser, bassist of Détente and Catalepsy, Lizzy Borden, Lunatic, The Douche Lords

Détente were formed in 1984 in Los Angeles, California as a crossover-adjacent the way that e.g. Hirax were and continue to be. They released three exciting demos, before releasing on Roadrunner Records their classic *Recognize No Authority* LP (1986) that was an energetic mix of thrash-speed metal with early Iron Maiden; the hardcore element comes from bands like Die Kreuzen with Dawn's vocals having a total Dan Kubinski style. The hardcore punk connotations don't end up here. Songs like the amazing 'Losers' or 'Blood I Bleed' have a total Broken Bones-meets-L.A. thrash touch, and the record cover itself has an anarcho-punk vibe. Criminally underrated to this day, *Recognize No Authority* has a massive charm, and once you get it, it sticks in your head! Détente disbanded in 1989, came back initially in 2007 and released *Decline* LP (2010), which was good, with a slightly more extended hardcore influence! You all must have already heard the story of Ross Robinson on how he later became one of the most famous producers; he was named in the 1990s as 'The Godfather of Nu-Metal', a term that he denounced, so I won't refer further to this. All though that I must add is that heavy metal needs bands like Détente, Sacred Reich, Znowhite more than ever; anti-establishment, political and with no commercial tendencies. Alongside, one of my favourite interactions with a musician ever, is the one I have held with Steve Hochheiser. Steve is one of a kind, a real gentleman with such a good will!

RANCID DECAY

(Rancid Decay first show flyer. Belair Rd. Assembly Hall, 29/03/1986)

"The influences of Rancid Decay early on were Death (their demos), Genocide [later changing their name to Repulsion], Attitude Adjustment, Sacrilege BC, Possessed, Sacrifice, Voivod. My fondest 1980s memory is when Sacrifice was touring for *Forward To Termination* and practiced in my parents' basement, that was awesome, they played a few songs they were working on *Soldier of Misfortune*. Also, meeting and opening for Death on the *Scream Bloody* Tour, they were great guys but also opening for Possessed and Dark Angel in Channel-One, Baltimore was amazing!" -- Matt Croco, guitarist of Rancid Decay, Ironboss, Lifetime Shitlist, Thee Iron Hand

Even though Rancid Decay lasted only four years, from 1985 to 1989, they released five demos, and one split cassette, the 1987 split release with Eureka, California's Mr. Bungle! While their first demos were crude, underproduced attempts of thrash- crossover, their split with Mr. Bungle as well as the 1988 demo headed for a style that somehow mixed the most extreme thrash metal (bordering with death metal sometimes) with crossover, both being pretty wild-songs like 'Toxic Death' or 'The Letdown' and 'Infested' actually sound like a blend of Death with Attitude Adjustment! Check their *Presumed Dead* LP (2004) compilation, really vicious and punishing stuff here!

CONCRETE SOX

(Concrete Sox band picture 1987. Courtesy unknown)

"Ah…we once played a gig in Vienna. I remember the guy who put the gig on, his name was Alex Wank…great guy, great name! Anyway, we played with a few other bands, and when we came on, everything seemed to be going great, the sound was good, and we were really into it. Then the bottles and other objects, and drinks started to be thrown at us by the audience. I remember smoke coming out of my amp. We all gave each other that look, it was time to bail out. We went back to the 'safety' of the dressing room, but not sure why we were being targeted. Turns out someone saw one of us loading some of their equipment into our van. It was a squat gig, so I imagine everything that had there was irreplaceable, or unaffordable for them. Some folks were trying to get to us, and some scuffles broke out. We eventually got out of there, I can't remember for sure, but I think we had a police escort! Anyway, the next day, we turned the van inside out, and the microphone was there. To this day I don't know who put it there, and if it was deliberate or a mistake. I remember me and Sean Cook though we're that angry, we decided to finish the tour and leave the band. Anyway, we did post the microphone back with a letter to apologise and that was that. We did finish the tour, and did some more shows in the UK, but it wasn't too long after that, that me and Sean departed" -- Rich Yellowman Button, guitarist of Concrete Sox

(Concrete Sox with Chaos U.K. and Antitoxin. Motte, Altona 4/10/1987)

One of the roughest, most fierce and brutal crossover acts, Concrete Sox, formed in 1984 in Nottingham, UK. Their crossover was a mental mix of UK hardcore with thrash metal and crust punk, always underproduced and fast as hell. In lyrics terms, they were always on the ecological awareness of anarcho-punk, into animal rights and anti-capitalism. Their first four full LP releases are mandatory if you are into this sound. *Your Turn Next* LP (1986), *Whoops Sorry Vicar!* LP (1987), the Concrete Sox/Heresy split LP (1987) and *Sewerside* LP (1989) are sheer classics of this sound, that could appeal both to crossover thrashers and anarcho-punks and crusties on the same time. My soft spot here is the split LP with Heresy which I consider it to be one of the best split LPs ever! Heresy side goes blast-after-blast of supersonic speed hardcore with a slight metal touch, whereas Concrete Sox side includes some of the best songs they ever written, 'Key To The Door', 'Speak Siberian or Die (for S.O.D.)' and 'Sustain The Orgy'. Concrete Sox through their existence released many demos, 7-inchs and one more LP with *No World Order* (1993); all of definite quality.

ENGLISH DOGS

(English Dongs band picture, 1986. Courtesy of Metal Forces)

"*To The Ends Of The Earth* 12-inch is my favourite English Dogs record. It was my first and I remember being in the practise room and hearing the tracks for the first time; I was blown away by them. I didn't know if my voice would fit to them, but it turned out it was perfect for it. I'm very proud of that record. My all-time favourite records must have been The Ruts - *The Crack*, Sex Pistols - *Never Mind The Bollocks*, Exodus - *Bonded By Blood*, Slayer - *Reign In Blood* and Metallica - *Ride The Lightning*.

(English Dogs with Substandard and Warwound at the Where House. 13/09/1983)

So many weird and crazy stories with English Dogs in the 1980s…we were on our last day of our first USA tour at a venue called 'The Loft' in Baltimore. It was a tiny little venue that was like a cave. I wasn't sure how it would be, but it turned out to be one of the best gigs of tour. Because it was the last night, we stayed at someone's house who was friend with the promoter and a mad party ensued. I had been drinking heavily and fell asleep in an armchair whilst the party went on. The next thing I knew was seeing a guy in front of me covered in blood and staggering all over the place. I couldn't understand it, I thought I was dreaming. Ten minutes later the place was full of cops. I was awoken by one of them and was asked if I saw anything. I couldn't even talk due the copious amounts of brandy I had drunk, and I just went back to sleep. It turned out the guy lived next door, and someone had robbed his house and stabbed him, and he had come to the house looking for help. Thinking back, it was quite scary as it could have been any of us. I know the journey back to the UK wasn't very nice due to having a nightmare hangover. I never found out what happened to him, but I can never unsee the vision of him covered in blood" -- Adie Bailey, vocalist of English Dogs and Unholy Alliance, Acid Age, Ultra-Violent

(English Dogs with The Destructors at the Golden Fleece. 12/03/1983)

English Dogs of Grantham, Lincolnshire, England formed in 1981. They were one of the first UK82 punk bands to crossover to metal; and also were one of the best, hands-down! I love both their eras, the pure punk as well as the more metal one. When I first got *Where Legend Began* LP (1986) I was confused; this was like epic metal, in the vein of e.g. Manilla Road! Anyway, if I had to pick my three favourite English Dogs records these would have been the excellent *Mad Punx & English Dogs* 12-inch EP (1983), *To the Ends of the Earth* 12-inch EP (1984) and *Forward into Battle* LP (1985). Their later records are definitely enjoyable, especially 1995's *All The World's a Rage* and 2014's *We Did, We Do, We Always Fucking Will!*.

I won't go into the whole dispute that created two bands (the punk English Dogs and the metal English Dogs), and instead I would suggest checking out Unholy Alliance, the band that Adie of the 'Metal Dogs' formed in 2017 with Nick Wynch, Richard Grizzwell and Michael Tatler, all of them musicians from the 'Punk Dogs', and their two excellent heavy metal-punk records! No matter the whole dispute, punk songs like 'Left Me For Dead' and metal punk songs like 'Ambassador Of Fear' are classics of their style, and only a quality band like English Dogs could pull out.

D.B.C.

(D.B.C. band picture 1987. Courtesy of Daniel Heon)

"I've often compared the evolution of my musical tastes to drug addiction. You start out with gateway bands like KISS, Rush, Van Halen, and AC/DC. But at some point, you want something heavier, and for me, Motörhead, Maiden, and Priest were the bands that eased me into the heavier stuff. Around the time I turned eighteen, bands like Raven and Venom came out, followed by Metallica and Slayer which was pretty much heroin at that point. This was pretty much as heavy as you could get. But then there were lateral moves to punk and hardcore, where the short, intense hit of the crack of hardcore was satisfying me. Discharge may have started me in that genre, but D.R.I. and Bad Brains just killed Ed [Sahini, guitarist] and me. We fell in love with that shit.

It was around then that D.B.C started, I think. Ed and I were pretty much aligned in our tastes, so our songwriting for the first album reflected that exact area. But you can see an evolution in the writing on that album. The simpler, hardcore songs like 'Outburst', 'Lies', and 'Power & Corruption' were written earlier, and you can see a progression through 'Trauma X' and 'Terrorist Mind' to more complicated metal riffs like 'Monument', 'Deadlock', and 'Tempest', all of which would have been written later. So, you can see the direction we were going already on that first album. Many of the songs for *Universe* existed in some form even while we were still writing the first album.

(D.B.C. with Diatribe and Nomeansno at Foufounes Electrique. 26/07/1986)

I always knew I was never going to write songs about blood, killing, and satanic nonsense. It had been done to death (and still is). But I think Rush may have been the single biggest, almost subliminal, influence on me, and at the time I didn't know it. Maiden also had a much more high-brow approach to lyrics, which I appreciated—basically writing about any book or movie they'd seen. For D.B.C., you can see earlier topics that were political ("Power & Corruption," "Terrorist Mind," "Deadlock," and "Negative Reinforcement"), but as I became a bit more experienced, I started tackling topics that were more personal to me. "Trauma X" came from my experience as a medical photographer, "Monument" was from an interest in Egyptology, and "Final Act" was almost dystopian sci-fi.

So, I guess the idea for the concept of *Universe* was also about another love of mine: science. I'd been reading books on the history of the universe and knew I could get a lot of cool song topics. The composing at this point was Ed bringing in tons of riffs, we might add something I did, but then we would just go off on tangents, bridges, and timing, making them even more complicated. (Pretty sure Hot Knives were also a huge influence). The songs were not written in the order of the album, of course. We knew 'Genesis Explosion' was going to start the album, and after that, I would pick songs that seemed to emanate the topic I was going to use for that song. The first side covered the Big Bang to the beginnings of humans.

The second side starts with 'Estuary', which is basically a metaphor for the human population up to our current time with 'Threshold', where we are right now. 'Infinite Universe' was a look into a future with the hope that humans can flourish in harmony with the planet and move out of religion into a positive future. Compositionally, the song 'Phobos and Deimos' was the most complicated. It was basically a big jerk-off finding the oddest timing and bridges. I think we realized we'd gone too far with this song, and it was losing listenability.

If you look at the following demos, you can see us pulling back from that precipice and writing songs that had a bit more of a groove to them.

I'd love to give you wild stories of those times when crossover was happening, but I'm afraid there are so many that it would require a lot of typing that I'm not prepared to do at this moment! Maybe it should even be a book!" -- Phil Dakin, bass player of D.B.C. and Kill of Rights, Final Chapter

(D.B.C. with The Nils and No Mind at the Silver Dollar, Ontario. 05/02/1988)

D.B.C. stands for Dead Brain Cells and they formed in 1985 in Montreal, Quebec as 'Final Chapter', only to change their name in 1986. Just like in the case of Chicago's Aftermath, D.B.C. started as a crossover thrash band (albeit more into hardcore), only to head for a progressive thrash metal style later! As you can imagine, I love their *'86 DBC* demo (maybe their most fierce recording), because it's messy and wild crossover, with a definite D.R.I. meets COC style. Seven ultra-speedcore songs with 'Pro-Choice' and 'Negative Reinforcement' being the definite highlights. Their first LP, the 1987 *Dead Brain Cells* included all demo songs minus 'Pro-Choice'. The slick production has taken away much of the power of the first demo-but anyway, it still sounds like a non-compromise blend of D.R.I., COC and Slayer; the new songs like 'M.I.A.' or 'The Vice' are excellent. Musical wise, D.B.C. were unbelievably proficient, just check the crazy drumming of Jeff St. Louis (RIP 2019) or the guitar playing of both Gerry Ouellette (RIP 1994) and Eddie Shahini, and the melodic bass lines of Phil Dakin. In their second LP, the 1988 *Universe*, DBC headed a progressive thrash direction, and metalheads consider this one to be their best LP; even I like it! It's weird and has a non-commercial edge, plus songs like 'Heliosphere' or 'Estuary' sound to me like a cross between anarcho-punk vibe and Voivod. DBC are still active since 2005, and they released two singles on 2024, 'Pendulum' and 'Sirens'.

DAYGLO ABORTIONS

(Dayglo Abortions band 1988. Courtesy unknown)

"A wild and crazy story from the eighties, eh! Well, these days you must be careful what you say. There was a lot of shit going on in the 1980s that would get your ass cancelled if it leaked out today. There are other issues to deal with these days also. The 1970s and 1980s were basically a drug-fuelled orgy. Back then kids could 'experiment' with all kinds of substances and partake in all manners of high-risk behaviour and for the most part...get away with it. It's nothing like that anymore. These days it seems that everything will kill you. I have stopped glorifying the hedonistic lifestyles that we used to get away with back then, because over the years I may have given some young impressionable people some very bad ideas that quite possibly contributed to their demise. These days I prefer to promote unity and understanding. I encourage people to be considerate of others' opinions, to help their friends, and be respectful of the world that they live in. There is too much infighting in the punk scene today. People are getting sucked into this false construct of right vs left politics and fighting with each other instead of uniting against the common enemy of mankind.... The multi death corporations and all the non-government thinktanks that want total control of the entire world. I know this might not be the answer you were hoping for but it's the way I see things now. We need to all put aside our differences. It's all just bullshit fake politics anyway. We need to develop strong communities that can support and protect themselves from the things to come" -- Murray Acton, vocalist and guitarist of Dayglo Abortions and Lummox, Sickfucks, Sikphuxz, The Colour Out of Space.

(Dayglo Abortions with Raw Power, Natas and Frightwig at the Cabaret Metro, Chicago. 09/11/1986)

Formed as early as 1979 (after the demise of the punk rock band Sikphuxz), Dayglo Abortions have been continuously striking the world with their shocking imagery and lyrics, not to mention their terrorizing hardcore punk with metal leanings. Initially a three-piece with Murray Acton (vocals, guitar), Trevor Hagen (bass) and Brian Whitehead (drums), they started off as a pure hardcore punk combo on the 1981 classic *Out Of The Womb* LP. They added some metal elements in the 1986 *Feed Us A Fetus* LP, that was crunchier, and included great and shockingly funny classics such as 'Argh Fuck Kill', 'Stupid Songs' or the mental 'Bedtime Story' that was later covered by Napalm Death. *Feed Us A Fetus* definitely has that snotty punk feeling, with a slight metal guitar riffage, and it's my most favourite Dayglo Abortions record. The 1988 *Here Today Guano Tomorrow* LP showcased the shift towards a more metal-punk sound, and it's still good, though not classic as the previous one. The later records like *Two Dogs Fucking* (1991) and *Little Man In A Canoe* (1995) kept up to this formula. Dayglo Abortions released several more LPs and are still (2025) active, offering their wild shows! Their latest record is the excellent *Hate Speech* (2021). If you get into them, I think that you will be a lifetime fan and enjoy all their records! Get also the Sikphuxz 7-inch EP that is out (2025) on Supreme Echo Records.

CLOWN ALLEY

"Much of the music around then had a lot of density to it and we also did some of that. I was interested in getting space and syncopation into some of the things we were doing and that might be one thing that separated us somewhat. We also did have a female bass player (Lori Black) who was probably the only woman playing music like that at the time in San Francisco. I was interested in different time signatures and silence as a rhythmic feature. We never really had much time to develop that or much else since we were a band for maybe two years at the most.

There're always odd things that are happening when you are traveling and it just becomes something that is routine after a while. I do remember once when we played at a place in Portland, Oregon called Satyricon that had a reputation for being a kind of nasty punk rock dive. During our set I became aware that our singer David Duran was playfully throwing these little plastic strips at me that bounced off me and landed on the floor. When I looked at them closely, I realized they were used syringes. People had been injecting drugs and then just throwing the syringes all over the place. I was lucky one didn't stick me. It's not really funny, but just the kind of thing that went on" -- Mark Deutrom, guitarist of Clown Alley as well as Mark Deutrom, and bassist of Melvins, Sunn O))), County Bucks. Also, producer and co-founder alongside Victor Hayden of Alchemy Records

(Clown Alley with Suicidal Tendencies and Maimed For Life at Fairgrounds Horticulture Bldg, Salt Lake City, UT. This was Clown Alley's last show. 24/04/1987)

A very eclectic crossover band, Clown Alley from San Francisco, California don't get so much mention nowadays, even though they were one of the innovators of this style. Adding to this, all the band members would have a massive story to narrate; guitarist Mark Deutrom founded Alchemy Records (among many others), Lori "Lorax" Black was the daughter of Shirley Temple, and later played in Melvins, vocalist David Duran played earlier in Jerry's Kidz, drummer Justin Clayton played later with Julian Lennon and Tears For Fears! Their 1985 demo was great hardcore punk with some metal leanings with catchy, fast thrashers like 'Bombs', 'Turn The Television On' and 'Brains', reminding me a more metal version of M.D.C. (which is of course, a compliment). Their sole LP, the 1986 *Circus Of Chaos* is more diverse, complex, with a progressive (!) edge: more metal this time, still on the hardcore punk tradition, but heading a more angular edge. Fantastic songs like the opening 'The Lie', 'Unplugged' and 'Pet Of A Pig'. Way ahead of its time, some of mathcore's roots are in *Circus Of Chaos*. Highly recommended for everyone that is fond of non-formulaic stuff.

CASTLE BLOOD/TRAVESTY

(Castle Blood band picture, 1987. Courtesy unknown)

"Early on, several things shaped my crossover journey. First was the underpinning of my secret love for metal since I was a teenager. Everyone says they loved Black Sabbath, but I did before discovering the Sex Pistols which led to everything UK82 and American punk and hardcore. My path wasn't the Clash and Ramones… it started with heavy rock and metal first.

I was all in abandoning most other types of music. However, the tone and heaviness are somethings that were missing from punk and to a lesser degree, hardcore. Of course, punk and hardcore had vitality, honesty and raw energy along with intelligence. I always felt lacking in metal at that time, so it was an intentional trade-off I was happy to make. However, for the bands I was in, I was always pushing this direction and a lot of other influences solidified and influenced me.

Being based in the Midwest, I was primarily in Pittsburgh and sometimes Cleveland. Pittsburgh had a sharp division between metal (even underground) and hardcore until crossover emerged. I believe Castle Blood is the first real crossover band in Pittsburgh and helped play a part in local convergence. Cleveland however always seemed more open to metal with bands like Integrity, Ringworm and countless others getting tighter and heavier…seeing shows at the PopShop. The first time I saw D.R.I. was at the Popshop where I bought the first EP from the band after the show. Surrounding Ohio clubs like Kent's JBs exposed me to a more diverse set of bands. Akron's Plasma Alliance was one that sticks out as being ahead of their time although clearly not as metal as the Cleveland bands.

(Travesty band picture 1986. Courtesy unknown)

Pittsburgh was a great spot for touring bands. Most of the great shows I saw were there…. some of the leading crossover bands came through such as Suicidal Tendencies in their parents' Winnebago, Nardcore early crossover bands such as Dr Know and Aggression, Seattle's Accüsed, and New York City legends such as Agnostic Front and the Cro-Mags. Exploited (Wattie lived in Pittsburgh for a year), Raw Power (not hugely attended but mind expanding!), D.R.I. and countless others.

Each time these bands passed through, there was a reset on local music and ripple effect. Unlike today with the internet and instant access to pre-filtered music, the infection of external underground music was limited. Without heavy distribution, shows and tape trading were how you'd learn about bands. However, I believe shows had the biggest impact. A great touring band's influence would wash through the scene like an almost subliminal wave.

The Detroit and Toledo, aka Maumee scenes had a big influence on me and Pittsburgh because of proximity as well. Bands from Ohio and Michigan passed through town much more frequently. One of the reasons is proximity and tours, tapes, people connected there…. Great bands from that area made an impact… at the time there was an active crossover and metal hardcore evolution happening: bands like

The Meatmen evolved musically (loved the one off with Brian Baker even if he didn't), Necros were ahead of their time, and other bands like The Stain (Ohio Version) with Jeff Kollman had similar qualities as Suicidal. As a note, Jeff went on to play with a lot of rock bands I hated back then like Alan Parson Project and some I always liked like UFO. If you never heard the Ohio version of The Stain, you should.

Additionally new metal was emerging that was influenced by the same underground music. I was an early fan of the expected thrash bands in there less polished state: Metallica (first three LPs ONLY!), Slayer, Motörhead, very early Megadeth, Sepultura, Zoetrope, Hallow's Eve, Post Mortem and many many others. However, the issue with metal (not all but lots) was the crappy lyrics…. that was generally a line that kept me on the punk/ hardcore side of crossover along with the coarse, roughness…

Finally, Pittsburgh had two additional sources at the time that helped shape crossover and underground music, in general. There was a great underground record store, Eides, where you could get stuff from the bands lucky enough to have records and distribution. It was here that I picked up transformative albums from the English Dogs, Jerry's Kids, Broken Bones, Crucifix, Battalion of Saints, and many others. This cacophony of bands was all part of my own musical evolution. I still listen to many frequently.

Current bands that keep it alive...Crossover is alive and, if anything, better - in terms of execution and musicianship, sound quality, and ability to connect with an audience. There are some amazing bands out there today like Dead Heat, Drain, Concrete, etc driving things forward. I think the internet has replaced the consolidation by local scene with a single connected global scene. As a result, to me, bands seem more similar. However, the advances and access to tools have allowed anyone and any band to record better quality music than anything - even in studios - we had in the eighties. One other bit difference is you have more people familiar with the music…. This means bands can find people to help record and mix that understand the goals. In the eighties, you would save your nickels and walk in a studio only to find a sound engineer that thought you couldn't play and weren't worth the time to get things right. This is why the underground labels delivered most of the better music of the era in my opinion.

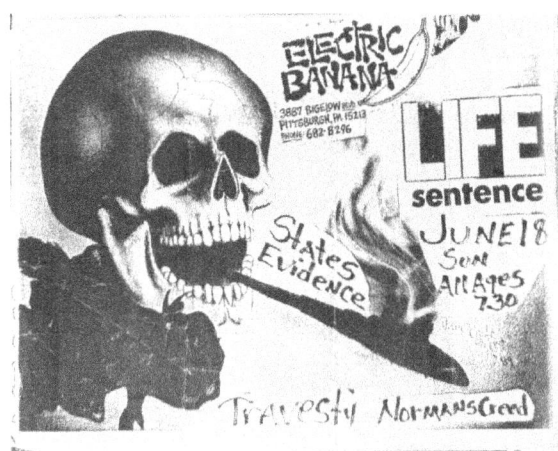

(Travesty with Life Sentence, Norman's Creed and State's Evidence at the Electric Banana. 18/06/1989)

In fact, since the eighties, there has been a steady stream of great bands.... the one's I've enjoyed including Madball (especially during the gap in Agnostic Front), Hatebreed, Terror, Crowd Deterrent, Trapped Under Ice, Cold World, Soul Search, Wolf Down, Broken Teeth, Bar Fight, Cold World, Brutality Will Prevail and many others.... every day, I get exposed to a new band through YouTube, Bandcamp, friends, etc. Although times have changed, it's exciting to see kids with the same drive and enthusiasm of the early days" -- Charles Griffith, bassist of Castle Blood as well as guitarist of Travesty and Heretics

(Castle Blood with Half Life, The Accüsed and G.B.H. at the City Limits, Pittsburgh. 16/09/1987)

Castle Blood is maybe the first ever band to pursue the crossover style in Pittsburgh, Pennsylvania; formed in 1986, they are still active today in 2026. Their *Land of the Lost* demo (1987) is as crude and nasty as you can imagine; fast and furious speedcore, in the early Accüsed tradition, lo-fi and crunchy, with great songs such as the chaotic 'Deceiver' and 'Another Day'. Their 1991 demo *Con*Fusion* was way better though, still fast speedcore with slight metal leanings, and The Accüsed influence now has been eliminated to a bare minimum, with some Attitude Adjustment in! This is my favourite demo off them, because of the songwriting; just check 'You Don't Care' and 'Power Play'.

Meanwhile, Charles has played also in the North Huntingdon, Pennsylvania crossover thrash band Travesty formed in 1987 and still active today too! Travesty released two demos of crossover thrash that was slightly more metal than Castle Blood; *Die Laughing* (1988) demo sounded like a cross between The Accüsed and early Nuclear Assault (*Game Over*-era), pretty enjoyable, with 'Future Man/Eyes of Glass' and 'Hope' being my favourite. *Destroyed from Within* demo (1989) was a better effort, snottier partly due to vocals of Jerry Petrosky. The song 'Your Kind' as well as '20th Century Lies' being fantastic songs. I guess that I enjoy more *Destroyed from Within* since it was a turn towards a more punkish crossover with mosh parts in-between!

Castle Blood and Travesty members played also in other bands, among them being Holocross, Eviction, Decadence, the crossover Hand of Doom, but I would like to focus on one more band, Heretics, a beloved garage punk group, with three full-length releases and many 7-inchs. Their 1988 *Heretics* LP is just top-notch garage punk with a slight Minnesota hardcore edge; while it's out of the scope of this book, you must get it!

BROKEN BONES

(Broken Bones 1987 band picture. Courtesy of Frank Skarth)

"I was still listening to stuff like UK Subs - *Endangered Species* LP, Ramones - *Too Tough To Die*, Dead Kennedys - *Bedtime For Democracy*, D.O.A., Circle Jerks etc. But by 1987 I also loved Metallica, Anthrax, Slayer, Voivod, Motörhead etc. Ha! I loved W.A.S.P. too lol and a bit of Motley n' Ratt! Saw W.A.S.P. on the *Electric Circus* tour! Slayer on the *Reign In Blood* tour, Metallica *Master Of Puppets* tour, Anthrax-quite a few gigs for them! I wasn't in Broken Bones for too long, and I was happy to get the fuck out of Stoke-On-Trent! I have no outstanding memories of that period though; the band was pretty much passive and quiet, Nobby kept to himself, and I only saw him at practice and gigs (there are a few daft stories but not for a book lol). However, I can remember a massive fight at a Birmingham gig but still my memories are really vague. It took place at the Mermaid, and I was outside when it kicked off...it escalated into a full riot!" -- Karl Morris, guitarist of Broken Bones as well as of Billyclub, Phantom Rockers, The Exploited and Xtract

(Broken Bones with The Unjust and Malignant Tumor at CBGB's. 27/01/1985)

(Broken Bones with G.B.H., Extreme Noise Terror and The Bad Men at The Dome, London. 17/07/1990)

Talking about TOP influential bands, Broken Bones are one of them. Originating from Stoke-On-Trent and formed in 1983 by brothers Tony 'Bones' Roberts and Terry 'Tezz' Roberts after they left Discharge. The mark that Broken Bones left in the worldwide hardcore, punk and thrash scene is endless. I used to see them all the time when I was living in U.K. in the 2010s, and a good friend that now is no longer with us used to make fun of me ('Alex, you have become their biggest fanboy!'). All their records (with the exception of the mediocre 1991 LP *Stitched Up*) are pure gold, and what is more exciting in their case is that in the 2000s and 2010s records they pushed the hardcore limits to an even more extreme approach, crazy! There are three Broken Bones records, that everyone should have in his collection: *Dem Bones* LP (1984), *Bonecrusher* LP (1986) LP and the 1987 *Decapitated* singles LP collection. That said, *Bonecrusher*'s second side is one of the best ever released by a punk-metal band. Songs like 'Treading Underfoot', 'Untamed Power' and 'Bonecrusher' are absolute bangers! There is a reason why bands like Metallica, Exodus, Sepultura, Voivod, S.O.D. sported the classic Broken Bones T-shirt logo all the time. On hold since the mid-2010s, hopefully they will be back someday soon!

SUDDEN IMPACT

(Sudden Impact live in Windsor 1988. Courtesy of Dave Poissant)

"What led to us in that direction was hearing early thrash metal bands coming along. We already knew Motörhead but when Metallica's *Kill 'em all*, Exodus' *Bonded by Blood* and Exciter's *Heavy Metal Maniac* and of course Slayer came out we were interested. We had a love for the new 'Speed Metal' style. At the same time, we were also getting better at playing out instruments. Around then COC's *Animosity* and D.R.I.'s *Dealing With It* came out. We were always a band that played what we were into and didn't follow any trends. As for how it was received in Toronto by our fans some said 'they are going to metal' and others liked the direction. We thought the new 'Crossover' scene was rad. As time went on the two scenes really became one, punks were going to metal shows and metal heads were coming to punk shows. We became good friends with Voivod from playing in Montreal, and Sacrifice. We played many shows with both those bands.

(Sudden Impact with Infamous Basturds at the Rising Sun. 07/03/1985)

I talked with our singer Johnny Borodenko and we could not really think of any real crazy stories, let's not forget it was almost forty years ago! There were lots of funny things happening, but they were mostly alcohol-induced stuff. Two funny things that came to mind both happened to our bass player Steve Milo and both happened in Montreal. The first was the time he passed out in the bathroom stall at a bar we were playing at. Woke up and the place was closed and dark, he proceeded to eat potato chips and drink the bar's booze until the workers came in to open the place up the next day. We had no idea what had happened to him, we thought maybe he met a girl and went back to her place, which brings me to the second funny story about Steve. He had brought a girl back to our hotel room, again in Montreal and went into the bathroom to bang. As they were going at it, he propped her up on the sink, the whole sink broke off the wall and hit the floor. I guess we were lucky no water pipes broke, we raced out of there the next morning and never went back!" -- Scott Fraser, drummer of Sudden Impact

(Sudden Impact with Razor and Dogs With Jobs at the Opera House, 29/09/1991)

Seeing a picture of John March (Heresy vocalist) flying onstage with a Sudden Impact T-shirt, really stroke me hard as a youngster. I had to find out who was the band that he was sporting, since the power of visuals in the pre-Internet days was massive. We discovered bands by the T-shirts that our favourite bands wore, the special thanks etc. and every detail mattered. Sudden Impact (Toronto, Ontario) kept the quality flag of Canada high (as most bands from the country do!), formed in 1984 and lasted up to 1991. Their 1984 *Freaked Out* demo is a major classic of Canadian hardcore with a slight metal touch, reminiscent of bands like Genetic Control or early Asexuals, this kind of snotty and superfast, but very catchy hardcore punk. I'm so happy that this demo has been re-issued by Supreme Echo on 7-inch, because a newer generation can check out blazing songs like 'Cat's Life' or 'Freaked Out'. Sudden Impact's first LP, the 1986 *No Rest From The Wicked* on Fringe Records, took a turn to a slightly more metal style. It was still hardcore, however now more metal partly due to the production. Another gem, a classic release with excellent musicianship and catchy songs like 'Keep On Truckin'', 'To Our Glorious Dead' or 'Continuing Saga', plus a frantic cover of 'I Got A Right'! Their final LP, the 1988 *Split Personality* was very good, albeit into an even more metal-thrash territory, more controlled and melodic, but still…it's highly enjoyable if you are into hardcore or/and thrash metal. Songs like 'Crossed Wire' or 'No Reason' are some highlights off this LP. My recommendation? Pick up the *Freaked Out* 7-inch re-release, as well as *No Rest From The Wicked* if you are into the more hardcore stuff, and *Split Personality* if you are more into thrash-crossover!

SOCIAL DECAY

(Social Decay band picture Seaside Heights NJ, 1985. Courtesy of Jimmy Tobin)

"Our top favourite crossover bands? Man, that's easy! We all loved D.R.I. (obviously), our mates Lethal Aggression, early COC, The Accüsed, English Dogs, Crumbsuckers and Ludichrist. Those bands was a common ground for everyone in Social Decay!

(Social Decay with Agnostic Front and The Psychos at CBGB's. 03/03/1984)

And many crazy stories from back in the day! It was such a wild time, and everything was new and there were all these factions pitted against each other. Punks had to fight with jocks, with white power jerkoffs and with cops and even in the beginning with metal dudes. Almost every show had problems back then. Cops were always called. But the big 'riot' at my house when the cops raided one of our shows (I used to have weekend shows in my basement) is the one I remember most. They arrested and beat up a bunch of people that day. We were all over the news, in the newspapers and shit. A bunch of us had to go to court and pay fines and all that bullshit. They literally beat the shit out of John Saltz from Lethal Aggression and fucking threw my little brother who was only like ten at the time into a tree! Someone wrote about it also in *Maximum Rocknroll*. I wish I had all the newspapers articles about it still, there was a picture of the cops grabbing Saltz by the throat. One kid crawled inside the bass drum and hid from the cops! The funny thing is we hid the keg in the shower and the dumb pigs never even looked behind the shower curtain!" -- Tommy Southard, guitarist of Social Decay and Solace, The Disease Concept, Robot Dicks, Sollubi, Godspeed, 3 Input Woman, Freak Theater, Gallery of Mites, Prunella Scales, Slaprocket

Party goers, police spar over fracas

Press Toms River Bureau

ISLAND HEIGHTS — Four young adults and three juveniles face numerous charges following a Saturday fracas that ensued when a borough police officer ordered a party featuring five rock bands stopped, police said.

Officers from Dover Township and the Ocean County Sheriff's Department had to be called in to assist Patrolman Jon Andrews in breaking up the party at a house at 35 Summit Avenue. Andrews was the lone borough officer on duty at the time.

Police Chief Thomas Grube said things "got out of hand" with an estimated 75 teen agers and young adults getting involved in the confrontation.

Grube said police were called initially to the party after receiving complaints that youths were urinating outside. Nearly 20 police eventually responded to the scene.

Andrews ordered those gathered to stop their party and disperse, after the department received numerous complaints from residents about the noise and disruption.

The owner of the house, Jackie Southard, said she was away on her honeymoon at the time and the party was arranged by her son, Thomas Kobi, 20.

"We don't stop people from having parties, (but) several residents complained," Grube said. "Subsequently arrests were made when they refused to disperse. They challenged the police."

Kenny Lund, Beachwood, who was at the party, said police overreacted and treated those they arrested with more force than necessary.

He said some of the suspects were already handcuffed and subdued and police officers were tugging on their hair and hitting them.

Kobi said several of the guests at his party plan to file charges against police for assault and using excessive force.

Kobi said the music from the rock bands was stopped when police arrived, and questioned what right police had to make his guests leave.

"We had beer, but no underage people were drinking," he said, denying that he had advertised a $3 admission to the party for five rock bands, beer and use of a skateboard ramp.

Grube said the arrests were wit See **FRACAS**, page C3

(The stories of Social Decay making the news, 1987! Courtesy of Tommy Southard)

Social Decay of Island Heights, New Jersey were another bombastic crossover group that emerged from the hardcore scene. Formed in 1984, their *Social Decay* (1984) and *NJHC* (1985) demos were frenetic attempts of mixing early D.R.I. with the NYHC style, a vicious attack to all senses, superfast ultracore with tiny metal influences. Songs like 'Everyday Habit' and 'Scared Youth' make me want to smash everything in sight! More demos and live cassettes followed always on the same style. Social Decay found themselves appearing in hardcore billings both in New Jersey as well as New York.

Social Decay's musical change took place on the *Hate* demo (1989), and on the brilliant *Life's Not Hard....*7-inch EP (1990) on Eightball Prod. What is funny in the case of *Life's Not Hard....* is that it also reminds me of a blend of the (new then) Youth Crew with Agnostic Front, with metal guitar solos! The power that derives from *Life's Not Hard....* is a major force to reckon with, while (finally!) the production is good; 'Dreams Of Reality' and 'Stepped On My Pride' are two of the best songs they ever written!

Social Decay called it quits in 1991 and returned in 2009, releasing in 2011 their *Sick Society* 10-inch on To The Point Records. This release sounded like a recollection of everything and every style they pursued in the past, with a modern production. Obviously, a rager, with total moshers like 'Sick Society' or 'Corporate Scum', and oddly enough, it reminds me of the Attitude Adjustment comeback records like *Terrorize*!

Members of Social Decay played also in the brother band Lethal Aggression (like Dave Gutierrez and Rob Hultz), as well as T.F.N. (Mike Roberts, Eddie and again, Dave Gutierrez), and in the thrashers Oblivion, as well as later in the stoner metal Solace (Tommy Southard, Tim Schoenleber, Rob Hultz). Fan of hardcore-oriented crossover? *Get Life's Not Hard....*at any cost, it's a minor classic!

WEHRMACHT

(Wehrmacht band picture 1987. Courtesy of New Renaissance Records)

"When we first started, our very first gig was up in Seattle, Washington in September 1985 at a club called the Gorilla Gardens Rock Theater. We played with a metal band Mayhem which was a few guys who later joined Poison Idea. That was great! Early on, in the underground in Portland we did a lot of DIY shows in basements and stuff. New Year's Eve 1985 we did a house party at the Death House in Portland. That was a blast! There was a recording of that show circulating among tape traders back in the day that is epic. If you find it get it! The crowds used to go wild back then. We played with Slayer, Possessed, Poison Idea, D.R.I., all those bands. It was amazing! Good times" -- Shannon Mortimer, bassist of Wehrmacht and Nervous Christians

The kings of 'beercore' as they self-referred their style, Wehrmacht formed in Portland, Oregon in 1985, and their musical terrorism stroke the underground scene since the early beginning. 'Sorry guys, but punk bands belong to the Satyricon club', was a Portland newspaper review that was dissing them for not being 'heavy metal', and Wehrmacht didn't give a toss about that, because they only wanted to have fun and play hardcore-thrash to its logical extreme. Their first five demos in 1985 to 1986 are as raw and unpolished as you can imagine, with the *Death Punk* demo (1986) being my favourite, fast-fast-and even faster! Their mental music was in-line with their frenzied shows, and their first release in 1987 *Shark Attack* sounded like a mishmash between early D.R.I. and Cryptic Slaughter, with some metal riffs. There is only one word to describe *Shark Attack*: it's NUTS! I dare you listen to 'Napalm Shower' or 'S.O.P.' and don't get out of control!

(Wehrmacht with Poison Idea and Corrosion Of Conformity at the Pine Street Theatre, 31/01/1986)

Wehrmacht kept it up releasing *Biērmächt* LP in 1988, that is somehow 'restrained'; I kind of miss the wild energy of the debut. *Biērmächt* has a much better production, and some great songs to boot like

'Munchies' or 'Night Of Pain'. Afterwards they changed their name to Macht and released in 1990 the *Vice Grip* demo that was more technical crossover thrash. They were back on various occasions since then, and they're currently active since 2023. Check also their grindcore-crossover alter ego of Spazztic Blurr and the 1988 *Before...and After* LP; plus they're active too today (2026)!

AMEBIX

(Amebix band picture, 1985. Courtesy unknown)

"These are records I bought when they first came out; I could name records for years that I like but these were kind of influential to me at the time: Iggy and the Stooges - *Raw Power*, Souxsie and the Banshees - *The Scream*, Wire - *Pink Flag*, Killing Joke – Self-Titled, The Ruts - *The Crack*. These are the albums that were highly influential at least for me, in the 1980s era of Amebix.

As for Amebix stories, there are so many I wouldn't know where to start. It has been a very wild ride for sure, and maybe I will pull some together for my memoirs one day!" -- Chris Miller, aka Stig Maximus, Amebix guitarist and founding member, as well as guitarist for Zygote, False Fed, Karnyx and The Band with No Name

OK, calm down; I know that the whole controversy that Rob 'The Baron' Miller has spawned the last decade, made many people somehow cancel Amebix. This is why I chose to have a very small chat, again with his brother, Stig. He has separated himself from any of his brother's conspiracy and racist theories, and he has distanced himself from him. The easy way for me would have been to ask for an interview from Baron (who is behind the Facebook page of Amebix NGNM), who now is yearning for any kind of publicity; but this, would have been totally unfair for both the history of the band, as well as for the other members. Amebix was an innovative and crucial band, and as this it should be treated.

(Amebix with C.C.M. and Concrete Sox at the Mermaid, Birmingham. 24/04/1987)

Formed in 1978 as The Band With No Name in Tavistock, Devon, England, then changed their name to Amebix in 1979, and a series of some of the most important records ever in the history of punk, with an influence on all extreme music genres, started.

I love all 1980s recorded material by Amebix; their gritty, rough and nasty sound that is reminiscent of post-war apocalyptic images will always be relevant in my book. Neither fast, nor melodic, Amebix created a sonic landscape that took its cues from Killing Joke, early Joy Division and Warsaw, PIL and Crass, only to be blended with some Black Sabbath. Their crossover wasn't the 'traditional' hardcore-meets-thrash (actually Amebix pre-dated all of that), but it was rather a musical digestion of the bleakest sounds of their youth. From the kick-off of *Who's The Enemy* 7-inch on their own, Spiderleg Records, as like most of their records were released on this label, to the crushing *Winter* 7-inch, then to the chaotic *Sanctuary* EP, to the major classic *Arise!* LP, and the more heavy metal-influenced *Monolith* LP. With all these releases, Amebix created the most influential stuff for a new punk genre (that was later baptised by Hellbastard): crust punk.

(Amebix with Depraved, Retaliate, Feed Your Head at Cloud 9, Manchester. 04/04/1987)

Their crazy ride stopped in the late 1980s. Stig, George Fletcher and Robert Richards formed the excellent Zygote in the late 1980s, lasting up to early 1990s. Amebix re-united with Ray Mayorga on drums from Nausea NYC and countless other bands. The re-united Amebix released again their own brand of inspired crust punk on *Redux* EP (2010), *Knights Of The Black Sun* single and *Sonic Mass* (LP) 2011.

Later in the 2010s, Baron formed alongside Away (Voivod), Andy Lefton (War//Plague), Jon (Misery) and Tom Radio (Frustration) as the brilliant band Tau Cross, that released three top-notch LPs. This is where it all ends, since Relapse Records dropped them because of Rob Miller thanking a Holocaust denier in the liner notes of *Messengers of Deception* LP (2020). Miller recruited new members, and Tau Cross seem somehow active (2025)-but in the case of Amebix there is no return. Stig took his distance from both his brother and his beliefs, and Amebix have split-up for good, with no chances of reforming soon. Rob Miller uses the Facebook page of Amebix NGNM as a place to expose his sad views, that border with conspiracy theories, racism, nationalism, anti-vaxx etc, only dragging the name of Amebix into the mud.

But no one can take away from Amebix the fact that songs like 'Largactyl', 'Drink and Be Merry', 'The Darkest Hour' and 'Battery Humans' are some of the most exceptional pieces of music written to externalize the feelings of despair that come from war, capitalism and modern world. *No Sanctuary* LP, *Arise!* LP and *Monolith* LP have a place in every punk kid's collection, every metalhead's. The influence of Amebix will live forever, and please, don't mention again that 'they sound like Venom' because they formed earlier than Venom, they don't have the rock 'n' roll composing styles, plus Stig always denied the influence of Venom!

MACE

(Mace band promotional picture, 1985. Courtesy unknown)

"Motörhead, Dead Kennedys, Black Flag, Slayer; these are the bands that I could acknowledge as influences for both me and Mace in the 1980s. As far as crazy stories go, my favourite was when Kirk (Verhey, vocals) was wearing a steel army helmet and he decided to throw it to the side stage. But instead, he hit me across the left eyebrow. Blood is spurting on the crowd which was going berserk. We finished the set; I went to the emergency room. Nine stitches, everyone laughing. Just another night in Mace!" -- Vern White, Mace bassist and The Pleasure Elite, Bondage Boys, Vendetta

(Mace with Raw Power, Dayglo Abortions and The Sea Monkeys at the New Gorilla Gardens, Seattle. 13/12/1985)

Another wild metal punk from Washington State, this time from Everett. Mace formed in 1982, making them one of the first bands that blended heavy metal and punk even though their approach wasn't the one of the classical speedcore crossover. Their 1984 *Metal Lust* demo is rough and underproduced heavy speed metal, while their first LP, the 1985 *Process of Elimination* is a very charming speed metal punk attempt, with great songs like 'S.U.B.C.' (that even reminds me of Misfits gone metal), and the California punk meets metal of 'Smoking Gun' and 'Drilling For Brains', that has a massive Poison Idea influence. Their second and last LP, the 1987 *The Evil In Good* is their hardest and roughest release, speed metal punk that sadly doesn't get much love; though songs like 'Intent To Kill' or 'Poison Gases' are major moshers. Forget the awful 'Daddy's Girl' and spin instead my favourite 'Thinning The Herd' with its ironic message and its brutal crossover style! Mace members later played in the thrash crossover bands Malevolence, Anticulture and Terrorist among others.

INFAMOUS SINPHONY

(Infamous Sinphony band picture. Courtesy unknown)

"Our main influences have always ranged from the raw aggression of Napalm Death and Corrosion of Conformity to the heaviness and precision of Black Sabbath and Iron Maiden. When it comes to our all-time favourite crossover shows of that era, those were by Excel, Crumbsuckers, Agnostic Front, D.R.I., and Ludichrist, bands that truly captured the spirit and energy of that era" -- Greg Raymond, vocalist of Infamous Sinphony

(Infamous Sinphony with Social Spit, Wrath and Dr. Know at the Club Mirage. 19/02/1989)

Infamous Sinphony from San Diego, California are still one of the heaviest crossover bands. They have been active since 1986 with three demos, five full-length LPs, one EP, one split, and all on the same style of heavy, brutal and extreme with the 1989 *Manipulation* LP on Wild Rags Records being my favourite. Their sound is fuzzy guitars, a mental vocalist, and sharp shocks like sticking your fingers in the electricity socket with songs 'Let's Move to Another Planet' or 'Executioner'. Not for the faint-hearted obviously, and even though they are way too extreme for my bag too, they have a certain charm. If you like *Manipulation*, feel free to check out and get all their other records!

HOLY TERROR

(Holy Terror 1989 picture. Courtesy unknown)

"In 1988 we were supporting D.R.I. and Kreator on the *4 of A Kind* tour, right after finishing the *Mind Wars* record, and by then I had a pretty good drug habit (my drug of choice was amphetamines and heroin mixed together…I really thought I had gotten away from that shit, all through 86 and 87, but this was not the case). We remixed the *Terror and Submission* record and recorded *Mind Wars* in the spring of 1988. We had already gone to Europe and hit the road in a motorhome with a roadie and my dog. The tour was long and great, and we were offered to do another month after getting home, but we had to turn in the motorhome and borrowed some money and bought a bus. But shit, the fucking thing didn't make it to the first gig in the Bay Area and began a complete nightmare where the band went ahead in the equipment truck and I stayed behind to try and get the bus fixed. We got towed to Fresno and tried to figure out what the hell was going on. Turned out we had grenaded the transmission and we sent someone to San Diego to get a used one. When we got the transmission, I tried and succeeded in changing it out…only to have it not work! So, we removed it again and looking inside realized they hadn't given us all the parts...This thing weighed over 900 pounds and every day the tour was getting farther and farther away. As the band got into the Midwest, we got the bus working and headed out to catch up. By the time we got to Vegas the power steering pump had sheared off and once again I'm out in the desert trying to repair the fucking thing. It would turn out that I would never catch up, and they did the better part of a month without me! We were broke but determined to get on tour in support of our new record through that fall. My drug problems increased and by the end of the year, we were offered to tour with Exodus and Nuclear Assault in Europe, where things started going bad immediately this time!" -- Kurt Kilfelt, guitarist of Holy Terror as well as a member of Old Dirty Buzzard, El Revengo, Hell Camano, Agent Steel, Midnight Idöls, Shark Chum, The Load Levelers, Zeke

(Holy Terror with D.R.I. and Toxic Reasons at The Union Francais, Montreal, QC. 17/11/1988)

Holy Terror formed in Los Angeles, California in 1985 after Kurt Kilfelt left Agent Steel and joined the forces of Keeth Deen (vocals), Floyd Flanary (bass), Mike Alvord (guitars) and Jack Schwartz on drums, who was replaced by Joe Mitchell. After one demo in 1986, released on Under One Flag Records their first LP, *Terror and Submission*, that metalheads worldwide consider one of the best hidden gems in speed and thrash metal. I find this style to be a little tedious and confined, so this isn't what I would consider as their best output. In 1988 they went on to release the excellent *Mind Wars* LP: this time they sound like a cross between Iron Maiden, D.R.I. Cro-Mags and Youth Of Today (yes, Keeth sounds like the metal version of Ray Cappo!). Songs like 'Do Unto Others' or ''No Resurrection' simply shred. Holy Terror in 1989, relocated to Seattle (minus Keith Deen and Mike Alvord) and continued for a short while as Holy

Terror, playing great punk rock. They recorded a demo with a much different sound than what they had played previously, and then changed their name to Shark Chum, recording demos of very enjoyable hardcore punk. They reformed from 2005 to 2008, and Keeth Deen's passing in 2012 (RIP) ended any thoughts of reformation. Get *Mind Wars*, it's their absolute best.

THE SKEPTIX

(The Skeptix 1978 picture. Courtesy unknown)

"After two name changes (Vermin and Chaos) The Skeptix formed in early 1982. We were gigging as Chaos in 1980-1981 but the record company wanted a name change due to other bands using the word 'Chaos'. We were all heavily influenced by the first wave of punk bands but as bands such as GBH and Discharge emerged, those bands had an influence on our sound. We began playing frequently locally and as our first release *Routine Machine* entered the alternative charts, we started to travel further afield playing cities across the UK. In December 1982 we travelled to Cologne, Germany to record our first album *So the Youth*. More gigs followed including a festival back in Germany. After further releases and gigs the band became less active but never split. We met to rehearse and chat as we were all friends from an early age. After quite a few years we were surprised to find that there was still a lot of interest in the band and London-based Captain Oi Records contacted us to see if we would allow our vinyl releases to be put out on CD format. We were humbled by this and of course we gave permission. This led to many tours across the USA and enabled us to play iconic venues including CBGB's in New York City. Our latest visit was in March 2025.

(The Skeptix at the Deutsch-Englisches hardcore festival, 27/08/1983)

Throughout the band's existence there have been many parties, arguments and even fights but we have always remained close friends. One of the strangest occurrences was when the tour van broke down in Death Valley, California. We were stranded roadside and unable to get to the next gig. As we pondered our next move, a massive and luxurious tour bus pulled up. The driver said he had just finished a tour with an American rock band, and the bus was empty so if we needed a lift, he would take us!!!! We arrived at the venue and the look on the faces of the punks in the queue was a picture! Many great times have been had by us all and we feel honoured and privileged to still be sharing festival stages with the likes of the U.K. Subs, GBH, Discharge, Chelsea, The Exploited to name a few. There will always be The Skeptix" -- Ian 'Chig' Chadwick, drummer of The Skeptix

Formed in Stoke-On-Trent, The Skeptix are one of the best, yet more unappreciated UK82 bands, something that can be attributed due to bad luck! The Skeptix should have been considered as a top five UK82 combo, up there with Discharge or G.B.H., because their musical output deserves it so.

The Skeptix are obviously a punk band by nature, however their inclusion in this book has the same mentality as GBH. They had a very Motörhead-driven sound, that could apply to metalheads and thrashers too, headbanging stuff! Their first three records were all self-released on their Zenon Records, *Routine Machine* 7-inch (1982), *Peace Force* 7-inch (1982 and *Return To Hell* 7-inch (1983) and will drive you nuts if you are into this sound. Songs like 'Routine Machine', 'Scarred For Life' and 'Return To Hell' are just hard-hitting bangers, total class! Everything seemed that the future would be brilliant for The Skeptix, but sadly this didn't happen...very soon.

Rock-O-Rama Records offered The Skeptix a contract for two releases, and the band flew to Germany to record their first full-LP, *...So The Youth*. Released in 1983, it was another excellent record in terms of songwriting, but it suffered of a terrible production by Jürgen Fickel and Herbert Egoldt, as well as a lack of decent support from Rock-O-Rama Records. Leftovers of those sessions were released on the split 7-inch with OHL in reference to *The Kids Are United* EP. The split 7-inch with The Insane in 1984 included one more great song, 'Vendetta'. Sadly, everything went downhill in 1984 for The Skeptix. The reason for that was that Rock-O-Rama Records in 1984 took a turn, and started releasing records by neo-Nazi bands. People were blaming The Skeptix all the time, but it wasn't their fault, since no one could ever expect from a label that was releasing chaotic punk bands' LPs, that they would turn in just one year to become the biggest and most notorious neo-Nazi promoting label.

The Skeptix returned in the late 1990s with the power of visuals that had a great impact on them while gaining popularity. The NYC punk band The Casualties were sporting their T-shirts and patches with the logo of The Skeptix, with a new generation of punks coming this way across their music! A new LP, *Hate And Fear* (2002) and a live one too (2004), and The Skeptix are still (2025) active, playing shows in the UK and US regularly. My recommendations are if you are into the motörpunk of GBH, or even the style that later Inepsy adopted, the 1980s records of The Skeptix are an excellent band to start with.

ALTERNATIVE ATTACK

(Alternative Attack band picture, 1986. Courtesy unknown)

"Basically, all three of us were huge Bad Brains fans; We even did a couple of gigs as a Bad Brains tribute called 'Destroy Babylon' (some footage of this exists on YouTube). We were influenced by American

Hardcore like Black Flag, Dead Kennedys and bizarrely enough as a three-piece, Rush! I learned a lot about timing through Spike's drumming and over the years if I play with a band, I tend to follow drums before anything, because I firmly believe if you lock in o the drums you have that machine that drives a song 100 percent.

We had some mad things happen on the road as you can imagine. Like the time we travelled around in my car, and we parked up near a building site. We got out of the car and the car started rolling down a ditch. We crashed on many floors after gigs as everyone did back then. We played a few gigs with Broken Bones where I first met seventeen-year-old Gizz (English Dogs) and Karl Morris (The Exploited, U.K. Subs). Me and Spike moved to Peterborough together after that tour and stayed at Gizz's parents until we rented our own house. The band obviously split up, and Spike joined Gizz's band Wardance.

But yes, the gigs with Broken Bones were an eye-opener for us. Like when the Nazi skinheads turned up and kicked off with the band. The next night at Adam & Eve's in Leeds, they came prepared with baseball bats expecting the skinheads to turn up…scary. I keep in touch with Tezz (Broken Bones and Discharge) now and then" --Burton, bassist of Alternative Attack

Alternative Attack from Holyhead, Anglesey, Wales were another one UK punk band that went for a metal thrash style later and did it with total class! Formed in 1985 by Burton (bass/vocals), Simon Lewis (vocals, guitar) and Spikey T. Smith (drums, vocals), they were included in *Crossover The Edge* with an extensive interview of Spikey T. Smith, so now it was Burton's turn for a few questions.

(Alternative Attack and The Desecrators at the Glasshouse. 17/05/1985)

Their first demo, the *85 Demo* (1985) includes twelve songs locking over 31 minutes of pure punk, that sounds like a cross of UK with US styles, snotty and belligerent, but not on the UK82 tradition of superfast songs! Most songs are mid-paced, anthemic and rough. Under the lo-fi production you can find so many gems like 'Police State', 'Alternative Attack' and 'All Systems Go'. As most punk bands of their era, Alternative Attack started touring extensively, supporting other bands (like Broken Bones), and were living their dream.

Their second demo named as *P.M.A.* (1986) followed a much different musical direction, with the American hardcore of Bad Brains blending in with speed metal. There were still straightforward punk tracks such as 'Metal Can' and 'Run Wild'. 'Avon Calling' and 'Wheels Wheels' were (fine) examples of this new direction! Their only vinyl release, the *No Turnin' Back* (1987) 7-inch on Active Minds' Loony Tunes Records was their most metal, and in fact their best; vicious and fast, like a blend of early Bad Brains with early Metallica, containing three songs ('No Turning Back' is a great tune!). After its release, and due to some problems (ahem…) that arose while they were touring, they changed their name to Destroy Babylon, playing mainly covers of Bad Brains!

Post-Alternative Attack drummer Spike went on to play in an unbelievable number of bands of diverse styles, something that isn't a surprise at all, since he's an exceptional drummer. Deep breath, here's a listing: he played in Sacrilege, English Dogs (live), Dub War (live), Memoriam, The More I See, War Dance, Atwar, Conflict, Destroy DC, HR of Bad Brains, Jolt, Morrissey, Sundance, The Damned, The Motivators, GBH (live), Killing Joke (live), New York Dolls (live), Sham 69 (live) and Steve Ignorant (live)!

EROSION

(Erosion band photo. Courtesy unknown)

"The bands and the records that Erosion totally loved, right? Well, we took inspiration from Cro-Mags - *Best Wishes*, Black Flag - *My War*, Voivod - *War and Pain*, Carnivore - *Retaliation* and Agnostic Front - *Victim in Pain*.

A crazy story from that era: Ille (the singer of The Emils) and I once had this pretty ridiculous moment during a show in Schwäbisch Gmünd [Germany]. We were both so fired up, completely lost in the chaos of the set. At one point, we stormed the stage together... and then suddenly, the whole thing gave way beneath us. The floor literally collapsed, just cracked open under our feet. We were way too heavy for that old, shaky stage. One second, we were screaming into the mic, and the next, we were stuck halfway through the floorboards, laughing like idiots. It took three people to pull us back up again, since we were too heavy!" -- Chris Zenk, vocalist of Erosion as well as of Black Laws, Minotaur and Schwanensee

(Erosion with Stengte Dorer, Angry Red Planet and Ludichrist at Netwerk. 04/12/1988)

Formed in 1987 as Black Laws (thrash metal), Erosion changed name and musical direction later that year. They released in 1988 on the hardcore label We Bite Records their first LP, *Mortal Agony*, that blended US thrash metal with Voivod and hardcore; good stuff, and 'Billharzia' alongside 'Nuclear Frost' are great numbers. They kept the same formula on their *Thoughts* LP (1989), with a slightly more hardcore approach blended in, as well as progressive thrash. Their *III* LP (1992) is the most hardcore-oriented, with a definite Cro-Mags edge, and maybe my favourite from Erosion. Tracks like 'Revenge' or 'Power Within' are enough to make me like this record. Their grand finale, the *Down...* CD (1995) incorporated elements from Biohazard in their usual mix, and it's OK.

MANIAC

(Maniac live onstage, 1987. Courtesy unknown)

"We loved English Dogs, especially one record (I think it was called *To The Ends Of The Earth* EP), but we also used to go and see them play at the 100 Club loads. They were there every couple of weeks or so it seemed. Also, regarding bands and records that all of us in Maniac loved, I have to add Discharge and *Hear Nothing, See Nothing, Say Nothing* LP, Motörhead - *No Sleep Til Hammersmith* LP, Metallica's *Kill 'em All* and *Ride The Lightning*. And for Barty (vocalist), his favourite record back then was Dead Kennedys - *Fresh Fruit For Rotting Vegetables*. The other guitarist Bill (who no one has ever seen or heard from in thirty years) was bang into hard rock, Thin Lizzy and Van Halen etc. Not sure we ever sounded as good as or anything like the above, but they made us change direction and want to be a better band.

As for the 'Punk Metal' thing on the back of the EP - that was put on there by the guy who put the EP out. I can't remember his name, but he was a lovely guy, very young, about the same age as us. He set up the label, Rentaracket Records. I was sending out cassettes to fanzines etc and somehow, he heard one and got in touch. Only met him a few times, lovely guy and to my shame can't remember his name. I remember at the time we wondered why he put the 'Punk Metal' tag on the cover, but I suppose it was punky with guitar solos so fair dos! He did all the artwork, paid for everything - all his work. We have no idea whether it sold or what, hope it did, and he made his money back - top man" -- Ed Glass, bassist of Maniac with contributions of Lee-drummer, Barty-vocalist and James 'Nozzle'-guitar

(Maniac with Bolt Thrower and Axegrinder at Fulham Greyhound. 08/07/1989)

Maniac from Surrey, UK formed in 1982. Their case is such a specialty in the history of crossover; while they can be considered both as a UK82 band and a metal punk combo, they were maybe the first band to coin the term 'Punk-Metal' on the back cover of their 1984 *Killing For Pleasure* 7-inch. And this term exactly applies into their music, that sounds like a cross between Subhumans and Motörhead, or NWOBHM bands like Holocaust (or even Saxon) with UK82 punk. The four songs of this 7-inch are catchy and fun, with 'Say No' bringing English Dogs in comparison, and 'Adrenalin Rush' being my favourite. Other tracks such as '1984' and 'Killing For Pleasure' balance perfectly between punk and metal! Prior to *Killing For Pleasure*, Maniac had two demos (that I sadly couldn't find anywhere), and in 2010 they released the *Is This What You Signed Up For?* CD-R, again in the same style, with a more modern production. They somehow seem to be still (2025) active, and I'll keep my eyes open if there's a chance to see them live! Any label out there to re-release their great musical output on a decent collection?

THE BONELESS ONES

(The Boneless Ones 1986 band picture. Courtesy of Boner Records)

"In 1984 Max Fox started The Boneless Ones with a few friends. Their first show they played three songs! Max singing, Ike on drums and Tom on guitar. The bass player, Dave Chavez, played in Code of Honor so he did not have time for another band. That is when I was asked to join. Soon we had a real set of 7-8 songs. But our guitarist, Tom, quit the band and we hired the amazing Luke Skeels. Luke was a truly amazing guitar player, much better than most punk rock bands ever had. With Luke we found our sound; rock 'n' roll and punk rock with thrash metal and head banging influences! A true crossover band. This is why our influences were Minor Threat and Bad Brains on the punk side and Iron Maiden and AC/DC on the metal side. Throw in some Metallica, Junkyard, Fang, Code of Honor, Ramones and Ozzy and turn on the blender!

Ike then quit and we added Tim Stiletto from Fang. So, the lineup for *Skate for the Devil* was Max, Troy, Luke and Tim. We played a lot, toured and had a ton of fun. Tim quit and we added Chris Kontos. However, six months later the band fell apart. It happens. We all joined other bands. The Boneless Ones was dead.

Thirty-two years later we came back from the dead. The Haight Ashbury Street Fair had a theme for the bands 'reunions of 1980 band'. They asked The Boneless Ones to play. I pulled my bass out of the garage and started playing it after twenty-nine years. After the concert we decided to keep playing. We hired Craig Locicero on guitar, and The Boneless Ones version 2.0 was born. 2021 still in COVID, we wrote the songs at Chris' house and recorded and released *Back to the Grind* LP. And of course, we started playing live again" -- Troy Takaki, bassist of The Boneless Ones, as well as of Hell's Kitchen

(The Boneless Ones with Sacrilege B.C., Attitude Adjustment, Clown Alley and Rabid Lassie at the Twilight Zone, Alameda. 10/04/1987)

The whole 'Skate Rock' style always had its fair share of bands that crossed over with metal and rock. In the case of The Boneless Ones, the metal influence into their hardcore sound is rough and heavy, taking its cues from bands like Tales Of Terror and Black Sabbath, with a twisted early Metallica edge. Formed in Berkeley, California, their first appearance was in the (classic) *Them Boners Be Poppin'* LP (1985) compilation, alongside Verbal Abuse, Special Forces, Fang, Bl'ast!, Fang and Tales Of Terror.

Their first LP, *Skate For The Devil* (1986) on Boner Records is scary, dark, powerful, but never too fast. The opening 'Give It To You' is a stormer, while 'Jason' is an ultra-heavy and dark stomper, with the nasty re-edition of 'Pipeline' and the chunky riffing of 'Skate For The Devil' being the real treats on a flawless record. Sadly, The Boneless Ones called it quits in 1987, only though to come back on 2019 with a new record, the exciting *Back To The Grind*. Now more clean-cut than before, but equally great in terms of songwriting, *Back To The Grind* holds all those qualities that make The Boneless Ones sounding so special with the vocal lines of Max Fox to the muddy rock and metal guitar riffs. 'We Ride The Night', 'Good Friends' and the headcrushing 'Faces Of Death' are my favourite anthems off this record.

(The Boneless Ones with D.R.I. at The Outhouse, Lawrence, KS. 26/06/1986)

The Boneless Ones are active (2025), and the lineup includes Max Fox (vocals), Troy Takaki (bass), Craig Locicero (guitar, of Forbidden fame) and Chris Kontos (drums, you know Chris and the countless great bands he played in, right?). *Skate For The Devil* is one hell of a Skate Rock record for punks and thrashers!

THE MENTORS

(Mentors in live action. Courtesy of Gary Leonard)

"Early on, we were on a steady diet of Van Halen and Wendy O. Williams and The Plasmatics, definitely.

Back then, there was a situation with me and Ella — she was living at my place in Riverside, California. I think it was around 1995 or 1996 when I got a call to go play a show in San Diego on a Saturday night. We were called maybe the day before, so we just packed up and went. It was a house party at a place with a pool, a few kegs, and a bunch of people- a really good crowd. We were supposed to get paid $500 for the gig. The show went great. Everyone was drinking from the kegs, and, as usual, I got totally wasted. Then the cops showed up and broke up the party. It was a drag, especially since we didn't even get paid, but we still had a great time. The cops weren't too harsh, but they told everyone to leave. We started loading our drums and amps back into the van, but El Duce didn't want to leave, he wanted to stay and keep drinking. Me and our roadie tried to get him out, but he resisted. We finally had to carry him out, one of us on each shoulder. There was a narrow pathway on the side of the house, and while carrying him out that way, he felt down hard and started screaming bloody murder.

(The Mentors with CH3 and The Pandoras at the Cathay De Grande. 07/04/1984)

Turned out, he'd fallen onto a piece of broken glass (maybe three or four inches long) and it sliced right into his butt cheek. There was blood everywhere. We rushed him to the hospital around three in the morning, and he was screaming the whole time while the doctors worked on him. You could hear him from down the hall, it was wild. Once they patched him up, we dragged him out to the car and headed home, straight up Highway 15 to Riverside. He was acting kind of stupid but not too bad. I actually felt guilty since, in a way, I was responsible for him getting hurt. So, I stopped at a Denny's for a Grand Slam breakfast.

It was Sunday morning, so the place was full with some drunk Mentors fans and a bunch of churchgoers. At first, everything was fine. El Duce was chatting with fans, but then someone had the brilliant idea to buy him a drink (I think a gin and tonic), since Denny's started serving alcohol at six in the morning. Of course, he got drunk all over again. We tried to get him out of there because we had another gig that night, but before we could leave, he suddenly dropped his pants right in the middle of Denny's, exposing his bandaged, bloody butt for everyone to see. It was horrifying and hilarious at the same time. I ran outside to the car, not knowing what to do, while our roadie somehow managed to convince El Duce to walk out. We barely made it out before the manager called the cops. We jumped in the van and drove off as fast as we could. And that's the story of how El Duce behaved that night" -- Steve Broy, aka Dr. Heathen Scum, bassist Mentors (1976 to present) and vocalist (2014 to present), as well as the bassist of Dr. Heathen Scum, Mantors, Mentorhawk, Church of El Duce, El Duce, Harsh, Kill Allen Wrench and The Milfhunters

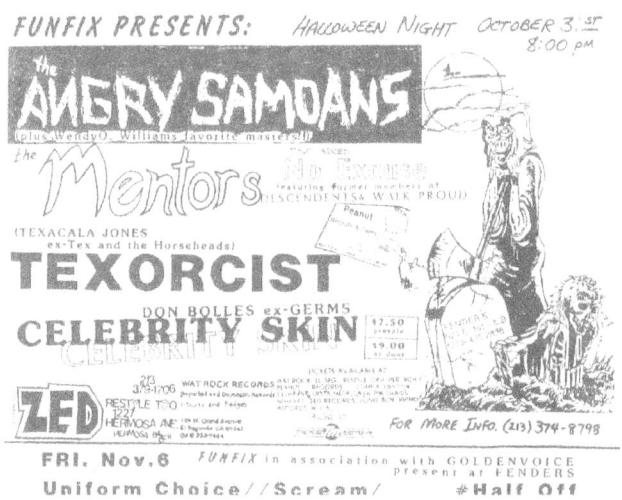

(The Mentors with Angry Samoans, No Excuse, Texorcist and Celebrity Skin at Fender's in Long Beach, California. 31/10/1987)

The Mentors began in Seattle, Washington, then relocating to Los Angeles, California formed in 1976 after being influenced by the punk explosion. Yes, there are many objections towards them in lyrics and visual terms, however one cannot omit that they were one of the first bands that blended punk with metal. Their first demo (1981) was a crude exercise on this style, almost bordering with art damage bands of the punk scene, sounding like Germs gone rock. The exact same things can be said about their *Mentors a.k.a.*

Trash Bag 7-inch (1982), that was released on the hardcore punk seminal Mystic Records label. It was totally deranged punk metal, with obscene lyrics with great songs like 'Get Up and Die' and 'Peepin' Tom'. Mentors were regulars of the L.A. punk scene, performing alongside bands like CH3, Angry Samoans or The Grim in places like Cathay De Grande, bombing the crowd with their sleaze metal punk. This was evident in their *Whisky a Go-Go / Cathay de Grande* live LP (1983). Later, they signed with Metal Blade Records, releasing their most known records, *You Axed For It!* (1985) and *Up The Dose* (1986). Totally offensive in lyrics and visual terms, however Mentors sound offensive the way bands like Fear or Steve Stiletto and Meatmen were. Sometimes things went too far as heard on 'Four F Club'. In strictly music terms, their crude metal punk rock is catchy and rough. The Mentors have been active since 1976 performing and touring too, even after the death of their frontman El Duce in 1997. My favourite moment off them is the 1982 *Mentors a.k.a. Trash Bag* 7-inch, however Mentors fans are very fanatic and hardcore, and seem to love all their stuff.

THE ICEMEN

(The Icemen third show at Pyramid Club, NYC, 1983. Courtesy unknown)

"I would say that without the Bad Brains, The Icemen probably wouldn't have existed. Especially early The Icemen.

It was Marco (Abularach) that insisted that I go with him to see the Bad Brains for my first time back in 1979 at CBGB's. And keep in mind we pre-date bands like the Cro-Mags so it was more like we all had similar influences rather than they influenced us. Another band was definitely The Damned! The song we had called 'The Icemen' wouldn't exist without The Damned! Later we were also into metal and speed metal and I think it's easy to hear the Motörhead influence on much of our material. For example, a song we had called 'Take you Down' wouldn't exist without Motörhead and speed metal influence.

For me the common thread was of course I loved great bass sounds and playing and the Bad Brains, The Damned and Motörhead all had great bass! We couldn't help but be influenced by so many bands. But those 3 I would put as the biggest influences on our songs and sound.

My favourite Bad Brains album is of course the ROIR cassette but people who never saw the Bad Brains live in the early eighties can't really hear from that recording how great they were because it's so underground it's hard to hear through the lo-fi aspect to understand how powerful they really were! For me, they were the best live band of all time or certainly the best live band I've ever seen!

The Damned I love *Machine Gun Etiquette* and the *Black Album* their earlier albums are also good. My favourite Motörhead album hands down is *Ace of Spades*, one of the best hard rock albums of all time! They have other good albums as well. For example, *Bomber* album for me is very underrated! It's I think the first time I heard double bass drum!

As far as my favourite shows, CBGB's was our home turf so we had a lot of good shows there and also some tough ones, but I would have to say that the [Washington] DC shows were some of my favourite because of the response and also because of how warm and welcoming they were to us. We developed some really close relationships with some of the people we met down there, and they really took care of us. We didn't need a hotel or to try to drive back after the shows we stayed at their houses. I think the others would agree we have many great memories from our DC trips!

Some of my favourite memories with the band were actually in the studio! Our first recordings were done at Nola Recording in New York City, the studio I worked at then. We used to record on holidays like Thanksgiving and Christmas Day so we could sneak into the studio and record because we didn't have the money to do recordings! I remember I would spend hours trying to get the snare sound and would get into disagreements with Mackie about it and I remember one time at Nola Marco said just wake me up when you guys are done and he went to sleep on the control room floor! I mostly got my way then as far as the snare sound but later Mackie finally won out and I guess you could argue that was a good thing because his snare sound, which basically came from Fishbone, influenced a ton of drummers and is on countless albums not just New York bands but I would argue bands like Rage Against the Machine and Deftones. Now it is possible that they got the influence from Fishbone also, but I don't really think of Fishbone as a hard rock band. Anyway, some of my best memories are of us in the studio and we did a lot of session even though we didn't release very much!" -- Noah Evans, bassist and founding member of The Icemen, as well as in Frontline and a well-known producer and engineer

(The Icemen with Raw Deal, Pagan Babies and Beyond at CBGB's. 28/08/1988)

Formed in New York City in 1982, The Icemen are maybe one of the very first, if not the first, NYHC bands to incorporate metal overtones into their hardcore. Formed by Noah Evans (bass), Mackie Jayson (drums, later of Cro-Mags, Leeway, Madball etc etc), Marco Abularach (guitars) and John Gamble (vocals), their musical approach sounds fresh and innovative even today, forty years later.

Their initial style can be found on the 2008 *The Icemen* 7-inch, that includes two songs from their early days: 'The Iceman' kicks off like a perfect blend of first-wave NYHC with Motörhead (and some Venom). The recording is a total rager that was recorded in 1984 at Nola Recording Studios, New York. The flipside of 'It'll Be Your Grave', sounds like a bone-crushing, street-cred version of early Bad Brains with a Motörhead bass solo, recorded later (in 1985 or 1986), again at Nola Recording Studios.

One of the original A7 and Pyramid bands, it is a damn shame that The Icemen didn't release anything on vinyl in the 1980s. In 1991 they released their first 7 inch, *Rest In Peace* on Blackout! Records (can somebody sell me a copy?) and this is a massive metal hardcore release. Neither too fast nor too extreme, it balances between the hard-hitting NYHC style and the perfectly executed metal riffing, with four songs that will leave you speechless! Each and every song is a ripper. I have to make a special mention on 'Shadow Out Of Time' for two reasons: first, it can make even the most technical progressive rock and metal band blush with its technical proficiency. Also, one of the bands that metalheads of today love so much, Eternal Champion, are always mentioning into their interviews that their unique (epic!) metal sound took its cues from Cro-Mags, Raw Deal/Killing Time and The Icemen. Hearing 'Shadow Out Of Time' is the perfect proof of that!

Their *Buried Alive* 7-inch (1995) on Twilite Records is their heaviest, angriest and nastiest release, with the title track being a pissed-off anthem, while the flipside of 'Fire N' Ice' maintains their metal hardcore approach, a real head-stomper.

The Icemen are one of the most unsung, yet significant bands that had their own brand of crossover out there since the early 1980s. Not active since 2008, hopefully a full discography of everything they recorded will someday see the light of day.

DEADHORSE

(Deadhorse with Devastation at the Axiom. 03/06/1989)

"At the time we all met in 1986 Metallica had broke, but we were listening to Sex Pistols, DEVO, Megadeth, Motorhead, even a touch of Slayer and Celtic Frost. Being from Texas, Southern rock and country were in our DNA and all were children of parents that has great tastes in music. So, it developed in us a musical dialect that we should never close the door on a style of music and not stick to just trash, heavy or death metal. We poked fun of all these styles at some point as well bring humour in; we loved comedy.

Seemed people loved us or hated us. We never claimed to be a great band we just wanted to have a great time and show while getting to know the crowd. It was all high tops jeans and cut off T-shirts. Oh, and beer!! For me Canada was always the big fun deal, we drank so much Canadian beer we got yeast sore in our mouths" -- Allen Price, bassist of Deadhorse

Deadhorse (Houston, Texas) are active since 1988 and are basically a thrash-death metal band with hardcore influences. Their first LP, the 1989 *Horsecore: An Unrelated Story That's Time Consuming* remains their brightest moment and sounds like a cross of Sadus and Slayer with D.R.I., with humorous jokes in-between, some crazy country riffs here and there, and weird changes all over! Their second LP *Peaceful Death and Pretty Flowers* is on the same style. Mr. Bungle fans will enjoy their approach-it's a bit too weird for me though.

PART TWO: But wait…there's more!

In this section I have added bands that I missed in *Crossover The Edge*. Bands that their demos couldn't be found earlier, as well as including bands that formed up to 1990. I wanted to include bands that formed up later like The Militants from Los Angeles, however things would have gone totally out of hand in terms of length.

USA

Johnny Vomit from South Side of Chicago, formed in December 1986 by Northern Illinois University friends, John Hanford, Roman Rokiciak. While initially, in their 1989 demo they sounded like a crazed D.R.I.-influenced band only to be fuelled by alcohol. In their later stuff, they also included more crossover elements heard on *Projectile* CD-R (1997) and *Extreme Championship Drinking* LP (2006), glorifying chaos, alcoholic destruction, hedonic living and being a total mess! The 1989 demo is just a whirlwind tornado of mental hardcore with a slight metal touch, and I'm totally on it! Johnny Vomit is still (2023) active. In the case of Atom West (Allentown, Pennsylvania), I sadly only found one song on the *Lehigh Valley Rocks! - The Best of 1984-1994* CD compilation; they included ex-members of Vicious Barreka, and the only song I heard off them ('Perkins Club') is just full-on power, raging crossover akin to early Nuclear Assault albeit with more hardcore vocals. A shame that their *One Day's Worth* demo is so rare. Noxious (Rochester, New York) derived from the thrash metal Twisted Cross, and were a mixed bag on their only release, the 1989 *A Big Sack o' Jaweeah* demo. They definitely had the power; however, it was just basic, ultra-fast uninspired hardcore thrash, with vocals reminiscent of what bands like Impaled Nazarene would later appropriate. I can't stand this kind of stuff, so sorry, I'll pass. Couldn't find anywhere two demos, *Demo 1*, 1986 and *Moment of Suffering* 1988 demo by Vae Victis (Lawrence, Kansas). They only get a reference as a hardcore speed metal band, and too bad that their output is scarce, because in their heyday they supported bands like The Accüsed, Beyond Possession and Agnostic Front. No idea on how Infested (St. Louis, Missouri) sounded like, only reported as a crossover band on *Final Holocaust* #2 zine, 1989. Their *Infestation of the Population* 1989 demo remains a mystery, and the band's bassist Ron Schodroski later played in the (much more known) Vacant Grave.

Die Theory (Providence, Rhode Island) went for a different approach in their crossover and thrash; highly technical, diverse, yet still brutal crossover (with an emphasis on thrash metal). Kind of reminds me of a more hardcore Violence, both their demos (1990 *Die Theory* and 1991 *Ice Cream Headache*) are ripping, but sadly they were too late for the crossover game. Anyway, songs like 'Inner City' or 'Cactus Man' are definite winners. Elimination (New Orleans, Louisiana) formed in 1988, and their 1989 demo *Process of Elimination* was rough and ultra-violent, sounding like a cross between early Slayer and The Accüsed, with some mental D.R.I. speed thrown in. Where Elimination lack inspiration, they gain in power, with songs like 'Toxic' or 'Disconsolent Apathy' are examples of that. No review on Menace (from Virginia Beach, Virginia) since I couldn't find their two demos (*Menace* 1989 and *Brainfood* 1990); reportedly, a crossover band. Social Deceit (Houston, Texas) were such a weird combo. Their crossover sounds sloppy and messed up, yet still it's a fun listen on their two demos (Demo 1990 and *Trials and Tribulations* 1990). Not something mandatory, still though decent goofy hardcore thrash, like an adrenalin-fuelled Mucky Pup, especially on songs like 'Murder Kit'.

Dark Carnival (San Mateo, California) included Josh Brock of Titanic, Dr. Know and Stigmata, and their sole offering, the 1987 36:05-minute demo includes some rapid-fire crossover thrash (emphasis on the metal side of things), with a weird, angular edge in places-cool stuff. Disarm (Virginia Beach, Virginia) on their 1985 *Existence* demo was re-issued on LP in 2024, took the Agnostic Front sound of *Victim in Pain* and blended it with Slayer (*Show no Mercy*) and this is so evident on songs like 'Blurred' and 'Freedom'. Still more on the hardcore side of things, *Existence* is just menacing and of course, a top release. The Final Demise (Mounds View, Minnesota) formed in 1988 and were pretty unlucky, because their only release, the 1992 *Power of Suggestion* CD was released while crossover had no luck in commercial terms. And it's a shame, because it's a good release, blending D.R.I. with Exodus and M.O.D. It was a bit too formulaic, yet songs like "One More Step Into Chaos" are a fun listen. The (Detroit) Meanies (Detroit, Michigan) on the other hand, are such a unique combo! Still active to this day (2024), they have released two demos (1989 and 1990 respectively), as well as a few more self-released stuff the subsequent decades, and their musical style can be described as a mix of heavy and power metal with a punk style of songwriting! Sometimes they sound like Warrior Soul, other times like the more metal version of the Misfits, definitely a band to check out if you enjoy more exotic stuff. 'Victim of Another Lie' is a killer song! Did you also know that vocalist Randy Cole played with Megadeth's Chuck Behler in Street Elite, a band that you can read more things about in my book, *Heroes of the Metal Underground*.

The Tranques (St. Paul, Minnesota) is basically the band that formed after the demise of the excellent Wilful Neglect (that you should all check out if you are into crazy frantic hardcore bands like DDT, Koro or even Adrenalin O.D.), and their *Heavy Whispers / Bleedin' Eyes* 1987 7-inch release is actually from the third Willful Neglect album that was recorded in 1984, only without Wade Calhoon on vocals. A wild mix of hard rock and punk, like The Stooges meets MC5 meets Black Sabbath and Deep Purple, and 'Heavy Whispers' is an amazing song. Pre-grunge? Get it! Apathy (Omaha, Nebraska) were such a weird case of band too! Their sole release, the 1988 *Out The Window* is a charming blend of metal, punk and alternative rock-and they definitely have a Motörhead meets garage sound, so you need to hear this! Rigor Mortis (hardcore punk band from Hollywood, California; not the thrash metal band from Texas) appeared in compilations such as BYO's *Something To Believe In* (1984), sporting a definite hardcore style, however their only release, the 1986 *The Conveyed Message* LP (as Rigormortis), was just a venomous and brutal metalpunk record. Rigor Mortis is reminiscent of Dr. Know both in terms of heaviness as well as the lyrical style. Songs like 'Bombscare' or 'Deathwish' are just pure madness. Reign Of Terror (Los Angeles, California) were formed by members of Würm and the Stains, and they called their sound as "Modern Metal" on their only (and super rare) *Don't Blame Me* 7-inch that was re-issued on Radio Raheem. The sound here is super catchy punk, with metal overtones and a fuzzy production, wholeheartedly recommended because 'Big Things' sounds like a more metal early Agent Orange!

(Apathy, Omaha 1998. Courtesy unknown)

Kurupsure from Goldsboro, North Carolina formed in 1987 and lasted up to 1991, releasing two demos that you can find on Heaven and Hell's compilation CD *Hello Cruel World Demos +6* that sounded like a cross between Metallica and hardcore, powerful stuff yet not something groundbreaking. The Elements (Buffalo, New York) were a short-lived project that included Jerome Augustyniak (of 10,000 Maniacs fame!), and their only release, the 1981 *Go Where The Women Go* 7-inch was a rough n' ready hard rock and punk crossover attempt. Rokker (San Antonio, Texas) had this same hard rock and punk crossover on their 1979 *Rokker* LP. Songs like 'Tall Girls' were definitely punk with hard rock vocals. While songs like 'Pigeon Hole Wankers' blended hard rock with punk with great results. Rokker was a very MC5 and Death influenced band, and this LP is totally recommended. Slaughterhouse from Detroit, Michigan were truly an outrageous act. Blending punk, industrial and doom metal in their 1985 demo and on their *Mommy's Little Panty Boy* 7-inch (1987). Not crossover in the classic style, yet crossing over different realms of punk and metal, Slaughterhouse were a vicious act. Detriment (Omaha, Nebraska) started off as I.O.D. (Implements of Destruction) and released in 1989 one cassette demo that contained raw and pissed off speedcore, more hardcore than metal, with great songs like 'Color War'. Through their existence they played with Sacred Reich, Ludichrist, Underdog, False Modulation, Warzone, and Say No More.

Radio Planet from Wantagh, New York, wow, such a story! They started off as a band that mixed power pop punk with hard rock on their excellent 1980 *I've Got No Use For You* 7-inch. They went full-on heavy metal on their 1989 *Radio Planet* cassette that was re-issued as a CD in 2020 by Heaven and Hell records. Tracks like 'Stormbringer's Curse' even remind me of a cross between Brocas Helm and Riot, metalheads will get the reference. Another case of hard rock and punk crossover was Ervin Berlin's sole release, the 1979 *Junior's Got Brain Damage* 7-inch; balancing between the two styles, one man band Ervin Berlin (originally named Erv Shuemake, from Florida), offers two quite interesting numbers of this combo. Hated Principles from Los Angeles, California, were initially a great hardcore act, in their semi-classic *The Curse Of Prince Hated* 7-inch (1983). Many releases since then and up to 2005. In terms of 1980s crossover, one should check out the 1987 *Storing Up Trouble* LP; it's fast, dark and highly unique mix of speed metal with hardcore punk, evident in songs like 'Lucifer's Legion' or 'Shoes'. A good one for sure, but oh those high-pitched vocals here and there! Joe Gizmo And The Spudmonsters (Cleveland, Ohio) were actually the band that pre-dated The Spudmonsters, and their only release, the self-titled 1988 cassette. You get their fierce, rhythmic crossover style in songs later famed by Spudmonsters such as 'Garbage Day' or 'Beer'. Solitude (Boston, Massachusetts) included John Alexander and John McCarthy (RIP 2009) of Post-Mortem, and their 1988 *Gristle* demo included two heavyweight doom and hardcore songs, heavy with a sound that was ahead of their time.

D.C. 3 was a hard rock group formed by one-time Black Flag vocalist Dez Cadena (vocals, guitar) and Paul Roessler (keyboards) in 1983, shortly after Cadena left Black Flag. Accompanied with Overkill L.A.'s drummer Kurt Markham, their first release was the 1985 *This Is the Dream* LP, a record that blended hard rock and metal (Sabbath, Hawkwind) with punk, a style that was later to be described as…stoner. We are talking here about the originals, *This Is the Dream* is just an exceptional record, full of great songs like 'We Feel The Sky' and 'This is the Dream'. Another three records followed in the 1980s for DC 3, all good stuff, in the same style, so if you're into *This Is the Dream* be sure to get them too! Slugworth (Pittsburgh, Pennsylvania) included later members of Submachine, Shiver, Speedgoat and Rising Seas (among many others), and their only offering, the *Demo '89* is just a forgotten jewel of crossover hardcore, taking its cues from the craziest days of The Accüsed, however with ridiculously idiotic lyrics. A pity, because their style in 'Big John Stud' or 'Booger Booger Booger' is mind-blowing. Certain Death (Chicago, Illinois) was a punk metal trio, and their crossover approach was more controlled, simple and mid-tempo metallic punk, as evident on the 1987 *Certain Death* demo and the 1988 *K.A.O.S. In Control* 7-inch; weird, and technically challenging crossover, I like it.

Atomic Gods (Bristol Way, Las Vegas, Nevada) was a crossover political punk metal band, that included drummer Alan Strong (later of Righteous Pigs). On their only release, the 1987 *Critical Mass* cassette, they exposed perfect crossover, that shared comparisons with bands like C.O.C, Ugly Americans and Attitude Adjustment. This is just a shredding release that hopefully will get an official re-release treatment.

All songs are winners, especially 'Walking Dead' and 'Wreck on the SS'. No Warning (San Jose, California) on their two tapes (1987 *F.U.N.* and *Slice of Death* 1988) they kind of blended Cryptic Slaughter and D.R.I. with Slayer, in a pretty raw and pissed-off mode; definitely good stuff (especially the first tape that was mixed by Neurosis Steve Von Toll), and No Warning through their existence played alongside bands ranging from Death and Forbidden to T.S.O.L., Circle Jerks and Operation Ivy. Assolt (Penn Valley, California) on their 1987 *Compression Exceeded* cassette they went for the metal- hardcore approach as this was reviewed of fanzines of the day, but sadly I couldn't find this release anywhere to review it. The same applies for Media Freak (Elizabeth, New Jersey) and their 1987 *Always Forward, Never Straight* cassette; metal hardcore (with some dodgy song titles such as 'My Bitch' and 'Cops are Gay'…come on guys), however this release was nowhere available to be reviewed.

(Atomic Gods live 1988. Courtesy unknown)

Dead Aim (Virginia Beach, Virginia) on their perfect 1986 *Dorks on Dope* cassette they headed for the 'Motörhead meets Poison Idea' slightly metal hardcore. This is one of my favourite unknown releases of that era! This is just flawless, fist-banging metal hardcore that's not superfast but it's super brutal. Songs like 'Fuck You' or 'Hometown Holocaust' are just frenetic, and Dead Aim went to release one more cassette of this top quality in 1986, *Blood is Sweet/Homeboy*. I think that they are still active because in 2014 they self-released the *Hellfire Stoked* mini-CD, and seem to be active on Bandcamp. All top releases for fans of late 1980s Poison Idea! Pleasington, California's Thrashing Hectic Circle on their 1987 *Christian Brainwash Demo* they shared a resemblance with the more metal-sounding California anarcho bands of their era (such as Final Conflict), and obviously as you might guessed it, it rules. Fast and heavy metal anarcho hardcore, with a great political message and bloody tunes like 'Blot Test' and 'Violently ill'. Suburban Death Trip (from Iowa City, Iowa) on their 1985 *Mind Shattering Power Blasts Demo* and their 1986 *Psychodelic Discore* LP are maybe one of the few bands that I could call as 'snotty crossover'; the ultra-snotty vocals of P.J. Partyhead, mixed with the total underproduced sonic approach are enough to prove this allegation. Their LP is weird, but great. It's totally recommended for those that can appreciate non-conformist stuff. Songs like 'Bang' are just so nasty!

Nuclear Jealousy (Fort Wayne, Indiana) on their sole release, the 1990 *Corrosive* demo went for a total COC (*Animosity* era) approach, and as you can imagine it's just brutal and heavy crossover, with no commercial tendencies whatsoever. Good stuff, and songs like 'Exceeding Corrosive' shows their approach. Demented (Noble County and DeKalb County, Indiana) formed in 1988 and included Ed Sawyer of Nuclear Jealousy. They released in 1991 the demo *Pacification By Violence*; blending doom and death and thrash metal with hardcore, this even reminds me of a heavier Dream Death-not a fan of this style but it's very powerful. Hatred (from West Orange, New Jersey) formed in 1984 and kept it up in the 1990s; up to 1998 with another name, as Planet Dread. They released about seven demos, from 1985 to 1987. Hatred's style was rough and heavy crossover with a strong Suicidal and Agnostic Front influence, and songs like 'Look What Have You Done' or 'No Control' that appeared on *Complete Death II* compilation from Death Records (1988) are just hard-hitters. Hatred members also played in the slightly more metal-sounding Corpse. Civilian Terrorists (Cleveland, Ohio) on the other hand released just one demo-the 1986 *Dark Inside* demo-but what a crazy release it was! Fast, pissed-off, full of mosh parts speedcore of the highest order, wish somebody re-releases this bad boy. Check out 'I'm Not' and find it out for yourselves.

Lethal Injection (Las Vegas, Nevada) formed in 1986 and contained Greg Falzone, later of Righteous Pigs. Their 1988 demo *Penetrate The Skin* was a lo-fi speedcore hit, reminiscent of bands like Desecration or the rawest output from Lethal Aggression; and I'm a sucker for this stuff. In the 1990s more releases followed, where they went for the death metal territory. Lethal Injection are still active (2025). Snag (Clifton, New Jersey) released two good demos of crossover thrash in the 1980s: *Ignorance is Bliss?* (1988) and *Rage in Unity* (1989), before heading for a more death metal style later in the 1990s. Again, good stuff, like the ultra-firing power of 'Thrash or Die' and 'Rage in Unity'. Some Snag members also played in the death metal act Solemn in the 1990s. Solitude (Boston, Massachusetts) included the late John McCarthy (of Post-Mortem) and John Alexander; their sole offering, *Gristle* demo (1988) was a punishing doom metal hardcore crossover, like a more hardcore Saint Vitus. Interesting stuff, even though it's not my cup of tea. On the same style, Parasite from Washington, DC on their *Gathering Strength* demo (1989) went for a doom metal meets hardcore combo too; again I think that this kind of blend is unique, but I can't go crazy over this.

Voluntary Manslaughter (Whittier, California) release only one demo (1985), and one known live appearance of them was with Dark Angel, Papsmear, and 5150 in January 1986. Scott Leonard (of Righteous Pigs) drummed for them but couldn't find the demo anywhere. Righteous Pigs (Las Vegas, Nevada) enjoy a cult fanbase all over the world for their musical mix of death metal with crossover and grindcore. Both their records, *Live and Learn* (1989) and *Stress Related* (1990) are considered classic releases especially from death metal and grindcore fans. I like them both, good, enjoyable and brutal stuff. Gut Instinct (Baltimore, Maryland) are such a unique case of crossover. They started in the 1980s with a style that was reminiscent of bands like Walk Proud or Bold, albeit more metal as heard on their two excellent demos: *Rage and Fury* (1989) and *D.T.P. Sessions* (1990). Then they headed off for a meatier, metal hardcore style in 1990 with *Disturbing the Peace* 7-inch and the *Off The Deep End* demo (1992). Their song 'Disturbing the Peace' was featured in the 2024 action film *Rebel Ridge*, and Gut Instinct have reunited in various occasions up to 2024 (now, in 2025 they are split). I love the sound of their first two demo, so nasty!

Allergic Reaction from Tewksbury, Massachusetts released an unbelievably professional demo in 1990, *Allergic Reaction* containing two songs in a total Ludichrist style (on their second LP), heavy, with weird rhythms and crazy musicianship-just check out 'New Kids'. Their style was a huge step forward from their early 1980s days as P.B.A. (and their *Peanut Butter and Anarchy* demo that was good). While they continued changing names, this time as Drawback in 1991, releasing the *Drawback* demo; now more bitter than before, with a total Cro-Mags from *Best Wishes* era-meets-Ludichrist. Still exciting, crunchy hardcore crossover stuff and 'Be Aware' is a great song. Augmentation (Chicago, Illinois) on their only demo (1990) played a more controlled crossover that was on the thrash metal side, with no speed outbursts, but more reminiscent of the chunkier sounds of NYHC like M.O.D. This is pretty enjoyable stuff and songs like 'The Dead' or 'Shattered Brains' are cool. Contortion Session (Austin, Texas) was born after a jam in 1985 at local punk rock band, Bark Hard's, practice space. Their only offering was the 1989 demo, into crossover hardcore style, good. Mosh Until Death (Hillsborough, California) formed by two members of the death thrashers Insanity in 1985. Their first effort was released in 1999, *One World Order* CD. Basic thrash hardcore, okay stuff, but nothing too special.

(Allergic Reaction 1990 picture. Courtesy unknown)

Sloppy, fast, raging and fun-these are the words to describe the musical output of Satan's Bake Sale (Camp Hill, Pennsylvania). Formed in 1985 by members that went later to play in the grindcore Exit-13, Satan's Bake Sale released two demos, one 7-inch and a split of weird, demented crossover hardcore, with a sound reminiscent of Hellhammer meets D.R.I. *We're Cookin Now* 1986 demo is just hilarious, while *Boombox tape 85* is almost reminiscent of musical atrocities like Kuolema, total noise. I was searching for the Stress (San Mateo, California) demo in *Crossover The Edge*, and happily found it now; their 1990 *This Ain't No Time to Be Doubtful* demo is just a top release, in the vein of bands like Excel, with the anarcho of Final Conflict and Dissension thrown in (plus some weirder jazzy parts), very enjoyable all over, especially tracks like 'Enough' or 'Literally'. 911 (Milwaukee, Wisconsin) on their *911* demo (1989) were just unbelievably brutal and inspired on the same time: taking their cues from D.R.I., Lethal Aggression and Dr. Know. One song, 'Little Girls' is an absolute disgrace, otherwise cuts like 'Faces of Death' and 'Am I Dead' are making up for one hell of a demo; just track it down. Sadly, couldn't find the Aftermath (Boulder, Colorado) *Demo-June 1989* (1989) to review it, I only have some info about some of their gigs with Dead Silence, Dissent, Soak, and Expatriate. And their favourite bands included Corrosion of Conformity, Violence, Cro-Mags, Agnostic Front, and Testament.

(911 band photo collage. Courtesy unknown)

Aggressive Injection (Flint, Michigan) sound as rough as you can imagine on their 1990 *Rehearsal Demo*; it has a certain charm, a major COC influence (especially songs like 'Cyclops' or 'Lifeless'). It's a pity that they didn't release something more. Couldn't find anywhere Apocalypse Culture's (Kansas City, Missouri) *Cycle of Existence* (1990) demo; no information about the band whatsoever. Arise (Chicago, Illinois) included Frank Ciampi (later of Devastation and Mindfunk) as well as Mike Le Gros (Jungle Rot). Their *Adrenalin* demo from 1990 focusses on the more thrash metal side of crossover in 50 percent of the songs, while the other 50 percent is more hardcore-oriented. 'Abducted' is an amazing song, and so is 'Only a Lie', both in the hardcore crossover camp. Betrayed S.B. (Sagamore Beach, Massachusetts) lasted from 1987 to 1992 and their weird mix of thrash and death metal with slight crossover tendencies isn't something memorable on the *1987-1992* compilation. On the contrary, Blasphemous (Mad Heights,

Michigan) were amazing; formed in 1985 and releasing their first cassette EP in 1987 (*Frustration*), they had a more hardcore sound initially with metal leanings. I can't recommend enough of *Frustration*, it's a thrash punk feast, a manic ride! Their first and only CD, the 1991 *Grooving With The Mutants* went for a more thrash metal direction, with crazy, and challenging musicianship, and it's just great stuff; and oh man, those crazy vocals of Rick Beard!

(Blasphemous with Ugly But Proud, Kriegs Legion and Major Dissapointment at Corktown Tavern. 14/01/1988)

Torment (Elizabeth, New Jersey) headed for a Nuclear Assault approach on their crossover that is riffy, thrash metal with hardcore tendencies, simple and brutal. Good stuff on their 1993 *Torment* demo, especially 'Protect and Serve'. They continued performing later in mid-1990s as Blasted, releasing two more demos. I imagined that a band named as Blind Justice (San Diego, California), would have a definitive Agnostic Front influence; I was wrong. Yes, there is some elements in songs like 'Revolution' on Blind Justice's 7-inch, *Don't Disturb Me Now/Egg on Your Head* (1991) and the *What Did I Do?* demo (1992) sound like late 1980s Suicidal Tendencies, okay stuff. No idea whatsoever about the musical approach of Bulimic Worms (Reading, Pennsylvania), only that they are reportedly a crossover band in their 1990 demo. Burnt Offerings (Boston, Massachusetts) included Kevin Norton that later played with Doom Loop and Serpent Saints (both sludge and doom). Their style was a sloppy metal punk, that had its charm on the Burnt Offerings demo (1988); 'Live Free' is a good song. C.C.S. (Anaheim, California) were a Christian crossover band. That's a pity, because in musical terms, their first demo (1988) is just fine metal punk, with songs as catchy as 'Two Hand Slam'. Their next two demos, *The Demo* (1989) and *A Prelude to a Sin* (1991) went for a more metal direction.

C.O.M.A. (Lynbrook, Long Island, New York) included later members of Vasaria, Sickness and Dem Brooklyn Bums, with their *Demo 1* (1989) and *Ask a Stupid Question... Get a Kick in the Head!!!* (1990) demo nowhere to be found. The same applies to Cerebral Meltdown Council (Orange County, California), who included members of Phantasm and Crucial Fixx. Released in 1990, their demo, *Pollution, Corruption and the American Way* wasn't available anywhere. Chaotic Evil's (Bakersfield, California) only demo released in 1986 was a real scorcher: fast and wild speedcore, a la early Excel! Chemakill (Eugene, Oregon) were formed by Mike Scheidt (of Vhol, Yob, Geistus, Middian, H.C. Minds, The Lumbar Endeavor, Soot) and both their *Chemical Playground* demo and their *The Power of Bob* 7-inch (1991) reminded me of a crude version of Leeway, heavy, hard-hitting and melodic crossover, with great guitar solos. Choke n' Gag'er (San Francisco Bay Area, California) on their 1990 demo tape they reminded me of D.R.I.'s *Thrash Zone* gone more metal; it's good! Songs like 'Spun' will bring in mind this comparison.

(Chaotic Evil band picture, 1986. Courtesy unknown)

Chronic Decay (Burlington, Vermont) formed in 1989 as Metally Insane until 1995. They only released one demo, but what a good release it was! The 1991 *Six Feet of Earth Makes All Men Equal* demo is weird, metal hardcore that never goes into lightning-fast speed but still has great moments. Not perfect, but still above par stuff. Contorted Souls (Kennesaw, Georgia) released just one four track demo in the late 1980s and it's of course, ridiculously rare to be found. Cornucopia of Death (Evansville, Indiana) included drummer Jeremy Spencer who played live with W.A.S.P. In musical terms, their two demos, the 1990 *Cornucopia of Death* and 1991 *Nip It in the Bud* were good, but in lyrics terms…avoid. Well-recorded though, with some great musical moments. Crucial Fix (Los Angeles, California) had too their good musical moments in their two releases, *1990 demo* and the *Racially Monitored* EP (1996) that is their best, with a very rough metalpunk sound. Get the latter, it could also appeal to gutter punks too!

Deelspeed (Yorktown Heights, New York), what a shame man, a Christian crossover band that in musical terms is amazing. Unbelievably rough, fast, with NYHC influences. Both their demos, *Faster than Death* (1991) and *Ludicrous Speed* (1992) are unbelievable. *Faster Than Death* took the early NYHC sound of bands like The Abused, Urban Waste and Kraut and blended it with crossover; but sadly, with Christian lyrics; come on, this is not fair! Ludicrous Speed is excellent too, so, can please someone take off the lyrics and replace them? Deelspeed will be an exception to my rule of 'no religious bands', as I will recommend their *Faster Than Death* demo (1991). Demented Aggressor (Clarkston, Michigan) on their only release, the *Demented Aggressor* demo (1988) went for the ultra-speed Cryptic Slaughter approach, mixed with The Accüsed; they were good. Democracide (Medford, Massachusetts) played several gigs at Boston's The Channel with Subjugator, Vio-lence, Flotsam and Jetsam, Defiance, Krash Palace, Dirt Cheap, Aggressor, Delusion, Crystal Myth (unclear which one), Dread, Zonehead, and Gang Green. However, their two 1980s demos were nowhere to be found.

Desolate Life (Cincinnati, Ohio) on their two demos, *Screaming Yellow* (1989) and *Understand?* (1990) went for the thrash hardcore approach being decent with more metal than other crossover bands of their era. Devious Misfortune (San Francisco Bay Area, California) played shows with Havoc, Terminus, Autopsy, Epidemic, and Epitaph. Their crossover was mostly metal-oriented on the 1987 *Meet The Disease* demo. I'm not such a fan of this style; it's way too heavy metal oriented. But still, this is good, especially the guitar riffs. But oh, these high-pitched vocals, Discourse (St. Louis, Missouri) existed for three years (1989-1992). Their only release, the 1991 *Discourse* demo sounded like a very rough cross between Slayer and The Accüsed. I like the brutality of this release, and the fact that it's very hardcore-oriented. Plus, 'Virus Afterlife' is a good song, with great lyrics. Doom Patrol (Easthampton, Massachusetts) formed in 1989 and lasted up until 1992, before changing name to Doom Nation and heading for a groove metal style. Their 1990 demo named as 'Fruit Jacks' is decent, basic, but very well recorded, crossover, reminiscent of Ludichrist and Mucky Pup. Heavy and catchy, check the song 'Cereal w/out milk'. Dread from Austin, Texas included Mike Peoples (later of Skrew and 3D House of Beef). Their 1988 *Dread Dread Dread* demo is crude and sloppy but has its charm; plus, I've been searching it for ages and finally got it.

Empty Grave (Chicago, Illinois) on their three releases: *New Year's Evil 1986* (1987), *Funeral Rates* (1990) and *Slaughter You to Sleep* (1991) sounded unbelievably rough and lo-fi, while their metal punk is pretty basic. Eternal Chaos (New York, New York) released the *Demo 1989*, reportedly a crossover demo, but was nowhere to be found. The same applies for F.C.A. (Ridgewood, New Jersey) and their ridiculously named 1987 demo *Blow It Out Your Hole!*; nowhere to be found. The only information found is that it was bassist Tim Scott (Methane, Revenant, HatePlow, Margrave, Volturyon, Parasyte) first band. F.U.B.A.R. (Webster, New York) on their 1991 *Beyond All Repair* demo had their good moments, especially on songs like 'Time To Play'; good, metal crossover, with mosh parts and controllable, much like early M.O.D.

with some Metallica influences, decent stuff. I couldn't though find the demos of F.U.B.A.R. from Long Beach, California, that Dark Angel's Gene Hoglan and Cris McCarthy played on, reportedly both filed under the crossover tag, especially the 1989 *The Drunk Undead* demo. Fatal Image from Connecticut released only one demo, the 1989 *Shock Therapy*, that is weird, amateurish, heavy…mostly metal crossover, with hardcore vocals, nothing to flip over, but mostly nostalgic stuff.

It is said that in Flembile (Oakley, California) Steve DiGiorgio played drums on the band's demo, and another member of Sadus may have been involved as well (not being confirmed though). Their 1988 *Ya! We Smoke Pot* sounds like a cross between Exodus, Cryptic Slaughter and The Accüsed, but more lo-fi, rough and punishing stuff. Forgotten Existence from Maryland released just one excellent demo in 1992, the *Demo '92* that was a metal approach heard on New York bands like Outburst, Alone in a Crowd or The Icemen. Super exciting stuff, especially songs like 'Scarred For Life'. Somebody should re-issue this gem! On the contrary, Fruit Salad from Racine, Wisconsin, in the 1991 demo *The Fruit Is Family* went on for a total Living Colour and Bad Brains worship, with a more metal sound, and obviously not as groundbreaking. Still decent though. Gardy-Loo! From Tampa, Florida, are active since 1989, and their metal punk is good in terms of music but, I can't stand their humour too on their extensive catalogue of releases. If you were to pick one of their records though, I guess that *Perverts on Parade* is the choice. No *Demo 1991* found by Gates of Delirium (New York, New York), reportedly crossover; Jon Burko later played on Cerebral Hemorrhage.

Grimace from Austin, Texas released in 1990 a near-perfect demo of snotty metal punk, and was re-issued in 2020 by Rockpile Records on an LP. I'm a sucker for this kind of stuff. So, as you can imagine, this one rules! Been on the hunt for Hedonistic Cravings' (Charlottesville, Virginia) two releases since the release of *Crossover The Edge*. Both are thrash metal with high-pitched vocals and very slight crossover leanings; plus, lyrics on Christianity. Well, you already know my view on this kind of stuff. Hostile Force (South Plainfield, New Jersey) had a demo of an allegedly crossover style, *The Sickness* (1991). As much I tried, I couldn't find it to review it. Ignorance (Apex, North Carolina) had definitely their great moment in the history of crossover with the 1991 *Ignorance Is Bliss* demo. It alternates from crunchy metal to fast crossover, and 'False Warning' is a good song. Invixous (St. Louis, Missouri) participated in the *This Is St. Louis Hardcore* compilation cassette (1988). They played gigs with Megalith, Heaven's Flame, W.T.G., Ultraman, Duck Duck Goose and other St. Louis bands. They released at least two demos, with the *1987 demo* being an excellent speedcore release, fast, wild, hardcore-based and out of control! Songs like 'Ronbo' just shred. Knucklehead (Santa Ana, California) are another one fine metal-punk band, with a driving force. They released a self-titled six track EP in 1992 and appeared on *Rikk Agnew Smash Demos-Vol. II* compilation with their song 'Phony Woman', which included members of Power Assault, Hirax, Corruption, Prison and Visual Discrimination. Knucklehead's style is reminiscent of the Venice scene, albeit with a NYHC edge, and obviously I love it!

I'll pass their sexist demo cover, and some insanely dumb lyrics, and say that Lappuss were a thrash hardcore from Williamsport, Pennsylvania. *Content To Lick* demo was their only offering, released on cassette by Hellpit Productions in 1992. The demo features some good musical ideas and it's a 52-minute demo FFS! The humour and lyrics are just disappointing; 'Pleatherface' is a good song. Likkra (Milwaukee, Wisconsin) released one demo in the late 1980s, again a rarity that isn't available anywhere (reported as a crossover band though). Another one Lost Because, this time from Austin, Texas, and their 1988 *Another Day, Another War* demo. It is basic metal crossover, not crucial, not bad though. Lunacy (Ann Arbor, Michigan) released two demos during 1989 and 1990 in ridiculously limited quantities. In 2005 these were re-released, and once again very limited numbers along with the demos from Head Factory and Road Kill on CD. I searched everywhere for this one but no luck, just an inactive link. Lycanthropy (unknown city of origin) released a demo named as *Tribes of the Moon*, that was rough, sounding like a cross between Carnivore and Misfits; 'Concubine' is a great song that's an example of this blend, while the other songs are more Carnivore-influenced, but not so inspired.

Meatlocker (Lake Worth, Florida) had a definite crossover sound in their early 1990s *Keep The Faith* and *1991 Demo*, while later they went for a more 'Biohazard-meets-crossover' sound on the 1994 *Triangle of Pain* CD released on Nuclear Blast Records, cool stuff. 'Who's Your God' is definitively a winner, and 'Oi Hate' is an antifascist anthem. Members of Meatlocker later played on Hellwitch and Disciples Of Icarus. Meatwagon (St. Petersburg, Florida) followed the 'D.R.I.-meets-Suicidal Tendencies' formula on their *Demo 1989*. While it is rather unpolished and lo-fi, the quality of band shines. 'Skitzoid' and 'Herve' are definitively good songs. Milk Toast (Freeville, New York) on their 1989 demo are reportedly a crossover band, but I couldn't find it to review it. Their continuation as Creeper was good, like a NYHC band on Celtic Frost; just check their demos and the unbelievably rare, self-financed 1992 *Creeper* CD. Monument (Beaver Dam, Wisconsin) on their 1991 *Be Slayin' Ya!* Demo attempted a mix of Metallica with some crossover, pretty generic, I think. Morbid Truth (Thousand Oaks, California) formed as Malicious Intent in late 1980s, with their two releases *Now What?* (1990) and *Living This Way* cassette (1991) are just brilliant, professionally executed crossover, with a slight Metallica influence. Listening to *Living This Way* and you'll be left speechless both with the band's crossover style, that the resemblance with Metallica, especially the intro. Mounds of Bullshit (West Orange, New Jersey) were more into the speedcore ferocity on their mid-1980s demo, obviously very Lethal Aggression meets Nuclear Assault, but not with the qualities of both bands, still okay.

(Morbid Truth with Adolescents at Mogz, Ventura, CA. 21/09/1991)

Negative Existence (Stratford, Connecticut) were on the sloppy and rough side of speedcore, more hardcore-oriented and as nasty as I love it on their *Victim of Life* demo with some great riffs here and there make it a worthy demo to listen to. Nickel Brains (Aurora, Illinois) were an amazing band, with just one cassette under their belts, the *Forward Message* (1990). Blending Suicidal Tendencies and the Venice Sound with NYHC and crazy musicianship, they pulled off great tunes such as 'Forward Message' or 'Modern Day Inquisition'. However, I'm not going to add *Forward Message* on the proposed list to the end, due to the sexist, misogynist lyrics of 'Toxic Bitch'; it's such a pity that a band that was nearly excellent, released this one. No Escape (Shirley, Long Island, New York) released two cassettes, the 1988 *Beyond Reality* and the 1990 *Lack of Life*, and while the former is more on the metal and thrash side, the latter reminded me of a weird mix between Crumbsuckers and Beyond Possession, in a more metal way. Crazy and highly unique stuff here, weird rhythms and brilliant musicianship. The songwriting skills are there, just check out 'Snow Melts Away' and 'Lack of Life' with its infectious melodies. Highly recommended!

Pestilence (Detroit, Michigan) released just one demo, *Empty Promises* cassette (1988) that I sadly couldn't find it. As reported, a crossover thrash band. Poser Patrol (Torrance, California) were one of the first crossover bands, led by Trevor Rick, and their sound on the *Demo '84* is like a mix of Venom with punk, albeit cruder and nastier, with songs like sharp shocks. A good one. Premonition (Bakersfield, California) were a thrash speed metal band, with some slight crossover overtones on their *Premonition* demo (1988). Not a fan of this total metal stuff, too technical, and they drag for too long, but I think that fans of e.g. early Testament and early Exodus, will enjoy it. Choosing a name like Punchin' Judy for your band is really nasty; but I found that they weren't misogynist, since their logo was a female punching another female. This band was from Bristol, Tennessee, were good in their metal speedcore on the 1991 *Punchin' Judy* cassette as well as in their more hardcore-oriented, *Figure IV* CD; wild stuff here, with some explosive riffs, and the brutal speed attacks that only bands from a hardcore background can offer. Just check songs like 'I've Got an Angle' or 'Nothing Sacred'.

With a name like Regurgitation you can't expect something cute and clean sounding, right? The Mesa, Arizona band had an unbelievably rough sound on their hardcore thrash demo, *Nothing Makes You Sick? Wait Until You Hear This!* (1987), however it was pretty uninspired. On the other hand, Retik (Seattle, Washington) were total class crossover in their 1989 *Choose Your Sentence* demo. There is a definite The Accüsed influence, however Retik are more clean-cut, and even though the constant use of double-bass drumming makes me sick, songs like 'Choose Your Sentence' and 'Spit The Skull' are more than good. Ripping Headaches (Ridge, Long Island, New York) on their 1989 demo went for the typical crossover thrash, not memorable or special at all. Three of their members later formed the true metal band Iron Rainbow that enjoyed some success in the heavy metal underground. Sarcasm (New York City, New York) included Eddie Cohen who went on to play with Altercation, Leeway, Sick of it All and Both Worlds and drummer Jimmy Williams who continued on to drum for Nausea, so you can expect that their sound must have been genuine and great, you are right. On their two demos, *Man of God?* (1986) and *War Song* (1986), Sarcasm released top-notch speedcore, wild and underproduced, with all that nasty NYHC sound, blended with guitar licks. Both demos are unbelievable and you have to get the Radio Raheem compilation LP (2019) because songs like 'Death Strike' and 'Back Off' will make you bounce on the wall! No idea what Scam (Plano, Texas) sounded like on their *Antiques* demo (1987); however, song titles like 'I'm Glad the Bitch Is Gone' are not intriguing at all.

Scum Lord (Akron, Ohio) are and were racist assholes, so I had no interest of listening to their crappy output. Scum of the Earth (Dallas, Texas) were a wild combo of COC meets Crumbsuckers on their nearly perfect *Introduction to Filth* demo (1989). Sadly, they have an unreleased recording, the *Infestation of Filth* full-length, later referred to as *Posthumous* (1991). Their demo is a real blast, check 'Metal Neck' and 'Color Blind'. Drummer Robert Knott narrates that "We listened to lots of punk and metal. Chris Thomas (guitar player) had a very deep music collection and was a DJ for KNON radio. The obvious ones were Slayer, Metallica and Suicidal but we were into more obscure stuff like Crumbsuckers, Accüsed, and Dr. Know. We were good friends with Dead Horse and toured with them a lot along with Morbid Scream. I really liked the Ramones but no one else in the band thought they were cool".

Self Destruct (New Jersey) included Keith Davies and Tim McMurtrie, both of M.O.D. and Angry Corpses, their 1990 Self Destruct demo is pissed-off hardcore thrash, a good one. I still recall the day I got Senslis Killin's (New London, Connecticut) *Chainsaw Boogie* 12-inch EP (1989). Initially I was disappointed by their motorpunk metal approach, just because I wanted more speed and less double-bass, but now, I enjoy it. Especially songs like 'Crime'. Members of the band worked as roadies for Nuclear Assault and released one more *It's Only Fun Until Someone Gets Hurt* cassette (1991), still on the same level, good stuff! Sgt. Billhead (Detroit, Michigan) follow the humorcore style of crossover, with such intelligent song titles as 'Santa's Got a Boner' or 'She Had A Dick' on their *Apocalypso* cassette (1990). Duh.

Socially Incorrect (Holbrook, Long Island, New York) included Tom Capone (1000 MPH, Antidote, Beyond, Bloodclot, Bold, Crippled Youth, Handsome and countless others) and Vic Dicara (Inner Strength, 108, Beyond, Burn, Inside Out, Reach Out, Shelter, etc). On their *Socially Incorrect* demo (1987) is, as you can imagine, a real speedcore fest. Catchy, crazy and to the point, it hits all the spots, with songs like 'Private Holocaust' and 'Prison of Glass'. Somebody should re-issue it! Sonic Lords (Jacksonville, Florida) have released five demos from 1987 to 1991, and one CD, *Mystery and Madness* (2004). On their 1991 *Scenes of Horror,* they sounded like Celtic Frost mixed with Cro-Mags; of course, not as inspired as both bands, but you get the point. A little too metal for my taste, this is heavy and menacing crossover thrash that will please fans of the heavier sounds. Check 'No Way', it's a good song. Speed Weenie (Portland, Oregon) included members of Macht and Wreck Creation (that will be referred later) and released three demos between 1987 to 1989 that sadly weren't available anywhere.

Stormbringer (Port Angeles, Washington) formed in 1989, and released just one good demo, the *Stormbringer* (1994), that was mostly into the mid-tempo metal hardcore style of that era (no speedcore shots here). Above par. Substance (Troy, Clifton Park and Albany, New York) were originally called Hard Times. They were heavily influenced by Cro-Mags and used to play Cro-Mags covers. Members went on to play in All Fall Down, Cutthroat, and Stigmata. Their 1989 demo had a definite character of their own, while they mixed in the Cro-Mags from their demo days as influences. Heavy, abrasive and punishing, the Substance demo kind of reminds me of bands like Outburst or Breakdown. 'Pressure Point' and 'Build Up' are great songs.

T.F.N. (Jackson, New Jersey) are referred in *Crossover The Edge*, on the Lethal Aggression section, since Dave Gutierrez played with them alongside with two members of Social Decay, Mike "Lunkhead" Roberts and Eddie Ramos. Their demo from 1986, *Political Death* is a mental barrage of noisy speedcore, ten songs in 9 minutes, blast after blast! The eponymous song is just a rager, and so is 'Life but Whos?'. This one needs a re-issue. At last, found the demo from Tarrasque (Kaneohe, Hawaii) from 1990, but sadly is nothing more than a pretty average crossover thrash, with a Suicidal Tendencies touch. 'Responsibility' is a very good tune. Technocide (Monrovia, California) released in 1990 their *Problems* demo that was reviewed in *Aaaarrghh* #7 (1991), where their sound is compared to that of Eviction, Faith or Fear and Ludichrist. I guess mostly metal crossover is their case, technical and more professional.

(T.F.N. band 1986, New Jersey. Courtesy unknown)

The Bang Gang (Atlanta, Georgia) were a three-piece band that split up in 1989 when Doyle Bright got recruited by Rigor Mortis and moved to Texas. Drummer Kelly Sanford soon moved to Texas as well and joined Arcane. Their only release was *The Bang Gang* demo (late-1980s), but I couldn't find it. Presumably, crossover thrash, on the metal side of things. The Council (Dallas, Texas) went on for a speed metal hardcore crossover on their decent *Live Demo* (1988). The Detrimentz from New Orleans, Louisiana, went on for a NYHC-fused crossover sound, like a cross between AF's *Cause For Alarm* with the Youth Crew on the 1989 *Face Reality* demo, which is simply fantastic! They also had a track on the *New Orleans Scene: Allow No Downfall* compilation 7-inch (1991) and disbanded. Check out 'Your time has come' and 'Morbid World'. The Killer Kitchen Utensils (Chicago, Illinois) released three demos from 1989 to 1992, with the 1989 *A Week To Live* being my favourite. Not as metal as other crossover bands of the time in 1989 and onwards, this one's into the speedcore style, with some crazy guitar licks. Tracks like 'A Soldier's Soul' or 'Man' are tasty.

The Not Wanteds (Rochester, New York) on the 1988 *Take Out the Trash* demo they went for a double-bass motorpunk approach, mixed with NYHC and NY crossover. I usually don't like the double-bass stuff, but in their case the hardcore element is very strong, and the songwriting is good too. Check out 'Political Prisoners' and 'Anxiety'. Throttle (Philadelphia, Pennsylvania) included Chuck Treece (Activate, Activator, Bad Brains, McRad) on drums and they released two demos, both in 1989; and the *New Freaks on the Block* 7-inch (1990). All their output sounded like a more metal thrash version of Bad Brains, and of course it's ace! Just listen to 'Thin Line'. Transgressor (San Jose, California) was one of the first bands of Steve Von Till (later in Neurosis among many others), and their 1987 *Transgressor* demo was a total holocaust of speedcore brutality as if Christ on Parade went slightly metal. Crucial stuff, and songs like

'Cold Storage' and 'DUI' have to be heard to be believed. Useless Degenerates (Santa Monica, California) formed in 1986 and their only release, the *Demo 1987*, suffered from an unbelievably bad production, however their total D.R.I. influence was evident, and it was good.

V.O.M. stands for Visions of Mortality (Brooklyn, New York). They got their name from the 1984 Celtic Frost song, being that they're one of the bands thanked in the j-card of their only known demo release, *Day Of Question* (1991). The demo follows the pattern 'Celtic Frost gone NYHC', and it's evil, heavy, and rough. Violent Carnage were a Bronx-based hardcore speed metal band, formed in the late 1980s; their 1990 *Violent Carnage* demo was nasty and rough, and more on the hardcore side of crossover, with great songwriting like 'Mistake' or 'Victory' (too bad that 'Lie Till You Die' is just a sexist crappy song). Violent Insanity (Chicago, Illinois) were rather a metal band with thrash death style and some slight crossover influences. Their sonic approach leaves me rather cold on *Final Chapter* demo (1989) and *Shadows of Doom* demo (1991), but I guess that metalheads will dig them. Wreck Creation (Portland, Oregon) released two demos, one split 7-inch with 90 Proof, and a full-length CD, *Wreck Creation*. Through their existence in 1990 to 1998, they had obviously a good The Accüsed influence! I love their 1991 *Steal this Tape!* demo, because it's well written and recorded, and still carries the hardcore influence all over. Sadly, the 1995 *Wreck Creation* CD went into the groove metal style that I detest with a passion. Maelstrom (Boston, Massachusetts) created a buzz with their groove and crossover thrash on their three releases, but I'll be honest: I couldn't stand this blend. Okay, it is musically challenging, but the whole 'groove' thing leaves me totally cold.

Ripped (North Canton, Ohio) formed in 1988 as RIPT. and after two very raw demos, they released the 1991 *Blotter* cassette, where their sound sounded like a cross between The Accüsed and Confessor, heavy and spastic, and very technical. I'm not a fan of this ultra-technical stuff, but I guess that some fans of techno-thrash will dig it. Their three next releases went for a more technical death metal sound. Skab (New Orleans, Louisiana) sounded to me just like Exhorder on their only release, the 1992 *Restrainer* demo; it's just a little bit more hardcore. Again, I am not a fan of this style. Terrorist (Seattle, Washington) formed in 1988 by Florida native James Dean (bass) and Washington natives Andy Massey (guitar) and Vence LaRose (drums). One of the unsung regulars of the Seattle metal scene, this power-trio had enough material for two albums, but regretfully only released a four-song demo, named as *Demo 1990*. It was a weird, but interesting mix of The Accüsed with technical thrash metal, it surely has its charm, especially in shorter songs like 'Detonate the Charge' and 'Tar'. Toxic Field Mice (Hartford, Connecticut) released one decent demo of crossover thrash with *Convulsion* demo (1992), before heading in for the dreaded groove/nu metal trend later on.

Attica (Grays Harbor, Washington) contained Aaron Burkhard who was the first drummer of Nirvana, and through their existence (1988-1991 and 2012-2013) they recorded twenty-seven tracks, all released on the *Don't Sleep Alone in the Dark* compilation CD. Metal crossover thrash is their style, like a more metal oriented The Accüsed (albeit not as crazy), still enjoyable, especially in more straightforward songs like 'Crack Attic' or 'JBJHA'. Bad Acid Trip (Los Angeles, California) had initially a more crossover hardcore style blended with grindcore heard in their 1989 to 1994 releases and then headed for a more grindcore approach-not really my thing, but kudos to them for being active up till today (2025). Bloodcum's (Los Angeles, California) story is pretty familiar for people into thrash metal, because bassist John Araya is Tom Araya of Slayer's brother. Bloodcum's musical output on the two demos from 1986 and 1987, as well as their 1988 *Death by a Clothes Hanger* LP could be described as 'Slayer gone crossover thrash'. Fast and wild, with a very rough sound. *Death by a Clothes Hanger* is totally recommended to people that want their crossover to be more metal with songs like 'Son of Sam' and 'Live to Kill' don't disappoint.

Charlotte's Webb (Bowling Green, Ohio) are one of the few exceptions to the 'no groove' rule that I have- and this is because their two demos, *Skeletons of South Street* and *Charlotte's Webb* are very powerful mosh metalcore, genuine stuff. Check 'Attain' and find it out for yourselves. After Dark (Sacramento, California) on their *1986 Demo* they went for a more traditional, mid-tempo approach of mixing heavy metal with punk. Interesting and unique, obviously with some Motörhead influences. Babylon (Anaheim, California) on their *Left To Die* Demo (1987) sounded amateurish (you can clearly hear drum programming), crude and with their ideas being not complete. Still though they have a certain charm, I mean it's okay hardcore thrash with a major punk influence. Bad Dog Bad (Bloomfield, New Jersey) formed in 1987 and are still active, up till today, with both the 1990 demo and the *Buried Alive* 1991 CD being metal punk, with the obvious Motörhead references, and some catchy tunes such as 'Danger Zone' or 'I Don't Give a Damn'. Okay stuff. Sadly, couldn't find Cremation's (Monterey, California) two demos, *The Burning* (1986) and *Three Faces* (1991); it's such a pity, because I'd love to listen to their 1986 (!) cover of 7 Seconds 'We're Going to Fight'.

Everybody's Problem (Collings Lake, New Jersey) formed in 1989 as Excruciating Pain and released three demos and one CD, *Crass* (1996). During their existence, they were decent metal punk, not something too special, still okay. Kilroc (Portland, Oregon) were another one metal punk combo, mid-tempo stuff mostly, with a good Motörhead influence on everything they released. Their *Demo 89* contains some catchy songs like 'Running Towards the Sun' and 'Sweet Sarah', and it also exists as a 2014 recording. Murder (San Francisco, California) have a very interesting story: Kurt Vanderhoof, Metal Church bassist for the Lewd originated the basic concept for Murder and wrote two songs in 1981: 'The Butcher', and 'Cease to Exist' before leaving the Lewd to eventually form Metal Church. He passed these songs on to then-Lewd guitarist Bob Clic. Bob approached bassist and long-time friend Ed, aka 'JU' MacNeill (Fuck-Ups, Legionnaires Disease) with the concept of a heavy metal band doing songs about serial killers, maniacs etc. and shared Kurt's two songs. Bob and JU conceptualized a splatter rock band and together wrote a set of songs in that genre. Drummer and graphic artist Danny DUI (Flyin' Fucking A-Heads) was then added, and he supplied poster art and the blood dripping Murder logo. Nyna Crawford (VKTMS) joined the band as singer and wrote lyrics for the songs. The result was the 1999 *Murder* 7-inch that contains two fantastic songs, 'Chainsaw Love/Slight Return' and 'Murder', metal punk of the highest order-get this now.

Vomitorium (Kensington, California) on their near-perfect *Ad Nauseam* demo (1987) had a fierce, lo-fi and unpolished sound, plus it is rumoured that the band that a few of the members were in some way related to other more established Bay Area metal bands. A // Solution (Long Beach, California) were an exceptional band of their era and place, because the followed the UK stenchcore style, blended with some crossover; fast and heavy, their 1989 *Butterfly* 7-inch sounded like Deviated Instinct mixed with Slayer and Celtic Frost, with some speedy moments reminiscent of Cryptic Slaughter. Political and raging, I can't recommend this enough for fans of this style. Check also their 1995 *Things to Come* CD. Pigmy Love Circus (Los Angeles, California) formed in 1987, are still active until today (2025) and have an extensive discography of hard rock and metal punk; not my cup of tea, still the 1989 *I'm the King of L.A. ...I Killed Axl Rose Today* 7-inch is a fun listen, but I guess that this kind of overproduced stuff is too 'rockish' for me.

House of Suffering (San Diego, California) formed in 1989 after Katon W. de Pena left Hirax and the demise of Phantasm. The rest of the lineup consisted in members of the hardcore punk band Amenity, and as you can imagine from their name, the Bad Brains influence is very vivid in their 1992 *Wired* 7-inch that is reminiscent of a more metal Downset. While Katon's vocals are simply unbelievable, maybe his best performances ever are evident on 'Wired' and 'Youth'. Mandatory of course! Forever Now (New Jersey) on their 1990 7-inch they went for a metal-thrash approach, with emo elements, and it's certainly interesting! Weird, but good, so check the song 'Burning Issue'. Kindred Idol (Ottokee, Ohio) started as a punk rock band in 1988, and their 1990 *In Memory Of...* cassette is rather typical, yet not memorable of this style. They went into sludge and doom metal later in the 1990s, releasing many records, but it's not my kind of thing at all.

Speed Demon (Monterey, California) formed as early as 1984, are still active today (2025) and released a good number of demos in 1980s, as well as the *Luna Demonics* CDEP in 2022. Their 1987 *Chemical Dependency* demo is a crude attempt to combine thrash-speed metal with some punk influences, with lots of force, but mediocre songwriting. However, 'D.S.F.P.H.' and 'Plastic Friends' are great blasts though, reminiscent of Attitude Adjustment, actually when they go for a crossover style, they are much better than when on thrash speed. The Assassins (Cupertino, California) on their *Demo 1982* attempted a crossover between hard rock, heavy metal and punk, decent stuff. I like this nostalgic tone a lot and 'Assassination' is a good song. Wharf Rats (Tacoma, Washington) formed in 1989 (featuring Dan Englund and Lonny Loomis later in Thrash Forward and Yuck Fou) and in their 1993 demo they had songs either on the thrash-speed style, or more crossover ones like, 'Cast a Spell'; good, powerful stuff, but not that crucial.

I was on the hunt for years to find any member from The Unjust (Bronx, New York) to get an interview, but with no luck. They started off as a NYHC band in their *1983 Demo* and the 1984 *Big City Don't Want*

No Pity! split 7-inch alongside Ultra Violence, Armed Citizens and No Control. As you can imagine you need songs like 'Ivan's Revenge' or 'No Justice' like air and water, if you are into the early 1980s NYHC sound (even though they still had a slight metal influence even then). Their only record, the 1987 *Hammerhead* LP was a move towards a power thrash style, with slight hardcore influences, and while the high-pitched vocals sometimes get on my nerves, this record is good, reminiscent of English Dogs mixed with Holy Terror. I still prefer their earlier output of course. *Hammerhead* is a record that people more into metal will enjoy. I just wanted to know how on Earth they went from NYHC to this power thrash style! Dunwich (St. Louis, Missouri) might have been one of the few crossover bands with female members, at one point they had three (Heather Koven, Kim Fahning, Dee Voyles); they formed in 1989 and their 1991 *Madman with a Headrush* demo was a sonic dynamite of hardcore thrash, with songs as brutal as 'Headrush/Madman' and 'Ashenland'. Their 1992 demo and the 1994 *Ignorance Powered by Greed* cassette went on a more metal thrash direction, still good, but I miss their early spark. Early Dunwich would even appeal to fans of Nausea or Sacrilege, as well as Znowhite.

Empty Tomb (Salem, Oregon) released seven demos from 1988 to 1993 of their own brand of splatter-rock, with a definite The Accüsed influence. I would recommend getting the *Eat It Like It Is (The Anthology)* 2012 compilation if you are into this sound. There are some good songwriting skills, especially in songs like 'Cheated (Welcome to the Human Race)' or 'They Say'. Grinchfist (Glendale, California) formed in 1990 as Termpatater and released four demos from 1993 to 1995, voted by *BAM* magazine and *Music Connection* magazine along with other magazines, more than once, as the best unsigned band in Los Angeles. They blended metal with hardcore through an alternative style, as evident in all their demos. There are good songs like 'B.A.', however when things move towards the groove metal in the Pantera style, well you know, I can't stand this kind of stuff. No idea how Hell Hound (Green Bay, Wisconsin) sound like on their 1988 *Burial Ground* demo. As reported, this is a thrash-hardcore release. Ruined (Van Nuys, California) formed in 1989 and included Bill Crooks (of Cryptic Slaughter) on vocals. As strange as it might sound, they were more into Pantera than in hardcore crossover on their *Inject Neglect* demo (1991), while their 1995 *Rule With An Iron Lung* cassette was by far better, fast hardcore thrash! Sad Reality (Westport, Connecticut) released a demo in 1990 reviewed in *Anti Poser* zine #8, where it's described as '...mid paced thrash, sorta like Armored Saint doing Cryptic Slaughter'. Couldn't find it anywhere to review it, and the comparison with Armored Saint wouldn't help much in my case, haha!

No idea what Sanguinairi (Holliston, Massachusetts) sound like on their 1988 *Learn to Live to Love to Hate* demo, that is described as 'hardcore thrash' on various databases; it seems to be a rarity to get hold of. Sinister (North Huntingdon, Pennsylvania) formed in 1985 and included Eric Good (Caustic Christ, The Sicks, Aus-Rotten) and Dave Fresch (Legendary Hucklebucks), so you can expect that their hardcore thrash sound was punk-oriented, fast, furious and very political on their *The Reich Is Dead* demo (1987), *Dawn of the Apocalypse* demo (1987), *Mark of the Deceiver* demo (1988) and *Crisis* demo (1989).

Excellent stuff all over, with *Crisis* demo being my favourite, because it sounds like UK82 and bands like Final Conflict gone hardcore thrash, as well as the songwriting. Tunes like 'Support No More' or 'Programmed Youth' are hard-hitters! Somebody please re-release all their demos?

It would be an overstretch to add Rorschach (New Jersey) in this book, however they formed in 1989, and their 1993 *Protestant* LP sounds like a cross between Die Kreuzen and Voivod. Not crossover in the strict sense of genres, but still, very metal-influence hardcore and unbelievably blinding as one of 1990s top records. Cottonmouth (St. Louis, Missouri) formed in 1989 and are active still (2025), having released three demos and five full-length CDs. Their sound is somewhere between Ludichrist's second LP and Scatterbrain, with way more metal touches. This is very technically challenging stuff so I won't slag them off, but their musical approach leaves me cold-Primus fans would maybe like them though. Apocalypse (Walnut, California) have been already referenced in the Transgression piece (due to their split 7-inch). They formed in 1984, and with a pause from 1990 to 2014 are back, still active (2025). In the 1980s, they sounded like a Californian take on Hellbastard and Deviated with Instinct and Axegrinder sound. Both their releases, *Krust* demo (1988) and *Earth* 7-inch (1989) being exceptional, highly inspired and political metallic crust. While in their later releases went a bit speedier, but still excellent stuff in the crust tradition. Start with *Earth* 7-inch and it's a sad fact that bands like A//Solution, Apocalypse and Glycine Max are still little known in both in punk and metal circles. Talking about Glycine Max (Long Beach, California), they formed in 1986, and they blended speedcore with stenchcore, rough, political and great stuff on their *Violent Mind/Peaceful Heart* LP (1990) and *Demo / Live* demo (1991). You can hear the echoes of Nausea, Amebix, Sacrilege in their sound; plus, some Doom and Hellbastard; you can't go wrong with songs like 'Take it Back'.

The Refuzors (Seattle, Washington) on their 1987 *Q. Why Do It, You'll Never Get Rich A. Cuz I'm A Refuser* cassette went for a hard rock and punk crossover, noisy, obnoxious and so much fun! They kept up this style to *Think I Lost My Faith* 7-inch (1993) and *Flashback* LP (1997), albeit with more garage edge. Listen to 'I'm a Refuzor' and go nuts! Brain Dead (Milwaukee, Wisconsin) formed in 1985 as Operation Beer Bound, and their only release was the 1989 *Sly Manila* demo, as well as two songs ('Zip My Pants' and 'Too Fat') on *Z-Rock 106.7 FM Classics 6* compilation LP. Nothing too special, just mediocre heavy thrash with a crossover edge. Leprosy (Hopewell Junction, New York) formed in 1986 and went for a thrash-doom and crossover blend, not too dissimilar than bands like Doom Watch, Dream Death or the slower Carnivore songs. Rough and heavy stuff as evident in their three demos, *Dripping Flesh* (1987), *Gangrene Intensification* (1987) and *Leprosy* (1988). Check songs like 'Atheism'. Okay.

Stonecrow (Bainbridge Island, Washington) released their great *Road Fauna* demo (1986) that is hardcore with slight metal influences before going on a full metal-crossover approach on their next two demos, the 1988 *Engulfed in Flames* and the 1990 *Island of Sorrow*. On their last demo, they took a massive Kreator influence and blended it with US crossover. While I'm not a fan of so metal stuff, this is just ace. Heavy and wild stuff, with songs like 'War Master' and 'Obstacles', Stonecrow sound like a mix of Kreator and Excel! Born Without A Face (Grand Rapids, Michigan) are filed under the hardcore bands with a slight metal edge. All their releases are exceptional, specifically their 1984 and 1985 cassettes, *Psych!* and *Freakshow* respectively were pure, frantic hardcore. On their two 7-inchs *The Unbecoming* (1986) and *Worship* (1987) incorporated metal riffs and solos in their crazy frantic hardcore, with lots of Discharge and Dr. Know influences; fast, heavy and wild stuff here. While *The Unbecoming* is more straightforward, *Worship* is more twisted, dark and vicious, and both belong to some of the best stuff ever released in the 1980s. Speaking of slightly metal hardcore, check songs like 'Teeth Machine', 'Black Narcissus' and 'Maelstrom' and get your head exploded! Mark Dancey later formed and played in Big Chief, another great band that mixed Black Sabbath with punk, but you are already familiar with them, right?

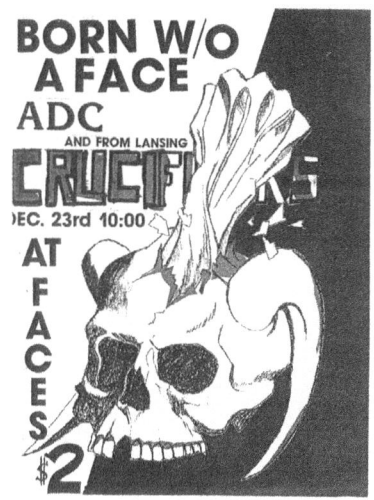

(Born Without A Face with Crucifucks at Faces Detroit, MI, 23/12/1985)

Have no idea where Frisky Archer are from, and their self-released *Patterns Of The Nighttime/Mystery Inside Tears* 7-inch (1980) is a crude attempt of mixing hard rock and metal with 1970s punk, inconsistent and uneven (but I guess that collectors of private records love to idolise this kind of stuff). Another band named Mayhem, this time from St. Louis, Missouri, who self-released two 7-inchs in the 1980s, in the same hard rock and punk style. Their 1981 *You Get What You Pay For* 7-inch is wild, and they mix The Stooges and Dead Boys with hard rock, with 'You Say/I Say' sounding like a cross between Stiff Little Fingers with Thin Lizzy! Sadly, I couldn't find anywhere their 1989 *Flight To The Sea* 7-inch. Dark Star formed in 1976 in Houston's Jacinto City suburb and disbanded in 1979, with their only release, they self-pressed 1000 copies *Spectre* 7-inch (1978). Dark Star being one of the earliest hard rock and punk crossovers when they cross Black Sabbath with the fuzzy punk guitars, with the biggest resemblance here being the early Wipers sound. As you can imagine this is just perfect. Just check out 'Sounds of the Sun'.

Thomas Lee Howell aka Tom "Major" Lazer (guitar/lead vocals) doesn't accept the term 'punk' in Dark Star's sound. This is way more punk than the typical hard rock or space rock of their day!

Blood (West Islip, New York) self-released two 7-inchs records on their own Blood Records, both in 1985. Their metal-hard rock blend with punk is average, mid-tempo and unmemorable, but I guess that fans of sleaze glam metal might enjoy *Teaser* 7-inch and *Fly All Night* 7-inch. Black Burn (Auburn, New Hampshire) followed too The Stooges, going hard rock style on their only release *Runaway / Head On To Hell* (1979). The track 'Runaway' being a hard rocker and 'Head On To Hell' going for the hard rock with punk crossover. Okay stuff, not something spectacular. Another one hard rock and punk crossover combo, Conzo Fury (Los Angeles, California) on their 1983 *Over The Edge* 7-inch. The eponymous song is good, representative of this style, while the flipside of 'Don't Do This To Me' is in the hard rock tradition. Crystal (Phoenix, Arizona) released on 1978 *I Gotta Go/You Shouldn't Be Loving Me* 7-inch, that is reported as a monster rarity of hard rock and punk crossover; sadly couldn't find it to review it. The same applies to Trilogy (Ft. Lauderdale, Florida) and their 1979 *The Top* 7-inch, that is described as a 'rock/punk' crossover. Nowhere to be found, plus there is also an unreleased LP by Trilogy named as *Find A New Star*. Again, a rarity, Skyhook's (no information available on their city of origin) and their 1981 *Low Life/Cronic Lateness* 7-inch, presumably a hard rock and punk crossover record. Abuse (Detroit, Michigan) took the Motörhead style, mixed in some Stooges, as well as classic heavy metal, and the result was the 1985 *Teacher's Pet / (I Wanna Be A) Cheerleader* 7-inch. The sound is powerful and catchy, but with awful lyrics. Such a shame, because in music terms this one rips. Have no idea what Lethal Dose sound like, while their 1987 demo named as *It's a Tough Life, But Someone Has to Live it* is described as 'slightly metallic hardcore'. I won't even discuss E.A.B. (Epileptic Albino Bullfrogs) and their 1987 *Epileptic Albino Bullfrogs* demo, because two idiots off them formed simultaneously two nazi bands, Arresting Officers and Elite Terror.

Exoteracy (Granada Hills, California) released one demo in 1989, and the perfect 1990 *Exoteracy* 7-inch; in their case, the crossover was way different. Exoteracy were a hardcore punk band with some slight metal leanings and brought also some elements of the (then) new powerviolence scene. *Exoteracy* was an ultra-fast rager, with seven blasts, and of course, it is totally recommended. Absence Of Malice (from Richmond, Virginia) on their 1985 *Awakening* 7-inch released six songs of ultra brutal, poisonous D-beat with a metal edge. Crushing stuff here! Abuse from Detroit, Michigan released on their label Thrash Records their sole effort, *Teacher's Pet / I Wanna be a Cheerleader* 7-inch (1985). A lo-fi, weird, but very enjoyable mix of Venom and Motorhead with Detroit hardcore punk. Against (Los Angeles), didn't release anything during their lifetime; however Grand Theft Audio released their 1984 unreleased album on the collection CD *No Arms* (1996). Like the Venice bands, Against had the Motörhead meets GBH catchiness with a huge added dose of Discharge. Fantastic stuff here, totally recommended for everyone into the Venice scene. Bam Bam from Seattle, Washington blended Motörhead with early 1980s US hardcore on their only release, *Stress* 7-inch (1984). The fantastic voice of Tina Bell is a scorcher, and Bam Bam sound so unique. Bam Bam's original lineup included Pearl Jam and Soundgarden drummer Matt Cameron and Tina Bell on vocals, who is the first black woman to front a hard rock, punk or grunge band in the US.

Bomb Squad from Washington D.C. went for a blend of punk rock with hard rock on their sole release, *Messin' Me* 7-inch (1982). Okay, nothing revolutionary here. Brunfuss from New Jersey were another band on Mutha Records band. Their only release, the 1984 self-titled LP includes some hardcore songs, some metal-fused punk such as 'Spandex Rock' and 'Old Too Soon', and a metal rap tune, 'Brunfuss Rap'. Enjoyable stuff here with the excellent vocals of Gail Jeanne. Bum Kon from Denver, Colorado released on 1983 the belligerent hardcore, *Drunken Sex Sucks* 7-inch, before going for a slight metal style on their next two releases, *Bum Kon* LP (1985) and *Ground Round* LP (1986). *Ground Round* is the better of this bunch, interesting mid-tempo metal hardcore with good songs like 'Tetracycline' and 'Butcher Block'. You are all familiar with the seminal NYHC band Cause For Alarm with a catalogue full of classic releases of course, all mandatory if you are into NYHC. Their band name was from the title of an Agnostic Front album by the same name. Their inclusion here is based on their 1983 demo that was released after *Cause For Alarm* 7-inch. Rockin' hardcore with lots of metal guitar licks, containing four excellent songs. 'Reflections' was re-released by Agnostic Front as 'Shoot His Load', while 'Time Will Tell' is one of the best songs Cause For Alarm ever written!

Cold Sweat from Bronx, New York on their *Chain Your Mind / Hide And Seek* 7-inch (1984) went for a brilliant mix of Dead Boys with heavy metal rock. Catchy as hell, mid-tempo metal punk. Can please somebody find me this one? Apparently only one hundred were made! Condemned to Death from San Francisco, California released in 1984 one of the most classic hardcore EPs of West Coast, *Condemned To Death*. Their first album and final release, *Diary of a Lone Monster* LP (1984) incorporated slower tempos and metal guitar licks and it was a great effort. Songs like 'Night of the Succubus' and 'The Assassin' just rip! Corporation Lounge from New Haven, Connecticut, released in 1984 the decent *Imported From America* 12-inch; a blend of mid-tempo punk with metal, okay. The Crewd from Long Beach, Los Angeles were balancing among the classic T.S.O.L. style and the Adolescents, with the addition of screaming vocals and some hard rock elements. Their *Gather 'Round* mini-LP (1983) is good. False Confession from Oxnard, California were one of the countless Mystic Records bands; their drummer Harry Misenheimer later played in Stalag 13 and The Cramps. Their 1984 *Left To Burn* 7-inch shares many commonalities with the metal hardcore of Dr. Know, and it's a stellar release. 'Left to Burn' and 'Just as I am' are my favourites songs off this 7-inch, while False Confession released a demo in 1983 with the same style. Freewill from New York City on their *Without Me / I Fought The Law* 7-inch (1985) took the Bad Brains approach, mixed it up with early Red Hot Chili Peppers and some metal guitar. It definitely sounded ahead of its time back then, but today it sounds generic.

Horrorshow from Northglenn, Colorado combined dark and horror metal with hardcore on their only release, *The Ed Sullivan Dance* 7-inch (1985). It is interesting, but not mandatory. Insanity Defense from Centerpoint, Long Island, and their alter ego, Satan's Cheerleaders get a special mention here. They are mostly a hardcore band with some metal influences. Their *Pilgrim State* LP (1985) is a really powerful release, while the demos of Satan's Cheerleaders are even wilder! Totally recommended stuff. Junior Achievement from Tempe, Arizona reminded me of D.I., albeit with a more metal crunch on the riffs and the guitar leads. Their *Fade to Black* LP (1984) is definitely highly enjoyable, especially songs like 'Dr. Cut Throat's Revenge' and 'Black Widow'. Knucklehead from Madison, Wisconsin released in 1985 their only LP, that was produced by Butch Vig; *I* includes eleven songs that balance between hardcore and speedcore, okay stuff, a few memorable songs such as 'P.O.W.' and 'You Dirty Kids'. Lad from Albuquerque, New Mexico had one of the cheesiest record covers on their *Downtrodden By Society* 12-inch (1985). The music though, is something else here! A solid mix of mid-tempo hardcore with metal, akin to Southern California bands, totally recommended.

L.D.S. from Salt Lake City, Utah went from the blazing hardcore of *On The Cross* 7-inch (1985) to the more metal-fused *Nightmare* LP (1986). *Nightmare* is unbelievably heavy and raging, and the faster songs remind me of Japanese hardcore bands! Okay, the horror lyrics leave me cold, but they add up to the whole frenzy. Manifest Destiny from San Diego, California had a definite metal edge in their venomous hardcore. Their 1983 mini-LP is good, however their next release, is even better. *We Love our Country* 7-inch is a sheer rager, just check out songs like 'Mr Jones' and 'Whose Power'. Modern Electrics from Cambridge, Massachusetts are a whole different story on their almost perfect *Kamikaze* 7-inch (1980). It is a blend of heavy metal riffs with punk, and the fantastic vocals of Soso Stoned, so, get it now. Musical Suicide from Cincinnati, Ohio and their cynical hardcore on the *Little Fish In The Big Sea* LP (1984) is a real treat for aficionados of this style, like me! It also incorporates some metal guitar licks and solos, even though it's not a crossover record.

The Prevaricators from Richmond, Virginia had a definite GBH influence into their sound, heard in early as 1983 when they released *No Kidding* 7-inch. Their first LP *Snubculture* (1985) integrated some more metal influences, still though very powerful and inspired. One more LP, *Détente* and a 7-inch, *Jihad* followed on the same style. Crossover-adjacent stuff? The same applies for Woburn, Boston band P.T.L. Klub. While they were never a crossover act, they always incorporated metal elements into their hardcore power. *13 Comandments* mini-LP (1985) is a stellar release. Also check out *Nobody Cares Anymore* 7-inch and *Living Death* 7-inch. I really love Rat Pack from Santa Barbara, California, and I wish I could get an interview from them. Their *Rat Pack* 7-inch (1985) is a fine example of muddy, rough and great speedcore; with the emphasis on 'core'. Their next two releases *Ice Cream, Acid & Cigarettes* 7-inch and *Rat Pack* LP (1990) headed towards a total Motörhead worship style with hardcore tendencies. Top stuff!

Secret Savior from Tonawanda, Buffalo, New York are fairly obscure, however this only adds up to the significance of their *First Love* 7-inch (1980); like Dead Boys gone NWOBHM, this is absolutely crucial! State from Ann Arbor, Michigan are one of the most classic first wave hardcore bands; their *No Illusions* 7-inch (1983) remains to this day a sheer exposure of ultra-core power, like The Fix or Negative Approach. State's *False Power* LP (1987) is heavy as hell, rough hardcore with a huge metal edge, and I love songs like 'Reign Of Terror' and 'Don't Tread On Me' that reminds me of Broken Bones! The State made a comeback in the 2000s and released seven 7-inchs on the old hardcore style, quality stuff. I think that most of you have heard the name of Vatican Commandos before, and that's because they were Moby's first band. Formed in Darien, Connecticut in 1982, they released two excellent hardcore 7-inchs (*Hit Squad For God* 1983 and *Just A Frisbee* 1983), reminiscent of C.I.A. and Reflex From Pain. On their last release, the *Point Me To The End* 12-inch they sounded like a more metal 76% Uncertain, still hardcore though, and always excellent.

Würm from Los Angeles were one of the very first examples of mixing heavy metal with punk; formed in the suburbs of Los Angeles 1974 by high school friends Gary McDaniel (later Chuck Dukowski) and Ed Danky, they were joined by drummer Lou Hinzo in 1976 and recorded an album around 1977 or 1978, but the record label failed to pay the studio bills and the tapes were recorded over. Their *We're Off* 7-inch (1982 on SST Records) is an unbelievable blend of punk with heavy metal, with 'We're Off' pre-dating even speed/thrash metal! *Feast* LP followed (1985) in a more mid-tempo style, and Würm were back in 2020 with a new 7'-inch (*Poison*).

CANADA

Moral Minority (Montréal, Quebec) included members of B.A.R.F. and Corrupted Reputation, and one or more members of the band also played in Les Rektums. They released two demos of underproduced, crazy speedcore, with the first one being the 1988 *Preaching For Profits*; crazy fast stuff, influenced by bands like Capitalist Alienation and Neos, but more metal with many Slayer influences. This one's a winner, and I wish I could get also the 1989 demo for review. Zero Hour (Calgary, Alberta) was Mike Davies's second band before he became Beyond Possession's final guitarist in 1989. Davies's first band was with Lyndon Johnson (vocalist of Zero Hour), Marc Pantella, and Rob Maker and was called Riot City IV. Zero Hour's only offering was the 1987 *Nature* demo, alongside with their track 'Speed Metal' on *Calgary Compelation* LP (1986); heavy and hard-hitting crossover that is slightly more metal. Still excellent stuff though, and just because songs like 'Talisman of Death' and 'Demon Seeds'.

No Rebate (Edmonton, Alberta) on their only offering, the 1986 *Dish Pig* cassette, they were just amazing; reminiscent of Beyond Possession's skate rock, they were highly proficient in terms of musicianship. *Dish Pig*'s production doesn't do justice to the amazing material. Get this re-issued at any cost, but first, check songs like 'Metal Maniac' and 'God Loves You'. I would also like to make a small reference to Karrion, even if their crossover elements into their thrash-speed metal are very few; they did offer the 'The King's Exile' song on the crossover compilation *Complete Death II* (1987), and overall, they were a good band. Down Syndrome from Edmonton, Alberta on their *Down Syndrome* 7-inch (1984) crossed political hardcore with GBH and slight metal overtones. The echoey production offers a feeling of nostalgia. All six songs crush, especially 'Pain and Hunger' and 'Values'. Eye on You from Calgary, Alberta released two 7-inchs of metal-fused punk in 1985: *Who's been Sleeping in my Head* and *Illusions of Freedom*, which have a melodic edge, that even sounds melancholic. Both recommended for those interested in a punk-meets-metal mix, but without the ferocity and speed of crossover.

House of Commons from Vancouver on their *Patriot* 12-inch (1983) were a rough hardcore band, reminiscent of California acts like Target Of Demand. Excellent stuff. Their *Guilty as Hell* demo (1985) went to incorporate heavy metal leanings, offering the band a slight speedcore edge. A must-have here! Songs like 'Ultimatum' and 'Attitude' are just spectacular.

UK

Coprolalia (Derby, Derbyshire) sounded like a cross between Venom and Discharge on their 1986 *Adapt Or Die* demo, not too dissimilar to what early Onslaught headed for. Definitely entertaining stuff here, songs like 'Schizophrenia' or 'Ritual Master' will apply to all metalpunks. Ex-members of Ardkore formed D.R. Korea (Stockton-on-Tees, Durham) in 1990, and their sole offering was the *It's Close Enough for Jazzz* demo (1990), above par crossover thrash. With a name like Helms Deep (Wombourne, Staffordshire) one should expect swords-and-sorcery heavy metal, but that's not the case for this band. Formed by ex-members of Genital Deformities with two demos of crazy rough speedcore, with 1990 *Anthem for Doomed Youth* being their best.

Konkrete Gerbil (London) released two demos and had one compilation inclusion with 'Unto the Bitter End' on *The Unspeakable Oath* cassette (1992). I would describe their sound as alternative metal crossover; it's melodic and mid-tempo mostly. Okay. War Dance (Peterborough, Cambridgeshire) started off as a hardcore thrash combo on their first two demos, *A Short Sharp Shock* (1988) and *None but the Brave* (1988) sounding professional from day one. Songs like 'Terminator' or 'Against the Grain' are just top stuff in the Suicidal and Venice sound, with some Bay Area thrown in. War Dance then headed for a more hardcore punk direction, starting off with their *Monkey See, Monkey Do* LP (1989) which is excellent, like a cross between HDQ and Dag Nasty. They kept up this style till their split in 1995. They were by far a better band on their hardcore days than in their crossover ones.

Couldn't find anywhere Daemaniac's (Sittingbourne, Kent) only demo (1988), reportedly a thrash punk mix. Damage, Inc. (Huddersfield, West Yorkshire) was formed in 1986 after members of the punk band Criminal Justice split-up. Their sound became more metal-oriented crossover on their 1986 *The New*

Realities! Demo. Hot stuff here, vicious and raging hardcore thrash, not that far away from the early Concrete Sox sound, great songwriting too. They changed name to Diekriest in 1987 (releasing one more demo and playing one show), and they are back as Criminal Damage in 2022, back to punk! Epidemic (Whitstable and Canterbury, Kent) formed as early as 1981. Initially they were a UK82 punk band, that later incorporated a more metal style on their two demos: the 1988 *Demo 1* and 1989 *Demo 2*; both good demos. I like their second one better, more fierce and powerful stuff here with songs like 'Bred To Fight' and 'Your Mistake'. Decline from Manchester formed in 1989, and their style is a weird combination of anarcho and crust with thrash metal on their three 7-inchs and one demo; *Blind* 1990 7-inch is an okay release with best song in is 'Zipper'. Zorro (Norwich) are a unique case of band. They formed in 1975, and their only release, the 1979 *Arrods Don't Sell 'em* 7-inch contains two punk songs 'Arrods Don't Sell 'em', 'Soldier Boy', and one NWOBHM-styled song, 'Starfight'; all good stuff.

Statement are still (2025) active since 1984, and they are a one-man-band of Patrick Poole (Anorexia, Arrogance, Carnivore Crusher, Cracked Cop Skulls, Eakra, La Masque, Riot/Clone, Squandered, The Apostles, The Children, The Rule, Unborn), with an enormous discography that obviously I'm not going to review. Their style changed from time to time, from anarcho-punk to metal punk, to folk punk and even crossover thrash as heard on their *Prepare For Battle* 7-inch EP (1990). *Prepare For Battle* is unbelievably amazing, punishing crossover, but sadly it was released on Sean Muttaqi's Hardline Records, known for anti-homosexuality beliefs. Still though, there's nothing against Statement, and pick up this rager; try their other discography too.

Heavy Discipline (Kettering, Northamptonshire) had a slight metal influence mostly coming from Venom and from Japancore bands on their hardcore punk *EMI Extreme Mutilation Increases* demo (1986), and the *Liberation Of Economics* 7-inch (1987). Obviously, this is stuff that enjoy, fast, heavy and political, with lots of Amebix influences in. 'Complete Annihilation' is just menacing. Bollweevil (Kent) on their only release, the 1981 *Rock Solid* are a NWOBHM band with obvious punk influences, especially on 'Rock Solid'. Okay, but it kind of lacks the power needed. On the contrary, A.R.C. Rockband on their only release, the 1979 *Home Made Wine* 7-inch they were amazing; total hard and heavy to punk crossover, rough, catchy, with a pub rock influence. Finally, I really loved Catharsis (Middlesbrough, North Yorkshire) and their crossover perspective on the *More Fun than Laughing* demo (1989) as well as *Beyond A Joke* 7-inch (1990); like crossing D.R.I. with Excel under a rougher UK sound, Catharsis just shred in anthems like 'Mad Slammer' or 'Laugh at Me'. Members later went to appear in hardcore acts like John Holmes and Jaded Eyes, and what is actually mind-blowing is that drummer Darren Moore played earlier in the very melodic NWOBHM band Millenium!

GERMANY

Scum (Bottrop, North Rhine-Westphalia) didn't follow the fuzz-ridden thrash metal and crossover of their country contemporaries. But rather went for an all-out attack hardcore with a metal edge on their *Hinder the Sadistic War* demo (1987) and their good *Imitation of Life* 7-inch (1988). Drowned In Surroundings (D.I.S.) from Freiburg, Baden-Württemberg released two demos: *Last Days Visions* (1988) and *Drowned in Surroundings!?* (1993); but they were nowhere available. The same applies for Hisn (Bavaria) that formed in 1989 and their *Modercore* demo (1994).

FRANCE

As you can imagine, Powertrip (Guipavas, Brittany) have a definite influence from Ludichrist on their most metal tunes though. Powertrip released two demos and one full-length CD, *Powertrip* (1993). Their sound can be described as power thrash metal with some hardcore influences. Okay, nothing too special. Bramstocker from Nice formed as early as 1978, and their *Il y a un ailleurs!* 7-inch (1979) mixed hard rock with punk, a highly enjoyable release. All the stuff they released can be found on *Plus d'illusions* LP (2019) that is totally recommended. Sadly, couldn't find the recordings of Coma Ethylique (Lille) anywhere; apparently, they had three or four demos.

ITALY

Atrox (Milan, Lombardy) formed in 1982 and were a classic Italian hardcore band of their era, with great releases with their 1990 *Fiori Neri* LP which included some slight metal influences; still hardcore though, and still great. It is songs like 'Citta Maledetta' or 'Se Fossi Re' that had this certain metal edge. Bandiera dell'Odio (Caserta, Campania) released a very rough demo in 1989, that sounded like Venom going Italian hardcore, but way more underproduced. Corroded (Catania, Sicily) formed in 1988 and released two demos of raw metal hardcore, fast, heavy but not that inspiring in terms of songwriting; check *Thrash Under the Volcano* demo (1988) and *Deep Inside in Your Mind* demo (1989). D.I.Y. (Catania, Sicily) released three demos, *Church Wants More* (1988), *Shadows of Grime* (1991) and *Therapy* (1992); I've only managed to get their first one. It's superfast speedcore with a strong metal element, actually they sound like Bulldozer going Declino, mental stuff! 'Factory Of Idiots' and 'Church Wants More' are the stand-out tracks here.

Illegal Ideas (Udine, Friuli-Venezia Giulia) formed in 1985 and started off as a hardcore combo, as evident from their three tracks on the 1986 *Weekend for Maniacs* cassette compilation. They recorded a 10-inch EP in 1988, *Quando La Musica Morirà*, that remained unreleased up to 1997, that went for a more metal approach, like speed metal going Italian hardcore. I think that its nearly flawless, especially songs like 'Paranoie' and 'Down'. Ipnosi (Ferrara, Emilia-Romagna) on their first demo, *Oltre l'Apparenza* (1989) are a great hardcore act with some metal elements; check the double-bass and solo in 'Clown'. While on their 1991 demo, *Delirium Tremens* went slightly more metal, but still hot stuff here. Later, they went from a more melodic hardcore and mid-tempo, and even alternative styles on their releases from *Ipnosi* 7-inch and onward.

Stige (Ascoli Piceno, Marche) was a crossover band created by ex-members of the hardcore bands Affluente, Dictatrista and Urban Power. They formed in 1985 as Befriend and released one demo, *Desperate Days* (1986), one EP in 1988, in 1989 *Uniti nell'abbraccio* LP and *Nuova Sensazione Freak* LP, unreleased (1991). I've only managed to get *Uniti nell'Abbraccio* and have to admit I was floored; ultra powerful speedcore, with a metal edge, not far from Raw Power's *After Your Brain* stuff, albeit faster. 'Come Assorto' is amazing, while 'Fede' is simply a crusher. Get this LP! Toxic Youth (Milan, Lombardy) formed in late 1989. Their first demo from 1993, Toxic Youth sounds like a Youth Crew band going slightly metal, and it's good. I enjoyed songs like 'Do It' and 'Survive'. Toxic Youth later headed for a beefier mid-tempo hardcore style reminiscent of NY bands of that era, still decent stuff. Plus, they are still active (2025).

Animal Farm (Naples, Campania) formed in 1987 and had some connections with Randall Flagg (thrash metal band) as two of their members provided backing vocals on the only demo. Animal Farm went on for a style that was mostly thrash metal. It was very unpolished, with many hardcore influences, on their only demo (*Demo '89*). There is a certain Voivod edge that makes this demo even more charming; they sound like a cross between COC's *Animosity* era with Voivod's *Killing Technology*, and for this they will end up in the top releases by Italy, ha! Absurd Conception (Genoa, Liguria) had already an established name in the underground due to two of the band members Marco and Fabio starting the first Italian extreme metal radio show in the late 1980s. Their 1990 *Receptacle of Nonsense* demo is a weird mix of thrash-death metal with hardcore. While I'm not fond of death metal, this is good when it enters the crossover territories.

Blacklisted (Milan, Lombardy) were an above par speed thrash band, with a huge Metallica influence, as well as crossover too, in their three demos: *Demo* (1991), *Demo 1992 - Grazie 1000 grazie di quore* (1992) and *The Broken Promise* (1993). Just listen to 'Live Fast Die Hard' song and check the Metallica and crossover influences for yourselves.

AUSTRIA

Räumungsalarm (Vienna) seem to be around forever, since they formed in 1985 and remain active ever since, having released one live demo in 1992, one CD, *Hart aber herzlich!* in 2001 and one live record in 2002. Massive respect for their anti-fascism stance. However, in musical terms, their heavy metal blended with punk leaved me totally cold. Maybe it's that Bavarian metal style with huge vocals, etc that puts me off. A special reference here to one excellent hardcore band on 1980s, Stand To Fall (Linz, Upper Austria), that later in the 1990s went into a more alternative metal hardcore style on the *Fear* CD (1993), but did it with gusto and style!

SWEDEN

Skull (Stockholm) included members of the thrash-speed metal band Contra, however their approach on *You're Dead* demo (1990) is totally different; wild and chaotic speedcore, very harsh sounding and fast, like early D.R.I. with a more metal edge. On 'Claustrophobia' they sound like Bad Brains gone Septic Death! Of course, this one rules. Publikförakt AB (Sollentuna, Stockholm) on their sole release, the 1982 *The Night Of Horror* 7-inch had one punk song ('The Night Of Horror') and one hard rock punk ('Young Rebel'); decent, but by no means mandatory stuff. TRP (Fjälkinge and Kristianstad, Skåne) had that same hard rock-punk blend, a bit above par on their 1982 *My Bike / Lady of the Night* 7-inch, enjoyable yet not crucial. T.S.T. was formed 1977 in Västerås by Jarmo Mäkkeli, Karri Mäkkeli (Zäba) and Nandor Hegedüs (Nalle), then renamed to Panic and later The Rats (or Rots). The name T.S.T. (The Schock Treatment) came from Ramones' *Leave Home* LP from the song 'Gimme Gimme Shock Treatment'; initially, they were a great punk band, in the 77 tradition, then headed into the hardcore punk style (on their 1983 *TST* LP, that is amazing), and finally, they went for a mix of 77 punk with heavy metal on their 1988 *All Through The Night* LP. Melodic and catchy, it's recommended, however pick up their hardcore stuff because it's their peak!

FINLAND

Massacre (Kuru, Pirkanmaa) formed in 1979 as Varaventtiili playing punk rock, then in 1982 they renamed to Maanvaiva continuing with punk rock. In 1983 they went to call themselves, Sotatila playing excellent hardcore; from 1984 to 1985 they incorporated more metal stuff into their sound. Sotatila reached its peak on the 1986 split 7-inch *Massacre / Miquel Co*. This is just great stuff (even though the high-pitched vocals now and then are irritating), and they kind of remind me of Raw Power going Finnish hardcore, 'Run For Your Life' is a great song, and so is the heavyweight 'The Last Dance' that kicks off with a speed outburst. They split in late 1989, and then returned in 2006, as a punk band, always top-quality stuff. Santa Lucia (Kemi, Lappi) formed in 1984 and are still active (2025), however their case is totally unique! This all-female band's crossover sometimes is between heavy metal and punk as heard on 'Viimeinen Aamu', sometimes is between power metal and punk, weird, but still intriguing. Five 7-inch EPs and one LP, *Arktista hysteria* (1990) you can try getting into their special sound!

NORWAY

Crossbreed formed in late 1980s, and their two 1990s CDs went for a total Cro-Mags mode; the 1994 EP and the 1995 EP *Ain't No Release From Fear* are in-line with *Best Wishes* and *Alpha Omega*, and obviously the fans of those records will like Crossbreed. Brutallika (Trondheim, Trøndelag) formed in late 1980s and their only appearance was on the *Evig Pine Tra La La* 4-way split LP (1989), including demo recordings in 1988 and 1989. Fantastic punkish thrash metal, like Stengte Dører gone metal, with great songs like 'Hva Gjør Det Meg' and 'Apathy No More'. I wish somebody will reissue their stuff.

From the same 4-way split LP comes Corporate Deathburger (Trondheim, Trøndelag), with Brutallika, TMB and 10-12 Søstre. Corporate Deathburger formed in 1987, took their name from MDC (obviously) and released two demos, *Sinsuck Insanity* and *Corporate Graves*, 1988 and 1990 respectively; as well as the 1992 *We're Just In Hell For Fun* LP. I can't recommend enough their offerings on the 4-way split; 'Deathburger' is an amazing song, as well as their early more hardcore-oriented demos. Their only LP release is just top-notch hardcore thrash. More hardcore crossover than thrash metal, this is just bouncing, catchy and weird stuff, that takes some cues from NYHC and crossover and blends it with Norwegian hardcore songs like 'They Shall Die' are crazy. They continued as Bud, adding industrial into their sound. Metal Rats (Borre, Vestfold og Telemark) formed in 1983, and their *Demo 1985* is amateurish, metal-punk, like Motörhead mixed with UK82 and classic heavy metal, it's so catchy and fun! 'Bang your Head' and 'Burn To Death' make me laugh and sing-along at the same time, just imagine!

DENMARK

Immortal Death (Copenhagen, Hovedstaden) formed in 1989 and released two demos, the 1990 *"Ihjel"* and the 1992 *Vomit* demo. I prefer the former one, because it's raw, basic, and Motörhead-driven crossover thrash, with a great punk influence, even though it isn't anything to flip over to. *Vomit* incorporated funk elements, so you know my views on this style already…*Scandal!...So What?* (Korsør, Sjælland) were a total disgrace in lyrics terms, so I won't even review them. Pathetic sexist stuff.

NETHERLANDS

Anarcrust (Rotterdam, South Holland) formed in 1987 and becoming in the 1990s one of the most known European anarcho-hardcore bands. Their style was also unique, like a techno-thrash metal band filtered through hardcore, and I think that their most 'crossover' release was the *Coalescence* CD (1990), while the 1993 *Progression Or Decline* LP went even further, towards a Voivod-Die Kreuzen sound, going post-hardcore. Not easy to digest stuff, challenging but rewarding. Ancestral Sin (Veenwouden, Friesland) formed in 1990 and are still active (2025), having released a good number of thrash hardcore records and demos; more into the mosh-metal style though, with lots of double-bass drumming and slow parts. I can't consider them as a crossover combo in the traditional sense, but more of a metal-thrash hardcore band that takes its cues from the 1990s style. Check their *Ancestral Sin* CD-EP (1994). Razende Roeland started as a punk band in the squat-scene in Leiden in 1984. Their sound went towards a more metal-punk approach on the 1987 *Gosh* demo that was reminiscent of the UK bands of the time, such as Concrete Sox; *Razende Roeland* LP (1991) went towards a more rock direction. Gosh is good, and songs like 'Let Us Live Our Way' are a proof of this.

Total Loss was a thrash crossover band from Hoorn, and sadly their 1990 *TV Zombie* demo suffered from an unbelievably bad production; a pity, because they presented some interesting ideas. Iron Fist (Alkmaar) started in 1986 as a Motörhead cover band but quickly evolved into a metal-punk combo. They were by far more punk than described in databases, and they were connected with Parkhof, a venue known for its various hardcore and punk concerts. Their first offerings were also included in the hardcore punk *Cheese Live* compilation (1987) with two excellent rough metalpunk songs. Other bands on the compilation: Vacuum Cleaner, Dutch Courage, Challenger, Daltons and Strange Day. In 1988, they self-released the *Sea Of Blood / Bitch* 7-inch EP, with 'Sea of Blood' being an excellent metal-punk anthem. The flipside of 'Bitch' suffers from terrible lyrics, however in musical terms it sounds like a cross between Discharge and Motörhead. Lots more CDs and demos followed, and the band in still (2025) active somehow. Finally, Break (Schijndel) on their 1981 *Drive My Car / Piece Of Shit* 7-inch they used two songs off their 1981 *Give Us A Break...* cassette, with 'Piece of Shit' as a hard rocker, 'Drive My Car' is a great song, in the punk tradition of the Heartbreakers.

BELGIUM

Knife Clatter (Brussels) formed in 1989 and released in the 1990s two full lengths of metal-rock n' roll punk. Knife Clatter started as a punk band, then evolved into a Motörhead style later heard on the *Burn It* CD (1992) and *Babylon* CD (1995); okay stuff. Legion of Metal (Scherpenheuvel-Zichem, Flemish Brabant) included members from different and varied musical backgrounds: Gerry Verstreken (Ostrogoth) and Burt Beyens (Agathocles, World Pollution). Their only release, *Faces Of Death* (1989) demo is a mediocre speedcore blast. Check 'With 100 They March' and 'Z.O.T.', decent yet not crucial stuff.

An honourable mention to Blast (Hainaut), and their crazy 1973(!) *Hope / Damned Flame* 7-inch, that sounds like a cross between hard rock and D-beat; it might have been totally unintentionally, however this 7-inch rules, it sounds like hardcore before hardcore!

GREECE

Oddly enough, the only crossover-related bands from 1980s I managed to track down from Greece, were neither from Athens nor Thessaloniki, the two biggest cities with the most progressive youth. In the region of East Macedonia and Thrace, the band Neurosis originated from Xanthi, a smaller and much more conservative city. From my experience it must have been really hard to be into the crossover stuff back then, in such a place. Anyway, their 1989 *The Day After* demo sounds like a blend between Kreator and Cryptic Slaughter, with some D.R.I. mosh parts, fast, wild and crazy stuff! 'Indignation' and 'KISS the Cross' are raging stuff.

The other one was Could be Worse, from Serres, Central Macedonia; Could be Worse were more hardcore-oriented in musicality, lyrics and visual terms on their *Uncontrolled Situations* demo (1988). Not perfect, but still raging, and with the same Kreator influence present on their metal side. Kreator were huge amongst thrashers and those ones that liked crossover in Greece. The common denominator for both bands was that they were included in *Decapitated Compilation* EP (1990), alongside Death Courier (thrash) and Septicemia (thrash-death).

In later years, some crossover bands appeared in Greece. A special mention to ZBR (Zmparalia from Thessaloniki), and their chaotic Ratos De Porao style, to Ripping Wounds (Athens) and their Integrity-meets-1990s Sepultura approach, and Offensive Attitude (Athens) and their 2018 7-inch of Cro-Mags-meets-Suicidal with Attitude Adjustment blast.

POLAND

Funeral of Brains (Lask, Lodz) on their 1990 *Nie-e* demo were crude, rough, but very charming in their hardcore thrash. There's still a melody, reminiscent of all Eastern European bands, and even though they could never change the world, this is enjoyable. Maggot (Zory, Silesia) released two demos on 1991: *Dla ludzi* and *Evil Dead;* however, I couldn't find them anywhere to review them. Sorrow (Bydgoszcz, Kujawy-Pomerania) formed as Morbid Tales in 1989, and kept it up until 1992, releasing one demo, the 1991 *Three Skulls*, like a cross between Celtic Frost and hardcore, okay. Afterwards, the guitarist Maciej Wacław (RIP 2022) joined the hardcore punk band Schizma, where he remained for fifteen years.

Confident (Szczecin, West Pomerania) had a hardcore thrash background, only that this was fuelled by some early grindcore influences, and while I'm not a fan of this stuff, their 1989 *Schizophrenia, War and Beer* demo is just belligerent! Even crazier was the 1990 *Who's Afraid of the Wind* demo, that sounded like all members were on helium and acid. A special mention here to Homomilitia (Lodz), who are one of the most classic 1990s Polish anarcho-hardcore bands, with some crust influences, that incorporated some metal elements later in the mid-1990s. Check their great *Twoje ciało - twój wybór* LP (1996), and check all of their discography.

I would also add the great Armia (Poznan) in the 'special mention' section; their 1980s and early 1990s stuff is just classic anarcho-hardcore. While on *Duch* (1997) and *Droga* LPs (1999), they added some experimental and metal elements into their own brand of hardcore. Crucial band. No idea what Mentor

(Lodz) sounded like, they are reported in fanzines of the day as 'thrash metal with some hardcore influences'. And the same applies in the case of Zembator (Lodz).

SWITZERLAND

Yukon (Lucerne) formed in 1986 however, their groove thrash mixed with hardcore was never my style. I don't want to sound nasty, however the whole 'groove' thing makes me nauseous. One EP, one demo and one CD *No Risk No Fun* (1997).

PORTUGAL

Incognita (Funchal, Madeira) had a massive Metallica influence on their first three demos, that sometimes slipped over the 'groove' tag…oh well. Later, from their 1995 *Madeirus Sarcasticus* CD and on, they went for a more Pantera sound. Meh. Alien Squad (Leiria, Leiria) are active since 1989, and their crossover approach is the one of thrash punk, highly reminiscent of Ratos De Porao *Brazil* era, blended with The Exploited' *Massacre*! And as you know, this kind of stuff drives me apeshit! Check their 1994 demo, as well as all their releases, and start with the *2000 From Alienation to an Alien Nation* CD. Just wild pogo-mosh stuff!

SPAIN

Kain (Lasarte-Oria, Basque Country) formed in 1985, and lasted up to 1989, when three members of the band formed the street punk band Kalean. Their 1988 demo blended punk a la RIP with heavy metal, and even though it sounds cheesy sometimes, it is catchy, especially in songs like 'Solo Por Ti' and 'Z.E.N. Tauro'. Fun stuff. Kontainer (L'Hospitalet de Llobregat, Catalonia) formed in 1987 and their heavy metal rock punk is always melodic in the 1991 *Kontainer* 7-inch, that contains some nice songs like 'Marinerito' and 'Ir Sobre Aguas'. Later in 1996 they released their *Sin Rumbo* cassette and *Analogicos* CD, adding some ska influences in. Mad Squad (Barcelona, Spain) formed in 1989 and initially their style was akin to a more crossover with Metallica influences. This is evident when listening to their 1993 demo *Revolució*. Later they went for a more melodic hardcore style especially on their 2019 self-titled CD; just OK stuff, not something outstanding.

Arsenal (Bellpuig, Catalonia) they headed for a more traditional crossover style, with a massive proportion of hardcore punk influences; formed in 1990, their two demos (1991 and *Epidemia*) reminiscent of bands like Lobotomia, Armagedom mixed with Cryptic Slaughter's early speed ferocity. Their 1994 *Pozo sin fondo* 7-inch is in-line with the above description, and all their stuff is recommended. Beer Mosh (Bilbao, Basque Country) formed in 1990, only lasted six years, yet they were very prolific with seven releases under their belt. Like Ratos De Porao's most metal moments, Beer Mosh's crossover is fast, heavy, and loud, and I would recommend the 1993 *A Todos Los Cerdos Les Llega Su San Martín* LP, may be their best release. Brain Washed (Lleida, Catalonia) are active since 1990, and their early 1990s demos, *Brain Washed* (1994) and *Irreal Realidad* (1996) are absolute scorchers; brutal and fast crossover, in the Latin American tradition. This is just stuff not for the faint-hearted. Gruff vocals, ultraspeed, *Irreal Realidad* is a top-class release! More releases followed in 2022, now more professional and calmed-down crossover.

Brutal Distracion (Pontevedra, Galicia) formed in 1990 and changed their name to Brutal in 2013, switching their style to metalcore. Their crossover on *Graves Consecuencias* demo (1993) and *7 Sueños* CD (1994) is very groove-metal oriented, so I'll pass. Last Generation from Barcelona formed in 1990. No idea what sound like on their *Last Generation* demo (1992) because nowhere can their music be found. Requien (Las Palmas de Gran Canaria, Canary Islands) sounded way too confused on their two demos, *Sin Fronteras* (1991) and *Víctimas de la Historia* (1992), weird stuff and way too lengthy. Sucio Sistema (Bilbao, Basque Country) went for an all-out vicious approach on their 1995 *La Propaganda del Kaos* demo and *El Vértigo del Progreso* CD (1997), that was very punk influenced, raw and basic stuff, like Disorder going metal (only of course not that great).

Thrash Tropical (Laudio, Basque Country) on their 1992 demo they followed the brutal Latin American crossover formula, decent stuff with at least one song, 'La Bomba', is good. Bastardos Del Metal (Illueca, Aragon) have been around since 1990, and I have to confess that I absolutely adore their mental crossover approach, that also blends crust and even the fastcore stuff like Heresy; their *Historias de Amor* demo (1991) is just nasty, however I'm not fond of the 2019 *Bombas De Odio* (Okay, it's good, but it sounds way too polished). Fumas Iskariote (Bilbao, Basque Country) was a mediocre speedcore combo as heard on their 1994 demos, *Fumas Iskariote* and *Panico,* but headed into rapcore in their 1998 *Ahí Tenéis Cabrones!!* CD. Finally, Trauma (Bilbao, Basque Country) formed in 1990, and they released one demo, one split and two full lengths, all more that decent crossover, with a death metal influence.

HUNGARY

Bandanas (Budapest) have been active since 1988, making them the longest-running Hungarian crossover band. Their story begins with the raw, but good 1988 demo, that might sound confused. However, when it headed to the crossover hardcore territory it surely had a charm, especially with songs like 'Hallgatnak a kövek' and 'Áldozd fel'. Next one was the 1992 demo, that was even worse recorded, again though, in the same style. Lots of releases followed, but I think that their 2008 *Is There Any Solution* CD is their best one, beefed-up brutal crossover hardcore, with a huge metal influence. Sújtólég (Budapest) sounded to me as an early black metal band with punk influences on their 1990 demo, and I'm not wild about this stuff, sorry.

YUGOSLAVIA

Brainstorm (Belgrade, Serbia) formed in 1988 and through their existence they were a top thrash-crust punk combo, with exciting releases all over. They are a bit too many to mention, but special reference should be made to the 1990 *The Nightmare Continues...* 7-inch. It is a shredding slab of vinyl, just check 'Help them out?'. Their split LP with Battle of Disarm is where Brainstorm went anarcho-hardcore, with a slight metal sound and their last LP, the 1995 *Milošević Is Dead,* again anarcho-hardcore, more melodic than before. Great band.

SINGAPORE

Global Chaos formed in 1987 as Unblessed and were into a death-thrash style. In 1990 on their first demo *And It's All Our Fault* they added some crossover influences, but still the death metal element is stronger here. Later in their career, they moved towards hardcore, especially on their final CD, the 2014 *Louder than Satan's Lollypop*. Can't get though into their stuff, sorry.

MEXICO

Corroxxxion (Mérida, Yucatán) have been active since 1990, yet they only managed to release some records and demos from 2012 and on; they are still active until today. I think that songs like 'El Grand Final' will apply to all crossover thrashers. They punk influence is apparent in the vocals by Ayuso; the guitar follows a very metal thrash- hardcore route. Check their 2016 *Virus Letales* CD, it may be their best work. Deathpils (Ciudad Juárez, Chihuahua) are the same case: they formed in 1990, they are still active today, however they released their music a bit later, starting from 2003 and onwards. Their style is vicious, punishing crossover thrash, that takes cues from Ratos De Porao's wildest days-even from their 1990s recordings that they were way noisier. Try the *Diablo Road* CD (2006).

PERU

Producto De Ira (P.D.I.) formed in Lima in 1989. As you can imagine their 1992 *No Entres a Circulo de Violencia* demo is not a slick recording; rough hardcore thrash that surely has its moments. However, their 2016 *Tempos De Furia* CD is top-notch: fast and heavy crossover, with influences ranging from Blood For Blood to Agnostic Front, and even The Casualties, all under a metal sound. Songs like 'El Tiempo Enseñara' or 'No Soy Un Criminal' are really inspiring.

ARGENTINA

Oxido (Elortondo, Santa Fe) went for a different kind of crossover; formed in 1988, their *Sueños Salvajes* 1992 demo includes highly enjoyable, heavy metal-punk crossover, melodic, slightly rough, but very catchy. Check out 'La calle esta pesada'. Karma (Haedo, Buenos Aires) are active since the 1990, and their thrash-death hardcore approach reminds me somehow of Sepultura; their 1992 demo was faster and crazier, while their 1994 *Fear of Destiny* CD is easier to digest, still on this style. Like their approach? Check also the 2018 *Persona Non Grata* CD. Finally, Argentina's longest-standing crossover band is Enot, active since 1986; a speed metal-hardcore blend, above par stuff on both their 1990s demos.

BRAZIL

Chacina (Piracicaba, São Paulo) even though they formed in 1990, they only released two demos in the 1990s: *Opening Eyes* (1993) and *Chacina* (1999). Their first demo was unbelievably poorly recorded and harsh. While *Chacina* sounds like a mix between Slayer and Sepultura's most hardcore moments. Later releases were in a modern thrash metal style, that fans will appreciate *Gaza* EP (2015) is a good one, and so are their other releases including their most recent from 2023 titled, *Lagoa Negra* CD. Gangrena Gasosa from São Paolo have quite an interesting story; they formed in 1990, with the sole intention to open a Ratos de Porão show. They labelled their music 'Saravá Metal'. 'Saravá' is string of words from of three mantras in Afro-Brazilian religions: "sá" (God's power), "rá" (movement of the Earth), and "vá" (energy), while actually they are a thrash-hardcore combo, with humorous and sarcastic lyrics. They've been active since their formation and are widely known in Brazil, however I can't stand either their humour or their musical approach. More Beer (São Paolo) were way above average on their two demos, the 1994 *Some Wrong?* and the 1995 *#3*. They were one of the few Brazilian bands that had such a US crossover influence, and they have a definite Cro-Mags and NYHC influence, especially in songs like 'One Nation'. Good stuff.

I wanted so much to find any of K.S.S.K.'s demos *Komsomoskaia* (1987) and *Demo '88* (1988) but with no luck. They were considered as one of the fastest bands in Brazil, and their influences included Rattus, Ratos de Porão, Kreator, Rövsvett, The Exploited and Sepultura. Nojo from São Paolo formed in 1989, and released only one demo, the 1991 *Feel the Carnage* that contained the eponymous song, a mix of death metal with grindcore and crossover; it's good, even though this extreme style is not my bag. Freax (Belo Horizonte) formed as early as 1983, and their story is quite interesting; they released one demo in 1987; a real disgrace in lyrical terms, named as *Fuckin' Whore;* even though their speedcore approach is crazy in musical terms, I won't recommend it. Freax split up when their guitarist Silvinho died by electrocution on a set of train tracks. About fifteen years later, original member Lou Ferriera reformed the band in Florida, recruiting an otherwise completely different lineup, and their style became industrial, releasing the 2002 *Freax* CD, with Keith Caputo (Life of Agony) on vocals!

Lethal Charge (Campinas, São Paulo) formed in 1990 and have also an interesting story: their vocalist Michel Viana was among the finalists to become the new Sepultura vocalist following the departure of Max Cavalera, but Derrick Green was chosen instead. Many demos and releases since their early formation, Lethal Charge are still active, and I believe that their 2010 *Convergence* CD will please thrashers with a fondness for some slight hardcore creeping in. Finally, Sacred Curse from São Paolo, formed in 1988 and had a more controlled heavy thrash-hardcore blend, except for their 1990 *An Abstract Way of Life* demo, that was speedy and rough. Their two CD releases, the 1992 *Sacral Age* and the 1996 *The Raw Truth Of Man* were enjoyable; nothing to flip over, still nice background music.

CHILE

As sweet sounding as you can imagine were Squad, from Santiago, formed in 1987. On their *Gallinazeous Death* demo (1989) they sound like a hardcore band with speed metal guitar licks, and guttural vocals. On their 2017 *Reconstitucion De Escena*, they sound like Varukers mixed with Slayer and Ratos De Porao, good stuff!

JAPAN

Slaver from Kanagawa did not release a record but only offered demos and contributions to compilations. F.O.A.D. records released on 2024 a compilation of their tracks, *Fighting Your A Go - Total Discography 1987-1990* LP. The LP is a great, power-driving metal-hardcore, catchy and crazy! Get this one now! Yellow Pearl (Nara) formed in 1995, and their 1995 demo is rare as hell-please, somebody help with finding this one? Reportedly, crossover hardcore. 24 Eyes are a long-standing Japanese (from Kobe) hardcore thrash band, formed in 1985, and currently (2025) active, offering shows. However, I couldn't find their 1988 demo, and what I saw from their live footage on YouTube, I can only say that currently they are going for an ultra-fast sound. G-Zet (Tokyo) formed in 1983 and their motorpunk sound will drive you wild! They were included in the classic 1983 *Great Punk Hits* compilation with G.I.S.M., The Execute, The Clay, Abudarako and Laughin Nose. Their real blast was the *G-Zet* 12-inch (1984), where they included Discharge and Black Sabbath influences into their crazy motorpunk. Five shredding songs, with 'Dog Eat Dog' and 'G-Motor-Zet' being my favourite, you need this ripper! War Painted City Indian (later City Indian) formed in Osaka in 1985, and while their 1980s stuff such as *W.P.C.I Warning* 7-inch (1985) and *Terror Boogie* 12-inch (1986) were an amazing amalgam of GBH with Motörhead. In 1990s they went for a more metal-rock a la Motörhead style with *Howling On Fire* CD (1991). Get their first two releases, mandatory for everyone into this sound.

Sadly, Deathmask's (Amagasaki, Hyogo Prefecture) three demos (1986, 1987 and *Cross My Mind* 1988) were nowhere available. I'd love to check them out someday. Finally, Geizz on their 1985 *We Wait For*

Song Of Geizz 7-inch sounded like a Japanese Discharge and Motörhead mix, four songs, all winners! Check out 'Song of Geizz' and 'Wild Boys'.

NEW ZEALAND

Post Mortem Depression was a pretty unique crossover band, formed in 1988 in New Plymouth, Taranaki. Their approach is diverse, the technical proficiency of the band is mental: just check out the bass lines of Nigel Brand or drummer's Ken Russel rhythms. The more I was listening to their 1990 *Addictions* cassette, the further I was digging it. It's always a great thing when you listen to a band and you can't spot their influences, and this is the case with Post Mortem Depression. Check it out, especially songs like 'Revenge' and 'Naked Doom', first class crossover. A re-issue maybe please? On his own words, Ken Russel narrates that "Sadly, the recording was done in a pretty simple studio for a couple of hundred bucks. The dude had a pretty good setup for the time, but his groove was recording bluegrass and country bands. We were a bit of a shock to him, but he gave it his best shot. Only had an eight-track tape machine, and not that many decent mics, so it was pretty hard to capture the double kicks (I had two kick drums), along with the snare and overheads. Was all pretty well done in a few takes and quick afternoon mix down, with no real mastering. Our influences were diverse. Frank was an all-out metal dude, Nigel was hardcore punk and death metal, Shaun was a bit more on the heavier side, and mine was more "Motörhead" type stuff. I also had the radical opposite as I was also a nightclub DJ at the time, playing heaps of early house type stuff. What we could have done with today's technology would be a thousand times better. I have no idea where the original masters ended up. Really, I don't think any of us had a 'label' on our style of music. Like a million other 'nobody' bands of the time, we were just letting out what came from our gut".

INTERNATIONAL NAMEDROPPING

Sadly, due to infringement rights, I couldn't add the bands that were included with a small review or reference in this chapter in *Crossover The Edge*. Instead, I will just namedrop them here. All the bands below they went to crossover somehow early or later in their existence or even adding slight metal or punk elements.

USA: SSD, DYS, YDI, Warzone, Meatmen, Jerry's Kids, Necros, Maimed For Life, Genocide, Rights Of The Accused, Kraut, Lost Generation, Saint Vitus, Token Entry, Sea Hags, TSOL, Poison Idea, Anthrax, Fear Itself, Disorderly Conduct, China White, Battalion Of Saints, Fearless Iranians From Hell, Mucky Pup, Evil Dead, Hallow's Eve, Sacred Reich, Rest In Pieces, RKL, Abandoned, Paranoia, Guillotine, Rancid (Flint, MI), The Uninvited (Louisiana), Slipknot (Connecticut), Legion Of Death, Knightmare (Manchester, NH), Insurgency (San Francisco), Herbicide, Chemical Waste (Fort, NJ), HVY DRT, Outcasts (Wild Rags band), School Of Violence, Elimination (New Orleans), Chronic Plague, Dysfunction, Base Apes, Sheer Terror, Judge, Afterbirth (Alabama), Afterbirth (Michigan), Eviction (Pittsburgh), Lunacy (Porter, TX), Saud, United Mutation, Cyanamid, Zombu (Georgia), Rednecks In Pain, Maximum Albacore Reekage, Malefice (DSI Records), U.Y.U.S., Ultraviolence (Flint, MI), Sordid Doctrine, Power Assault, Iron Fist (Minneapolis), Avarice, Neurosis, Beer On Tap, Axite (Rhode Island), Damaged (Massapequa Park, New York), Desecration (Arizona), Flagrantz, Hearing Impaired (MA), Formicide (MA), Doomwatch, Chaotic Plague (Pittsburgh), Manikin (NJ), Academy Black (Houston), Broadax (Culver City, CA), Sins Of The Flesh, Mortis (Fullerton, CA), Manitoba's Wild Kingdom, False Liberty, Diddly Squat, Aftermath (NJ), Krangkorr, Humanicide (Huntsville, Alabama), Bad Attitude (Connecticut), Blatant Disregard, Affliction (Huntington Beach), C.F.I. (Connecticut), Conspiracy Of Equals (Arizona), Imminent Attack (Madison, Wisconsin), Hardcore 918V, Jim Jones and the Kool-Ade Kids, Haunted Garage (L.A.), Godsent Humans (Texas), The Crucified (Fresno), The Lead (Miami), Hellfire (Stirling City, CA), Expatriate (Colorado Springs), Suicidal Overdose (New Orleans), Morbid Life Society, Knifedance (Cleveland), Blatant Frustration (New Orleans), Shell Shock (New Orleans), Pap Smear, Spastik Children, Nevermore (NYC), No Warning (San Jose, CA), Scum of the Earth (Dallas), Selective Outrage (NY), Xyster (South Dakota), Romper Room Rejects, S.I.K. (Marrero, Louisiana), Sewer Puppets (Charlotte, NC), Refractory Period, Maniacal Genocide (Rosemead, CA), Pitbulls on Crack (Tulsa), S.O.S.A. (San Francisco), Canonical Destruction (Raritan, NJ), Cannibal (Seattle, WA), Death Moshing Assholes, Cholos on Acid (West Hills, CA), Dead Orchestra (Wichita, KS), Insanity (Pittsburgh), Malicious Grind (El Segundo, CA), Random Draw (Pennsylvania), Ripchord (Scottsdale, AZ), THC (Livermore, CA), Slaughter Shack (Boston), SGM (Seattle), Geneticide (Mechanicsburg, Pennsylvania), Santa Claus (San Diego, CA), Violent Encounter (Port Clyde, Maine), Vehemence (L.A.), Uglor (El Paso, Texas), Self-Infliction (Bellflower, California), The Bastard Squad (Cleveland), Spare Change (Chicago),

Death Squad (Saint Paul, MN), Slambodians (Fremont, CA), Social Disease (Long Island, NY), Warhead (Saint Paul, MN), Virgin Destroyers, Speed Freaks (Milwaukee, WI), Rabid Lassie, Hypertribe, Dread (Austin, TX), Leprosy (Hopewell Junction, NY), Nuclear Crucifixion (New Orleans), Tarrasque (Hawaii), The Bleeding Hemeroids (Woodheaven, NY), and The Bag Men (Ohio), Whoppers Taste Good (St. Louis, Missouri), Decomposed (Corpus Christi), Distemper (Atlanta), Hedonistic Cravings, Mosh Until Death (CA), Repulsa, Stress (San Mateo, CA), Violent Insanity (Chicago),The Log, The Guff (Florida), The Final Demise (Minnesota), Domestic Crisis (Parma, OH), Destroyed Youth (La Puente, California), Demented (Noble-DeKalb County, Indiana), Demented (Daly City, CA), Social Disorder (New York), Corruption (Fullerton, CA), DDT (Atlanta, Georgia), Primal Scream NYC, Bitter End (Seattle), Distorted World (Pennsylvania), Graveyard Rodeo, DUMT (Mountlake Terrace, Washington), F.C.D.N. Tormentor, No Empathy (Chicago), Sacred Denial (Clifton, New Jersey), Sik Mentality (Houston, Texas), Nocturnal Fear (Pennsauken, New Jersey), False Hope (Ohio), Dmize (NYC), Terrorizer (L.A.), Repulsion (Flint, MI), F.U.C.T. (Nashville), Radiation Sickness (Indianapolis).

UK: The Exploited, Attak, Gemage, Cockney Rejects, Varukers/Arbitrater, Annihilator (Birmingham, UK), Red Rage, Oral (Brighton), Girlschool, Antisect, Bolt Thrower, Terrorain, Heresy, Antichrist (London), Bomb Disneyland/Bomb Everything, Extreme Noise Terror, Napalm Death, Genital Deformities, Energetic Krusher, Anti-System, Unseen Terror, Sic Boy Federation, Cerebral Fix, Life Cycle (Wales), Execrate (Nottingham).

Canada: Voivod, D.O.A., Razor, Adversity, Slayed Nekros, Specters Of Madness, Visible Minority, Senile Decay, Machiavellian Regression, Infamous Basturds, Organized Kaos, Fanatical Views, Groovy Aardvark, Degenerate Youth, Dark Legion, Iron Gypsy, Death Sentence, Soothsayer, Alazif, Damnation (Quebec), Epileptic Brain Surgeons, Lizard, Genetic Error, Noslom, Burned Brain, Morbid Decapitation, Corpus Vile, Matricide, Lab Animals.

France: Razzle Dazzle, Krull, M.S.T., Asshole, Phobia (Grenoble), Fly's Fuckers, Deconciator, Endless Diatribe.

Czech: Bastard, Barricade, Insania, Gradually Insania, Sebastian, Detrom, Erebus.

Brazil: Psychic Possessor, Skarnio, Angel Butcher, Krofader, Explicit Repulsion, S.T.I., Realidade Encoberta, BSB-H, W.C.H.C., DeFalla, Mortuario.

Slovakia: Acheron, Akant.

Italy: Negazione, Crash Box, Disper-Azione, Rock Train Band, Upset Noise, Peggio Punx, Jester Beast, Warhead, Contropotere, Convulsed, Schizo, Depressione (Abruzzo), Silence (Trieste) Blacklisted (Milan), D.I.Y. (Catania).

Singapore: Opposition Party.

Poland: The Corpse, Od Jutra, Inkwizycja, SKTC, Acid Drinkers, Smirnoff, Thermodon, Confident, Poison Mosh, D.I.R.T., Kara Smierci, E.C.H. IX, Neuroleprosy, Psychiatrist, Sorrow's Three Skulls, Paymon.

Mexico: Arkanhell, Escape (Aguascalientes), Corroxxxion, Evil.

Colombia: Sacrilegio, La Pestilencia.

Switzerland: Celtic Frost/Hellhammer, Messiah, M.I.S., Yukon, Exxor, Bloodstar, Non Konform.

Portugal: D.O.M. (Defacement Of Malfunction), Paranoia (Leiria).

South Africa: Urban Assault.

Japan: The Clay, G.I.S.M., The Comes, 666 Triangle Six of Death, Beyond Description, Ghoul, Inzest, Clod, Gastunk, Quest Object Project, Rose Rose, Xenolith Oger, Crisis Kill, Rapes, Final Bombs, Poison Arts, Genoa, S.O.B., Bat Bones, Kathabuta, Drastic Gunsmith, Front Guerrilla, Airraid, Vathokija, Brain, Whiplash.

Slovenia: III Kategorija.

Belgium: X-Creta, Damaged Corpse, Dead Serious, Creep Insanity, Jerbees Jam, Deadly Intentions, Mistress Of Pain, Something Horrible In Town.

Spain: Soziedad Alkoholika, MG-15, Anestesia, Desvirgheitors, Tropel Nat, Orgon, Crusher, Carpe Diem, Juicio Final, Reaccion Corrupta, Histeria Colectiva.

Chile: Betrayed, Drosera, Squad, Fornicadores Unidos Contra Los Kuicos.

Sweden: Anti-Cimex, Black Uniforms, Flegma, Tribulation, Brejn Dedd, D.T.A.L., Cemetarium, The Krixhjälters, Misery, Kazjurol.

Finland: Rattus, Faff-Bey, Dirty Damage, Rytmihairio, W.D.M. (World Disarmament Movement), Damage.

Yugoslavia: Amnesia (Belgrade), Crist (Belgrade), Pneumonia, Condition Critical, Kerozin, Mortus.

Austria: Blitzgemetzel.

Netherlands: Vopo's, Cry Of Terror, Brutal Obscenity, Swampsurfers, Disabuse, Soaking Wet, Disturbing Foresights, Noisy Act of Protest, Egghead, Blatant Yobs.

Australia: Depression, Permanent Damage, Insane Hombres, S.I.C. (Screaming In Churches), Vicious Circle, Massappeal, Belial.

Greece: Chaotiko Telos, Panikos, Naftia (all hardcore/crust with slight metal leanings), Industrial Suicide.

Peru: Curriculum Mortis, Situacion Hostil, Feretro.

Philippines: Deceased (Viejo).

Denmark: The Brats, Geronimo, Sliced Pimples.

Argentina: 7mo Regimiento, Militia (Buenos Aires), Intense Mosh, Raw Meat.

Venezuela: Laberinto.

Hungary: Anarchia, Despot.

Germany: Inferno, Mottek, OHL, Emils, Vellocet, Chronical Diarrhoea, Children of Riot, Rostok Vampires, Antimon, Cox-Orange, Suckspeed, Uncounted Faces Of Death, Tokatta, Breeding Fear, Collaps, Der Rib, Solitary Confinement, Phobic Instinct, Death In Action, Charley's War, Inhuman Conditions, Theresa Lynn, Mega Mosh, Lavatory, Antitoxin, Total Mosh Project, Atrocity, Die Ausgebombten, Bottled, Deadlock, Eternal Trash, Wicked Power, Megatherion, BOPW.

NO INTERVIEW, NO WORRY

In this small sub-chapter, I decided to include a few words about bands that I have taken interviews of in *Crossover The Edge* but sadly couldn't get in *Tear It Down*.

You all know Suicidal Tendencies (Venice, California) was one of the blueprints of crossover sound, the 'original metal skate thrash' as they were referred in the mail-order catalogue of *Vinyl Solution*. Alongside D.R.I. and S.O.D. they were the ones to spread the crossover style in the 'mainstream'. My favourite record of ST will always be their 1983 debut, a hysterical hardcore attack with metal solos. I also love *Join The Army* LP (1987); even though the energy of the debut is missing, and I also like *How Will I Laugh Tomorrow*…LP, that sounds like a long-jam of emocore metal (!) or something like that. They totally lost me when they incorporated too much funk into their music, and the re-recording in 1993 of their debut, *Still Cyco After All These Years* is one of the most atrocious re-editions a band ever did. However, I have a soft spot for *Freedumb* LP (1999), it was a comeback to their hardcore punk roots (minus the awful slap-bass style…duh!). Many records followed, Suicidal Tendencies are still (2026) active offering shows and recording/releasing music, and their 1980s stuff is a great way for a newcomer to find out both hardcore and crossover.

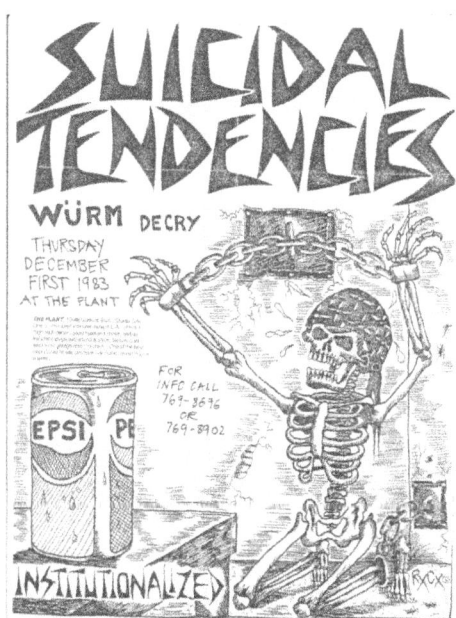

(Suicidal Tendencies with Wurm and Decry at the Plant, CA. 01/12/1983)

No Mercy also from Venice, California started off as a side-project of Mike Clark (who later joined Suicidal Tendencies) and formed in 1982. After three kick-ass hardcore demos, they were included in the seminal *Welcome To Venice* LP compilation, with a more metal sound. Their first LP, the 1987 *Widespread Bloodshed Love Runs Red* is a sheer metal hardcore rager. Just think of *Join The Army* but way more vicious, rough and demonic. Songs off this LP were later re-recorded by Suicidal Tendencies on their *Controlled By Hatred* LP. No Mercy continue today (2026) as Waking The Dead.

(No Mercy with Beowülf, Powertrip, Tormentor, Abandoned, Bloodcum and Sanktum at the Balboa Theater, San Diego. 14/12/1985)

I wish I could include Beowülf (Venice, California) with an interview and a great chapter, like in *Crossover The Edge*; sadly, all founding members passed away, so obviously this wasn't feasible. Formed in 1981, Beowülf alongside Excel are my favourite Venice bands-their sound on *Beowülf* LP (1986) and *Lost My Head... But I'm Back On The Right Track* LP (1988) is reminiscent of a cross between Motörhead, GBH and Californian punk, catchy as hell! Both records are unbelievable classics, while they changed their style later on the next LPs: *Un-sentimental* (1993), *2c* (1995), *Westminster & 5th* (2007) and *Jesus Freak* (2011) towards a rockier hardcore style, still cool.

The Beast from New York-ah man, I was so sad when I learned about Anthony Bernardo's passing away in 2020. He was a real sweetheart, always so kind. The Beast released two records of highly enjoyable punk metal, the 1986 *...Has Arrived* LP and the 1988 *Carnival of Souls* LP. Maybe I should have find a way to contact Pete Brasino, aka Guitar Peter, I bet he had many stories to share. Don't be fooled by the bad record covers of The Beast, this is just top-notch punk metal.

(The Beast live in CBGB's 1992. Courtesy of Anthony Bernardo)

Since the founding members of Carnivore (Brooklyn, New York) have either passed away or never bothered to offer me an interview, there's sadly no separate sub-chapter for them. While I have many objections towards their lyrics, I have to admit that in music terms, Carnivore just ripped; their first LP (1985) is mostly a metal album with doom and hardcore influences, while their second one, *Retaliation* (1987) is my favourite-fast and furious crossover with thrash and doom elements; totally out of control. Pete Steele's bass sound on this one still haunts my dreams!

(Carnivore with Sheer Terror and Shok at CBGB's. 12/01/1986)

Scum rock or rockin' crossover? Either way, Norman Bates and The Showerheads (Queens, New York) formed in 1984 and they appeared in various compilations including, *New York Hardcore: Where The Wild Things Are* before releasing their excellent 1989 *Norman Bates & The Showerheads* LP. The album is mental, rockin' crossover hardcore, with a definite Motörhead edge, always loved this record. The 1990 *Sinus* cassette follows the same winning formula, and I think that you should get the *Psycho Too! 1987-1996 Discography* CD that contains all their stuff. Just blast 'Mailman' and 'Tarantula' and find it out for yourself.

(Norman Bates and The Showerheads, 1985 Queens, NY. Courtesy of Nick Plaitakis)

You are all familiar with Prong (New York City) and their massive career, so this is just a review. Prong in the 1980s went on to release some totally classy crossover stuff, based on their love for Bad Brains. I have a soft spot for *Primitive Origins* EP (1987), and not only because of Pushead's artwork, but it is also because of its brutal power. The 1988 *Force Fed* LP was equally good, and somehow more mature, while the 1990 *Beg To Differ* LP was a minor disappointment; may be their worst record in their extensive discography. After *Beg To Differ* Prong re-invented their sound, added groove and industrial into the mix, leading to the greatness of records like *Cleansing*.

(Prong with Sheer Terror, Stillborn, Schizoid, Kruciform and Mutilator at Streets, New Rochelle, NY. 02/10/1988)

Final Conflict (Long Beach, California) are hands-down one of my favourite anarcho-hardcore bands. Formed in 1983 by Jeff Harp (and still going), they have released some tremendous hardcore stuff, however they always had a slight metallic edge into their sound. Loud, political and uncompromising, Final Conflict's best stuff can be found on the 1985 demo and the 1987 *Ashes To Ashes* LP. Songs like 'Self-righteous Pigs' or 'The Last Sunrise' will drive you nuts, and I believe that they can have an appeal to people both into e.g. Iconoclast and Cryptic Slaughter on the same time, while they are neither as noisy as the former, nor as fast as the latter. Already Confused? Check them out!

(Final Conflict with R.K.L., The Grim, Bulimia Banquet and No Comment live at the Country Club, Reseda. 15/04/1989)

The Brood (Venice, California) have no connection whatsoever with the eponymous garage-revival band from Portland, Oregon. They formed right after Jon Nelson and Amery Smith had both left Suicidal Tendencies in 1984. They went initially by the name Screaming Fetus. In 1985 the changed their name to The Brood and released a demo with four songs of metal-punk, with a huge NWOBHM dose. Their first- and only-LP, the 1986 The Brood on Profile Records, sounds like a cross between Motörhead, NWOBHM and punk. With songs as great as 'Going Out In Style', 'Good vs. Evil' or 'Born To Lose', get it. Uncle Slam were kind of the continuation of The Brood, in a more hardcore style; their 1988 *Say Uncle* LP is good crossover thrash, with songs like 'The Ugly Dude' or 'The Executioner'. Uncle Slam headed for a more metal-thrash approach in the subsequent releases, *Will Work for Food* CD (1993) and *When God Dies* CD (1995); commercial crossover thrash, not too crazy or too fast, but still very good.

(No Mercy with Megadeth, Dark Angel and Agent Steel at the Balboa, L.A. 28/02/1986)

Virulence (San Clemente, California) had a very different approach in their crossover. Highly influenced by Minor Threat, Black Flag and Bl'ast!, their 1986 *Promise Is Shot* demo is just a snotty hardcore ripper, fast and sweet, while their only LP, the 1989 *If This Isn't A Dream...* incorporated elements from the Melvins, and Black Flag's *My War*-era, heavy and punishing stuff. After Ken Pucci departure and his replacement by Glen Chivens, they changed their name to Fu Manchu and became famous for their stoner rock style.

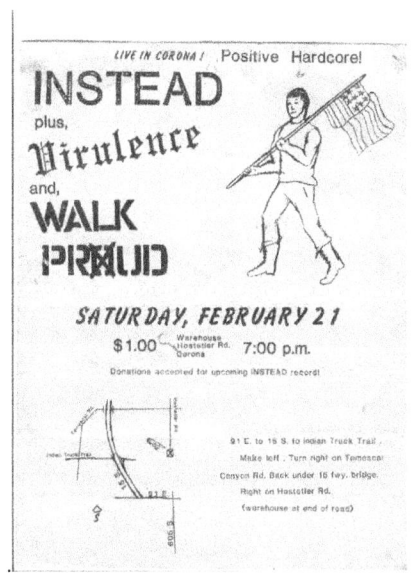

(Virulence with Insted and Walk Proud at the Warehouse Hostetler, Corona. 21/02/1986)

Crossover-adjacent, Mind Over Four (Los Angeles, California) went from the garage and experimental rock of *Desperate Expression* EP (1983) to progressive and alternative metal, performing though alongside hardcore and punk bands most of the time. Spike Xavier on the same time played in Doggy Style (hardcore punk) with his brother Brad and Lou Gaez, while guitarist Dan Colburn also played in Adolescents, D.I., Tender Fury and The Detours. Crossover-adjacent also applies to Nasty Savage that played alongside hardcore and crossover bands, D.R.I., Sick Of It All, etc. On several times they even toured with D.R.I. Nasty Savage's *Indulgence* 12-inch (1987) remains my favourite with a slight punk metal touch!

(Mind Over 4 with Angry Samoans, Youth Of Today and Brotherhood at Babylon Music, WA. 30/07/1988)

My interview with Troy Takaki was exclusively regarding The Boneless Ones, while later on he was a member of Hell's Kitchen (Oakland, California). Their first LP, the *If You Can't Take the Heat...* (1989) followed the approach that The Boneless Ones had, that is tuneful and rocking crossover, with the faster songs such as, 'Crystal Wasteland', 'War Of The Gerbils' or 'Farm Animals' being the better ones. There is a definite Motörhead influence, and it's blended through the skate rock sound and Verbal Abuse *Rocks Your Liver* era. Their second LP, *Fistful Of Chicken* (1990) kept up the same formula, enjoyable stuff all over but nothing too mandatory; though 'Concord Is A Beast' and 'Intoxicated Madman' are pretty wild songs. A live LP followed in 1990, and the band folded.

Void (Columbia, Maryland) might have been the very first band that incorporated metal into hardcore; formed in 1980, their manic approach was totally revolutionary on the (now classic) split LP with The Faith (1982), with songs like 'Who Are You', 'War Hero' and 'Organized Sports'. Some of the most belligerent classic hardcore ever recorded, with a slight metal touch, Void pre-dated crossover while being 100 percent hardcore. Their 1984 *Potion For Bad Dreams* cassette went for an even more metal approach, but equally extreme and poisonous. You have to hear songs like 'Blood Lust', or the frantic 'Breakaway' that sounds like Venom gone out of control DC hardcore and the pumping 'Start The Night'. A mandatory band for everyone into extreme music in general.

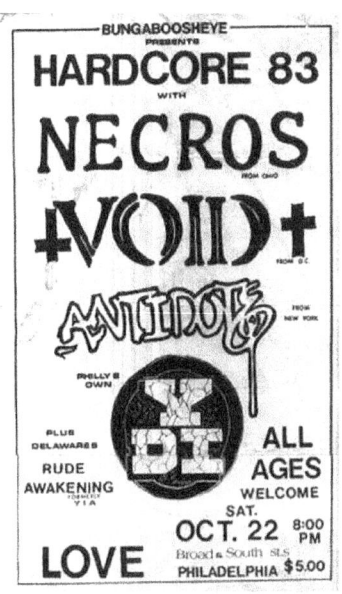

(Void with Necros, Antidote, YDI and Rude Awakening at Broad South, Philadelphia. 22/10/1983)

Tortoise Corpse (Swansea, Wales) were a thrash metal band with slight crossover tendencies that were mostly on the punk side of things, not hardcore. They formed in 1988 and released three demos, before their first LP, the 1991 *World's Got A Problem*. While their straightforward metal songs leave me cold, it is when they add punk into the blend, they are very enjoyable. Such are songs like the excellent 'Visions Of Lust', 'Psychotaff' and 'We Kill' with is blatant Motörhead fusion. Their second LP, the 1996 *Standard Of Misery* headed towards a more metal-thrash style with a Megadeth influence, surely more technical, but way outside the scope of this book. As aforementioned, their first one is pretty enjoyable.

Virus (Eastbourne, UK) formed in 1986 by Keith 'Henry Heston' Hazelden and Terry 'Tez' Kaylor, members of the excellent Oi! punk band Criminal Damage ('Oi! Oi! Criminal Crew!'). John Damien Hess joined on bass, and Coke Finlay on guitar, with this first lineup released the 1987 *Pray For War* LP. I know that quite a few people are not fond of this record, however I love it. It's absolutely raw punk metal, reminiscent of early Onslaught with a touch of Japanese hardcore, fast, heavy, political and wild. The opener 'Pray For War' is just a sheer rager, while 'Thermo-Nuclear-Thrash' is as raw as you can imagine and 'Risen From Death' sounds like it's coming straight from hell. Okay, the musicianship isn't top notch, and there are flaws, however no one can refuse its sheer power. Virus later moved to a more thrash metal direction on *Force Recon* LP (1988) that most people believe is their best and *Lunacy* LP (1989). They disbanded in 1990 and came back in 2008 and active today (2025). Their last LP, *Evilution Apocalypse* is good, again on the thrash metal formula. Did I mention that Criminal Damage are back again and active too? Oi! Oi!

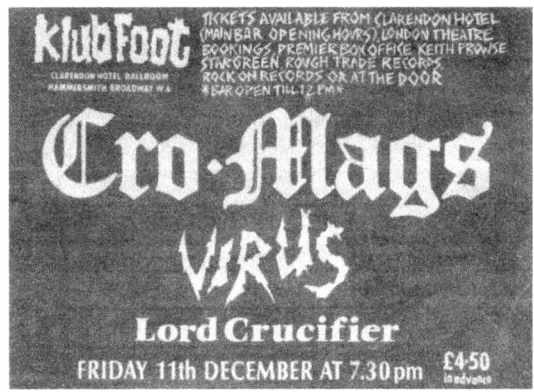

(Virus with Cro-Mags and Lord Crucifier at the Klubfoot, London. 11/12/1987)

I wish I could have an interview (again) with Paul 'Evo' Evans, mastermind behind Warfare, and one of the first and original UK metalpunks, alongside Algy Ward; sadly, this wasn't the case. So, I will just note here that Evo has a massive story both in UK punk and metal, being a member of The Blood, Angelic Upstarts, Major Accident, Warfare and Warhead. From his punk days, everyone should check out The Blood's 1983 *False Gestures For A Devious Public* LP, that is a real masterpiece of mental Oi! punk with NWOBHM riffs. Imagine a mix between Oi!, The Damned, Alice Cooper and Motörhead, everything though on 78 RPM! And what can I say about Warfare? All their records up to and including *A Conflict Of Hatred* (1988) are mandatory for metalpunks worldwide, even if I have a soft spot for *Hammer Horror* LP (1990) too, because of The Damned influences! Start though with their 1984 *Pure Filth*, their nastiest, noisiest ever. Warfare is currently (2026) active.

Doom (Birmingham, UK) formed in 1987 by Bri Doom (guitar), John Pickering (bass/vocals) and Jason 'Hog' Hodges (drums) and were initially named as The Subverters, with their music approach being the one of crossover (imagine something like e.g. Concrete Sox). Soon, they changed name and dropped the crossover style, heading for a different kind of 'crossover', blending in Celtic Frost, the gruff vocals of early Brazilian scene (Ratos De Porao, Olho Seco) with D-beat, creating their own style of crust punk that became highly popular both in crust punks and anarcho-punks worldwide. Still active today with several lineup changes, Doom have released an impressive back catalogue of classic D-beat crust punk releases. If I was to choose two for somebody not familiar with them, this would have been the excellent 1989 split

LP with the Swedish No Security titled, *Bury The Debt Not The Dead / No Security* LP and *Police Bastard* 7-inch (1989). Both are utter menacing ultra-power with great political lyrics. The force of Doom continues to drive wild punks and metalheads around the world.

(Doom ad-drummer wanted, late 1986)

Axegrinder (London, UK) was another crossover-adjacent combo; formed initially as Tyrants Of Hate in 1985, they changed name in 1986, releasing their chaotic demo *Grind The Enemy* (1987), taking the influence of Amebix to a whole new level. One of the best demos ever released in the crust punk scene, it definitely included many metal riffing, taking cues from early Venom, early Bathory and Celtic Frost. Songs like 'Master Race' or 'Thelphobia' are just unbelievably nasty and demonic. Their first LP, the 1989 *Rise Of Serpent Men* not only included some great artwork, but it's a crust punk masterpiece from start to finish. Slightly more metal than before, with better production, and with a gloomy atmosphere that grabs you by the throat. It includes terrific songs like 'Hellstorm', 'War Machine' and 'Final War', setting up the blueprint for the neo-crust bands that appeared later in 1990s-00s. Their comeback after a long hiatus, *Satori* LP (2018) is again, jaw-dropping; more melodic than before, with highly inspired songs like 'Rain' and 'Under The Sun', they again reached epic levels of greatness. Sadly, Axegrinder disbanded in 2024.

(Axegrinder with Maniac and Throbs at the William Morris Club, Wimbledon, South West London. 04/01/1987)

We need more bands like Civilised Society? (Batley, West Yorkshire); melodic, fast, slightly metal anarcho-hardcore with dual vocals, with the great female voice of Bev Carter. Formed in 1983 as Rapide 79, in their first period up to 1988 they released just top-notch demos and records, with the 1986 *Scrap Metal* being one of the best records of the (then) emerging Britcore scene; fast, melodic, slightly metal hardcore with excellent songs from start to finish. 'Tonight' is an unbelievable tune, while other highlights include 'Pansies' and the frantic 'Star Wars'. The 1987 *Violence Sucks!* LP headed for a more metal style, less melodic, but without losing their catchiness. This is the record that would appeal most to the crossover crowd. All their output is recommended, due to songs like 'Violence Sucks', 'Treedoom' and 'Tooth & Claw'. They broke up in 1988, with member creating the thrash metal act Karrion, releasing one demo, and then back together again in 2017 until 2024. They released in 2021, *The Third (Dimension)* LP, their most furious and metal release to date, with excellent songs like 'Cage' or 'Ten Number 6' (with its Slayer riffs!). Sadly, they are not together as a band, but this isn't a reason not to check their discography.

(Civilised Society? with Conflict, A.O.A., Exit-Stance, Oi Polloi, Chumbawamba at Leeds University Riley Smith Hall. 20/10/1985)

Deviated Instinct (Norwich, Norfolk, UK) were one of the most innovative bands that derived from the crust sound, aptly offering their sonic approach a new name: 'stenchcore'. They took the classic crust style to a whole new level of ferocity, even from the very beginning. Formed in 1984, their 1986 *Terminal Filth Stench-Core* is still a crust classic of the demo era, while their first 7-inch, *Welcome to the Orgy*, 1987 spawned a more metal edge. With guttural vocals and songs as heavy as 'Cancer Spreading' and 'Disciplines Of The Storm'. However, what was about to follow later, exceeded all expectations: the 1988 *Rock n' Roll Conformity* LP blended the crust punk sound with extreme hardcore on songs 'Pearls Before Swine', 'Putrid Scum' or 'Return of Frost', and some crossover thrash akin to The Accüsed heard on, 'Conquest for Eternity' and 'Laugh In Your Face'. This recording making it their most extreme record to date! Their next LP, the 1990 *Guttural Breath* even incorporated some death metal, while it was back into the mid-tempo crust punk! They split-up in 1991 and are back since 2007 releasing great records; their 2024 *Dance of the Plague Bearer* 12-inch EP being a heavyweight crusher-just check 'Conquest (Into the Void)' to find it out for yourselves!

(Deviated Instinct with Decadence Within and Prophecy of Doom UK Tour 1991)

The Accüsed (Seattle, Washington) have somehow their own reference on the Toe Tag/The Accüsed A.D. section. It would have been totally unfair not to get some more mention, since they are one of the most influential crossover bands, especially for the US West Coast scene. They are active since 1981 and are non-stop. They started as a pure hardcore band; they were daring enough to even cover Deep Purple's 'Highway Star' on the *What Syndrome?* compilation (1982)! They have an impressive back catalogue of great and diverse releases. Starting with their 1983 split LP with Rejectors being their first release, it is crazy off-the-rails hardcore attack. Their first 12-inch *Martha Splatterhead* (1985) as well as *The Return of Martha Splatterhead* LP (1986) are some of the most bombastic crossover ever released, manic speedcore riffing over hardcore brutality, with frenzied vocals by Blaine Cook. Songs like 'She's The Killer' or 'Lonely Place' are beyond any level of extremity, nasty and blistering stuff. Many more records followed, all with definite quality, ranging from very good, *Grinning Like An Undertaker* LP, *Splatter Rock* LP to great, *Martha Splatterhead's Maddest Stories Ever Told* LP. By far one of the more consistently great crossover bands ever, or should I say splatter rock?

(The Accüsed with G.B.H. at The Anthrax, Norwalk, CT. 05/11/1987)

Ratos De Porao (São Paulo, Brazil) formed in 1981 and have been active since then other than with a small pause in 1984 till 1985). Ratos De Porao is blueprint for the South American hardcore and crossover sound as R.D.P. have been storming the world with some of the roughest and noisiest stuff ever. Their debut LP, *Crucificados Pelo Sistema* (1984) remains one of the most influential hardcore punk records ever released, taking its cues from the UK82 sound of Varukers, Discharge, Chaos UK blending it with some of the nastiest Swedish and Finnish hardcore such as Rattus, Kaaos and Anticimex, with a heavy, down-tuned sound and gruff vocals. A masterpiece from start to finish, this is one of the most significant records in extreme music in general. Their crossover trip started in the next LP, the excellent *Descanse Em Paz* (1986), that incorporated a heavier sound, longest songs, adding some Onslaught and Slayer influences into their hardcore style, however this is way rougher and dirtier than you can imagine. Their 1987 *Cada Dia Mais Sujo E Agressivo* LP headed for the speedcore style, with a more clean-cut approach, still its bouncing power is great. Their two most metal crossover and that sold most were released by RoadRunner Records. Starting with *Brasil* (1989), this one sounds like a cross between D.R.I. and Slayer, albeit with the rough and fast(er) Brazilian edge, and it's a masterpiece. Their next one, *Anarkophobia* LP (1991) is their most complex, metal and melodic, it's a good one. However, I miss the spark and energy of their past releases. Did I say, 'I miss'? Miss no more! Ratos De Porao abandoned this melodic approach right afterwards, and gradually, they became heavier, faster and more extreme, only to reach levels of hardcore and crust in records such as *Onisciente Coletivo* (2002) and *Homem Inimigo do Homem* (2006). Of course, you can't expect me to cover all their records, however, all punks and metalpunks should have in their record collection at least two R.D.P. records (*Crucificados Pelo Sistema* and *Descanse Em Paz*), while crossover kids would love *Brasil*! Try also their last one, *Necropolitica* LP (2022), good return to hardcore thrash.

(Ratos De Porao with Sepultura, Anthares and more at Sao Paolo. 27/02/1988)

Rumble Militia (Bremen, Germany) are the longest-running German crossover band, having formed in 1985. Their case is of major significance and unique, because they were the first German band with a metal background to refer to issues of antifascism, anti-commercialism and anti-capitalism almost exclusively in their lyrics. And while their music has a certain thrash metal background, they went to incorporate hardcore punk elements even from the early beginning, from their 1986 *Treason* demo. I have a very soft spot for Rumble Militia, because I believe that it was very difficult for them to gain acceptance in the (then) conservative German metal scene, as well as to fight with the neo-Nazis all the time. Rumble Militia were a constant target for them. They have released a good number of records since their formation, with my favourite ones being the crazy, *En Nombre Del Ley* 12' EP (1988), *Destroy Fascism* 12-inch EP (1991) and their most current, *Set The World On Fire* LP (2020). Songs like 'Chile Under Pinochet', 'Rise And Fight' and 'Liebe' still give me the chills after all these years. In musical terms, they have a definite, more complex, thrash metal approach, with lots of guitar riffs, however they slide constantly into the hardcore and crossover catchiness and directness.

(Rumble Militia promotional flyer, 1992. Courtesy of the band)

Jingo De Lunch (Berlin, Germany) formed in 1987 and were a band comprised of already known musicians of the German hardcore punk scene. Vocalist Yvonne Ducksworth was a member of Combat Not Conform and Manson Youth (both excellent German hardcore bands-check out the Manson Youth and Hostages of Ayatollah split LP); in Manson Youth with guitarist Sepp Ehrensberger (formerly of Vorkriegsjugend), while Tom Schwoll (guitarist) played in Terstörte Jugend. With the inclusion of drummer Steve Hahn and bassist Henning Menke, the first lineup of Jingo De Lunch was formed in 1987. With this lineup, they released *Perpetuum Mobile* LP, one of the best and most diverse records of the (then) German punk scene. It is melodic, taking its cues from anarcho punk and blending it with metal and rock riffs; songs like 'Utopia' and 'Illusions' are such a breath of fresh air! Equally exciting was their 1988 *Cursed Earth* EP, containing five superb metal punk songs such as 'No One Can Reach You' and a cover of 'Pay To Cum' by Bad Brains. On the 1989 *Axe To Grind* LP are songs like 'Did You Ever' and 'Chill Out' took a total Bad Brains influence to a more melodic style, with Yvonne's amazing vocals. Their next three LPs: *Underdog* (1990), *B.Y.E.* (1992) and *Deja Voodoo* (1994), were under the umbrella of a major label, Vertigo Records. While they were good, they kind of missed the early spark and energy. The broke up in 1994, and were back in 2007, releasing a new LP on 2010 with *Land Of The Free-ks* and back in the early sound, then a live LP, and finally breaking up again, with Yvonne currently being the vocalist of the doom sludge Treedeon.

(Jingo De Lunch band picture, 1989. Courtesy of Tom Neitzke)

Aversion, from Orange County, California, formed in 1987 and remained active until 1996. They began as a power trio, with guitarist Dash handling both guitar and lead vocal duties, alongside brothers Ed Tatar and Joe Tatar (both formerly of the classic hardcore band D.I.). This initial line-up played a number of parties and gigs.

In 1988, Christian Fuhrer joined as lead vocalist, and shortly thereafter the band recorded their first demo, followed by the *In the Dead of Night* demo (1989). Their first official release, *The Ugly Truth* (Medusa Records, 1990), is a highly enjoyable crossover CD that balances metal and fast punk—not traditional speedcore, but rather a punk-meets-metal approach with a strong emphasis on melody and songwriting. There is certainly a Suicidal Tendencies feel, particularly on tracks such as *'Modern Day Martyr'* and *'In Dead of Night'*, yet Aversion clearly maintain their own identity. Their next release, the *Fit to Be Tied* CD (1992), is nothing short of apocalyptic. Here, the band successfully blended a wide range of influences into their sound: from the Venice-style crossover frenzy of *'Hung'*, to the semi-thrash metal attack of *'Falling Full Circle'*, and finally to *(S.M.F.) Obligatory Obsolescence*, which incorporates blast beats. *Fit to Be Tied* stands as their brightest moment. I also have a soft spot for their next and final release, *Fall from Grace* CD (1995), which is notably diverse in scope and approach. On a final note, vocalist Christian Fuhrer is an absolute sweetheart—a true gentleman.

(Aversion 1995 band picture. Courtesy of DJ Davis)

White Pigs from Hartford, Connecticut, are one of the most ferocious first-wave hardcore bands, having formed as early as 1980. On this occasion, I was unable to secure an interview with the band's founding member, Keith Grave, due to his medical condition. This is a real shame, as Keith is one of the most significant yet largely unheard figures in US underground music. Keith has an extensive musical career, having played in bands such as Blastmat, Chicken McHead, Cruel Lies, Dennis Most and the Instigators, Found Dead in Trunk, Free Love Society, Mailorder Brides, Sanity Assassins, The Dispossessed, Tutsis, and, of course, White Pigs.

Their first 7-inch, the excellent *White Pigs* (1984), was released on their own Swinch Kwilsen Record Productions and contained eight songs in just under nine minutes. Fast, wild, Neanderthal hardcore that makes you want to smash everything in sight. Totally recommended for fans of The Fix and Negative Approach-you get the idea. Their next release, *Live: Evil Stalks the Innocent* 7-inch (1985), took a more metal-oriented approach to their already feral hardcore sound. This was not classic crossover, but rather a more vile, dark, and menacing hybrid of metal and hardcore. It is rough as hell, and tracks like *'Satan Sparrows'* and *'Early Grave'* still give me the creeps. The *White Pigs* 12-inch (1986) was released on Combat Records as part of the Combat Boot Camp series, which also featured Powermad, Napalm, and Have Mercy. This record represents White Pigs at their peak in terms of crossover—simply their finest moment. Just listen to tracks like *'Body Parts'* and *'Deathway'*. *Songs of Sin* LP (1989) was also a strong release; however, this time the band leaned more heavily towards thrash metal, with punk elements still present. Regardless, tracks such as *'Leave Me'* and *'Live for the Fire'* absolutely shred. The band split shortly afterwards, and the final 1988 White Pigs line-up played a private party in late July 2015. As of early 2016, White Pigs were discussing the possibility of playing a few more shows. It remains unclear how long the band continued from that point, or whether any public performances ultimately took place.

(White Pigs with Demonax at the Old Queens St. Cinema, Connecticut. 10/02/1985)

THE LIST SESSIONS

It must be mentioned that all the lists don't follow any kind of order of preference. After all, lists can change any day!

50 You Have To Get

1. D.R.I., *Dealing With It!* LP
2. Corrosion of Conformity, *Animosity* LP
3. Beyond Possession, *Is Beyond Possession* LP
4. Agnostic Front, *Cause For Alarm* LP
5. Beowülf, Self-titled LP
6. Attitude Adjustment, *American Paranoia* LP
7. Sacrilege B.C., *Party With God* LP
8. Gang Green, *Another Wasted Night* LP
9. Broken Bones, *Bonecrusher* LP
10. Nuclear Assault, *Game Over* LP
11. Cryptic Slaughter, *Convicted* LP
12. Manimals, *Blood is the Harvest* LP
13. Suicidal Tendencies, Self-titled LP
14. Hogan's Heroes, Self-titled LP
15. Wehrmacht, *Shark Attack* LP
16. Accused, *The Return of Martha Splatterhead* LP
17. English Dogs, *Forward Into Battle* LP
18. Leeway, *Born to Expire* LP
19. Crumbsuckers, *Life of Dreams* LP
20. Lobotomia, Self-titled LP
21. Excel, *Split Image* LP
22. Prong, *Primitive Origins* LP
23. Norman Bates and the Showerheads, Self-titled LP
24. Aftermath, *Killing the Future* demo
25. Zoetrope, *A Life of Crime* LP
26. Wrecking Crew, *Balance of Terror* LP
27. Dissension, *Why Work For Death?* LP
28. FU's, *Do We Really Want To Hurt You* LP
29. Sacrilege, *Behind The Realms of Madness* 12-inch
30. Ratos De Porao, *Descanze em Paz* LP
31. Dr. Know, *This Island Earth* LP

32. Lethal Aggression, *Life Is Hard... But That's No Excuse At All!* LP
33. The Boneless Ones, *Skate for the Devil* LP
34. Subvert, *Free Your Mind!* LP
35. Carnivore, *Retaliation* LP
36. Gastunk, *Under the Sun* LP
37. Ludichrist, *Immaculate Deception* LP
38. No Mercy, *Widespread Bloodshed / Love Runs Red* LP
39. Impulse Manslaughter, *He Who Laughs Last... Laughs Alone* LP
40. Concrete Sox, *Your Turn Next!* LP
41. Depression/Gash, split-LP
42. Civilised Society?, Violence Sucks! LP
43. Acrophet, *Corrupt Minds* LP
44. Rest In Pieces, *My Rage* LP
45. Armagedom, *Silencio Funebre* LP
46. DBC, Self-titled LP
47. Uncle Slam, *Say Uncle* LP
48. Final Warning, Self-titled 7-inch
49. The Brood, Self-titled LP
50. Powertrip, *When Cut We Bleed* LP
51. Clown Alley, *Circus of Chaos* LP

Under Their Influence
1. GBH, *City Baby Attacked by Rats* LP
2. Discharge, *Hear Nothing, See Nothing, Say Nothing* LP
3. Bad Brains, *Rock for Light* LP
4. Cro-Mags, *Age of Quarrel* LP
5. Motörhead, *Ace of Spades* LP
6. Anti-Nowhere League, *We Are The League* LP
7. Plasmatics, *New Hope for the Wretched* LP
8. Black Flag, *My War* LP
9. S.O.D, *Speak English or Die* LP
10. Venom, *Welcome to Hell* LP
11. The Exploited, *Troops of Tomorrow* LP
12. NYC Mayhem, *Violence* demo
13. Raw Power, *Screams From the Gutter* LP
14. Amebix, *Arise!* LP

15. Void/Faith, split-LP
16. Onslaught, *Power From Hell* LP
17. China White, *Danger Zone* LP
18. Inferno, *Todd und Wahsinn* LP
19. Verbal Abuse, *Just An American Band* LP
20. Overkill L.A,, *Triumph of the Will* LP
21. The Blood, *False Gestures For a Devious Public* LP

The Ones For Everybody
1. The Worst, Self-titled 7-inch (1982)
2. Killing Time, *Brightside* LP
3. RKL, *Rock 'n' Roll Nightmare* LP
4. Jingo De Lunch, *Perpetuum Mobile* LP
5. McRad, *Absence of Sanity* LP
6. Heresy/Concrete Sox, Split-LP
7. Varukers, *One Struggle, One Fight* LP
8. Negazione, *Lo Spirito Continua* LP
9. Hirax, *Hate, Fear and Power* LP
10. Septic Death, *Now That I Have The Attention What Do I Do With It?* LP
11. Final Conflict, *Ashes to Ashes* LP
12. Doom/No Security, Split-LP
13. White Pigs, *1984* 7-inch
14. Offenders, *Endless Struggle* LP
15. Skeptix, *So The Youth* LP
16. Anti-System, *No Laughing Matter* LP
17. Bl'ast!, *Power of Expression* LP
18. Nausea, *Extinction* LP
19. Poison Idea, *War All The Time* LP
20. Attak, *Zombies* LP
21. Battalion of Saints, *Second Coming* LP
22. Holy Terror, *Mind Wars* LP

Going Underground
1. Capitalist Alienation, *Same-titled* LP
2. Deadspot, *Adios Dude* LP

3. Expatriate, *No Sleep 'til Chugwater* demo
4. Schizoid, *Beer Thief* 7-inch
5. AMQA, *Cats Are Neat* 7-inch
6. Whoppers Taste Good, *Don't They?* 7-inch
7. X-Creta, *Patronizing the Heterodox* LP
8. Fear Itself, *'Til Death Do Us Part* LP
9. Ugly but Proud, *Knuckles From Nowhere* 7-inch
10. Aversion, *The Ugly Truth* LP
11. Groovy Aardvark, *One Fine Day* demo
12. Inzest, *Another Religion... Another Violence* 7-inch
13. Methedrine, *Crawl Before You Walk* demo
14. Desecration, *Who's In Control* LP
15. Haywire, *Private Hell* LP
16. Ardkore, *Apocalypso* demo
17. Guillotine, *Bring Down The Curtain* LP
18. Black Uniforms, *Faces of Death* LP
19. Permanent Damage, *End of Innocence* LP
20. The Clay, *The Middle East Combat Area* 7-inch
21. Santa Claus, *Rocks In Your Stocking* demo
22. No Warning, *Back From The Dead* CD

There's More List….Part 2

1. Born Without A Face, *The Unbecoming* 7-inch (1986)
2. Statement, *Prepare for Battle* 7-inch (1990)
3. Geizz, *We Wait For Song Of Geizz* 7-inch (1985)
4. Stillborn, *Scorn of Absence* demo (1989)
5. Throttle, *New Freaks on the Block* 7-inch (1990)
6. Arise, *Adrenalin* demo (1988)
7. G-Zet, *G-Zet* 12-inch EP (1984)
8. Heavy Discipline, *Liberation of Economics* 7-inch (1987)
9. No Rebate, *Dish Pig* cassette (1986)
10. Exoteracy, *Exoteracy* 7-inch (1990)
11. T.F.N., *Political Death* demo (1986)
12. Forgotten Existence, *Demo '92* (2020)

13. Slaver, *Fighting Your A Go - Total Discography 1987-1990* LP (2024)

14. Apocalypse, *Earth* 7-inch (1989)

15. Glycine Max, *Violent Mind / Peaceful Heart* LP (1990)

16. Transgressor, *Demo* (1987)

17. Animal Farm, *Demo '89* (1989)

18. Dead Aim, *Dorks on Dope* cassette (1986)

19. Post Mortem Depression, *Addictions* LP (1990)

20. Mayhem, *You Get What You Pay For* 7-inch (1981)

21. House of Suffering, *Wired* 7-inch (1990)

22. Stige, *Uniti nell'abbraccio* LP (1989)

23. Catharsis, *More Fun than Laughing* demo (1989)

24. Thrashing Hectic Circle, *Christian Brainwash* demo (1987)

25. Civilian Terrorists, *Dark Inside* cassette (1986)

26. Socially Incorrect, *Demo* demo (1987)

27. Massacre, *Massacre / Miquel Co.*, Split LP (1989)

28. Apathy, *Out the Window* LP (1988)

29. Dark Star, *Spectre* 7-inch (1978)

30. Skull, *You're Dead* demo (1990)

31. City Indian, *Terror Boogie* 12-inch EP (1986)

32. Blasphemous, *Frustration* demo (1987)

33. No Escape, *Lack of Life* cassette (1990)

34. Deelspeed, *Faster Than Death* demo (1991)

35. Sarcasm, *Warsong Compilation* LP (2019)

36. Damage, Inc., *The New Realities!* demo (1986)

37. At All Cost, *Demo 90* demo (1990)

38. Dunwich, *Madman with a Headrush* demo (1991)

39. Sinister, *Crisis* demo (1989)

40. Epidemic, *Demo 2* (1989)

41. Brain Washed, *Irreal realidad* demo (1996)

EPILOGUE: Final Daze

"Crossover began for me with Agnostic Front's *Cause For Alarm* LP and curiously enough; I heard that album before listening to their seminal *Victim In Pain* LP because when I got into the scene in early 1986, *Victim In Pain* was long out of print and signing to Combat Core made their second LP a lot easier to obtain. I was seeing local bands like Leeway that had a pronounced crossover vibe so from the beginning NYHC for me had a metal element, but it was sort of taboo to mention any association to what 'longhairs' listened to even though the Crumbsuckers, Ludichrist, Sheer Terror had definite heavy metal vibes, riffs, and grooves. The second wave of NYHC circa 1986-87 tried to erase any connection to metal via back to basics hardcore exemplified by the straight edge brigade of Youth Of Today, Straight Ahead, Side by Side even though the bands they worshipped from the first wave of NYHC like The Abused, Antidote all had riffs that referenced classic metal. I think the crossover influence strengthened the NYHC sound in general by having more technically proficient players that cut their teeth by playing in local garage outfits that covered classic Priest and Maiden tunes as well as the current Slayer-Metallica sound. This new batch of converts went on to form seminal bands like Raw Deal, Beyond, Breakdown, Outburst in what I call the 2.5 wave. What is considered the 'NYHC Sound' these days can be traced back to when crossover came into the picture, but metal has been present since day one in the NYC Hardcore scene". -- Freddy Alva, writer of the book *Urban Styles: Graffiti in New York Hardcore* book and zines *NYHC Black Book*, *American Hardcore Black Book* and Wardance Records

"I think both worlds were very similar in ways. The carefree 'fuck the world' attitude, along with the barbaric volume speed and power of the music was fitting. They were like blood brothers in a lot of ways". -- King Fowley, Deceased

"Although, many fans from both scenes merged very well, there was also a strong culture class that could not be denied. Many punks resented the 'long-hairs' invading their shows and some of the more aggressive metalheads looked down on the punks and used the mosh pit as an opportunity to rough up the more passive kids at the shows. One of the things I always found to be hypocritical within the punk scene was that although punk rock was supposed to be all about non-conformity, if you didn't look like a punk, you were often rejected or ostracized at the shows". -- Kenn Nardi, Anacrusis

"There was a group of kids calling themselves FSU who used to go to metal shows just to beat people up. And at one of the shows we played with the Cro-Mags, the audience there was very anti-metal and someone threw a bottle at the stage while we were playing". -- Bob Mayo, Wargasm

"Around 1982–83, I was hanging out with people who were mainly into classic rock. I had already been listening to bands like Rush and Judas Priest, but what was coming next felt completely different. I went to high school with Nick Benetos from Cold Front in 1985; we were in the same class. Later on in 1985, I got a job at a supermarket, where my colleagues were Tony 'the Greek' and Foti.

In 1985, Tony and I started spending time together in Astoria Park South, and he made me a cassette tape with just four tracks: one by Anthrax, one by Metallica, one by Accept, and one by Raven. That tape was my real introduction to heavy metal.

At the same time, A.J. Novello from Leeway lived across Tony 'the Greek', and the band's original drummer, Saso Montroni, lived just a few blocks away. When I began visiting Tony's house, I realised he had an incredible record collection: metal and hardcore alike. He owned everything that mattered at the time, from Mercyful Fate and Metallica to Bad Brains and Agnostic Front. That's when I started buying records myself. I bought the first Youth of Today 7-inch the moment it was released.

Nick Benetos and I used to go to Venus Records, where I bought S.O.D.'s *Speak English or Die*, which was my very first LP. Through Benetos, I also got the Leeway demo (1985) and Kraut's *An Adjustment to Society*, which remains one of my top three hardcore records of all time. After that, I started going to record shops on my own; places like Record Factory, Bleecker Bob's, and Venus Records.

My first show was Leeway at the Ritz in 1986, with GBH, Agnostic Front, and Crumbsuckers. I really connected with Agnostic Front through *Cause for Alarm*, which was the first record of theirs I owned. It completely blew my mind and is still my favourite release by them. I also loved Crumbsuckers' *Life of Dreams*, and from the first time I saw them perform "Prelude", I was hooked.

There was a lot of tension back then. Many metalheads ended up becoming skinheads, turning into tough guys who went around beating up metalheads. I never chose sides, I embraced both metal and hardcore, and of course crossover. Early on, metalheads often got beaten up. There's a story I always tell that sums up how intense things were. I owned an Iron Maiden "Trooper" jacket, and one day I said to Nick Benetos, "Let's go to CBGB's," wearing that jacket. He immediately replied, "Lou, if you're going to CBGB's, you can't wear that jacket, we'll get our heads kicked in!" That's how crazy the scene was at the time". -- Lou Gatzaris, NYHC stalwart

"Well, when D.R.I. released an album called *Crossover*, it was when the term was first coined-but there are loads of bands who can claim to be the first, English Dogs, Discharge. It's a good pub argument". -- H, Acid Reign

I wanted so much to have a big book that would merge this book with *Crossover The Edge*, but this sadly didn't happen for various reasons; one being the obvious one, length. I won't refer to some other reason, even though it's hands-down disappointing, because *Crossover The Edge* has been out of print since forever. The great David Gamage and Earth Island Publications saved the day, and loved the idea of a separate, new book, so you now hold it in your hands.

A lot of things and changes took place in the world, as well in the hardcore crossover musical scene since the release of *Crossover The Edge* (2019); COVID, War in Ukraine, Trump, Palestine, AI for the masses.

We have now entered the New World, where everything is faster, everything is created and consumed faster than ever before. Societies are under pressure like never before in the last thirty or forty years, with the days of wine and roses and innocence are lost. Most people aren't bothered to read an interesting post in (anti) social media, and there's a whole new generation swamped into their smartphones, scrolling through the next 10-second video to satisfy their mania for dopamine.

So, what's more punk than being creative at the moment, than being original, than being anti-war, anti-oppression and against the neoliberal agenda that is already being in full force, with your everyday life being supressed into 'Work-Eat-Sleep'? That's right: the only way to escape is not escapism. Escape means action against a vicious circle.

While writing this book I suffered from (minor) depression for the first time in my life, as a result of being crushed every day at work, putting ridiculously many things under my belt, and finally collapsing. But now, with the help of my beloved ones, my favourite music, and obviously a psychiatrist, the future looks bright (even though some days really suck). And I won't forget the words of a good friend of mine, a much elder punk, that used to tell me that "if you take what happens in the world real seriously, you'll either go crazy or depressed". Well, here you are, haha!

But let's stick to the good side of things. Crossover is back, in another form obviously, but it's back. And I'm not talking about the goofy 'pizza thrash' bands that will bore you to death if you are older than fifteen years old, but the good crossover, that comes from the underground of the hardcore scene. Bands like Mindforce, Pest Control, Inhuman Nature, Combust or more metal ones like Fugitive, Enforced, Foreseen, Judiciary, and High Command have been ripping it up for quite a while. You can see that they gain following from both camps worldwide. And here, it must be mentioned the influence of two bands on this current crossover wave: Cro-Mags and Leeway. It took a while, but their legacy, especially Leeway's, is finally finding a more extensive recognition. I wish though that there were more Attitude Adjustment, more Excel, more Beowülf, more Beyond Possession and more Gang Green today, but hopefully their time will come too!

"I remember one time going to see the Bad Brains and being really fucked up on acid and PCP at the same time, this was 1986. We went down to this real ghetto club in Washington D.C. and all of us were so fucked up we saw paintings on the wall singing the lyrics. We even jumped onstage and rocked with the Bad Brains. Smoking bowls of hash with them. That's a classic moment for me!" -- King Fowley, Deceased

"I don't recall any specific incidents at our shows, but one of the first hardcore shows I attended was Corrosion of Conformity back in 1985. There was a group of skinheads who were targeting mainly the long-haired metalheads in the pit. Someone was even stabbed that night though I was not a witness and only heard about it after the fact. I did witness plenty of dirty looks and trash-talking from both sides in the earlier days though. I don't think most of the metal heads really understood the idea of the mosh pit at first and basically saw it as an excuse to take out their aggression on others. Metal always had a more macho element, and this attitude caused a lot of problems when the two crowds first began to mix". -- Kenn Nardi, Anacrusis

And at last, great labels are treating crossover re-issues with honesty and passion: Radiation Records, F.O.A.D. Records, Generation Records, Beer City Records. Oh, and Metal Blade re-released classic crossover LPs produced on burgundy and vomit wax. What a treat after nearly forty years! So, now COC and D.R.I. are the good guys for them, haha!

We lost too many good people those years. To the loving memory of Chris 'Papi' and Nikos Lambadas, who sadly passed away way too soon, leaving us with great memories; both had huge hearts that offered their love without any compromise. And of course, Steven Hanford (I miss our conversations so much…), Michael Gibbons (a class of his own, a real gentleman), the kind human being of Josh Pappe and Dale Henderson of Beowülf (I never made it to Venice my homie…).

This book is dedicated firstly and foremost to my partner, Nikoletta, and our daughter, Amaryllis. To Ian Glasper, for he is the one that offered me the opportunity to start writing books. To David Gammage of Earth Island, because he was super-excited since the day that we met at a Negative Approach show in London, and because he offered me the chance to release my books on his label. To Tim Cundle, real brother, awesome human being. Our families that always supported us. Mike Gitter, what a big heart. Brian Walsby for offering his great art on my past and forthcoming. Musicians, from the kind soul of Phil Pobran (of Beyond Possession), to Billy Lo (The Worst), to Bill Reeves (Random Conflict), to Scott Helland (The Outpatients), to Steve Hochheiser (Détente), always massively supporting my books.

Friends, worldwide. From the ones you met and have great times with, such as Stevil Minta and James Sherry, Christopher Owens, Theodor Papp, Mario Take The City Records, Marco Sannino, Mike Fury, Stefano Lumetta, Freddy Alva and Heidi, to the ones that you can't wait to meet: Scott Feinstein and Shadow 15, Michele Giorgi, Hugo Higgins, Patrick Grindstaff, Todd Norin, Mark Prindle and so many more especially from New York City area. Friends in Greece, all of you, especially the ones that supported me through very hard times: Makis and Irene, Tati-Kika-Michaela, Gregory Tsol, Polis, Leon, Tolis Tzotzoulini., George Virvilis and Elena, Kyriaki Karag, Periklis-Lena-Jordan, Stelios P., Professor Yiannis Skarpelos for the sheer support and love, Prof. Pantelis Vatikiotis, Niki Polymeri and Aristoteles, Foivos T., Foivos K., Misail, Beloved Dimitris Periergos, Kostis Giov, Peter Bakidis, Stavros Kouvaris, Yanni Zikidis, Moof Porotic, Elen Sui and Sofia 4, Marselos family (good luck), Vlospa, Bob and family, Minmin, Tzouvalekis, Elmer, Iskender and Ntelos, George Pirounakis, Achilleas Bock and Dimosthenis Miliaras (for his help and guidance) and Karakostas family of course. Great people like Haris Tsak, Vic, Nick Banger, Giannis Koul, Apostolis Themelis, Vagelis Kamaretsos, George Liverpool, Chris Gkoutzi, Peter Mario, Jim Vassis and all of The Antinormals (best punk band in Greece). The antifascists of P.A.O.K, Stergios…everybody. Professor Waksman for inspiration. Scarecrow Records (both Darek and

George) for keeping it alive in Greece. Generation Records NYC and Mark Yoshitomi. Bulldog Oi! from Kavala (Sakis and Stelios), and everybody that set things straight. Sorry if I forgot someone. Oh, and of course, Jennifer Beckwith for doing an excellent job while proofreading this! And absolutely pissed with myself for not having a chat with Jim Martin, an amazing artist that so many of his flyers/work are included in this book.

No love for scammers, people that rip-off bands and promoters that hi-jack the hardcore scene to make money. No love for the close-minded too. And obviously, no love for fascists.

A huge thank you to all the bands that are included in this book with an interview. Thank you for your kindness and willingness to spend some time talking to a freak!

Never Surrender-Never Give In

About the author

Alexandros Anesiadis is a writer and researcher whose work explores the intersections of underground music, culture, and identity. He is the author of Crossover The Edge, We Can Be The New Wind, and Heroes of the Metal Underground. He also holds a Ph.D. in Media and Communications. Yes, a Dr. too.

Musically, he balances between hardcore punk, crossover, and punk rock, with flavours ranging from thrash to post-punk and Oi! to garage rock. He is a lifelong devotee of bands as diverse as Naked Raygun, Wipers, Cro-Mags, D.R.I., Discharge, and Varukers. An unapologetic and borderline manic record collector, he is always willing to sell minor (or not-so-minor) body parts in pursuit of essential vinyl, such as Antidote's Thou Shalt Not Kill 7-inch.

Alex (his preferred name) is a massive PAOK fan, a proud partner to an exceptional person (remarkably tolerant of his record-collecting and gig-going mania), and the father of a daughter whose passion for K-Pop constantly reminds him that underground culture evolves in the most unexpected ways.

WE CAN BE THE NEW WIND

by Alexandros Anesiadis

'We Can Be The New Wind' captures the era when bands throughout the world were blending more melodic and experimental styles whilst heading in an alternative rock direction for hardcore punk. It is the early encyclopaedia of powerful pop-punk. Including in-depth profiles of both the bigger names and more underground players that helped push this new sound forward and interviews with over 150 bands, such as 7 Seconds, Husker Du, Dream Syndicate, Hard-Ons, Camper Van Beethoven, The Plimsouls and To Damascus. More than 900 bands from all over the world, active from 1980 to 1989, get an interesting and insightful mention. Cover artwork by Brian Walsby.

Available now at www.earthislandbooks.com

A HARDCORE HEART
Adventures in a D.I.Y. scene

David is a 'lifer' - he's been around the block and earnt his stripes – and 'A Hardcore Heart' is not only a fascinating insight into the reality of touring with an underground hardcore band, but an invigorating time capsule of a punk scene before Instagram, Facebook and MySpace, even before mobile phones, sat navs and Google Maps. It's a veritable ode to being in the wrong place at the wrong time, an underdog story with (spoiler alert!) no happy ending, yet that won't stop its bittersweet narrative from putting a wry smile on your face.
Ian Glasper - Down For Life (and author of 'The Scene That Would Not Die' +)

Want to know what it was really like to submerge yourself in the nineties Hardcore scene? To live, eat, breathe, and be consumed by punk rock? Or what the reality of being in a touring band that lived hand to mouth and played more shows than the author cares to, or probably can remember, for the sheer joy of playing and not a whole lot else? Then you need to read 'A Hardcore Heart', a book that's a love letter to the intoxicating joy of music, the enduring power of friendship, loyalty, and the overwhelming desire to create something from nothing and forge a better tomorrow. Thoroughly recommended.
Tim Cundle - Mass Movement (and author of 'What Would Gary Gygax Do?'

Available now at
www.earthislandbooks.com

Raccoon Starts A Band

By Alex CF

From Alex CF, the creator of 'Punks In The Willows', the beautiful new book, 'Raccoon Starts A Band' is a semi-autobiographical tale of discovering punk. Amongst the difficulties that come with growing up; from the anguish of being bullied, to lack of self-esteem, yet ultimately finding a community that will stoke a passion for music, politics and kindle many life-long friendships. A full colour, illustrated exploration of the many iterations of punk rock, and the greater punk rock community as a force for positive change in the world.

Available now at www.earthislandbooks.com

THE FIRE STILL BURNS

Music inspired by the post-punk message
By David Gamage

WWW.EARTHISLANDBOOKS.COM

AVAILABLE FROM

www.earthislandbooks.com

www.ingramcontent.com/pod-product-compliance
Lightning Source LLC
Chambersburg PA
CBHW040514220526
45357CB00052B/1181